Brief Edition

BUSINESS MATHEMATICS

TWELFTH EDITION

Gary Clendenen
Siena College

Stanley A. Salzman
American River College

Charles D. Miller

Prentice Hall

Boston   Columbus   Indianapolis   New York   San Francisco   Upper Saddle River
Amsterdam   Cape Town   Dubai   London   Madrid   Milan   Munich   Paris   Montréal   Toronto
Delhi   Mexico City   São Paulo   Sydney   Hong Kong   Seoul   Singapore   Taipei   Tokyo

Editorial Director: Vernon Anthony
Executive Editor: Gary Bauer
Development Editor: Linda Cupp
Editorial Assistant: Tanika Henderson
Director of Marketing: David Gessel
Senior Marketing Manager: Stacey Martinez
Marketing Assistant: Les Roberts
Senior Managing Editor: JoEllen Gohr
Project Manager: Christina Taylor

Senior Operations Specialist: Pat Tonneman
Senior Art Director: Diane Ernsberger
Cover Art: iStock
Full-Service Project Management: Trish O'Kane, PreMediaGlobal
Composition: PreMediaGlobal
Printer/Binder: RR Donnelley/Willard
Cover Printer: Lehigh-Phoenix Color/Hagerstown
Text Font: 10/12 Times Roman

Credits appear on page CR-1.

Microsoft® and Windows® are registered trademarks of the Microsoft Corporation in the U.S.A. and other countries. Screen shots and icons reprinted with permission from the Microsoft Corporation. This book is not sponsored or endorsed by or affiliated with the Microsoft Corporation.

Library of Congress Cataloging-in-Publication Data
Clendenen, Gary.
   Business mathematics / Gary Clendenen, Stanley A. Salzman, Charles D. Miller.—12th ed.
      p. cm.
   Miller's name appears first on the ealier editions.
   Includes bibliographical references and index.
   ISBN 978-0-13-510978-6 (student ed.: alk. paper)—ISBN 978-0-13-254564-8 (annotated instructor's ed.: alk. paper)—ISBN 978-0-13-254587-7 (breif ed.: alk. paper)
   1. Business mathematics.   2. Business mathematics—Programmed instruction.   I. Salzman, Stanley A.
II. Miller, Charles David, 1942-   III. Title.
   HF5691.M465 2012
   650.01'513—dc22
                                                                                     2010049927

Prentice Hall
is an imprint of

www.pearsonhighered.com

10 9 8 7 6 5 4 3

ISBN 10:   0-13-254587-X
ISBN 13: 978-0-13-254587-7

contents

preface

FROM THE AUTHORS

The twelfth edition of *Business Mathematics* has been extensively revised to improve readability and currency and to motivate students by using interesting examples from business and personal finance. Additional focus has been placed on real-world business applications. A different, well-known company is highlighted at the beginning of each chapter and used throughout that chapter in discussions, examples, exercises, and a case. Each chapter ends with two new business application cases that help students integrate the concepts using a business setting. Numerous new graphs, news clippings, and photographs have been added to increase the relevance of the material to the world that students know and discussion of the recent financial crisis has been added to help students better understand what has happened. The globalization of our society is also emphasized through examples and exercises that highlight foreign countries and international topics.

This text strives to teach students math calculations in the context of business applications. An important goal of the text is to develop student's understanding of both to the point where they can figure out which calculations apply when presented with an unfamiliar situation. In this sense, we seek to develop a level of business "intuition" by having them work through the integrative cases, a wide-range of application exercises, writing and investigate questions, and discussions about current and relevant data.

The new edition reflects the extensive business and teaching experience of the authors, college faculty who have previously worked in and owned businesses. It also incorporates ideas for improvement from reviewers nationwide as well as students who have taken the course. We focus on providing solid, practical, and up-to-date coverage of business mathematics topics beginning with a brief review of basic mathematics and on to introduce key business topics, such as bank services, payroll, business discounts and markups, simple and compound interest, stocks and bonds, consumer loans, taxes and insurance, depreciation, financial statements, and business statistics. In this edition we have moved the Equations material that was previously included in an appendix into a new Chapter 4: Equations and Formulas. It was moved up based upon requests from reviewers who want to cover this topic early in the course. Coverage of this chapter is optional.

The traditional concept of learning has evolved based on knowledge that students learn in a variety of ways and that many classes are at least partly taught online or in labs. To support student learning in this multidimensional world, we have developed an outstanding supplemental learning package of print and electronic products including the industry leading MyMathLab. Numerous studies have shown that it can greatly increase student learning and retention by presenting material in a variety of formats to suit all types of student learning styles.

Our state-of-the-art supplements package includes revised video lectures, case study videos, an enhanced PowerPoint package, student solutions manual, an extensive instructor's manual, printed quick reference tables, an Excel project manual, and a wealth of online resources for instructors and students including MathXL online, Math XL on CD, MyMathLab, MyCourse, and InterActMath. We hope this text and package satisfies all of your classroom needs. Please feel free to contact us with any questions or concerns.

Gary Clendenen
gclendenen@siena.edu

Stanley Salzman
stan.salzman@comcast.net

about the authors

Gary Clendenen received bachelor's and master's degrees in mathematics before going into business for himself in the oil industry. He returned to academia and earned his Ph.D. in Business Management in 1993 and has been a faculty member since then. His business experience includes working as an actuary for an insurance company and owning commercial real estate. He has published papers in numerous refereed journals and does volunteer work with several organizations. His hobbies include long bicycle rides, traveling, and reading on diverse topics such as the history of the Apache Indians of the Southwest, economics, and issues related to potential shortages of energy, water, and minerals. He has two sons and four grandchildren.

Stanley A. Salzman has taught Business Math, Marketing, and Real Estate courses at American River College in Sacramento for 35 years. He says, "Some of my greatest moments in teaching have been seeing the look on the face of a student who understands a business math concept or idea for the first time." Stan and his wife have four children and eight grandchildren. The grandchildren (all 8 of them) with whom he has enjoyed playing "math class," where they practice simple arithmetic using chocolate raisins. Stan likes outdoor activities, exercising, and collecting antique toy trains.

Charles D. Miller (deceased) was instrumental in writing the early editions of this book as well as several other books. We continue to find inspiration and guidance in his passion for excellence.

learning tips for students

SUCCESS IN BUSINESS MATHEMATICS

This text applies mathematics to solve problems in business. Your success in future business courses and pursuits will be enhanced by the knowledge and skills you will gain in this course. It is very important to realize that your future employer is far more interested in your ability to solve problems than whether you remember a particular formula or how to work one type of problem. So, the goal of this book is both to educate you about business mathematics and importantly to also help you become a better problem solver.

Studying business mathematics is different from studying subjects like English or history. The key to success is *regular practice*. This should not be surprising. After all, can you learn to ski or play a guitar without regular practice? The same is true for learning mathematics. Working problems nearly every day *is the key to becoming successful*. Here are some suggestions to help you succeed in business mathematics.

1. **Attend class regularly. Try to pay careful attention and take notes.** In particular, write down the problems the instructor works on the board.

2. **Ask questions in class.** It is not a sign of weakness, but of strength. There are always other students with the same question who are too shy to ask.

3. **Read the book carefully, maybe twice, and spend time using the online materials.** Studying each topic will help you solve the homework problems. Most exercises are keyed to specific examples or objectives that will explain the procedure for working them.

4. **Before doing your homework, look at the problems the teacher worked in class.** This will reinforce what you have learned. Many students say, "I understand it perfectly when you do it, but I get stuck when I try to work the problem myself."

5. **Read the section and review your notes before starting your homework.** Check your work against the answers in the back of the book. If you get a problem wrong and are unable to understand why, mark that problem and ask your instructor about it. Then practice working additional problems of the same type to reinforce what you have learned.

6. **Work as neatly as you can using a pencil, and organize your work carefully.** Write your symbols clearly, and make sure the problems are clearly separated from each other. Working neatly will help you to think clearly and also make it easier to review the homework before a test.

7. **After you complete a homework assignment, look over the text again.** Try to identify the main ideas that are in the lesson. Often they are clearly highlighted or boxed in the text.

8. **Use the chapter test at the end of each chapter as a practice test.** Work through the problems under test conditions, without referring to the text or the answers until you are finished. You may want to time yourself to see how long it takes you. When you finish, check your answers against those in the back of the book, and study the problems you missed.

9. **Keep all quizzes and tests that are returned to you, and use them when you study for future tests and the final exam.** These quizzes and tests indicate what concepts your instructor considers to be most important. Be sure to correct any problems on these tests that you missed so you will have the corrected work to study.

10. **Don't worry if you do not understand a new topic right away.** As you read more about it and work through the problems, you will gain understanding. Each time you review a topic, you will understand it a little better. Few people understand each topic completely right from the start.

business mathematics pretest

This pretest will help you determine your areas of strength and weakness in the business mathematics presented in this book.

1. Round 5.46 to the nearest tenth.

2. Round $.064 to the nearest cent.

3. Round $399.49 to the nearest dollar.

4. Multiply: 7801
   $\times$ 1758

5. Divide: $35\overline{)11,032}$

6. Change $8\frac{7}{8}$ to an improper fraction.

7. Change $\frac{40}{26}$ to a mixed number.

8. Write $\frac{15}{21}$ in lowest terms.

9. Add: $\frac{3}{4}$
   $\frac{1}{2}$
   $+\frac{7}{8}$

10. Add: $2\frac{2}{3}$
    $7\frac{1}{4}$
    $+10\frac{1}{2}$

11. Subtract: $\frac{3}{8} - \frac{7}{24}$

12. Subtract: $83\frac{3}{4}$
    $-21\frac{2}{5}$

13. Multiply: $\frac{3}{8} \times \frac{3}{5}$

14. Divide: $15\frac{1}{4} \div 5\frac{1}{8}$

15. Express .625 as a common fraction.

16. Express $\frac{3}{5}$ as a decimal.

17. Subtract: 598.316
    $-$ 79.839

18. Multiply: 30.67
    $\times$ 5.39

19. Divide: $1.2\overline{)309.6}$

20. Express $\frac{7}{8}$ as a percent.

21. Intelnet spent 5.2% of its sales on advertising. If sales amounted to $864,250, what amount was spent on advertising?

22. What annual rate of return is needed to receive $930 in one year on an investment of $18,600?

23. Home Entertainment Systems offers a 60-inch LCD HDTV at a list price of $2459 less trade discounts of 20/10. What is the net cost?

24. A department head at Old Navy is paid $16.80 per hour with time and a half for all hours over 40 in a week. Find the employee's gross pay if she worked 43 hours in one week.

25. How long will it take an investment of $12,500 to earn $125 in interest at 4% per year? (*Hint:* Use Bankers Interest, i.e., assume 360 day year.)

26. An invoice from Collier Windows amounting to $20,250 is dated October 6 and offers terms of 3/10, n/30. If the invoice is paid on October 14, what amount is due?

27. Find the percent of markup based on selling price if some home exercise equipment costing $1584 is sold for $1980.

28. Find the single discount equivalent to a series discount of 30/20.

29. Using the straight-line method of depreciation, find the annual depreciation on a Bobcat loader that has a cost of $18,750, an estimated life of six years, and a scrap value of $750.

30. Whiting's Oak Furniture sells a dining room set for $1462.98 after deducting 26% from the original price. Find the original price.

1. _____
2. _____
3. _____
4. _____
5. _____
6. _____
7. _____
8. _____
9. _____
10. _____
11. _____
12. _____
13. _____
14. _____
15. _____
16. _____
17. _____
18. _____
19. _____
20. _____
21. _____
22. _____
23. _____
24. _____
25. _____
26. _____
27. _____
28. _____
29. _____
30. _____

index of applications

Whole Numbers and Decimals

case IN point ▶

JESSICA FERNANDEZ began working part time for SUBWAY® when she was a student at a nearby community college. After graduation, she applied for, and was hired, to be a store manager. She now manages 17 people and must continually recruit and train new people to replace those that leave. As the Case in Point Summary Exercise at the end of the chapter shows, Fernandez uses whole numbers and decimals on a daily basis to schedule employees, do the payroll, compute sales and taxes, order inventory, and pay bills.

Often, the most difficult part of solving a problem is knowing how to set the problem up and then deciding on the steps to solve it. The first two chapters of this book review the mathematical concepts of whole numbers, decimals, and fractions. The rest of the chapters apply these concepts to actual business situations.

1.1   Whole Numbers

OBJECTIVES

1   Define whole numbers.
2   Round whole numbers.
3   Add whole numbers.
4   Round numbers to estimate an answer.
5   Subtract whole numbers.
6   Multiply whole numbers.
7   Multiply by omitting zeros.
8   Divide whole numbers.

case IN point

To improve the efficiency of workers at the SUBWAY store she manages, Jessica Fernandez cross-trains each employee so that he or she can do several tasks, including food preparation, cleanup, and operating the cash register. After watching an employee give a customer too much change for a second time, a frustrated Jessica Fernandez decided that any new hire must pass a basic math test.

OBJECTIVE 1   Define whole numbers. The **decimal system** uses the ten one-place **digits:** 0, 1, 2, 3, 4, 5, 6, 7, 8, and 9. Combinations of these digits represent any number needed. The starting point of this system is the **decimal point (.).** This section considers only the numbers made up of digits to the left of the decimal point—the **whole numbers**. The following diagram names the first fifteen places held by the digits to the left of the decimal point.

Recently, the Department of Transportation estimated that there were 250,851,833 motor vehicles in the United States. To help read this number, a **comma** is used at every third place, starting at the decimal point and moving to the left. However, commas are not necessary for four-digit numbers such as 5679 and 1204. Even though we always use commas when writing larger numbers, some calculators do not show commas.

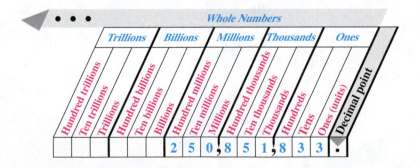

The number 250,851,833 is read as

two hundred fifty million, eight hundred fifty-one thousand, eight hundred thirty-three

Notice that the word "*and*" is not used with whole numbers. The word "*and*" is used for the decimal place, as discussed in Section 1.3.

Expressing Whole Numbers in Words **EXAMPLE 1**

Write the following numbers in words.

(a) 7835 (b) 111,356,075 (c) 17,000,017,000

SOLUTION

(a) seven thousand, eight hundred thirty-five

(b) one hundred eleven million, three hundred fifty-six thousand, seventy-five

(c) seventeen billion, seventeen thousand

> **Quick TIP ▼**
> Do not use the word "and" when reading or writing a whole number.

QUICK CHECK 1

At one point in 2010, the national debt of the United States was $13,663,945,047,118. However, the debt was increasing rapidly as the federal government spent more than it earned to offset the financial crisis. Write the number in words.

OBJECTIVE 2 Round whole numbers. Business applications often require **rounding** numbers. For example, money amounts are commonly rounded to the nearest cent. However, money amounts can also be rounded to the nearest dollar, hundred dollars, thousand dollars, or even hundreds of thousands of dollars and beyond. Use the following steps for **rounding whole numbers**.

Rounding Whole Numbers

Step 1   Locate the **place** to which the number is to be rounded. Draw a line under that place.

Step 2   If the first digit to the *right* of the underlined place is **5 or more, increase** the digit in the place to which you are rounding by 1.

         If the first digit to the right of the underlined place is **4 or less, do not change** the digit in the place to which you are rounding.

Step 3   **Change** all digits to the right of the underlined digit to zeros.

Rounding Whole Numbers **EXAMPLE 2**

Round each number as indicated.

(a) 579 to nearest ten

(b) 34,127 to nearest thousand

(c) 498,712 to nearest ten thousand

(d) 69,965,130 to nearest hundred thousand

SOLUTION

(a) Step 1   Locate the tens place and underline.

579
  ↑ —— Round to this place.

Step 2   The first digit to the right of the underlined digit is 9, which is in the category of 5 or more. Therefore, increase the digit in the tens place by 1, from 7 to 8.

Step 3   Change all digits to the right of the tens place to zero. In other words, change the 9 in the ones place to a zero.

579 rounded to the nearest ten is 580.

(b) Step 1   Locate the thousands place and underline. 34,127

Step 2   The first digit to the right of the thousands place is 1, which is in the category of 4 or less. Thus, do not change the number in the thousands place.

Step 3   Change all digits to the right of the thousands place to zeros.

34,127 rounded to the nearest thousand is 34,000

> **Quick TIP ▼**
> When rounding a number, look at the first digit to the right of the digit being rounded. Do not look beyond this digit.

(c) Step 1   Locate the ten thousands place and underline. 4<u>9</u>8,712

Step 2   Since the digit to the right of the ten thousands place is 8, which is 5 or more, increase the 9 in the ten thousands place by one. Increasing 9 by 1 results in 10, so put a 0 in the ten thousands place and carry 1 to the hundred thousands place, changing it from 4 to 5.

Step 3   Change all digits to the right of the ten thousands place to zeros.

498,712 rounded to the nearest ten thousand is 500,000.

(d) Step 1   Locate the hundred thousands place and underline. 69,<u>9</u>65,130

Step 2   Since the number to the right of the hundred thousands place is 6, which is 5 or more, round the 9 in the hundred thousands place up to 10. Put a 0 in the hundred thousands place and carry one to the millions place, making it 10. So, put a 0 in the millions place and carry 1 to the ten millions place, changing the 6 to 7.

Step 3   Change all digits to the right of the hundred thousands place to zeros.

69,965,130 rounded to the nearest hundred thousand is 70,000,000.

QUICK CHECK 2

Round each number.

(a) 653,781 to the nearest ten thousand   **(b)** 6,578,321 to the nearest million

(c) 499,100 to the nearest thousand   **(d)** 499,100 to the nearest hundred thousand

---

We will now review four basic **operations** with whole numbers: **addition**, **subtraction**, **multiplication**, and **division**.

OBJECTIVE 3 Add whole numbers. In **addition**, the numbers being added are **addends**, and the answer is the **sum**, or **total**, or **amount**.

$$
\begin{array}{rl}
8 & \text{addend} \\
+\ 9 & \text{addend} \\
\hline
17 & \text{sum (answer)}
\end{array}
$$

Add numbers by arranging them in a column with units above units, tens above tens, hundreds above hundreds, thousands above thousands, and so on. Use the decimal point as a reference for arranging the numbers. If a number does not include a decimal point, the decimal point is assumed to be at the far right. For example, 85 = 85. and 527 = 527.

Adding with Checking

To find the one-day total amount of purchases at the SUBWAY store, manager Jessica Fernandez needed to add the following amounts.

Quick TIP ▼

Always be sure to check your work.

$$
\begin{array}{r}
\textbf{\$4028} \\
\hline
\$738 \\
63 \\
125 \\
2617 \\
+\quad 485 \\
\hline
\$4028
\end{array}
$$

First, add down the columns   **Then, check by adding up.**

Adding from the top down results in an answer of $4028. Check for accuracy by adding again—this time from the bottom up. If the answers are the same, the sum is probably correct. If the answers are different, there is an error in either adding down or adding up, and the problem should be reworked. Both answers agree in this example, so the sum is correct.

QUICK CHECK 3

Find the total of the following expenses.

$2805 + $871 + $28 + $169 + $1196

OBJECTIVE 4 Round numbers to estimate an answer. **Front-end rounding** is used to estimate an answer. With front-end rounding, each number is rounded so that all the digits are changed to zero, except the first digit, which is rounded. Only one nonzero digit remains.

Using Front-end Rounding to Estimate an Answer **EXAMPLE 4**

Experts that are worried about the world's supply of energy study data such as that shown here. Apply front-end rounding to the data in the figure to estimate the total amount of oil produced per year in the United States.

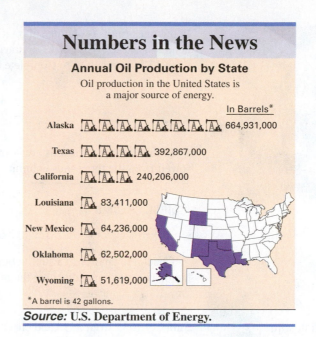

Numbers in the News

Annual Oil Production by State

Oil production in the United States is a major source of energy.

In Barrels*

Alaska		664,931,000
Texas		392,867,000
California		240,206,000
Louisiana		83,411,000
New Mexico		64,236,000
Oklahoma		62,502,000
Wyoming		51,619,000

*A barrel is 42 gallons.

Source: U.S. Department of Energy.

SOLUTION

> **Quick TIP ▼**
>
> In front-end rounding, only one nonzero digit (first digit) remains. All digits to the right are zeros.

	Actual		Front-end Rounded
Alaska	664,931,000	→	700,000,000
Texas	392,867,000	→	400,000,000
California	240,206,000	→	200,000,000
Louisiana	83,411,000	→	80,000,000
New Mexico	64,236,000	→	60,000,000
Oklahoma	62,502,000	→	60,000,000
Wyoming	+ 51,619,000	→	+ 50,000,000
			1,550,000,000

The estimate is 1,550,000,000 barrels of oil. As an aside, the United States uses more than 7,000,000,000 barrels of oil per year, so the remainder of the oil needed must be imported from other countries, such as Saudi Arabia. This has become very expensive.

> **QUICK CHECK 4**
>
> Use front-end rounding to estimate the total of the following numbers.
>
> 621,150; 38,400; 9682; 27,451; 435,620

OBJECTIVE 5 Subtract whole numbers. A **subtraction** problem is set up much like an addition problem. The top number is the **minuend**, the number being subtracted is the **subtrahend**, and the answer is the **difference**.

$$
\begin{array}{r}
23 \\
- 7 \\
\hline
16
\end{array}
$$
minuend
subtrahend
difference

Subtract one number from another by placing the subtrahend directly under the minuend. Be certain that units are above units, tens above tens, and so on. Then begin at the right column and subtract the subtrahend from the minuend.

When a digit in the subtrahend is **larger** than the corresponding digit in the minuend, use **borrowing**, as shown in the next example.

Subtracting with Borrowing   EXAMPLE 5

Subtract 2894 SUBWAY drink cups from 3783 SUBWAY drink cups in inventory. First, write the problem as follows.

$$\begin{array}{r} 3783 \\ -\ 2894 \end{array}$$

In the ones (units) column, subtract 4 from 3 by borrowing a 1 from the tens column in the minuend to get 1 ten + 3, or 13, in the units column with 7 now in the tens column. Then subtract 4 from 13 for a result of 9. Complete the subtraction as follows.

$$\begin{array}{cccc} 2 & 16 & 17 & 13 \\ \cancel{3} & \cancel{7} & \cancel{8} & \cancel{3} \\ -\ 2 & 8 & 9 & 4 \\ \hline 8 & 8 & 9 \end{array}\ \text{drink cups}$$

In this example, the tens are borrowed from the hundreds column, and the hundreds are borrowed from the thousands column.

> **QUICK CHECK 5**
>
> Subtract 7832 customers from 9511 customers.

Check the answer to a subtraction problem by adding the answer (difference) to the subtrahend. The result should equal the minuend.

Subtracting with Checking   EXAMPLE 6

Subtract 1635 from 5383 and check the answer.

	Problem		**Check**	
Problem	5383	minuend	5383 ↑	This result should equal the minuend.
(subtract down) ↓	− 1635	subtrahend	+ 1635	
	3748	**difference**	3748	Check (add up)

> **QUICK CHECK 6**
>
> Subtract 2374 from 4165, and check the answer.

OBJECTIVE 6 Multiply whole numbers. Multiplication is actually a quick method of addition. For example, 3 × 4 can be found by adding 3 a total of 4 times, since 3 × 4 means 3 + 3 + 3 + 3 = 12. However, it is not practical to use the addition method for large numbers. For example, 103 × 92 would be found by adding 103 a total of 92 times. Instead, find this result with multiplication. The multiplication of 103 by 92 can be written in any of the following ways:

$$103 \times 92 = 103 \cdot 92 = 103 * 92 = (103)(92)$$

The number being multiplied is the **multiplicand**, the number doing the multiplying is the **multiplier**, and the answer is the **product**.

$$\begin{array}{r} 3 \quad \text{multiplicand} \\ \times\ 4 \quad \text{multiplier} \\ \hline 12 \quad \text{product} \end{array}$$

When the multiplier contains more than one digit, **partial products** must be used, as in the next example, which shows the product of 25 and 34.

Multiplying Whole Numbers 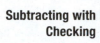 EXAMPLE 7

On a recent trip to visit grandparents, a college student averaged 25 miles per gallon while using 34 gallons of gasoline. To find the total number of miles traveled, multiply 25 miles traveled per gallon of gasoline by 34 gallons of gasoline used.

$$\begin{array}{r} 25 \quad \text{multiplicand} \\ \times\ 34 \quad \text{multiplier} \\ \hline 100 \quad \text{partial product } (4 \times 25) \\ 75 \quad \text{partial product } (3 \times 25, \text{ one position to the left}) \\ \hline 850 \quad \text{product} \end{array}$$

Find the product of 25 and 34 by first multiplying 25 by 4. The product of 25 and 4 is 100, which is a partial product. Next multiply 25 by 3 (from the tens column of the multiplier) and get 75 as a partial product. Since the 3 in the multiplier is from the tens column, write the partial product 75 one position to the left so that 5 is under the tens column. Finally, add the partial products to find the product 850.

QUICK CHECK 7

Multiply 18 telemarketers by 36 phone calls per telemarketer per hour to estimate the number of calls made in one hour.

OBJECTIVE 7 Multiply by omitting zeros. If the multiplier or multiplicand or both end in zero, save time by first omitting any zeros at the right of the numbers and then replacing omitted zeros at the right of the final answer. This shortcut is useful even with calculators. For example, find the product of 240 and 13 as follows.

$$
\begin{array}{r}
24\cancel{0} \\
\times\ 13 \\
\hline
72 \\
24\ \downarrow \\
\hline
3120
\end{array}
$$

Omit the zero in the calculation.

Replace the omitted zero at the right of 312 for a final answer (product) of 3120.

Multiplying, Omitting Zeros   EXAMPLE 8

In the following multiplication problems, omit zeros in the calculation and then replace omitted zeros to obtain the product.

(a)
$$
\begin{array}{r}
150 \\
\times\ 70
\end{array}
\qquad
\begin{array}{r}
15 \\
\times\ 7 \\
\hline
105 \\
10{,}500
\end{array}
$$
attach 2 zeros
answer

(b)
$$
\begin{array}{r}
300 \\
\times\ 90
\end{array}
\qquad
\begin{array}{r}
3 \\
\times\ 9 \\
\hline
27 \\
27{,}000
\end{array}
$$
attach 3 zeros
answer

QUICK CHECK 8

Multiply 400 by 50. Omit zeros in the calculation and replace them in the product.

Quick TIP ▼

A shortcut for multiplying by 10, 100, 1000, and so on is to just attach the number of zeros to the number being multiplied. For example,

$$33 \times 10 = 33 \text{ and } 1 \text{ zero} = 330$$
$$56 \times 100 = 56 \text{ and } 2 \text{ zeros} = 5600$$
$$732 \times 1000 = 732 \text{ and } 3 \text{ zeros} = 732{,}000$$

OBJECTIVE 8 Divide whole numbers. The **dividend** is the number being divided, the **divisor** is the number doing the dividing, and the **quotient** is the answer. **Division** is indicated in any of the following ways.

$$15 \div 5 = 3$$

dividend divisor **quotient (answer)**

$$\begin{array}{r} 3 \\ 5\overline{)15} \end{array}$$

divisor **quotient (answer)** dividend

$$\frac{15}{5} = 3$$

dividend divisor **quotient (answer)**

Dividing Whole Numbers   **EXAMPLE 9**

To divide 1095 baseball cards evenly among 73 collectors, divide 1095 by 73 as follows.

$$73\overline{)1095}$$

Since 73 is larger than 1 or 10, but smaller than 109, begin by dividing 73 into 109. There is one 73 in 109, so place 1 *over the digit 9* in the dividend as shown. Then multiply 1 and 73.

$$\begin{array}{r} 1 \\ 73\overline{)1095} \\ \underline{73} \quad 1 \times 73 = 73 \\ 36 \end{array}$$

Then subtract 73 from 109 to get 36. The next step is to bring down the 5 from the dividend, placing it next to the remainder 36. This gives the number 365. The divisor, 73, is then divided into 365 with a result of 5, which is placed to the right of the 1 in the quotient. Since 73 divides into 365 exactly 5 times, the final answer (quotient) is exactly 15.

$$\begin{array}{r} 15 \\ 73\overline{)1095} \\ \underline{73} \\ 365 \\ \underline{365} \\ 0 \end{array}$$

Check the answer by multiplying.

$$\begin{array}{r} 73 \\ \times 15 \\ \hline 365 \\ 73 \\ \hline 1095 \end{array}$$ **Since this is the original number of cards, the answer checks.**

QUICK CHECK 9

Divide $7506 evenly among 18 winners. How much will each receive?

Often, the divisor does not divide evenly into the dividend, leaving a remainder. The next example shows that remainders can be also be written using fractions or decimals. Fractions and decimals are covered in the next chapter. For now, write a remainder such as 6 as R6, as shown in Example 10.

Dividing with a Remainder in the Answer   **EXAMPLE 10**

Divide 126 by 24. Express the remainder in each of the three forms.

Remainder	**Fraction**	**Decimal**

$$\begin{array}{r} 5\,\text{R6} \\ 24\overline{)126} \\ \underline{120} \\ 6 \end{array} \qquad \begin{array}{r} 5\frac{6}{24} \\ 24\overline{)126} \\ \underline{120} \\ 6 \end{array} \qquad \begin{array}{r} 5.25 \\ 24\overline{)126.00} \\ \underline{120} \\ 6\,0 \\ \underline{4\,8} \\ 1\,20 \\ \underline{1\,20} \\ 0 \end{array}$$

QUICK CHECK 10

Divide 19 by 5.

If a divisor contains zeros at the far right, as in 30, 300, or 8000, first drop the zeros in the divisor. Then move the decimal point in the dividend the same number of positions to the left as there were zeros dropped from the divisor. For example, divide 108,000 by 900 by letting

$$900\overline{)108,000} \qquad \text{becomes} \qquad 9\overline{)1080}$$

Drop 2 zeros. ———↑   ↑——— Move decimal point 2 places left.

Divide 7320 by 30 by letting

$$30\overline{)7320} \qquad \text{become} \qquad 3\overline{)732}$$

Dropping Zeros to Divide **EXAMPLE 11**

For each of the following, first drop zeros, and then divide.

(a) $40\overline{)11{,}000}$ (b) $3500\overline{)31{,}500}$ (c) $200\overline{)18{,}800}$

SOLUTION

Quick TIP ▼

After dropping zeros and dividing, do not add trailing zeros back to the answer.

(a)
```
      275
  4)1100
    8
    30
    28
     20
     20
      0
```

(b)
```
      9
 35)315
    315
      0
```

(c)
```
      94
  2)188
    18
     8
     8
     0
```

Do not add the zeros back in the answer.

QUICK CHECK 11

First drop zeros, and then divide $19{,}200 \div 300$.

Checking Division Problems **EXAMPLE 12**

In a division problem, check the answer by multiplying the quotient (answer) and the divisor. Then add any remainder. The result should be the dividend. If the result is not the same as the dividend, an error exists and the problem should be reworked. Check the following division problems.

(a)
```
      22
 19)418
    38
    38
    38
     0   match
```

(b)
```
       37
716)26,492
    21 48
     5 012
     5 012
         0
```

(c)
```
      85 R6
418)35,536
    33 44
     2 096
     2 090
         6   remainder
```

Quick TIP ▼

When checking a division problem that has a remainder, as in part (c) of this example, be sure to add the remainder to the product.

SOLUTION

(a)
```
      19
   ×  22
      38
      38
     418   correct
```

(b)
```
      716
   ×   37
     5012
     2148
   26,492   correct
```

(c)
```
       418
   ×    85
      2090
      3344
     35,530
   +     6   add remainder
     35,536   correct
```

QUICK CHECK 12

Divide 9897 by 215. Check the answer by multiplying the quotient (answer) by the divisor.

1.1 Exercises

  PRACTICE WATCH DOWNLOAD READ

The QUICK START exercises in each section contain solutions to help you get started.

Write the following numbers in words. (See Example 1.)

QUICK START

1. 7040 <u>seven thousand, forty</u>

2. 5310 <u>five thousand, three hundred ten</u>

3. 37,901 _____

4. 725,069 _____

5. 4,650,015 _____

6. 3,765,041,000 _____

*Round each of the following numbers first to the nearest ten, then to the nearest hundred, and finally to the nearest thousand. Go back to the **original number** each time before rounding to the next position. (See Example 2.)*

QUICK START

		Nearest Ten	Nearest Hundred	Nearest Thousand
7.	2065	2070	2100	2000
8.	8385	8390	8400	8000
9.	46,231			
10.	55,175			
11.	106,054			
12.	359,874			

13. Explain the three steps needed to round a number when the digit to the right of the place to which you are rounding is 5 or more. (See Objective 2.)

14. Explain the three steps needed to round a number when the digit to the right of the place to which you are rounding is 4 or less. (See Objective 2.)

Add each of the following. Check your answers. (See Example 3.)

QUICK START

15.	75	16.	57	17.	875	18.	135
	63		26		364		594
	45		43		171		415
	+ 27		+ 18		+ 776		+ 276
	210						

19.	750	20.	371	21.	311,479	22.	803,526
	91		45		77,631		759,991
	8		839		+ 594,383		+ 36,024
	540		3				
	+ 7		+ 47				

Subtract each of the following. Check your answers. (See Examples 5 and 6.)

23.	896	24.	757	25.	3715	26.	6215
	− 228		− 286		− 838		− 767

27.	65,198	28.	445,193	29.	7,025,389	30.	9,807,943
	− 43,652		− 62,785		− 936,490		− 959,489

Solve the following problems. To serve as a check, the vertical and horizontal totals must be the same in the lower right-hand corner.

31. PRODUCT PURCHASES   The following table shows monthly purchases at a Best Buy by product line for each of the first six months of the year. Complete the totals by adding horizontally and vertically.

QUICK START

PRODUCT	JAN.	FEB.	MAR.	APR.	MAY	JUNE	TOTALS
Software	$49,802	$36,911	$47,851	$54,732	$29,852	$74,119	**$293,267**
Computers	$86,154	$72,908	$31,552	$74,944	$85,532	$36,705	
Printers	$59,854	$85,119	$87,914	$45,812	$56,314	$91,856	
Mobile Phones	$73,951	$72,564	$39,615	$71,099	$72,918	$42,953	
Totals							

32. DEPARTMENT SALES   The following table shows Jansen's Pipe & Supply expenses by department for the last six months of the year. Complete the totals by adding horizontally and vertically.

DEPARTMENT	JULY	AUG.	SEPT.	OCT.	NOV.	DEC.	TOTALS
Office	$29,806	$31,712	$40,909	$32,514	$18,902	$23,514	
Production	$92,143	$86,599	$97,194	$72,815	$89,500	$63,754	
Sales	$31,802	$39,515	$58,192	$32,544	$41,920	$48,732	
Warehouse	$15,746	$12,986	$32,325	$41,983	$39,814	$20,605	
Totals							

Multiply each of the following. (See Example 7.)

QUICK START

33. 218
  × 43
  654
  872
  9374

34. 672
  × 56

35. 1896
  × 62

36. 7318
  × 38

37. 6452
  × 263

38. 7143
  × 295

39. 1109
  × 7311

40. 9503
  × 3411

Estimate answers using front-end rounding. Then find the exact answers. (See Example 4.)

QUICK START

41. **Estimate**   **Exact**
  8000 ←rounds 8215
  60 ←to 56
  700 ← 729
  + 4000 ← + 3605
  12,760   12,605

42. **Estimate**   **Exact**
  ← 2685
  ← 73
  ← 592
  +   ← + 7183

43. **Estimate**   **Exact**
  ← 783
  −   ← − 238

44. **Estimate**   **Exact**
  ← 942
  −   ← − 286

45. **Estimate**   **Exact**
  ← 638
  ×   ← × 47

46. **Estimate**   **Exact**
  ← 864
  ×   ← × 74

Multiply, omitting zeros in the calculation and then replacing them at the right of the product to obtain the final answer. (See Example 8.)

QUICK START

47. 370
  × 180
  37
  × 18
  666   2 zeros
          ↙
  66,600

48. 520
  × 400

49. 3760
  × 6000

50. 7200
  × 1300

Divide each of the following. (See Examples 9 and 10.)

QUICK START

51.   1241 R1
  4)4965
  4
  09
  8
  16
  16
  05
  4
  1

52. 7)13,214

53. 43)19,715

54. 93)81,452

55. Explain why checking the answer is a very important step in solving math problems.

56. In your personal and business life, when is it most important to check your math calculations? Why?

Divide each of the following, dropping zeros from the divisor. (See Examples 10 and 11.)

QUICK START

57. 180)429,350

$$
\begin{array}{r}
2\ 385\ R5 \\
18)\overline{42,935} \\
\underline{36} \\
6\ 9 \\
\underline{5\ 4} \\
1\ 53 \\
\underline{144} \\
95 \\
\underline{90} \\
5
\end{array}
$$

58. 320)360,990

59. 1300)75,800

60. 1600)253,100

Rewrite the following numbers in words. (See Example 1.)

61. TOTAL BUSINESSES There are 29,671,300 business enterprises in the United States. (*Source:* A. G. Edwards.)

62. WOMEN IN BUSINESS There are 8,534,350 businesses owned by women in the United States. (*Source:* A. G. Edwards.)

63. PARACHUTE JUMPS There are 3,200,000 parachute jumps in the United States each year. (*Source:* History Channel.)

64. GROSS NATIONAL PRODUCT The annual gross national product or sum of all goods and services produced was $14,243,600,000,000. (*Source:* U.S. Department of Commerce.)

Rewrite the numbers from the following sentences using digits. (See Example 1.)

QUICK START

65. JELL-O SALES The average number of boxes of Jell-O gelatin sold each day is eight hundred fifty-four thousand, seven hundred ninety-five. (*Source:* Kraft Foods.)

65. 854,795 boxes

66. CRAYON SALES The Binney & Smith Company makes about two billion Crayola Crayons each year. (*Source:* Binney & Smith Company.)

66. _____

67. SALVATION ARMY During the past year, the Salvation Army served fifty-five million, five hundred seventy-two thousand, six hundred thirty-three meals to hungry men, women, and children. (*Source:* The Salvation Army National Annual Report.)

67. _____

68. HURRICANE KATRINA At a New Orleans pumping station, one of the pumps designed by Alexander Baldwin Wood pumped six hundred forty-eight million gallons of flood water (7500 gallons per second) in one day. (*Source:* Modern Marvels, Hurricane Katrina, History Channel.)

68. _____

Solve the following application problems.

QUICK START

69. **HERSHEY MINI CHIPS** There are approximately 5000 Mini Chips semisweet chocolate chips in 1 pound. How many chips are in 40 pounds? (*Source:* Hershey Foods Corporation.)

    $5 \times 4 = 20$ 4 zeros

    200,000

    69. **200,000 chips**

70. **HERSHEY KISSES** Each day 33,000,000 Hershey Kisses can be produced. Find the number of Hershey Kisses that can be produced in 30 days. (*Source:* Hershey Foods Corporation.)

    70. _____

71. **CAMPUS VENDING MACHINES** On a normal weekday, the vending machines at American River College dispense 900 sodas, 400 candy bars, 500 snack items, and 200 cups of coffee. If it takes Jim Wilson four hours to restock the vending machines, how many items does he restock each hour?

    71. _____

72. **IPAD SALES** The numbers of iPads sold each day in one city were 1801, 927, 2088, 580, and 1049. Find the average number sold per day.

    72. _____

WHITE WATER RAFTING *American River Raft Rentals lists the following daily raft rental fees. Notice that there is an additional $3 launch fee payable to the park system for each raft rented. Use this information to solve Exercises 73 and 74.*

AMERICAN RIVER RAFT RENTALS		
SIZE	RENTAL FEE	LAUNCH FEE
4 persons	$50	$3
6 persons	$72	$3
10 persons	$128	$3
12 persons	$143	$3

(*Source:* American River Raft Rentals.)

73. On a recent Sunday, the following rafts were rented: 6 4-person rafts, 15 6-person rafts, 10 10-person rafts, and 5 12-person rafts. Find the total receipts, including the $3-per-raft launch fee.

    73. _____

74. During the July 4th weekend, the following rafts were rented: 38 4-person rafts, 73 6-person rafts, 58 10-person rafts, and 46 12-person rafts. Find the total receipts including the $3-per-raft launch fee.

    74. _____

MILK PRODUCTION   *The following pictograph shows the states with the most milk production. Use this information to answer Exercises 75–78.*

Numbers in the News

MILK PRODUCTION

Top Milk-Producing States (millions of pounds)

California	3,433
Wisconsin	2,060
New York	1,040
Idaho	990
Pennsylvania	900
Texas	778
Minnesota	753
New Mexico	687
Michigan	662
Washington	460

Source: **National Agricultural Statistics Service.**

QUICK START

75. Find the combined milk production from California, Wisconsin, and New York.

$3433 + 2060 + 1040 = 6533$ million pounds or 6,533,000,000 pounds

75. 6533 million pounds, or 6,533,000,000 pounds

76. Use front-end rounding to estimate the total amount of milk produced from all the states shown. Find the total amount of milk produced from all the states listed.

76. _____

77. How much more milk is produced in California than in Michigan?

77. _____

78. How much more milk is produced in Wisconsin and Minnesota combined compared to Texas and New Mexico combined?

78. _____

RETAIL GIANTS   *The following pictograph shows the number of retail stores worldwide for the seven companies with the greatest number of outlets. Use the pictograph to answer Exercises 79–84.*

Numbers in the News

The Retail Giants

Dollar General	
Wal-Mart	
7-Eleven	
CVS	
Family Dollar	
Walgreens	
Rite-Aid	

🛒 = 1000 stores

Source: **Company Web sites.**

QUICK START

79. Find the number of Family Dollar retail stores.

$6.5 \times 1000 = 6500$ stores

79. 6500 stores

80. Estimate the number of stores for 7-Eleven.

80. _____

81. Which company has the largest number of retail stores? How many does it have?

81. _____

82. Which of the seven retailers has the fewest number of retail stores? How many does it have?

82. _____

83. How many more retail stores does Dollar General have than Walgreens?

83. _____

84. How many more stores does CVS have compared to its competitor Walgreens?

84. _____

QUICK CHECK ANSWERS

1. thirteen trillion, six hundred sixty-three billion, nine hundred forty-five million, forty-seven thousand one hundred eighteen
2. (a) 650,000, (b) 7,000,000, (c) 499,000 (d) 500,000
3. $5069
4. 1,080,000
5. 1679 customers
6. 1791
7. 648 phone calls
8. 20 attach 3 zeros = 20,000
9. $417
10. 3 R4
11. 64
12. 46 R7

1.2 Application Problems

OBJECTIVES

1 Find indicator words in application problems.
2 Learn the four steps for solving application problems.
3 Learn to estimate answers.
4 Solve application problems.

case IN point

When Jessica Fernandez became a manager at a SUBWAY store, she had to brush up on her math skills. She remembered that certain words indicate addition, subtraction, multiplication, and division.

Many business-application problems require mathematics. You must read very carefully to decide how to solve the problem.

OBJECTIVE 1 Find indicator words in application problems. Look for **indicator words** in the application problem—words that indicate the necessary operations: addition, subtraction, multiplication, or division. Some of these words appear below.

Addition	Subtraction	Multiplication	Division	Equals
plus	less	product	divided by	is
more	subtract	double	divided into	the same as
more than	subtracted from	triple	quotient	equals
added to	difference	times	goes into	equal to
increased by	less than	of	divide	yields
sum	fewer	twice	divided equally	results in
total	decreased by	twice as much	per	are
sum of	loss of			
increase of	minus			
gain of	take away			
	reduced by			

The word *and* is not listed above since it can have many different meanings, including all the following:

1. sum of 3 **and** 4,
2. product of 6 **and** 8,
3. seventeen **and** one-half, or
4. six **and** seven tenths.

OBJECTIVE 2 Learn the four steps for solving application problems. When working difficult problems, try to take your time and relax as if you were at the gym or a pool. Believe it or not, you are training your brain when working problems. It is okay if you do NOT know how to solve a problem when first reading it.

Quick TIP ▼
Do NOT make the mistake that some students do, which is to try and solve a problem before knowing what is being asked.

Solving Application Problems

Step 1   Read the problem carefully, two or three times if needed. Be sure that you understand what is being asked.

Step 2   Identify given facts and *look for indicator words*. Then work out a plan to solve the problem.

Step 3   Estimate a *reasonable answer* using rounding.

Step 4   Solve the problem. Does the answer make sense? If not, work it again.

OBJECTIVE 3 Learn to estimate answers. Each of the steps in solving an application problem is important, but special emphasis should be placed on step 3, estimating a reasonable answer. Many times an answer just *does not fit* the problem.

What is a *reasonable answer*? Read the problem and estimate the approximate size of the answer. Should the answer be part of a dollar, a few dollars, hundreds, thousands, or even millions of dollars? For example, if a problem asks for the retail price of a shirt, would an answer of $20 be reasonable? $1000? $.65? $65?

Always make an estimate of a reasonable answer. Always look at the answer and decide if it is reasonable. These steps will give greater success in problem solving.

Using Word Indicators to Help Solve a Problem **EXAMPLE 1**   Total sales at a neighborhood yard sale were $3584. The money was divided equally among the boys soccer club, the girls soccer club, the boys softball team, and the girls softball team. How much did each group receive?

SOLUTION

Sales of $3584 are to be *divided equally* among the four groups. Estimate the answer by first rounding $3584 to the nearest hundred ($3600); then divide by 4.

$$\$3600 \div 4 = \$900 \text{ estimate of amount to each group}$$

Divide to find the exact answer.

$$\begin{array}{r} \$896 \\ 4\overline{)3584} \end{array} \quad \text{Each group should get \$896.}$$

The answer is reasonable, so check the work.

$$\begin{array}{r} \$896 \\ \times \quad 4 \\ \hline \$3584 \end{array} \quad \text{The answer is correct.}$$

QUICK CHECK 1

A library budget surplus of $13,280 is divided evenly among four branch libraries. How much did each receive?

OBJECTIVE 4 Solve application problems. To improve your accuracy, use the four steps and estimate answers when solving application problems.

Solving an Application Problem **EXAMPLE 2**   One week, Jessica Fernandez decided to total her sales at SUBWAY. The daily sales figures were $2358 on Monday, $3056 on Tuesday, $2515 on Wednesday, $1875 on Thursday, $3978 on Friday, $3219 on Saturday, and $3008 on Sunday. Find the total sales for the week.

case IN point

SOLUTION

The sales for each day are given, and the total sales are needed. The word indicators *total sales* tell you to add the daily sales to arrive at the weekly total. Since the sales are about $3000 each day for a week of 7 days, a reasonable estimate would be around $21,000 (7 × $3000 = $21,000). Find the actual answer by adding the sales for each of the 7 days.

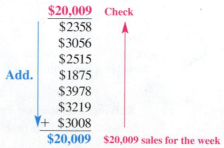

The answer of $20,009 is reasonable.

QUICK CHECK 2

The numbers of visitors to a war veterans' memorial during one week are 5318, 2865, 4786, 1898, 3899, 2343, and 7221. First estimate the total attendance for the week. Then calculate exactly.

Solving an Application Problem

EXAMPLE 3

Many experts believe that water shortages will soon be a major problem. The chart below shows an estimate of fresh water resources per person, by country. For example, the photo at the side shows people waiting for a water truck in India where some families spend several hours each day trying to find water needed for the day.

(a) Find the difference in the water resources per person between China and India.

(b) Use division to compare water per person in the United States to that in India.

Numbers in the News

Who Has Water?
(cubic meters per person per year)

Country	cubic meters
Brazil	43,028
Russia	31,763
United States	6,816
France	3,342
China	2,125
India	1,670
Saudi Arabia	93

Data: CIA

(a) The indicator word *difference* suggests a subtraction problem.

$$\begin{array}{r} 2125 \\ -\ 1670 \\ \hline 455 \end{array}$$ cubic meters per person per year

(b) $6816 \div 1670 = 4.08$ (rounded), or about 4 times as much water per person in the United States as in India.

Note that the figure suggests nothing about the geographic distribution of water within a country or whether the water is clean enough for human consumption. Clearly, some countries have far fewer water resources than others. In addition, water pollution is a terrible problem in many poor countries.

QUICK CHECK 3

Find the difference in the water resources per person for Brazil and Saudi Arabia.

Solving a Two-Step Problem

EXAMPLE 4

In May, the landlord of an apartment building received $940 from each of eight tenants. After paying $2730 in expenses, how much money did the landlord have left?

SOLUTION

Multiply the amount of rent by the number of tenants to arrive at the monthly income. Since the rent is about $900 and there are eight tenants, a *reasonable estimate* would be around $7200 ($900 × 8 = 7200).

$$\begin{array}{r} \$940 \\ \times\quad 8 \\ \hline \$7520 \end{array}$$ monthly income (this is reasonable)

Now subtract the expenses from the monthly income.

$$\begin{array}{r} \$7520 \\ -\ 2730 \\ \hline \$4790 \end{array}$$ amount remaining

QUICK CHECK 4

A homeowner's association collected $385 from each of 62 homeowners. If the association paid $18,280 in expenses, how much remained?

SUBWAY promotes healthy, low-fat food choices and fresh vegetables. The chain offers eight sandwiches that are low in fat, containing 6 grams of fat or less. Perhaps you have seen the SUBWAY advertising featuring Jared Fogle. As a college student, he weighed 425 pounds. By eating just two (a 6-inch and a foot-long) SUBWAY sandwiches each day, he lost 225 pounds in one year.

The nutritional information shown below is printed on all SUBWAY napkins.

Solving Application Problems   **EXAMPLE 5**

Using the nutritional information shown for SUBWAY, answer each question.

(a) How many fewer calories and grams of fat are in a 6-inch Veggie Delite sandwich than a Big Mac Value Meal?

(b) How much less calories and fat are in a 6-inch Turkey Breast and Ham sandwich than in a Whopper Value Meal?

SOLUTION

The word indicator in part **(a)** is *fewer,* and the word indicator in part **(b)** is *less.* These words indicate that we must subtract.

(a)   940 Big Mac Value Meal   50
       − 265 Veggie Delite   − 3
       675 fewer calories   **47 fewer fat grams**

(b)   1030 Whopper Value Meal   58
       − 325 Turkey Breast and Ham   − 5
       705 less calories   **53 less fat grams**

QUICK CHECK 5

From the SUBWAY nutritional information, how many fewer calories and grams of fat are in a Sweet Onion Chicken Teriyaki sandwich than in a Whopper Value Meal?

1.2 Exercises

The **QUICK START** *exercises in each section contain solutions to help you get started.*

Solve the following application problems.

QUICK START

 1. **SUBWAY SANDWICHES** Last week, SUBWAY sold 602 Veggie Delite sandwiches, 935 ham sandwiches, 1328 turkey breast sandwiches, 757 roast beef sandwiches, and 1586 SUBWAY Club sandwiches. Find the total number of sandwiches sold.
$602 + 935 + 1328 + 757 + 1586 = 5208$ sandwiches

1. <u>5208 sandwiches</u>

2. **COMPETITIVE CYCLIST TRAINING** During a week of training, Rob Andrews rode his bike 80 miles on Monday, 75 miles on Tuesday, 135 miles on Wednesday, 40 miles on Thursday, and 52 miles on Friday. What is the total number of miles he rode in the five-day period?
Total miles traveled $= 80 + 75 + 135 + 40 + 52 = 382$ miles

2. <u>382 miles</u>

3. **MILES DRIVEN** The Federal Highway Administration estimates that total miles driven fell from 3020 billion miles last year to 2920 billion miles this year due to the recession. Find the reduction in miles driven.

3. _____

4. **SUV SALES** In a recent three-month period, there were 81,465 Ford Explorers and 70,449 Jeep Grand Cherokees sold. How many more Ford Explorers were sold than Jeep Grand Cherokees? (*Source:* J. D. Power and Associates.)

4. _____

5. **WORLD WAR II VETERANS** World War II veterans, part of what is now called "the greatest generation," are dying at the rate of 1050 each day. How many World War II veterans are projected to die in the next year of 365 days? (*Source:* Department of Veterans Affairs.)

5. _____

6. **TOTAL WORLD WAR II VETERANS** There are an estimated 2,933,310 World War II veterans alive today. If only 1 in 6 is still alive, find the total number of people who were World War II veterans. Round to the nearest hundred thousand. (*Source:* Department of Veterans Affairs.)

6. _____

7. **FISHING BOAT** A fishing boat weighs 8375 pounds. If its 762-pound engine is removed and replaced with a 976-pound engine, find the weight of the boat after the engine change.

7. _____

8. **PRESCHOOL MANAGER** Bobby Benson has $2324 in his preschool operating account. After he spends $734 from this account, the class parents raise $568 in a rummage sale. Find the balance in the account after the money from the rummage sale is deposited.

8. _____

9. **NOTEBOOK COMPUTER** The price of a mini notebook was lowered from $499 to $435. Find the decrease in price.

9. _____

10. **WEIGHING FREIGHT** A truck weighs 9250 pounds when empty. After being loaded with firewood, the truck weighs 21,375 pounds. What is the weight of the firewood?

10. _____

 indicates an exercise that is related to the Case in Point feature.

11. LAND AREA   There are 43,560 square feet in 1 acre. How many square feet are there in 140 acres?

11. _____

12. CHECK PROCESSING   Bank of America processes 40 million checks each day. Find the number of checks processed by the bank in a year. (Use a 365-day year.) (*Source:* Bank of America.)

12. _____

13. HOTEL ROOM COSTS   In a recent study of hotel–casinos, the cost per night at Harrah's Reno was $45, while the cost at Harrah's Lake Tahoe was $99 per night. Find the amount saved on a seven-night stay at Harrah's Reno instead of staying at Harrah's Lake Tahoe. (*Source:* Harrah's Casinos and Hotels.)

13. _____

14. LUXURY HOTELS   A luxury hotel room at the Ritz-Carlton in San Francisco costs $645 per night, while a nearby room at a Motel 6 costs $74 per night. What amount will be saved in a four-night stay at Motel 6 instead of staying at the Ritz-Carlton? (*Source:* Ritz-Carlton; Motel 6.)

14. _____

15. PHYSICALLY IMPAIRED   The Enabling Supply House purchased 6 wheelchairs at $1256 each and 15 speech compression recorder-players at $895 each. Find the total cost.

15. _____

16. KITCHEN EQUIPMENT   Find the total cost if SUBWAY buys 32 baking ovens at $1538 each and 28 warming ovens at $887 each.

16. _____

17. YOUTH SOCCER   A youth soccer association raised $7588 through fund-raising projects. There were expenses of $838 that had to be paid first, and the remaining money was divided evenly among the 18 teams. How much did each team receive?

17. _____

18. EGG PRODUCTION   Feather Farms Ranch collects 3545 eggs in the morning and 2575 eggs in the afternoon. If the eggs are packed in flats containing 30 eggs each, find the number of flats needed for packing.

18. _____

19. THEATER RENOVATION   A theater owner is remodeling to provide enough seating for 1250 people. The main floor has 30 rows of 25 seats in each row. If the balcony has 25 rows, how many seats must be in each row of the balcony to satisfy the owner's seating requirements?

19. _____

20. CALL CENTER   Beverly Stratton was hired to manage a call center for a market research firm that makes calls asking about consumer preferences. She anticipates about 82 outgoing calls per hour, 8 hours per day, 5 days a week, 50 weeks a year. Estimate the total number of calls per year. Also estimate the minimum number of call center operators needed if each can make about 17,000 calls a year. Round up to the next larger whole number.

20. _____

QUICK CHECK ANSWERS

1. $3320   **2.** 28,000; 28,330 visitors   **3.** 42,935 cubic meters per person per year
4. $5590   **5.** 625 fewer calories; 53 fewer fat grams

1.3 Basics of Decimals

OBJECTIVES

1. Read and write decimal numbers.
2. Round decimal numbers.

OBJECTIVE 1 Read and write decimal numbers. A **decimal number** is any number written with a decimal point, such as 6.8, 5.375, or .000982. Decimals, like fractions, can be used to represent parts of a whole. These parts are "less than 1." **Section 1.1** discussed how to read the digits to the *left* of the decimal point (whole numbers). Now we will see how to read the digits to the right of the decimal point, which always end in the letters "th" or "ths."

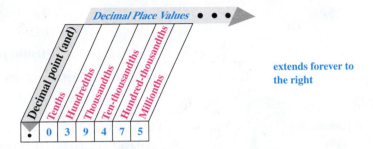

Read the decimal number .039475 as "39475 millionths," where millionths comes from the fact that the last digit of this number falls in the millionths place. Write this number using words as follows.

thirty-nine thousand, four hundred seventy-five millionths

When reading a number with digits both to the left and the right of the decimal place, use the word *and* to show the location of the decimal point. Here are some examples.

9.7	nine **and** seven tenths
11.59	eleven **and** fifty-nine hundredths
1045.658	one thousand, forty-five **and** six hundred fifty-eight thousandths
5,600,000.0072	five million, six hundred thousand **and** seventy-two ten thousandths

Reading Decimal Numbers | **EXAMPLE 1**

Write the following decimals in words.

(a) 19.08   (b) .097   (c) 7648.9713   (d) 3,068,001.7

SOLUTION

(a) nineteen **and** eight hundredths

(b) ninety-seven thousandths

(c) seven thousand, six hundred forty-eight **and** nine thousand, seven hundred thirteen ten-thousandths

(d) three million, sixty-eight thousand, one **and** seven tenths

> **Quick TIP ▼**
> Use the word *"and"* only when writing a number to separate the whole number from the fractional (decimal) part.

QUICK CHECK 1

Write (a) 0.068 and (b) 4,370.15 in words.

OBJECTIVE 2 Round decimal numbers. It is important to be able to round decimals. For example, Walgreens sells two candy bars for $.79, but you want to buy only one candy bar. The price of one bar is $.79 ÷ 2, which is $.395, but you cannot pay part of a cent. So the store rounds the price up to $.40 for one bar. The steps to round decimal numbers are the same as those used to round whole numbers, which have already been discussed.

> **Rounding Decimals**
>
> **Step 1**   Find the **place** to which the number is to be rounded. Draw a vertical line after that place to show that you are cutting off the rest of the digits.
>
> **Step 2**   Look at only the first digit to the right of your cut-off line. If the first digit is **5 or more, increase** the digit in the place to which you are rounding by 1.
>
> If the first digit to the right of the line is **4 or less, do not change** the digit in the place to which you are rounding.
>
> **Step 3**   **Drop** all digits to the right of the place to which you have rounded.

To round 97.3892 to the nearest tenth, first draw a vertical line to the right of the 3 in the tenths place. The digit to the right of the vertical line is 5 or more, so round the 3 in the tenths position up to 4 and drop all digits to the right.

$$\begin{array}{c} \text{digit to the right of tenths place} \\ \downarrow \\ 97.3\,|\,892 \\ \uparrow \;\textbf{tenths place} \end{array}$$

97.3892 rounded to the nearest tenth is 97.4.

Rounding Decimal Numbers **EXAMPLE 2**

Round each as indicated.

(a) 87.562 to the nearest tenth   (b) 3678.5928 to the nearest hundredth

SOLUTION

(a) **Step 1**   Locate the tenths place and put a vertical line immediately to the right.

$$\begin{array}{c} 87.5\,|\,62 \\ \uparrow \;\textbf{tenths place} \end{array}$$

Step 2   The number to the right of the line is 6, which is 5. Therefore, round the 5 in the tenths place up to 6.

Step 3   Drop all digits to the right of the tenths place.

87.562 rounded to the nearest tenth is 87.6.

(b) **Step 1**   Locate the hundredths place and put a vertical line to the right.

$$3678.59\,|\,28$$

Step 2   The number to the right of the line is 2, or less than 5. Therefore, leave the 9 as it is in the hundredths place.

Step 3   Drop all digits to the right of the hundredths place.

3678.5928 rounded to the nearest hundredth is **3678.59**.

Rounding 3678.5928 to the nearest tenth would result in 3678.6, and rounding it to the nearest whole number would result in 3679.

> **QUICK CHECK 2**
>
> Round 72.8479 to the nearest thousandth.

Rounding the Same Decimal Number to Different Places **EXAMPLE 3**

Round 24.998 to the nearest **(a)** hundredth, **(b)** tenth, and **(c)** whole number.

SOLUTION

Use the method just described.

(a) 24.998 rounded to the nearest hundredth is 25.00.

(b) 24.998 rounded to the nearest tenth is 25.0.

(c) 24.998 rounded to the nearest whole number is 25.

Interestingly, in this particular situation all three round to the same number. However, that will usually not be the case.

> **Quick TIP** ▼
>
> Always refer back to the original number before rounding.

> **QUICK CHECK 3**
>
> Round 518.4464 to the nearest **(a)** thousandth, **(b)** hundredth, and **(c)** tenth.

1.3 Exercises

MyMathLab   **Math XL** PRACTICE   WATCH   DOWNLOAD   READ

The **QUICK START** *exercises in each section contain solutions to help you get started.*

Write the following decimals in words. (See Example 1.)

QUICK START

1. .38 <u>thirty-eight hundredths</u>

2. .91 <u>ninety-one hundredths</u>

3. 5.61 _____

4. 6.53 _____

5. 7.408 _____

6. 1.254 _____

7. 37.593 _____

8. 20.903 _____

9. 4.0062 _____

10. 9.0201 _____

11. "My answer is right, but the decimal point is in the wrong place." Can this statement ever be correct? Explain. (See Objective 1.)

12. In your own words, explain the difference between thousands and thousandths.

Write the following decimals, using numbers.

QUICK START

13. four hundred thirty-eight and four tenths <u>438.4</u>

14. six hundred five and seven tenths <u>605.7</u>

15. ninety-seven and sixty-two hundredths _____

16. seventy-one and thirty-three hundredths _____

17. one and five hundred seventy-three ten-thousandths _____

18. nine and three hundred eight ten-thousandths _____

19. three and five thousand eight hundred twenty-seven ten-thousandths _____

20. two thousand seventy-four ten-thousandths _____

GROCERY SHOPPING   *Alan Zagorin is grocery shopping. The store will round the amount he pays for each item to the nearest cent. Write the rounded amounts. (See Examples 2–4.)*

21. Claim Jumper apple pies are two for $11.99. So one pie is $5.995. Zagorin pays _____.

22. Four 12-packs of soda cost $11.90. So one 12-pack costs $2.975. Zagorin pays _____.

23. Muffin mix is three packages for $1.75. So one package is $.58333. Zagorin pays _____.

24. Candy bars are six for $2.99. So one bar is $.4983. Zagorin pays _____.

25. Barbeque sauce is three bottles for $3.50. So one bottle is $1.1666. Zagorin pays _____.

26. Tony's Pizzas are five for $18.73. So one pizza is $3.746. Zagorin pays _____.

 indicates an exercise that is related to the Case in Point feature.

Round each of the decimals to the nearest tenth, the nearest hundredth, and the nearest thousandth. Remember to use the original number each time before rounding. (See Examples 2–4.)

QUICK START

	Nearest Tenth	Nearest Hundredth	Nearest Thousandth
27. 3.5218	3.5	3.52	3.522
28. 4.836	4.8	4.84	4.836
29. 2.54836			
30. 7.44652			
31. 27.32451			
32. 89.53796			
33. 36.47249			
34. 58.95651			
35. .0562			
36. .0789			

Round each of the dollar amounts to the nearest cent.

QUICK START

37. $5.056 $5.06   **38.** $16.519 $16.52   **39.** $32.493 _____

40. $375.003 _____   **41.** $382.005 _____   **42.** $12,802.965 _____

43. $42.137 _____   **44.** $.846 _____   **45.** $.0015 _____

46. $.008 _____   **47.** $1.5002 _____   **48.** $7.6009 _____

49. $1.995 _____   **50.** $28.994 _____   **51.** $752.798 _____

Round each of the dollar amounts to the nearest dollar (nearest whole number).

QUICK START

52. $8.58 $9   **53.** $26.49 $26   **54.** $.57 _____

55. $.49 _____   **56.** $299.76 _____   **57.** $12,836.38 _____

58. $268.72 _____   **59.** $395.18 _____   **60.** $666.66 _____

61. $4699.62 _____   **62.** $11,285.13 _____   **63.** $378.59 _____

64. $233.86 _____   **65.** $722.38 _____   **66.** $8263.47 _____

67. Explain what happens when you round $.499 to the nearest dollar. (*See Objective 2.*)

68. Review Exercise 67. How else could you round $.499 to obtain a result that is more helpful? What kind of guideline does this suggest about rounding to the nearest dollar?

--- QUICK CHECK ANSWERS ---

1. (a) sixty-eight thousandths, (b) four thousand, three hundred seventy and fifteen hundredths

2. 72.848

3. (a) 518.446
(b) 518.45
(c) 518.4

1.4 Addition and Subtraction of Decimals

OBJECTIVES

1 Add decimals.

2 Estimate answers.

3 Subtract decimals.

case IN point ▶

As manager of a SUBWAY, Jessica Fernandez is responsible for making bank deposits to the company checking account. These banking activities require the ability to accurately add and subtract decimal numbers.

OBJECTIVE 1 Add decimals. To add, write the numbers so that the decimal points are aligned, which causes the place values to be aligned. As with adding whole numbers, add decimal numbers in columns, beginning on the right and moving to the left.

You may wish to add **trailing zeros** to the right of the decimal point so that each number being added has the same number of digits to the right of the decimal point. This does not change the number and can make it easier to keep track of things.

$$45.93 = 45.930 = 45.9300$$

two trailing zeros added
one trailing zero added

Adding Decimal Numbers   **EXAMPLE 1**

Add $45.93 + 14.017 + 96.5432$.

SOLUTION

First, align place values by lining up the decimal points.

decimals aligned

$$
\begin{array}{r}
45.93 \\
14.017 \\
96.5432
\end{array}
$$

Although not required, you can add trailing zeros if you wish so that each number has the same number of digits to the right of the decimal point. Then, add from right to left.

trailing zeros added

$$
\begin{array}{r}
45.9300 \\
14.0170 \\
96.5432 \\
\hline
156.4902
\end{array}
$$

QUICK CHECK 1

Add 3.8, 14.604, 5.76, and 27.152.

OBJECTIVE 2 Estimate answers. Check that the numbers in Example 1 were correctly added by estimating the answer. Apply front-end rounding to the numbers as follows.

Problem		Estimate
45.93	$\longrightarrow$	50
14.017	$\longrightarrow$	10
$+\ 96.5432$	$\longrightarrow$	$+\ 100$
156.4902		160

The answer is relatively close to the actual value found of 156.4902 providing confidence that the original decimal numbers were added correctly.

Another option is to round each of the numbers to the nearest whole number and then compare as follows.

Problem		Estimate
45.93	⟶	46
14.017	⟶	14
+ 96.5432	⟶	+ 97
156.4902		157

The sum of 156.4902 is very close to the estimate of 157, so it appears the addition was done correctly.

Adding Dollars and Cents  **EXAMPLE 2**

During a recent week, a manager made the following bank deposits to a business account: $1783.38, $4341.15, $2175.94, $896.23, and $2562.53. Use front-end rounding to estimate the total deposits and then find the total deposits.

SOLUTION

Estimate		Problem
$ 2000	⟵	$ 1783.38
4000	⟵	4341.15
2000	⟵	2175.94
900	⟵	896.23
+ 3000	⟵	+ 2562.53
$11,900		$11,759.23

The total deposits for the week were $11,759.23, which is close to our estimate.

QUICK CHECK 2

The following bills were paid last week; $1268.72, $228.35, $2336.19, $176.68, and $1560.75. Use front-end rounding to estimate the total amount of the bills paid, and then find the total bills paid.

OBJECTIVE 3 Subtract decimals. Subtraction is done in much the same way as addition. Line up the decimal points and place as many zeros after each decimal as needed. For example, subtract 17.432 from 21.76 as follows.

21.76**0**   Place one trailing zero after the top decimal.
− 17.432
4.328

Estimating and Then Subtracting Decimals **EXAMPLE 3**

First estimate using front-end rounding and then subtract.

(a)   11.7
    − 4.923

(b)   39.428
    − 27.98

SOLUTION

Attach zeros as needed and then subtract.

(a) Estimate | Problem
10 ⟵ 11.700
− 5 ⟵ − 4.923
5 | 6.777

(b) Estimate | Problem
40 ⟵ 39.428
− 30 ⟵ − 27.980
10 | 11.448

QUICK CHECK 3

First estimate using front-end rounding, and then subtract 5.32 from 26.952.

1.4 Exercises

MyMathLab Math XL PRACTICE WATCH DOWNLOAD READ

The **QUICK START** *exercises in each section contain solutions to help you get started.*

First use front-end rounding to estimate and then add the following decimals. (See Examples 1 and 2.)

QUICK START

1. Estimate	Problem	2. Estimate	Problem	3. Estimate	Problem
40 ←	43.36	600 ←	623.15		6.23
20 ←	15.8	700 ←	734.29		3.6
+ 9 ←	+ 9.3	+ 700 ←	+ 686.26		5.1
69	68.46	2000	2043.70		7.2
					+ 1.69

4. Estimate	Problem	5. Estimate	Problem	6. Estimate	Problem
	12.79		2156.38		1889.76
	2.15		5.26		21.42
	16.28		2.791		19.35
	4.39	+	6.983	+	8.1
	+ 7.61				

7. Estimate	Problem	8. Estimate	Problem	9. Estimate	Problem
	6133.78		743.1		1798.419
	506.124		3817.65		68.32
	18.63		2.908		512.807
+	7.527		4123.76		643.9
		+	21.98	+	428.

Place each of the following numbers in a column and then add. (See Example 1.)

QUICK START

10. 45.631 + 15.8 + 7.234 + 19.63 = **88.295**

11. 12.15 + 6.83 + 61.75 + 19.218 + 73.325 = **173.273**

12. 197.4 + 83.72 + 17.43 + 25.63 + 1.4 =

13. 27.653 + 18.7142 + 9.7496 + 3.21 =

14. 73.618 + 19.18 + 371.82 + 355.125 =

15. It is a good idea to estimate an answer before actually solving a problem. Why is this true? (See Objective 2.)

16. Explain why placing zeros after any digits to the right of the decimal point does not change the value of a number. (See Objective 1.)

Solve the following application problems.

 17. SUBWAY SALES Sales for each day of the week at the SUBWAY managed by Jessica Fernandez were $1815.79, $2367.34, $1976.22, $2155.81, $1698.14, $2885.26, and $2239.63. Find the total weekly sales.

17. _____

 indicates an exercise that is related to the Case in Point feature.

18. RESTAURANT TIPS   Becky Waterton wants to know what her total tips were for the three days she worked as a waitress at a Spanish tapas restaurant. Her tips for Thursday, Friday, and Saturday were $85.25, $114.60, and $129.40. Find the total.

18. _____

19. BEEF/TURKEY COST   The average cost of T-bone steak is $6.71 per pound, while the average cost of turkey is $1.39 per pound. How much more per pound is the price of T-bone steak than turkey? (*Source:* U.S. Bureau of the Census.)

19. _____

20. CHILD DAY CARE   The number of hours spent in day care by an infant averages 30.5 hours a week, while the number of hours spent in day care by four-year-olds averages 27.75 hours a week. How much more time is spent in day care each week by infants than by four-year-olds?

20. _____

First use front-end rounding to estimate the answer and then subtract. (See Example 3.)

QUICK START

21. Estimate	Problem	22. Estimate	Problem	23. Estimate	Problem
20	19.74	40	35.86		51.215
− 7	− 6.58	− 8	− 7.91		− 19.708
13	**13.16**	**32**	**27.95**		

24. Estimate	Problem	25. Estimate	Problem	26. Estimate	Problem
	27.613		325.053		3974.61
	− 18.942		− 85.019		− 892.59

27. Estimate	Problem	28. Estimate	Problem	29. Estimate	Problem
	7.8		27.8		5
	− 2.952		− 13.582		− 1.9802

⚠ CHECKING-ACCOUNT RECORDS   *Jessica Fernandez, manager of SUBWAY, had a bank balance of $5382.12 on March 1. During March, she deposited $60,375.82 received from sales, $3280.18 received as credits from suppliers, and $75.53 as a county tax refund. She paid out $27,282.75 to suppliers, $4280.83 for rent and utilities, and $12,252.23 for salaries and miscellaneous. Find each of the following.*

QUICK START

30. How much did Fernandez deposit in March?

$60,375.82 (sales) + $3280.18 (credits) + $75.53 (refund) = $63,731.53

30. $63,731.53 _____

31. How much did she pay out?

31. _____

32. What was her final balance at the end of March?

32. _____

1.5 Multiplication and Division of Decimals

case IN point

OBJECTIVES

1 Multiply decimals.
2 Divide a decimal by a whole number.
3 Divide a decimal by a decimal.

Managing a business requires the ability to multiply and divide decimal numbers. The manager at SUBWAY applies these skills in many ways to find payroll, purchasing, and sales.

OBJECTIVE 1 **Multiply decimals.** Decimals are multiplied as if they were whole numbers. It is not necessary to line up the decimal points. The decimal point in the answer is then found using the following steps.

Positioning the Decimal Point

Step 1   Count the total number of digits to the *right* of the decimal point in each of the numbers being multiplied.

Step 2   In the answer, count from *right to left* the number of places found in step 1 and write the decimal point. It may be necessary to attach zeros to the left of the answer in order to correctly place the decimal point.

Multiplying Decimals  **EXAMPLE 1**   Multiply each of the following.

(a) 8.34×4.2 (b) $.032 \times .07$

SOLUTION

(a) First multiply the given numbers as if they were whole numbers.

$$
\begin{array}{r}
8.34 \quad \longleftarrow \text{2 decimal places} \\
\times \quad 4.2 \quad \longleftarrow \text{1 decimal place} \\
\hline
1668 \\
3336 \quad\quad \\
\hline
35.028 \quad \longleftarrow \text{3 decimal places in answer}
\end{array}
$$

There are two decimal places in 8.34 and one in 4.2. This means that there are $2 + 1 = 3$ decimal places in the final answer. Find the final answer by starting at the right and counting three places to the left:

35.028   3 places to the left

(b) Here, it is necessary to attach zeros at the left in the answer:

$$
\begin{array}{r}
.032 \quad \longleftarrow \text{3 decimal places} \\
\times \quad .07 \quad \longleftarrow \text{2 decimal places} \\
\hline
.00224 \quad \longleftarrow \text{5 decimal places in answer}
\end{array}
$$

⬑ Attach 2 zeros.

QUICK CHECK 1

Multiply each of the following

(a) 6.7×4.32 (b) $.086 \times .05$

The next example uses the formula for the gross pay or pay before deductions.

Gross pay = Number of hours worked × Pay per hour

Multiplying Two Decimal Numbers   **EXAMPLE 2**

Find the gross pay of a SUBWAY employee working 31.5 hours at a rate of $8.65 per hour.

SOLUTION

Find gross pay by multiplying the number of hours worked by the pay per hour.

$$
\begin{array}{r}
31.5 \quad \longleftarrow \text{1 place} \\
\times\ 8.65 \quad \longleftarrow \text{2 places} \\
\hline
1575 \\
1890\ \\
2520\ \ \\
\hline
272.475 \quad \longleftarrow \text{3 places in answer}
\end{array}
$$

This worker's gross pay, rounded to the nearest cent, is $272.48.

QUICK CHECK 2

A college student earns $9.28 per hour. How much is earned for 26.5 hours of work?

Applying Decimal Multiplication   **EXAMPLE 3**

Assume the cost of each 30-second television ad at the 2011 Super Bowl game was $2.7 million. If there were 60 advertising spots of 30 seconds during the game, find the total amount charged for advertising.

SOLUTION

Find the total amount charged for advertising during the 2011 Super Bowl by multiplying the number of 30-second advertising spots during the game by the charge for each advertisement.

$$
\begin{array}{r}
2.7 \quad \longleftarrow \text{1 place} \\
\times\ 60 \quad \longleftarrow \text{0 places} \\
\hline
00\ \\
162\ \ \\
\hline
162.0 \quad \longleftarrow \text{1 place}
\end{array}
$$

The total amount charged for advertising was $162 million ($162,000,000).

QUICK CHECK 3

Find the total amount charged for Super Bowl ads in 2011 if two advertisers canceled, resulting in fifty-eight 30-second ads.

OBJECTIVE 2 Divide a decimal by a whole number. Divide the decimal 21.93 by the whole number 3 by first writing the division problem as usual. Place the decimal point in the quotient directly above the decimal point in the dividend and perform the division.

Place a decimal point directly above dividend's decimal point.

$$
\begin{array}{r}
7.31 \\
3\overline{)21.93}
\end{array}
$$

Check by multiplying the divisor and the quotient. The answer should equal the dividend.

$$
\begin{array}{r}
7.31 \\
\times\quad 3 \\
\hline
21.93 \quad \longleftarrow \text{matches dividend}
\end{array}
$$

Sometimes it is necessary to place zeros after the decimal point in the dividend. Do this if a remainder of 0 is not obtained. Attaching zeros *does not change* the value of the dividend. For example, divide 1.5 by 8 by dividing and placing zeros as needed.

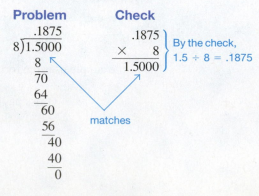

Problem

$$
\begin{array}{r}
.1875 \\
8\overline{)1.5000} \\
8\ \ \\
\hline
70 \\
64 \\
\hline
60 \\
56 \\
\hline
40 \\
40 \\
\hline
0
\end{array}
$$

matches

Check

$$
\begin{array}{r}
.1875 \\
\times\quad\ 8 \\
\hline
1.5000
\end{array}
$$

By the check, $1.5 \div 8 = .1875$

Sometimes, a remainder of 0 is never obtained when dividing. For example, dividing 4.7 by 3 results in repeating 6s that continue without end, as you can see from the following division. Continue the division to one decimal place more than needed so that you can round to the desired place. In this case, the division is carried out to the nearest ten thousandth so that the final answer can be rounded to the nearest thousandth.

$$
\begin{array}{r}
1.5666 \\
3\overline{)4.7000} \\
\underline{3} \\
17 \\
\underline{15} \\
20 \\
\underline{18} \\
20 \\
\underline{18} \\
20 \\
\underline{18} \\
2 \\
\end{array}
$$

The number 1.5666 rounded to the nearest thousandth is 1.567.

Dividing a Decimal by a Whole Number **EXAMPLE 4**

Divide the following; then check using multiplication.

(a) 27.52 ÷ 32   **(b)** 153.4 ÷ 8

Quick TIP ▼

Carry the division one place further than the position to which you wish to round.

SOLUTION

Problem	Check
.86	.86
(a) 32$\overline{)27.52}$	× 32
25 6	172
1 92	258
1 92	**27.52**
0	

Problem	Check
19.175	19.175
(b) 8$\overline{)153.400}$	× 8
8	**153.400**
73	
72	
1 4	
8	
60	
56	
40	
40	
0	

QUICK CHECK 4

Divide the following; then check using multiplication.

(a) 15$\overline{)823.26}$ **(b)** 78.562 ÷ 4

OBJECTIVE 3 Divide a decimal by a decimal. To divide by a decimal, first convert the divisor to a whole number. For example, to divide 27.69 by .3, convert .3 to a whole number by moving the decimal one place to the right. Then move the decimal point in the dividend, 27.69, one place to the right so that the value of the problem does not change. You may need to attach one or more trailing zeros to do this.

$$.3\overline{)27.6.9}$$

First, convert the decimal to a whole number.

Then move the decimal point in the dividend the same number of places to the right as done in the divisor.

Then divide as follows:

$$
\begin{array}{r}
92.3 \\
3\overline{)276.9} \\
\underline{27} \\
06 \\
\underline{6} \\
0\,9 \\
\underline{9} \\
0 \\
\end{array}
$$

Dividing a Decimal by a Decimal   **EXAMPLE 5**

Divide and check the answers.

(a) 17.6 ÷ .25   (b) 5 ÷ .42

SOLUTION

	Check		Check

(a)
```
       70.4
 .25,)17.60,0
      17 5
         10
          0
        100
        100
          0
```

Check
```
    70.4
  ×  .25
   3520
   1408
  17.600
```

(b)
```
        11.9047
 .42,)5.00,0000
      42
       80
       42
       38 0
       37 8
         200
         168
         320
         294
          26
```

Rounding the answer to the nearest thousandth gives 11.905.

Check
```
   11.905
  ×   .42
   23810
   47620
  5.00010
```

(The check is off a little due to rounding.)

> **Quick TIP** ▼
>
> For an answer that has been rounded, the check answer will not be exactly equal to the original dividend.

QUICK CHECK 5

Divide; then check using multiplication.

(a) 22.5 ÷ .8   (b) 8.6 ÷ .32

1.5 Exercises

The **QUICK START** *exercises in each section contain solutions to help you get started.*

First estimate using front-end rounding and then multiply. (See Example 1.)

QUICK START

1.	Estimate	Problem	2.	Estimate	Problem
	100 ←	96.8		20 ←	16.6
	× 4 ←	× 4.2		× 4 ←	× 4.2
	400	406.56		80	69.72

3. Estimate	Problem	4. Estimate	Problem
	34.1		70.35
	× 6.8		× 8.06

5. Estimate	Problem	6. Estimate	Problem
	43.8		69.3
	× 2.04		× 2.81

Multiply the following decimals.

QUICK START

7. .532	8. .259	9. 21.7
× 3.6	× 6.2	× .431
.532 ← 3 decimals	.259 ← 3 decimals	
× 3.6 ← 1 decimal	× 6.2 ← 1 decimal	
1.9152 ← 4 decimals	1.6058 ← 4 decimals	

10. 76.9	11. .0408	12. 2481.9
× .903	× .06	× .003

CALCULATING GROSS EARNINGS *Find the gross pay for each employee at the given rate. Round to the nearest cent. (See Examples 2 and 3.)*

QUICK START

13. 18.5 hours at $8.25 per hour

    18.5 × $8.25 = $152.63

13. $152.63 _____

14. 36.6 hours at $9.85 per hour

14. _____

15. 27.9 hours at $11.42 per hour, and 6.8 hours at $14.63 per hour

15. _____

16. 11.4 hours at $8.59 per hour, and 23.9 hours at $10.06 per hour

16. _____

△ indicates an exercise that is related to the Case in Point feature.

Divide the following, and round your answer to the nearest thousandth. (See Examples 4 and 5.)

17. 6)‾48.45

18. 5)‾62.38

19. 411.63 ÷ 15

20. 2.43)‾9.6153

21. .65)‾37.6852

22. 15.62 ÷ .28

23. In your own words, write the rule for placing the decimal point in the answer of a decimal multiplication problem. (See Objective 1.)

24. Describe what must be done with the decimal point in a decimal division problem. Include the divisor, dividend, and quotient in your description. (See Objectives 2 and 3.)

Solve the following application problems:

QUICK START

25. **REAL ESTATE FEES** Robert Gonzalez recently sold his home for $246,500. He paid a commission of .06 times the price of the house. What was the amount of the commission?

$246,500 × .06 = $14,790

25. $14,790

26. **CROWN MOLDING** Mazie Chauvin bought 9.5 yards of crown molding to complete her bathroom remodeling. If she paid $5.68 per yard for the trim, what was her total cost?

26. _____

27. **HYBRID TOYOTA** To reduce his driving costs as a salesperson, Bill Chen bought a Toyota Prius. One week, he drove 519 miles in and around the city and used 10.2 gallons of gasoline. Find the miles per gallon to the nearest tenth.

27. _____

28. **MANAGERIAL EARNINGS** A SUBWAY assistant manager earns $2528 each month for working a 48-hour week. Find **(a)** the number of hours worked each month and **(b)** the assistant manager's hourly earnings (1 month = 4.3 weeks). Round to the nearest cent.

(a) _____

(b) _____

29. **BIG RIMS AND TIRES** Henry Barnes has a loan balance of $2872.26 on the new 23-inch rims and tires he bought for his SUV. If his payments are $106.38 per month, how many months will it take to pay off the balance? (*Source:* Less Schwab Tire.)

29. _____

30. **MEDICINE DOSE** Each dose of a medication contains 1.62 milligrams of a certain ingredient. Find the number of doses that can be made from 57.13 milligrams of the ingredient. Round to the nearest whole number.

30. _____

31. U.S. PAPER MONEY   The thickness of a $100 bill is .0043 inch.

    (a) If you had a pile of 100 bills, how high would it be?

    (b) How high would a pile of 1000 bills be?

(a) _____

(b) _____

32. (a) Use the information from Exercise 31 to find the number of $100 bills in a pile that is 43 inches high.

    (b) How much money would you have if the pile was all $20 bills, which have the same thickness as a $100 bill?

(a) _____

(b) _____

Use the information from the Look Smart online catalog to answer Exercises 33–36.

43-2A 43-2B 43-3A 43-3B

KNIT SHIRT ORDERING INFORMATION	
43–2A Short sleeve, solid colors	$14.75 each
43–2B Short sleeve, stripes	$16.75 each
43–3A Long sleeve, solid colors	$18.95 each
43–3B Long sleeve, stripes	$21.95 each

XXL size, add $2 per shirt.

Monogram, $4.95 each. Gift box, $5 each.

TOTAL PRICE OF ALL ITEMS (EXCLUDING MONOGRAMS AND GIFT BOXES)	SHIPPING, PACKING, AND HANDLING
$0–25.00	$3.50
$25.01–75.00	$5.95
$75.01–125.00	$7.95
$125.01+	$9.95

Shipping to each additional address add $4.25.

33. Find the total cost of ordering four long-sleeve, solid-color shirts and two short-sleeve, striped shirts, all size XXL and all shipped to your home.

33. _____

34. What is the total cost of eight long-sleeve shirts, five in solid colors and three striped? Include the cost of shipping the solid shirts to your home and the striped shirts to your brother's home.

34. _____

35. (a) What is the total cost, including shipping, of sending three short-sleeve, solid-color shirts, with monograms, in a gift box to your aunt for her birthday?

    (b) How much did the monogram, gift box, and shipping add to the cost of your gift?

(a) _____

(b) _____

36. (a) Suppose you order one of each type of shirt for yourself, adding a monogram on each of the solid-color shirts. At the same time, you order three long-sleeve, striped, size-XXL shirts to be shipped to your father in a gift box. Find the total cost of your order.

    (b) What is the difference in total cost (excluding shipping) between the shirts for yourself and the gift for your father?

(a) _____

(b) _____

QUICK CHECK ANSWERS

1. (a) 28.944   **(b)** .0043

2. $245.92

3. $156.6 million or $156,600,000

4. (a) 54.884   **(b)** 19.6405

5. (a) 28.125   **(b)** 26.875

Chapter 1 | Quick Review

Chapter Terms *Review the following terms to test your understanding of the chapter. For each term you do not know, refer to the page number found next to that term.*

addends [p. 4]
addition [p. 4]
amount [p. 4]
borrowing [p. 5]
comma [p. 2]
decimal number [p. 23]
decimal part [p. 23]
decimal point [p. 2]
decimal system [p. 2]

difference [p. 5]
digits [p. 2]
dividend [p. 7]
dividing decimals [p. 32]
division [p. 4]
divisor [p. 7]
front-end rounding [p. 4]
indicator words [p. 17]
minuend [p. 5]

multiplicand [p. 6]
multiplication [p. 6]
multiplier [p. 6]
multiplying decimals [p. 31]
operations [p. 4]
partial products [p. 6]
product [p. 6]
quotient [p. 7]
rounding [p. 3]

rounding decimals [p. 4]
rounding whole numbers [p. 3]
subtraction [p. 4]
subtrahend [p. 5]
sum [p. 4]
total [p. 4]
trailing zeros [p. 27]
whole numbers [p. 2]

CONCEPTS

1.1 Reading and writing whole numbers

The word *and* is not used. Commas help divide thousands, millions, and billions. A comma is not needed with a four-digit number.

1.1 Rounding whole numbers

Rules for rounding:

1. Identify the position to be rounded. Draw a line under that place.
2. If the digit to the right of the underlined place is 5 or more, increase by 1. If the digit is 4 or less, do not change.
3. Change all digits to the right of the underlined digit to zero.

1.1 Front-end rounding

Front-end rounding leaves only the first digit as a nonzero digit. All other digits are changed to zero.

1.1 Addition of whole numbers

Add from top to bottom, starting with the ones place and working to the left. To check, add from bottom to top.

1.1 Subtraction of whole numbers

Subtract the subtrahend from the minuend to get the difference, borrowing when necessary. To check, add the difference to the subtrahend to get the minuend.

EXAMPLES

Write 795 and 9,650,036 using words.

seven hundred ninety-five
nine million, six hundred fifty thousand, thirty-six

Round:

726 to the nearest ten

5 or more, so add 1 to tens position

tens position

So, 726 rounds to 730.

1,498,586 to the nearest million

4 or less, so do not change

millions position

So, 1,498,586 rounds to 1,000,000.

Round each of the following, using front-end rounding.

76 rounds to 80
348 rounds to 300
6512 rounds to 7000
23,751 rounds to 20,000
652,179 rounds to 700,000

$$
\begin{array}{r}
\mathbf{1140} \\
687 \\
\text{Problem} \quad 26 \quad \text{Check} \\
\text{(add down)} \quad 9 \quad \text{(add up)} \\
+\,418 \\
\hline
\mathbf{1140}
\end{array}
$$

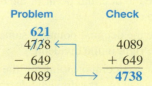

Problem   Check

621
4738   4089
− 649   + 649
4089   4738

CONCEPTS	**EXAMPLES**

1.1 Multiplication of whole numbers

The multiplicand is multiplied by the multiplier, giving the product. When the multiplier has more than one digit, partial products must be used and then added.

$$
\begin{array}{r}
78 \\
\times\ 24 \\
\hline
312 \\
156 \\
\hline
1872
\end{array}
$$

78   multiplicand
× 24   multiplier
312   partial product
156   partial product (one position left)
1872   product

1.1 Division of whole numbers

÷ and $\overline{)}$ mean divide.

A —, as in $\frac{25}{5}$, means divide 25 by 5.

Also, the /, as in 25/5, means to divide 25 by 5.

Remainders are usually expressed as decimals.

$$
\begin{array}{r}
44 \\
2\overline{)88} \\
88 \\
\hline
0
\end{array}
$$

44   quotient
divisor 2)88   dividend

If answer is rounded, the check will not be perfect.

1.2 Application problems

Follow these steps.

1. Read the problem carefully.
2. Work out a plan using *indicator words* before starting.
3. Estimate a reasonable answer.
4. Solve the problem. If the answer is reasonable, check. If it is not, start over.

Shauna Gallegos earns $118 on Sunday, $87 on Monday, and $63 on Tuesday. Find her total earnings for the three days. Total means to add. An estimate using front-end rounding is $100 + $90 + $60 is $250.

$$
\begin{array}{r}
\$268 \quad \text{Check}\\
\$118 \\
\$\ 87 \\
+\ \$\ 63 \\
\hline
\$268 \quad \text{total earnings are reasonable}
\end{array}
$$

1.3 Reading and rounding decimals

1.3 is read as "one and three tenths."

Round .073265 to the nearest ten-thousandth.

.0732|65

↑ ten-thousandth position

Since the digit to the right is 6, increase the ten-thousandths digit by 1 and drop all digits to the right. So, .073265 rounds to .0733.

1.4 Addition and subtraction of decimals

Decimal points must be in a column. Attach zeros to keep digits in their correct columns.

Add: 5.68 + 785.3 + .007 + 10.1062
Line up the decimal points and add from right to left.

$$
\begin{array}{r}
5.6800 \leftarrow \\
785.3000 \leftarrow \text{Attach zeros.}\\
.0070 \leftarrow \\
+\ 10.1062 \\
\hline
801.0932
\end{array}
$$

1.5 Multiplication of decimals

Multiply as if decimals are whole numbers. Place the decimal point as follows.

1. Count digits to the right of decimal points.
2. Count from right to left the same number of places as in step 1. Zeros must be attached on the left if necessary.

Multiply: .169 × .21

$$
\begin{array}{r}
.169 \quad \text{3 decimal places}\\
\times\ .21 \quad \text{2 decimal places}\\
\hline
169 \\
338 \\
\hline
.03549 \quad \text{5 decimal places in answer}
\end{array}
$$

Attach one zero.

1.5 Division of decimals

1. Move the decimal point in the divisor all the way to the right.
2. Move the decimal point the same number of places to the right in the dividend.
3. Place a decimal point in the answer position directly above the dividend decimal point.
4. Divide as with whole numbers.

Divide 52.8 by .75

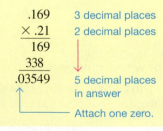

Check

$$
\begin{array}{r}
70.4 \\
\times\ .75 \\
\hline
3520 \\
4928 \\
\hline
52.800
\end{array}
$$

case study

THE TOLL OF WEDDING BELLS

The Wedding Report recently released statistics showing the average wedding costs in the United States in 2010. In 2005, the cost of the average wedding was $24,168. This cost has increased as the average number of wedding guests has grown to over 200. The graph gives most of the costs involved in a wedding. Use this information to answer the questions that follow.

With over 200 guests, the cost of an average wedding has continued to grow. Most of the money is spent on the following:

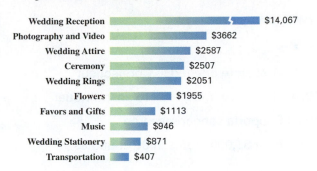

Wedding Reception	$14,067
Photography and Video	$3662
Wedding Attire	$2587
Ceremony	$2507
Wedding Rings	$2051
Flowers	$1955
Favors and Gifts	$1113
Music	$946
Wedding Stationery	$871
Transportation	$407

DATA: The Wedding Report, Shane McMurray

1. What is the total of the costs shown in the graph?

    1. _____

2. How much more expensive was a wedding in 2010 compared with 2005?

    2. _____

3. If you budget $6000 for the wedding reception and the cost per person is $37, how many guests can you invite and how much of your budgeted amount will be left over?

    3. _____

4. If 150 guests are invited to the wedding and $11,000 is budgeted for the reception, find the amount that can be spent per person. Round to the nearest cent.

    4. _____

5. The bridal party will need five bouquets that cost $36.25 each and five boutonnieres, each costing $7.50. If a total of $863 is budgeted for flowers, find the amount that remains to be spent for other floral arrangements.

    5. _____

INVESTIGATE

List five expenses associated with a wedding that are not mentioned. List five things that could be changed to bring the cost of the wedding down.

case in point summary exercise

SUBWAY

www.subway.com

Facts:

- 1965: First store opened in Connecticut
- 1974: First store franchised to an individual
- 1995: Supports cancer research
- 2010: Over 31,000 stores in 90 countries

With the help of a family friend, seventeen-year-old Freed DeLuca opened the first SUBWAY store in 1965. DeLuca believed in using only the freshest ingredients and drove many miles each week in his Volkswagen bug to buy fresh produce. Later management decided to "give back" to the community and now supports research related to both heart disease and cancer. The firm differs from many other fast-food firms by offering healthy, fresh foods.

Profit margins are surprisingly small in most businesses, so managers must work very hard to control costs. A primary responsibility of a store manager at SUBWAY is to control costs. Of course, the store manager is also responsible for many issues related to employees, the quality of food and service, and also sales.

1. Jessica Fernandez is the manager of a SUBWAY store. Help her find the total of an invoice with the following costs: produce, $486.12; meat and cheese, $1236.14; bread dough, $364.76; shipping charges, $103.75.

    1. _____

2. One employee worked the following hours during the week: Thursday, 3.5 hours; Friday, 4.5 hours; Saturday, 6 hours; and Sunday, 5.5 hours. He is paid $8.65 per hour. Find the total number of hours worked and the pay for the week rounded to the nearest cent.

    2. _____

3. Fernandez notes that meat and cheese costs went up from $1864.92 last week to $2065.48 this week and attributes it to additional customers. Find the difference between the two. If the average cost of meat and cheese per sub sandwich is $.94, estimate the number of additional customers this week compared to last week, rounded to the nearest whole number.

    3. _____

4. This month, Fernandez plans to spend four times as much on advertising as the $168.32 spent last week. Find the amount spent on advertising. If the increased advertising brings in 1.3 times last week's revenue of $10,984.76, estimate the revenue.

    4. _____

Discussion Question: *If sales increase by $1500 in a week, do you think profit for the week will also increase by about $1500? Why or why not?*

Chapter 1 Test

To help you review, the bracketed numbers indicate the section in which the topic is discussed.

Round as indicated. **[1.1]**

1. 844 to the nearest ten

2. 21,958 to the nearest hundred

3. 671,529 to the nearest thousand

Round each of the following, using front-end rounding. **[1.1]**

4. 50,987

5. 851,004

6. One week, Katie Nopper earned the following commissions: Monday, $124; Tuesday, $88; Wednesday, $62; Thursday, $137; Friday, $195. Find her total amount of commissions for the week. **[1.2]**

7. A rental business buys three airless sprayers at $1540 each, five rototillers at $695 each, and eight 25-foot ladders at $38 each. Find the total cost of the equipment purchased. **[1.2]**

Round as indicated. **[1.3]**

8. $21.0568 to the nearest cent

9. $364.345 to the nearest cent

10. $7246.49 to the nearest dollar

Solve each problem. **[1.4 and 1.5]**

11. $9.6 + 8.42 + 3.715 + 159.8 =$ ____

12.
$$
\begin{array}{r}
2.715 \\
32.78 \\
426.3 \\
+\ 37 \\
\hline
\end{array}
$$

13.
$$
\begin{array}{r}
341.4 \\
-\ 207.8 \\
\hline
\end{array}
$$

14. $3.8 - .0053$

15.
$$
\begin{array}{r}
21.98 \\
\times\ \ .72 \\
\hline
\end{array}
$$

16.
$$
\begin{array}{r}
218.6 \\
\times\ \ .037 \\
\hline
\end{array}
$$

17. $21.8\overline{)252.008}$

18. $57.358 \div 2.41 =$ ____

19. $79.135 \div 18.62 =$ ____

1. _____
2. _____
3. _____
4. _____
5. _____
6. _____
7. _____
8. _____
9. _____
10. _____

20. A manager at SUBWAY wants to find the total cost of 24.8 pounds of sliced turkey at $1.89 a pound and 38.2 pounds of provolone cheese at $2.05 a pound.   **[1.4 and 1.5]**

20. _____

21. Roofing material costs $84.52 per square (10 ft × 10 ft). The roofer charges $55.75 per square for labor, plus $9.65 per square for supplies. Find the total cost for 26.3 squares of installed roof. Round to the nearest cent.   **[1.4 and 1.5]**

21. _____

22. A federal law requires that all residential toilets sold in the United States use no more than 1.6 gallons of water per flush. Prior to this legislation, conventional toilets used 3.4 gallons of water per flush. Find the amount of water saved in one year by a family flushing the toilet 22 times each day (1 year = 365 days).   **[1.4 and 1.5]**

22. _____

23. Steve Hamilton bought 135.5 meters of steel rod at $.86 per meter and 12 meters of brass rod at $2.18 per meter. How much change did he get from eight $20 bills?   **[1.4 and 1.5]**

23. _____

24. The Capital Hills Supermarket in Washington, DC, sells bananas for $1.74 per kilogram (2.2 pounds). Find the price of bananas per pound. Round to the nearest cent. (*Source:* Associated Press.)   **[1.5]**

24. _____

25. A concentrated fertilizer must be applied at the rate of .058 ounce per seedling. Find the number of seedlings that can be fertilized with 14.674 ounces of fertilizer.   **[1.5]**

25. _____

Fractions

2

case IN point

KARA OAKS has been employed at The Home Depot for several years. During this time, she has worked in the hardware and plumbing departments and now manages the cabinetry department. She has been managing this department for a year and a half and enjoys helping contractors and homeowners plan and design new and replacement cabinets for their kitchens and bathrooms. Knowing and using fractions is a key part of Oaks's job. As shown in the Summary Case at the end of the chapter, she must be extremely accurate when determining the specifications for building and installing cabinets.

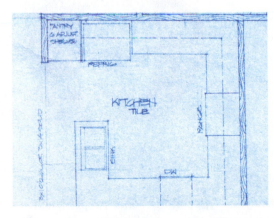

Chapter 1 discussed whole numbers and decimals. This chapter looks at *fractions*—numbers, such as decimals, that can be used to represent parts of a whole. Fractions and decimals are two ways of representing the same quantity. Fractions are used in business and our personal lives.

2.1 Basics of Fractions

OBJECTIVES

1   Recognize types of fractions.

2   Convert mixed numbers to improper fractions.

3   Convert improper fractions to mixed numbers.

4   Write a fraction in lowest terms.

5   Use the rules for divisibility.

case in point ▶

The employees in the cabinetry department at Home Depot must be able to use decimals, fractions, and mixed numbers in order to work with customers. The measurements of cabinets, trim pieces, and room sizes never seem to be an even number of inches—they often involve fractions.

A **fraction** represents part of a whole. Fractions are written in the form of one number over another, with a line between the two numbers, as in the following.

$$\frac{5}{8} \quad \frac{1}{4} \quad \frac{9}{7} \quad \frac{13}{10} \quad \begin{array}{l} \leftarrow \text{numerator} \\ \leftarrow \text{denominator} \end{array}$$

The number above the line is the **numerator**, and the number below the line is the **denominator**. In the fraction $\frac{2}{3}$, the numerator is 2 and the denominator is 3. The denominator is the number of equal parts into which something is divided. The numerator tells how many of these parts are needed. For example, $\frac{2}{3}$ is "2 parts out of 3 equal parts," as shown in the figure.

$\frac{2}{3}$ means 2 parts
out of 3 equal parts

OBJECTIVE 1 Recognize types of fractions. Proper fractions, also called **common fractions**, have numerators that are smaller than their denominators. Proper fractions have a value of less than 1. **Improper fractions** have numerators that are equal to or greater than the denominators. Improper fractions have a value of 1 or more. Here are some examples.

$$\text{Proper fractions:} \quad \frac{1}{2}, \frac{3}{4}, \frac{7}{13}, \frac{91}{100}$$

$$\text{Improper fractions:} \quad \frac{3}{3}, \frac{9}{7}, \frac{125}{4}, \frac{13}{12}$$

To write a whole number as a fraction, place the whole number as the numerator on top of a denominator of 1, as shown here.

$$8 = \frac{8}{1} \qquad 25 = \frac{25}{1} \qquad 4 = \frac{4}{1} \qquad 135 = \frac{135}{1}$$

A **mixed number** is the sum of a whole number and a fraction. So, $5\frac{3}{8}$ is a mixed number that means $5 + \frac{3}{8}$. It is even read as *five and three-eighths* or as the sum of a whole number and a fraction. Here are some other mixed numbers.

$$17\frac{3}{5} \quad \text{seventeen and three-fifths}$$

$$92,407\frac{3}{4} \quad \text{ninety-two thousand, four hundred seven and three-fourths}$$

It is important to realize that the number 0 is never used in the denominator of any fraction, since division by 0 is not defined.

OBJECTIVE 2 Convert mixed numbers to improper fractions. Follow the steps shown to convert a mixed number to an improper fraction.

Converting a Mixed Number to an Improper Fraction

Step 1   Multiply the whole number by the denominator of the fraction.

Step 2   Add the product to the numerator of the fraction to find the new numerator.

Step 3   Keep the same denominator.

Here is an example.

Step 1 Multiply the whole number by the denominator.
Step 2 Add the product to the numerator.

$$4\frac{5}{8} = \frac{(4 \times 8) + 5}{8} = \frac{37}{8}$$

Step 3 Keep the same denominator.

Converting Mixed Numbers to Improper Fractions

EXAMPLE 1

Kara Oaks read the instructions that came with a new microwave oven. She discovered that the opening in the kitchen cabinet needed to be $25\frac{3}{4}$ inches wide by $16\frac{1}{2}$ inches tall in order to install the microwave oven. Convert both of these mixed numbers to improper fractions.

(a) $25\frac{3}{4}$ **(b)** $16\frac{1}{2}$

SOLUTION

(a) Multiply the whole number 25 by the denominator 4 to find 100. Add the product to the numerator of the fraction 3 to find 103. Keep the same denominator of 4.

$$25\frac{3}{4} = \frac{103}{4} \quad (4 \times 25) + 3$$

(b) Follow these same steps using $16\frac{1}{2}$.

$$16\frac{1}{2} = \frac{(2 \times 16) + 1}{2} = \frac{33}{2}$$

QUICK CHECK 1

Convert to improper fractions.

(a) $15\frac{1}{3}$ **(b)** $21\frac{3}{8}$

OBJECTIVE 3 Convert improper fractions to mixed numbers. Use the steps shown here to convert an improper fraction to a mixed number.

Converting an improper fraction to a mixed number

Step 1   Divide the numerator of the fraction by the denominator.

Step 2   The quotient is the whole-number part of the mixed number.

Step 3   The remainder is the numerator of the fraction.

Step 4   Keep the same denominator in the fraction part of the mixed number.

For example, to convert $\frac{17}{5}$ to a mixed number, first divide 17 by 5. The quotient is the whole-number part and the remainder is the numerator of the fraction. Keep the same denominator.

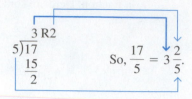

$$\begin{array}{r} 3\text{ R2} \\ 5\overline{)17} \\ \underline{15} \\ 2 \end{array} \qquad \text{So, } \frac{17}{5} = 3\frac{2}{5}.$$

Check the calculation by converting the mixed number $3\frac{2}{5}$ back to an improper fraction.

$$3\frac{2}{5} = \frac{3 \times 5 + 2}{5} = \frac{17}{5}$$

The answer checks, so the fraction $\frac{17}{5}$ equals the mixed number $3\frac{2}{5}$. These are two different ways to write the same number.

Converting Improper Fractions to Mixed Numbers Convert the following improper fractions to mixed numbers.

(a) $\frac{27}{4}$ (b) $\frac{29}{8}$ (c) $\frac{42}{7}$

SOLUTION

(a) Convert $\frac{27}{4}$ to a mixed number by dividing 27 by 4.

$$\begin{array}{r} 6 \\ 4\overline{)27} \\ \underline{24} \\ 3 \end{array} \qquad \frac{27}{4} = 6\frac{3}{4}$$

The whole-number part of the mixed number is 6. The remainder 3 is used as the numerator of the fraction. Keep 4 as the denominator.

$$\frac{27}{4} = 6\frac{3}{4}$$

(b) Divide 29 by 8 to convert $\frac{29}{8}$ to a mixed number.

$$\begin{array}{r} 3 \\ 8\overline{)29} \\ \underline{24} \\ 5 \end{array} \qquad \frac{29}{8} = 3\frac{5}{8}$$

(c) Divide 42 by 7 to convert $\frac{42}{7}$ to a mixed number.

$$\begin{array}{r} 6 \\ 7\overline{)42} \\ \underline{42} \\ 0 \end{array} \qquad \frac{42}{7} = 6$$

> **QUICK CHECK 2**
>
> Convert to mixed numbers.
>
> (a) $\frac{73}{4}$ (b) $\frac{32}{5}$

OBJECTIVE 4 Write a fraction in lowest terms. If both the numerator and denominator of a fraction cannot be divided without a remainder by any number other than 1, then the fraction is in **lowest terms**. For example, 2 and 3 cannot be divided without a remainder by any number other than 1, so the fraction $\frac{2}{3}$ is in lowest terms. In the same way, $\frac{1}{9}$, $\frac{4}{11}$, $\frac{12}{17}$, and $\frac{13}{15}$ are in lowest terms.

When both numerator and denominator *can* be divided without a remainder by a number other than 1, the fraction is *not* in lowest terms. For example, both 15 and 25 may be divided by 5, so the fraction $\frac{15}{25}$ is not in lowest terms. Write $\frac{15}{25}$ in lowest terms by dividing both numerator and denominator by 5, as follows.

$$\frac{15}{25} = \frac{15 \div 5}{25 \div 5} = \frac{3}{5} \qquad \text{lowest terms}$$

Divide by 5.

Writing Fractions in Lowest Terms Write the following fractions in lowest terms.

(a) $\dfrac{15}{40}$ (b) $\dfrac{33}{39}$

SOLUTION

Look for a number that can be divided without a remainder into both the numerator and denominator.

(a) Both 15 and 40 can be divided by **5**.

$$\frac{15}{40} = \frac{15 \div \mathbf{5}}{40 \div \mathbf{5}} = \frac{3}{8} \qquad \text{lowest terms}$$

(b) Divide both numbers by 3.

$$\frac{33}{39} = \frac{33 \div \mathbf{3}}{39 \div \mathbf{3}} = \frac{11}{13} \qquad \text{lowest terms}$$

QUICK CHECK 3

Write in lowest terms.

(a) $\dfrac{36}{45}$ (b) $\dfrac{48}{66}$

OBJECTIVE 5 Use the rules for divisibility. It is sometimes difficult to tell which numbers will divide evenly into another number. The following rules can sometimes help.

Rules for Divisibility

A number can be evenly divided by

2   if the last digit is an even number, such as 0, 2, 4, 6, or 8

3   if the sum of the digits is divisible by 3 with no remainder

4   if the last two digits are divisible by 4 with no remainder

5   if the last digit is 0 or 5

6   if the number is even and the sum of the digits is divisible by 3 with no remainder

8   if the last three digits are divisible by 8 with no remainder

9   if the sum of all the digits is divisible by 9 with no remainder

10 if the last digit is 0

Using the Divisibility Rules Determine whether the following statements are true.

(a) 3,746,892 is evenly divisible by 4.

(b) 15,974,802 is evenly divisible by 9.

SOLUTION

(a) The number 3,746,892 is evenly divisible by 4, since the last two digits form a number divisible by 4.

$$3,746,8\underline{\mathbf{92}}$$

92 is divisible by 4.

Quick TIP ▼

Testing for divisibility by adding the digits works only for 3 and 9.

(b) See if 15,974,802 is evenly divisible by 9 by adding the digits of the number.

$$1 + 5 + 9 + 7 + 4 + 8 + 0 + 2 = \mathbf{36}$$

36 is divisible by 9.

Since 36 is divisible by 9, the given number is divisible by 9.

The rules for divisibility help determine only whether a number is evenly divisible by another number. They cannot be used to find the result. The division must actually be done to find the quotient.

QUICK CHECK 4

Determine **(a)** whether 628,375,210 is evenly divisible by 5, and **(b)** whether 825,693,471 is evenly divisible by 3.

2.1 Exercises

  WATCH DOWNLOAD READ

The **QUICK START** *exercises in each section contain solutions to help you get started.*

Convert the following mixed numbers to improper fractions. (See Example 1.)

QUICK START

1. $3\dfrac{5}{8} = \dfrac{29}{8}$

   $\dfrac{(8 \times 3) + 5}{8} = \dfrac{29}{8}$

2. $2\dfrac{4}{5} = \dfrac{14}{5}$

   $\dfrac{(5 \times 2) + 4}{5} = \dfrac{14}{5}$

3. $4\dfrac{1}{4} = $ _____

4. $3\dfrac{2}{3} = $ _____

5. $12\dfrac{2}{3} = $ _____

6. $2\dfrac{8}{11} = $ _____

7. $22\dfrac{7}{8} = $ _____

8. $17\dfrac{5}{8} = $ _____

9. $7\dfrac{6}{7} = $ _____

10. $21\dfrac{14}{15} = $ _____

11. $15\dfrac{19}{23} = $ _____

12. $7\dfrac{9}{16} = $ _____

Convert the following improper fractions to mixed or whole numbers and write in lowest terms.
(See Examples 2 and 3.)

QUICK START

13. $\dfrac{13}{4} = 3\dfrac{1}{4}$

   $\begin{array}{r} 3 \\ 4\overline{)13} \\ 12 \\ \hline 1 \end{array}$ $3\dfrac{1}{4}$

14. $\dfrac{9}{5} = 1\dfrac{4}{5}$

   $\begin{array}{r} 1 \\ 5\overline{)9} \\ 5 \\ \hline 4 \end{array}$ $1\dfrac{4}{5}$

15. $\dfrac{8}{3} = $ _____

16. $\dfrac{23}{10} = $ _____

17. $\dfrac{38}{10} = $ _____

18. $\dfrac{56}{8} = $ _____

19. $\dfrac{40}{11} = $ _____

20. $\dfrac{78}{12} = $ _____

21. $\dfrac{125}{63} = $ _____

22. $\dfrac{195}{45} = $ _____

23. $\dfrac{183}{25} = $ _____

24. $\dfrac{720}{149} = $ _____

25. Your classmate asks you how to change a mixed number to an improper fraction. Write a couple of sentences explaining how this is done. (See Objective 2.)

26. Explain in a sentence or two how to change an improper fraction to a mixed number. (See Objective 3.)

 indicates an exercise that is related to the Case in Point feature.

Write the following in lowest terms. (See Example 3.)

QUICK START

27. $\dfrac{8}{16} = \dfrac{1}{2}$

$\dfrac{8 \div 8}{16 \div 8} = \dfrac{1}{2}$

28. $\dfrac{15}{20} = \dfrac{3}{4}$

$\dfrac{15 \div 5}{20 \div 5} = \dfrac{3}{4}$

29. $\dfrac{25}{40} = $ _____

30. $\dfrac{36}{42} = $ _____

31. $\dfrac{27}{45} = $ _____

32. $\dfrac{112}{128} = $ _____

33. $\dfrac{165}{180} = $ _____

34. $\dfrac{12}{600} = $ _____

UNDERSTANDING GOLD KARATS The fineness (purity) of gold is regulated by law and is the same in all parts of the world. The scale below shows the fineness in 24-karat, 18-karat, 14-karat, and 10-karat gold. Write each fraction in lowest terms. (*Source:* Costco Wholesale.)

QUICK START

35. 24 karat = (24 parts gold, no alloy) $\dfrac{24}{24} = 1$

35. 1 _____

36. 18 karat = (18 parts gold, 6 parts alloy)

36. _____

37. 14 karat = (14 parts gold, 10 parts alloy)

37. _____

38. 10 karat = (10 parts gold, 14 parts alloy)

38. _____

39. What does it mean when a fraction is expressed in lowest terms? (See Objective 4.)

40. Eight rules of divisibility were given. Write the three rules that are most useful to you. (See Objective 5.)

Put a check mark in the blank if the number at the left is evenly divisible by the number at the top. Put an X in the blank if the number is not divisible. (See Example 4.)

QUICK START

	2	3	4	5	6	8	9	10
41. 32	✓	X	✓	X	X	✓	X	X
42. 45	X	✓	X	✓	X	X	✓	X
43. 60	–	–	–	–	–	–	–	–
44. 72	–	–	–	–	–	–	–	–
45. 90	–	–	–	–	–	–	–	–
46. 105	–	–	–	–	–	–	–	–
47. 4172	–	–	–	–	–	–	–	–
48. 5688	–	–	–	–	–	–	–	–

QUICK CHECK ANSWERS

1. (a) $\dfrac{46}{3}$ (b) $\dfrac{171}{8}$
2. (a) $18\frac{1}{4}$ (b) $6\frac{2}{5}$
3. (a) $\frac{4}{5}$ (b) $\frac{8}{11}$

4. (a) 628,375,210 is evenly divisible by 5
   (b) 825,693,471 is evenly divisible by 3

2.2 Addition and Subtraction of Fractions

OBJECTIVES

1 Add and subtract like fractions.

2 Find the least common denominator.

3 Add and subtract unlike fractions.

4 Rewrite fractions with a common denominator.

OBJECTIVE 1 Add and subtract like fractions. Fractions with the same denominator are called **like fractions**. Such fractions have a **common denominator**. For example, $\frac{3}{4}$ and $\frac{5}{4}$ are *like* fractions with a common denominator of 4, while $\frac{4}{7}$ and $\frac{4}{9}$ are *not like* fractions. Add or subtract like fractions by adding or subtracting the numerators, and then place the result over the common denominator.

Adding and Subtracting Like Fractions Add or subtract.

(a) $\dfrac{3}{4} + \dfrac{1}{4} + \dfrac{5}{4}$ (b) $\dfrac{11}{15} - \dfrac{4}{15}$

SOLUTION

The fractions in both parts of this example are like fractions. Add or subtract the numerators and place the result over the common denominator.

(a) $\dfrac{3}{4} + \dfrac{1}{4} + \dfrac{5}{4} = \dfrac{3 + 1 + 5}{4}$ ⟵ Add the numerators.

                   ⟵ Write the common denominator.

           $= \dfrac{9}{4} = 2\dfrac{1}{4}$ ⟵ Write the answer as a mixed number.

(b) $\dfrac{11}{15} - \dfrac{4}{15} = \dfrac{11 - 4}{15} = \dfrac{7}{15}$

> **Quick TIP ▼**
>
> When adding or subtracting like fractions, keep the same denominator.

> **QUICK CHECK 1**
>
> Add or subtract.
>
> (a) $\dfrac{5}{8} + \dfrac{7}{8} + \dfrac{1}{8}$ (b) $\dfrac{17}{21} - \dfrac{4}{21}$

OBJECTIVE 2 Find the least common denominator. Fractions with different denominators, such as $\frac{3}{4}$ and $\frac{2}{3}$, are **unlike fractions**. Add or subtract unlike fractions by first writing the fractions with a common denominator. The **least common denominator (LCD)** for two or more fractions is the smallest whole number that can be divided, without a remainder, by all the denominators of the fractions. For example, the LCD of the fractions $\frac{3}{4}$, $\frac{5}{6}$, and $\frac{1}{2}$ is 12, since 12 is the smallest number that can be divided evenly by 4, 6, and 2.

Notice that the fractions shown in the shelf-end base drawing below are *like fractions*, $23\frac{3}{16}$, $10\frac{9}{16}$, and $11\frac{3}{16}$. However, in the drawing of the shelf-end peninsula base, the fractions are *unlike fractions*, $22\frac{7}{16}$, $11\frac{3}{32}$, and $11\frac{5}{8}$.

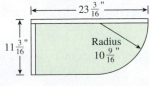 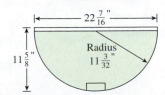

Shelf-End Base: Cross Section

Shelf-End Peninsula Base: Cross Section

There are two methods of finding the least common denominator.

Inspection. With small denominators, it may be possible to find the least common denominator by inspection. For example, the LCD for $\frac{1}{3}$ and $\frac{1}{5}$ is 15, the smallest number that can be divided evenly by both 3 and 5.

Method of prime numbers. If the LCD cannot be found by inspection, use the method of prime numbers, as shown in the next two examples. First, we will define a prime number.

A **prime number** is a number that can be divided without a remainder by exactly two distinct numbers: itself and 1. Prime numbers are 2, 3, 5, 7, 11, 13, 17, and so on. The number 1 is *not* prime because it can be divided evenly by only *one* number: the number 1.

Finding the Least Common Denominator

Use the method of prime numbers to find the least common denominator for $\frac{5}{12}$, $\frac{7}{18}$, and $\frac{11}{20}$.

SOLUTION

First write the three denominators: 12   18   20

Begin by trying to divide the three denominators by the smallest prime number, 2. Write each quotient directly above the given denominator as follows.

$$
\begin{array}{r}
\mathbf{6}\quad \mathbf{9}\quad \mathbf{10} \\
2\overline{)12\quad 18\quad 20}
\end{array}
$$

> **Quick TIP ▼**
>
> It does not matter which prime number you start with; the final list of prime numbers will be the same.

This way of writing the division is just a handy way of writing the separate problems $2\overline{)12}$, $2\overline{)18}$, and $2\overline{)20}$. Two of the new quotients, 6 and 10, can still be divided by 2, so perform the division again. Since 9 cannot be divided evenly by 2, just bring up the 9.

$$
\begin{array}{r}
\mathbf{3}\quad \mathbf{9}\quad \mathbf{5} \qquad \text{Just bring 9 up.}\\
2\overline{)6\quad 9\quad 10} \\
2\overline{)12\quad 18\quad 20}
\end{array}
$$

None of the new quotients in the top row can be divided by 2, so try the next prime number, 3. The numbers 3 and 9 can be divided by 3, and one of the new quotients can still be divided by 3, so the division is performed again.

$$
\begin{array}{r}
\mathbf{1}\quad \mathbf{1}\quad \mathbf{5} \\
3\overline{)1\quad 3\quad 5} \\
3\overline{)3\quad 9\quad 5} \\
2\overline{)6\quad 9\quad 10} \\
2\overline{)12\quad 18\quad 20}
\end{array}
$$

Since none of the new quotients in the top row can be divided by 3, try the next prime number, 5. The number 5 can be used only once, as shown.

$$
\begin{array}{r}
1\quad 1\quad 1 \\
5\overline{)1\quad 1\quad 5} \\
3\overline{)1\quad 3\quad 5} \\
3\overline{)3\quad 9\quad 5} \\
2\overline{)6\quad 9\quad 10} \\
2\overline{)12\quad 18\quad 20}
\end{array}
$$

Now that the top row contains only 1s, find the least common denominator by multiplying the prime numbers in the left column.

The least common denominator is **2 × 2 × 3 × 3 × 5** = 180.

QUICK CHECK 2

Use prime numbers to find the least common denominator for $\frac{3}{5}$, $\frac{5}{6}$, and $\frac{3}{20}$.

Finding the Least Common Denominator

Find the least common denominator for $\frac{3}{8}$, $\frac{5}{12}$, and $\frac{9}{10}$.

SOLUTION

Write the denominators in a row and use the method of prime numbers.

$$
\begin{array}{r}
1\quad 1\quad 1 \\
5\overline{)1\quad 1\quad 5} \\
3\overline{)1\quad 3\quad 5} \\
2\overline{)2\quad 3\quad 5} \\
2\overline{)4\quad 6\quad 5} \\
\text{Start here} \longrightarrow 2\overline{)8\quad 12\quad 10}
\end{array}
$$

The least common denominator is **2 × 2 × 2 × 3 × 5** = 120.

QUICK CHECK 3

Find the least common denominator for $\frac{4}{9}, \frac{5}{24}$, and $\frac{3}{4}$.

OBJECTIVE 3 Add and subtract unlike fractions. Unlike fractions may be added or subtracted using the following steps.

> **Adding or Subtracting Unlike Fractions**
> Step 1   Find the least common denominator (LCD).
> Step 2   Rewrite the unlike fractions as like fractions having the least common denominator.
> Step 3   Add or subtract numerators, placing answers over the LCD and reducing to lowest terms.

To add or subtract unlike fractions, rewrite the fractions with a common denominator. Since Example 2 shows that 180 is the least common denominator for $\frac{5}{12}, \frac{7}{18}$, and $\frac{11}{20}$, these three fractions can be added if each fraction is first written with a denominator of 180.

Step 1 $$\frac{5}{12} = \frac{}{180} \qquad \frac{7}{18} = \frac{}{180} \qquad \frac{11}{20} = \frac{}{180}$$

OBJECTIVE 4 Rewrite fractions with a common denominator. To rewrite the preceding fractions with a common denominator, first divide each denominator from the original fractions into the common denominator.

Step 2 $$12\overline{)180}^{\,15} \qquad 18\overline{)180}^{\,10} \qquad 20\overline{)180}^{\,9}$$

Next multiply each quotient by the original numerator.

$$15 \times 5 = 75 \qquad 10 \times 7 = 70 \qquad 9 \times 11 = 99$$

Now, rewrite the fractions.

$$\frac{5}{12} = \frac{75}{180} \qquad \frac{7}{18} = \frac{70}{180} \qquad \frac{11}{20} = \frac{99}{180}$$

Add the fractions.

Step 3 $$\frac{5}{12} + \frac{7}{18} + \frac{11}{20} = \frac{75}{180} + \frac{70}{180} + \frac{99}{180} = \frac{75 + 70 + 99}{180}$$

$$= \frac{244}{180} = 1\frac{64}{180} = 1\frac{16}{45} \qquad \text{Write the answer as a mixed number with the fraction in lowest terms.}$$

Adding and Subtracting Unlike Fractions   **EXAMPLE 4**

Add or subtract.

(a) $\frac{3}{4} + \frac{1}{2} + \frac{5}{8}$ (b) $\frac{9}{10} - \frac{3}{8}$

SOLUTION

(a) Inspection shows that the least common denominator is 8. Rewrite the fractions so each has a denominator of 8. Then add.

$$\frac{3}{4} + \frac{1}{2} + \frac{5}{8} = \frac{6}{8} + \frac{4}{8} + \frac{5}{8} = \frac{6 + 4 + 5}{8} = \frac{15}{8} = 1\frac{7}{8}$$

(b) The least common denominator is 40. Rewrite the fractions so each has a denominator of 40. Then subtract.

$$\frac{9}{10} - \frac{3}{8} = \frac{36}{40} - \frac{15}{40} = \frac{36 - 15}{40} = \frac{21}{40}$$

Fractions can also be added or subtracted vertically, as shown in the next example.

Adding and Subtracting Unlike Fractions   **EXAMPLE 5**

Add or subtract.

(a) $\dfrac{2}{9} + \dfrac{3}{4}$ (b) $\dfrac{11}{16} + \dfrac{7}{12}$ (c) $\dfrac{7}{8} - \dfrac{5}{12}$

SOLUTION

First rewrite the fractions with a least common denominator.

(a)
$$\begin{aligned}\frac{2}{9} &= \frac{8}{36}\\ +\frac{3}{4} &= \frac{27}{36}\\ \hline &\frac{35}{36}\end{aligned}$$

(b)
$$\begin{aligned}\frac{11}{16} &= \frac{33}{48}\\ +\frac{7}{12} &= \frac{28}{48}\\ \hline &\frac{61}{48} = 1\frac{13}{48}\end{aligned}$$

(c)
$$\begin{aligned}\frac{7}{8} &= \frac{21}{24}\\ -\frac{5}{12} &= \frac{10}{24}\\ \hline &= \frac{11}{24}\end{aligned}$$

All calculator solutions are shown using a basic calculator. The calculator solution to part (b) uses the fraction key on the calculator.

$$11 \; \boxed{a^{b/c}} \; 16 \; \boxed{+} \; 7 \; \boxed{a^{b/c}} \; 12 \; \boxed{=} \; 1\tfrac{13}{48}$$

Note: Refer to Appendix B for calculator basics.

2.2 Exercises

The **QUICK START** *exercises in each section contain solutions to help you get started.*

Convert each fraction so that it has the indicated denominator. (See Objective 3.)

QUICK START

1. $\dfrac{4}{5} = \dfrac{16}{20}$

   $20 \div 5 = 4$
   $4 \times 4 = 16$

2. $\dfrac{3}{4} = \dfrac{12}{16}$

   $16 \div 4 = 4$
   $4 \times 3 = 12$

3. $\dfrac{9}{10} = \dfrac{}{40}$

4. $\dfrac{7}{8} = \dfrac{}{56}$

5. $\dfrac{6}{5} = \dfrac{}{40}$

6. $\dfrac{7}{8} = \dfrac{}{64}$

7. $\dfrac{6}{7} = \dfrac{}{49}$

8. $\dfrac{11}{15} = \dfrac{}{120}$

Find the least common denominator for each group of denominators using the method of prime numbers. (See Example 2.)

QUICK START

9. 3, 8, 24

   ```
       1  1
   3) 3  1
   2) 3  2
   2) 3  4
   2) 3  8
   ```
   $2 \times 2 \times 2 \times 3 = 24$

10. 18, 24, 72

    ```
         1   1
    3)  3   1
    3)  9   3
    2)  9   6
    2)  9  12
    2) 18  24
    ```
    $2 \times 2 \times 2 \times 3 \times 3 = 72$

11. 12, 18, 20, _____

12. 18, 20, 24, _____

13. 15, 24, 32, _____

14. 6, 8, 10, 12, _____

15. 10, 35, 50, 60, _____

16. 5, 18, 25, 30, 36, _____

17. 3, 5, 8, 12, 18, _____

18. Prime numbers are used to find the least common denominator. Write the definition of a prime number in your own words. (See Objective 2.)

19. Explain how to write a fraction with an indicated denominator. Give the example of changing $\frac{3}{4}$ to a fraction having 12 as a denominator. (See Objective 4.)

Add or subtract. Write answers in lowest terms. (See Examples 4 and 5.)

QUICK START

20. $\dfrac{2}{5} + \dfrac{1}{5} = \dfrac{3}{5}$

    $\dfrac{2+1}{5} = \dfrac{3}{5}$

21. $\dfrac{2}{9} + \dfrac{4}{9} = \dfrac{2}{3}$

    $\dfrac{2+4}{9} = \dfrac{6}{9} = \dfrac{2}{3}$

22. $\dfrac{5}{8} + \dfrac{7}{12} =$ _____

23. $\dfrac{11}{12} - \dfrac{5}{12} =$ _____

⚠ indicates an exercise that is related to the Case in Point feature.

24. $\dfrac{5}{7} - \dfrac{1}{3} =$ _____

25. $\dfrac{5}{12} - \dfrac{1}{16} =$ _____

26. $\dfrac{2}{3} - \dfrac{3}{8} =$ _____

27. $\dfrac{3}{4} + \dfrac{5}{9} + \dfrac{1}{3} =$ _____

28. $\dfrac{1}{4} + \dfrac{1}{8} + \dfrac{1}{12} =$ _____

29. $\dfrac{3}{7} + \dfrac{2}{5} + \dfrac{1}{10} =$ _____

30. $\dfrac{5}{6} + \dfrac{3}{4} + \dfrac{5}{8} =$ _____

31. $\dfrac{7}{10} + \dfrac{8}{15} + \dfrac{5}{6} =$ _____

32. $\dfrac{3}{10} + \dfrac{2}{5} + \dfrac{3}{20} =$ _____

33.
$$\begin{array}{r} \dfrac{3}{4} \\[4pt] \dfrac{2}{3} \\[4pt] +\dfrac{8}{9} \\ \hline \end{array}$$

34.
$$\begin{array}{r} \dfrac{7}{12} \\[4pt] \dfrac{5}{8} \\[4pt] +\dfrac{7}{6} \\ \hline \end{array}$$

35.
$$\begin{array}{r} \dfrac{8}{15} \\[4pt] \dfrac{3}{10} \\[4pt] +\dfrac{3}{5} \\ \hline \end{array}$$

36.
$$\begin{array}{r} \dfrac{1}{6} \\[4pt] \dfrac{5}{9} \\[4pt] +\dfrac{13}{18} \\ \hline \end{array}$$

37.
$$\begin{array}{r} \dfrac{7}{10} \\[4pt] -\dfrac{1}{4} \\ \hline \end{array}$$

38.
$$\begin{array}{r} \dfrac{4}{5} \\[4pt] -\dfrac{2}{3} \\ \hline \end{array}$$

39.
$$\begin{array}{r} \dfrac{5}{8} \\[4pt] -\dfrac{1}{3} \\ \hline \end{array}$$

40.
$$\begin{array}{r} \dfrac{19}{24} \\[4pt] -\dfrac{5}{16} \\ \hline \end{array}$$

41. Where are fractions used in everyday life? Think in terms of business applications, hobbies, and personal finance. Give three examples.

42. With the exception of the number 2, all prime numbers are odd numbers. However, not all odd numbers are prime numbers. Explain why these statements are true. (See Objective 2.)

Solve the following application problems.

43. **GARDENING**   Zalia Todd is planting her flower bed and has ordered $\frac{1}{4}$ cubic yard of sand, $\frac{3}{8}$ cubic yard of mulch, and $\frac{1}{3}$ cubic yard of peat moss. Find the total cubic yards that she has ordered.

43. _____

44. **AUTO REPAIR**   Chuck Manly has used his savings to repair his car. He spent $\frac{1}{4}$ of his savings for new tires, $\frac{1}{6}$ of his savings for brakes, $\frac{1}{10}$ of his savings for a tune-up, and $\frac{1}{12}$ of his savings for new belts and hoses. What fraction of his total savings has he spent?

44. _____

45. **COMPUTER ASSEMBLY**   When installing a printer cable to a computer, Ann Kuick must be certain that the proper type and size of mounting hardware are used. Find the total length of the bolt shown.

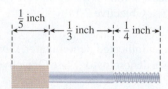

45. _____

46. **CABINET INSTALLATION**   When installing cabinets for The Home Depot, Kara Oaks must be certain that the proper type and size of mounting screw are used. Find the total length of the screw.

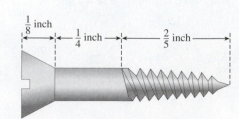

46. _____

47. PETROLEUM TRANSPORT Ken Faulk drives a tanker truck for Chemlake Transport. He leaves the refinery with his tanker filled to $\frac{7}{8}$ of capacity. If he delivers $\frac{1}{4}$ of the tank's contents at the first stop and $\frac{1}{3}$ of the tank's contents at the second stop, find the fraction of the tanker's contents remaining.

47. _____

48. HYDRAULIC SYSTEM The hydraulic system on a fork lift contains $\frac{7}{8}$ gallon of hydraulic fluid. A cracked seal resulted in a loss of $\frac{1}{6}$ gallon of fluid in the morning and another $\frac{1}{3}$ gallon in the afternoon. Find the amount of fluid remaining.

48. _____

49. DEBT REDUCTION Dave Chwalik paid $\frac{1}{8}$ of a debt in January, $\frac{1}{3}$ in February, $\frac{1}{4}$ in March, and $\frac{1}{12}$ in April. What fraction of the debt was paid in these four months?

49. _____

50. NATURAL-FOODS STORE Joan McKee wants to open a natural-foods store and has saved $\frac{2}{5}$ of the amount needed for start-up costs. If she saves another $\frac{1}{8}$ of the amount needed and then $\frac{1}{6}$ more, find the total portion of the start-up costs she has saved.

50. _____

51. CABINET INSTALLATION The mounting bracket shown was purchased at The Home Depot. Find the diameter of the hole which is the distance across it.

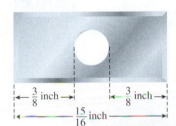

51. _____

52. SPRINT TRAINING Ron Martin competes in 100-meter sprints in high school. At this time of the year, he sprints $\frac{3}{4}$ mile every day. After stretching to warm up, his trainer has Martin sprint $\frac{1}{8}$ mile, $\frac{1}{4}$ mile, and $\frac{1}{4}$ mile. Find the additional distance he must run.

52. _____

STUDENT TIME MANAGEMENT *Refer to the circle graph to answer Exercises 53–56.*

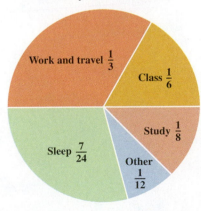

53. What fraction of the day was spent in class and study?

53. _____

54. What fraction of the day was spent in work and travel and other?

54. _____

55. In which activity was the greatest amount of time spent? What fraction of the day was spent on this activity and class time?

55. _____

56. In which activity was the least amount of time spent? What fraction of the day was spent on this activity and study?

56. _____

Use the newspaper advertisement for this four-piece chisel set to answer Exercises 57 and 58. (*Source:* Harbor Freight Tools.)

57. Find the difference in the cutting-edge width of the narrowest chisel and the second to widest chisel. The symbol " is for inches.

57. _____

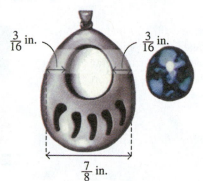

4-Piece Chisel Set   Lot NO. 42429
- sizes: $\frac{1}{4}$ ", $\frac{1}{2}$", $\frac{3}{4}$", and 1"
- Heat-treated, high-carbon steel
- $7\frac{1}{4}$" overall length
- Straight bevel

SALE!
$4⁹⁷   REGULAR PRICE $7.99

58. Find the difference in the cutting-edge width of the two chisels with the narrowest blades. The symbol " is for inches.

58. _____

59. PERIMETER OF FENCING   A hazardous-waste site will require $\frac{7}{8}$ mile of security fencing. The site has four sides, three of which measure $\frac{1}{4}$ mile, $\frac{1}{6}$ mile, and $\frac{3}{8}$ mile. Find the length of the fourth side.

59. _____

60. NATIVE-AMERICAN JEWELRY   Chakotay is fitting a turquoise stone into a bear-claw pendant. Find the diameter of the hole in the pendant. (The diameter is the distance across the center of the hole.)

60. _____

$\frac{3}{16}$ in. $\frac{3}{16}$ in.

$\frac{7}{8}$ in.

2.3 Addition and Subtraction of Mixed Numbers

OBJECTIVES

1 Add mixed numbers.
2 Add with carrying.
3 Subtract mixed numbers.
4 Subtract with borrowing.

Total customer satisfaction is very important to managers at The Home Depot. Some important aspects of quality include:

1. quality products,
2. excellent prices and a wide selection,
3. making sure customers feel comfortable in the store, and
4. accuracy in design and installation.

OBJECTIVE 1 Add mixed numbers. To add mixed numbers, first add the fractions. Then add the whole numbers and combine the two answers. For example, add $16\frac{1}{8}$ and $5\frac{5}{8}$ as shown.

$$\text{First add the fractions: } \frac{1}{8} + \frac{5}{8} = \frac{1+5}{8} = \frac{6}{8} = \frac{3}{4} \quad \textbf{reduced}$$

$$\text{Then add the whole numbers: } 16 + 5 = 21$$

Finally, write the sum of the fraction and whole-number parts as a mixed number.

$$21 + \frac{3}{4} = 21\frac{3}{4}$$

So, $16\frac{1}{8} + 5\frac{5}{8} = 21\frac{3}{4}$.

To add mixed numbers, change the mixed numbers, if necessary, so that the fraction parts have a common denominator.

Adding Mixed Numbers **EXAMPLE 1**

Add $9\frac{2}{3}$ and $6\frac{1}{4}$.

SOLUTION

Inspection shows that 12 is the least common denominator. Write $9\frac{2}{3}$ as $9\frac{8}{12}$, and write $6\frac{1}{4}$ as $6\frac{3}{12}$. Then add. The work can be organized as follows.

$$9\frac{2}{3} = 9\frac{8}{12}$$
$$+6\frac{1}{4} = 6\frac{3}{12}$$
$$\overline{\qquad\quad 15\frac{11}{12}}$$

QUICK CHECK 1

Add $5\frac{3}{4}$ and $8\frac{3}{8}$.

OBJECTIVE 2 Add with carrying. If the sum of the fraction parts of mixed numbers is greater than 1, carry the excess from the fraction part to the whole-number part.

Adding with Carrying **EXAMPLE 2**

A rubber gasket must extend around all four edges (perimeter) of the dishwasher door panel shown on the following page before it is installed. Find the length of gasket material needed. Add $34\frac{1}{2}$ inches, $23\frac{3}{4}$ inches, $34\frac{1}{2}$ inches, and $23\frac{3}{4}$ inches.

case IN point

SOLUTION

Write using the least common denominator and then add.

$$34\frac{1}{2} = 34\frac{2}{4}$$

$$23\frac{3}{4} = 23\frac{3}{4}$$

$$34\frac{1}{2} = 34\frac{2}{4}$$

$$+\ 23\frac{3}{4} = 23\frac{3}{4}$$

$$114\frac{10}{4} = 114 + \frac{10}{4} = 114 + 2\frac{2}{4} = 116\frac{2}{4} = 116\frac{1}{2} \text{ inches}$$ length of gasket needed

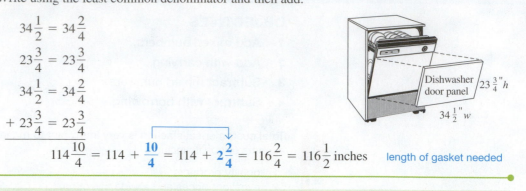

Dishwasher door panel $23\frac{3}{4}"\,h$

$34\frac{1}{2}"\,w$

> **Quick TIP ▼**
>
> To add mixed numbers:
> 1. add fractions,
> 2. add whole numbers, and
> 3. combine the two.

QUICK CHECK 2

The four sides of a vegetable garden are $15\frac{1}{2}$ feet, $18\frac{3}{4}$ feet, $24\frac{1}{4}$ feet, and $30\frac{1}{2}$ feet. How many feet of fencing are needed to go around the garden?

OBJECTIVE 3 Subtract mixed numbers. To subtract two mixed numbers, change the mixed numbers, if necessary, so that the fraction parts have a common denominator. Then subtract the fraction parts and the whole-number parts separately. For example, subtract $3\frac{1}{12}$ from $8\frac{5}{8}$ by first finding that the least common denominator is 24. Then rewrite the problem as shown.

$$8\frac{5}{8} - 3\frac{1}{12}$$

use 24 as a common denominator

$$8\frac{15}{24} - 3\frac{2}{24}$$

$$8\frac{15}{24}$$ First subtract the fraction parts. Then subtract the whole-number parts.

$$-\ 3\frac{2}{24}$$

$$5\frac{13}{24}$$ ← Subtract fractions.

← Subtract whole numbers.

OBJECTIVE 4 Subtract with borrowing. The following example shows how to subtract when borrowing is needed.

Subtracting with Borrowing   **EXAMPLE 3**

(a) Subtract $6\frac{3}{4}$ from $10\frac{1}{8}$.   **(b)** Subtract $15\frac{7}{12}$ from 41.

SOLUTION

Start by rewriting each problem with a common denominator.

(a)
$$10\frac{1}{8} = 10\frac{1}{8}$$
$$-\ 6\frac{3}{4} = 6\frac{6}{8}$$

Subtracting $\frac{6}{8}$ from $\frac{1}{8}$ requires borrowing from the whole number 10.

$$10\frac{1}{8} = 9 + 1 + \frac{1}{8}$$

$$= 9 + \frac{8}{8} + \frac{1}{8} = 9\frac{9}{8} \quad 1 = \frac{8}{8}$$

Rewrite the problem as shown. Check by adding $3\frac{3}{8}$ and $6\frac{3}{4}$. The answer should be $10\frac{1}{8}$.

$$10\frac{1}{8} = 9\frac{9}{8}$$
$$-\ 6\frac{6}{8} = 6\frac{6}{8}$$
$$3\frac{3}{8}$$

(b)
$$41$$
$$-15\frac{7}{12}$$

To subtract the fraction $\frac{7}{12}$ requires borrowing 1 whole unit from 41.

$$41 = 40 + 1 = 40 + \frac{12}{12} = 40\frac{12}{12} \quad 1 = \frac{12}{12}$$

Rewrite the problem as shown. Check by adding $25\frac{5}{12}$ and $15\frac{7}{12}$. The answer should be 41.

$$41\ = 40\frac{12}{12}$$
$$-\ 15\frac{7}{12} = 15\frac{7}{12}$$
$$25\frac{5}{12}$$

> **Quick TIP ▼**
>
> You do not have to write fractions using the least common denominator when adding or subtracting on a calculator.

The calculator solution to part (a) uses the fraction key.

10 $\boxed{a^{b/c}}$ 1 $\boxed{a^{b/c}}$ 8 $\boxed{-}$ 6 $\boxed{a^{b/c}}$ 3 $\boxed{a^{b/c}}$ 4 $\boxed{=}$ $3\frac{3}{8}$

QUICK CHECK 3

Subtract **(a)** $5\frac{2}{3}$ from $12\frac{3}{8}$ and **(b)** $17\frac{5}{9}$ from 73.

2.3 Exercises

The **QUICK START** *exercises in each section contain solutions to help you get started.*

Add. Write each answer in lowest terms. (See Examples 1 and 2.)

QUICK START

1.
$82\frac{3}{5}$ $82\frac{3}{5}$

$+15\frac{1}{5}$ $+15\frac{1}{5}$

$97\frac{4}{5}$ $97\frac{4}{5}$

2.
$25\frac{2}{7}$ $25\frac{2}{7}$

$+14\frac{3}{7}$ $+14\frac{3}{7}$

$39\frac{5}{7}$ $39\frac{5}{7}$

3.
$41\frac{1}{2}$

$+39\frac{1}{4}$

4.
$28\frac{1}{4}$

$23\frac{3}{5}$

$+19\frac{9}{10}$

5.
$46\frac{3}{4}$

$12\frac{5}{8}$

$+37\frac{4}{5}$

6.
$26\frac{5}{8}$

$17\frac{3}{14}$

$+32\frac{2}{7}$

7.
$32\frac{3}{4}$

$6\frac{1}{3}$

$+14\frac{5}{8}$

8.
$16\frac{7}{10}$

$26\frac{1}{5}$

$+\ 8\frac{3}{8}$

9.
$46\frac{5}{8}$

$21\frac{1}{6}$

$+\ 38\frac{1}{10}$

Subtract. Write each answer in lowest terms. (See Example 3.)

QUICK START

10.
$16\frac{3}{4}$ $16\frac{6}{8}$

$-12\frac{3}{8}$ $-12\frac{3}{8}$

$4\frac{3}{8}$ $4\frac{3}{8}$

11.
$25\frac{13}{24}$ $25\frac{13}{24}$

$-18\frac{5}{12}$ $-18\frac{10}{24}$

$7\frac{1}{8}$ $7\frac{3}{24}=7\frac{1}{8}$

12.
$9\frac{7}{8}$

$-6\frac{5}{12}$

13.
374

$-211\frac{5}{6}$

14.
19

$-12\frac{3}{4}$

15.
$71\frac{3}{8}$

$-62\frac{1}{3}$

16.
$6\frac{1}{3}$

$-2\frac{5}{12}$

17.
$72\frac{3}{10}$

$-25\frac{8}{15}$

18.
$23\frac{1}{2}$

$-18\frac{3}{4}$

19.
$5\frac{1}{10}$

$-4\frac{2}{5}$

20.
$15\frac{3}{18}$

$-12\frac{8}{9}$

21. In your own words, explain the steps you would take to add two large mixed numbers.
(See Objective 1.)

22. When subtracting mixed numbers, explain when you need to borrow. Explain how to borrow using an example. (See Objective 4.)

Solve the following application problems.

QUICK START

23. WINDOW INSTALLATION   A contractor who installs windows for The Home Depot must attach a lead strip around all four sides of a custom-made stained glass window. If the window measures $34\frac{1}{2}$ by $23\frac{3}{4}$ inches, find the length of lead stripping needed.

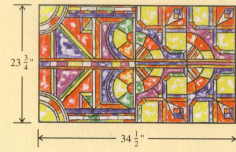

23. $116\frac{1}{2}$ inches

$$34\frac{1}{2} + 23\frac{3}{4} + 34\frac{1}{2} + 23\frac{3}{4} =$$

$$34\frac{2}{4} + 23\frac{3}{4} + 34\frac{2}{4} + 23\frac{3}{4} = 114\frac{10}{4} = 116\frac{1}{2} \text{ inches}$$

24. MEASURING BRASS TRIM   To complete a custom order, Kara Oaks of The Home Depot must find the number of inches of brass trim needed to go around the four sides of the lamp base plate shown. Find the length of brass trim needed.

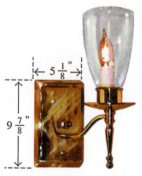

24. _____

25. SECURITY FENCING   The exercise yard at the correction center has four sides and is enclosed with $527\frac{1}{24}$ feet of security fencing around it. If three sides of the yard measure $107\frac{2}{3}$ feet, $150\frac{3}{4}$ feet, and $138\frac{5}{8}$ feet, find the length of the fourth side.

25. _____

26. PARKING LOT FENCING   Three sides of a parking lot are $108\frac{1}{4}$ feet, $162\frac{3}{8}$ feet, and $143\frac{1}{2}$ feet. If the distance around the lot is $518\frac{3}{4}$ feet, find the length of the fourth side.

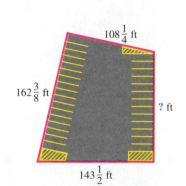

26. _____

27. DELIVERING CONCRETE   Chuck Stone has $8\frac{7}{8}$ cubic yards of concrete in a truck. If he unloads $2\frac{1}{2}$ cubic yards at the first stop, 3 cubic yards at the second stop, and $1\frac{3}{4}$ cubic yards at the third stop, how much concrete remains in the truck?

27. _____

28. TAILORED CLOTHING   Marv Levenson bought 15 yards of Italian silk fabric. He made two tops with $3\frac{3}{4}$ yards of the material, a suit for his wife with $4\frac{1}{8}$ yards, and a jacket with $3\frac{7}{8}$ yards. Find the number of yards of material remaining.

28. _____

29. **PART-TIME WORK** Loren Kabakov, a college student, works part time at the Cyber Coffeehouse. She worked $3\frac{3}{8}$ hours on Monday, $5\frac{1}{2}$ hours on Tuesday, $4\frac{3}{4}$ hours on Wednesday, $3\frac{1}{4}$ hours on Thursday, and 6 hours on Friday. How many hours did she work altogether?

29. _____

30. **TRAILER LOAD** A trailer is to be loaded with plasma televisions weighing $2\frac{5}{8}$ tons, DVD players weighing $6\frac{1}{2}$ tons, personal computers weighing $1\frac{5}{6}$ tons, and computer monitors weighing $3\frac{1}{4}$ tons. If the truck weighs $7\frac{3}{8}$ tons empty, find the total weight after it has been loaded.

30. _____

QUICK CHECK ANSWERS

1. $13\frac{9}{8} = 14\frac{1}{8}$

2. $87\frac{8}{4} = 89$ feet

3. (a) $6\frac{17}{24}$ (b) $55\frac{4}{9}$

2.4 Multiplication and Division of Fractions

OBJECTIVES

1 Multiply proper fractions.
2 Use cancellation.
3 Multiply mixed numbers.
4 Divide fractions.
5 Divide mixed numbers.
6 Multiply or divide by whole numbers.

case IN point ▶

Most of the cabinets sold by The Home Depot are standard size units and modules that can be combined to satisfy varied applications and room sizes. However, all too often, Kara Oaks finds that various components and trim pieces must be custom sized. In order to custom size items, she must multiply and divide fractions.

OBJECTIVE 1 Multiply proper fractions. To multiply two fractions, first multiply the numerators to form a new numerator and then multiply the denominators to form a new denominator. Write the answer in lowest terms if necessary. For example, multiply $\frac{2}{3}$ and $\frac{5}{8}$ by first multiplying the numerators and then the denominators.

Multiply numerators.

$$\frac{2}{3} \times \frac{5}{8} = \frac{2 \times 5}{3 \times 8} = \frac{10}{24} = \frac{5}{12} \quad \text{in lowest terms}$$

Multiply denominators.

OBJECTIVE 2 Use cancellation. This problem can be simplified by **cancellation**, a modification of the method of writing fractions in lowest terms. For example, find the product of $\frac{2}{3}$ and $\frac{5}{8}$ by canceling as follows.

$$\frac{\overset{1}{\cancel{2}}}{3} \times \frac{5}{\underset{4}{\cancel{8}}} = \frac{1 \times 5}{3 \times 4} = \frac{5}{12}$$

Divide 2 into both 2 and 8. Then multiply the numerators and, finally, multiply the denominators.

Note: Any numerator can cancel with any denominator as long as both are divisible without remainder by the same number other than 1.

Multiplying Common Fractions   **EXAMPLE 1**

Multiply.

(a) $\dfrac{8}{15} \times \dfrac{5}{12}$ **(b)** $\dfrac{35}{12} \times \dfrac{32}{25}$

SOLUTION

Use cancellation in both of these problems.

(a) $\dfrac{\overset{2}{\cancel{8}}}{\underset{3}{\cancel{15}}} \times \dfrac{\overset{1}{\cancel{5}}}{\underset{3}{\cancel{12}}} = \dfrac{2 \times 1}{3 \times 3} = \dfrac{2}{9}$

Divide 4 into both 8 and 12.
Divide 5 into both 5 and 15.

(b) $\dfrac{\overset{7}{\cancel{35}}}{\underset{3}{\cancel{12}}} \times \dfrac{\overset{8}{\cancel{32}}}{\underset{5}{\cancel{25}}} = \dfrac{7 \times 8}{3 \times 5} = \dfrac{56}{15} = 3\dfrac{11}{15}$

Divide 4 into both 12 and 32.
Divide 5 into both 35 and 25.

> **Quick TIP ▼**
>
> When canceling, be certain that the numerator and the denominator are both divided by the same number.

QUICK CHECK 1

Multiply using cancellation.

(a) $\dfrac{7}{8} \times \dfrac{4}{21}$ **(b)** $\dfrac{36}{15} \times \dfrac{45}{24}$

OBJECTIVE 3 Multiply mixed numbers. To multiply mixed numbers, change the mixed numbers to improper fractions, cancel, and then multiply. For example, multiply $6\frac{1}{4}$ and $2\frac{2}{3}$ as follows.

Cancel.

$$6\frac{1}{4} \times 2\frac{2}{3} = \frac{25}{4} \times \frac{8}{3} = \frac{25}{4} \times \frac{\overset{2}{8}}{3} = \frac{25 \times 2}{1 \times 3} = \frac{50}{3} = 16\frac{2}{3}$$

Change to improper fractions.

Multiplying Mixed Numbers **EXAMPLE 2**

Multiply.

(a) $3\frac{3}{4} \times 8\frac{2}{3}$ **(b)** $1\frac{3}{5} \times 3\frac{1}{3} \times 1\frac{3}{4}$

SOLUTION

(a) $3\frac{3}{4} = \frac{15}{4}$ and $8\frac{2}{3} = \frac{26}{3}$

$$\frac{\overset{5}{15}}{\underset{2}{4}} \times \frac{\overset{13}{26}}{\underset{1}{3}} = \frac{5 \times 13}{2 \times 1} = \frac{65}{2} = 32\frac{1}{2}$$

(b) $1\frac{3}{5} = \frac{8}{5}, 3\frac{1}{3} = \frac{10}{3}$, and $1\frac{3}{4} = \frac{7}{4}$

$$\frac{\overset{2}{8}}{\underset{1}{5}} \times \frac{\overset{2}{10}}{3} \times \frac{7}{\underset{1}{4}} = \frac{2 \times 2 \times 7}{1 \times 3 \times 1} = \frac{28}{3} = 9\frac{1}{3}$$

The calculator solution to part (b) uses the fraction key.

1 $\boxed{a^{b/c}}$ 3 $\boxed{a^{b/c}}$ 5 $\boxed{\times}$ 3 $\boxed{a^{b/c}}$ 1 $\boxed{a^{b/c}}$ 3 $\boxed{\times}$ 1 $\boxed{a^{b/c}}$ 3 $\boxed{a^{b/c}}$ 4 $\boxed{=}$ $9\frac{1}{3}$

> **Quick TIP ▼**
> Be sure to change each mixed number to a fraction before multiplying.

QUICK CHECK 2

Multiply.

(a) $3\frac{3}{5} \times 1\frac{2}{3}$ **(b)** $2\frac{2}{3} \times 1\frac{5}{9} \times 3\frac{3}{4}$

The recipe shown next is easy to follow using proper measuring cups and spoons. Sometimes you may want to double or triple a recipe, or perhaps you need to cut the recipe in half. To double the recipe, multiply the amount of each ingredient by 2. To triple the recipe, multiply by 3. To halve the recipe you'll need to divide by 2.

Chocolate/Oat-Chip Cookies

1 cup (2 sticks) margarine or butter, softened
$1\frac{1}{4}$ cups firmly packed brown sugar
$\frac{1}{2}$ cup granulated sugar
2 eggs
2 tablespoons milk
2 teaspoons vanilla
$1\frac{3}{4}$ cups all-purpose flour
1 teaspoon baking soda

$\frac{1}{2}$ teaspoon salt (optional)
$2\frac{1}{2}$ cups uncooked oats
One 12-ounce package (2 cups) semi-sweet chocolate morsels
1 cup coarsely chopped nuts (optional)

Heat oven to 375°F. **Beat** margarine and sugars until creamy.
Add eggs, milk, and vanilla; beat well.
Add combined flour, baking soda, and salt; mix well. **Stir** in oats, chocolate morsels, and nuts; mix well.
Drop using rounded measuring tablespoonfuls onto ungreased cookie sheet.
Bake 9 to 10 minutes for a chewy cookie or 12 to 13 minutes for a crisp cookie.
Cool 1 minute on cookie sheet; remove to wire rack. Cool completely.

MAKES ABOUT 5 DOZEN

Multiplying a Mixed Number by a Whole Number   **EXAMPLE 3**

(a) Find the amount of uncooked oats needed if the preceding recipe for chocolate/oat-chip cookies is doubled (multiplied by 2).

(b) How many cups of all-purpose flour are needed when the recipe is tripled (multiplied by 3)?

SOLUTION

(a) $2\frac{1}{2} \times 2 = \frac{5}{\overset{1}{\cancel{2}}} \times \frac{\overset{1}{\cancel{2}}}{1} = \frac{5 \times 1}{1 \times 1} = \frac{5}{1} = 5 \text{ cups}$

(b) $1\frac{3}{4} \times 3 = \frac{7}{4} \times \frac{3}{1} = \frac{7 \times 3}{4} = \frac{21}{4} = 5\frac{1}{4} \text{ cups}$

QUICK CHECK 3

(a) Find the amount of brown sugar needed if the preceding recipe is tripled.

(b) How many teaspoons of salt are needed if the recipe is multiplied 15 times?

OBJECTIVE 4 **Divide fractions.** To divide two fractions, first invert the divisor, which is the fraction following the ÷ sign. To invert a fraction, exchange the numerator and denominator. Then multiply the two fractions.

$$\overset{\textbf{dividend}}{\frac{3}{8}} \quad \overset{\textbf{divisor}}{\frac{7}{12}}$$

For example, to divide $\frac{3}{8}$ by $\frac{7}{12}$:

First, invert the divisor, $\frac{7}{12}$:   The inverse of $\frac{7}{12}$ is $\frac{12}{7}$.

Then multiply the fractions: $\frac{3}{8} \times \frac{12}{7}$

$$\frac{3}{8} \times \frac{12}{7} = \frac{3}{\underset{2}{\cancel{8}}} \times \frac{\overset{3}{\cancel{12}}}{7} = \frac{3 \times 3}{2 \times 7} = \frac{9}{14}$$

So, $\frac{3}{8} \div \frac{7}{12} = \frac{9}{14}$.

Dividing Common Fractions   **EXAMPLE 4**

Divide.

(a) $\frac{7}{8} \div \frac{1}{4}$ (b) $\frac{25}{36} \div \frac{15}{18}$

SOLUTION

First, invert the second fraction, and then multiply.

Quick TIP ▼

Only invert the second fraction, the divisor, when dividing fractions.

(a) $\frac{7}{8} \div \frac{1}{4} = \frac{7}{\underset{2}{\cancel{8}}} \times \frac{\overset{1}{\cancel{4}}}{1} = \frac{7 \times 1}{2 \times 1} = \frac{7}{2} = 3\frac{1}{2}$ (b) $\frac{25}{36} \div \frac{15}{18} = \frac{\overset{5}{\cancel{25}}}{\underset{2}{\cancel{36}}} \times \frac{\overset{1}{\cancel{18}}}{\underset{3}{\cancel{15}}} = \frac{5 \times 1}{2 \times 3} = \frac{5}{6}$

QUICK CHECK 4

Divide.

(a) $\frac{2}{3} \div \frac{1}{2}$ (b) $\frac{12}{21} \div \frac{18}{24}$

OBJECTIVE 5 **Divide mixed numbers.** To divide mixed numbers, first change all mixed numbers to improper fractions. Then divide as above by inverting the divisor and, finally, multiplying the fractions. The divisor is the number that follows the ÷ sign.

To divide $3\frac{5}{9}$ by $2\frac{2}{5}$:

First, convert to improper fractions: $3\frac{5}{9} \div 2\frac{2}{5} = \frac{32}{9} \div \frac{12}{5}$

Next, invert the divisor: $\frac{32}{9} \div \frac{12}{5} = \frac{32}{9} \times \frac{5}{12}$ **Change ÷ to ×.**

Finally, multiply the fractions:

$$\frac{32}{9} \times \frac{5}{12} = \frac{\overset{8}{\cancel{32}}}{9} \times \frac{5}{\underset{3}{\cancel{12}}} = \frac{8 \times 5}{9 \times 3} = \frac{40}{27} = 1\frac{13}{27}$$

So, $3\frac{5}{9} \div 2\frac{2}{5} = 1\frac{13}{27}$.

OBJECTIVE 6 Multiply or divide by whole numbers. To multiply or divide a fraction by a whole number, write the whole number as a fraction over 1.

Multiply: $3\frac{3}{4} \times 16 = 3\frac{3}{4} \times \frac{\mathbf{16}}{\mathbf{1}} = \frac{15}{4} \times \frac{16}{1} = \frac{15}{\underset{1}{\cancel{4}}} \times \frac{\overset{4}{\cancel{16}}}{1} = 15 \times 4 = 60$

———— **Write as a whole number over 1.**

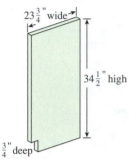

Base-End Panel

$23\frac{3}{4}''$ wide

$34\frac{1}{2}''$ high

$\frac{3}{4}''$ deep

Divide: $2\frac{2}{5} \div 3 = \frac{12}{5} \div \frac{\mathbf{3}}{\mathbf{1}} = \frac{\overset{4}{\cancel{12}}}{5} \times \frac{1}{\underset{1}{\cancel{3}}} = \frac{4 \times 1}{5 \times 1} = \frac{4}{5}$

———— **Write 3 as $\frac{3}{1}$.**

Mills Pride manufactures cabinets for kitchens and baths. The specifications for base-end panels are shown in the diagram. The lumber used is $\frac{3}{4}$ inch deep and is cut down from 24 inches to a $23\frac{3}{4}$-inch width. The panel is then cut to a height of $34\frac{1}{2}$ inches. The materials used in the manufacture of cabinets, solid oak in this case, are very expensive. Every precaution is taken to ensure a minimum of wasted material.

Multiplying a Whole Number by a Mixed Number   **EXAMPLE 5**

A cabinetmaker will need 80 base-end panels, shown above and to the left, to complete a job. If each panel is $34\frac{1}{2}$ inches in length, how many inches of oak material are needed, assuming no waste?

SOLUTION

Multiply the number of panels needed by the length of each panel: $34\frac{1}{2}$ (which is $\frac{69}{2}$).

$$80 \times \frac{69}{2} = \frac{\overset{40}{\cancel{80}}}{1} \times \frac{69}{\underset{1}{\cancel{2}}} = \frac{40 \times 69}{1 \times 1} = \frac{2760}{1} = 2760 \text{ inches}$$

The length of material needed by the cabinetmaker is 2760 inches.

QUICK CHECK 5

A plumber needs 68 pieces of 1-inch-diameter copper tubing. If each piece of tubing must be $28\frac{1}{2}$ inches long, how many total inches of tubing are needed?

Dividing a Whole Number by a Mixed Number   **EXAMPLE 6**

To complete a custom-designed cabinet, oak trim pieces must be cut exactly $2\frac{1}{4}$ inches long so that they can be used as dividers in a spice rack. Find the number of pieces that can be cut from a piece of oak that is 54 inches in length.

SOLUTION

To divide the length of the piece of oak by $2\frac{1}{4}$, first change the mixed number $2\frac{1}{4}$ to the fraction $\frac{9}{4}$. Then invert the divisor and multiply. The divisor is the number that follows the $\div$ sign.

$$54 \div 2\frac{1}{4} = 54 \div \frac{9}{4} = \frac{\overset{6}{\cancel{54}}}{1} \times \frac{4}{\underset{1}{\cancel{9}}} = \frac{6 \times 4}{1 \times 1} = \frac{24}{1} = 24$$

The number of trim pieces that can be cut from the oak stock is 24.

QUICK CHECK 6

A welder needs angle iron pieces that are $3\frac{1}{3}$ inches long. Find the number of pieces that can be cut from a piece of angle iron that is 70 inches in length, assuming no waste.

2.4 Exercises

  PRACTICE   WATCH   DOWNLOAD   READ

The **QUICK START** *exercises in each section contain solutions to help you get started.*

Multiply. Write each answer in lowest terms. (See Examples 1–3.)

QUICK START

1. $\frac{3}{4} \times \frac{2}{5} = \frac{3}{10}$

   $\frac{3}{\overset{2}{\cancel{4}}} \times \frac{\overset{1}{\cancel{2}}}{5} = \frac{3}{10}$

2. $\frac{2}{3} \times \frac{5}{8} = \frac{5}{12}$

   $\frac{\overset{1}{\cancel{2}}}{3} \times \frac{5}{\underset{4}{\cancel{8}}} = \frac{5}{12}$

3. $\frac{9}{10} \times \frac{11}{16} = $ _____

4. $\frac{2}{3} \times \frac{3}{8} = $ ___

5. $\frac{9}{22} \times \frac{11}{16} = $ _____

6. $\frac{5}{12} \times \frac{7}{10} = $ _____

7. $1\frac{1}{4} \times 3\frac{1}{2} = $ _____

8. $1\frac{2}{3} \times 2\frac{7}{10} = $ _____

9. $3\frac{1}{9} \times 3 = $ _____

10. $\frac{3}{4} \times \frac{8}{9} \times 2\frac{1}{2} = $ _____

11. $\frac{1}{4} \times 6\frac{2}{3} \times \frac{1}{5} = $ _____

12. $\frac{2}{3} \times \frac{9}{8} \times 3\frac{1}{4} = $ _____

13. $\frac{5}{9} \times 2\frac{1}{4} \times 3\frac{2}{3} = $ _____

14. $3 \times 1\frac{1}{2} \times 2\frac{2}{3} = $ ___

15. $5\frac{3}{5} \times 1\frac{5}{9} \times \frac{10}{49} = $ _____

Divide. Write each answer in lowest terms. (See Example 4.)

QUICK START

16. $\frac{1}{4} \div \frac{3}{4} = \frac{1}{3}$

   $\frac{1}{\cancel{4}} \times \frac{\overset{1}{\cancel{4}}}{3} = \frac{1}{3}$

17. $\frac{3}{8} \div \frac{5}{8} = \frac{3}{5}$

   $\frac{3}{\cancel{8}} \times \frac{\overset{1}{\cancel{8}}}{5} = \frac{3}{5}$

18. $\frac{13}{20} \div \frac{26}{30} = $ ___

19. $\frac{9}{10} \div \frac{3}{5} = $ ___

20. $\frac{7}{8} \div \frac{3}{4} = $ ___

21. $2\frac{1}{2} \div 3\frac{3}{4} = $ ___

22. $1\frac{1}{4} \div 4\frac{1}{6} = $ ___

23. $5 \div 1\frac{7}{8} = $ ___

24. $3 \div 1\frac{1}{4} = $ ___

25. $\dfrac{3}{8} \div 2\dfrac{1}{2} =$ _____   **26.** $1\dfrac{7}{8} \div 6\dfrac{1}{4} =$ _____   **27.** $2\dfrac{5}{8} \div \dfrac{5}{16} =$ _____   **28.** $5\dfrac{2}{3} \div 6 =$ _____

29. In your own words, explain the rule for multiplying fractions. Make up an example problem of your own showing how this works.

30. A useful shortcut when multiplying fractions involves dividing a numerator and a denominator before multiplying. This is often called cancellation. Describe how this works and give an example of cancellation. (See Objective 2.)

Find the time-and-a-half pay rate for each of the following regular pay rates. (See Example 5.)

QUICK START

31. $8 **$12** _____

$8 \times 1\dfrac{1}{2} =$ **$12**

32. $17 _____

33. $12.50 _____

(*Hint:* $12.50 = $12\dfrac{1}{2}$)

34. $9.50 _____

35. Your classmate is confused about how to divide by a fraction. Write a short explanation telling how this should be done.

36. If you multiply two proper fractions, the answer is smaller than the fractions multiplied. When you divide by a proper fraction, is the answer smaller than the numbers in the problem? Show some examples to support your answer.

Solve the following application problems.

37. ELECTRICITY RATES   The utility company says that the cost of operating a hair dryer is $\dfrac{1}{5}$¢ per minute. Find the cost of operating the hair dryer for 30 minutes. (*Source:* Pacific Gas and Electric Company.)

37. _____

38. ELECTRICITY RATES   The cost of electricity for brewing coffee is $\dfrac{2}{5}$¢ per minute. What is the cost of brewing coffee for 90 minutes? (*Source:* Pacific Gas and Electric Company.)

38. _____

39. PRODUCING CRAFTS   Matthew Genaway wants to make 16 holiday wreaths to sell at the craft fair. Each wreath needs $2\dfrac{1}{4}$ yards of ribbon. How many yards does he need?

39. _____

40. EARNINGS CALCULATION   Jack Horner worked $38\dfrac{1}{4}$ hours at $10 per hour. How much money did he make?

40. _____

41. FINISH CARPENTRY Kara Oaks at The Home Depot estimates that a certain design for a kitchen and bathroom needs $109\frac{1}{2}$ feet of cabinet trim. How many homes can be fitted with cabinet trim if there are 1314 feet of cabinet trim available?

41. _____

42. COMMERCIAL FERTILIZER For 1 acre of a crop, $7\frac{1}{2}$ gallons of fertilizer must be applied. How many acres can be fertilized with 1200 gallons of fertilizer?

42. _____

43. A manufacturer of floor jacks is ordering steel tubing to make the handles for this jack. How much steel tubing is needed to make 135 of these jacks? (The symbol for inch is ".) (*Source:* Harbor Freight Tools.)

43. _____

CENTRAL HYDRAULICS
2-Ton Compact Floorjack
4000 LB CAPACITY

- $19\frac{1}{2}$" handle
- Lifts 5" to $15\frac{1}{4}$"
- Fully rolled edge for added tray strength
- 21" L × $9\frac{1}{2}$" W × 6" H
- Compact & lightweight for portability—perfect for the trunk

44. A wheelbarrow manufacturer uses handles made of hardwood. Find the amount of wood that is needed to make 182 handles. The longest dimension shown is the handle length. (*Source:* Harbor Freight Tools.)

44. _____

6.0 CUBIC FT
WHEELBARROW

- Steel construction with hardwood handles
- 14" tubeless pneumatic tire
- Fully rolled edge for added strength
- Overall dimensions: $61\frac{1}{2}$" L × 27" W × 24.9" H

45. STEEL FABRICATION A fishing boat anchor requires $10\frac{3}{8}$ pounds of steel. Find the number of anchors that can be manufactured with 25,730 pounds of steel.

45. _____

46. COMMERCIAL CARPETING The manager of the flooring department at The Home Depot determines that each apartment unit requires $62\frac{1}{2}$ square yards of carpet. Find the number of apartment units that can be carpeted with 6750 square yards of carpet.

46. _____

47. FUEL CONSUMPTION   A fishing boat uses $12\frac{3}{4}$ gallons of fuel on a full-day fishing trip   47. _____
and $7\frac{1}{8}$ gallons of fuel on a half-day trip. Find the total number of gallons of fuel used in
28 full-day trips and 16 half-day trips.

48. MAKING JEWELRY   One necklace can be completed in $6\frac{1}{2}$ minutes, while a bracelet takes   48. _____
$3\frac{1}{8}$ minutes. Find the total time that it takes to complete 36 necklaces and 22 bracelets.

49. DISPENSING EYEDROPS   How many $\frac{1}{8}$-ounce eyedrop dispensers   49. _____
can be filled with 11 ounces of eyedrops?

50. CONCRETE FOOTINGS   Each building footing requires $\frac{5}{16}$ cubic yard of concrete. How   50. _____
many building footings can be constructed from 10 cubic yards of concrete?

51. ALASKA WILDERNESS   "Grizzly" Hanson needs 40 crates of   51. _____
trapping and other supplies to make it through the winter at his
remote cabin. If he can carry only $8\frac{1}{2}$ crates with each load
behind his snowmobile, find the number of round trips required.
You may need to round up.

52. WEATHER STRIPPING   Bill Rhodes, an employee at The Home Depot, sells a 200-yard   52. _____
roll of weather stripping material. Find the number of pieces of weather stripping $\frac{5}{8}$ yard in
length that may be cut from the roll.

QUICK CHECK ANSWERS

1. (a) $\frac{1}{6}$ **(b)** $\frac{9}{2} = 4\frac{1}{2}$ **4. (a)** $\frac{4}{3} = 1\frac{1}{3}$ **(b)** $\frac{16}{21}$

2. (a) 6   **(b)** $15\frac{5}{9}$ **5.** 1938 inches

3. (a) $3\frac{3}{4}$ cups   **(b)** $7\frac{1}{2}$ teaspoons   **6.** 21 pieces

2.5 Converting Decimals to Fractions and Fractions to Decimals

OBJECTIVES

1 Convert decimals to fractions.
2 Convert fractions to decimals.
3 Know common decimal equivalents.

OBJECTIVE 1 Convert decimals to fractions. To convert a decimal to a fraction, first simply. Think of writing the decimal number using words, as you did in Chapter 1. Then write the fraction. Here are some examples in which the fractions have been reduced to lowest terms.

Decimal	Read as	Fraction equivalent
0.6	six tenths	$\dfrac{6}{10} = \dfrac{3}{5}$
0.38	thirty-eight hundredths	$\dfrac{38}{100} = \dfrac{19}{50}$
0.875	eight hundred seventy-five thousandths	$\dfrac{875}{1000} = \dfrac{7}{8}$

Another method of converting a decimal to a fraction is by first removing the decimal point. The remaining number is the numerator of the fraction. The denominator of the fraction is 1 followed by as many zeros as there were digits to the right of the decimal point in the original number.

Converting Decimals to Fractions   **EXAMPLE 1**

Convert the following decimals to fractions.

(a) .3   (b) .98   (c) .654

SOLUTION

(a) After removing the decimal point in .3, you can see that the numerator of the fraction is 3. Since there is only one digit to the right of the decimal point, the denominator is 1 followed by one zero, or 10.

$$.3 = \frac{3}{10}$$

1 followed by 1 zero

(b) The numerator of the fraction is 98. Since there are two digits to the right of the decimal point, the denominator is 1 followed by two zeros, or 100.

$$.98 = \frac{98}{100} = \frac{49}{50} \text{ (lowest terms)}$$

1 followed by 2 zeros

(c) Since there are three digits to the right of the decimal point, the denominator is 1 followed by three zeros, or 1000.

$$.654 = \frac{654}{1000} = \frac{327}{500} \text{ (lowest terms)}$$

1 followed by 3 zeros

QUICK CHECK 1

Convert the following decimals to fractions.

(a) .75   (b) .64   (c) .875

OBJECTIVE 2 Convert fractions to decimals. Convert a fraction to a decimal by dividing the numerator of the fraction by the denominator. Place a decimal point after the numerator and attach one zero at a time to the right of the decimal point as the division is performed. Keep going until the division produces a remainder of zero or until the desired degree of accuracy is reached.

Converting Fractions to Decimals

EXAMPLE 2

Convert the following fractions to decimals.

(a) $\frac{1}{8}$ (b) $\frac{2}{3}$

Decimal Equivalents

$\frac{1}{16} = .0625$

$\frac{1}{10} = .1$

$\frac{1}{9} = .1111$ (rounded)

$\frac{1}{8} = .125$

$\frac{1}{7} = .1429$ (rounded)

$\frac{1}{6} = .1667$ (rounded)

$\frac{3}{16} = .1875$

$\frac{1}{5} = .2$

$\frac{1}{4} = .25$

$\frac{3}{10} = .3$

$\frac{1}{3} = .3333$ (rounded)

$\frac{3}{8} = .375$

$\frac{2}{5} = .4$

$\frac{1}{2} = .5$

$\frac{3}{5} = .6$

$\frac{5}{8} = .625$

$\frac{2}{3} = .6667$ (rounded)

$\frac{7}{10} = .7$

$\frac{3}{4} = .75$

$\frac{4}{5} = .8$

$\frac{5}{6} = .8333$ (rounded)

$\frac{7}{8} = .875$

$\frac{9}{10} = .9$

SOLUTION

(a) Convert $\frac{1}{8}$ to a decimal by dividing 1 by 8. Since 8 will not divide into 1, place a 0 to the *right* of the decimal point. Now 8 goes into 10 once, with a remainder of 2.

$$\begin{array}{r} .1 \\ 8\overline{)1.0} \\ \underline{8} \\ 2 \end{array}$$ Be sure to move the decimal point up.

Continue placing zeros to the *right* of the decimal point and continue dividing until the remainder is 0.

$$\begin{array}{r} .125 \\ 8\overline{)1.000} \\ \underline{8} \\ 20 \\ \underline{16} \\ 40 \\ \underline{40} \\ 0 \end{array}$$ Keep attaching zeros.

remainder of 0   Therefore, $\frac{1}{8} = .125$.

(b) Divide 2 by 3.

$$\begin{array}{r} 0.6666 \\ 3\overline{)2.0000} \\ \underline{1\,8} \\ 20 \\ \underline{18} \\ 20 \\ \underline{18} \\ 20 \\ \underline{18} \\ 2 \end{array}$$ Keep attaching zeros.

This division results in a repeating decimal and is often written as $.\overline{6}$, $.6\overline{6}$, or $.66\overline{6}$. Rounded to the nearest thousandth, $\frac{2}{3} = .667$. Do not use both a decimal and a fraction in the same number.

The calculator solution to this example is

2 ÷ 3 = 0.666666667

QUICK CHECK 2

Convert the following fractions to decimals.

(a) $\frac{4}{5}$ (b) $\frac{5}{8}$

OBJECTIVE 3 Know common decimal equivalents. Some of the more common **decimal equivalents** of fractions are listed in the margin. These decimals appear from least to greatest value and are rounded to the nearest ten-thousandth.

2.5 Exercises

The **QUICK START** *exercises in each section contain solutions to help you get started.*

Convert the following decimals to fractions, and write each in lowest terms. (See Example 1.)

QUICK START

1. $.75 = \dfrac{3}{4}$

$\dfrac{75}{100} = \dfrac{3}{4}$

2. $.55 = \dfrac{11}{20}$

$\dfrac{55}{100} = \dfrac{11}{20}$

3. $.24 = $ _____

4. $.64 = $ _____

5. $.73 = $ _____

6. $.33 = $ _____

7. $.85 = $ _____

8. $.68 = $ _____

9. $.34 = $ _____

10. $.288 = $ _____

11. $.444 = $ _____

12. $.125 = $ _____

13. $.625 = $ _____

14. $.875 = $ _____

15. $.805 = $ _____

16. $.791 = $ _____

17. $.096 = $ _____

18. $.012 = $ _____

19. $.0375 = $ _____

20. $.0875 = $ _____

21. $.1875 = $ _____

22. $.9845 = $ _____

23. $.0016 = $ _____

24. $.0085 = $ _____

25. A classmate of yours is confused about how to convert a decimal to a fraction. Write an explanation of this for your classmate, including changing the fraction to lowest terms. (See Objective 1.)

26. Explain how to convert a fraction to a decimal. Be sure to mention rounding in your explanation. (See Objective 2.)

Convert the following fractions to decimals. If a division does not come out evenly, round the answer to the nearest thousandth. (See Example 2.)

QUICK START

27. $\dfrac{1}{4} = .25$

$$\begin{array}{r} .25 \\ 4\overline{)1.00} \\ \underline{8} \\ 20 \\ \underline{20} \\ 0 \end{array}$$

28. $\dfrac{7}{8} = $ _____

29. $\dfrac{3}{8} = $ _____

30. $\dfrac{5}{8} =$ _____

31. $\dfrac{2}{3} =$ _____

32. $\dfrac{5}{6} =$ _____

33. $\dfrac{7}{9} =$ _____

34. $\dfrac{1}{9} =$ _____

35. $\dfrac{7}{11} =$ _____

36. $\dfrac{8}{25} =$ _____

37. $\dfrac{22}{25} =$ _____

38. $\dfrac{14}{25} =$ _____

39. $\dfrac{181}{205} =$ _____

40. $\dfrac{1}{99} =$ _____

41. $\dfrac{148}{149} =$ _____

42. GAMBLING WITH HEALTH   A hospital study of 1521 heart-attack patients found that 1 out of 8 quit taking the life-saving drugs prescribed to them. **(a)** What fraction stopped taking their medicine? **(b)** Convert this fraction to a decimal. **(c)** How many patients in the study quit taking their medicine? Round to the nearest whole number. (**Source:** Associated Press.)

(a) _____

(b) _____

(c) _____

43. SMOKING   A study was done using 272 smokers to see if a specific chewing gum would help them quit smoking. After three months, 2/3 of those in the group were still smoking. **(a)** Convert the fraction to a decimal and round to the nearest thousandth. **(b)** Find the number of people in the study that quit smoking rounded to the nearest whole number.

(a) _____

(b) _____

QUICK CHECK ANSWERS

1. (a) $\dfrac{3}{4}$ **(b)** $\dfrac{16}{25}$ **(c)** $\dfrac{7}{8}$ **2. (a)** .8 **(b)** .625

Chapter 2 Quick Review

Chapter Terms *Review the following terms to test your understanding of the chapter. For each term you do not know, refer to the page number found next to that term.*

cancellation **[p. 67]**

common denominator **[p. 53]**

common fraction **[p. 46]**

decimal equivalent **[p. 76]**

denominator **[p. 46]**

dividend **[p. 69]**

divisor **[p. 69]**

fraction **[p. 46]**

improper fraction **[p. 46]**

inspection **[p. 53]**

least common denominator (LCD) **[p. 53]**

like fractions **[p. 53]**

lowest terms **[p. 48]**

method of prime numbers **[p. 53]**

mixed number **[p. 47]**

numerator **[p. 46]**

prime number **[p. 54]**

proper fraction **[p. 46]**

quotient **[p. 48]**

unlike fractions **[p. 43]**

CONCEPTS

EXAMPLES

2.1 Types of fractions

Proper: Numerator smaller than denominator
Improper: Numerator equal to or greater than denominator
Mixed: Whole number plus proper fraction

$$4 + \frac{2}{3} = 4\frac{2}{3}$$

proper fractions $\quad \frac{2}{3}, \frac{3}{4}, \frac{15}{16}, \frac{1}{8}$

improper fractions $\quad \frac{17}{8}, \frac{19}{12}, \frac{11}{2}, \frac{5}{3}, \frac{7}{7}$

mixed numbers $\quad 2\frac{2}{3}, 3\frac{5}{8}, 9\frac{5}{6}$

2.1 Converting fractions

Mixed to improper: Multiply denominator by whole number and add numerator.
Improper to mixed: Divide numerator by denominator and place remainder over denominator.

$$7\frac{2}{3} = \frac{(7 \times 3) + 2}{3} = \frac{23}{3}$$

$$\frac{17}{5} = 3\frac{2}{5} \qquad 5\overline{)17} \atop \underline{15} \atop 2$$

2.1 Writing fractions in lowest terms

Divide the numerator and denominator by the same number.

$$\frac{30}{42} = \frac{30 \div 6}{42 \div 6} = \frac{5}{7}$$

2.2 Adding like fractions

Keep the same denominator, add numerators, and reduce to lowest terms.

$$\frac{3}{4} + \frac{1}{4} + \frac{5}{4} = \frac{3 + 1 + 5}{4} = \frac{9}{4} = 2\frac{1}{4}$$

2.2 Finding a least common denominator (LCD)

Inspection method: Look to see if the LCD can be found.
Method of prime numbers: Use prime numbers to find the LCD.

$$\frac{1}{3} + \frac{1}{4} + \frac{1}{10}$$

$$\begin{array}{r} & 1 \quad 1 \quad 1 \\ 5\overline{)} & 1 \quad 1 \quad 5 \\ 3\overline{)} & 3 \quad 1 \quad 5 \\ 2\overline{)} & 3 \quad 2 \quad 5 \\ 2\overline{)} & 3 \quad 4 \quad 10 \end{array}$$

Multiply the prime numbers.

$$2 \times 2 \times 3 \times 5 = 60 \text{ LCD}$$

2.2 Adding unlike fractions

1. Find the LCD.
2. Rewrite fractions using the LCD.
3. Add numerators, placing answers over the LCD, and reduce to lowest terms.

$$\frac{1}{3} + \frac{1}{4} + \frac{1}{10} \text{ LCD} = 60$$

$$\frac{1}{3} = \frac{20}{60}, \frac{1}{4} = \frac{15}{60}, \frac{1}{10} = \frac{6}{60}$$

$$\frac{20 + 15 + 6}{60} = \frac{41}{60}$$

2.2 Subtracting fractions

1. Find the LCD.
2. Rewrite fractions using the LCD.
3. Keep the same denominator and subtract numerators.
4. Reduce to lowest terms.

$$\frac{5}{8} - \frac{1}{3} = \frac{15}{24} - \frac{8}{24} = \frac{15 - 8}{24} = \frac{7}{24}$$

CONCEPTS	EXAMPLES

2.3 Adding mixed numbers

1. Find the LCD, then add fractions and reduce.
2. Add whole numbers.
3. Combine the sums of whole numbers and fractions.

$$9\frac{2}{3} = 9\frac{8}{12}$$
$$+ \ 6\frac{3}{4} = 6\frac{9}{12}$$ LCD = 12
$$15\frac{17}{12} = 16\frac{5}{12}$$

2.3 Subtracting mixed numbers

1. Find the LCD and subtract fractions, borrowing if necessary.
2. Subtract whole numbers.
3. Combine the differences of whole numbers and fractions.

$$8\frac{5}{8} = 8\frac{15}{24}$$
$$- \ 3\frac{1}{12} = 3\frac{2}{24}$$ LCD = 24
$$5\frac{13}{24}$$

2.4 Multiplying proper fractions

1. Multiply numerators and multiply denominators.
2. Reduce the answer to lowest terms if cancelling was not done.

$$\frac{6}{11} \times \frac{7}{8} = \frac{\overset{3}{6}}{11} \times \frac{7}{\underset{4}{8}} = \frac{21}{44}$$

2.4 Multiplying mixed numbers

1. Change mixed numbers to improper fractions.
2. Cancel if possible.
3. Multiply fractions.

$$1\frac{3}{5} \times 3\frac{1}{3} = \frac{8}{\underset{1}{5}} \times \frac{\overset{2}{10}}{3} = \frac{8}{1} \times \frac{2}{3}$$
$$= \frac{16}{3} = 5\frac{1}{3}$$

Always reduce to lowest terms.

2.4 Dividing proper fractions

Invert the divisor, multiply as proper fractions, and reduce the answer to lowest terms.

$$\frac{25}{36} \div \frac{15}{18} = \frac{\overset{5}{25}}{\underset{2}{36}} \times \frac{\overset{1}{18}}{\underset{3}{15}} = \frac{5}{2} \times \frac{1}{3} = \frac{5}{6}$$

2.4 Dividing mixed numbers

Change mixed numbers to improper fractions. Invert the divisor, cancel if possible, and then multiply fractions.

$$3\frac{5}{9} \div 2\frac{2}{5} = \frac{32}{9} \div \frac{12}{5} = \frac{\overset{8}{32}}{9} \times \frac{5}{\underset{3}{12}}$$
$$= \frac{40}{27} = 1\frac{13}{27}$$

2.5 Converting decimals to fractions

Think of the decimal as being written in words and write in fraction form. Reduce to lowest terms.

Convert .47 to a fraction.
Think of .47 as **"forty-seven hundredths."**
Then write as $\frac{47}{100}$.

2.5 Converting fractions to decimals

Divide the numerator by the denominator. Round if necessary.

Convert $\frac{1}{8}$ to a decimal.

$$\begin{array}{r} .125 \\ 8\overline{)1.000} \\ \underline{8} \\ 20 \\ \underline{16} \\ 40 \\ \underline{40} \\ 0 \end{array} \qquad \frac{1}{8} = .125$$

case study

OPERATING EXPENSES AT WOODLINE MOLDINGS AND TRIM

It is often said that a picture is worth a thousand words. Visual presentation of data is often used in business in the form of graphs. A commonly used graph that shows the relationships of various data is the circle graph, also called a pie chart. The circle, which contains 360 degrees, is divided into slices, or fractional parts. The size of each slice helps to show the relationship of the various slices to each other and to the whole.

The annual operating expenses for Woodline Moldings and Trim are shown below. Use this information to answer the questions that follow.

WOODLINE MOLDINGS AND TRIM OPERATING EXPENSES

Expense Item	Monthly Amount	Annual Amount	Fraction of Total Expenses
Salaries	$10,000	_____	_____
Rent	$6,000	_____	_____
Utilities	$2,000	_____	_____
Insurance	$1,500	_____	_____
Advertising	$1,500	_____	_____
Miscellaneous	$3,000	_____	_____
Total Expenses		_____	

1. Find the total annual operating expenses for Woodline Moldings and Trim.   1. _____

2. What fraction should be used to represent each expense item as part of the total expenses?   2. _____

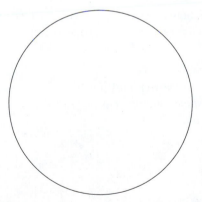

3. Draw a circle (pie) graph using the fractions you found in part (b) to represent each expense item. Approximate the fractional part of the circle needed for each expense item. Label each segment of the circle graph with the fraction and the expense item.

4. Since there are 360 degrees in a circle, find the number of degrees that would be used to represent each expense item in the circle graph.   4. _____

INVESTIGATE

Business and economic data are often shown using pie charts. Find two pie charts with business or economic data and explain the contents. Look in newspapers such as *USA Today* or on the Internet.

case 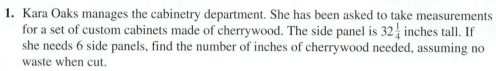 point summary exercise

HOME DEPOT

www.homedepot.com

Facts:

- 1978: Founded in Atlanta, Georgia
- 2005: More than $80 billion in annual sales
- 2010: More than 2200 retail stores

The Home Depot is the world's largest home-improvement retailer, employing more than 300,000 employees called associates. Its goal is to provide a very high level of service, broad selection of products, and very competitive prices in a one-stop shopping environment. Management also believes in taking care of its employees by offering many benefits. It even has a program that matches employee charitable donations. Management also tries to encourage employees to donate their time to needy organizations.

1. Kara Oaks manages the cabinetry department. She has been asked to take measurements for a set of custom cabinets made of cherrywood. The side panel is $32\frac{1}{4}$ inches tall. If she needs 6 side panels, find the number of inches of cherrywood needed, assuming no waste when cut.

1. _____

2. The width of each side panel is $14\frac{1}{2}$ inches. Find the area of each panel by multiplying the height of the panel given in (a) by the width. The resulting area is in square inches.

2. _____

3. Find the total area of cherrywood needed for all six side panels in square inches.

3. _____

4. Ignoring waste, how many side panels can be made if the cabinetmaker has only 2250 square inches of cherrywood panels of the appropriate width?

4. _____

Discussion Question: *Do you think that exact measurements are an important component of quality from the standpoint of a customer at The Home Depot? What are other important components of quality?*

Chapter 2   Test

To help you review, the numbers in brackets show the section in which the topic was discussed.

Write the following fractions in lowest terms.   **[2.1]**

1. $\dfrac{25}{30} = $ _____

2. $\dfrac{875}{1000} = $ _____

3. $\dfrac{84}{132} = $ _____

Convert the following improper fractions to mixed numbers, and write using lowest terms.   **[2.1]**

4. $\dfrac{65}{8} = $ _____

5. $\dfrac{56}{12} = $ _____

6. $\dfrac{120}{45} = $ _____

Convert the following mixed numbers to improper fractions.   **[2.1]**

7. $7\dfrac{3}{4} = $ _____

8. $18\dfrac{4}{5} = $ _____

9. $18\dfrac{3}{8} = $ _____

Find the LCD of each of the following groups of denominators.   **[2.2]**

10. $2, 6, 5,$ _____

11. $6, 8, 15,$ _____

12. $6, 9, 12, 24,$ _____

Solve the following problems.   **[2.2–2.4]**

13.
$$\begin{array}{r} \dfrac{1}{5} \\ \dfrac{3}{10} \\ + \dfrac{3}{8} \\ \hline \end{array}$$

14.
$$\begin{array}{r} 32\dfrac{5}{16} \\ - 17\dfrac{1}{4} \\ \hline \end{array}$$

15.
$$\begin{array}{r} 126\dfrac{3}{16} \\ - 89\dfrac{7}{8} \\ \hline \end{array}$$

16. $67\dfrac{1}{2} \times \dfrac{8}{15} = $

17. $33\dfrac{1}{3} \div \dfrac{200}{9} = $

Solve the following application problems.

18. Becky Finnerty, a pastry chef, used $23\frac{1}{2}$ pounds of powdered sugar for one recipe, $34\frac{3}{4}$ pounds powdered sugar for another recipe, and $17\frac{5}{8}$ pounds of powdered sugar for a third recipe. If Finnerty started with two 50-pound sacks of powdered sugar, find the amount of powdered sugar remaining.   **[2.3]**

18. _____

19. Rhonda Goedeker received her Social Security check of $1275. After paying $\frac{1}{3}$ of this amount for rent, she paid $\frac{3}{5}$ of the remaining amount for food, utilities, and transportation. How much money does she have left?

19. _____

20. A painting contractor arrived at a 6-unit apartment complex with $147\frac{1}{2}$ gallons of paint. If his crew sprayed $68\frac{1}{2}$ gallons on the interior walls, rolled $37\frac{3}{8}$ gallons on the masonry exterior, and brushed $5\frac{3}{4}$ gallons on the window trim, find the number of gallons of paint remaining.   **[2.3]**

20. _____

21. A seamstress uses $1\frac{1}{4}$ yards of material to make a blouse. Find the number of blouses that can be made from $80\frac{1}{2}$ yards of material.

21. _____

Convert the following decimals to fractions.   **[2.5]**

22. $.625 =$ 23. $.82 =$

*Use the advertisement for this four-piece chisel set to answer Exercises 24 and 25. The symbol " is for inches. (**Source**: Harbor Freight Tools.)*   **[2.5]**

24. Convert the cutting-edge width of the smallest chisel from a fraction to a decimal.

24. _____

25. Convert the cutting-edge width of the largest chisel from a fraction to a decimal.

25. _____

Percent

3

case in point ▶

TOM DUGALLY has been a real estate agent with Century 21® for 20 years. He loves the business since it allows him to be his own boss and schedule his own time, but there are downsides. For example, during the recent serious recession, which caused home sales to plummet to record lows, Dugally's income dropped "like a rock," as he told a friend. However, he had been through recessions before and his income suffered through every one of them. He knew that there were good years and bad years in the real estate business. So, he and his wife made it a practice for life to save and invest during the good years. Now, he hopes he has enough money so that his family can outlast the current recession.

Dugally uses percents every day to calculate monthly payments on homes, determine his commission from a sale, calculate the fee that must be paid to finance a loan and estimate real estate taxes. In fact, the exam he had to pass to get his real estate license required calculations using percents. He simply _could not do his job_ without using percents.

As you can see from these examples, percents are very common in business.

Markdown on an iPod is 10% of the original price.

Interest rate on a certificate of deposit is 3.5% of amount on deposit.

Sales taxes in one city are 8.5% of the total amount of the sale.

Real estate commission is 6% of the selling price of a house.

Unemployment is 8.3% of the workforce.

Learn the topics in this chapter well—percents will be used throughout this course and you will see them throughout your life!

3.1 Writing Decimals and Fractions as Percents

OBJECTIVES

1 Write a decimal as a percent.
2 Write a fraction as a percent.
3 Write a percent as a decimal.
4 Write a percent as a fraction.
5 Write a fractional percent as a decimal.

Similar to fractions and decimals, **percents** represent parts of a whole. However, percents (**hundredths**) mean parts out of 100. They are written using a percent sign (%). For example 1% means 1 of 100 equal parts. The number 12% is read "twelve percent."

	Fraction Form	**Decimal Form**
12% = 12 out of 100 equal parts	$= \dfrac{12}{100}$	$= .12$
25% = 25 out of 100 equal parts	$= \dfrac{25}{100}$	$= .25$
50% = 50 out of 100 equal parts	$= \dfrac{50}{100}$	$= .50$
100% = 100 out of 100 equal parts	$= \dfrac{100}{100}$	$= 1.00$
150% = 150 out of 100 equal parts	$= \dfrac{150}{100}$	$= 1.50$

Since 100% is 1, it is the whole or entire amount. Any percent greater than 100% is more than the whole. You can make 100% on a test, but not 150%, unless there is extra credit of some type. However, an athlete may eat $1\frac{1}{2}$ granola bars, thereby eating 150% of a granola bar.

OBJECTIVE 1 Write a decimal as a percent. Reading the first row of the preceding table, from the right to the left, shows that:

$$.12 = \frac{12}{100} = 12\% \quad \text{or} \quad .12 = 12\%$$

Effectively, the decimal number .12 was changed from a decimal to a percent by moving the decimal point two places to the right and adding a percent (%) sign.

> **Converting Decimals to Percents**
>
> Change a decimal to a percent by moving the decimal point two places to the right and attaching a percent sign (%).
>
> .75   original decimal
> .75.   Move decimal point 2 places to the right.
> 75%   Attach a percent sign.

Changing Decimals to Percents

Change the following decimals to percents.

(a) .35 (b) .42 (c) .58

SOLUTION

Move the decimal point two places to the right and attach a percent sign.

(a) 35% (b) 42% (c) 58%

> **QUICK CHECK 1**
>
> Change the decimals to percents.
>
> (a) .72 (b) .25 (c) .67

If there is no digit in the hundredths position, place zeros to the right of the number to hold the hundredths position. For example, the decimal .5 is expressed as 50%, and the whole number 1.2 is expressed as 120%.

$$.5 = .50.\% = 50\% \qquad 1.2 = 1.20.\% = 120\%$$

attach zero   attach zero

Writing Decimals as Percents

Write the following decimals as percents.

(a) .8 (b) 2.6 (c) .1 (d) 4

SOLUTION

It is necessary to attach zeros here.

(a) 80% (b) 260% (c) 10% (d) 400%

attach zero   attach zero   attach zero   attach 2 zeros

> **QUICK CHECK 2**
>
> Write the decimals as percents.
>
> (a) .6 (b) 3.5 (c) 8

If the decimal extends past the hundredths position, the resulting percent includes decimal parts of whole percents.

Writing Decimals as Percents

Write these decimals as percents.

(a) .625 (b) .0057 (c) .0018

SOLUTION

(a) 62.5% (b) .57% (c) .18%

> **QUICK CHECK 3**
>
> Write the decimals as percents.
>
> (a) .875 (b) .0038 (c) .0056

It is important to notice that in part (b) of the last example, the percent .57% is less than 1%, so .57% is less than 1 part out of 100 equal parts. In fact, .57% = .0057 is *a very small* fraction, as is .18% = .0018 in part (c).

OBJECTIVE 2 Write a fraction as a percent. There are two ways to write a fraction as a percent. One way is to write the fraction first as a decimal. For example, to express the fraction $\frac{2}{5}$ as a percent, write $\frac{2}{5}$ as a decimal by dividing 2 by 5. Then write the decimal as a percent by moving the decimal point two places to the right and adding a percent sign.

$$\begin{array}{ccc} \text{fraction} & \text{decimal} & \text{percent} \\ \dfrac{2}{5} & = \quad .4 \quad = & 40\% \end{array}$$

Writing Fractions as Percents

EXAMPLE 4

A marketing manager is given the following data in fraction form and must change the data to percents.

(a) $\dfrac{1}{4}$ (b) $\dfrac{3}{8}$ (c) $\dfrac{4}{5}$

SOLUTION

First write each fraction as a decimal, and then write the decimal as a percent.

(a) $\dfrac{1}{4} = .25 = 25\%$ (b) $\dfrac{3}{8} = .375 = 37.5\%$ (c) $\dfrac{4}{5} = .8 = 80\%$

QUICK CHECK 4

Change the fractions to percents.

(a) $\dfrac{3}{4}$ (b) $\dfrac{2}{5}$ (c) $\dfrac{5}{8}$

A second way to write a fraction as a percent is by multiplying the fraction by 100%. For example, write the fraction $\frac{4}{5}$ as a percent by multiplying $\frac{4}{5}$ by 100%.

$$\frac{4}{5} = \frac{4}{5} \times 100\% = \frac{400\%}{5} = 80\%$$

OBJECTIVE 3 Write a percent as a decimal.

Converting Percents to Decimals

Change a percent to a decimal by moving the decimal point two places to the left and dropping the percent sign (%).

25%	original percent
.25.%	Move decimal point 2 places to the left.
.25	Drop the percent sign.

Writing Percents as Decimals

EXAMPLE 5

To calculate some insurance claims, an insurance agent must change the following percents to decimals.

(a) 35%   (b) 50%   (c) 325%   (d) $37\frac{1}{2}\%$ $\left(\textit{Hint: } 37\frac{1}{2}\% = 37.5\%.\right)$

SOLUTION

Move the decimal point two places to the left and drop the percent sign.

(a) .35   (b) .5   (c) 3.25   (d) .375

Quick TIP ▼

Change any fraction part of a percent to a decimal before converting from a percent to a decimal.

QUICK CHECK 5

Change the percents to decimals.

(a) 75%   (b) 40%   (c) 280%

OBJECTIVE 4 Write a percent as a fraction. To write a percent as a fraction, first change the percent to a decimal, then write the decimal as a fraction in lowest terms.

Writing Percents as Fractions   **EXAMPLE 6**

Even though smoking is believed to account for 1 of every 5 deaths in the United States, more than 45 million Americans smoke. The bar chart shows the percent of people in each age group that smoke. Convert each percent to a fraction and reduce to lowest terms.

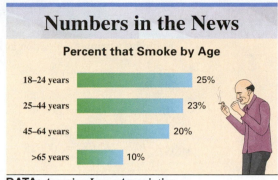

Numbers in the News

Percent that Smoke by Age

18–24 years	25%
25–44 years	23%
45–64 years	20%
>65 years	10%

DATA: *America Lung Association*

SOLUTION

Write each percent as a decimal and then as a fraction in lowest terms.

(a) $25\% = .25 = \dfrac{25}{100} = \dfrac{1}{4}.$

(b) $23\% = .23 = \dfrac{23}{100}$

(c) $20\% = .20 = \dfrac{20}{100} = \dfrac{1}{5}$

(d) $10\% = .10 = \dfrac{10}{100} = \dfrac{1}{10}$

QUICK CHECK 6

Change the percents to fractions. Reduce to lowest terms.

(a) 35%   **(b)** 22%   **(c)** 88%

We did not always believe that smoking was harmful. During World War II, cigarettes were given to soldiers, who often traded them as currency. By the 1960s, a lot of scientific evidence indicated that smoking had serious negative consequences related to heart and lung disease, in particular. Today, smoking is considered to be *the* leading cause of preventable death in the world killing more people than HIV/AIDS, tuberculosis, and malaria combined.

OBJECTIVE 5 **Write a fractional percent as a decimal.** A fractional percent such as $\frac{1}{2}\%$ is smaller than 1%. In fact, $\frac{1}{2}\%$ is equal to $\frac{1}{2}$ of 1%. Write a fractional percent as a decimal by first changing the fraction to a decimal, followed by the percent sign. Then, write that number as a decimal by moving the decimal point two places to the left and dropping the percent sign.

$$\frac{1}{2}\% = .5\% = .005$$

                      ↑ written as a decimal with percent sign remaining

**Writing Fractional
Percents as Decimals**

The following percents appear in a newspaper article. Write each fractional percent as a decimal.

(a) $\frac{1}{5}\%$ **(b)** $\frac{3}{4}\%$ **(c)** $\frac{5}{8}\%$

SOLUTION

Begin by writing the fraction as a decimal percent.

(a) $\frac{1}{5}\% = .2\% = .002$

(b) $\frac{3}{4}\% = .75\% = .0075$

(c) $\frac{5}{8}\% = .625\% = .00625$

QUICK CHECK 7

Write the fractional percents as decimals.

(a) $\frac{1}{2}\%$ **(b)** $\frac{1}{4}\%$ **(c)** $\frac{7}{8}\%$

The following chart shows many fractions as well as their decimal and percent equivalents.

Fraction, Decimal, and Percent Equivalents

$\frac{1}{100} = .01 = 1\%$	$\frac{9}{16} = .5625 = 56.25\%$ or $56\frac{1}{4}\%$
$\frac{1}{50} = .02 = 2\%$	$\frac{3}{5} = .6 = 60\%$
$\frac{1}{25} = .04 = 4\%$	$\frac{5}{8} = .625 = 62\frac{1}{2}\%$
$\frac{1}{20} = .05 = 5\%$	$\frac{2}{3} = .66\overline{6} = 66\frac{2}{3}\%$
$\frac{1}{16} = .0625 = 6.25\%$ or $6\frac{1}{4}\%$	$\frac{11}{16} = .6875 = 68.75\%$ or $68\frac{3}{4}\%$
$\frac{1}{12} = .083\overline{3} = 8\frac{1}{3}\%$	$\frac{7}{10} = .7 = 70\%$
$\frac{1}{10} = .1 = 10\%$	$\frac{3}{4} = .75 = 75\%$
$\frac{1}{9} = .111\overline{1} = 11\frac{1}{9}\%$	$\frac{4}{5} = .8 = 80\%$
$\frac{1}{8} = .125 = 12.5\%$ or $12\frac{1}{2}\%$	$\frac{13}{16} = .8125 = 81.25\%$ or $81\frac{1}{4}\%$
$\frac{1}{7} = .1428 = 14\frac{2}{7}\%$	$\frac{5}{6} = .833\overline{3} = 83\frac{1}{3}\%$
$\frac{1}{6} = .166\overline{6} = 16\frac{2}{3}\%$	$\frac{7}{8} = .875 = 87\frac{1}{2}\%$
$\frac{3}{16} = .1875 = 18\frac{3}{4}\%$	$\frac{9}{10} = .9 = 90\%$
$\frac{1}{5} = .2 = 20\%$	$\frac{15}{16} = .9375 = 93.75\%$ or $93\frac{3}{4}\%$
$\frac{1}{4} = .25 = 25\%$	$1 = 1.00 = 100\%$
$\frac{3}{10} = .3 = 30\%$	$1\frac{1}{10} = 1.1 = 110\%$
$\frac{5}{16} = .3125 = 31.25\%$	$1\frac{1}{4} = 1.25 = 125\%$
$\frac{1}{3} = .333\overline{3} = 33\frac{1}{3}\%$	$1\frac{1}{3} = 1.13333 = 133\frac{1}{3}\%$
$\frac{3}{8} = .375 = 37\frac{1}{2}\%$	$1\frac{1}{2} = 1.5 = 150\%$
$\frac{2}{5} = .4 = 40\%$	$1\frac{2}{3} = 1.66666 = 166\frac{2}{3}\%$
$\frac{7}{16} = .4375 = 43.75\%$ or $43\frac{3}{4}\%$	$1\frac{3}{4} = 1.75 = 175\%$
$\frac{1}{2} = .5 = 50\%$	$2 = 2.00 = 200\%$

3.1 Exercises

The QUICK START *exercises in each section contain solutions to help you get started.*

Write the following decimals as percents. (See Examples 1–3.)

QUICK START

1. .25 = **25%**   2. .4 = **40%**   3. .72 = _____   4. 1.3 = _____

5. 2.034 = _____   6. .625 = _____   7. 3.625 = _____   8. 4.6 = _____

9. .875 = _____   10. .005 = _____   11. .0005 = _____   12. .0012 = _____

13. 3.45 = _____   14. .2108 = _____   15. .0308 = _____

Write the following as decimals. (See Examples 4–6.)

QUICK START

16. $\frac{1}{5}$ = **.2**   17. $\frac{5}{8}$ = **.625**   18. 64% = _____   19. 65% = _____

20. $\frac{1}{100}$ = _____   21. $\frac{1}{8}$ = _____   22. $8\frac{1}{2}\%$ = _____   23. $12\frac{1}{2}\%$ = _____

24. $\frac{1}{200}$ = _____   25. $\frac{1}{400}$ = _____   26. $50\frac{3}{4}\%$ = _____   27. $84\frac{3}{4}\%$ = _____

28. $3\frac{3}{8}$ = _____   29. $1\frac{3}{4}$ = _____   30. 350% = _____

Determine the fraction, decimal, or percent equivalents for each of the following, as necessary.
Write fractions in lowest terms.

QUICK START

	Fraction	Decimal	Percent
31.	$\frac{1}{2}$	.5	50%
32.	$\frac{3}{50}$	.06	6%
33.	_____	.875	_____
34.	$\frac{4}{5}$	_____	_____
35.	_____	_____	.8%
36.	_____	.00625	_____
37.	$10\frac{1}{2}$	_____	_____
38.	_____	_____	675%
39.	_____	.65	_____
40.	$4\frac{3}{8}$	_____	_____
41.	_____	.005	_____
42.	_____	_____	$\frac{1}{8}\%$

Fraction	Decimal	Percent
43. $\dfrac{1}{3}$	_____	_____
44. _____	_____	12.5%
45. _____	2.5	_____
46. $\dfrac{7}{20}$	_____	_____
47. _____	_____	$4\dfrac{1}{4}\%$
48. _____	.7	_____
49. $\dfrac{3}{200}$	_____	_____
50. _____	5.125	_____
51. _____	_____	1037.5%
52. _____	_____	$\dfrac{3}{4}\%$
53. _____	.0025	_____
54. $\dfrac{5}{8}$	_____	_____
55. _____	_____	$37\dfrac{1}{2}\%$
56. _____	_____	$6\dfrac{3}{4}\%$

57. Fractions, decimals, and percents are all used to describe a part of something. The use of percents is much more common than fractions and decimals. Why do you suppose this is true?

58. List five uses of percent that are or will be part of your life. Consider the activities of working, shopping, saving, and planning for the future.

59. Select a decimal percent and write it as a fraction. Select a fraction and write it as a percent. Write an explanation of each step of your work. (See Objectives 2 and 3.)

60. The fractional percent $\frac{1}{2}\%$ is equal to .005. Explain each step as you change $\frac{1}{2}\%$ to its decimal equivalent. (See Objective 4.)

QUICK CHECK ANSWERS

1. (a) 72%   **(b)** 25%   **(c)** 67%

2. (a) 60%   **(b)** 350%   **(c)** 800%

3. (a) 87.5%   **(b)** .38%   **(c)** .56%

4. (a) 75%   **(b)** 40%   **(c)** 62.5%

5. (a) .75   **(b)** .4   **(c)** 2.8

6. (a) $\dfrac{7}{20}$ **(b)** $\dfrac{11}{50}$ **(c)** $\dfrac{22}{25}$

7. (a) $\dfrac{1}{2}\% = .5\% = .005$

(b) $\dfrac{1}{4}\% = .25\% = .0025$

(c) $\dfrac{7}{8}\% = .875\% = .00875$

3.2 Finding Part

OBJECTIVES

1 Know the three components of a percent problem.
2 Learn the basic percent formula.
3 Solve for part.
4 Recognize the terms associated with base, rate, and part.
5 Calculate sales tax.
6 Learn the standard format of percent problems.

case point IN ▶

As a real estate agent, Tom Dugally is paid on commission. When he produces income as a result of a sale, a sale of his listing by someone else, or a rental agreement that is completed, he is paid a portion of this income. Currently, Dugally is looking for a home in the $210,000 price range for Scott and Andrea Abriani, a couple he met at an open house. He believes this is the most they can reasonably afford.

OBJECTIVE 1 Know the three components of a percent problem. Problems in percent contain three main components. Usually, two of these components are given, and the third component must be found.

> **Three components of a percent problem**
>
> 1. **Base:** The whole or total, starting point, or that to which something is being compared.
> 2. **Rate:** A number followed by % or **percent**.
> 3. **Part:** The result of multiplying the base and the rate. The part is a *part* of the base. For example, sales tax is a part of total sales.

OBJECTIVE 2 Learn the basic percent formula. The base, rate, and part are related by the basic **percent formula.**

> $$P = B \times R \qquad P = R \times B$$
> **Part = Base × Rate   or   Part = Rate × Base**

OBJECTIVE 3 Solve for part. Tom Dugally finds a house that the Abrianis purchase for $210,000. A 6% real estate commission must be paid. The $210,000 price of the house is the whole (or base), and the 6% percent commission is the rate. The unknown is the actual commission, which is the part. Find the commission as follows.

$$P = \quad B \quad \times R$$
$$P = \$210,000 \times 6\%$$
$$= \$210,000 \times .06 \quad \text{Change percent to decimal.}$$
$$= \$12,600$$

The real estate commission of $12,600 will be split between the listing agent, the selling agent, and their two brokers. So, only part of it goes to Dugally.

Solving for Part   EXAMPLE 1

Solve for part, using $P = B \times R$.

(a) 4% of 50   (b) 1.2% of 180   (c) 140% of 225   (d) $\frac{1}{4}$% of 560

(*Hint:* $\frac{1}{4}$% = .25%.)

SOLUTION

	50		180		225		560
(a)	× .04	(b)	× .012	(c)	× 1.4	(d)	× .0025
	2.00		2.160		315.0		1.4000

EXAMPLE 2

The bar graph shows the unemployment rate by category in the midst of a serious recession. Use the data provided to estimate the number of unemployed teenagers out of a total of roughly 32,000 working-age teenagers in one city.

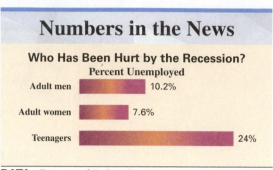

Numbers in the News

Who Has Been Hurt by the Recession?
Percent Unemployed

Adult men	10.2%
Adult women	7.6%
Teenagers	24%

DATA: *Bureau of Labor Statistics*

SOLUTION

The base is 32,000. The rate for unemployed teenagers is 24%. The number of unemployed teenagers is part of the whole, so part (P) is the unknown.

$$P = \quad B \quad \times \quad R$$
$$P = 32{,}000 \times 24\%$$
$$= 32{,}000 \times .24$$
$$= 7680$$

About 7680 of the 32,000 working-age teenagers in the city are unemployed.

The calculator solution to this example is

32000 ⊠ 24 %️ =️ 7680

Note: Refer to Appendix B for calculator basics.

OBJECTIVE 4 **Recognize the terms associated with base, rate, and part.** Percent problems have certain similarities. For example, some phrases are associated with the base in the problem. Other phrases lead to the part, while % or *percent* following a number identifies the rate. The following chart helps distinguish between the base and the part.

Words and Phrases Associated with Base and Part

Usually indicates the base (B)	Usually indicates the part (P)
Sales ────────────────→	Sales tax
Investment ──────────→	Return on investment
Savings ─────────────→	Interest
Retail price ─────────→	Discount
Last year's figure ───→	Increase or decrease
Old salary ──────────→	Raise
Earnings ────────────→	Expenditures

OBJECTIVE 5 Calculate sales tax. Calculating **sales tax** is a good example of finding part. States, counties, and cities often collect taxes on retail sales to the consumer. The sales tax is a percent of the sale. This percent varies from as low as 3% in some states to 8% or more in other states. The formula used for finding sales tax follows.

$$P = B \times R$$
Sales tax = Sales × Sales tax rate

Calculating Sales Tax

Becky Smith finally saved enough to buy the guitar she had dreamed about. Her goal was to start a band with her two sisters as backup and a friend as a drummer. The list price on the guitar was $1199.99 and the sales tax was 8.5%. Find the sales tax and total cost.

SOLUTION

The whole (B) is $1199.99, and the rate ($R$) is 8.5%.

$$P = B \times R$$
$$P = \$1199.99 \times 8.5\%$$
$$= \$1199.99 \times .085$$
$$= \$101.99915, \textbf{ or \$102.00 rounded to the nearest cent}$$

Now, add the sales tax cost to the cost of the guitar to find the total.

$$\text{Total} = \$1199.99 + \$102 = \textbf{\$1301.99}$$

QUICK CHECK 3

One day, the Lock Shoppe had sales of $1485 and charged a sales tax of 6%. Find the sales tax and the total sales including the tax.

Identify the rate, base, and part with the following hints.

Base tends to be preceded by the word *of* or *on*; tends to be the *whole*.
Rate is followed by a percent sign or the word *percent*.
Part is in the same units as the base and is usually a portion of the base.

OBJECTIVE 6 Learn the standard format of percent problems. Percent problems can be written in the form "% of whole is/are part," as shown by these common examples.

Rate	Whole		Part
7.5% of the	total	is	the sales tax
8.5% of the	workers	are	unemployed
74% of the	students	are	full-time students
18% of the	children	are	obese

The following data shows the percent of 1582 people surveyed that purchased each type of ice cream. To find the number out of 1582 surveyed that bought Breyers, multiply the whole (B) of 1582 by the rate (R) of 14.7%.

$$1582 \times 14.7\% = 232.554, \text{ or } 233 \text{ people (rounded)}$$

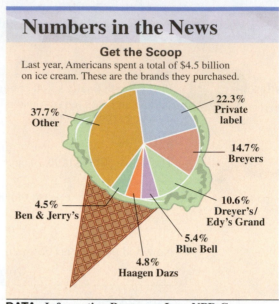

Numbers in the News

Get the Scoop

Last year, Americans spent a total of $4.5 billion on ice cream. These are the brands they purchased.

22.3% Private label

37.7% Other

14.7% Breyers

4.5% Ben & Jerry's

10.6% Dreyer's/ Edy's Grand

5.4% Blue Bell

4.8% Haagen Dazs

DATA: Information Resources Inc.; NPD Group

Since $B \times R = R \times B$, it makes no difference which term is used first in multiplication. To prove the point, the same data is used, but with rate first, giving the same results as above.

$$14.7\% \times 1582 = 232.554, \text{ or } 233 \text{ people (rounded)}$$

Identifying the Pieces in Percent Problems **EXAMPLE 4**

Identify the whole and rate in the following; then find the part.

(a) A refrigerator with an original price of $949 was marked down 10%.

(b) Expenses for the weekend were 92% of total sales of $1850.

(c) Corporate income taxes were 30% of total profit of $18,240,000.

SOLUTION

	Base	×	Rate	=	Part
(a)	$949	×	10%	=	$94.90 discount
(b)	$1850	×	92%	=	$1702 expenses
(c)	$18,240,000	×	30%	=	$5,472,000 corporate income taxes

QUICK CHECK 4

A video game is priced at $280 less a 15% discount. First, identify the whole and rate; then calculate the part (the discount).

3.2 Exercises

The **QUICK START** *exercises in each section contain solutions to help you get started.*

Solve for part in each of the following. Round to the nearest hundredth. (See Example 1.)

QUICK START

1. 10% of 620 homes = **62 homes**

2. 25% of 3500 Web sites = **875 Web sites**

3. 75.5% of $800 = _____

4. 20.5% of $1500 = _____

5. 4% of 120 feet = _____

6. 125% of 2000 products = _____

7. 175% of 5820 miles = _____

8. 15% of 75 crates = _____

9. 17.5% of 1040 cell phones = _____

10. 52.5% of 1560 trucks = _____

11. 118% of 125.8 yards = _____

12. 110% of 150 apartments = _____

13. $90\frac{1}{2}$% of $5930 = _____

14. $7\frac{1}{2}$% of $150 = _____

15. Identify the three components in a percent problem. In your own words, write one sentence telling how to identify each of these three components. (See Objective 1.)

16. There are words and phrases that are usually associated with base and part. Give three examples of words that usually identify the base and the accompanying word for the part. (See Objective 4.)

Solve for part in each of the following application problems. Round to the nearest cent unless otherwise indicated. (See Examples 2 and 3.)

QUICK START

17. **SUMMER VACATION** Of 350 people surveyed recently in New York, 68% said they prefer to vacation in the beautiful Caribbean islands. Find the number preferring the Caribbean.

    $P = B \times R$
    $P = 350 \times .68 = 238$

    17. **238 people**

18. **ICE CREAM SALES** In a poll of 1582 people, 4.5% said that they prefer to purchase Ben and Jerry's brand ice cream. Find the number of people who said they prefer Ben and Jerry's ice cream. Round to the nearest whole number. (*Source:* Information Resources Inc., NPD Group.)

    18. _____

19. **SALES TAX** A real estate broker wants to purchase a new iPhone priced at $399. If the sales tax rate is 7.75%, find the total price including the sales tax. (*Source:* Real Estate Technology.)

    19. _____

20. Thomas Dugally of Century 21 Real Estate is working with a mortgage company that charges borrowers $350 plus 2% of the loan amount. What is the total charge to get a home loan of $190,000?

    20. _____

indicates an exercise that is related to the Case in Point feature.

21. **WOMEN IN THE NAVY**   The navy guided-missile destroyer USS *Sullivans* has a 335-person crew of which 13% are female. Find the number of female crew members. Round to the nearest whole number. (*Source:* U.S. Navy.)

21. _____

22. **SUPERMARKET SHOPPING**   The Point of Purchase Advertising Institute says that 55% of all supermarket shoppers have a written list of their needs. If 3680 shoppers enter the supermarket that you manage in one day, what number of shoppers would you expect to have a written shopping list?

22. _____

23. **BAR SOAP**   A bar of Ivory Soap is $99\frac{44}{100}$% pure. If the bar of soap weighs 9 ounces, how many ounces are pure? Round to the nearest hundredth.

23. _____

24. **CANNED-MEAT SALES**   According to Hormel Foods Corporation, Spam® and Spam Lite together held 62.2% of the $148-million canned lunchmeat category over a 52-week period (the entire year). Find the total annual sales of these Hormel products. Round to the nearest hundredth of a million.

24. _____

25. **DRIVING DISTRACTIONS**   It is estimated that 29.5% of automobile crashes are caused by driver distractions, such as mobile communications devices. If there are 16,450 automobile crashes in a study, what number would be caused by driver distractions? Round to the nearest whole number. (*Source:* National Conference of State Legislatures.)

25. _____

26. **SMOKING AND LUNG DISEASE**   According to one study by Danish scientists, at least 25% of all long-term smokers get a chronic lung disease known as COPD. Out of every 1000 smokers, find the minimum number expected to get COPD.

26. _____

27. **FEMALE LAWYERS**   There are 1,094,751 active lawyers living in the United States. If 71.4% of these lawyers are male, find **(a)** the percent of the lawyers who are female and **(b)** the number of lawyers who are female. Round to the nearest whole number. (*Source:* American Bar Association.)

(a) _____
(b) _____

28. **OVERWEIGHT**   About 65% of Americans are overweight. In a city of 1 million, estimate the number that are overweight. (*Source:* National Health Institute.)

28. _____

29. **DIGITAL CAMERA**   A Sony 6.0 megapixel digital camera priced at $319 is marked down 25%. Find the price of the camera after the markdown. (*Source:* RC Willey.)

29. _____

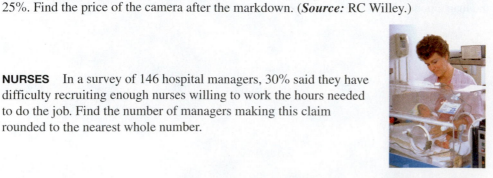

30. **NURSES**   In a survey of 146 hospital managers, 30% said they have difficulty recruiting enough nurses willing to work the hours needed to do the job. Find the number of managers making this claim rounded to the nearest whole number.

30. _____

31. **NEW PRODUCT FAILURE** Marketing Intelligence Service says that there were 15,401 new products introduced last year. If 86% of the products introduced last year failed to reach their business objectives, find the number of products that did reach their objectives. Round to the nearest whole number.

31. _____

32. **FAMILY BUDGET** A family of four with a monthly income of $5150 spends 90% of its earnings and saves the balance for the down payment on a house. Find (a) the monthly savings and (b) the annual savings of this family.

(a) _____
(b) _____

33. **GM SALES IN CHINA** General Motors auto sales in China this year were 38% greater than last year's sales of 1,180,358 units. Find this year's sales. Round to the nearest whole number. (**Source:** General Motors Corporation.)

33. _____

34. **SUPER BOWL ADVERTISING** The average cost of 30 seconds of advertising during the Super Bowl 6 years ago was $2.3 million. If the increase in cost over the last 6 years has been 17%, find the average cost of 30 seconds of advertising during the Super Bowl this year. Round to the nearest tenth of a million. (**Source:** NFL Research.)

34. _____

35. **SALES-TAX COMPUTATION** As the owner of a copy and print shop, you must collect $6\frac{1}{2}\%$ of the amount of each sale for sales tax. If sales for the month are $48,680, find the combined amount of sales and tax.

35. _____

36. **TOTAL COST** A NuVac is priced at $524 with an allowed trade-in of $125 for an old unit. If sales tax of $7\frac{3}{4}\%$ is charged on the price of the new NuVac unit, find the total cost to the customer after receiving the trade-in. (*Hint:* Trade-in is subtracted last.)

36. _____

37. **REAL ESTATE COMMISSIONS** Thomas Dugally of Century 21 Real Estate sold a home for $174,900. The commission was 6% of the sale price. Since Dugally both listed and sold the home, he receives 60% of the commission, and his broker receives the remainder. Find the amount received by Dugally.

37. _____

38. **BUSINESS OWNERSHIP** Jimmy Ruiz has an 82% ownership in a company called Jimmy's Cell Phones. If the company has a value of $98,400 and Ruiz receives an income of 45% of the value of his ownership, find the amount of his income.

38. _____

CONSUMER INTERNET SALES   *Country Store has a unique selection of merchandise that it sells by catalog and over the Internet. Use the shipping and insurance delivery chart below and a sales tax rate of 5% to solve Exercises 39–42. There is no sales tax on shipping and insurance. (***Source:*** *Country Store catalog.)*

Shipping and Insurance Delivery Chart

Up to $15.00	add $3.95
$15.01 to $25.00	add $5.95
$25.01 to $35.00	add $6.95
$35.01 to $50.00	add $7.95
$50.01 to $70.00	add $8.95
$70.01 to $99.99	add $9.95
$100.00 or more	add $10.95

39. Find the total cost of 6 Small Fry Handi-Pan electric skillets at a cost of $29.99 each.

39. _____

40. A customer ordered 5 sets of flour-sack towels at a cost of $12.99 each. What is the total cost?

40. _____

41. Find the total cost of 3 pop-up hampers at a cost of $9.99 each and 4 nonstick minidonut pans at $10.99 each.

41. _____

42. What is the total cost of 5 coach lamp bird feeders at a cost of $19.99 each and 6 garden weather centers at $14.99 each?

42. _____

3.3 Finding Base

OBJECTIVES

1 Use the basic percent formula to solve for base.
2 Find sales when tax amount and tax rate are known.
3 Find the investment when interest payment and rate of interest are known.

Thomas Dugally of Century 21 Real Estate helps buyers select properties that they can afford. Real estate lenders have strict guidelines that determine the maximum loan that they will give a buyer. Usually, the lender will limit the borrowers' monthly house payment to no more than about 28% of their monthly income.

OBJECTIVE 1 Use the basic percent formula to solve for base. In some problems, the rate and part are given, but the base, or starting point, must be found. The formula $P = B \times R$ can be used to get the **formula for base**. The following circle diagram can be used to learn how to use this formula. To find the formula for base, cover B with your finger. This leaves P divided by R, so $B = \dfrac{P}{R}$.

$$\text{Base} = \frac{\text{Part}}{\text{Rate}} \quad \text{or} \quad B = \frac{P}{R}$$

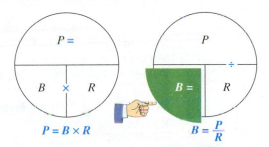

$$P = B \times R \qquad\qquad B = \frac{P}{R}$$

Scott and Andrea Abriana can afford a monthly house payment of only 28% of their income, or $1386. To find their monthly income, insert the rate of 28% and the part, or monthly payment of $1386, into the formula. Be sure to first convert 28% to its decimal equivalent, .28.

$$B = \frac{P}{R}$$

$$B = \frac{1386}{.28} = 4950$$

Their monthly income is $4950.

Solving for Base EXAMPLE 1

Solve for base, using the formula $B = \frac{P}{R}$.
(a) 8 is 4% of _____.   (b) 135 is 15% of _____.   (c) 1.25 is 25% of _____.

SOLUTION

(a) $\dfrac{8}{.04} = 200$ (b) $\dfrac{135}{.15} = 900$ (c) $\dfrac{1.25}{.25} = 5$

QUICK CHECK 1

Solve for base, using $B = \frac{P}{R}$.
(a) 15 is 10% of _____.   (b) 62 is 1% of _____.   (c) 1.6 is 40% of _____.

OBJECTIVE 2 Find sales when tax amount and tax rate are known. In business problems involving sales tax, the amount of sales is always the base.

Finding Sales When
Sales Tax Is Given

EXAMPLE
2

One week, a Famous Footware store collected sales taxes of $780. If the sales tax rate is 5%, find total sales for the week.

SOLUTION

Here, the rate of tax collection is 5%, and taxes collected are a part of total sales. The rate in this problem is 5%, the part is $780, and the base, or total sales, must be found. Arrange the problem in standard form.

$$R \quad \times \quad B \quad = \quad P$$

%	of	**something**	is	**something**
5%	of	**total sales**	is	**$780 (tax)**

Using the formula $B = \frac{P}{R}$, we get

$$B = \frac{780}{.05} = \$15,600 \text{ total sales}$$

The calculator solution to this example is

$$780 \boxed{\div} .05 \boxed{=} 15600$$

QUICK CHECK 2

The number of people who passed the real estate license exam was 832. If this was a 65% pass rate, how many took the exam?

It is very important to check the reasonableness of an answer. Intuitively, total sales should be much higher than the sales tax. This is true in the last example because the sales tax is $780 and total sales are $15,600. If $780 had mistakenly been used as the base, the resulting answer would be $780 × 5% = $39, which would not be a reasonable figure for total sales.

OBJECTIVE 3 Find the investment when interest payment and rate of interest are known.

Finding the Amount
of an Investment

EXAMPLE
3

Roberta Gonzales received $162.50 in interest from an account that paid 3.25% interest for the year. Find the amount of money invested in the account.

SOLUTION

The part (P) is the $162.50 in interest and the rate (R) is 3.25%. The whole, or base (B), is unknown.

$$B = \frac{P}{R}$$
$$B = \frac{\$162.50}{3.25\%}$$
$$= \frac{\$162.50}{.0325}$$
$$= \$5000$$

The original investment was $5000.

QUICK CHECK 3

One quarter, the administrator of a school district's retirement funds received $37,500 interest from an investment in bonds that paid 1.5% for the quarter. Find the amount invested.

3.3 Exercises

The **QUICK START** *exercises in each section contain solutions to help you get started.*

Solve for base in each of the following. Round to the nearest hundredth. (See Example 1.)

QUICK START

1. 530 firms is 25% of __2120__ firms.

2. 240 letters is 80% of __300__ letters.

3. 130 salads is 40% of _____ salads.

4. 32 shipments is 8% of _____ shipments.

5. 110 lab tests is 5.5% of _____ lab tests.

6. $850 is $4\frac{1}{4}$% of _____.

7. 36 students is .75% of _____ students.

8. 23 workers is .5% of _____ workers.

9. 66 files is .15% of _____ files.

10. 54,600 boxes is 60% of _____ boxes.

11. 50 doors is .25% of _____ doors.

12. 39 bottles is .78% of _____ bottles.

13. $33,870 is $37\frac{1}{2}$% of _____.

14. $8500 is $27\frac{1}{2}$% of _____.

15. $12\frac{1}{2}$% of _____ people is 135 people.

16. $18\frac{1}{2}$% of _____ circuits is 370 circuits.

17. 375 crates is .12% of _____ crates.

18. 3.5 quarts is .07% of _____ quarts.

19. .5% of _____ homes is 327 homes.

20. 6.5 barrels is .05% of _____ barrels.

21. 12 audits is .03% of _____ audits.

22. 8 banks is .04% of _____ banks.

23. The basic percent formula is $P = B \times R$. Show how to find the formula to solve for B (base). (See Objective 1.)

24. A problem includes amount of sales, sales tax, and a sales-tax rate. Explain how you could identify the base, rate, and part in this problem. (See Objective 2.)

Solve for base in the following application problems. (See Examples 2 and 3.)

QUICK START

25. **HOME OWNERSHIP** The number of U.S. households owning homes last year was 72.6 million—a record-setting 67.8% of all households. What is the total number of U.S. households? Round to the nearest tenth of a million. (***Source: Habitat World.***)

    $$B = \frac{P}{R} = \frac{72.6}{.678} = 107.07 = 107.1 \text{ million (rounded)}$$

    25. __107.1 million households__

26. **EMPLOYEE POPULATION BASE** In a large metropolitan area, 81% of the employed population is enrolled in a health maintenance organization (HMO). If 700,650 employees are enrolled, find the total number of people in the employed population.

    26. _____

27. **COLLEGE ENROLLMENT** This semester there are 1785 married students on campus. If this figure represents 23% of the total enrollment, what is the total enrollment? Round to the nearest whole number.

    27. _____

28. VOTER REGISTRATION Registered voters make up 13.8% of the county population. If there are 345,000 registered voters in the county, find the total population in the county.

28. _____

29. LOAN QUALIFICATION Thomas Dugally found a home for Scott and Andrea Abriani that will require a monthly loan payment of $1350. If the lender insists that the buyer's monthly payment not exceed 30% of the buyer's monthly income, find the minimum monthly income required by the lender.

29. _____

30. DRIVING TESTS In analyzing the success of driver's license applicants, the state finds that 58.3% of those examined received a passing mark. If the records show that 8370 new driver's licenses were issued, what was the number of applicants? Round to the nearest whole number.

30. _____

31. PERSONAL BUDGETING Jim Lawler spends 28% of his income on housing, 15% on food, 11% on clothing, 15% on transportation, 11% on education, 7% on recreation, and saves the balance. If his savings amount to $266.50 per month, what are his monthly earnings?

31. _____

32. FAMILY SIZE One survey among college students found that 28.4% grew up in a home with two or more siblings and 44.7% grew up in a home with one sibling. If 194 students grew up in a home with no siblings, find the size of the survey group.

32. _____

33. MAN'S BEST FRIEND In a recent survey of dog owners, it was found that 901, or 34%, of the owners take their dogs on vacation with them. Find the number of dog owners in the survey who do not take their dogs on vacation. (*Source:* American Animal Hospital Association.)

33. _____

34. COMMUNICATIONS INDUSTRY LAYOFFS Telecommunications equipment maker Nortel Networks says it will lay off 4000 workers globally. If this amounts to 4% of its total workforce, how many workers will remain after the layoffs? (*Source:* Nortel Networks.)

34. _____

35. GAMBLING PAYBACK An Atlantic City casino advertises that it gives a 97.4% payback on slot machines, and the balance is retained by the casino. If the amount retained by the casino is $4823, find the total amount played on the slot machines.

35. _____

36. SMOKING OR NONSMOKING A casino hotel in Barbados states that 45% of its rooms are for nonsmokers. If the resort allows smoking in 484 rooms, find the total number of rooms.

36. _____

Supplementary Application Exercises on Base and Part

Solve the following application problems. Read each problem carefully to determine whether base or part is being asked for.

1. **SHAMPOO INGREDIENTS**   Most shampoos contain 75% to 90% water. If there are 12.5 ounces of water in a bottle of shampoo that contains 78% water, what is the size of the bottle of shampoo? Round to the nearest whole number.

   1. _____

2. **HOUSEHOLD LUBRICANT**   The lubricant WD-40 is used in 82.3 million U.S. homes, which is 79% of all homes in the United States. Find the total number of homes in the United States. Round to the nearest tenth of a million. (*Source:* WD-40.)

   2. _____

3. **PROPERTY INSURANCE**   Thomas Dugally of Century 21 Real Estate sold a commercial building valued at $423,750. If the building is insured for 68% of its value, find the amount of insurance coverage.

   3. _____

4. **FLU PANDEMIC OF 1918**   The Spanish Flu epidemic of 1918 killed more than 50 million people worldwide. Among others, Eskimos had little resistance to this flu strain. Ninety percent of the 80 villagers of Brevig Mission, Alaska, died of the flu within five days, killing entire families. Find the number of villagers that died in five days.

   4. _____

5. **CAMAROS AND MUSTANGS**   The Chevrolet Camaro was introduced in 1967. Camaro sales that year were 220,917, which was 46.2% of the number of Ford Mustangs sold in the same year. Find the number of Mustangs sold in 1967. Round to the nearest whole number.

   5. _____

6. **CHILD SUPPORT**   Sean Eden has 12.4% of his earnings withheld for child support. If this amounts to $396.80 per month, find his annual earnings.

   6. _____

7. **CALORIES FROM FAT**   Häagen-Dazs vanilla ice cream has 270 calories per serving. If 60% of these calories come from fat, find the number of calories coming from fat. (*Source:* Häagen-Dazs.)

   7. _____

8. **BLOOD-CHOLESTEROL LEVELS**   At a recent health fair, 32% of the people tested were found to have high blood-cholesterol levels. If 350 people were tested, find the number having a high blood-cholesterol level.

   8. _____

9. **RETIREMENT ACCOUNT**   Erin Joyce has 9.5% of her earnings deposited into a retirement account. If this amounts to $308.75 per month, find her annual earnings.

   9. _____

10. **COLLEGE ENDOWMENT** During a recession in which stock prices fell, one community college endowment fund lost $1,016,760, or 14.8% of the total, at the start of the recession. Find the amount in the endowment at the start of the recession.

10. _____

AIDING DISABLED EMPLOYEES *The bar graph below shows how companies have accommodated their employees with disabilities. The data were collected from personnel directors, human resource directors, and executives responsible for hiring at 501 companies. Use this information to solve Exercises 11–14. Round to the nearest whole number.*

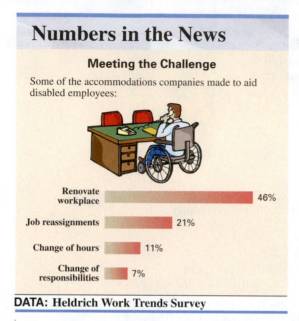

Numbers in the News

Meeting the Challenge

Some of the accommodations companies made to aid disabled employees:

Renovate workplace	46%
Job reassignments	21%
Change of hours	11%
Change of responsibilities	7%

DATA: Heldrich Work Trends Survey

11. How many companies have renovated the workplace to aid employees with disabilities?

11. _____

12. How many companies changed worker responsibilities to aid employees with disabilities?

12. _____

13. Find the number of companies that changed worker hours to aid employees with disabilities.

13. _____

14. Find the number of companies that made job reassignments to aid employees with disabilities.

14. _____

3.4 Finding Rate

OBJECTIVES

1 Use the basic percent formula to solve for rate.

2 Solve for the rate in application problems.

case IN point

As managing broker at a Century 21 Real Estate office, Tom Dugally must prepare monthly, quarterly, and annual reports. He often calculates each expense item as a percent of income. He watches these numbers carefully to better control costs.

OBJECTIVE 1 Use the basic percent formula to solve for rate. In this type of percent problem, the part and base are given, and the rate must be found. The **formula for rate** is found from the formula $P = B \times R$. The diagram shows that to find the formula for rate, cover R to get $\frac{P}{B}$, or part ÷ base.

$$\text{Rate} = \frac{\text{Part}}{\text{Base}} \quad \text{or} \quad R = \frac{P}{B}$$

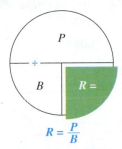

$$R = \frac{P}{B}$$

Actually, the formula $P = B \times R$ can be used to find either P, B, or R as long as the values of two of the three components are known.

To find P:
$$\text{Use } P = B \times R.$$

To find R:
$$P = B \times R$$
$$\frac{P}{B} = \frac{B \times R}{B} \quad \textbf{Divide both sides by B.}$$
$$\frac{P}{B} = R, \quad \text{or} \quad R = \frac{P}{B}$$

To find B:
$$P = B \times R$$
$$\frac{P}{R} = \frac{B \times R}{R} \quad \textbf{Divide both sides by R.}$$
$$\frac{P}{R} = B, \quad \text{or} \quad B = \frac{P}{R}$$

Solving for Rate **EXAMPLE 1**

Solve for rate.

(a) 26 is _____ % of 104. (b) _____ % of 300 is 60. (c) 54 is _____ % of 12.

Quick TIP ▼

When finding rate, be sure to change your decimal answer to a percent.

SOLUTION

(a) $\frac{26}{104} = .25 = 25\%$ (b) $\frac{60}{300} = .2 = 20\%$ (c) $\frac{54}{12} = 4.5 = 450\%$

OBJECTIVE 2 Solve for the rate in application problems. Total revenue at Thomas Dugally's busy Century 21 Real Estate office one month was $113,000. The $9884 cost of maintaining the computer system that month was unusually high due to a system crash. Find the percent of revenue that went to maintain the computer system. Note first that the base is $113,000 and the part is $9884. The unknown is rate.

$$R = \frac{P}{B}$$

$$R = \frac{\$9884}{\$113,000}$$

$$= .0875 \quad \text{(rounded)}$$

$$= 8.75\%$$

Investors constantly try to invest funds where they can get the best rate of return on investment. The rate of return is found using the basic percent formula.

Finding the Rate of Return   **EXAMPLE 2**   An investment officer at Graham Bank placed $3,000,000 in a government security. It remained there for one year and earned $96,000 in interest. Find the rate of return.

SOLUTION

The whole is $3,000,000 and the part is $96,000. Find the rate as follows.

$$R = \frac{P}{B}$$

$$R = \frac{\$96,000}{\$3,000,000}$$

$$= .032, \quad \text{or} \quad 3.2\%$$

The investment earned 3.2% for the year.

Solving for the Percent Remaining   **EXAMPLE 3**   One of the toughest races in the world is the 26.2-mile-long Boston marathon. After running 22 miles, Sheila James is exhausted. Find the percent of the race that she must still run.

SOLUTION

$$\text{Distance yet to be run} = 26.2 - 22 = 4.2 \text{ miles}$$

$$R = \frac{P}{B}$$

$$R = \frac{4.2}{26.2}$$

$$= .160 \quad \text{(rounded)}$$

$$= 16\%$$

James still has to run 16% of the total distance.

3.4 Exercises

The QUICK START *exercises in each section contain solutions to help you get started.*

Solve for rate in each of the following. Round to the nearest tenth of a percent. (See Example 1.)

QUICK START

1. __10__ % of 2760 listings is 276 listings.

2. __40__ % of 850 showings is 340 showings.

3. 35 rail cars is _____ % of 70 rail cars.

4. 144 desks is _____ % of 300 desks.

5. _____ % of 78.57 ounces is 22.2 ounces.

6. _____ % of 728 miles is 509.6 miles.

7. 114 tuxedos is _____ % of 150 tuxedos.

8. $310.75 is _____ % of $124.30.

9. _____ % of $53.75 is $2.20.

10. _____ % of 850 liters is 3.4 liters.

11. 46 shirts is _____ % of 780 shirts.

12. 5.2 vats is _____ % of 28.4 vats.

13. _____ % of 600 acres is 7.5 acres.

14. _____ % of $8 is $.06.

15. 170 cartons is _____ % of 68 cartons.

16. _____ % of 425 orders is 612 orders.

17. _____ % of $330 is $91.74.

18. _____ % of 752 employees is 470 employees.

19. The basic percent formula is $P = B \times R$. Show how to find the formula to solve for R (rate). (See Objective 1.)

20. A problem includes last year's sales and this year's sales and asks for the percent of increase. Explain how you would identify the base, rate, and part in this problem. (See Objective 4.)

Solve for rate in the following application problems. Round to the nearest tenth of a percent. (See Examples 2–5.)

QUICK START

 21. **ADVERTISING EXPENSES** Thomas Dugally of Century 21 Real Estate reports that office income last month was $315,600, while advertising expenses were $19,567.20. What percent of last month's income was spent on advertising?

$$R = \frac{P}{B} = \frac{19,567.20}{315,600} = .062 = 6.2\%$$

21. __6.2%__

22. **JOB CUTS** Beutler Heating and Air Conditioning will lay off 45 of its 1215 workers. What percent of the workers will be laid off? (*Source:* Beutler Heating and Air Conditioning.)

22. _____

23. **WOMEN IN THE MILITARY** A recent study by Rand's National Defense Research Institute examined 48,000 military jobs, such as Army attack-helicopter pilot and Navy gunner's mate. It was found that only 960 of these jobs are filled by women. What percent of these jobs are filled by women?

23. _____

 indicates an exercise that is related to the Case in Point feature.

24. **VOCABULARY** There are 55,000-plus words in *Webster's Dictionary*, but most educated people can identify only 20,000 of these words. What percent of the words in the dictionary can these people identify?

24. _____

25. **ADVERTISING EXPENSES** Advertising expenditures for Bailey's Roofers are as follows.

Newspaper	$2250	Television	$1425
Radio	$954	Yellow Pages	$1605
Outdoor	$1950	Miscellaneous	$2775

What percent of the total advertising expenditures is spent on radio advertising?

25. _____

26. **ANTIQUE SALES** Country Bear's Antiques says that of its 3800 items in inventory, 3344 are just plain junk, while the rest are antiques. What percent of the total inventory is antiques?

26. _____

27. **TANNING SALON** One week, 860 customers tanned at Carib Beach. If 559 of those customers were under 28 years old, find the percent under age 28.

27. _____

28. **MOTORCYCLISTS** Of the 2380 motorcycle riders that participated in a recent bike rally through the California mountains, 2041 were men. Find the percent who were men.

28. _____

29. **NURSING** In a recent survey of 230 nurses, 159 were unhappy with their jobs due to the difficult working hours and work-related stresses. Find the percent unhappy with their jobs.

29. _____

30. **WIND ENERGY** In the early 1980s, wind-generated electricity cost about 30 cents per kilowatt hour. Today, the best wind systems can produce electricity for 5 cents per kilowatt hour. Find today's cost as a percent of the cost in the 1980s.

30. _____

QUICK CHECK ANSWERS

1. (a) 75%   **(b)** 425%   **3.** 17%
2. 2.5%

Supplementary Application Exercises on Base, Rate, and Part

In the equation P = B × R, P = part, B = base, or whole, and R = rate, or percent. Use the following forms of the equation to solve the application problems.

$$P = B \times R \qquad B = \frac{P}{R} \qquad R = \frac{P}{B}$$

You will first need to read the problem carefully to determine whether base, part, or rate is unknown. Round rates to the nearest tenth of a percent.

1. **VACATION MISTAKES** Out of 571 employees interviewed, 17% said they thought about work while on vacation. How many people thought about work? (*Source:* Office Team survey.)

   1. _____

2. **AMERICAN CHIROPRACTIC ASSOCIATION** There are 60,000 licensed chiropractors in the United States. If 25% of these chiropractors belong to the American Chiropractic Association (ACA), find the number of chiropractors in the ACA.

   2. _____

3. **MOTORCYCLE SAFETY** Only 20 of the 50 states require motorcycle riders to wear helmets. What percent of the states require motorcycle riders to wear helmets? (*Source:* National Highway Traffic Safety Administration.)

   3. _____

4. **DANGER OF EXTINCTION** Scientists tell us that there are 9600 bird species and that 1227 of these species are in danger of extinction. What percent of the bird species are in danger of extinction?

   4. _____

5. **LOST OVERBOARD** In a recent insurance company study of boaters who had lost items overboard, 88 boaters or 8% said that they lost their cell phones. Find the total number of boaters in the survey. (*Source:* Progressive Groups of Insurance Companies.)

   5. _____

6. **LIGHTS OUT** There are still 100,000 households in the United States that do not have electricity. If this is .08% of the homes, find the total number of households. (*Source: Time* magazine.)

   6. _____

7. **COST AFTER MARKDOWN** A copier and fax machine priced at $398 is marked down 7% to promote the new model. Find the reduced price.

   7. _____

8. **BOOK DISCOUNT** College students are offered a 6% discount on a dictionary that sells for $18.50. Find the reduced price.

   8. _____

A monthly sales report for the top four salespeople at Active Sports is shown below. Use this information to answer Exercises 9–12.

Employee Commission	Sales	Rate of Commission	
Strong, A.	$18,960	3%	_____
Ferns, K.	$21,460	3%	_____
Keyes, B.	$17,680	_____	$707.20
Vargas, K.	$23,104	_____	$1152.20

9. Find the commission for Strong.

9. _____

10. Find the commission for Ferns.

10. _____

11. What is the rate of commission for Keyes?

11. _____

12. What is the rate of commission for Vargas?

12. _____

13. **BIKER HELMET LAWS** There were 2.48 million motorcycle riders in the country who supported biker helmet laws. If this was 62% of the total motorcycle riders in the country, what is the total number of motorcycle riders? (*Source:* National Highway Traffic Safety Administration.)

13. _____

14. **HOME PRICES** In one city, the average selling price of a home increased 2.4%, or by $5088, compared to last year. Find the average selling price of a house last year.

14. _____

15. **HIGH SCHOOL DROPOUTS** In one inner city school district in a large city, 257 out of 414 entering students dropped out before graduating. Find the percent of dropouts.

15. _____

16. **LAYOFF ALTERNATIVE** Instead of laying off workers, a company cut all employee hours from 40 hours a week to 30 hours a week. By what percent were employee hours cut?

16. _____

POPULATION FORECASTS The figure shows current population with a forecast of population for 2050 for the six most populated countries of the world. Use the data to answer Exercises 17–20.

Numbers in the News

Population with a Forecast

	2000 Population	Increase in Population Forecast for 2050
China	1267	150
India	1043	571
United States	288	116
Indonesia	205	80
Brazil	174	43
Pakistan	148	187

Source: World Population Prospects, United Nations.

17. For each country, find the percent increase in population forecast for 2050 rounded to the nearest percent.

18. List the countries from those growing most rapidly (in percent growth) to those growing slowest.

19. Find the 2050 forecast population for China and India, and write using digits.

20. China was the most populous country in the world in 2000. What country is forecast to be the most populous by 2050? What is the difference between the forecast population of this country and China in 2050?

20. _____

21. HEALTH IN A MACHINE   Vending machines on campus must include healthy food choices such as fruits, fruit juices, and healthy snacks. Of the total items sold in the machines this past month, 1440 or 25% have been in the healthy foods group. Find the total number of items sold in the vending machines.

21. _____

22. TOTAL SALES   If the sales tax rate is $7\frac{1}{2}$% and the sales tax collected is $942.30, find the total sales.

22. _____

23. SAVING TO BUY A HOME   Shamus and Kathleen McCoy are motivated to buy a home and set up the following budget based on percent of take-home income: 25% for rent and utilities, 22% for food and pharmacy, 12% for health care, and 32% for other, with the remainder to savings. Their take-home pay after taxes is $5450 per month. Find the annual savings.

23. _____

24. CHICKEN NOODLE SOUP   In one year, there were 350 million cans of chicken noodle soup sold (all brands). If 60% of this soup is sold in the cold-and-flu season (October through March), find the number of cans sold in the cold-and-flu season.

24. _____

25. BUDGETING   The owner of Omni Web Designs decides to save in order to purchase the small building he currently rents. Currently, after tax income averages $6800 per month. The owner budgets the following: 35% for rent, 17% for utilities and insurance, and 40% for salaries and supplies, with the remainder to savings. Find the annual savings.

25. _____

26. BENEFIT INCREASE   One 80-year-old couple gets $1582 in monthly Social Security benefits. They receive a letter saying that their benefits will go up by 2.4% per month. Find the amount of the increase and the new total monthly benefit, both to the nearest dollar.

26. _____

27. SIDE-IMPACT COLLISIONS   Automobile accidents involving side-impact collision resulted in 9000 deaths last year. If automobiles were manufactured to meet a side-impact standard, it is estimated that 63.8% of these deaths would have been prevented. How many deaths would have been prevented?

27. _____

28. NEW-HOME PRICES   The average price of a new home in one area dropped 1.2%. If the average price of a new home was $240,000, find the average price after the decrease.

28. _____

29. U.S. PATENT RECIPIENTS   Among the 50 companies receiving the greatest number of U.S. patents last year, 18 were Japanese companies. **(a)** What percent of the top 50 companies were Japanese companies? **(b)** What percent of the top 50 companies were not Japanese companies?

(a) _____
(b) _____

30. BLOOD-ALCOHOL LEVELS   In the United States, 15 of the 50 states limit blood-alcohol levels for drivers to .08%. The remaining states limit these levels to .10%. **(a)** What percent of the states have a blood-alcohol limit of .08%? **(b)** What percent have a limit of .10%?

(a) _____
(b) _____

3.5 Increase and Decrease Problems

OBJECTIVES

1 Learn to identify an increase or decrease problem.
2 Apply the basic diagram for increase word problems.
3 Use the basic percent formula to solve for base in increase problems.
4 Apply the basic diagram for decrease word problems.
5 Use the basic percent formula to solve for base in decrease problems.

case IN point ▶

Tom Dugally of Century 21 Real Estate knows that real estate values are always changing, usually going up, occasionally going down, but never staying the same. Dugally needs to keep track of the market and must be able to calculate increases and decreases in value on a regular basis.

OBJECTIVE 1 **Learn to identify an increase or decrease problem.** Businesses commonly look at how amounts change, either up or down. For example, a manager might need to know the percent by which sales have **increased** or costs have **decreased**. A consumer might want to know the percent by which the price of an item has changed. Identify these **increase** and **decrease** problems as follows.

> **Identifying Increase and Decrease Problems**
>
> **Increase problem.** The base (100%) *plus* some portion of the base gives a new value, which is the part. Phrases such as *after an increase of, more than,* or *greater than* often indicate an increase problem. The basic formula for an increase problem is
>
> $$\text{Original} + \text{Increase} = \text{New value}$$
> $$\quad\;\;\text{(base)} \qquad\qquad\qquad\quad\text{(part)}$$
>
> **Decrease problem.** The part equals the base (100%) *minus* some portion of the base, giving a new value. Phrases such as *after a decrease of, less than,* or *after a reduction of* often indicate a decrease problem. The basic formula for a decrease problem is
>
> $$\text{Original} - \text{Decrease} = \text{New value}$$
> $$\quad\;\;\text{(base)} \qquad\qquad\qquad\qquad\text{(part)}$$

Using a Diagram to Understand an Increase Problem

EXAMPLE 1

The value of a home sold by Tom Dugally this year is $203,500, which is 10% more than last year's value. Find the value of the home last year.

SOLUTION

Remember that base is the starting point, or that to which something is compared. In this case the base is last year's value. Call base 100%, and remember that

$$\text{Original (base)} + \text{Increase} = \text{New value}$$

case IN point ▶

OBJECTIVE 2 **Apply the basic diagram for increase word problems.**

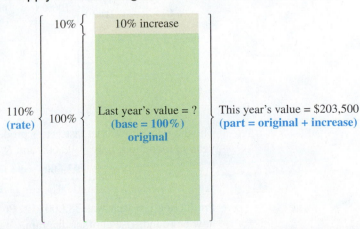

This diagram shows that the 10% increase is based on last year's value, which is unknown, and not on this year's value of $203,500. To get this year's value, 10% of last year's value was added to the amount of last year's value.

OBJECTIVE 3 Use the basic percent formula to solve for base in increase problems.

Original	+	Increase	=	New value
100%	+	10%	=	110%

Substituting in the percent formula with part = $203,500 and rate = 110% results in the following.

$$\$203{,}500 = B \times 110\%$$

Solving for B results in the following equation, which is solved for B.

$$B = \frac{\$203{,}500}{110\%}$$

$$B = \frac{\$203{,}500}{1.1}$$

$$B = \$185{,}000$$

Quick TIP ▼

The common error in solving an increase problem is thinking that the base is given and that the solution can be found by solving for part.

So the value of the house last year was $185,000. Now check the answer.

$185,000	⟵ last year's value
+ 18,500	⟵ 10% of $185,000
$203,500	⟵ this year's value

$203,500 is 110% of $185,000.

QUICK CHECK 1

The total sales at Office Products this year are $713,340, which is 35% more than last year's sales. What is the amount of last year's sales?

Finding Base after Two Increases **EXAMPLE 2**

Due to increased demand for a patented process that will help analyze the DNA of mice, Biotics Genome has increased production of testing kits by 20% per year for each of the two past years. This year's production is 93,600 kits. Find the number of kits produced two years ago.

SOLUTION

The two increases cannot be added together because the increases are from two different years, or two separate bases. The problem must be solved in two steps. First, use a diagram to find last year's production.

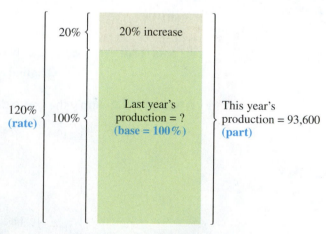

The diagram shows that last year's production plus 20% of last year's production equals this year's production. If $P = 93{,}600$ and $R = 100\% + 20\% = 120\%$, the formula $B = \frac{P}{R}$ gives

$$B = \frac{93{,}600}{120\%} = \frac{93{,}600}{1.2} = 78{,}000 \quad \text{last year's production}$$

Production last year was 78,000 kits. Production for the preceding year (two years ago) must now be found. Use another diagram.

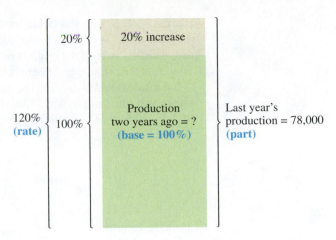

Thus, production two years ago added to 20% of production two years ago equals last year's production. Use the formula $B = \frac{P}{R}$ with P equal to 78,000 and R equal to 120%.

$$B = \frac{78,000}{120\%} = \frac{78,000}{1.2} = 65,000 \qquad \text{production 2 years ago}$$

The calculator solution to this example is done by dividing in a series.

$$93600 \; \boxed{\div} \; 1.2 \; \boxed{\div} \; 1.2 \; \boxed{=} \; 65000$$

Check the answer.

65,000	production 2 years ago
+ 13,000	20% increase
78,000	production last year
+ 15,600	20% increase
93,600	production this year

QUICK CHECK 2

Due to a large gift from a donor, Blalock College has increased scholarships by 10% per year for each of the past two years. If 1815 scholarships will be offered this year, find the number offered two years ago.

Using a Diagram to Understand a Decrease Problem

EXAMPLE 3

After Nike deducted 10% from the price of a pair of competition running shoes, Katie Small paid $135. What was the original price of the shoes?

SOLUTION

Use a diagram again, and remember that base is the starting point, which is the original price. As always, the base is 100%. Use the decrease formula.

$$\begin{array}{ccccc} \textbf{Original} & - & \textbf{Decrease} & = & \textbf{New value} \\ 100\% & - & 10\% & = & 90\% \end{array}$$

OBJECTIVE 4 Apply the basic diagram for decrease word problems.

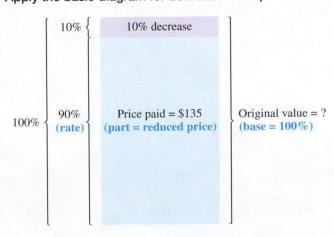

OBJECTIVE 5 Use the basic percent formula to solve for base in decrease problems.
The diagram shows that 10% was deducted from the original price. The result equals the price
paid, which is 90% of the original price. Since the original price is needed, and the diagram
shows that the original price here is the base, use the formula $B = \frac{P}{R}$.

But what should be used as the rate? The rate 10% cannot be used because the original price
is unknown (the price to which the 10% reduction was applied). The rate 90% (the difference,
$100\% - 10\% = 90\%$) must be used, since 90% of the original price is the $135 price paid.
Now find the base.

$$B = \frac{P}{R}$$

$$B = \frac{135}{90\%} = \frac{135}{.9} = \$150 \qquad \text{original price}$$

Check the answer.

$$\begin{array}{rl} \$150 & \text{original price} \\ -\quad 15 & \text{10\% discount} \\ \hline \$135 & \text{price paid} \end{array}$$

QUICK CHECK 3

A 40-inch HD LCD television is discounted 25% from the original price. If the discounted
price is $1799.99, what was the original price of the television?

3.5 Exercises

The **QUICK START** exercises in each section contain solutions to help you get started.

Solve for base in each of the following. Round to the nearest cent.
(Hint: Original + Increase = New value.) (See Examples 1 and 2.)

QUICK START

Part (after increase)	Rate of Increase	Base
1. $450	20%	$375
2. $800	25%	_____
3. $30.70	10%	_____
4. $10.09	5%	_____

Solve for base in each of the following. Round to the nearest cent.
(Hint: Original − Decrease = New value.) (See Example 3.)

QUICK START

Part (after decrease)	Rate of Decrease	Base
5. $20	20%	$25
6. $1530	15%	_____
7. $598.15	30%	_____
8. $98.38	15%	_____

9. Certain words or word phrases help to identify an increase problem. Discuss how you identify an increase problem. (See Objective 1.)

10. Certain words or word phrases help to identify a decrease problem. Discuss how you identify a decrease problem. (See Objective 1.)

indicates an exercise that is related to the Case in Point feature.

Solve the following application problems. Read each problem carefully to decide which are increase or decrease problems, and work accordingly. (See Examples 1–3.)

QUICK START

 11. **HOME-VALUE APPRECIATION** Thomas Dugally of Century 21 Real Estate just listed a home for $205,275. If this is 5% more than what the home sold for last year, find last year's selling price.

$$B = \frac{P}{R} = \frac{205{,}275}{1.05} = \$195{,}500$$

11. $195,500 _____

12. **DEALER'S COST** Cruz Electronics sold an Xbox 360 Gaming and Entertainment System for $345, a loss of 8% of the dealer's original cost. Find the original cost.

$$B = \frac{P}{R} = \frac{345}{.92} = \$375$$

12. $375 _____

13. **FAMILY RESTAURANT** Santiago Rowland owns a small restaurant and charges 8% sales tax on all orders. At the end of the day he has a total of $1026 including the sales and sales tax in his cash register. **(a)** What were his sales not including sales tax? **(b)** Find the amount that is sales tax.

(a) _____

(b) _____

14. **SALES TAX** Tom Dugally of Century 21 Real Estate purchased a new GPS for $639, including $6\frac{1}{2}\%$ sales tax. Find **(a)** the price of the GPS and **(b)** the amount of sales tax.

(a) _____

(b) _____

15. **EATING OUT** There are 177,000 fast-food restaurants in the United States. If fast food represents 21% of the total restaurants, find the total number of restaurants. Round to the nearest whole number. (*Source:* Contra Costa Times/Knight Ridder Newspapers.)

15. _____

16. **ANTILOCK BRAKES** In a recent test of an automobile antilock braking system (ABS) on wet pavement, the stopping distance was 114 feet. If this was 28.75% less than the distance needed to stop the same automobile without the ABS, find the distance needed to stop without the ABS.

16. _____

17. **FOOD INFLATION** Food inflation refers to the annual rate of increase in food prices. Food inflation in one African country was 10% for each of the past two years. Estimate the cost, two years ago, of a large basket of food that costs $80 today. Round each calculation to the nearest cent before proceeding.

17. _____

18. **DELI SALES** Sara Rasic, owner of Sara's Deli, says that her sales have increased exactly 20% per year for the last two years. Her sales this year are $170,035.20. Find her sales two years ago.

18. _____

19. **DVD RENTALS** Netflix, a DVD-rental company, has 11,000,000 subscribers, an increase of 220% from five years ago. Find the number of subscribers five years ago. Round to the nearest whole number. (*Source:* Netflix.)

19. _____

20. **FARMLAND PRICES** The value of Iowa farmland increased 4.3% this year to a statewide average value of $4450 per acre. How much per acre did Iowa farmland increase this year? Round to the nearest dollar.

20. _____

21. **AUTO SALES** Automobile sales in Asia were 23.4 million this year, a 9.4% increase over last year. Find the number of auto sales in Asia last year, rounded to the nearest tenth of a million.

21. _____

22. **EXPENSIVE RESTAURANTS** Among New York City's 20 most expensive restaurants, the average per-meal cost, excluding drinks, increased 5.5% to $90.13 in the last year. Find the price of this meal before the increase.

22. _____

23. **SURPLUS-EQUIPMENT AUCTION** In a three-day public auction of Jackson County's surplus equipment, the first day brought $5750 in sales and the second day brought $4186 in sales, with 28% of the original equipment left to be sold on the third day. Find the value of the remaining surplus equipment.

23. _____

24. **COLLEGE EXPENSES** After spending $3450 for tuition and $4350 for dormitory fees, Edgar Espina finds that 35% of his original savings remains. Find the amount of his savings that remains.

24. _____

25. **PAPER PRODUCTS MANUFACTURING** The world's largest paper-manufacturing company reported a 16% drop in third-quarter earnings. If earnings had dropped to $122 million, find the earnings before the drop. Round to the nearest hundredth of a million.

25. _____

26. **NATIONAL HOME SALES** During the recession, sales of existing homes decreased 2.3% to an annual number of 4.87 million units. Find the annual number of homes sold before the decrease. Round to the nearest hundredth of a million. (*Source:* National Association of Realtors.)

26. _____

27. **WINTER-WHEAT PLANTING** Even though wheat prices rose during the planting season, farmers planted only 50.2 million acres of winter wheat varieties. If this is 2% fewer acres than last year, find the number of acres planted last year. Round to the nearest tenth of a million.

27. _____

28. **CHIQUITA BRANDS INTERNATIONAL** Shares of Chiquita Brands stock fell 14%, to close at $13.35 per share. What was the value of the stock before the fall? Round to the nearest cent. (*Source:* Associated Press.)

28. _____

29. **COLLEGE ENROLLMENT** The enrollment at one college has grown 6% per year for the past two years. If the current enrollment is 33,708 students, find the number of students enrolled two years ago.

29. _____

30. **UNIVERSITY FEES** Students at one state university are outraged. The annual university fees were 30% more last year than they were the year before. If the fees are $3380 per year this year, which is 30% more than they were last year, find the annual student fees two years ago.

30. _____

31. **CONE ZONE DEATHS** This year there were 1181 deaths related to road construction zones in the United States. If this is an increase of 70% in the last five years, what was the number of deaths five years ago? Round to the nearest whole number. (*Source:* American Road and Transportation Builders Association.)

31. _____

32. **MINORITY LOANS** A large mortgage lender made 52% more loans to minorities this year than last year. If the number of loans to minorities this year is 2660, find the number of loans made to minorities last year.

32. _____

33. **UNEMPLOYMENT** The unemployment rate among workers under 25 in a populous state went from 8.2% to 7.1% in one year. Assume an average of 1,340,200 workers and estimate the decrease in the number unemployed.

33. _____

34. **STOCK VALUE** The stock value of drugstore operator CVS dropped 7.4% to close at $29.06 per share. Find the value of each share of stock before the drop. Round to the nearest cent.

34. _____

Chapter 3   Quick Review

Chapter Terms   *Review the following terms to test your understanding of the chapter. For each term you do not know, refer to the page number found next to that term.*

base [p. 93]	formula for rate [p. 107]	part [p. 93]	percents [p. 86]
decrease problem [p. 115]	hundredths [p. 86]	percent [p. 86]	rate [p. 93]
formula for base [p. 101]	increase problem [p. 115]	percent formula [p. 93]	sales tax [p. 95]

CONCEPTS

EXAMPLES

3.1 Writing a decimal as a percent

Move the decimal point two places to the right and attach a percent sign (%).

$$.75(.75.) = 75\%$$

3.1 Writing a fraction as a percent

First change the fraction to a decimal. Then move the decimal point two places to the right and attach a percent sign (%).

$$\frac{2}{5} = .4$$
$$.4(.40.) = 40\%$$

3.1 Writing a percent as a decimal

Move the decimal point two places to the left and drop the percent sign (%).

$$50\% (.50.\%) = .5$$

3.1 Writing a percent as a fraction

First change the percent to a decimal. Then write the decimal as a fraction in lowest terms.

$$15\% (.15.\%) = .15 = \frac{15}{100} = \frac{3}{20}$$

3.1 Writing a fractional percent as a decimal

First change the fraction to a decimal, keeping the percent sign. Then move the decimal point two places to the left and drop the percent sign (%).

$$\frac{1}{2}\% = .5\%$$
$$.5\% = .005$$

3.2 Solving for part, using the percent formula

$$\textbf{Part = Base} \times \textbf{Rate}$$
$$P = B \times R$$
$$P = BR$$

A company offered a 15% discount on all sales. Find the discount on sales of $1850.

$$P = B \times R$$
$$P = \$1850 \times 15\%$$
$$P = \textbf{\$1850} \times .15 = \$277.50 \text{ discount}$$

3.2 Using the standard format to solve percent problems

Express the problem in the format

$$R \quad \times \quad B \quad = \quad P$$
$$\underline{\hphantom{xxx}}\% \text{ of } \underline{\hphantom{xxx}} \text{ is } \underline{\hphantom{xxx}}$$

Notice that *of* means × and *is* means =.

A shop gives a 10% discount on all repairs. Find the discount on a $175 repair.

Rate = 10%, Base = $175, and discount is unknown.

$$P \quad = \quad R \times B$$
$$\text{Discount} = 10\% \times \$175 = \$17.50$$

3.3 Using the percent formula to solve for base

Use $P = B \times R$.

$$B = \frac{P}{R}$$

If the sales tax rate is 4%, find amount of sales when the sales tax is $18.

$$R \times B = P, \quad \text{or} \quad B = \frac{P}{R}$$

$$B = \frac{18}{.04} = \$450 \text{ sales}$$

CONCEPTS   **EXAMPLES**

3.4 Using the percent formula to solve for rate

Use $P = B \times R$.

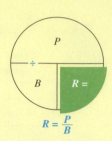

$$R = \frac{P}{B}$$

The return is $307.80 on an investment of $3420. Find the rate of return.

$$R \times B = P, \quad \text{or} \quad R = \frac{P}{B}$$

$$R = \frac{307.8}{3420} = .09 = 9\%$$

3.5 Drawing a diagram and using the percent formula to solve increase problems

Solve for the base when given the rate (110%) and the part (after increase).

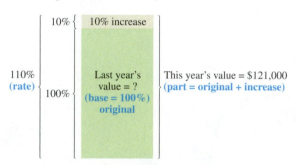

This year's sales are $121,000, which is 10% more than last year's sales. Find last year's sales.

Original + Increase = New value
$$100\% + 10\% = 110\%$$

Use $B = \dfrac{P}{R}$.

$$B = \frac{\$121{,}000}{110\%} = \frac{\$121{,}000}{1.1}$$

$$= 110{,}000 \text{ last year's sales}$$

Check: $\begin{array}{ll} \$110{,}000 & \text{last year's sales} \\ + \quad 11{,}000 & \text{10\% of \$110,000} \\ \hline \$121{,}000 & \text{this year's sales} \end{array}$

3.5 Drawing a diagram and using the percent formula to solve decrease problems

Solve for the base when given the rate (90%) and the part (after decrease).

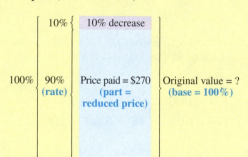

After a deduction of 10% from the price, a customer paid $270. Find the original price.

Original − Decrease = New value
$$100\% - 10\% = 90\%$$

Use $B = \dfrac{P}{R}$.

$$B = \frac{270}{.9} = \$300 \text{ original price}$$

Check: $\begin{array}{ll} \$300 & \text{original price} \\ - \quad 30 & \text{10\% discount} \\ \hline \$270 & \text{price paid} \end{array}$

case study

SELF EMPLOYED RETIREMENT PLAN

Betty and Juan Martinez are self-employed and have a retirement plan. They have decided to invest in stocks in the plan and are looking at the companies listed below trying to figure out which to buy. Find the stock price last year, the percent of change from last year, or the stock price this year as indicated. Round dollar amounts to the nearest cent and percents to the nearest tenth. Note that some of the stock prices in the table increased dramatically during the 2009–2010 time period shown in the table. This occurred since the financial crisis of 2008–09 resulted in abnormally low stock prices in the base year shown which is 2009.

Numbers in the News

Many Stock Prices Increase after Sharp Recession Wanes

Company	Stock Symbol	Stock Price Last Year	Stock Price This Year	% Change from Last Year
Amazon.com	AMZN	$70.48	$138.50	_____
Bank of America	BAC	$10.50	_____	64.2%
McDonald's	MCD	_____	$63.55	13.4%
Wal-Mart Stores	WMT	$50.72	_____	6.7%

INVESTIGATE

List five large publicly held companies that you know or whose products and services you enjoy. Then use the Web to find the most recent closing stock price. Ignoring commissions, estimate the cost if you purchased 10 shares of each of the five companies at the close price for the day.

case ≈ point summary exercise

CENTURY 21

www.century21.com

Facts:

- 1971: Founded in California
- 1977: Went Public
- 1984: Purchased by Metropolitan Life Insurance
- 2006: Offices and Listings in over 60 countries

Century 21 Real Estate Corporation franchises real estate offices. It has more than 8500 independently owned and operated offices, with locations in all 50 states and more than 60 countries. The firm's Web site, Century21.com, is the fifth most visited real estate Web site on the Internet.

    Tom Dugally worked as an agent for Century 21 for several years before he received his broker's license. A few years later, he contacted Century 21 and they helped him set up his own real estate office under a Century 21 franchise. He uses percents on a daily basis to find real estate commissions, monitor costs, follow interest rates, estimate property taxes, and keep up with home prices.

1. Dugally owned a small apartment complex that was worth $865,000 last year. He sold it for $892,680 this year. Find the percent increase in value.

    1. _____

2. Mr. Makin wants Dugally's agency to sell a similar property. Last year, this property had a value of $1,145,000. Use the percent increase from (1) to estimate the current value of this property.

    2. _____

3. A home owner has a large home overlooking a river that is currently valued at $435,000. If his home price has increased by the amount indicated in (1), find the amount by which it increased in value compared to one year ago. Round all dollar values to the nearest dollar.

    3. _____

4. The total real estate commissions paid to Dugally's real estate agency for the quarter were $237,075. If 65% of those funds are paid directly to the self-employed real estate agents that work in the office under Dugally, find the amount the real estate office keeps. He uses these funds to pay for office, computer, advertising expenses, unilities, etc.

    4. _____

Discussion Question: *It is very difficult for a new real estate agent to earn enough to live on while learning the business. What can Dugally do to train and help a new agent?*

Chapter 3 Test

To help you review, the numbers in brackets show the section in which the topic was discussed.

Determine the fraction, decimal, or percent equivalent for each of the following as necessary.
Write fractions in lowest terms. **[3.1]**

	FRACTION	DECIMAL	PERCENT
1.	$\dfrac{3}{8}$	.375	_____
2.	_____	.35	35%
3.	$\dfrac{3}{125}$	_____	2.4%
4.	_____	.14	14%
5.	$5\dfrac{7}{8}$	5.875	_____

Solve the following problems. **[3.1–3.4]**

6. 36 home sales is 12% of what number of home sales?

6. _____

7. What is $\frac{1}{4}$% of $1260?

7. _____

8. Find the fractional equivalent of 24%.

8. _____

9. 48 purchase orders is $2\frac{1}{2}$% of how many purchase orders?

9. _____

10. Change 87.5% to its fractional equivalent.

10. _____

11. One share of Microsoft Corporation stock sells for $29.60. It currently pays an annual dividend of 1.8% of that selling price. Find the dividend per share to the nearest cent. **[3.2]**

11. _____

12. A supervisor at Barrett Manufacturing finds that 1120 cabinet door hinges are rejected each month. If this amounts to .5% of total monthly production, find the total monthly production of door hinges. **[3.3]**

12. _____

13. The Honda Civic GX is the only car offered to consumers in the United States that runs on natural gas and *uses no gasoline*. It gets 36 miles per gallon of natural gas on the highway and is the cleanest burning automobile engine in the country. Although it is listed at $25,189, it is offered at a discount (including rebate on federal taxes) of 18%. Find the sale price.

13. _____

14. There are 41 million Americans 65 or older, and they make up 13 percent of the U.S. population. What is the total population of the United States? Round to the nearest tenth of a million. (*Source:* AARP.) **[3.2]**

14. _____

15. A retail store with a monthly advertising budget of $3400 decides to set up a media budget. It plans to spend 22% for television advertising, 38% for newspaper advertising, 14% for outdoor signs, 15% for radio advertising, and the remainder for bumper stickers.

  (a) What percent of the total budget do they plan to spend on bumper stickers?
  (b) How much do they plan to spend on bumper stickers for the entire year? **[3.2]**

(a) _____

(b) _____

16. Americans lose about 300 million golf balls each year, and about 225 million of these are recovered and resold in what has become a $200-million annual business. What percent of the lost golf balls are recovered and resold? (*Source: USA Today.*) **[3.4]**

16. _____

17. A Digital Media Player is marked "Reduced 20%, Now Only $149." Find the original price of the media player. **[3.5]**

17. _____

18. Last year's backpack sales were 10% more than they were the year before. This year's sales are 1452 units, which is 10% more than last year. Find the number of backpacks sold two years ago. **[3.5]**

18. _____

19. The local real estate board reports that the number of condominium listings last month was 379. If 357 condominiums were listed in the same month last year, find the percent of increase. Round to the nearest tenth of a percent. (*Source:* Sacramento *Realtor.*) **[3.4]**

19. _____

20. Proctor & Gamble, the maker of Tide detergent, Pampers diapers, and Clairol hair-care products, had quarterly earnings that rose 20% to $1.76 billion. Find the earnings in the previous quarter. Round to the nearest hundredth of a billion. (*Source:* Proctor & Gamble.) **[3.4]**

20. _____

Equations and Formulas

4

case IN point ▶

BEN JAMES works in the research department of General Motors (GM) as a statistician. Among other things, his duties include making forecasts of demand for individual vehicle models produced by the company. He uses a variety of tools, including equations, to make the forecasts.

It is very important that management have an accurate forecast of demand. A forecast of demand that is too low results in lost sales, since customers often will not wait to buy. A forecast that is too high results in too much inventory, which is expensive to carry in stock. Sometimes, excess inventory must be marked down in order to sell it. Either way, the firm loses money, potentially a *lot* of money. So, James has a very important job at GM.

Equations and formulas are often used in business. For example, they are used to find markup, interest, depreciation, the future value of annuities, and many other things. In this chapter, we show how to solve and work with basic equations and formulas.

4.1 Solving Equations

OBJECTIVES

1   Learn the basic terminology of equations.
2   Use basic rules to solve equations.
3   Solve equations requiring more than one operation.
4   Combine like terms in equations.
5   Use the distributive property to simplify equations.

OBJECTIVE 1 Learn the basic terminology of equations. Some of the basic terms related to equations are given in the table.

Definitions	Examples
A **variable** is a letter used to represent an unknown value. Any letter can be used for a variable.	$x, t, s, z, R, y,$ or A
A **term** is a number, a variable, or the product or quotient of a number and a variable.	$53, y, 6x, 9.5z, \dfrac{4}{5}y, \dfrac{s}{3}$
An **expression** can be a single term, but it is often the sum or difference of two or more terms. An expression does not contain an *equal* sign.	$7b, 6x + 9, z - \dfrac{1}{2}y, 19.4t - 5$
An **equation** is two expressions that are equal to one another.	$x + 5 = 9$
Each equation has a **left side** and a **right side**.	$x + 5 = 9$
A **solution** to an equation is the number that can be substituted in place of a variable that makes the equation true.	$x = 4$ is a solution to the equation $x + 5 = 9$.

To see that $x = 4$ is a solution to the equation $x + 5 = 9$, **substitute** 4 in place of x and determine if the resulting equation is true.

$$x + 5 = 9$$
$$4 + 5 = 9 \qquad \text{\textbf{Substitute 4 in place of } } x \textbf{ in the equation.}$$
$$9 = 9 \qquad \text{\textbf{Replace } } 4 + 5 \textbf{ with 9 on the left side.}$$

Since the final equation is true, we know that $x = 4$ is a solution to the equation.

OBJECTIVE 2 Use basic rules to solve equations. To solve a basic equation for the unknown, change it so that:

1. all terms with a variable are on one side of the equation and
2. all terms with only numbers are on the other side of the equation.

It makes no difference whether the variables are on the left side or the right side of the equation.

To move a term to the other side of the equation, do the opposite operation, or "undo," as shown in Example 1, using the following two rules. It is important that what you do to one side of the equation is done to the other side.

> **Rules for Solving Equations**
>
> **Addition Rule**   The same number (or term) may be added or subtracted on both sides of an equation.
>
> **Multiplication Rule**   Both sides of an equation may be multiplied or divided by the same nonzero number (or term).

Solving a Linear Equation Using Addition **EXAMPLE 1**

Solve $x - 9 = 15$ for the unknown.

SOLUTION

The goal is to end up with an equation equivalent to the original equation in which the variable x is isolated on one side and the numbers are on the opposite side. The number 9 is being subtracted from the x on the left side. Undo this operation and move 9 to the other side of the equation by adding 9 to both sides.

$$x - 9 = 15$$
$$x - 9 + 9 = 15 + 9 \qquad \text{Add 9 to both sides.}$$
$$x + 0 = 24$$
$$x = 24$$

To confirm that the value of the unknown is 24, substitute 24 for x in the original equation.

$$x - 9 = 15 \qquad \text{Original equation}$$
$$24 - 9 = 15 \qquad \text{Let } x = 24.$$
$$15 = 15 \qquad \text{True}$$

Therefore, x is equal to 24. This is the solution to the equation.

QUICK CHECK 1

Solve $y - 22 = 45$.

Solving a Linear Equation Using Subtraction **EXAMPLE 2**

Solve $k + 7 = 18$.

SOLUTION

To isolate k on the left side, do the opposite of adding 7, which is *subtracting* 7 from both sides.

$$k + 7 = 18$$
$$k + 7 - 7 = 18 - 7 \qquad \text{Subtract 7 from both sides.}$$
$$k = 11$$

QUICK CHECK 2

Solve $m + 19 = 32$.

Solving a Linear Equation Using Division **EXAMPLE 3**

Solve $5p = 60$.

SOLUTION

The term $5p$ indicates the multiplication of 5 and p. Since division is the inverse of multiplication, solve the equation by *dividing* both sides by 5.

$$5p = 60$$
$$\frac{5p}{5} = \frac{60}{5} \qquad \text{Divide both sides by 5.}$$
$$p = 12$$

Check by substituting 12 for p in the original equation.

QUICK CHECK 3

Solve $17g = 153$.

Solving a Linear Equation Using Multiplication **EXAMPLE 4**

Solve $\frac{y}{3} = 9$.

SOLUTION

The bar in $\frac{y}{3}$ means to divide. Since multiplication is the opposite of division, multiply both sides by 3.

$$\frac{y}{3} = 9$$
$$\frac{y}{3} \cdot 3 = 9 \cdot 3 \qquad \text{Multiply both sides of the equation by 3.}$$
$$y = 27$$

Example 5 shows how to solve an equation using a reciprocal. To get the **reciprocal** of a nonzero fraction, exchange the numerator and the denominator. For example, the reciprocal of $\frac{7}{9}$ is $\frac{9}{7}$. The product of two reciprocals is 1.

$$\frac{\overset{1}{\cancel{7}}}{\underset{1}{\cancel{9}}} \cdot \frac{\overset{1}{\cancel{9}}}{\underset{1}{\cancel{7}}} = 1$$

So, $\frac{9}{7}$ is the reciprocal of $\frac{7}{9}$.

Solving a Linear Equation Using Reciprocals **EXAMPLE 5**

Solve $\frac{3}{4}z = 9$.

SOLUTION

Solve this equation by multiplying both sides by $\frac{4}{3}$, the reciprocal of $\frac{3}{4}$. This process will give $1z$, or just z, on the left.

$$\frac{3}{4}z = 9$$

$$\frac{3}{4}z \cdot \frac{4}{3} = 9 \cdot \frac{4}{3} \qquad \text{Multiply both sides by } \frac{4}{3}.$$

$$z = 12$$

OBJECTIVE 3 Solve equations requiring more than one operation. The equation in Example 6 requires two steps to solve.

Solving a Linear Equation Using Several Steps **EXAMPLE 6**

Solve $2m + 5 = 17$.

SOLUTION

To solve equations that require more than one step, first isolate the terms involving the unknown (or variable) on one side of the equation and the constants (or numbers) on the other side by using addition and subtraction.

$$2m + 5 = 17$$

$$2m + 5 - 5 = 17 - 5 \qquad \text{Subtract 5 from both sides.}$$

$$2m = 12$$

Now divide both sides by 2.

$$\frac{2m}{2} = \frac{12}{2} \qquad \text{Divide both sides by 2.}$$

$$m = 6$$

As before, check by substituting 6 for m in the original equation.

The unknown can be on either side of the equal sign, so $6 = m$ is the same as $m = 6$.

Solving a Linear Equation Using Several Steps **EXAMPLE 7**

Solve $3y - 12 = 52$.

SOLUTION

$$3y - 12 = 52$$

$$3y - 12 + 12 = 52 + 12 \qquad \text{Add 12 to both sides.}$$

$$3y = 64$$

$$\frac{3y}{3} = \frac{64}{3} \qquad \text{Divide both sides by 3.}$$

$$y = 21\frac{1}{3}$$

QUICK CHECK 7

Solve $9q - 14 = 58$.

OBJECTIVE 4 Combine like terms in equations. Some equations have more than one term with the same variable. Terms with the same variables are called **like terms**. They can be *combined* by adding or subtracting the coefficients just as 5 apples + 2 apples can be combined to be 7 apples.

$$5y + 2y = (\mathbf{5 + 2})y = 7y$$
$$11k - 8k = (\mathbf{11 - 8})k = 3k$$
$$12p - 5p + 2p = (\mathbf{12 - 5 + 2})p = 9p$$
$$2z + z = 2z + 1z = (\mathbf{2 + 1})z = 3z$$

Terms with different variables in them *cannot* be combined into a single term just as 5 apples + 2 bananas cannot be combined to be either 7 apples or 7 bananas. These are called **unlike terms**. For example, $12y + 5x$ cannot be combined to make one term, since y and x are different variables and may have different values.

Solving a Linear Equation Using Several Steps **EXAMPLE 8**

Solve $8y - 6y + 4y = 24$.

SOLUTION

Start by combining terms on the left: $\mathbf{8y - 6y} + 4y = 2y + 4y = 6y$.

$$8y - 6y + 4y = 24$$
$$(8 - 6 + 4)y = 24 \qquad \text{Combine like terms.}$$
$$6y = 24$$
$$\frac{6y}{6} = \frac{24}{6} \qquad \text{Divide both sides by 6.}$$
$$y = 4$$

QUICK CHECK 8

Solve $17z - 12z = 42$.

Solving a Linear Equation **EXAMPLE 9**

Solve $7z - 3z + .5z = 15$.

SOLUTION

$$7z - 3z + .5z = 15$$
$$(7 - 3 + .5)z = 15 \qquad \text{Combine like terms.}$$
$$4.5z = 15$$
$$\frac{4.5z}{4.5} = \frac{15}{4.5} \qquad \text{Divide both sides by 4.5.}$$
$$z = 3\frac{1}{3}$$

QUICK CHECK 9

Solve $3t - .5t = 17$.

OBJECTIVE 5 Use the distributive property to simplify equations. Some of the equations used in this book involve a number in front of terms in parentheses. These formulas often require use of the *distributive property*. According to the **distributive property**, a number on the outside of the parentheses can be multiplied by each term inside the parentheses, as shown here.

$$a(b + c) = ab + ac$$

The following diagram may help in remembering the distributive property.

Multiply a by b and by c.

$$a(b + c) = ab + ac$$

More examples:

Multiply 2 by m and 7.

$$2(m + 7) = 2m + 2 \cdot 7 = 2m + 14$$
$$8(k - 5) = 8k - 8 \cdot 5 = 8k - 40$$

Solving a Linear Equation Using the Distributive Property

EXAMPLE 10

Solve $8(t - 5) = 16$.

SOLUTION

First use the distributive property on the left to remove the parentheses.

$$8(t - 5) = 16$$
$$8t - 40 = 16$$
$$8t - 40 + \mathbf{40} = 16 + \mathbf{40} \qquad \text{Add 40 to both sides.}$$
$$8t = 56$$
$$\frac{8t}{\mathbf{8}} = \frac{56}{\mathbf{8}} \qquad \text{Divide both sides by 8.}$$
$$t = 7$$

QUICK CHECK 10

Solve $9(s - 16) = 135$.

Use the following steps to solve an equation.

Solving an Equation

Step 1   Remove all parentheses on both sides of the equation using the distributive property.

Step 2   Combine all like terms on both sides of the equation.

Step 3   Place all terms containing a variable on the same side of the equation and all terms not containing a variable on the other side of the equation.

Step 4   Multiply or divide the variable term by numbers as needed to produce a term with a coefficient of 1 in front of the variable.

Solving a Linear Equation Using the Distributive Property

Solve $5r - 2 = 2(r + 5)$.

SOLUTION

$$5r - 2 = 2(r + 5) \qquad \text{Use the distributive property on the right side.}$$
$$5r - 2 = 2r + 10$$
$$5r - 2 + \mathbf{2} = 2r + 10 + \mathbf{2} \qquad \text{Add 2 to both sides to get all terms with only numbers on the right side.}$$
$$5r = 2r + 12$$
$$5r - \mathbf{2r} = 2r + 12 - \mathbf{2r} \qquad \text{Subtract 2r from both sides to get all terms with only variables on the left side.}$$
$$5r - 2r = 12$$
$$3r = 12 \qquad \text{Combine like terms on the left side.}$$
$$\frac{3r}{\mathbf{3}} = \frac{12}{\mathbf{3}} \qquad \text{Divide both sides by 3.}$$
$$r = 4$$

> **Quick TIP ▼**
>
> Be sure to check the answer in the *original* equation.

Check by substituting 4 for r in the original equation.

QUICK CHECK 11

Solve $5(s - 4) = 3(s + 9)$.

Solving a Linear Equation Using the Distributive Property

EXAMPLE 12

Solve $3(t - .8) = 14 + t$.

SOLUTION

$$3(t - .8) = 14 + t$$
$$3t - 2.4 = 14 + t \qquad \text{Use the distributive property.}$$
$$3t - 2.4 - \mathbf{t} = 14 + t - \mathbf{t} \qquad \text{Subtract t from both sides.}$$
$$2t - 2.4 = 14 \qquad \text{Combine like terms on the left side.}$$
$$2t - 2.4 + \mathbf{2.4} = 14 + \mathbf{2.4} \qquad \text{Add 2.4 to both sides.}$$
$$2t = 16.4$$
$$\frac{2t}{\mathbf{2}} = \frac{16.4}{\mathbf{2}} \qquad \text{Divide both sides by 2.}$$
$$t = 8.2$$

QUICK CHECK 12

Solve $12u - 8 = 8(u + 4)$.

4.1 Exercises

The **QUICK START** exercises in each section contain solutions to help you get started.

Solve each equation for the unknown.

QUICK START

1. $s + 12 = 15$ __3__
$$s + 12 = 15$$
$$s + 12 - 12 = 15 - 12$$
$$s = 3$$

2. $k + 15 = 22$ __7__
$$k + 15 = 22$$
$$k + 15 - 15 = 22 - 15$$
$$k = 7$$

3. $b - 7 = 24$ _____

4. $P - 13 = 52$ _____

5. $12 = b + 9$ _____

6. $7 = m - 3$ _____

7. $8k = 56$ _____

8. $3q = 120$ _____

9. $60 = 30m$ _____

10. $94 = 2z$ _____

11. $\dfrac{m}{5} = 6$ _____

12. $\dfrac{r}{7} = 1$ _____

13. $\dfrac{2}{3}a = 5$ _____

14. $\dfrac{3}{4}m = 18$ _____

15. $\dfrac{9}{5}r = 18$ _____

16. $2x = \dfrac{5}{3}$ _____

17. $3m + 5 = 17$ _____

18. $2y - 5 = 39$ _____

19. $4r + 3 = 9$ _____

20. $2p + \dfrac{1}{2} = \dfrac{3}{2}$ _____

21. $11r - 5r + 6r = 84$ _____

△c indicates an exercise that is related to the Case in Point feature.

22. $5m + 6m - 2m = 72$ _____   **23.** $3(2x + 3) = 3x + 12$ _____   **24.** $4z + 2 = 2(z + 3)$ _____

25. Define variable, term, expression, and equation.

26. Explain the difference between an expression and an equation. Then explain what is meant by the *solution to an equation*.

4.2 Applications of Equations

OBJECTIVES

1 Translate phrases into mathematical expressions.

2 Write equations from given information.

3 Solve application problems.

At General Motors, Ben James studies historical sales, looking for trends and patterns. He also analyzes the current economic conditions that affect those who buy vehicles produced by General Motors. He uses the knowledge gained to develop equations that help him make forecasts of demand. Without a good forecast, managers would not know how many cars to build.

OBJECTIVE 1 Translate phrases into mathematical expressions. Most problems in business are expressed in words. Before these problems can be solved, they must be converted into mathematical language.

Word problems often have certain phrases that occur again and again. The key to solving word problems is to correctly translate these expressions into mathematical expressions. The next few examples illustrate this process.

Translating Verbal Expressions Involving Addition

EXAMPLE 1

Write the following verbal expressions as mathematical expressions. Use x to represent the unknown quantity. Note that other letters can also be used to represent this unknown quantity.

SOLUTION

VERBAL EXPRESSION	MATHEMATICAL EXPRESSION	COMMENTS
(a) 5 plus a number	$5 + x$	x represents the number, and *plus* indicates **addition**.
(b) Add 20 to a number	$x + 20$	x represents the number, and *add* indicates **addition**.
(c) The sum of a number and 12	$x + 12$	x represents the number, and *sum* indicates **addition**.
(d) 6 more than a number	$x + 6$	x represents the number, and *more than* indicates **addition**.

QUICK CHECK 1

Write a number plus 7 as a mathematical expression using y for the unknown.

Translating Verbal Expressions Involving Subtraction

EXAMPLE 2

Write each of the following verbal expressions as a mathematical expression. Use p as the variable.

SOLUTION

VERBAL EXPRESSION	MATHEMATICAL EXPRESSION	COMMENTS
(a) 3 less than a number	$p - 3$	p represents the number, and *less than* indicates **subtraction**.
(b) A number decreased by 14	$p - 14$	p represents the number, and *decreased by* indicates **subtraction**.
(c) 10 fewer than p	$p - 10$	p represents the number, and *fewer than* indicates **subtraction**.

QUICK CHECK 2

Use s for the unknown, and write a mathematical expression for 19 minus an unknown.

Translating Verbal Expressions Involving Multiplication and Division

EXAMPLE 3

Write the following verbal expressions as mathematical expressions. Use y as the variable.

SOLUTION

VERBAL EXPRESSION	MATHEMATICAL EXPRESSION	COMMENTS
(a) The product of a number and 3	$3y$	y represents the number, and *product* indicates **multiplication**.
(b) Four times a number	$4y$	y represents the number, and *times* indicates **multiplication**.
(c) Two-thirds of a number	$\frac{2}{3}y$	y represents the number, and *of* indicates **multiplication**.
(d) The quotient of a number and 2	$\frac{y}{2}$	y represents the number, and *quotient* indicates **division**.
(e) The sum of 3 and a number is multiplied by 5	$5(3 + y)$	This requires **parentheses**.
(f) 7 is multiplied by the difference of an unknown number and 14	$7(y - 14)$	This requires **parentheses**.

> **QUICK CHECK 3**
>
> Use t for the variable, and write an expression for the product of 7 and the sum of 9 plus an unknown.

When multiplying or adding, it does not make any difference which variable is written first, as you can see from the examples.

$$15 \times y = y \times 15 \qquad x + 3 = 3 + x$$

However, the order *does* make a difference when dividing or subtracting, as you can see.

$$\frac{10}{x} \neq \frac{x}{10} \quad (\text{unless } x = 10) \qquad z - 150 \neq 150 - z \quad (\text{unless } z = 150)$$

OBJECTIVE 2 Write equations from given information. Read the problem carefully as you develop the equation(s) needed to solve it.

Writing an Equation from Words

EXAMPLE 4

Translate "the product of 5 and a number decreased by 8 is 100" into an equation. Then, solve the equation.

SOLUTION

Use the letter y as the variable and translate as follows.

Simplify and complete the solution of the equation.

$$5 \cdot (y - 8) = 100$$
$$5y - 40 = 100 \qquad \text{Apply the distributive property.}$$
$$5y = 140 \qquad \text{Add 40 to both sides.}$$
$$y = 28 \qquad \text{Divide by 5.}$$

> **QUICK CHECK 4**
>
> Write "ninety-four is the product of 12 and the sum of a number and 2.5" as an equation, using p for the variable.

Writing an Equation from Words

Write "the sum of an unknown and 6, when divided by 15, is equal to 7" as an equation, using r as the variable.

SOLUTION

The sum of an unknown and 6	when divided by 15	is equal to	7.
↓	↓	↓	↓
$(r + 6)$	$\div 15$	$=$	7

Simplify and solve the equation.

$$(r + 6) \div 15 = 7$$
$$(r + 6) \div 15 \cdot \mathbf{15} = 7 \cdot \mathbf{15} \qquad \text{Multiply both sides by 15.}$$
$$r + 6 = 105$$
$$r + 6 - \mathbf{6} = 105 - \mathbf{6} \qquad \text{Subtract 6 from both sides.}$$
$$r = 99$$

QUICK CHECK 5

Write "the quantity 17 minus an unknown, divided by 12, is equal to 14" as an equation, using r as the variable.

OBJECTIVE 3 Solve application problems. Now that statements have been translated into mathematical expressions, you can use this knowledge to solve problems.

Solving Application Problems

Step 1	Read the problem carefully. A sketch may help.
Step 2	Identify the unknown and choose a variable to represent it. If possible, write any other unknowns in terms of the same variable.
Step 3	Translate the problem into an equation.
Step 4	Solve the equation.
Step 5	Answer the question(s) asked in the problem.
Step 6	Check your solution using the original words of the problem.
Step 7	Be sure your answer is reasonable.

Step 3 is often the most difficult. To write an equation from the information given in the problem, convert the facts stated in words into mathematical expressions. These expressions are used to build a *mathematical model* of the situation.

Solving a Business Problem   **EXAMPLE 6**

case IN point

Ben James is studying monthly demand for Chevrolet Impalas in two different regions of the country. He has 14,200 new Impalas to ship to the two regions, and he decides to ship 3350 more to the Southeast region than to the mid–Atlantic Coast region. Find the number to be shipped to the mid–Atlantic Coast region.

SOLUTION

If m = number of Impalas to be shipped to the mid–Atlantic Coast region, then $(m + 3350)$ = number to be shipped to the Southeast region. The sum of the two shipments is 14,200.

Number to mid–Atlantic Coast region	+	Number to Southeast region	=	Total
m	+	$(m + 3350)$	=	$14,200$

$$m + m + 3350 = 14,200 \qquad \text{Remove parentheses}$$
$$2m + 3350 = 14,200 \qquad \text{Combine like terms.}$$
$$2m + 3350 - \mathbf{3350} = 14,200 - \mathbf{3350} \qquad \text{Subtract 3350 from both sides.}$$
$$2m = 10,850 \qquad \text{Simplify.}$$
$$\frac{2m}{2} = \frac{10,850}{2} \qquad \text{Divide both sides by 2.}$$
$$m = 5425$$

So, the numbers to be shipped are:

$$m = 5425 \text{ to the mid–Atlantic Coast region}$$
$$(m + 3350) = \underline{8775} \text{ to the Southeast region}$$
$$= \overline{14{,}200} \text{ to be shipped}$$

Since this agrees with the total to be shipped, the answer checks.

> **QUICK CHECK 6**
>
> A professor was taking 28 students to Guadalajara, Mexico, on a two-week, travel-study program. If there were 14 more women than men, find the number of men and the number of women.

Applying Equation Solving **EXAMPLE 7**

A mattress for a single bed is on sale for $200, which is $\frac{4}{5}$ of its original price. Find the original price.

SOLUTION

Let p represent the original price, $200 is the sale price, and the sale price is $\frac{4}{5}$ of the original price. Use all this information to write the equation.

Sale price	is	$\frac{4}{5}$	of	original price.
↓	↓	↓	↓	↓
$200	=	$\frac{4}{5}$	×	p

Solve the equation.

$$200 = \frac{4}{5} \cdot p$$
$$\frac{5}{4} \cdot 200 = \frac{5}{4} \cdot \frac{4}{5} \cdot p \qquad \textcolor{blue}{\text{Multiply by reciprocal.}}$$
$$\frac{1000}{4} = \mathbf{1} \cdot p$$
$$250 = p$$

The original price is $250.

> **QUICK CHECK 7**
>
> Fearful of bankruptcy, the top manager of a company laid off enough people so that the workforce was only $\frac{2}{3}$ of the original workforce. Find the original number of employees if there were 34 employees after the layoff.

Solving a Business Problem **EXAMPLE 8**

The Eastside Nursery ordered 27 tree seedlings. Some of the seedlings were elms, costing $17 each. The remainder of the seedlings were maples at $11 each. The total cost of the seedlings was $375. Find the number of elms and the number of maples.

SOLUTION

Let x represent the number of elm seedlings in the shipment. Since the shipment contained 27 seedlings, the number of maples is found by subtracting the number of elms from 27.

$$27 - x = \text{number of maples}$$

If each elm seedling costs $17, then x elm seedlings will cost $17x$ dollars. Also, the cost of $(27 - x)$ maple seedlings at $11 each is $11(27 - x)$. The total cost of the shipment was $375.

A table can be very helpful in identifying the knowns and unknowns.

	COST PER SEEDLING	NUMBER OF SEEDLINGS	TOTAL COST
Elms	$17	x	$17x$
Maples	$11	$(27 - x)$	$11(27 - x)$
Totals		27	375

The information in the table is used to develop the following equation.

$$\textcolor{blue}{\textbf{Cost of elms} + \textbf{Cost of maples} = \textbf{Total cost}}$$
$$17x + 11(27 - x) = 375$$

Now solve this equation.

$$17x + 297 - 11x = 375 \quad \text{Use distributive property.}$$
$$6x + 297 = 375 \quad \text{Combine terms.}$$
$$6x = 78 \quad \text{Subtract 297 from each side.}$$
$$x = 13 \quad \text{Divide each side by 6.}$$

There were $x = 13$ elm seedlings and $(27 - 13) = 14$ maple seedlings.

QUICK CHECK 8

A beer-bottling company ordered 2100 more 12-ounce bottles than 1-quart bottles. The cost of the 12-ounce bottles was $.08 each, and the cost of the 1-quart bottles was $.11 each. The total cost was $310.50 not including shipping. Find the number of each type of bottle ordered.

Solving Investment Problems

EXAMPLE 9

Laurie Zimmerman has $15,000 to invest. She places a portion of the funds in a passbook account and $3000 more than twice this amount in a retirement account. How much is put into the passbook account? How much is placed in the retirement account?

SOLUTION

Let z represent the amount invested in the passbook account. To find the amount invested in the retirement account, translate as follows.

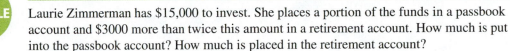

3000	more than	2 times the amount
↓	↓	↓
3000	+	$2z$

Since the sum of the two investments must be $15,000, an equation can be formed as follows.

Amount invested in passbook	+	Amount invested in retirement account	=	Total amount invested
z	+	$(3000 + 2z)$	=	$15,000

Now solve the equation.

$$z + (3000 + 2z) = 15,000$$
$$3z + 3000 = 15,000$$
$$3z = 12,000 \quad \text{Subtract 3000.}$$
$$z = 4000 \quad \text{Divide by 3.}$$

The amount invested in the passbook account is z, or $4000. The amount invested in the retirement account is $3000 + 2z$ or $3000 + 2(4000) = \$11,000$.

QUICK CHECK 9

A mutual fund company has $24 million to invest. They place part of the funds in the bonds of a utility company and $4 million more than three times that amount in New York City bonds. Find the amount placed in utility bonds and the amount in New York City bonds.

PRACTICE WATCH DOWNLOAD READ

The **QUICK START** exercises in each section contain solutions to help you get started.

Write the following as mathematical expressions. Use x as the variable.

QUICK START

1. 27 plus a number   **27 + x**
2. the sum of a number and $16\frac{1}{2}$ **x + $16\frac{1}{2}$**

3. a number added to 22 _____
4. 6.8 added to a number _____

5. 4 less than a number _____
6. 12 fewer than a number _____

7. subtract $3\frac{1}{2}$ from a number _____
8. subtract a number from 5.4 _____

9. triple a number _____
10. the product of a number and 9 _____

11. three-fifths of a number _____
12. four-thirds of a number _____

13. the quotient of 9 and a number _____
14. the quotient of a number and 11 _____

15. 16 divided by a number _____
16. a number divided by 4 _____

17. the product of 2.1 and the sum of 4 and a number _____

18. the quantity of a number plus 4, divided by 9 _____

19. 7 times the difference of a number and 3 _____

20. the difference of a number and 2, multiplied by 7 _____

Write mathematical expressions for each of the following.

QUICK START

21. **PURCHASING CDs**   Find the cost of 12 CDs at *y* dollars each.   **12y**

22. **TUITION FEES**   Find the cost of *x* students paying tuition of $2800 each.   **2800x**

23. **LIVESTOCK FEED**   The demand forecast for next month is 472 tons of livestock feed. Find the amount that should be ordered if inventory is *x* tons. _____

24. **COMPUTER USERS**   Eighty-three of the *x* employees have computers. How many do not have computers? _____

25. **UNION MEMBERSHIP**   A company has 73 employees of whom *x* are members of a union. How many employees are not union members? _____

26. **CARD SALES**   The inventory of a small card shop is valued at $73,000. The value of the greeting cards is *x*. Find the value of the rest of the inventory. _____

27. **TEXTBOOK PURCHASES**   A college bookstore paid $20,210 to purchase *x* textbooks for a biology class. Find the cost of one textbook. _____

28. **ADMISSION FEES**   A lodge paid $1853 for tickets for its *x* members to visit the state capitol. Find the cost of one ticket. _____

29. **CHARITABLE DONATIONS**   Robin has 21 books on computers. She donates *x* of them to the school library. How many does she have left? _____

30. **VIDEO STORE**   A video rental store is *x* years old. How old will it be in 8 years? _____

⚠ indicates an exercise that is related to the Case in Point feature.

Solve the following application problems. Steps 1–7 are repeated here for your convenience—use them.

Solving Applied Problems

Step 1   Read the problem carefully. A sketch may help.

Step 2   Identify the unknown and choose a variable to represent it. If possible, write any other unknowns in terms of the same variable.

Step 3   Translate the problem into an equation.

Step 4   Solve the equation.

Step 5   Answer the question(s) asked in the problem.

Step 6   Check your solution using the original words of the problem.

Step 7   Be sure your answer is reasonable.

QUICK START

31. Four times a number, plus 6 equals 58. Find the number.

$$4x + 6 = 58$$
$$4x = 52$$
$$x = 13$$

31. <u>13</u>

32. Seventeen times a number, plus 5 equals 107. Find the number.

$$17x + 5 = 107$$
$$17x = 102$$
$$x = 6$$

32. <u>6</u>

33. Six times the quantity of 4 minus a number is 15. Find the number.

33. _____

34. Twelve times the quantity of a number less 1 is 72. Find the number.

34. _____

35. When 6 is added to a number, the result is 7 times the number. Find the number.

35. _____

36. If 6 is subtracted from three times a number, the result is 4 more than the number. Find the number.

36. _____

37. When 5 times a number is added to twice the number, the result is 10. Find the number.

37. _____

38. If 7 times a number is subtracted from 11 times the number, the result is 9. Find the number.

38. _____

39. CAR STEREO Last month, Ben Jamison sold 17 more car stereos than did the other salesperson at the store. If the two salespeople sold a total of 101 stereos, find the number sold by Jamison.

39. _____

40. SODA SALES A grocery store sold 19 more cases of Coke than Sprite. Given that 43 cases were sold, find the number of cases of Coke sold.

40. _____

41. _____

41. SHIP BUILDING One hundred eighty-five more people work in building the ships than are in management, accounting, finance, and marketing. Given a total of 229 employees, find the number working in building the ships.

42. EXCHANGE PROGRAM Twenty-one students went on a student exchange program to Hong Kong. There were 11 more women than men. Find the number of women.

42. _____

43. AUTOMOBILE A one-year-old automobile is marked "on sale" for $18,450, which is $\frac{9}{10}$ of its original price. Find the original price.

43. _____

44. INTERNATIONAL SHIPMENTS Because of unusually high handling and freight charges, Western Oil Equipment charges $\frac{5}{4}$ of the list price for an item shipped to Indonesia. Find the list price of an item that was charged at $725.

44. _____

45. COMMERCIAL BUILDING Jane Anderson purchased a rundown, empty commercial building and plans to fix it up. The building can be used for both retail stores and office space. She thinks she can get a total annual rent of $135,000, with $3\frac{1}{2}$ times as much rent coming from retail stores as from office space. Find the rent she expects from office space and also the rent she expects from retail stores.

45. _____

46. MATERIAL Karen Cherie has a piece of fabric that is 106 inches long. She wishes to cut it into two pieces so that one piece is 12 inches longer than the other. What should be the length of each piece?

46. _____

47. HARLEY DAVIDSON Excluding managers, there are 22 full-time employees working at a large Harley Davidson shop. New employees receive $9.50 per hour, while more experienced workers average $12.90 per hour. The company spends $273.60 per hour in wages, not counting benefits. Find the number of each type of worker.

47. _____

48. VEGETABLE SALES Jumbo Market makes $0.10 on a head of lettuce and $0.08 on a bunch of carrots. Last week, a total of 12,900 heads of lettuce and bunches of carrots were sold, with a total profit of $1174. How many heads of lettuce and how many bunches of carrots were sold?

48. _____

49. NISSAN SALES Profits on Nissan Altimas and Sentras average $1200 and $850, respectively, at one dealership. The total profit in a month in which they sold 120 of these models was $130,350. Find the number of each sold.

49. _____

50. AUTO REPAIR One week, revenue from the 95 repairs at an auto repair shop totaled $20,040. The average charges for repairs on personal and commercial vehicles were $250 and $180 respectively. Find the number of each type of vehicle repaired.

50. _____

51. Are the problems in this section difficult for you? Explain why or why not. Explain two things you would recommend to a classmate who is having difficulty.

52. Write out the steps necessary to solve an applied problem. (See Objective 3.)

QUICK CHECK ANSWERS

1. $y + 7$
2. $19 - s$
3. $7(9 + t)$
4. $94 = 12(p + 2.5)$
5. $\dfrac{17 - r}{12} = 14$

6. 7 men, 21 women
7. 51 employees
8. 2850 12-ounce bottles; 750 1-quart bottles
9. utility bonds, $5 million; New York City bonds, $19 million

4.3 Business Formulas

OBJECTIVES

1. Evaluate formulas for given values of the variables.
2. Solve formulas for a specific variable.
3. Use standard business formulas to solve word problems.
4. Evaluate formulas containing exponents.

OBJECTIVE 1 Evaluate formulas for given values of the variables. Many of the most useful rules and procedures in business are given as **formulas**: equations showing how one number is found from other numbers. One of the single most useful formulas in business is the one for simple interest.

$$\text{Interest} = \text{Principal} \times \text{Rate} \times \text{Time}$$

When written out in words, as shown, a formula can take up too much space and be hard to remember. For this reason, it is common to *use letters as variables for the words* in a formula. Many times the first letter in each word of a formula is used, to make it easier to remember the formula. By this method, the formula for simple interest is written as follows.

$$\text{Interest} = \text{Principal} \times \text{Rate} \times \text{Time}$$
$$I = P \times R \times T$$

By using letters to express the relationship among interest, principal, rate, and time, we have generalized the relationship so that any value can be substituted into the formula. Once, three values are substituted into the formula, we can find the value of the remaining variable.

Evaluating a Formula Use the formula $I = PRT$ to find I if $P = \$7000$, $R = .09$, and $T = 2$.

SOLUTION

Substitute $\$7000$ for P, $.09$ for R, and 2 for T in the formula $I = PRT$. Remember that writing P, R, and T together as PRT indicates the product of the three letters.

$$I = PRT$$
$$I = \$7000(.09)(2)$$

Multiply on the right to get the solution.

$$I = \$1260$$

> **QUICK CHECK 1**
>
> Use $F = ma$ to find F if $m = 1700$ and $a = 9.8$.

Evaluating a Formula Use $I = PRT$ to find P if $I = \$5760$, $R = .16$, and $T = 3$.

SOLUTION

Substitute the given numbers for the letters of the formula.

$$I = PRT$$
$$\$5760 = P(.16)(3)$$
$$5760 = .48P \qquad \text{\small{P(.16)(3) = .48P}}$$
$$\frac{5760}{.48} = \frac{.48P}{.48} \qquad \text{\small{Divide both sides by .48.}}$$
$$\$12,000 = P$$

> **QUICK CHECK 2**
>
> Use the formula $I = PRT$ to find T if $I = \$3000$, $P = \$40,000$, and $R = .75$.

Evaluating a Formula **EXAMPLE 3**

Solve for rate (R) given $M = \$12{,}540$, $P = \$12{,}000$, and $T = .5$ in the equation $M = P(1 + RT)$.

SOLUTION

$$M = P(1 + RT)$$
$$\$12{,}540 = \$12{,}000(1 + R \cdot .5)$$
$$12{,}540 = 12{,}000 + 12{,}000 \cdot R \cdot .5 \qquad \text{Use the distributive property.}$$
$$12{,}540 = 12{,}000 + 6000 \cdot R$$
$$12{,}540 - \mathbf{12{,}000} = 12{,}000 + 6000 \cdot R - \mathbf{12{,}000} \qquad \text{Subtract 12,000 from each side.}$$
$$540 = 6000 \cdot R$$
$$\frac{540}{\mathbf{6000}} = \frac{6000 \cdot R}{\mathbf{6000}} \qquad \text{Divide by 6000.}$$
$$.09 = R$$

Rate is .09, or 9%.

QUICK CHECK 3

Solve for rate (R) if $M = \$8300$, $P = \$8000$, and $T = .5$ in the equation $M = P(1 + RT)$.

OBJECTIVE 2 **Solve formulas for a specific variable.** Sometimes, you may need to rearrange a formula to solve for a particular variable. For example, rearrange the formula $I = PRT$ to solve for the variable P as follows.

$$I = PRT$$
$$\frac{I}{RT} = \frac{P\cancel{RT}}{\cancel{RT}} \qquad \text{Divide both sides by } RT.$$
$$\frac{I}{RT} = P, \quad \text{or} \quad P = \frac{I}{RT}$$

Solving a Formula for a Specific Variable **EXAMPLE 4**

Solve for T in the formula $M = P(1 + RT)$. This formula gives the maturity value (M) of an initial amount of money (P) invested at a specific rate (R) for a certain period of time (T).

SOLUTION

Start by using the distributive property on the right side.

$$M = P(1 + RT)$$
$$M = P + PRT$$

Now subtract P from both sides.

$$M - P = P + PRT - P$$
$$M - P = PRT$$

Divide each side by PR.

$$\frac{M - P}{PR} = \frac{\cancel{PR}T}{\cancel{PR}}$$
$$\frac{M - P}{PR} = T, \quad \text{or} \quad T = \frac{M - P}{PR}$$

QUICK CHECK 4

Solve $S = (kT - 12)$ for T.

Solving a Formula for a Specific Variable

EXAMPLE 5

Solve for T in the formula $D = \dfrac{B}{MT}$.

SOLUTION

This formula gives the discount rate (D) of a note in terms of the face value (B), the time of a note (T), and the maturity value (M). Solve for T.

$$D = \frac{B}{MT}$$

$$DMT = \frac{B}{\cancel{MT}}\cancel{MT} \qquad \text{Multiply both sides by } MT.$$

$$DMT = B$$

$$\frac{\cancel{D}MT}{\cancel{D}M} = \frac{B}{DM} \qquad \text{Divide both sides by } DM.$$

$$T = \frac{B}{DM}$$

QUICK CHECK 5

Solve $T = \dfrac{R}{JK}$ for J.

OBJECTIVE 3 Use standard business formulas to solve word problems. In the following examples, application problems that use some common business formulas are solved.

Finding Gross Sales

EXAMPLE 6

Find the gross sales amount from selling 481 fishing lures at $2.65 each.

SOLUTION

The formula for gross sales is $G = NP$, where N is the number of items sold and P is the price per item. To find the gross sales from selling 481 fishing lures at $2.65 each, use the formula.

$$G = NP$$
$$G = 481(\$2.65)$$
$$G = \mathbf{\$1274.65}$$

The gross sales will be $1274.65.

QUICK CHECK 6

Find the gross revenue from selling 27 cases of wine at $156 each.

Finding Selling Price

EXAMPLE 7

A retailer purchased a personal computer with special speakers for $1265. It then adds a markup of $150 before placing it on the shelf to sell. Find the selling price.

SOLUTION

The selling price is found by adding the cost of the item and the markup.

$$S = C + M$$

The variable C is the cost and M is the markup, which is the amount added to the cost to cover expenses and profit. The selling price is found as shown.

$$S = \$1265 + \$150$$
$$S = \mathbf{\$1415}$$

The selling price is $1415.

QUICK CHECK 7

A discount Web retailer buys software packages for $26.92 each and marks them up by $8.07 each. Find the selling price.

OBJECTIVE 4 Evaluate formulas containing exponents. Exponents are used to show repeated multiplication of a quantity called the *base*. For example,

Exponent: the number of times the
base appears as a factor

$$x^2 = x \cdot x$$

Base: the quantity being multiplied.

Similarly,

$$z^3 = z \cdot z \cdot z \qquad \text{and} \qquad 5^4 = 5 \cdot 5 \cdot 5 \cdot 5 = 625$$

Forecasting Monthly Sales

EXAMPLE 8

After significant research, Ben James believes that the number of Chevrolet vehicles that can be sold in one state can be forecast as follows.

$$S = \$40 + 16.2 \times A^2$$

Both advertising (A) and sales (S) are in millions of dollars. Estimate sales for July if advertising is $1.4 million.

SOLUTION

Substitute $1.4 into the equation for advertising and solve for S to find the forecast.

$$\begin{aligned}
S &= \$40 + 16.2 \times A^2 \\
S &= \$40 + 16.2 \times (\$1.4)^2 \\
S &= 40 + 16.2 \times 1.96 \qquad \textbf{Evaluate exponent first.} \\
S &= 40 + 31.752 \\
S &= 71.752
\end{aligned}$$

Based on the model, July sales are forecast to be $71,752,000.

QUICK CHECK 8

Stress on a suspension cable on a bridge can be estimated using $S = 7.2(\text{weight})^2 + 3480$. Find the stress if the weight is 29 tons.

4.3 Exercises

The **QUICK START** *exercises in each section contain solutions to help you get started.*

In the following exercises a formula is given, along with the values of all but one of the variables in the formula. Find the value of the variable that is not given. Round to the nearest hundredth, if applicable.

QUICK START

1. $I = PRT$; $P = \$4600$, $R = .085$, $T = 1\frac{1}{2}$ **$586.50**

2. $F = ma$; $m = 820$, $a = 12$ **9840**

3. $P = B \times R$; $B = \$168{,}000$, $R = .06$ _____

4. $B = \dfrac{P}{R}$; $P = \$1200$, $R = .08$ _____

5. $s = c + m$; $c = \$14$, $m = \$2.50$ _____

6. $m = s - c$; $s = \$24{,}200$, $c = \$2800$ _____

7. $P = 2L + 2W$; $P = 40$, $W = 6$ _____

8. $P = 2L + 2W$; $P = 340$, $L = 70$ _____

9. $P = \dfrac{I}{RT}$; $T = 3$, $I = 540$, $R = .08$ _____

10. $M = P(1 + RT)$; $R = .15$, $T = 2$, $M = 481$ _____

11. $y = mx^2 + c$; $m = 3$, $x = 7$, $c = 4.2$ _____

12. $C = \$5 + \$.10N$; $N = 38$ _____

13. $M = P(1 + i)^n$; $P = \$640$, $i = .02$, $n = 8$ _____

14. $M = P(1 + i)^n$; $M = \$2400$, $i = .05$, $n = 4$ _____

15. $E = mc^2$; $m = 7.5$, $c = 1$ _____

16. $x = \dfrac{1}{2}at^2$; $t = 5$, $x = 150$ _____

17. $A = \dfrac{1}{2}(b + B)h$; $A = 105$, $b = 19$, $B = 11$ _____

18. $A = \dfrac{1}{2}(b + B)h$; $A = 70$, $b = 15$, $B = 20$ _____

19. $P = \dfrac{S}{1 + RT}$; $S = 24{,}600$, $R = .06$, $T = \dfrac{5}{12}$ _____

20. $P = \dfrac{S}{1 + RT}$; $S = 23{,}815$, $R = .09$, $T = \dfrac{11}{12}$ _____

Solve each formula for the indicated variable.

QUICK START

21. $A = LW$; for L

$$A = LW$$
$$\frac{A}{W} = \frac{LW}{W}$$
$$L = \frac{A}{W}$$

22. $d = rt$; for t

$$d = rt$$
$$\frac{d}{r} = \frac{rt}{r}$$
$$t = \frac{d}{r}$$

21. $L = \dfrac{A}{W}$

22. $t = \dfrac{d}{r}$

23. $PV = nRT$; for V

24. $I = PRT$; for R

23. _____

24. _____

25. $M = P(1 + i)^n$; for P

26. $R(1 - DT) = D$; for R

25. _____

26. _____

indicates an exercise that is related to the Case in Point feature.

27. $P = \dfrac{A}{1 + i}$; for i

28. $M = P(1 + RT)$; for R

27. _____

28. _____

29. $P = M(1 - DT)$; for D

30. $P = \dfrac{M}{1 + RT}$; for R

29. _____

30. _____

31. $A = \dfrac{1}{2}(b + B)h$; for h

32. $P = 2L + 2W$; for L

31. _____

32. _____

Solve the following application problems.

33. CARNIVAL A carnival purchases 1800 stuffed animals to give to people who win at carnival games. Given a total cost of $4320, find the cost per stuffed animal.

    $y =$ cost per stuffed animal
    1800 · y = $4320
    $\dfrac{1800y}{1800} = \dfrac{4320}{1800}$
    y = $2.40

33. $2.40 _____

34. WEB PAGES A retailer paid $1305 to a college student who built and added 15 pages to the firm's Web site. Find the cost per Web page.

    $c =$ cost per Web page
    15 · c = $1305
    $\dfrac{15c}{15} = \dfrac{1305}{15}$
    c = $87

34. $87 _____

35. **MUSICAL INSTRUMENTS** The Guitar Shoppe bought 6 sets of bongo drums and 7 quality Alvarez guitars for $2445.80. The guitars cost $269 apiece. Find the cost for a set of bongo drums.

35. _____

36. **REFRIGERATORS** An appliance store bought 8 large refrigerators and 10 washer/dryer combination sets. The store's cost for a washer/dryer was $462 and the total paid for all of the appliances was $10,860. Find the cost of a refrigerator.

36. _____

37. **CLOTHING STORE** The weekly salary for each salesperson at a clothing store is found using the formula $S = \$280 + .05x$, where x = employee's total sales for the week. Find the salary of two employees with the following weekly sales: **(a)** $2940 and **(b)** $4450.

37. _____

38. **LENGTH OF AN INVESTMENT** A principal (P) of $3500 invested in stocks over an unknown amount of time (T) at 9.5% ($R = 0.095$) yields $748.13 in interest ($I$). Use $I = PRT$ to find the time rounded to the nearest hundredth of a year.

38. _____

39. **COMPUTER CHIPS** A computer chip manufacturer had net sales of $230 million with returns equal to $\frac{1}{40}$ of gross sales. Find gross sales rounded to the nearest million given that net sales equals gross sales less returns.

39. _____

40. **BRIDAL SHOP** One month, the Bridal Shop had net sales of $33,000 and return(s) of $\frac{1}{12}$ of gross sales. If net sales equal gross sales minus returns, find gross sales.

40. _____

41. **MOVIES** The manager of one theatre marks up the cost of chocolate covered raisins by $\frac{3}{4}$ of the cost of the raisins. Find the cost to the nearest cent if the theatre sells a box of raisins for $4.00. (*Hint*: Selling price is cost plus markup.)

41. _____

42. **TEXTBOOK COSTS** A college book store marks their textbooks up by $\frac{1}{2}$ the cost of the book. Find the cost to the bookstore of a book they sell for $162 where selling price is cost plus markup.

42. _____

43. **PIZZA** Last year, the expenses at Mack's Pizzeria were $\frac{5}{6}$ of the total revenue and the remainder was profit. The profit, or the total revenue less expenses, was $107,400. Find the total revenue.

43. _____

44. **COMPUTER SALES** Computerworld has expenses that run $\frac{15}{16}$ of revenue. One month's profit (the difference between revenue and expenses) was $18,000. Find the revenue.

44. _____

In Exercises 45–49, use the formula $I = PRT$, where I = interest in dollars, P = principal or loan amount, R = interest rate written as a decimal, and T = time in years.

45. **FINDING INTEREST** Find the interest if principal of $5200 is invested at $7\frac{1}{2}\%$ (or .075) for one year.

45. _____

46. **LOAN TO AN UNCLE** Ben Cross loaned $8000 to his uncle for 4 years and received $1920 in interest. Find the interest rate.

46. _____

47. **AUTO PARTS STARTUP** Terry Twitty made a $22,000 loan so that Melissa Graves could start an auto parts business. The loan was for 2 years, and interest was $5720. Find the rate of interest.

47. _____

48. FINDING TIME   Fred Tausz loaned $39,000 to his sister. The loan was at 7% (or 0.07), with interest of $13,650. Find the time for the loan.

48. _____

49. STUDENT LOAN   Joan Summers borrowed $5850 (*P*) from her brother to help pay for her last year in college. They agreed to an interest rate (*R*) of 3% and a final interest amount (*I*) of $702. Find the Time.

49. _____

In Exercises 50–54, M = maturity value at the end of the loan, P = principal or loan amount, I = interest rate written as a decimal, n is the number of years, and R = annual interest rate written as a decimal.

50. MATURITY VALUE   Mary Scott invets $1000 in a bond fund that she hopes will yield 8% per year (or .08) for 5 years. What maturity value (*M*) will she have in her account at the end of 5 years?

50. _____

51. SAVING   John Wood had $4560 in his retirement account after 2 years. If the account paid 7% (or .07) per year. How much did John initially deposit in his account?
$[M = P(1 + RT)]$

51. _____

52. ANTIQUES   Jan Reus borrowed $12,500 from her uncle to help start an antique shop. She repaid $14,750 exactly 2 years later. Find the interest rate. $[M = P(1 + RT)]$

52. _____

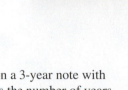

53. LOAN AMOUNT   Bill Abel paid a maturity value of $5989.50 on a 3-year note with annual interest of 10% (or .10). Use $M = P(1 + i)^n$, where *n* is the number of years in this problem, to solve for the amount borrowed.

53. _____

54. INHERITANCE Maybelle Jackson inherited $8500 when her grandfather died. She placed the money in a bank certificate of deposit that paid 3.5% per year and plans to leave it there for 20 years until she retires. Use $M = P(1 + i)^n$ to solve for the maturity value.

54. _____

55. Write a step-by-step explanation of the procedure you would use to solve the equation $A = P + PRT$ for R. (See Objective 2.)

56. Formulas are used in business, physics, biology, chemistry, engineering, and many other places. Why are formulas so commonly used? (See Objective 1.)

QUICK CHECK ANSWERS

1. $F = 16,660$
2. $T = .1$
3. $R = 7.5\%$
4. $T = \dfrac{(S + 12)}{k}$

5. $J = \dfrac{R}{KT}$
6. 4212
7. 34.99

4.4 Ratio and Proportion

OBJECTIVES

1 Define a ratio.
2 Set up a proportion.
3 Solve a proportion for unknown values.
4 Use proportions to solve problems.

OBJECTIVE 1 Define a ratio. A **ratio** is a quotient of two quantities that is used to *compare* the quantities. The ratio of the number *a* to the number *b* is written in any of the following ways.

$$a \text{ to } b, \qquad a:b, \qquad \frac{a}{b}$$

All are pronounced "*a* to *b*" or "*a* is to *b*." This last way of writing a ratio is most common in mathematics, while *a:b* is perhaps more common in business.

Writing Ratios **EXAMPLE 1**

Write a ratio in the form $\frac{a}{b}$ for each word phrase. Notice in each example that the number mentioned first is always the numerator.

SOLUTION

(a) The ratio of 5 hours to 3 hours is $\frac{5}{3}$.

(b) To find the ratio of 5 hours to 3 days, *first convert* 3 *days* to *hours*. Since there are 24 hours in 1 day, **3 days** = 3·24 = **72 hours**. Then the ratio of 5 hours to 3 days is the quotient of 5 and 72.

$$\frac{5}{72}$$

(c) The ratio of $700,000 in sales to $950,000 in sales is written this way.

$$\frac{\$700{,}000}{\$950{,}000}$$

Reduce to write this ratio in lowest terms.

$$\frac{\$700{,}000}{\$950{,}000} = \frac{14}{19}$$

QUICK CHECK 1

Write 40 sheep to 15 goats as a ratio.

Writing Ratios **EXAMPLE 2**

Burger King sold the following items in a one-hour period last Friday afternoon.

   70 bacon cheeseburgers
   15 plain hamburgers
   30 salad combos
   45 chicken sandwiches
   40 fish sandwiches

Write ratios for the following items sold:

(a) bacon cheeseburgers to fish sandwiches

(b) salad combos to chicken sandwiches

(c) plain hamburgers to salad combos

(d) fish sandwiches to total items sold

SOLUTION

(a) $\dfrac{\text{bacon cheeseburgers}}{\text{fish sandwiches}} = \dfrac{70}{40} = \dfrac{7}{4}$

(b) $\dfrac{\text{salad combos}}{\text{chicken sandwiches}} = \dfrac{30}{45} = \dfrac{2}{3}$

(c) $\dfrac{\text{plain hamburgers}}{\text{salad combos}} = \dfrac{15}{30} = \dfrac{1}{2}$

(d) $\dfrac{\text{fish sandwiches}}{\text{total items sold}} = \dfrac{40}{200} = \dfrac{1}{5}$

OBJECTIVE 2 Set up a proportion. A ratio is used to compare two numbers or amounts. A **proportion** says that two ratios are equal, as shown here.

$$\frac{3}{4} = \frac{15}{20}$$

A proportion can be simplified by multiplying both sides of the equation by the product of the two denominators. Look at the following proportion, which uses variables.

$$\frac{a}{b} = \frac{c}{d}$$

$$\frac{a}{\cancel{b}} \cdot \cancel{b}d = \frac{c}{\cancel{d}} \cdot b\cancel{d} \qquad \textbf{Multiply both sides by the product of two denominators.}$$

$$ad = bc$$

Thus, $\frac{a}{b} = \frac{c}{d}$ only if the cross products $a \cdot d$ and $b \cdot c$ are equal to one another. This **method of cross products** can be used to determine if a proportion is true.

Method of Cross Products

The proportion

$$\frac{a}{b} = \frac{c}{d}$$

is true if the cross products $a \cdot d$ and $b \cdot c$ are equal (that is, if $ad = bc$).

Determining If a Proportion Is True   Decide whether the following proportions are true.

(a) $\dfrac{3}{5} = \dfrac{12}{20}$ **(b)** $\dfrac{2}{3} = \dfrac{9}{16}$

SOLUTION

(a) Find each cross product.

$$\frac{3}{5} = \frac{12}{20}$$
$$3 \times 20 \overset{?}{=} 5 \times 12$$
$$60 = 60$$

Since the cross products are equal, the proportion is true.

(b) Find the cross products.

$$\frac{2}{3} = \frac{9}{16}$$
$$2 \times 16 \overset{?}{=} 3 \times 9$$
$$32 \neq 27$$

> **Quick TIP ▼**
>
> The symbol $\neq$ means "not equal to."

This proportion is false, so $\dfrac{2}{3} \neq \dfrac{9}{16}$.

OBJECTIVE 3 Solve a proportion for unknown values. Four numbers and/or variables are used in a proportion. If any three of the values are known, the fourth can be found. The two methods to solve a proportion are to:

1. multiply both sides by the product of the two denominators or

2. use the method of cross products.

Solving a Proportion **EXAMPLE 4**

Find the value of the unknowns. Use the first method for **(a)** and the second method for **(b)**.

(a) $\dfrac{3}{5} = \dfrac{x}{40}$ (b) $\dfrac{3}{10} = \dfrac{5}{k}$

SOLUTION

(a) Solve for the unknown by multiplying both sides of the equation by the product of the denominators.

$$\frac{3}{5} = \frac{x}{40}$$

$$\frac{3}{5} \cdot (5 \cdot 40) = \frac{x}{40} \cdot (5 \cdot 40) \qquad \textbf{\color{blue}{Multiply both sides by product of denominators.}}$$

$$120 = 5x$$

$$\frac{120}{5} = \frac{5x}{5} \qquad \textbf{\color{blue}{Divide both sides by 5.}}$$

$$24 = x, \quad \text{or} \quad x = 24$$

(b) Solve for the unknown using the method of cross products.

$$\frac{3}{10} = \frac{5}{k}$$

$$3k = 50 \qquad \textbf{\color{blue}{Use method of cross products.}}$$

$$\frac{3k}{3} = \frac{50}{3}$$

$$k = \frac{50}{3} = 16\frac{2}{3}$$

QUICK CHECK 4

Find y in the following proportion: $\dfrac{7}{y} = \dfrac{84}{228}$.

Solving Proportions **EXAMPLE 5**

A food wholesaler charges a restaurant chain \$83 for 3 crates of fresh produce. How much should it charge for 5 crates of produce?

SOLUTION

Let x be the cost of 5 crates of produce. Set up a proportion with one ratio the number of crates and the other ratio the costs. Use this pattern.

$$\frac{\text{Crates}}{\text{Crates}} = \frac{\text{Cost}}{\text{Cost}}$$

Now substitute the given information.

$$\frac{3}{5} = \frac{83}{x}$$

Use the cross-products to solve the proportion.

$$3x = 5(83)$$

$$3x = \$415$$

$$x = \$138.33 \qquad \text{(rounded to the nearest cent)}$$

The 5 crates cost \$138.33.

OBJECTIVE 4 Use proportions to solve problems. Proportions are used in many practical applications, as shown in the next two examples.

Solving Applications EXAMPLE 6

A firm in Hong Kong and one in Thailand agree to jointly develop an engine-control microchip to be sold to North American auto manufacturers. They agree to split the development costs in a ratio of 8:3 (Hong Kong firm to Thailand firm), resulting in a cost of $9,400,000 to the Hong Kong firm. Find the cost to the Thailand firm.

SOLUTION

Let x represent the cost to the Thailand firm, then

$$\frac{8}{3} = \frac{9,400,000}{x}$$

$$8x = 3 \cdot 9,400,000 \qquad \text{Cross multiply.}$$

$$8x = 28,200,000$$

$$x = \mathbf{3,525,000} \qquad \text{Divide by 8.}$$

The Thailand firm's share of the costs is $3,525,000.

Solving Applications EXAMPLE 7

Bill Thomas wishes to estimate the amount of timber on some forested land that he owns. One value he needs to estimate is the average height of the trees. One morning, Thomas notices that his own 6-foot body casts an 8-foot shadow at the same time that a typical tree casts a 34-foot shadow. Find the height of the tree.

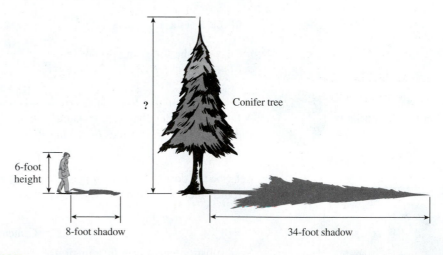

?   Conifer tree

6-foot height

8-foot shadow   34-foot shadow

SOLUTION

Set up a proportion in which the height of the tree is given the variable name x.

$$\frac{6}{8} = \frac{x}{34}$$

$$6 \cdot 34 = 8 \cdot x \qquad \text{Cross multiply.}$$

$$\frac{204}{8} = \frac{\cancel{8} \cdot x}{\cancel{8}} \qquad \text{Divide by 8.}$$

$$x = 25.5 \text{ feet}$$

The height of the tree is 25.5 feet.

4.4 Exercises

The **QUICK START** *exercises in each section contain solutions to help you get started.*

Write the following ratios. Write each ratio in lowest terms.

QUICK START

1. 18 kilometers to 64 kilometers $\dfrac{9}{32}$

2. 18 defects out of 580 items $\dfrac{9}{290}$

3. 216 students to 8 faculty _____

4. \$80 in returns to \$8360 in sales _____

5. 8 men to 6 women _____

6. 12 feet to 1 inch _____

7. 30 kilometers (30,000 meters) to 8 meters _____

8. 30 inches to 5 yards _____

9. 90 dollars to 40 cents _____

10. 148 minutes to 4 hours _____

11. 4 dollars to 10 quarters _____

12. 35 dimes to 6 dollars _____

13. 20 hours to 5 days _____

14. 6 days to 9 hours _____

15. \$.80 to \$3 _____

16. \$1.20 to \$.75 _____

17. \$3.24 to \$.72 _____

18. \$3.57 to \$.42 _____

Decide whether the following proportions are true or false.

QUICK START

19. $\dfrac{3}{5} = \dfrac{21}{35}$ T _____

20. $\dfrac{6}{13} = \dfrac{30}{65}$ T _____

21. $\dfrac{9}{7} = \dfrac{720}{480}$ _____

22. $\dfrac{54}{14} = \dfrac{270}{70}$ _____

23. $\dfrac{69}{320} = \dfrac{7}{102}$ _____

24. $\dfrac{17}{19} = \dfrac{72}{84}$ _____

25. $\dfrac{19}{32} = \dfrac{33}{77}$ _____

26. $\dfrac{19}{30} = \dfrac{57}{90}$ _____

27. $\dfrac{110}{18} = \dfrac{160}{27}$ _____

28. $\dfrac{46}{17} = \dfrac{212}{95}$ _____

29. $\dfrac{32}{75} = \dfrac{61}{108}$ _____

30. $\dfrac{28}{75} = \dfrac{224}{600}$ _____

31. $\dfrac{7.6}{10} = \dfrac{76}{100}$ _____

32. $\dfrac{95}{64} = \dfrac{320}{217}$ _____

33. $\dfrac{2\frac{1}{4}}{5} = \dfrac{9}{20}$ _____

34. $\dfrac{\frac{3}{4}}{80} = \dfrac{\frac{9}{8}}{120}$ _____

35. $\dfrac{4\frac{1}{5}}{6\frac{1}{8}} = \dfrac{27}{41}$ _____

36. $\dfrac{1\frac{1}{2}}{12} = \dfrac{5\frac{1}{4}}{42}$ _____

37. $\dfrac{8.15}{2.03} = \dfrac{61.125}{15.225}$ _____

38. $\dfrac{423.88}{17.119} = \dfrac{330.6264}{13.35282}$ _____

Solve the following proportions.

QUICK START

39. $\dfrac{x}{15} = \dfrac{49}{105}$ 7 _____

40. $\dfrac{y}{35} = \dfrac{27}{315}$ 3 _____

41. $\dfrac{6}{9} = \dfrac{r}{108}$ _____

42. $\dfrac{16}{41} = \dfrac{112}{I}$ _____

43. $\dfrac{63}{s} = \dfrac{3}{5}$ _____

44. $\dfrac{260}{390} = \dfrac{x}{3}$ _____

45. $\dfrac{1}{2} = \dfrac{r}{7}$ _____

46. $\dfrac{2}{3} = \dfrac{5}{s}$ _____

47. $\dfrac{\frac{3}{4}}{6} = \dfrac{3}{x}$ _____

48. $\dfrac{3}{x} = \dfrac{11}{9}$ _____

49. $\dfrac{12}{P} = \dfrac{23.571}{15.714}$ _____

50. $\dfrac{86.112}{57.408} = \dfrac{k}{15}$ _____

△C indicates an exercise that is related to the Case in Point feature.

51. Explain the difference between ratio and proportion. (See Objective 2.)

52. Explain cross products using the rules of algebra. (See Objective 2.)

Solve the following application problems.

QUICK START

53. TICKET SALES One Ticketmaster outlet sold 350 rock-concert tickets in 2 days. At that rate, find the number of tickets it can expect to sell in 9 days.

$$\frac{350}{2} = \frac{x}{9}$$
$$350 \cdot 9 = 2x$$
$$2x = 3150$$
$$x = 1575 \text{ tickets}$$

53. 1575 tickets

54. BLOOD CELLS A 170-pound person has about 30 trillion blood cells. Estimate the number of blood cells in a 140-pound person to the nearest tenth of a trillion.

$$\frac{170}{30} \text{ trillion} = \frac{140}{x} \text{ trillion}$$
$$170x = 30 \cdot 140$$
$$170x = 4200$$
$$x = 24.7 \text{ trillion}   \text{(rounded)}$$

54. 24.7 trillion

55. REAL ESTATE DEVELOPMENT Mike George paid $215,000 for a 5-unit apartment house. Find the cost for a 12-unit apartment house.

55. _____

56. TIGER FOOD A 450-pound circus tiger eats 15 pounds of meat per day. How many pounds of meat would you expect a 360-pound tiger to eat per day?

56. _____

57. SEWING If 22 children's dresses cost $660, what is the cost of 12 dresses?

57. _____

58. BISCUITS A biscuit recipe that feeds 7 requires 2 cups of flour. How much flour is needed for enough biscuits to feed a church group of 125? Round to the nearest whole number.

58. _____

59. GLOBAL WARMING   The concentration of carbon dioxide in the atmosphere has increased from 315 parts per million to 380 parts per million in the past 48 years. During the same period of time, the global average temperature increased by 1°F. Estimate the amount of further increase in global average temperature to the nearest tenth of a degree, if the concentration of carbon dioxide (CO_2) in the atmosphere increases from 380 parts per million up to 550 parts per million, as predicted by some.

59. _____

60. FERTILIZER COVERAGE   Suppose that 7 sacks of fertilizer cover 3325 square feet at a rose farm. Find the number of sacks needed for 7125 square feet.

60. _____

61. MAP READING   The distance between two cities on a road map is 2 inches. Actually, the cities are 120 miles apart. The distance between two other cities is 17 inches. How far apart are these cities?

61. _____

62. WOMAN'S CLOTHING SHOP   Martha Vinn opened a woman's clothing shop and had sales of $3720 during the first 3 weeks. At that rate, estimate sales for the first 4 weeks.

62. _____

63. SALES OF HEALTH FOOD   Natural Harvest had sales of $274,312 for the first 20 weeks of the year. Estimate sales for the entire 52-week year.

63. _____

64. PARTNERSHIP PROFITS   Chester and Gaines have a partnership agreement that calls for profits to be paid in the ratio of 2:5, respectively. Find the amount that goes to Chester if Gaines receives $45,000.

64. _____

65. OIL PROFITS   The two partners in Alamo Energy agreed to split profits in a ratio of 3:8. If the first partner received $48,000 in profits one year, find the profit earned by the second partner.

65. _____

66. PRODUCTION EMPLOYEES The owner of a factory has always kept the ratio of salespeople to production employees at 2:7. If she currently has 24 salespeople, how many production employees are there?

66. _____

67. SONGBIRD MIGRATION Small songbirds in one area migrate at about 20 miles per hour whereas eider ducks migrate at 35 miles per hour. How far would the eider ducks migrate in the same amount of time it would take songbirds to migrate 200 miles?

67. _____

68. ISLAND AREA Indonesia has an area of 741,101 square miles and is made up of 13,677 islands. Assume the United States, with an area of 3,618,770 square miles, were similarly broken up into islands. How many islands would there be (to the nearest whole number)?

68. _____

69. ICEBERG VOLUME Seven-eighths of an iceberg is below the water since icebergs are made up of freshwater, which is not as dense as seawater. Find the amount of an iceberg that is under water if the amount above water has a volume of 500,000 cubic meters. (*Hint:* $1 - \frac{7}{8} = \frac{1}{8}$ above water.)

69. _____

70. AUTO PRODUCTION An auto plant produces 3 red sports models for every 7 blue family models. Find the number of red sports models produced if the plant produces 868 blue family models.

70. _____

71. JAPANESE YEN Benjamin Lopez was in Japan for 2 months on a business trip. Find the number of U.S. dollars he will receive for 20,355 Japanese yen if $1 U.S. can be exchanged for 95 yen. Round to the nearest cent.

71. _____

72. WORKING IN CHINA Gina Harden was offered a job as a teacher at an elite private high school in Beijing at an annual salary of 471,200 yuan. Find the salary in U.S. dollars if 6.70 yuan can be exchanged for $1 U.S. Round to the nearest cent.

72. _____

Chapter 4 Quick Review

Chapter Terms *Review the following terms to test your understanding of the chapter. For each term you do not know, refer to the page number found next to that term.*

addition rule **[p. 130]**
cross product **[p. 158]**
distributive property **[p. 133]**
equation **[p. 130]**
left side **[p. 130]**

like terms **[p. 132]**
method of cross product **[p. 158]**
multiplication rule **[p. 130]**
proportion **[p. 158]**

ratio **[p. 157]**
reciprocal **[p. 131]**
right side **[p. 130]**
solution **[p. 130]**

substitute **[p. 130]**
term **[p. 130]**
unlike terms **[p. 133]**
variable **[p. 130]**

CONCEPTS

EXAMPLES

4.1 Use the addition rule to solve basic equations.

Add or subtract the same number from both sides of the equation.

Solve $x - 17.5 = 50$.

$$x - 17.5 = 50$$
$$x - 17.5 + 17.5 = 50 + 17.5 \quad \textbf{Add 17.5}$$
$$x = 67.5$$

4.1 Use the multiplication rule to solve basic equations.

Multiply or divide both sides of the equation by the same number.

Solve $6x = 72$.

$$6x = 72$$
$$\frac{6x}{6} = \frac{72}{6} \quad \textbf{Divide by 6}$$
$$x = 12$$

4.1 Solve more complicated equations.

Use the preceding addition and multiplication rules. Move all terms with only numbers to one side of the equation and all terms with variables to the other side.

Solve $10y = 8y + 42$.

$$10y = 8y + 42$$
$$10y - 8y = 8y + 42 - 8y \quad \textbf{Subtract 8y}$$
$$2y = 42$$
$$\frac{2y}{2} = \frac{42}{2} \quad \textbf{Divide by 2}$$
$$y = 21$$

4.1 Solve equations with parentheses.

First use the distributive property to remove the parentheses; then solve.

Solve $15(p - 1) = 3p + 2$.

$$15(p - 1) = 3p + 2$$
$$15p - 15 = 3p + 2$$
$$15p - 15 - 3p = 3p + 2 - 3p \quad \textbf{Subtract 3p}$$
$$12p - 15 = 2$$
$$12p - 15 + 15 = 2 + 15 \quad \textbf{add 15}$$
$$12p = 17$$
$$\frac{12p}{12} = \frac{17}{12} \quad \textbf{Divide by 12}$$
$$p = 1\frac{5}{12}$$

4.2 Translate phrases into expressions.

7 plus a number
sum of a number and 12
a number minus $\frac{1}{2}$
product of 2 and a number
a number multiplied by 19

a number divided by .68

8 times the sum of a number and 1

Any letter can be used as a variable.

$7 + x$
$y + 12$
$z - \frac{1}{2}$
$2A$
$19t$

$\dfrac{T}{.68}$

$8(P + 1)$

CONCEPTS	EXAMPLES
4.2 Solve a basic application problem. Read problem carefully. Define variables. Write an equation and solve for the unknown. Check to make sure the answer is reasonable.	The sum of two consecutive odd numbers is 96. Find both numbers. Let x be the smaller number. Then $(x + 2)$ is the larger number. $$x + (x + 2) = 96$$ $$2x + 2 = 96$$ $$2x = 94$$ $$x = 47 \quad \text{and} \quad (x + 2) = 49$$
4.3 Evaluate a formula given values. Substitute known values into the formula and solve for the unknown.	Use $I = PRT$ to find I when $P = \$10{,}000$, $R = 4.5\%$, and $T = 1$. $$I = PRT$$ $$I = \$10{,}000 \cdot .045 \cdot 1$$ $$I = \$450$$
4.3 Solve a formula for a variable. Isolate the variable of interest on one side of the equation.	Solve $I = PRT$ for P. $$I = PRT$$ $$\frac{I}{RT} = \frac{PRT}{RT}$$ $$\frac{I}{RT} = P, \quad \text{or} \quad P = \frac{I}{RT}$$
4.3 Evaluate formulas with exponents. Substitute known values into the formula and solve for the unknown.	Use $M = P(1 + i)^n$ with $P = \$5000$, $i = 5\%$, and $n = 3$ to find M. $$M = P(1 + i)^n$$ $$M = \$5000\,(1 + .05)^3$$ $$M = 5000\,(1.05)^3$$ $$M = 5000 \cdot 1.157625$$ $$M = \$5788.13 \quad \text{(rounded)}$$
4.4 Determine if a proportion is true. Check to see that cross products are equal to one another.	Is $\dfrac{4}{5} = \dfrac{28}{35}$ true? $$4 \cdot 35 \stackrel{?}{=} 5 \cdot 28 \quad \textbf{Use cross products}$$ $$140 = 140$$ The proportion is true.
4.4 Solve a proportion for an unknown. Use the method of cross products and solve the resulting equation.	Find x: $\dfrac{35}{17} = \dfrac{x}{153}$. $$35 \cdot 153 = 17x \quad \textbf{Use cross products}$$ $$5355 = 17x$$ $$\frac{5355}{17} = \frac{17x}{17}$$ $$x = 315$$
4.4 Use a proportion to solve a problem. 1. Define the unknown variable. 2. Set up the proportion. 3. Use the method of cross products. 4. Solve the equation.	A hiker walked 5.8 miles in 2 hours. At this rate, estimate the number of hours needed to hike 10 miles. Let $x =$ number of hours needed. $$\frac{5.8 \text{ miles}}{2 \text{ hours}} = \frac{10 \text{ miles}}{x \text{ hours}}$$ $$5.8x = 2 \cdot 10 \quad \textbf{Use cross products}$$ $$5.8x = 20$$ $$\frac{5.8x}{5.8} = \frac{20}{5.8}$$ $$x = \textbf{3.4 hours} \quad \text{(rounded)}$$

case study

FORECASTING SALES AT ALCORN'S BOUTIQUE

Jane Alcorn had sold items on eBay for several years but felt it was time to open a retail store once her son Benton graduated from college. After thinking about the options and competition, she decided to open a shop specializing in women's clothing. Sales were slow for her first few months and she began to wonder how much she should be spending on advertising. So, she decided to do an experiment and keep track of the monthly amount spent on advertising and the monthly sales. The actual data is shown in the following graph.

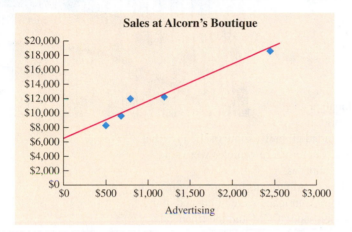

Benton used statistics to help find the equation that was a best fit for the data. The equation is shown as the straight line in the graph. He told his mother it might not help much since it did not take into account factors such as seasonality or competition. And of course, Alcorn still had to decide where to advertise and exactly what the advertisements should look like. But she thought the equation might give her some idea of how much she should spend on advertising each month. The equation for the best-fit line for actual sales data found by Benton is given next. It is the equation of the straight line in the graph.

1. Estimate sales for advertising of $800 and $2000.

    1. _____

2. Ah, Alcorn thought, this easy. If you increase advertising from $800 up to $2000, then sales go up from $10,500 to $16,500. So an increase in advertising expenses of $1200 results in an increase in sales of $6000. Her gross profit margin on the fashion goods she carried in her tiny boutique was 50%. Find the increased gross profit by multiplying the 50% by the increase in sales.

    2. _____

3. So an increase in advertising of $1200 results in $3000 more gross profit. Given this information, Alcorn's first thought was to borrow $5000 from a bank and advertise a lot. Then she began to wonder. What suggestions do you have for her? Should she borrow $5000 and advertise? Why or why not (based on your intuition)?

    3. _____

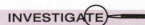 **INVESTIGATE**

List all of the factors you can think of that can influence sales at a small, local store. You may wish to talk to the manager or owner of store and compare to your list.

case ▾ in ▾ point summary exercise

GENERAL MOTORS

www.GM.com

Facts:

- 1908: Founded
- 1970s: Massive redesign of cars for better gas mileage
- 1982: Built huge factory in Spain
- 2009: Files for bankruptcy
- 2010: Emerges from bankruptcy

In some respects, General Motors (GM) *is* the story of globalization. It was one of the most successful companies in the world in the 1960s under the gifted manager Alfred Sloan. As it expanded globally, some of the jobs that had gone to Americans were moved overseas, partly to be closer to where vehicles were sold but also to cut costs. Labor costs were much lower in other countries.

Gasoline prices increased sharply during the 1970s and many Americans turned away from GM products and bought cars from Toyota, Honda, or Nissan. Americans were interested in the smaller, high-quality cars built by the Japanese. The weakened state of GM and the financial crisis of 2008–2010 forced the company to file for bankruptcy in 2009 when the U.S. government stepped in to help.

Ben James received a bachelor's degree in statistics and a master's degree in business administration. He has worked at GM for several years. Among other things, he studies data such as that shown in the following two figures and develops equations to forecast demand.

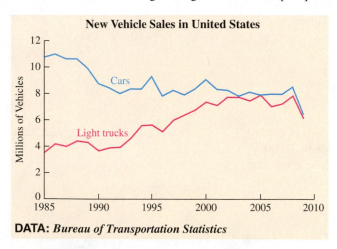

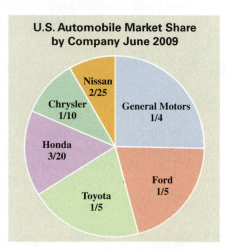

1. What can you learn from the two figures?

2. Many factors are involved in making a forecast. To illustrate, use the following equation to make a monthly forecast of car sales (in thousands) in one area given Advertising = $6.2 (millions), Economic Growth = 2.8% (.028), and Level of Competition = .6. (See Section 4.2, Examples 1–8.)

   Sales = 34.8 + 5.3 · Advertising + 485 · Economic Growth − 34.2 · Level of Competition

2. _____

3. GM has responded to increasing competition, and rapid economic growth in China by building and selling cars in China. About 1 out of every 8 vehicles sold in China is built by GM. Since the conditions in China differ greatly from those in the United States, a somewhat different model must be used to forecast sales. Forecast monthly GM sales in China using the following equation (in thousands) when Advertising = $5.3 (millions), Economic Growth = 6.5%, and Level of Competition = .7. (See Section 4.3, Examples 1–8.)

Sales = 50.9 + 9.6 · Advertising + 720 · Economic Growth − 28.7 · Level of Competition

3. _____

4. In one European country, the sales of GM products increased from 23,850 to 36,400 in the third year that GM was in that market. Use a proportion to estimate the number of sales in the third year in a neighboring country with a very similar economy, if year two sales were 14,910. (See Section 4.4, Examples 5–7.)

4. _____

Discussion Question: Many factors other than those listed here affect sales of new automobiles. Think about your own family or a family you know and list things that influence the purchase of an automobile, new or used.

Chapter 4 Test

To help you review, the numbers in brackets show the section in which the topic was discussed.

Solve each equation for the unknown. **[4.1]**

1. $x + 45 = 96$ _____

2. $r - 36 = 14.7$ _____

3. $8t + 45 = 175.4$ _____

4. $4x - 6 = 15$ _____

5. $\dfrac{s}{6} = 43$ _____

6. $\dfrac{5z}{8} = 85$ _____

7. $\dfrac{m}{4} - 5 = 9$ _____

8. $5(x - 3) = 3(x + 4)$ _____

9. $6y = 2y + 28$ _____

10. $3r - 7 = 2(4 - 3r)$ _____

11. $.15(2x - 3) = 5.85$ _____

12. $.6(y - 3) = .1y$ _____

In Exercises 13–22, a formula is given, along with the values of all but one of the variables in the formula. Find the value of the variable that is not given. **[4.3]**

13. $I = PRT; P = 2800, R = .09, T = 2$ _____

14. $S = C + M; C = 275, M = 49$ _____

15. $G = NP; N = 840, P = 3.79$ _____

16. $M = P(1 + RT); P = 420, R = .07, T = 2\dfrac{1}{2}$ _____

17. $R = \dfrac{D}{1 - DT}; D = .04, T = 5$ _____

18. $A = \dfrac{S}{1 + RT}; S = 12,600, R = .12, T = \dfrac{5}{12}$ _____

19. $T = \dfrac{D}{S}; T = 100, S = 2$ _____

20. $\dfrac{I}{PR} = T; P = 1000, R = .05, T = 1\dfrac{1}{2}$ _____

21. $d = rt; r = .07, t = 12$ _____

22. $I = PRT; P = 500, R = .08, T = 3$ _____

In Exercises 23–28, solve for the indicated variables. **[4.3]**

23. $A = LW;$ for W _____

24. $d = rt;$ for r _____

25. $I = PRT;$ for T _____

26. $P = 1 + RT;$ for R _____

27. $A = P + PRT;$ for T _____

28. $R(1 - DT) = D;$ for R _____

In Exercises 29–34, write the ratio in lowest terms. **[4.4]**

29. 250 pesos to 1250 pesos _____

30. 45 women to 110 men _____

31. \$1.20 to 75¢ _____

32. 20 hours to 5 days _____

33. 35 dimes to 6 dollars _____

34. 30 inches to five yards _____

In Exercises 35–40, decide whether the proportions are true or false. **[4.4]**

35. $\dfrac{2}{3} = \dfrac{42}{63}$ _____

36. $\dfrac{6}{9} = \dfrac{36}{52}$ _____

37. $\dfrac{18}{20} = \dfrac{56}{60}$ _____

38. $\dfrac{12}{18} = \dfrac{8}{12}$ _____

39. $\dfrac{420}{600} = \dfrac{14}{20}$ _____

40. $\dfrac{7.6}{10} = \dfrac{76}{100}$ _____

In Exercises 41–48, solve the proportions for the unknown. **[4.4]**

41. $\dfrac{y}{35} = \dfrac{25}{5}$ _____

42. $\dfrac{15}{s} = \dfrac{45}{117}$ _____

43. $\dfrac{a}{25} = \dfrac{4}{20}$ _____

44. $\dfrac{6}{x} = \dfrac{4}{18}$ _____

45. $\dfrac{z}{20} = \dfrac{80}{200}$ _____

46. $\dfrac{25}{100} = \dfrac{8}{m}$ _____

47. $\dfrac{1}{2} = \dfrac{r}{7}$ _____

48. $\dfrac{2}{3} = \dfrac{5}{s}$ _____

Solve the following application problems.   [4.2–4.4]

49. The sum of an unknown and eight is twenty. Find the unknown.

49. _____

50. The sum of four plus an unknown equals fifty-one. Find the unknown.

50. _____

51. An unknown times thirty equals one thousand eight hundred. Find the unknown.

51. _____

52. Twenty-four equals three times an unknown. Find the unknown.

52. _____

53. Three times an unknown plus five is equal to fifty. Find the unknown.

53. _____

54. Four plus seven times an unknown is eighteen. Find the unknown.

54. _____

55. The sum of two consecutive whole numbers is equal to ninety-one. Find the numbers.

55. _____

56. The sum of two consecutive odd whole numbers is equal to two hundred forty. Find both numbers.

56. _____

57. Tom throws some coins onto a table. His twin brother Joe throws coins worth twice as much onto the table. The total value of the coins on the table is $2.61. How much money did Joe place on the table?

57. _____

58. A business math class has 47 students, with 9 more women than men. Find the number of men and women in the class.

58. _____

59. Cajun Boatin' Inc. bought 5 small boats and 3 skiffs for $14,878. A small boat costs $1742. Find the cost of a skiff.

59. _____

60. Mike Anderson bought a 4-unit apartment house for $172,000. Use ratios to find the cost of a 10-unit apartment house.

60. _____

61. The tax on a $40 item is $3. Find the tax on a $160 item.

61. _____

62. Sam bought 17 table-model television sets for $1942.25. Find the cost of one set.

62. _____

63. The bookstore at Hudson Community College has a markup that is $\frac{1}{4}$ its cost on a book. Find the cost to the bookstore of a paperback book selling for $20.

63. _____

64. An unknown principal (P) loaned out at 8% for $1\frac{3}{4}$ years yields a maturity value (M) of $1368. Use $M = P(1 + RT)$ to find the principal.

64. _____

65. Explain why all terms with a variable should be placed on one side of the equation, and all terms without a variable should be placed on the other side, when solving an equation.   [4.1]

66. In your own words, explain the terms *formula, ratio,* and *proportion.*   [4.3–4.4]

Chapters 1–4 / Cumulative Review

CHAPTERS 1–4

To help you review, the numbers in brackets show the section in which the topic was introduced.

Round each of the following numbers as indicated. **[1.1, 1.3]**

1. 65,462 to the nearest hundred

2. 4,732,489 to the nearest thousand

3. 78.35 to the nearest tenth

4. 328.2849 to the nearest hundredth

1. _____

2. _____

3. _____

4. _____

Solve the following problems. **[1.1–1.5]**

5.
```
   351
   763
  2478
+   17
```

6.
```
  45,867
− 37,985
```

7.
```
  634
×  38
```

8.
```
  2450
×  320
```

9. $6290 \div 74 =$ _____

10. $22,899 \div 102 =$ _____

11. $.46 + 9.2 + 8 + 17.514 =$ _____

12.
```
  45.36
− 23.7
```

13.
```
  29.8
× .41
```

14.
$$21.8\overline{)396.76}$$

Solve the following application problems.

15. Felix Schmid decides to establish a budget. He will spend $700 for rent, $325 for food, $420 for child care, $182 for transportation, $300 for other expenses, and he will put the remainder in savings. If his monthly take-home pay is $2025, find his savings. **[1.1]**

15. _____

16. Clancy Strock wrote a feature article called "I know . . . I was there" for each issue of *Reminisce* magazine. He has written an article for each monthly issue of the magazine from 1993 through 2008 (16 years). How many of these monthly articles has he written? (*Source:* Reiman Publications.) **[1.1]**

16. _____

17. Software Depot had a bank balance of $29,742.18 at the beginning of April. During the month, the firm made deposits of $14,096.18 and $6529.42. A total of $18,709.51 in checks was paid by the bank during the month. Find the firm's checking account balance at the end of April. **[1.4]**

17. _____

18. Cara Groff pays $128.11 each month to the Bank of Bolivia. How many months will it take her to pay off $4099.52? **[1.5]**

18. _____

Solve the following problems. **[2.1–2.4]**

19. Write $\dfrac{48}{54}$ in lowest terms. _____

20. Write $8\frac{1}{8}$ as an improper fraction. _____

21. Write $\dfrac{107}{15}$ as a mixed number. _____

22. $1\frac{2}{3} + 2\frac{3}{4} =$ _____

23. $5\frac{7}{8} + 7\frac{2}{3} =$ _____

24. $6\frac{1}{3} - 4\frac{7}{12} =$ _____

25. $8\frac{1}{2} \times \frac{9}{17} \times \frac{2}{3} =$ _____

26. $3\frac{3}{4} \div \frac{27}{16} =$ _____

Solve the following application problems.

27. The size of a prison cell at Alcatraz Prison in the San Francisco Bay is 5 feet by 9 feet. The average size of a shark cage is 5 feet by $6\frac{1}{2}$ feet. How many more square feet are there in the prison cell than in the shark cage? (**Source:** Discovery Channel, Monster Garage Factoid.)

27. _____

28. To prepare for the state real estate exam, Mia Dawson studied $5\frac{1}{2}$ hours on the first day, $6\frac{1}{4}$ hours on the second day, $3\frac{3}{4}$ hours on the third day, and 7 hours on the fourth day. How many hours did she study altogether? **[2.3]**

28. _____

29. The storage area at American River Raft Rental has four sides and is enclosed with $527\frac{1}{24}$ feet of security fencing around it. If three sides of the yard measure $107\frac{2}{3}$ feet, $150\frac{3}{4}$ feet, and $138\frac{5}{8}$ feet, find the length of the fourth side. **[2.3]**

29. _____

30. Play-It-Now Sports Center has decided to divide $\frac{2}{3}$ of the company's profit-sharing funds evenly among the eight store managers. What fraction of the total amount will each receive? **[2.4]**

30. _____

Solve the following problems. **[2.5]**

31. Change .65 to a fraction.

31. _____

32. Change $\frac{2}{3}$ to a decimal. Round to the nearest thousandth.

32. _____

Solve the following problems. **[3.1–3.4]**

33. Change $\frac{7}{8}$ to a percent. _____

34. Change .25% to a decimal. _____

35. Find 35% of 6200 home loans. _____

36. Find 134% of $80. _____

37. 275 sales is what percent of 1100 sales? _____

38. 375 patients is what percent of 250 patients? _____

Solve the following application problems.

39. Currently there are 38,990 movie screens in the United States. It is expected that only 400 screens will be added in the next five years. Find the percent to be added.

39. _____

40. A Bose Home Theater System normally priced at $2499.99 is on sale for 15% off. Find the amount of discount and the sales price. Round to the nearest cent. **[3.2]**

40. _____

41. Bookstore sales of the *Physicians' Desk Reference*, which contains prescription drug information, rose 13.7% this year. If sales this year were 111,150 copies, find last year's sales. Round to the nearest whole number. **[3.5]**

41. _____

42. After deducting 11.8% of total sales as her commission, George-Ann Hornor, a salesperson for Marx Toy Company, deposited $35,138.88 to the company account. Find the total amount of her sales. **[3.5]**

42. _____

43. Tumaro's Gourmet Tortillas saw sales increase 450 times in the past few years. What percent increase did they experience? Show your work, explaining how you arrived at your answer. (*Source: Los Angeles Times.*) **[3.1]**

43. _____

44. The value of a stock used to be 6 times what it is worth today. The value today is what percent of the past value? Round to the nearest tenth of a percent. Show your work, explaining how you arrived at your answer. **[3.1]**

44. _____

WHERE'S THE BEEF? *The United States exported 2.3 billion pounds of beef. Use the circle graph below to solve Exercises 45–48.* **[3.2]**

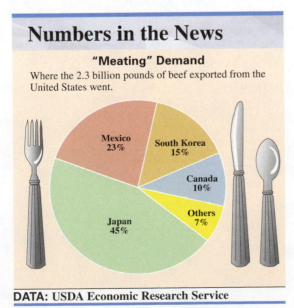

Numbers in the News

"Meating" Demand

Where the 2.3 billion pounds of beef exported from the United States went.

Mexico 23%
South Korea 15%
Canada 10%
Others 7%
Japan 45%

DATA: USDA Economic Research Service

45. (a) What percent of the exported beef was shipped to Japan, Mexico, and South Korea combined? **(b)** Find the total number of pounds exported to these three countries.

(a) _____

(b) _____

46. (a) What percent of the exported beef was shipped to countries other than Japan, Mexico, and South Korea combined? **(b)** Find the total number of pounds exported to these three countries.

(a) _____

(b) _____

47. How much more beef was exported to Japan than to South Korea?

47. _____

48. How much more beef was exported to Mexico than to Canada?

48. _____

Solve each equation for the unknown. **[4.1]**

49. $9r - 23 = 31$ _____

50. $\dfrac{3}{4}t = 120$ _____

51. $5y - 10 = 26$ _____

52. $20 + 5x = 83 - x$ _____

Find the value of the variable that is not given. **[4.3]**

53. $I = PRT; P = \$45,000, R = .015,$ $T = .5$ _____

54. $d = rt; r = 378, t = 8.5$ _____

55. $A = P + PRT; A = 1368, P = 1200,$ $T = 2$ _____

56. $M = P(1 + i)^n; n = 6, i = 0.02,$ $M = \$42,231.09$ _____

Solve the equation for the variable indicated. **[4.3]**

57. Solve $I = PRT$ for T. _____

58. Solve $PV = nRT$ for P. _____

59. Solve $M = P(1 + i)^n$ for P. _____   **60.** $A = \dfrac{S}{1 + RT}$ for R. _____

Write the ratio in lowest terms. [4.4]

61. 500 euros to 725 dollars _____   **62.** 24 ounces to 15 gallons _____

63. 14 lockers to 40 minutes _____   **64.** 630 apples to 168 cans _____

Solve the following application problems.

65. The sum of an unknown and 47 is 93. Find the unknown. [4.2]   **65.** _____

66. The sum of two consecutive odd numbers is 228. Find the numbers. [4.2]   **66.** _____

67. A community college bookstore marks up the price of a book by 42%. Find the cost to the bookstore if the selling price is $159. [4.2]   **67.** _____

68. Forty-seven students signed up for a two-week travel/study trip to Greece. There were 9 more women than men. Find the number of men and women. [4.2]   **68.** _____

69. The cost of replacing a roof on a 1450 square foot house is $6600. Find the cost to replace the roof on a 2400 square foot house. Round to the nearest dollar. [4.4]   **69.** _____

70. A 32 unit apartment complex generates total monthly rents of $21,920. Assuming comparable rents, estimate the total monthly rent generated by a 70 unit complex. [4.4]   **70.** _____

Bank Services

5

case IN point ▶

BARBARA WIFFY owns and operates a small nursery named Rose Gardens. Although she sells all types of outdoor trees and shrubs, her specialty is roses. For the best quality roses, she has always bought from Jackson & Perkins Wholesale, Inc. This firm has research scientists who experiment with hybridizing roses with the goal of creating new, beautiful flowers. Wiffy also likes the fact that Jackson & Perkins guarantees the quality of their roses.

As her business began to grow, Barbara Wiffy carefully looked at several different banks. She even talked to bank managers before choosing a bank because she wanted to make sure the bank managers and employees would work with her needs as an entrepreneur. She knows how important the right bank and bankers are for a business owner.

Historically, banks offered checking and savings accounts and made loans. Today, they also offer home banking, electronic funds transfer, automated teller machines (ATMs), credit cards, debit cards, investment securities services, collection on notes, guaranteed bank checks, and even payroll services for business owners. In this chapter, we discuss some banking services, including **electronic banking**, and show how to use check registers and reconcile bank accounts. We also show how credit-card transactions are handled by businesses.

5.1 Electronic Banking, Checking Accounts, and Check Registers

OBJECTIVES

1 Compare traditional versus electronic banking.
2 Know the types of checking accounts.
3 Identify the parts of a check.
4 Calculate the monthly service charges.
5 Identify the parts of a deposit slip.
6 Identify the parts of a check stub.
7 Complete the parts of a check register (transaction register).

case IN point

As a business owner, Barbara Wiffy receives payments in all these ways: cash, checks, credit cards, debit cards, electronic payments, and even traveler's checks. In turn, she pays bills using checks, credit cards, debit cards, and electronic payments. She chose a bank that will support her growing company by efficiently handling all these types of payments.

OBJECTIVE 1 Compare traditional versus electronic banking. Traditional banking involves the use of paper checks and check registers to record deposits and checks. Many people still use the traditional system, as do some small businesses. Quite a few people use both traditional banking and electronic banking. However, increasing numbers of people are moving toward electronic banking.

Electronic banking allows customers to make financial transactions on secure Web sites through computer networks such as the Internet. Electronic banking may be referred to as **home banking, online banking**, or **Internet banking**. The table that follows shows some of the many features of electronic banking. **Electronic commerce (EC)** refers to the buying or selling of products or services over the Internet or other computer networks.

FEATURE	DESCRIPTION
Automated Teller Machine (ATM)	Worldwide network of electronic machines with 24-hour-a-day access. Used to make deposits, transfer money, or get cash. Use of the ATM machine at a bank at which you are not an account holder often results in a charge.
Direct Deposit/Direct Payment	Allows you to authorize regularly occurring deposits (e.g., payroll checks) directly into your checking account. It also allows you to authorize direct payments from your accounts (e.g., house payment or utility bills).
Electronic Funds Transfer (EFT)/ Electronic Payment	Allows you to electronically make transfers of funds and pay bills. Many small and most large businesses use this feature extensively.
Pay by Phone	Allows you to use the phone to transfer money.
Personal Computer Banking	Allows you to use a computer hooked up to the Internet to remotely check balances, pay bills, and transfer funds.

FEATURE	DESCRIPTION
Debit Card	A card that looks very similiar to a credit card. When used, the payment amount is immediately subtracted from the account, even if late at night. It requires a **personal identification number (PIN)**.
Prepaid Card	A card upon which a user has stored monetary value before making any purchases.
Smart Card	A card with a microchip that receives electronic signals, makes calculations, and sends signals. Some can be used for identification.
Point of Sale (POS)	Refers to the checkpoint register where a transaction occurs in a business.

Let's compare the three common payment systems for a customer making a purchase at a merchant such as a Wal-Mart store.

PAYMENT METHOD	
Check	Depending on the amount of the check, the teller may ask for identification and write on the back of the check. The check is soon deposited in Wal-Mart's local bank, which electronically requests payment from the customer's bank through a clearing house.
Credit Card	The customer swipes the card through the card reader. Depending on factors such as the amount of the charge and whether the customer has purchased there before, he or she may be asked to sign the credit slip. Often, the merchant's system will electronically check to make sure the credit card is valid.
Debit Card	The customer swipes the card through the reader and enters his or her personal identification number (PIN) when requested. Wal-Mart immediately routes the charge to a bank, which authorizes payment and debits the account balance.

In the past, it took a week to process a check. But now, checks are often processed in just a few days. However, the percent of all consumer payments made by check has fallen from 50% in 2000 to about 18% in 2010. So, the era of the check is slowly but surely coming to an end as checks are replaced by credit cards, debit cards, and **electronic payments**.

A credit-card transaction is not completely settled until the end of the customer's billing cycle. A debit-card transaction is completed in a few seconds or a few minutes at most. The cheapest and fastest of the three is the debit card, which is often processed over a network such as the Internet. The graphic shows the cost of various transactions at a bank. As you can see, the Internet is by far the lowest-cost option.

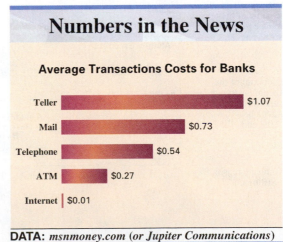

Numbers in the News

Average Transactions Costs for Banks

Teller	$1.07
Mail	$0.73
Telephone	$0.54
ATM	$0.27
Internet	$0.01

DATA: *msnmoney.com (or Jupiter Communications)*

However, electronic banking is not without problems. For example, it is relatively easy to authorize a payment(s) for which you do not have available funds. This may occur when a payroll check is for less than expected, yet the date for a scheduled payment arrives. This has resulted in up to ten charges for insufficient funds in one day for some individuals. Clearly, you need to monitor your account balances carefully and continuously.

Thief from the Past

Another problem is unauthorized use of your account, or even identity theft. **Identity theft** occurs when someone gathers enough information about you to fraudulently establish credit cards or borrow money using your name and personal information. It can be very difficult to stop the thief since it is difficult to find him or her. It is extremely important to protect your financial information as well as your log-on ID and password to all financial accounts. Experts recommend using complex passwords that cannot easily be discovered by criminals. They also recommend destroying documents that include credit-card numbers, account numbers, Social Security numbers, and all bank records.

Thief of Today

A newer trend in Asia and Europe called **mobile payments** uses specially equipped cell phones instead of cash, checks, credit cards, or debit cards to make payments. For example, in some places you can pay charges for a commuter train simply by holding your phone as you walk through the turnstile. Some banks in the United States allow customers to use cell phones to check account balances on credit cards, pay bills, transfer money, and view transactions. Some banks even communicate balances using **texting**. Expect more applications in the future as banks look to both satisfy customers and cut costs.

OBJECTIVE 2 **Know the types of checking accounts.** Checking accounts are used by individuals and businesses for many daily transactions. The two basic types of checking accounts are discussed here. There are dozens of variations of these account types.

Personal checking accounts are used by individuals. The bank supplies printed checks (normally charging a check-printing fee) for the customer to use. Some banks offer the checking account at no charge to the customer, but most require that a minimum monthly balance remain in the checking account. If the minimum balance is not maintained during any month, a service charge is applied to the account. Today, the **flat-fee checking account** is common. For a fixed charge per month, the bank supplies the checking account, a supply of printed checks, a bank charge card, an ATM card, a debit card, and a host of other services. **Interest paid** on checking-account balances is common with personal checking accounts. These accounts are offered by savings-and-loan associations, credit unions, and banks and are available to individuals as well as to a few business customers.

Business checking accounts often receive more services and have greater activity than do personal accounts. For example, banks often arrange to receive payments on debts due to business firms. The bank automatically credits the amount to the business account.

OBJECTIVE 3 **Identify the parts of a check.** Although many transactions are done electronically today, there are still hundreds of millions of checks written each year. So it is important to understand checks. The diagram explains the parts of a check.

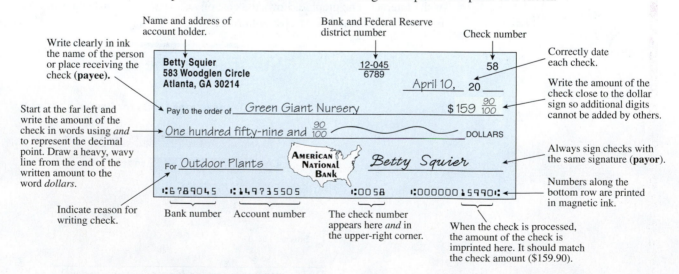

OBJECTIVE 4 Calculate the monthly service charges. Service charges for business checking accounts are based on the average balance for the period covered by the statement. This average balance determines the **maintenance charge per month**, to which a **per-debit charge** (per-check charge) is added. The charges generally apply without regard to the amount of account activity. The following table shows typical bank charges for a business checking account.

AVERAGE BALANCE	MAINTENANCE CHARGE PER MONTH	PER-CHECK CHARGE
Less than $500	$12.00	$.20
$500–$1999	$7.50	$.20
$2000–$4999	$5.00	$.10
$5000 or more	0	0

Some banks reduce charges for customers who pay bills electronically and make few deposits. Use the information in the table above for the following examples, and for the relevant exercises at the end of this chapter.

Finding the Checking-Account Service Charge

EXAMPLE 1

Find the monthly service charge for the following business accounts.

(a) Omni Computer, 38 checks written, average balance $983

Based on the average balance of $983, the maintenance charge is $7.50 and the per-check charge is $.20.

$$\text{Charge} = \textbf{Maintenance charge} + \textbf{Per-check charge}$$
$$= \qquad \$7.50 \qquad + 38 \text{ checks} \times \$.20$$
$$= \qquad \$7.50 \qquad + \$7.60$$
$$= \qquad \$15.10$$

(b) Jamison Auto Repair, 62 checks written, average balance $4632.25

Based on the average balance, the maintenance charge is $5.00 and the per-check charge is $.10.

$$\text{Charge} = \text{Maintenance charge} + \text{Per-check charge}$$
$$= \qquad \$5.00 \qquad \textbf{+ 62 checks} \times \textbf{\$.10}$$
$$= \qquad \$5.00 \qquad + \$6.20$$
$$= \qquad \$11.20$$

The calculator solutions to this example use chain calculations, with the calculator observing the order of operations.

(a) 7.5 [+] 38 [×] .2 [=] 15.1   (b) 5 [+] 62 [×] .1 [=] 11.2

Note: Refer to Appendix B for calculator basics.

QUICK CHECK 1

Find the monthly service charge for the following business accounts.

(a) Towne Florist, 76 checks written, average balance $2180
(b) On-Line Books, 58 checks written, average balance $1850

OBJECTIVE 5 Identify the parts of a deposit slip. Cash and checks are placed into an account using a **deposit slip** or **deposit ticket**, as shown here. The account number is printed at the bottom in magnetic ink. The slip contains blanks for entering any currency (bills) or coins (change) as well as any checks that are to be deposited.

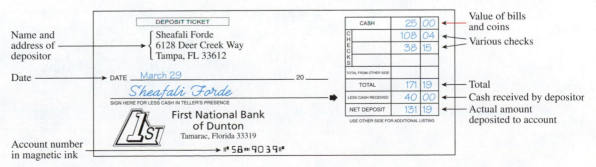

When a check is deposited, it should have "for deposit only" and either the depositor's signature or the company stamp placed on the back within 1.5 inches of the trailing edge (as seen in the following figure). In this way, if a check is lost or stolen before it is deposited, it will be worthless to anyone finding it. Such an endorsement, which limits the ability to cash a check, is called a **restricted endorsement**. An example of a restricted endorsement is shown below along with two other types of endorsements. The most common endorsement by individuals is the **blank endorsement**, where only the name of the person being paid is signed. This endorsement should be used only at the moment of cashing the check. The **special endorsement**, used to pass on the check to someone else, might be used to pay a bill on another account.

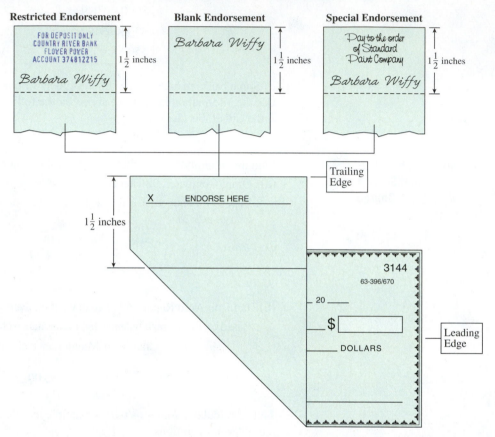

After a check is endorsed, it is deposited or cashed at a bank. Originally, the actual checks were returned to the check writer's bank and, finally, to the writer of the check. However, in 2004, a federal law known as **Check 21** was passed that resulted in numerous changes. Under this law, banks can take electronic photos of all **canceled checks** and then exchange the photos of checks electronically. The bank retains the photos but destroys the paper checks. This law greatly reduced the amount of time needed for a check to clear, thereby reducing the **float time**. Float time refers to the time between writing a check and the time funds are transferred out of the payee's account. However, even photos of the canceled checks contain the following types of **processing** information on them.

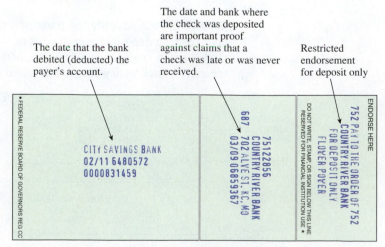

OBJECTIVE 6 Identify the parts of a check stub. Businesses must keep careful records of all deposits and payments so that they know how much money they have. Managers must have accurate information to prepare tax returns and financial statements. Businesses that use checks often keep such information by using a **check stub** for each check, as shown here. The check stub includes space for the date, **balance brought forward**, amount deposited, amount of this check, and **balance forward**, or **current balance**, at the bottom of the stub. Reading down the bottom half of the check stub, add the *Bal. Bro't. For'd.* to *Am't. Deposited*, to find *Total*. Then subtract *Am't. this Check* to find the *Bal. For'd.* at the bottom. Write this number at the top of the next check stub. Paying the bills at a business is tedious, but accuracy is very important. In fact, fast and accurate processing of bill payments forms the backbone of electronic commerce.

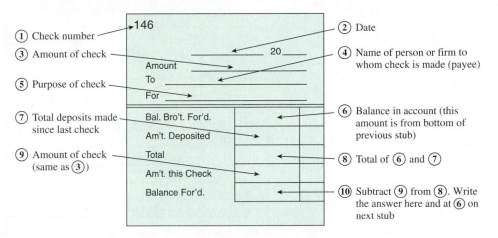

Completing a Check Stub **EXAMPLE 2**

Check number 2724 was made out on June 8 to Lillburn Utilities as payment for water and power. Assume that the check was for $182.15, that the balance brought forward is $4245.36, and that deposits of $337.71 and $193.17 have been made since the last check was written. Complete the check stub.

SOLUTION

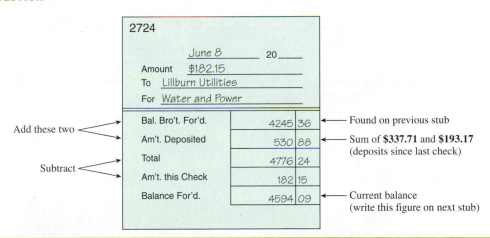

QUICK CHECK 2

Use the check stub to find the balance forward. Check number 3502 is made out on April 4 to City Hall for $273.28. The balance brought forward was $6750.17 and deposits of $1876.22 and $879.65 have been made since the last check was written.

3502		
_____ 20 ___		
Amount		
To		
For		
Bal. Bro't. For'd.		
Am't. Deposited		
Total		
Am't. this Check		
Balance For'd.		

OBJECTIVE 7 Complete the parts of a check register (transaction register). Some depositors prefer a check register to check stubs, while others use both. A **check register**, also called a **transaction register**, is shown here. It lists the checks written and deposits made at a glance. The column headed with a check mark is used to record each check after it has cleared or when it is received back from the bank. Check registers of one form or another are also used by many individuals who use electronic banking. Be sure to write down all electronic transactions and any ATM fees and charges.

Check Register

CHECK NO.	DATE	TRANSACTION DESCRIPTION	AMOUNT OF WITHDRAWAL		✓	DATE OF DEP.	AMOUNT OF DEPOSIT/CREDIT		BALANCE	
		BALANCE BROUGHT FORWARD →							3518	72
e*	5/8	Swan Brothers	378	93					3139	79
1436	5/8	Class Acts	25	14					3114	65
1437	5/9	Mirror Lighting	519	65					2595	00
		Deposit				5/10	3821	17	6416	17
e	5/10	Woodlake Auditorium	750	00					5666	17
		Deposit				5/12	500	00	6166	17
1438	5/12	Rick's Clowns	170	80					5995	37
1439	5/14	Y.M.C.A.	219	17					5776	20
	5/14	ATM	120	00					5656	20
		Deposit				5/15	326	15	5982	35
e	5/16	Stage Door Playhouse	825	00					5157	35
e	5/17	Gilbert Eckern	1785	00					3372	35
		Deposit				5/19	1580	25	4952	60

e refers to electronic payment.

5.1 Exercises

MyMathLab   Math XL PRACTICE   WATCH   DOWNLOAD   READ

The QUICK START *exercises in each section contain solutions to help you get started.*

CHECKING CHARGES   *Use the table on page 185 to find the monthly checking-account service charge for the following accounts. (See Example 1.)*

QUICK START

1. Rose Gardens, 92 checks, average balance $4618   1. $14.20
   $5.00 + (92 × $.10) = $5.00 + $9.20 = $14.20

2. Fresh Choice Restaurant, 114 checks, average balance $3318   2. $16.40
   $5.00 + (114 × $.10) = $5.00 + $11.40 = $16.40

3. Pest-X, 40 checks, average balance $491   3. _____

4. Kent's Keys, Inc., 76 checks, average balance $468   4. _____

5. Budget Dry Cleaning, 48 checks, average balance $1763   5. _____

6. Direct Connection, 272 checks, average balance $8205   6. _____

7. Software and More, 72 checks, average balance $516   7. _____

8. Mart & Bottle, 74 checks, average balance $875   8. _____

MAINTAINING BANK RECORDS   *Use the following information to complete each check stub.*
(See Example 2.)

	DATE	TO	FOR	AMOUNT	BAL. BRO'T. FOR'D.	DEPOSITS
9.	Mar. 8	Nola Akala	Tutoring	$380.71	$3971.28	$79.26
10.	Oct. 15	Corinn Berman	Rent	$850.00	$2973.09	$1853.24
11.	Dec. 4	Paul's Pools	Chemicals	$37.52	$1126.73	

9.

857

_____ 20 _____

Amount _____
To _____
For _____

Bal. Bro't. For'd.		
Am't. Deposited		
Total		
Am't. this Check		
Balance For'd.		

10.

1248

_____ 20 _____

Amount _____
To _____
For _____

Bal. Bro't. For'd.		
Am't. Deposited		
Total		
Am't. this Check		
Balance For'd.		

11.

735

_____ 20 _____

Amount _____
To _____
For _____

Bal. Bro't. For'd.		
Am't. Deposited		
Total		
Am't. this Check		
Balance For'd.		

 indicates an exercise that is related to the Case in Point feature.

12. List and explain at least six parts of a check. Draw a sketch showing where these parts appear on a check. (See Objective 3.)

13. Discuss the advantages and disadvantages of electronic banking. (See Objective 1.)

14. Write an explanation of two types of check endorsements. Describe where these endorsements must be placed. (See Objective 5.)

15. Explain in your own words the factors that determine the service charges on a business checking account. (See Objective 4.)

◢ **COMPLETING CHECK STUBS**   *Using the information provided, complete the following check stubs for Rose Gardens.* ***The balance brought forward for check stub 5311 is $7223.69.*** *(See Example 2.)*

CHECKS WRITTEN					DEPOSITS MADE	
NUMBER	DATE	TO	FOR	AMOUNT	DATE	AMOUNT
5311	Oct. 7	Julie Davis	Seeds	$1250.80	Oct. 8	$752.18
5312	Oct. 10	County Clerk	License	$39.12	Oct. 9	$23.32
5313	Oct. 15	United Parcel	Shipping	$356.28	Oct. 13	$1025.45

16.

5311 **Rose Gardens**	
_____ 20 _____	
Amount _____	
To _____	
For _____	
Bal. Bro't. For'd.		
Am't. Deposited		
Total		
Am't. this Check		
Balance For'd.		

17.

5312 **Rose Gardens**	
_____ 20 _____	
Amount _____	
To _____	
For _____	
Bal. Bro't. For'd.		
Am't. Deposited		
Total		
Am't. this Check		
Balance For'd.		

18.

5313 **Rose Gardens**	
_____ 20 _____	
Amount _____	
To _____	
For _____	
Bal. Bro't. For'd.		
Am't. Deposited		
Total		
Am't. this Check		
Balance For'd.		

BANK BALANCES   *In Exercises 19–22, complete the balance column in the following company check registers after each check or deposit transaction. Electronic payments are indicated by* **e**. *(See Objective 7.)*

 19. Rose Gardens

CHECK NO.	DATE	TRANSACTION DESCRIPTION	AMOUNT OF WITHDRAWAL	✓	DATE OF DEP.	AMOUNT OF DEPOSIT/CREDIT	BALANCE
		BALANCE BROUGHT FORWARD →					9628 35
1221	10/4	Delta Contractors	215 71				
e	10/5	Hand Fabricating	573 78				
1222	10/5	Photo Specialties	112 15				
		Deposit			10/6	753 28	
		Deposit			10/8	1475 69	
e	10/9	Young Marketing	426 55				
e	10/11	Wholesale Supply	637 93				
	10/11	ATM (fuel)	65 62				
e	10/14	Light and Power Utilities	248 17				
		Deposit			10/16	335 85	
1223	10/16	License Board	450 50				

20. Ontime Marketing

CHECK NO.	DATE	TRANSACTION DESCRIPTION	AMOUNT OF WITHDRAWAL	✓	DATE OF DEP.	AMOUNT OF DEPOSIT/CREDIT	BALANCE
		BALANCE BROUGHT FORWARD →					1629 86
e	7/3	Ahwahnee Hotel	250 45				
862	7/5	Willow Creek	149 00				
863	7/5	Void					
		Deposit			7/7	117 73	
e	7/9	Del Campo High School	69 80				
		Deposit			7/10	329 86	
		Deposit			7/12	418 30	
864	7/14	Big 5 Sporting Goods	109 76				
865	7/14	Dr. Yates	614 12				
866	7/16	Office Supplies	32 18				
		Deposit			7/16	520 95	

21. Stencils by Loree

CHECK NO.	DATE	TRANSACTION DESCRIPTION	AMOUNT OF WITHDRAWAL	✓	DATE OF DEP.	AMOUNT OF DEPOSIT/CREDIT	BALANCE
		BALANCE BROUGHT FORWARD →					832 15
e	3/17	AirTouch Cellular	257 29				
e	3/18	Curry Village	190 50				
		Deposit			3/19	78 29	
		Deposit			3/21	157 42	
1123	3/22	San Juan District	38 76				
e	3/23	Macy's Gourmet	175 88				
		Deposit			3/23	379 28	
1124	3/24	Class Video	197 20				
1125	3/24	Water World	25 10				
1126	3/25	Bel Air Market	75 00				
		Deposit			3/28	722 35	

22. Beverly's Event Planning

CHECK NO.	DATE	TRANSACTION DESCRIPTION	AMOUNT OF WITHDRAWAL		✓	DATE OF DEP.	AMOUNT OF DEPOSIT/CREDIT		BALANCE	
		BALANCE BROUGHT FORWARD →							3852	48
e	12/6	Web Masters	143	16						
e	12/7	Water and Power	118	40						
		Deposit				12/8	286	32		
	12/10	ATM (cash)	80	00						
2312	12/11	Ann Kuick	986	22						
e	12/11	Account Temps	375	50						
		Deposit				12/14	1201	82		
e	12/14	Central Chevrolet	735	68						
2313	12/15	Miller Mining	223	94						
		Deposit				12/17	498	01		
2314	12/18	Federal Parcel	78	24						

5.2 Checking Services and Credit-Card Transactions

OBJECTIVES

1 Identify bank services available to customers.

2 Understand interest-paying checking plans.

3 Understand credit-card sales and calculate the fee.

OBJECTIVE 1 Identify bank services available to customers. Most business checking-account charges are determined by either the average balance or the minimum balance in the account, together with specific charges for each service performed by the bank. Some of the services provided by banks, along with the *typical charges*, are listed here.

- **ATM cards** are used as debit cards when making point-of-sale purchases. The fee for purchases varies from $.10 per transaction to $1 per month for unlimited transactions. When the card is used at the ATM machine, there is usually no fee at any branch of your bank, a fee as high as $2.50 at other banks, and an international fee as high as $5.
- An **overdraft** occurs when a check is written for which there are nonsufficient funds (NSF) in the checking account and the customer has no overdraft protection, also referred to as bouncing a check. The typical charge to the writer of the "bad" check is $25 to $35 per bad check. The same charge occurs when a check is returned because it was improperly completed.
- **Overdraft protection** is given when an account balance is insufficient to cover the amount of a check and an overdraft occurs. Charges for overdraft protection vary among banks.
- A **returned-deposit item** is a check that was deposited and then returned to the bank, usually because of lack of funds in the account of the person or firm writing the check. A common charge to the depositor of the check is $25. At least one bank in New York charges $35.
- A **stop-payment order** is a request by a depositor that the bank not honor a check the depositor has written ($30 per request).
- A **cashier's check** is a check written by the financial institution itself and is viewed as being as good as cash ($8 per check).
- A **money order** is a purchased instrument that is often used in place of cash and is sometimes required instead of a personal or business check ($4 each).
- A **notary service** (official certification of a signature on a document) is a service that is required on certain business documents. Occasionally this service is free to customers, but there is usually a charge ($10).
- **Online banking** or banking on the Internet allows customers to perform many banking functions from their home or place of business. This service is usually free.

OBJECTIVE 2 Understand interest-paying checking plans. Federal regulations allow both personal and business checking accounts that pay interest. Some of the plans combine two accounts, a savings and checking account, whereas others are simply checking accounts that pay interest. The interest rates paid on checking accounts are typically very low, but funds can be withdrawn without notice.

Money market accounts offered by banks pay somewhat higher rates depending on the market rates at the time. Money market accounts often require a higher balance than regular checking accounts and also often limit the number of transactions (checks, electronic transfers, and deposits) in the account each month. The advantage of a money market account over a regular checking account is that it earns a higher interest rate, yet funds are still easily accessible without giving advance notice to the bank. Banks also offer savings accounts and longer-term investments called certificates of deposit (CDs), which are discussed in Chapter 10.

OBJECTIVE 3 Understand credit-card sales and calculate the fee. Credit-card sales are very common in business. Even customers that are not comfortable using the Web for purchases often use credit cards without hesitation. The customer swipes his or her credit card at the **point-of-sale terminal**, which scans information from the card. The system seeks authorization for the charge, which is quickly given or denied. Credit charges are accumulated by the

Undergrads Love Their Plastic	
Undergrads with a credit card	78%
Average number of cards owned	3
Average student card debt	$2748
Students with four or more cards	32%
Balances of $3000 to $7000	13%
Balances over $7000	13%
Pay off card balance in full each month	39%

Source: Nellie Mae (college loan provider)

financial institution in batches and then submitted for funding, which takes a few days. The customer receives a bill at the end of the month and has the option to pay all or part of the balance due.

"How It Works" Diagram

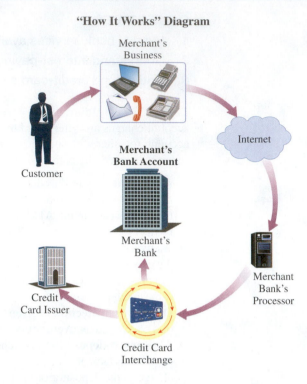

The cost to the merchant of processing credit-card transactions is often higher than processing debit-card transactions. In fact, merchants must pay a fee averaging about 2% on credit-card sales made on VISA® and MasterCard®. The merchant is willing to pay the fee since it increases sales. The banks that offer the credit cards like this business because it generates a lot of income. Many consumers like to use credit cards since it allows them to either delay the payment until the end of the billing cycle or spread the cost out over several months. To avoid the fee charged by the issuer of the credit card, some merchants offer discounts to customers who pay using cash, debit, or check. Still, most merchants take payments in any form to maximize sales.

> **Finding Net Deposit for Credit-Card Sales:**
> 1. Net credit card sales = Total credit card sales − Total credit card refunds
> 2. Total fee = Appropriate percent × Net credit card sales
> 3. Net deposit = Total credit card sales − Total fee

Find the Fees and Net Deposit on Credit-Card Sales — **EXAMPLE 1**

Here are some credit-card sales and credit-card refunds made one afternoon at Rose Gardens. Find the total credit card sales, the total credit card refunds, and the net credit card sales. Then find the bank fee charged, assuming a fee of 2% of the net credit card sales. Finally, find the amount deposited to Rose Garden's checking account.

CREDIT-CARD SALES		CREDIT-CARD REFUNDS
$82.31	$146.50	$43.83
$38.18	$78.80	$85.95
$249.33	$470.15	
$46.80	$320.90	

SOLUTION

Add the preceding to find total credit-card sales of $1432.97 and total credit-card refunds of $129.78. Then find the net credit-card sales as follows.

$$
\begin{array}{rl}
\text{Total sales} & = \$1432.97 \\
\text{Total refunds} & = -129.78 \\
\hline
\text{Net sales} & \quad \$1303.19
\end{array}
$$

The bank fee is 2% of net credit card sales.

$$\text{Bank fee} = 2\% \text{ of } \$1303.19$$
$$= \$26.06 \quad \text{(rounded)}$$

Finally, find the amount deposited to Rose Garden's checking account.

$$\text{Amount} = \$1303.19 - \$26.06 = \$1277.13$$

QUICK CHECK 1

Assume a fee of 2.25% and find the amount deposited to a business owner's account based on the following credit-card transactions.

Sales: $532.15, $650.19, $127.45, $314.98
Refunds: $120.15

Interestingly, some banks that issue MasterCard® and Visa® give rewards to credit-card users. When you receive cash back or some other reward based on your credit-card use, you are really getting a small rebate based on your previous credit-card use.

Some small-business owners have aggressively challenged the charges levied by the banks on credit cards, saying they are far too high. Congress is now exploring the fee structures of the financial institutions, and it may pass legislation that restricts the amount of the fee that can be charged to merchants.

5.2 Exercises

MyMathLab   Math XL PRACTICE   WATCH   DOWNLOAD   READ

The **QUICK START** exercises in each section contain solutions to help you get started.

CREDIT-CARD DEPOSITS *Mak's Tune and Smog accepts cash, checks, and credit cards from customers for auto repair and the sale of parts. The following credit-card transactions occurred one day.*

SALES		REFUNDS
$66.68	$18.95	$62.16
$119.63	$496.28	$106.62
$53.86	$21.85	$38.91
$178.62	$242.78	
$219.78	$176.93	

QUICK START

1. What is the total amount of the credit-card sales?

   $66.68 + $119.63 + $53.86 + $178.62 + $219.78 + $18.95 + $496.28 + $21.85 + $242.78 + $176.93 = $1595.36

   1. **$1595.36**

2. Find the total of the credit-card refunds.

   $62.16 + $106.62 + $38.91 = $207.69

   2. **$207.69**

3. Find credit-card sales less refunds.

   3. _____

4. If the fee paid by the business is 2.5%, find the amount of the charge at the statement date.

   4. _____

5. Find the amount of the credit given to Mak's Tune and Smog after the fee is subtracted.

   5. _____

 CREDIT-CARD DEPOSITS *Rose Gardens does most of its business on the Internet and accepts credit cards. In a recent period, the business had the following credit-card charges and credits. (See Examples 1 and 2.)*

SALES		REFUNDS
$78.56	$38.15	$29.76
$875.29	$18.46	$102.15
$330.82	$22.13	$71.95
$55.24	$707.37	
$47.83	$245.91	

6. What is the total amount of the credit-card sales?

   6. _____

7. Find the total of the credit-card refunds.

   7. _____

8. Find credit-card sales less refunds.

   8. _____

9. If the bank charges Rose Gardens a 3% fee, find the amount of the charge at the statement date.

   9. _____

10. Find the amount of the credit given to Rose Gardens after the fee is subtracted.

    10. _____

 indicates an exercise that is related to the Case in Point feature.

CREDIT-CARD DEPOSITS *Jay Jenkins owns Campus Bicycle Shop near a college campus. The shop sells new and used bicycle parts and does a major portion of its business in adjustments and repairs. The following credit-card charges and credits took place during a recent period.*

SALES		REFUNDS
$7.84	$98.56	$13.86
$33.18	$318.72	$58.97
$50.76	$116.35	
$12.72	$23.78	
$9.36	$38.95	
$118.68	$235.82	

11. Find the total amount of the credit-card sales.

11. _____

12. Find the total of the credit-card refunds.

12. _____

13. Find credit-card sales less refunds.

13. _____

14. If the fee paid by the shop is 2%, find the amount of the charge at the statement date.

14. _____

15. Find the amount of the credit given to Campus Bicycle Shop after the fee is subtracted.

15. _____

CREDIT-CARD DEPOSITS *Kaare Taylor Photo Studios had the following credit-card transactions during a recent period.*

SALES		REFUNDS
$14.86	$76.15	$43.15
$49.70	$226.17	$17.06
$183.60	$63.95	
$238.75	$111.10	
$18.36	$77.86	
$52.08	$132.62	

16. Find the total amount of the credit-card sales.

16. _____

17. Find the total of the credit-card refunds.

17. _____

18. Find credit-card sales less refunds.

18. _____

19. If the fee paid by the shop is 2.5%, find the amount of the charge at the statement date.

19. _____

20. Find the amount of credit given to Kaare Taylor Studios after the fee is subtracted.

20. _____

21. List and describe in your own words four services offered to business checking-account customers. (See Objective 1.)

22. The merchant accepting a credit card from a customer must pay a fee of 2% or more of the transaction amount. Why is the merchant willing to do this? Who really pays this fee? (See Objective 3.)

─── **QUICK CHECK ANSWER** ───

1. $1470.77

5.3 Bank Statement Reconciliation

OBJECTIVES

1 Know the importance of reconciling a checking account.

2 Reconcile a bank statement with a checkbook.

3 List the outstanding checks.

4 Find the *adjusted bank balance* or *current balance*.

case IN point ▶

Barbara Wiffy, owner of Rose Gardens, knows the importance of keeping accurate checking-account records. She has received customers' checks drawn on accounts with nonsufficient funds (NSF), but with great pride she says, "I have never bounced a business check."

OBJECTIVE 1 **Know the importance of reconciling a checking account.** Once a month, a bank creates a bank statement that shows all activity for each account. Some customers want the bank to mail them a copy. Others prefer to look at the **bank statement** on the bank's Web site, where it can also be printed out if desired. The bank statement shows all deposits and credits as well as disbursements, such as checks, debits, electronic payments, ATM cash withdrawals, and any fees. Here is a list of a few reasons for an account owner to look at the bank statement every month.

1. The fee charged by the bank often varies from month to month.
2. A deposited check may be returned due to insufficient funds. The amount of the check and any fees must be deducted. **Returned checks** are also called **bounced checks**.
3. A scheduled deposit may or may not have been made.
4. The account holder may have made an error in the check register.

If someone owed you money and was supposed to make an automatic payment into your checking account but did not do so one month, would you be concerned? Of course; funds in a bank account are an asset that individuals and business managers should manage carefully.

OBJECTIVE 2 **Reconcile a bank statement with a checkbook.** The process of checking the bank statement against the check register is called **reconciliation**. The following bank statement is for **Rose Gardens**. Two columns of information on the bank statement are further explained at the top of the next page.

```
BANK STATEMENT

                                  3/31    STATEMENT PERIOD    4/30

COUNTRY RIVER BANK                         PAGE    1

  Rose Gardens
  #6 Highway 17
  Crossville, GA 38555
```

ACCOUNT NUMBER	PREVIOUS BALANCE	CREDITS COUNT	CREDITS AMOUNT	DEBITS COUNT	DEBITS AMOUNT	FEE	PRESENT BALANCE
ODA 110004565	5218.29	4	10406.71	10	8732.59		6892.41

CHECK NUMBER	PAYMENTS		DEPOSITS	DATE	BALANCE
			Beginning Balance		5218.29
e	1836.71 debit			4/3	3381.58
847	79.26			4/4	3302.32
e	2625.10 elec. pmt.			4/5	677.22
			4137.80	4/5	4815.02
e	1498.92 elec. pmt.			4/10	3316.10
838	478.63			4/15	2837.47
	37.75 ATM			4/19	2799.72
e	1626.63 elec. pmt.			4/19	1173.09
			3279.62	4/22	4452.71
e	142.45 debit			4/25	4310.26
854	400.72			4/25	3909.54
			2984.51	4/28	6894.05
	6.42 SC			4/30	6887.63
			4.78 IC	4/30	6892.41

Codes Used Above	RC = Returned Check	SC = Service Charge
	IC = Interest Credit	ATM = Automated Teller Machine

> **PAYMENTS**—include checks, electronic payments, debits, electronic transfers of funds to other accounts, ATM withdrawals, returned checks, and fees.
>
> **DEPOSITS**—include regular deposits, electronic deposits, transfers of money into the account, and interest credited during the month.

Electronic transfers are easy to track since they show up very quickly on the bank's computer system. Checks are different. For example, you may send your aunt a check for her birthday that she does not deposit for 5 weeks. A firm often has written checks that do not yet show up on the bank statement. These unpaid checks are called **checks outstanding**. The next example shows how to identify checks outstanding and reconcile an account.

Reconciling a Checking Account **EXAMPLE 1**

case IN point

The most recent bank statement for Rose Gardens shows a balance of $6892.41 after a bank service charge of $6.42 and an interest credit of $4.78. The check register for Rose Gardens shows a current balance of $7576.38. Reconcile the account as follows.

OBJECTIVE 3 List the outstanding checks. Find the checks outstanding by comparing the list of checks on the bank statement against the list of checks written by the firm. You may wish to put a check mark on the bank statement and/or check register as you compare them. In particular, note any differences in the amounts for any check. Here are the outstanding checks.

NUMBER	AMOUNT
846	$42.73
852	$598.71
853	$68.12
857	$79.80
858	$160.30

After listing the outstanding checks in the space provided on the form, total them. The total is $949.66.

OBJECTIVE 4 Find the *adjusted bank balance* or *current balance*. Follow the steps listed here and shown on the reconciliation form on the next page.

Step 1 Enter the new balance of $6892.41 in the space at the top of the reconciliation form.

Step 2 List any deposits that have not yet been recorded by the bank. These are called **deposits in transit (DIT)**. Suppose that Rose Gardens has deposits of $892.41 and $739.58 that are not yet recorded. These numbers are written at step 2 on the form.

Step 3 Add the numbers from steps 1 and 2. At this point, the total is $8524.40.

Step 4 Write the total of outstanding checks. The total is $949.66.

Step 5 Subtract the total in step 4 from the number in step 3. The result here is $7574.74, which is the **adjusted bank balance**, or the current balance. This number should represent the current checking-account balance.

Now look at the firm's own records.

Step 6 List the firm's check register balance of $7576.38 on line 6 on the form.

Step 7 Enter total service charges of $6.42 on line 7.

Step 8 Subtract the charges on line 7 from the checkbook balance on line 6 to get $7569.96.

Step 9 Enter the interest credit of $4.78 on line 9. This is interest paid on money in the account.

Step 10 Add the interest on line 9 to line 8 to get $7574.74, the same result as in step 5.

Since the result from step 10 is the same as the result from step 5, the account is **balanced** (reconciled). The correct current balance in the account is $7574.74.

Reconciliation

Checks Outstanding	
Number	Amount
846	$ 42 73
852	598 71
853	68 12
857	79 80
858	160 30
Total	$ 949 66

Compare the list of checks paid by the bank with your records. List and total the checks not yet paid.

(1) Enter new balance from bank statement: $ 6892.41

(2) List any deposits made by you and not yet recorded by the bank: + 892.41
    + 739.58
    +
    +

(3) Add all numbers from lines above.
    Total: 8524.40

(4) Write total of checks outstanding: − 949.66

(5) Subtract (4) from (3).
    This is adjusted bank balance: $ 7574.74

To reconcile your records:

(6) List your checkbook balance: $ 7576.38

(7) Write the total of any fees or charges deducted by the bank and not yet subtracted by you from your checkbook: − 6.42

(8) Subtract line (7) from line (6).   7569.96

(9) Enter interest credit: (Add to your checkbook)   + 4.78

(10) Add line (9) to line (8).
    Adjusted checkbook balance. $ 7574.74

New balance of your account; this number should be same as (5).

QUICK CHECK 1

Find the current balance for a checking account given the following: balance from bank statement, $7622.18; checks outstanding of $318.36, $1752.44, $738.35, $66.78; and deposits in transit of $1197.22 and $578.91.

There are several typical reasons checking accounts do not balance.

Why Checking Accounts Do Not Balance

- Forgetting to enter a check in the check register.
- Forgetting to enter a deposit in the check register.
- Transposing numbers (writing $961.20 as $916.20, for example).
- Making addition or subtraction errors.
- Forgetting to subtract one of the bank service fees, such as those charged for using your debit card or for ATM use.
- Charging the customer an amount different from the check amount.
- Having checks that are altered or forged.

If an account does not reconcile, employees must slowly work through the transactions, comparing the company's check register to the bank statement, until the error is found. It can be a pain to find the error, and often there will be more than one error or discrepancy in a very active business account. Usually, the errors are made by the account owner rather than the bank, but banks sometimes make mistakes too.

The following graph shows how much consumers pay for monthly banking fees. The business person, as well as the consumer, must look for the best value and convenience when selecting a banking-services provider.

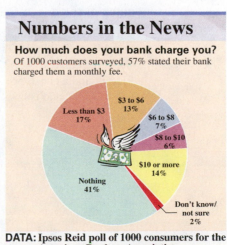

Numbers in the News

How much does your bank charge you?
Of 1000 customers surveyed, 57% stated their bank charged them a monthly fee.

Less than $3 17%
$3 to $6 13%
$6 to $8 7%
$8 to $10 6%
$10 or more 14%
Nothing 41%
Don't know/not sure 2%

DATA: Ipsos Reid poll of 1000 consumers for the American Bankers Association

Reconciling a Checking Account **EXAMPLE 2**

Using the information on the following check register and the bank statement, reconcile the checking account. Compare the items appearing on the check register to the bank statement a check ✓ indicates that the transaction was on the prior months bank statement, so does not need to be added or subtracted again. (Codes indicate the following: RC means returned check; SC means service charge; IC means interest credit; ATM means automated teller machine.)

Check Register

CHECK NO.	DATE	TRANSACTION DESCRIPTION	AMOUNT OF WITHDRAWAL	✓	DATE OF DEP.	AMOUNT OF DEPOSIT/CREDIT	BALANCE	
		BALANCE BROUGHT FORWARD →					2782	95
e	7/11	Miller's Outpost	138 50	✓			2644	45
e	7/12	Barber Advertising	73 08				2571	37
723	7/18	Wayside Lumber	318 62	✓			2252	75
		Deposit			7/20	980 37	3233	12
724	7/25	I.R.S.	836 15				2396	97
e	7/26	John Lessor	450 00				1946	97
e	7/28	Sacramento Bee	67 80				1879	17
726	8/2	T.V.A.	59 25				1819	92
727	8/3	Carmichael Office	97 37				1722	55
		Deposit			8/6	875 45	2598	00
ATM	8/5	ATM Cash	80 00				2518	00

Bank Statement

```
************************************************************
CHECK     WITHDRAWALS              DEPOSITS     DATE   BALANCE
NUMBER
************************************************************
                                                7/20   2325.83
          73.08 elec. pmt.                      7/22   2252.75
                                 980.37         7/24   3233.12
724      836.15                                 7/28   2396.97
e        450.00 debit  49.07  RC                7/30   1897.90
726       59.25              80.00 ATM  3.22 IC 8/4    1761.87
                             7.60  SC           8/5    1754.27
```

Reconciliation

Checks Outstanding

Number	Amount	
725	$ 67	80
727	97	37
Total	$ 165	17

Compare the list of checks paid by the bank with your records. List and total the checks not yet paid.

(1) Enter new balance from bank statement: $ 1754.27

(2) List any deposits made by you and not yet recorded by the bank:
+ 875.45
+
+
+

(3) Add all numbers from lines above. Total: 2629.72

(4) Write total of checks outstanding: − 165.17

(5) Subtract (4) from (3). This is adjusted bank balance: $ 2464.55

To reconcile your records:

(6) List your checkbook balance: $ 2518.00

(7) Write the total of any fees or charges deducted by the bank and not yet subtracted by you from your checkbook: − 56.67 (Returned check and service charge)

(8) Subtract line (7) from line (6). 2461.33

(9) Enter interest credit: (Add to your checkbook) + 3.22

(10) Add line (9) to line (8). Adjusted checkbook balance. $ 2464.55

New balance of your account; this number should be same as (5).

Since the adjusted bank balance from step 5 is the same as the new balance from step 10, the account is reconciled (balanced). The correct current balance in the account is $2464.55.

QUICK CHECK 2

Use the form in Example 2 to reconcile the following account. The checkbook of Dottie Fogel Furnishings shows a balance of $7779. When the bank statement was received, it showed a balance of $6237.44, a returned check amounting to $246.70, a service charge of $15.60, and a check-printing charge of $18.50. There were unrecorded deposits of $1442.44 and $479.50, and checks outstanding of $146.36, $91.52, $43.78, and $379.52.

5.3 Exercises

The **QUICK START** *exercises in each section contain solutions to help you get started.*

CURRENT CHECKING BALANCE   *Find the current balance for each of the following accounts.*
(See Example 1.)

QUICK START

	Balance from Bank Statement	Checks Outstanding		Deposits Not Yet Recorded	Balance
1.	$4572.15	$225.23 $97.68	$418.25 $348.17	$816.14 $571.28	$4870.24

$4572.15 − $225.23 − $97.68 − $418.25 − $348.17 + $816.14 + $571.28 = $4870.24

2.	$6274.76	$381.40 $875.14	$681.10 $83.15	$346.65 $198.96	$4799.58

$6274.76 − $381.40 − $875.14 − $681.10 − $83.15 + $346.65 + $198.96 = $4799.58

3.	$7911.42	$52.38 $95.42	$528.02 $76.50	$492.80 $38.72	_____
4.	$9343.65	$840.71 $78.68	$665.73 $87.00	$971.64 $3382.71	_____
5.	$19,523.20	$6853.60 $795.77	$340.00 $22.85	$6724.93 $78.81	_____
6.	$32,489.50	$3589.70 $263.15	$18,702.15 $7269.78	$7110.65 $2218.63	_____

7. Explain in your own words the significance of writing a bad check. What might the cost be in dollars? What are the other consequences? (See Objective 1.)

8. What are the financial costs to a business owner who receives a bad check? What would the business owner likely do regarding this customer? (See Objective 1.)

9. Briefly describe the importance of reconciling a checking account. What benefits are derived from keeping good checking records? (See Objective 2.)

10. Suppose your checking account does not balance. Name four types of errors that you will look for in trying to correct this problem. (See Objective 4.)

 indicates an exercise that is related to the Case in Point feature.

RECONCILING CHECKING ACCOUNTS   *For Exercises 11 and 12, use the following table to reconcile each account and find the current balance. (See Example 1.)*

		EXERCISE 11.		EXERCISE 12.
Balance from bank statement		$6875.09		$14,928.42
Checks outstanding	421	$371.52	112	$84.76
(check number is given first)	424	$429.07	115	$109.38
	427	$883.69	117	$42.03
	429	$35.62	119	$1429.12
Deposits not yet recorded		$701.56		$54.21
		$421.78		$394.76
		$689.35		$1002.04
Bank charge		$8.75		$7.00
Interest credit		$10.71		$22.86
Checkbook balance		$6965.92		$14,698.28
Current balance				

11.

Reconciliation

Checks Outstanding	
Number	Amount
Total	

Compare the list of checks paid by the bank with your records. List and total the checks not yet paid.

(1) Enter new balance from bank statement: _____

(2) List any deposits made by you and not yet recorded by the bank:
+ _____
+ _____
+ _____
+ _____

(3) Add all numbers from lines above. Total:

(4) Write total of checks outstanding: − _____

(5) Subtract (4) from (3). This is adjusted bank balance: _____

To reconcile your records:

(6) List your checkbook balance: _____

(7) Write the total of any fees or charges deducted by the bank and not yet subtracted by you from your checkbook: − _____

(8) Subtract line (7) from line (6). _____

(9) Enter interest credit: (Add to your checkbook) + _____

(10) Add line (9) to line (8). Adjusted checkbook balance. _____

New balance of your account; this number should be same as (5).

12.

Reconciliation

Checks Outstanding	
Number	Amount
Total	

Compare the list of checks paid by the bank with your records. List and total the checks not yet paid.

(1) Enter new balance from bank statement: _____

(2) List any deposits made by you and not yet recorded by the bank:
+ _____
+ _____
+ _____
+ _____

(3) Add all numbers from lines above. Total:

(4) Write total of checks outstanding: − _____

(5) Subtract (4) from (3). This is adjusted bank balance: _____

To reconcile your records:

(6) List your checkbook balance: _____

(7) Write the total of any fees or charges deducted by the bank and not yet subtracted by you from your checkbook: − _____

(8) Subtract line (7) from line (6). _____

(9) Enter interest credit: (Add to your checkbook) + _____

(10) Add line (9) to line (8). Adjusted checkbook balance. _____

New balance of your account; this number should be same as (5).

C ***CHECKING-ACCOUNT RECONCILIATION*** *Reconcile the checking accounts for the following companies. Compare the items appearing on the bank statement with the check register. A ✔ indicates that the transaction appeared on the previous month's statement. (Codes indicate the following: RC means returned check; SC means service charge; IC means interest credit; CP means check printing charge; ATM means automated teller machine.) (See Example 2.)*

13. Rose Gardens

CHECK NO.	DATE	TRANSACTION DESCRIPTION	AMOUNT OF WITHDRAWAL	✔	DATE OF DEP.	AMOUNT OF DEPOSIT/CREDIT	BALANCE
		BALANCE BROUGHT FORWARD →					6669 34
e	2/8	Floors to Go	248 96				6420 38
762	2/9	Healthways Dist.	125 63				6294 75
		Deposit			2/11	618 34	6913 09
763	2/12	Franchise Tax	770 41	✔			6142 68
764	2/14	Foothill Repair	22 86	✔			6119 82
e	2/15	Yellow Pages	91 24				6028 58
		Deposit			2/17	826 03	6854 61
e	2/17	Morning Herald	71 59				6783 02
765	2/18	San Juan Electric	63 24				6719 78
ATM	2/22	ATM Gas	15 26				6704 52
766	2/23	West Construction	405 07				6299 45
767	2/24	Heater Repairs	525 00				5774 45
		Deposit			2/26	220 16	5994 61
768	2/28	Capital Alarm	135 76				5858 85

Bank Statement

```
****************************************************************
CHECK          WITHDRAWALS              DEPOSITS      DATE      BALANCE
NUMBER
****************************************************************
                                                      2/14      5876.07
               91.24  elec. pmt.        618.34        2/16      6403.17
              248.96  debit             826.03        2/17      6980.24
               71.59  elec. pmt.                      2/19      6908.65
762           125.63                                  2/21      6783.02
              198.17  RC                              2/22      6584.85
               15.26  ATM               8.12   IC     2/24      6577.71
766           405.07    4.85  CP                      2/26      6167.79
                        6.28  SC                      2/27      6161.51
767           525.00                                  2/28      5636.51
```

Reconciliation

Checks Outstanding	
Number	Amount
Total	

Compare the list of checks paid by the bank with your records. List and total the checks not yet paid.

(1) Enter new balance from bank statement: _____

(2) List any deposits made by you and not yet recorded by the bank:
+ _____
+ _____
+ _____
+ _____

(3) Add all numbers from lines above. Total: _____

(4) Write total of checks outstanding: − _____

(5) Subtract (4) from (3). This is adjusted bank balance: _____

To reconcile your records:

(6) List your checkbook balance: _____

(7) Write the total of any fees or charges deducted by the bank and not yet subtracted by you from your checkbook: − _____

(8) Subtract line (7) from line (6). _____

(9) Enter interest credit: (Add to your checkbook) + _____

(10) Add line (9) to line (8). Adjusted checkbook balance. _____

New balance of your account; this number should be same as (5).

14. Play It Again Sports

CHECK NO.	DATE	TRANSACTION DESCRIPTION	AMOUNT OF WITHDRAWAL		✔	DATE OF DEP.	AMOUNT OF DEPOSIT/CREDIT		BALANCE	
		BALANCE BROUGHT FORWARD →							7682	07
e	3/3	Action Packing Supplies	451	16					7230	91
663	3/3	Crown Paper	954	29	✔				6276	62
664	3/5	ATM Cash	80	00	✔				6196	62
		Deposit				3/7	913	28	7109	90
e	3/10	Fairless Water District	72	37					7037	53
665	3/12	Audia Temporary	340	88					6696	65
e	3/13	Lionel Toys	618	65					6078	00
666	3/14	Fairless Hills Power	100	50					5977	50
		Deposit				3/16	450	18	6427	68
		Deposit				3/18	163	55	6591	23
667	3/20	Hunt Roofing	238	50					6352	73
668	3/22	Standard Brands	315	62					6037	11
669	3/23	Penny-Saver Products	67	29					5969	82
		Deposit				3/24	830	75	6800	57

Bank Statement

```
************************************************************************
CHECK           WITHDRAWALS              DEPOSITS        DATE      BALANCE
NUMBER
************************************************************************
                                                         3/5      6647.78
                                         913.28          3/7      7561.06
                451.16  elec. pmt.                       3/11     7109.90
665             340.88    82.15  RC      450.18          3/16     7137.05
                 72.37  debit            22.48  IC       3/20     7087.16
                618.65  elec. pmt.       163.55          3/22     6632.06
667             238.50    12.70  SC                      3/26     6380.86
```

Reconciliation

Checks Outstanding	
Number	Amount
Total	

Compare the list of checks paid by the bank with your records. List and total the checks not yet paid.

(1) Enter new balance from bank statement: _____

(2) List any deposits made by you and not yet recorded by the bank:
  + _____
  + _____
  + _____
  + _____

(3) Add all numbers from lines above. Total: _____

(4) Write total of checks outstanding: − _____

(5) Subtract (4) from (3). This is adjusted bank balance: _____

To reconcile your records:

(6) List your checkbook balance: _____

(7) Write the total of any fees or charges deducted by the bank and not yet subtracted by you from your checkbook: − _____

(8) Subtract line (7) from line (6). _____

(9) Enter interest credit: (Add to your checkbook) + _____

(10) Add line (9) to line (8). Adjusted checkbook balance. _____

New balance of your account; this number should be same as (5).

Chapter 5 Quick Review

Chapter Terms Review the following terms to test your understanding of the chapter. For each term you do not know, refer to the page number found next to that term.

adjusted bank balance [p. 200]
ATM cards [p. 193]
automated teller machine (ATM) [p. 182]
balance brought forward [p. 187]
balance forward [p. 187]
balanced [p. 200]
bank statement [p. 199]
blank endorsement [p. 186]
bounced checks [p. 199]
business checking account [p. 184]
canceled (check) [p. 186]
cashier's check [p. 193]
Check 21 [p. 186]
check register [p. 188]
check stub [p. 187]
checks outstanding [p. 200]
credit-card sales [p. 193]

current balance [p. 187]
debit cards [p. 183]
deposit slip [p. 185]
deposit ticket [p. 185]
deposits in transit (DIT) [p. 200]
direct deposit [p. 182]
direct payment [p. 182]
electronic banking [p. 182]
electronic payments [p. 183]
electronic commerce (EC) [p. 182]
electronic funds transfer (EFT) [p. 182]
electronic payment [p. 183]
flat-fee checking account [p. 184]
float [p. 186]
home banking (Internet banking) [p. 182]

identity theft [p. 184]
interest paid (accounts) [p. 184]
Internet banking [p. 182]
maintenance charge per month [p. 185]
mobile payments [p. 184]
money market account [p. 193]
money order [p. 193]
nonsufficient funds (NSF) [p. 193]
notary service [p. 193]
online banking [p. 193]
overdraft [p. 193]
overdraft protection [p. 193]
pay by phone [p. 182]
per-debit charge [p. 185]
personal checking account [p. 184]

personal computer banking [p. 182]
personal identification number (PIN) [p. 183]
point of sale (POS) [p. 183]
prepaid card [p. 183]
processing (check) [p. 186]
reconciliation [p. 199]
restricted endorsement [p. 186]
returned check [p. 199]
returned-deposit item [p. 193]
smart card [p. 183]
special endorsement [p. 186]
stop-payment order [p. 193]
texting [p. 184]
traditional banking [p. 182]
transaction register [p. 188]

CONCEPTS

5.1 Checking-account service charges

A checking-account maintenance fee is usually charged and there is often a per-check charge.

5.2 Bank services offered

The checking account customer must be aware of various banking services that are offered.

5.2 Deposits with credit-card transactions

All credit-card refunds must be subtracted from total credit-card sales to find the net deposit. The discount charge is then subtracted from this total.

EXAMPLES

Find the monthly checking-account service charge for a business with 36 checks and transactions, given a monthly maintenance charge of $7.50 and a $.20 per check charge.

$$\$7.50 + 36(\$.20) = \$7.50 + \$7.20 =$$
$$\$14.70 \text{ monthly service charge}$$

Overdraft protection Offered to protect the customer from bouncing a check (NSF)

ATM card Used at an automated teller machine to get cash or used as a debit card to make purchases

Stop-payment order Stops payment on a check written in error

Cashier's check A check written by a financial institution, such as a bank, and that is viewed to be as good as cash

Money order An instrument used in place of cash

Notary service An official certification of a signature or document

Online banking Allows customers to perform many banking functions on the Internet

The following are credit-card charges and credits.

CHARGES		CREDITS
$28.15	$78.59	$21.86
$36.92	$63.82	$19.62

(a) Find total charges.

$$\$28.15 + \$36.92 + \$78.59 + \$63.82 = \$207.48$$

(b) Find total credits.

$$\$21.86 + \$19.62 = \$41.48$$

CONCEPTS	EXAMPLES
	(c) Find gross deposit.
	$$\$207.48 - \textbf{\$41.48} = \$166$$
	(d) Given a 3% fee, find the amount of the charge.
	$$\$166 \times \textbf{.03} = \$4.98$$
	(e) Find the amount of credit given to the business.
	$$\$166 - \textbf{\$4.98} = \$161.02$$

5.3 Reconciliation of a checking account

A checking-account customer must periodically reconcile checking-account records with those of the bank or financial institution. The bank statement is used for this.

The accuracy of all checks written, deposits made, service charges incurred, and interest paid is checked and verified. The customer's checkbook balance and bank balance must be the same for the account to reconcile, or balance.

case study

BANKING ACTIVITIES OF A RETAILER

Tiny Waterton owns and operates an automobile repair shop. Many of his customers use credit cards for their purchases, and his credit-card sales during a recent week were $8752.40. During the same period, he had $573.94 in credit refunds, and he pays credit-card fees of 2½% on the net credit-card sales.

The balance at the beginning of the week was $4228.34. Checks outstanding were $758.14, $38.37, $1671.88, $120.13, $2264.75, $78.11, $3662.73, $816.25, and $400. Waterton had credit-card and bank deposits of $458.23, $771.18, $235.71, $1278.55, $663.52, and $1475.39 that were not recorded.

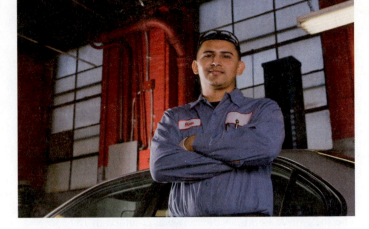

1. Find the net deposit given credit-card sales and refunds.

   1. _____

2. Find the fee on the net credit-card sales.

   2. _____

3. What is the total of the checks outstanding?

   3. _____

4. Find the total of the deposits that were not recorded.

   4. _____

5. Find the current balance in the account.

   5. _____

INVESTIGATE

Look at your bank statement and identify any fees you pay and interest you earn. Name three factors other than cost that are important to you when selecting a bank. Does your bank meet your needs, or can you find one better suited to your situation?

case ➤ point summary exercise

JACKSON & PERKINS

www.jacksonandperkins.com

Facts:

- 1872: Founded
- 1901: Sold first hybridized rose
- 1939: Began selling using mail order
- 1960s: Moved growing operations to California
- 2010: Shipped more than 2 million roses and plants

The Jackson & Perkins Company was founded in 1872 to wholesale strawberry and grape plants. But it quickly found its specialty in roses. Today, the firm's research scientists grow and evaluate more than 300,000 rose seedlings each year. It takes 7 to 10 years of hybridizing work to find a handful of the best and hardiest new varieties of roses. In order to help sell flowers, marketing at Jackson & Perkins has given fun or recognizable names to specific hybridized roses, including Sweet Intoxication and Pope John Paul II.

Barbara Wiffy at Rose Gardens does not grow her own roses. Rather, she buys them from Jackson & Perkins Wholesale, Inc., marks up the prices of the roses, and then sells them to her customers. Rose Gardens is an established customer that buys a lot of roses. Wiffy often places several orders with the company during a month but usually only makes one electronic payment to them each month. Following are copies of Rose Gardens' check register for the month and also the bank statement. Help Wiffy reconcile the business account to see what other charges should be added and subtracted from her balance and see if there are any errors in her check register.

Check Register—Rose Gardens

Check Num.	Date	Amount of Withdrawal	Amount of Deposit	Comment	Balance
				Balance Brought Forward	$9,277.59
	6/24	$1,000.00	-	Online Transfer to Savings	$8,277.59
761	6/25	$195.00	-	Wal-Mart	$8,082.59
	6/26	$2,446.82	-	Electronic—Mortgage Payment	$5,635.77
	6/26	$4,080.97	-	Electronic—Office Max	$1,554.80
	6/27	$395.07	-	Electronic—Utilities	$1,159.73
	6/28	-	$4,500.00	Online Transfer from ***5332	$5,659.73
762	6/29	$32.34	-	CVS—Pharmacy	$5,627.39
	6/29	-	$7,550.80	Direct deposit—debit	$13,178.19
	6/30	$2,153.93	-	Electronic—Dice Plants	$11,024.26
	7/1	-	$5,781.48	Regular Deposit	$16,805.74
763	7/3	$723.35	-	Max's Remodeling	$16,082.39
	7/14	$6,230.19	-	Electronic—Jackson & Per.	$9,852.20
764	7/15	$3,290.41	-	Bacon Farms	$6,561.79
	7/15	-	$2,705.00	Regular Deposit	$9,266.79

CITIZENS BANK

Bank Statement

Period: June 17 through July 16
Year: 2011

Checking Summary		Checks	
Balance Calculation		#761	195.00
Previous Balance	9,277.59	#762	32.34
Checks	227.34		
Withdrawals	16,315.93		
Deposits	20,537.28	**Interest**	
Interest Paid	0.57	7/16	0.57
Current Balance	**13,272.17**		

Date	Description	Withdrawals	Deposits	Balance
6/24	Online Transfer—to savings	1,000.00		
6/26	Online Pmt.—Mtge. Pymt.	2,446.82		
6/26	Debit Pmt.—Office Max	4,080.97		
6/27	Online Pmt.—Utilities	395.07		
6/28	Online Transfer—from checking		4,500.00	
6/29	Direct Deposit—Numerous Debit Purchases		7,550.80	
6/30	Online Pmt.—Dice Plants	2,153.93		
7/01	Regular Deposit		5,781.48	
7/14	Online Pmt.—Jackson & Per.	6,230.19		
7/15	Regular Deposit		2,705.00	
7/16	Fee to Bank	8.95		

Reconciliation

Checks Outstanding	
Number	Amount
Total	

(1) Enter new balance from bank statement: _____

(2) List any deposits made by you and not   { + _____
    yet recorded by the bank: + _____
                                                 + _____
                                                 + _____

(3) Add all numbers from lines above.   _____
(4) Write total of checks outstanding: − _____
(5) Subtract (4) from (3).   _____

To reconcile your records:

(6) List your checkbook balance: _____

(7) Write the total of any fees.   − _____

(8) Subtract line (7) from line (6).   _____

(9) Enter interest credit: + _____   New balance

(10) Add line (9) to line (8).
     Adjusted checkbook balance.   _____

So, Wiffy's check register balances this month. The only items not recorded in her check register were the bank fee of $8.95 and the interest credit of $.57. She was relieved that none of her customer checks bounced since she often has 1 or 2 bounced checks each month.

Discussion Question: *Some people no longer reconcile their checking account, effectively trusting the bank. Is it reasonable for a business with a large volume of banking activity to not reconcile its checking account? Why or why not?*

Chapter 5 Test

To help you review, the numbers in brackets show the section in which the topic was discussed.

Use the table on page 185 to find the monthly checking-account service charge for the following accounts. **[5.1]**

1. Tino's Italian Grocery, 62 checks, average balance $1834

2. Gifts Galore, 44 checks, average balance $2398

3. Batista Tile Works, 27 checks, average balance $418

1. _____

2. _____

3. _____

Complete the following three check stubs for Advertising Specialists. Find the balance forward at the bottom of each stub. **[5.1]**

CHECKS WRITTEN

NUMBER	DATE	TO	FOR	AMOUNT
2261	Aug. 6	WBC Broadcasting	Airtime	$6892.12
2262	Aug. 8	Lakeland Weekly	Ad	$1258.36
2263	Aug. 14	W. Wilson	Freelance art	$416.14

Deposits made: $1572 on Aug. 7, $10,000 on Aug. 10.

4. 2261

_____ 20___
Amount _____
To _____
For _____

Bal. Bro't. For'd.	$16,409 82
Am't. Deposited	
Total	
Am't. this Check	
Balance For'd.	

5. 2262

_____ 20___
Amount _____
To _____
For _____

Bal. Bro't. For'd.	
Am't. Deposited	
Total	
Am't. this Check	
Balance For'd.	

6. 2263

_____ 20___
Amount _____
To _____
For _____

Bal. Bro't. For'd.	
Am't. Deposited	
Total	
Am't. this Check	
Balance For'd.	

John Hendrick owns Outdoor Machines. The shop sells new and used jet skis, snowmobiles, and other outdoor recreation equipment. The following credit-card transactions occurred during a recent period. **[5.2]**

SALES		REFUNDS
$218.68	$135.82	$45.63
$37.84	$67.45	$36.36
$33.18	$461.82	
$20.76	$116.35	
$12.72	$23.78	
$8.97	$572.18	

7. Find the total amount of credit-card sales.

7. _____

8. What is the total amount of the refunds?

8. _____

9. Find credit-card sales less refunds.

9. _____

🔺 indicates an exercise that is related to the Case in Point feature.

10. Assuming that the bank charges the retailer a $3\frac{1}{2}$% discount charge, find the amount of the discount charge at the statement date.

10. _____

11. Find the amount of the credit given to Outdoor Machines after the fee is subtracted.

11. _____

12. Weddings by Bobbi is a regular customer of Rose Gardens. Use the information in the following table to reconcile her checking account on the form that follows. **[5.3]**

12. _____

Balance from bank statement		$4721.30
Checks outstanding	3221	$82.74
(check number is given first)	3229	$69.08
	3230	$124.73
	3232	$51.20
Deposits not yet recorded		$758.06
		$32.51
		$298.06
Bank charge		$2.00
Interest credit		$9.58
Checkbook balance		$5474.60
Current balance		_____

Reconciliation

Checks Outstanding	
Number	Amount
Total	

Compare the list of checks paid by the bank with your records. List and total the checks not yet paid.

(1) Enter new balance from bank statement: _____

(2) List any deposits made by you and not yet recorded by the bank:
  + _____
  + _____
  + _____
  + _____

(3) Add all numbers from lines above. Total: _____

(4) Write total of checks outstanding: − _____

(5) Subtract (4) from (3). This is adjusted bank balance: _____

To reconcile your records:

(6) List your checkbook balance: _____

(7) Write the total of any fees or charges deducted by the bank and not yet subtracted by you from your checkbook: − _____

(8) Subtract line (7) from line (6). _____

(9) Enter interest credit: (Add to your checkbook) + _____

(10) Add line (9) to line (8). Adjusted checkbook balance. _____

New balance of your account; this number should be same as (5).

Payroll

6

case IN point ▶

SARAH BRYNSKI enjoyed working at Starbucks when in college and was happy to be promoted to manager of a company-owned store. She quickly discovered that payroll for her 15 employees was far more complicated than she had anticipated, with many deductions. She decided to look at the history of two programs that involved deductions.

Brynski found that many elderly people suffered greatly during the Great Depression of the 1930s. The Social Security Act was passed in 1935 to help supplement the retirement income of the elderly as well as provide income for the disabled. Medicare was established in 1965 to help people 65 and over pay for hospital care, medical care, and, later, prescriptions. Experts believe that without Social Security and Medicare, poverty would be greatly increased in the United States, especially among the elderly.

In her reading, Sarah also discovered that both Social Security and Medicare are projected to have financial problems. Without changes to the system, current projections forecast financial problems for Social Security by 2037 and for Medicare by 2017. Sarah realizes that these two programs are far too important to go away, so she expects there will be some changes to both of them in the next few years.

Preparing the payroll is one of the most important jobs in any business. Payroll records must be accurate, and the payroll must be prepared on time so that the necessary checks can be written.

6.1 Gross Earnings: Wages and Salaries

OBJECTIVES

1 Understand the methods of calculating gross earnings for salaries and wages.
2 Find overtime earnings for over 40 hours of work per week.
3 Use the overtime premium method of calculating gross earnings.
4 Find overtime earnings for over 8 hours of work per day.
5 Understand double time, shift differentials, and split-shift premiums.
6 Find equivalent earnings for different pay periods.
7 Find overtime for salaried employees.

case in point As a manager of a Starbucks store, Sarah Brynski hires employees and makes sure they are paid appropriately. In fact, she had to make sure overtime can be paid to an employee before asking one person to work more than 40 hours in a week when someone else did not show up. She was a little surprised to learn that her employees would receive overtime, but as a manager she would not.

The first step in preparing the payroll is to determine the **gross earnings** (the total amount earned). There are many methods used to find gross earnings, and several of these are discussed in this chapter. A number of **deductions** may be subtracted from gross earnings to arrive at the **net pay**, the amount the employee actually receives. These various deductions also are discussed in this chapter. Finally, the employer must keep records to maintain an efficient business and to satisfy legal requirements. Many businesses use the services of a company such as Automatic Data Processing (ADP) to professionally prepare their payroll. Other businesses use computer software such as QuickBooks to help them complete this task.

OBJECTIVE 1 Understand the methods of calculating gross earnings for salaries and wages. Several methods are used to find an employee's pay. Salaries and wages are discussed in this section, and piecework and commission are discussed in the next section. As shown in the Numbers in the News, many employees live from paycheck to paycheck. Understanding how net pay is calculated can eliminate unwanted surprises.

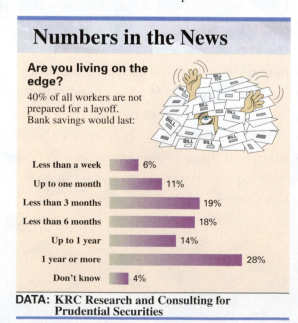

Numbers in the News

Are you living on the edge?

40% of all workers are not prepared for a layoff. Bank savings would last:

Less than a week	6%
Up to one month	11%
Less than 3 months	19%
Less than 6 months	18%
Up to 1 year	14%
1 year or more	28%
Don't know	4%

DATA: KRC Research and Consulting for Prudential Securities

In some businesses, the first step in preparing the payroll is to look at the **time card** maintained for each employee. The following time card shows the dates of the pay period; the employee's name and other personal information; the days, times, and hours worked; the total number of hours worked; and the signature of the employee as verification of the accuracy of the card. While the card shown is filled in by hand, many companies use a time clock that automatically stamps days, dates, and times on the card. The information on these cards is then transferred to a **payroll ledger** (a chart showing all payroll information) such as the one shown in Example 1.

Katie Nopper, whose payroll card is shown, is a shift manager at Starbucks and is paid an **hourly wage** of $14.80. Her gross earnings can be calculated with the following formula.

> Gross earnings = Number of hours worked × Rate per hour

For example, if Nopper works 8 hours at $14.80 per hour, her gross earnings are

$$\text{Gross earnings} = 8 \times \$14.80 = \$118.40$$

PAYROLL CARD
NO TIME CLOCK REQUIRED

EMPL. NO. 1375   CARD NO. _____

FULL NAME   Katie Nopper   AGE (IF UNDER 18)

ADDRESS 412 Fawndale Drive   SOCIAL SECURITY NO. 123–45–6789

DATE EMPLOYED   POSITION Shift MGR   RATE $14.80

PAY PERIOD STARTING 7/23   ENDING 7/27

| DATE | REGULAR TIME | | | | | OVER TIME | | |
	IN	OUT	IN	OUT	DAILY TOTALS	IN	OUT	DAILY TOTALS
7/23	8:00	11:50	12:20	4:30	8	4:30	6:30	2
7/24	7:58	12:00	12:30	4:30	8	5:00	7:30	2.5
7/25	8:00	12:00	12:30	4:32	8			
7/26	7:58	12:05	12:35	4:30	8	4:30	5:00	.5
7/27	8:01	12:00	1:00	5:00	8			
APPROVED BY			TOTAL REGULAR TIME		40			5

REGULAR DAYS WORKED 5 @   8 HRS. @ EARNINGS 14.80 $ 592.00
ADDITIONAL COMPENSATION:
VALUE OF MEALS, LODGING, GIFTS, ETC.   AMOUNT $ _____
COMMISSIONS, FEES, BONUSES, GOODS, ETC. OT 5 @ 22.²⁰   AMOUNT $ 111.00
OTHER REMUNERATIONS (KIND) $ _____
      TOTAL EARNINGS $ 703.00
DEDUCTIONS:

I CERTIFY THE FOREGOING TO BE A CORRECT ACCOUNT OF THE TIME WORKED AND WAGES RECEIVED:
SIGNATURE _____   DATE PAID _____

Completing a Payroll Ledger · **EXAMPLE 1**   Sarah Brynski is doing the payroll for two employees, Nelson and Orr. She must first complete a payroll ledger.

| | HOURS WORKED | | | | | | | TOTAL HOURS | RATE | GROSS EARNINGS |
EMPLOYEE	S	M	T	W	TH	F	S			
Nelson, L.	—	2	4	8	6	3	—		$8.40	
Orr, T.	—	3.5	3	7	6.75	7	—		$9.12	

case in point

SOLUTION

First, find the total number of hours worked by each person.

Nelson: 2 + 4 + 8 + 6 + 3 = **23 hours**
Orr: 3.5 + 3 + 7 + 6.75 + 7 = **27.25 hours**

Then multiply the number of hours worked by the rate per hour to find the gross earnings.

Nelson: Orr:
  23   27.25
× $8.40   × $9.12
$193.20   **$248.52**

The payroll ledger can now be completed.

	HOURS WORKED							TOTAL HOURS	RATE	GROSS EARNINGS
EMPLOYEE	S	M	T	W	TH	F	S			
Nelson, L.	—	2	4	8	6	3	—	23	$8.40	$193.20
Orr, T.	—	3.5	3	7	6.75	7	—	27.25	$9.12	$248.52

QUICK CHECK 1

Ellie Kugler worked 6 hours on Monday, 4.5 hours on Tuesday, 4 hours on Wednesday, 5.75 hours on Thursday, and 3 hours on Friday. If she is paid $10.18 per hour, find her gross earnings for the week.

Workers' pay varies around the world. The list below shows how long it takes an average worker around the world to earn enough to buy a Big Mac.

Numbers in the News

Where to Buy a Big Mac Fast

Here is a new way to measure economic health. The UBS Bank calculated how long it takes an average worker around the world to earn enough to buy a Big Mac.

Tokyo	10 minutes
New York	13 minutes
London	16 minutes
Hong Kong	17 minutes
Paris	21 minutes
Rome	39 minutes
Beijing	44 minutes
Jakarta	86 minutes

DATA: *Parade Magazine*

OBJECTIVE 2 Find overtime earnings for over 40 hours of work per week. The **Fair Labor Standards Act** covers the majority of full-time employees in the United States. It establishes a workweek of 40 hours and sets the minimum hourly wage. The law states that an **overtime** wage (a higher-than-normal wage) must be paid for all hours worked over 40 hours per workweek. Also, many companies not covered by the Fair Labor Standards Act have voluntarily followed the practice of paying a **time-and-a-half rate** ($1\frac{1}{2}$, or 1.5, times the normal rate) for any work over 40 hours per week. With the time-and-a-half rate, gross earnings are found with the following formula.

> Gross earnings = Earnings at regular rate + Earnings at time-and-a-half rate

Completing a Payroll Ledger with Overtime

EXAMPLE 2

Complete the following payroll ledger.

	HOURS WORKED							TOTAL HOURS		REG. RATE	GROSS EARNINGS		
EMPLOYEE	S	M	T	W	TH	F	S	REG.	O.T.		REG.	O.T.	TOTAL
Lanier, D.	6	9	8.25	8	9	4.5	—			$8.30			
Morse, T.	—	10	6.75	9	6.25	10	4.25			$9.48			

SOLUTION

First, find the total number of hours worked.

Lanier: $6 + 9 + 8.25 + 8 + 9 + 4.5 = $ **44.75 hours**
Morse: $10 + 6.75 + 9 + 6.25 + 10 + 4.25 = $ **46.25 hours**

Both employees worked more than 40 hours. Gross earnings at the regular rate can now be found as discussed earlier. Lanier earned 40 × $8.30 = $332 at the regular rate, and Morse earned 40 × $9.48 = $379.20 at the regular rate. To find overtime earnings, first find the number of overtime hours worked by each employee.

Lanier: 44.75 − **40** = **4.75 overtime hours**
Morse: 46.25 − **40** = **6.25 overtime hours**

The regular rate given for each employee can be used to find the time-and-a-half rate.

Lanier: **1.5** × $8.30 = $12.45
Morse: **1.5** × $9.48 = $14.22

Now find the overtime earnings.

Lanier: 4.75 hours × **$12.45** per hour = **$59.14**   (rounded to the nearest cent)
Morse: 6.25 hours × **$14.22** per hour = **$88.88**   (rounded)

The ledger can now be completed.

EMPLOYEE	HOURS WORKED							TOTAL HOURS		REG. RATE	GROSS EARNINGS		
	S	M	T	W	TH	F	S	REG.	O.T.		REG.	O.T.	TOTAL
Lanier, D.	6	9	8.25	8	9	4.5	—	**40**	**4.75**	$8.30	**$332**	**$59.14**	**$391.14**
Morse, T.	—	10	6.75	9	6.25	10	4.25	**40**	**6.25**	$9.48	**$379.20**	**$88.88**	**$468.08**

QUICK CHECK 2

Joseph Monti works 5 hours on Monday, 10 hours on Tuesday, 9.5 hours on Wednesday, 8.25 hours on Thursday, 6 hours on Friday, and 7.5 hours on Saturday. Monti is paid $9.85 per hour and time and a half for all hours over 40 per week. Find his gross earnings.

OBJECTIVE 3 Use the overtime premium method of calculating gross earnings. Gross earnings with overtime is sometimes found using the **overtime premium method**. This method produces the same result as the method used in Example 2. Add the total hours at the regular rate to the overtime hours at one-half the regular rate to arrive at gross earnings.

Overtime Premium Method

Straight-time earnings ⟵ total hours worked × regular rate
+ Overtime premium   ⟵ overtime hours worked × $\frac{1}{2}$ regular rate
Gross earnings

Using the Overtime Premium Method This week, Holly Kelly worked 40 regular hours and 12 overtime hours. Her regular rate of pay is $17.40 per hour. Find her total gross pay, using the overtime premium method.

SOLUTION

Kelly's total hours are 40 + 12 = 52, and her overtime premium rate is .5 × $17.40 = $8.70.

52 hours × $17.40 = $904.80   regular rate earnings
12 overtime hours × $8.70 = $104.40   overtime premium
$1009.20   gross earnings

The calculator solution uses the order of operations to find the regular earnings and the overtime earnings, and then adds these together.

52 ⊠ 17.4 ⊞ 12 ⊠ 17.4 ⊠ .5 ⊜ 1009.2

Note: Refer to Appendix B for calculator basis.

QUICK CHECK 3

Janice Garinger worked 40 regular hours and 10 overtime hours this week. If her regular pay is $12.10 per hour, find her gross earning using the overtime premium method.

OBJECTIVE 4 Find overtime earnings for over 8 hours of work per day. Some companies pay the time-and-a-half rate for all time worked over 8 hours in any one day no matter how many hours are worked in a week. This **daily overtime** is shown in the next example.

One week, Jason Polanski worked the hours shown. Given that his regular pay is $10.10 per week, find gross earnings.

	S	M	T	W	TH	F	S	TOTAL HOURS
Reg.	—	8	5	7	8	—	—	28
O.T.	—	2	—	—	4	—	—	6

SOLUTION

Polanski worked fewer than 40 hours this week. Still, his company pays time and a half for any hours over 8 in a day, so he will earn some overtime. The table shows that he worked 28 regular hours and 6 overtime hours.

$$\text{Overtime hourly pay } = \$10.10 \times 1\tfrac{1}{2} = \textbf{\$15.15 per hour}$$

Wages at regular rate: 28 hours $\times$ \$10.10 = \$282.80
Wages at overtime rate: 6 hours $\times$ **\$15.15** = \$90.90
Total gross earnings   **\$373.70**

Some careers require unusual hours and do not pay overtime for over 40 hours worked in a week or 8 hours in a day. An example is a firefighter, who may work 24 hours and then get 48 hours off.

> **QUICK CHECK 4**
>
> Luke Stansbury is paid $9.60 per hour and time and a half for all hours over 8 worked per day. He worked 9 hours on Monday, 6 hours on Tuesday, 12 hours on Wednesday, and 3 hours on Friday. Find his gross earnings for the week.

OBJECTIVE 5 Understand double time, shift differentials, and split-shift premiums. In addition to premiums paid for overtime, other **premium payment plans** include **double time** for holidays and, in some industries, for Saturdays and Sundays. A **shift differential** is often given to compensate employees for working less-desirable hours. For example, an additional amount per hour or per shift might be paid to swing shift (4:00 P.M. to midnight) and graveyard shift (midnight to 8:00 A.M.) employees.

Restaurant employees and nursing home employees often receive a **split-shift premium**. Hours are staggered so that the employees are on the job during only the busiest times. For example, an employee may work 4 hours, be off 4 hours, and then work another 4 hours. The employee is paid a premium because of this less-desirable schedule.

Some employers offer **compensatory time**, or **comp time**, for overtime hours worked. Instead of additional money, an employee is given time off from the regular work schedule as compensation for overtime hours already worked. Quite often, the compensatory time is calculated at $1\tfrac{1}{2}$ times the overtime hours worked. For example, 12 hours might be given as compensation for 8 hours of previously worked overtime. Occasionally, an employee is given a choice of overtime pay or comp time. Many companies reserve the use of compensatory time for their supervisory or managerial employees.

OBJECTIVE 6 Find equivalent earnings for different pay periods. The second common method of finding gross earnings uses a **salary**, a fixed amount given as so much per **pay period** (time between paychecks). Common pay periods are weekly, biweekly, semimonthly, and monthly.

> **Common Pay Periods**
>
> | Monthly | 12 paychecks each year |
> |---------|------------------------|
> | Semimonthly | Twice each month; 24 paychecks each year |
> | Biweekly | Every 2 weeks; 26 paychecks each year |
> | Weekly | 52 paychecks each year |

Determining Equivalent Earnings **EXAMPLE 5**

You are a career counselor and want to compare the earnings of four clients you have helped to find jobs. Scott Perrine receives a weekly salary of $546, Tonya McCarley receives a biweekly salary of $1686, Julie Circle receives a semimonthly salary of $736, and Bill Leonard receives a monthly salary of $1818. For each worker, find the following: **(a)** earnings per year, **(b)** earnings per month, and **(c)** earnings per week.

SOLUTION

Scott Perrine:

(a) $546 × **52** = $28,392 per year

(b) $28,392 ÷ **12** = $2366 per month

(c) $546 per week

Tonya McCarley:

(a) $1686 × **26** = $43,836 per year

(b) $43,836 ÷ **12** = $3653 per month

(c) $1686 ÷ **2** = $843 per week

Julie Circle:

(a) $736 × **24** = $17,664 per year

(b) $736 × **2** = $1472 per month

(c) $17,664 ÷ **52** = $339.69 per week

Bill Leonard:

(a) $1818 × **12** = $21,816 per year

(b) $1818 per month

(c) $21,816 ÷ **52** = $419.54 per week

QUICK CHECK 5

Glen Lewis receives a weekly salary of $852. Find his **(a)** earnings per year, **(b)** earnings per month, and **(c)** semimonthly earnings.

The data that follows shows that higher levels of education are usually associated with higher incomes. As you look at the data, ask yourself if you should go further in your education than you have planned.

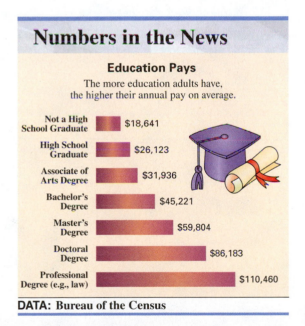

Numbers in the News

Education Pays

The more education adults have, the higher their annual pay on average.

Not a High School Graduate	$18,641
High School Graduate	$26,123
Associate of Arts Degree	$31,936
Bachelor's Degree	$45,221
Master's Degree	$59,804
Doctoral Degree	$86,183
Professional Degree (e.g., law)	$110,460

DATA: Bureau of the Census

OBJECTIVE 7 Find overtime for salaried employees. A salary is ordinarily paid for the performance of a certain job, regardless of the number of hours worked. However, the Fair Labor Standards Act requires that employees in certain salaried positions receive additional compensation for overtime. Similar to a wage earner, such salaried workers are paid time and a half for all hours worked over 40 hours per week.

Finding Overtime for Salaried Employees **EXAMPLE 6** Monica Gonzales earns $936 a week as an assistant to the vice president of a community bank. A normal workweek for her is 40 hours. Find her gross earnings if she works 45 hours one week and is paid time and a half for everything over 40 hours.

SOLUTION

$$\text{Hourly equivalent to salary} = \frac{\$936}{40 \text{ hours}} = \$23.40$$

$$\text{Overtime rate} = 1\tfrac{1}{2} \times \$23.40 = \textbf{\$35.10}$$

Find gross earnings as follows.

Regular wages		$936.00
Overtime wages	**5 hours × $35.10** =	$175.50
		$1111.50 Gross earnings

The calculator solution to this example is

936 [+] 936 [÷] 40 [×] 1.5 [×] 5 [=] 1111.5

QUICK CHECK 6

Elinor Nunes has a normal workweek of 35 hours and is paid $675.50 each week. What are her gross earnings in a week in which she works 42 hours?

The **QUICK START** *exercises in each section contain solutions to help you get started.*

Find the number of regular hours and the overtime hours (any hours over 40) for each employee. Then calculate the overtime rate (time and a half) for each employee. (See Examples 1 and 2.)

QUICK START

EMPLOYEE	S	M	T	W	TH	F	S	REG. HRS.	O.T. HOURS	REG. RATE	O.T. RATE
1. Burke, E.	—	7	4	7	10	8	4	40	0	$8.10	$12.15
2. Elbern, J.	—	6.5	9	7.5	8	9.5	7			$8.24	
3. Kling, J.	3	5	8.25	9	8.5	5	—			$18.70	
4. Scholz, K.	8.5	9	7.5	8	10	8.25	—			$9.50	
5. Tomlin, M.	—	9.5	7	9	9.25	10.5	—			$11.48	

Using the information from Exercises 1–5, find the earnings at the regular rate, the earnings at the overtime rate, and the gross earnings for each employee. Round to the nearest cent. (See Example 2.)

QUICK START

EMPLOYEE	EARNINGS AT REG. RATE	EARNINGS AT O.T. RATE	GROSS EARNINGS
6. Burke, E.	$324	$0	$324
7. Elbern, J.			
8. Kling, J.			
9. Scholz, K.			
10. Tomlin, M.			

Find the overtime rate, the amount of earnings at regular pay, the amount at overtime pay, and the total gross wages for each employee. Round to the nearest cent. (See Example 2.)

QUICK START

	TOTAL HOURS				GROSS EARNINGS		
EMPLOYEE	REG.	O.T.	REG. RATE	O.T. RATE	REGULAR	OVERTIME	TOTAL
11. Deining, M.	39.5	—	$8.80	$13.20	$347.60	$0	$347.60
12. Demaree, D.	36.25	—	$10.20				
13. Snow, P.	40	4.5	$14.40				
14. Taylor, O.	40	6.75	$12.08				
15. Weyers, C.	40	4.25	$9.18				

 indicates an exercise that is related to the Case in Point feature.

Some companies use the overtime premium method to determine gross earnings. Use this method to complete the following payroll ledger. Overtime is paid at the time-and-a-half rate for all hours over 40. (See Example 3.)

QUICK START

	HOURS WORKED							TOTAL HOURS	REG. RATE	O.T. HOURS	O.T. PREMIUM RATE	GROSS EARNINGS		
EMPLOYEE	S	M	T	W	TH	F	S					REG.	O.T.	TOTAL
16. Averell, B.	10	9	8	5	12	7	—	51	$11.40	11	$5.70	$581.40	$62.70	$644.10
17. Brownlee, K.	7.75	10	5	9.75	8	10	—		$9.50					
18. Carter, M.	—	12	11	8	8.25	11	—		$8.60					
19. Parks, K.	—	8.5	5.5	10	12	10.5	7		$12.50					
20. Parr, J.	—	10	9.75	9	11.5	10	—		$10.20					

Some companies pay overtime for all time worked over 8 hours in a given day. Use this method to complete the following payroll ledger. Overtime is paid at the time-and-a-half rate. (See Example 4.)

QUICK START

	HOURS WORKED							TOTAL HOURS		REG. RATE	O.T. RATE	GROSS EARNINGS		
EMPLOYEE	S	M	T	W	TH	F	S	REG.	O.T.			REG.	O.T.	TOTAL
21. Bailey, M.	—	10	9	11	6	5	—	35	6	$9.40	$14.10	$329.00	$84.60	$413.60
22. Campbell, C.	—	9	8.75	7	8.5	10	—			$9.85				
23. Ruhkala, B.	—	7.5	8	9	10.75	8	—			$10.80				
24. Salorin, B.	—	9	10	8	6	9.75	—			$17.20				
25. Warren, L.	—	9.5	8.5	7.75	8	9.5	—			$21.50				

26. Explain what premium payment plans are in your own words. Select a premium payment plan and describe it. (See Objective 5.)

27. If you were given a choice of overtime pay or compensatory time, which would you choose? Why? (See Objective 5.)

Find the equivalent earnings for each of the following salaries as indicated. (See Example 5.)

QUICK START

	EARNINGS			
WEEKLY	BIWEEKLY	SEMIMONTHLY	MONTHLY	ANNUAL
28. $496	$992	$1074.67	$2149.33	$25,792
29. $443.08	$886.15	$960	$1920	$23,040
30.	$852			
31.		$5200		
32.				$26,100
33. $830				
34.				$27,600

Find the weekly gross earnings for the following people who are on salary and normally work a 40-hour week. Overtime is paid at the time-and-a-half rate. (See Example 6.)

EMPLOYEE	WEEKLY SALARY	HOURS WORKED	WEEKLY GROSS EARNINGS
35. Beckenstein, J.	$360	42	
36. de Bouchel, V.	$468	45	
37. Feist-Milker, R.	$420	43	
38. Johnson, J.	$520	56	
39. Mader, C.	$640	48	

Solve the following application problems.

QUICK START

40. RETAIL EMPLOYMENT Last week, Frank Nicolazzo worked 48 hours at Starbucks. Find his gross earnings for the week if he is paid $8.40 per hour and earns time and a half for all hours over 40 worked in a week.

40. $436.80

$48 - 40 = 8$ overtime hours
$1.5 \times \$8.40 = \$12.60$ overtime rate
$40 \times \$8.40 = \$336$ regular
$8 \times \$12.60 = \$100.80$ overtime
$\$336 + \$100.80 = \$436.80$

41. INSIDE SALES Sheila Spinney is an inside salesperson at Radio Shack and is paid $13.60 per hour for straight time and time and a half for all hours over 40 worked in a week. Find her gross earnings for a week in which she worked 52 hours.

41. _____

42. CRIMINOLOGY LAB Benito Zamora earns $12.80 per hour at his job as a lab assistant in a criminology lab. He is paid time and a half for everything worked over 8 hours in one day. Find his gross earnings for a week in which he worked the following hours: Monday, 9.5; Tuesday, 7; Wednesday, 10.75; Thursday, 4.5; and Friday, 8.75.

42. _____

43. OFFICE ASSISTANT Michelle Small is an office assistant and worked 10 hours on Monday, 9.75 hours on Tuesday, 5.5 hours on Wednesday, 12 hours on Thursday, and 7.25 hours on Friday. Her regular rate of pay is $11.50 an hour, with time and a half paid for all hours over 8 worked in a given day. Find her gross earnings for the week.

43. _____

44. INSURANCE OFFICE MANAGER Alicia Klein is paid $728 a week as an insurance office manager. Her normal workweek is 40 hours. She gets paid time and a half for overtime. Find her gross earnings for a week in which she works 46 hours.

44. _____

45. OFFICE EMPLOYEE   An office employee earns $630 weekly. Find the equivalent earnings if the employee is paid **(a)** biweekly, **(b)** semimonthly, **(c)** monthly, and **(d)** annually.

(a) _____

(b) _____

(c) _____

(d) _____

46. STORE MANAGER   Michelle Renda is assistant manager at Barnes and Noble and is paid $42,900 annually. Find the equivalent earnings if this amount is paid **(a)** weekly, **(b)** biweekly, **(c)** semimonthly, and **(d)** monthly.

(a) _____

(b) _____

(c) _____

(d) _____

47. Semimonthly pay periods result in 24 paychecks per year. Biweekly pay periods result in 26 paychecks per year. Which of these pay periods results in three checks in two months of the year? Will it always be the same two months? Explain.

48. Which would you prefer: a monthly pay period or a weekly pay period? What special budgetary issues might you consider regarding the pay period that you choose?

6.2 Gross Earnings: Piecework and Commissions

OBJECTIVES

1. Find the gross earnings for piecework.
2. Determine the gross earnings for differential piecework.
3. Find the gross pay for piecework with a guaranteed hourly wage.
4. Calculate the overtime earnings for piecework.
5. Find the gross earnings using commission rate times sales.
6. Determine a commission using the variable commission rate.
7. Find the gross earnings with a salary plus commission.

OBJECTIVE 1 Find the gross earnings for piecework. The salaries and wages of the preceding section are **time rates** because they depend only on the actual time an employee is on the job. The methods described in this section are **incentive rates** because they are based on production and pay an employee for actual performance on the job. The ten help-wanted ads from the classified section of the newspaper are for jobs offering incentive rates of pay. The ad for lathers and stucco construction workers offers piecework and hourly compensation, while the ad for truck drivers lists piece rates of 43 cents per mile (cpm). The ads for bill collectors and commercial roofing, health insurance, Better Business Bureau membership, automobile, swimming pool, and home security system sales positions pay on a commission plan.

A **piecework rate** pays an employee a given amount per item produced. Gross earnings are found with the following formula.

$$\text{Gross earnings} = \text{Pay per item} \times \text{Number of items}$$

For example, a truck driver who drives 680 miles in one day and is paid a piecework rate of $.43 per mile has total gross earnings as follows.

$$\text{Gross earnings} = \$.43 \times 680 = \$292.40$$

Finding Gross Earnings for Piecework **EXAMPLE 1**

Stacy Arrington is paid $.73 for sewing a jacket collar, $.86 for a sleeve with cuffs, and $.94 for a lapel. One week she sewed 318 jacket collars, 112 sleeves with cuffs, and 37 lapels. Find her gross earnings.

SOLUTION

Multiply the rate per item by the number of that type of item.

ITEM	RATE		NUMBER		TOTAL
Jacket collars	$.73	×	318	=	$232.14
Sleeves with cuffs	$.86	×	112	=	$96.32
Lapels	$.94	×	37	=	$34.78

Find the gross earnings by adding the three totals from the table.

$$\$232.14 + \$96.32 + \$34.78 = \mathbf{\$363.24}$$

QUICK CHECK 1

A production worker is paid $.58 for assembling a ceiling lamp, $1.23 for assembling a ceiling fan, and $.86 for assembling a box fan. One week a worker assembled 220 ceiling lamps, 318 ceiling fans, and 174 box fans. Find the worker's gross earnings.

OBJECTIVE 2 Determine the gross earnings for differential piecework. There are many variations to the straight piecework rate just described. For example, some rates have **quotas** that must be met, with a premium for each item produced beyond the quota. These plans offer an added incentive within an incentive. A typical **differential piece rate** plan is one where the rate paid per item depends on the number of items produced.

Using Differential Piecework **EXAMPLE 2**

Suppose Metro Electric pays assemblers as follows:

1–100 units	$2.10 each
101–150 units	$2.25 each
151 or more units	$2.40 each

Find the gross earnings of a worker producing **214 units**.

SOLUTION

> **Quick TIP** ▼
>
> With differential piecework, the highest amount paid applies to only the last units produced.

$$\begin{array}{r} 214 \\ -100 \\ \hline 114 \\ -50 \\ \hline 64 \end{array}$$

⟵ total units
⟵ first 100 units ⟶
⟵ next 50 units ⟶
⟵ number over 150 ⟶

100 units at $2.10 each = $210.00
50 units at $2.25 each = $112.50
64 units at $2.40 each = $153.60
214 total units = $476.10

The gross earnings are $476.10.

QUICK CHECK 2

Scooter Frame Company pays welders as follows: 1–150 frames, $2.85 each; 151–250, $3.20 each; and 251 or more, $3.45 each. Find the gross earnings of a worker who welds 282 frames.

OBJECTIVE 3 Find the gross pay for piecework with a guaranteed hourly wage. The piecework and differential piecework rates are frequently modified to include a guaranteed hourly pay rate. This is often necessary to satisfy federal and state laws concerning minimum wages. With this method, the employer must pay either the minimum wage or the piecework earnings, whichever is higher.

Finding Earnings with a Guaranteed Hourly Wage   **EXAMPLE 3**

A tire installer at the Tire Center is paid $10.50 per hour for an 8-hour day or $1.15 per tire installed, whichever is higher. Find the weekly earnings for an employee having the following rate of production.

Monday	85 tires
Tuesday	70 tires
Wednesday	88 tires
Thursday	68 tires
Friday	82 tires

> **Quick TIP** ▼
>
> The worker *cannot* earn less than $10.50 per hour or $84 ($10.50 × 8) for the day. Since the piecework earnings on Tuesday and Thursday in Example 3 fall below the hourly minimum, the hourly rate, or $84 for the day, is paid on those days.

SOLUTION

The hourly earnings for an 8-hour day are **$84 (8 × $10.50)**. The larger of hourly earnings or the piecework earnings is paid each day.

Monday	85 × $1.15 = $97.75 piece rate
Tuesday	70 × $1.15 = **$84 hourly (piece rate is $80.50)**
Wednesday	88 × $1.15 = $101.20 piece rate
Thursday	68 × $1.15 = **$84 hourly (piece rate is $78.20)**
Friday	82 × $1.15 = $94.30 piece rate

$461.25 weekly earnings

> **QUICK CHECK 3**
>
> A cabinet door finisher is paid $14.70 per hour for an 8-hour day or $.95 per cabinet door finished, whichever is higher. Find the gross earnings for a worker who finished 106 doors on Monday, 127 doors on Tuesday, 152 doors on Wednesday, 120 doors on Thursday, and 138 doors on Friday.

OBJECTIVE 4 Calculate the overtime earnings for piecework. Piecework employees, like other workers, are paid time and a half for overtime. It is common for the overtime rate to be $1\frac{1}{2}$ times the regular rate per piece.

Calculating Earnings with Overtime Piecework   **EXAMPLE 4**

Eugene Smith is paid $.98 per child's tricycle assembled. During one week, he assembled 480 tricycles on regular time and 104 tricycles during overtime hours. Find his gross earnings for the week if time and a half per assembly is paid for overtime.

SOLUTION

Gross earnings = Earnings at regular piece rate + Earnings at overtime piece rate
= (480 × $.98)   + 104 × (1.5 × $.98)
= $470.40 + $152.88
= **$623.28**

> **QUICK CHECK 4**
>
> An assembler is paid $.84 for each child car seat assembled. During a recent week, she assembled 400 car seats on regular time and 138 car seats during overtime hours. If time and a half is paid for each overtime assembly, find the gross earnings for the week.

A **commission rate** pays a salesperson either a fixed percent of sales or a fixed amount per item sold. Commissions are designed to produce maximum output from the salesperson, since pay is directly dependent on sales. All of the types of sales commission arrangements are discussed here.

OBJECTIVE 5 Find the gross earnings using commission rate times sales. With **straight commission**, the salesperson is paid a fixed percent of sales. Gross earnings are found with the following formula.

> Gross earnings = Commission rate × Amount of sales

The following data shows average incomes for some sales positions. However, the average probably does not mean a lot since some salespeople make far more than others. You can imagine that a mother of two young children who just started working as a real estate agent probably does not make anything near the income shown in the table, whereas a real estate agent who has worked in the business for years may make quite a bit more than that shown.

Numbers in the News

Average Salaries for Sales Positions

Position	Salary
Telemarketers	$24,770
Retail Sales	$25,050
Parts Sales	$30,850
Travel Agents	$32,470
Real Estate Agents	$54,410
Insurance Sales	$60,400

DATA: Bureau of Labor Statistics

Determining Earnings Using Commission **EXAMPLE 5**

A real estate broker charges a 6% commission. Find the commission on a house selling for $268,500.

SOLUTION

The commission is 6% × $268,500 = **.06** × $268,500 = $16,110. The **6%** is called the commission rate, or the **rate of commission**.

QUICK CHECK 5

An advertising sales representative is paid a 5% commission. Find the commission earned on sales of $9473.60.

Before the commission is calculated, any **returns** from customers, or any **allowances**, such as discounts, must be subtracted from sales.

Subtracting Returns When Using Commission **EXAMPLE 6**

Amanda Roach, a food-supplements sales representative, had sales of $10,230 one month, with returns and allowances of $1120. If her commission rate is 12%, find her gross earnings.

SOLUTION

The returns and allowances must first be subtracted from gross sales. Then multiply the difference, net sales, by the commission rate.

$$\text{Gross earnings} = (\$10{,}230 \text{ gross sales} - \$1120 \text{ returns and allowances}) \times \mathbf{12\%}$$
$$= \$9110 \text{ net sales} \times .12$$
$$= \$1093.20 \text{ gross earnings}$$

QUICK CHECK 6

Nate Sellers, an Avon salesperson, had sales of $45,350 one month, with returns and allowances of $432. If his commission rate is 18%, find his gross earnings.

OBJECTIVE 6 Determine a commission using the variable commission rate. The **sliding scale**, or **variable commission**, is a method of pay designed to retain top-producing salespeople. Under such a plan, a higher rate of commission is paid as sales get larger and larger.

Finding Earnings Using a Variable Commission

EXAMPLE 7

Maureen O'Connor sells food and bakery products to businesses such as Starbucks and is paid as follows based on monthly sales.

SALES	RATE
Up to $10,000	6%
$10,001–$20,000	8%
$20,001 and up	9%

Find O'Connor's earnings if she has sales of $32,768 one month.

SOLUTION

$32,768 ⟵ total sales
− 10,000 ⟵ first $10,000 ⟶ $10,000 at 6% = $600.00
$22,768
− 10,000 ⟵ next $10,000 ⟶ $10,000 at 8% = $800.00
$12,768 ⟵ over $20,000 ⟶ $12,768 at 9% = $1149.12
$32,768 total sales **$2549.12 total commissions**

QUICK CHECK 7

Timmy Heslin sells office copiers to businesses and is paid a variable commission rate. His commission rate on sales up to $20,000 is 2%; sales of $20,001 to $30,000, 2.5%, and sales of $30,001 and up, 3%. If he has sales of $38,400, find the commission earned.

OBJECTIVE 7 Find the gross earnings with a salary plus commission. With a **salary plus commission**, the salesperson is paid a fixed sum per pay period, plus a commission on all sales. This method of payment is commonly used by large retail stores. Gross earnings with salary plus commission are found with the following formula.

> Gross earnings = Fixed amount per pay period + Amount earned on commission

Many salespeople like this method. It is especially attractive to beginning salespeople who lack selling experience. While providing an incentive, it offers the security of a guaranteed income to cover basic living costs. Occasionally, this income is an earnings advance or a **draw**, which is a loan against future commissions. This loan is paid back when future commissions are earned.

Adding Commission to a Salary

EXAMPLE 8

Jaime Bailey is paid $325 per week by Beverly's Creations, plus 3% on all sales over $500. During one week, her total sales were $2972. Find her gross earnings.

SOLUTION

Gross earnings = Weekly salary + 3% on sales above $500
= $325 + .03($2972 − $500)
= $325 + (.03 × $2472)
= $325 + $74.16
= $399.16

QUICK CHECK 8

Sanford Howard is paid a salary of $290 a week, plus a 4% commission on all sales over $750. Find his gross earnings for a week in which his total sales were $1870.

Commission-based earning plans may be a strong deterrent to attracting new salespeople. Many companies offer the salary plus commission and draw plans to help fill sales positions.

Subtracting a Draw to Find Earnings **EXAMPLE 9**

Craig Johnson has office product sales of $36,850 for the month and is paid an 8% commission on all sales. He had draws of $850 for the month. Find his gross earnings after repaying the drawing account.

SOLUTION

$$\text{Gross earnings} = \text{Commissions} - \text{Draw}$$
$$= (.08 \times \$36,850) - \$850$$
$$= \$2948 - \$850$$
$$= \$2098$$

QUICK CHECK 9

Bob Smith has toy train sales of $18,540 for the month and is paid a 10% commission on all sales. If he had draws of $975 for the month, find his gross earnings after repaying the drawing account.

The graph shows the median weekly wages for a variety of careers.

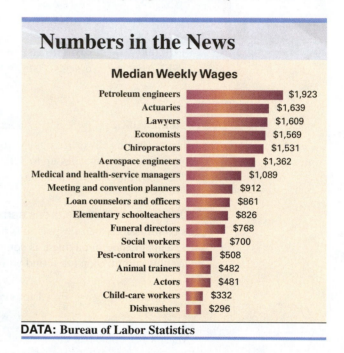

Numbers in the News

Median Weekly Wages

Petroleum engineers	$1,923
Actuaries	$1,639
Lawyers	$1,609
Economists	$1,569
Chiropractors	$1,531
Aerospace engineers	$1,362
Medical and health-service managers	$1,089
Meeting and convention planners	$912
Loan counselors and officers	$861
Elementary schoolteachers	$826
Funeral directors	$768
Social workers	$700
Pest-control workers	$508
Animal trainers	$482
Actors	$481
Child-care workers	$332
Dishwashers	$296

DATA: Bureau of Labor Statistics

6.2 Exercises

The QUICK START exercises in each section contain solutions to help you get started.

RECYCLING *Earth Plus pays workers $.48 per container for sorting recyclable materials. Find the daily gross earnings for each worker. (See Example 1.)*

QUICK START

Employee	Number of Containers	Gross Earnings	Employee	Number of Containers	Gross Earnings
1. Crossett, J.	194	$93.12	2. Biron, C.	292	_____
194 × $.48 = $93.12					
3. Campbell, K.	320	_____	4. Halcomb, J.	243	_____

AGRICULTURAL WORKERS *Find the daily gross earnings for each employee. (See Example 2.) Suppose that avocado pickers are paid as follows.*

1–500 avocados	$.05 each
501–700 avocados	$.07 each
Over 700 avocados	$.09 each

QUICK START

Employee	Number of Avocados	Gross Earnings	Employee	Number of Avocados	Gross Earnings
5. Hoch, R.	820	$49.80	6. Leonard, M. K.	907	_____
(500 × $.05) + (200 × $.07) + (120 × $.09) = $49.80					
7. Matysek, J.	852	_____	8. Panunzio, K.	1108	_____

9. Wages and salaries are known as *time rates*, while commissions are called *incentive rates of pay*. Explain in your own words the difference between these payment methods. (See Objective 5.)

10. Explain in your own words the difference between a piecework rate and differential piece rate. (See Objective 2.)

GUARANTEED HOURLY WORK *Find the gross earnings for each employee by first finding the daily hourly earnings and then finding the daily piecework earnings. Each employee has an 8-hour workday and is paid $.75 for each unit of production or the hourly rate, whichever is higher. (See Example 3.)*

QUICK START

EMPLOYEE	UNITS PRODUCED M	T	W	TH	F	HOURLY RATE	GROSS EARNINGS
11. Coughlin, S.	95	90	74	98	101	$8.20	$353.60 $71.25 + $67.50 + $65.60 + $73.50 + $75.75 = $353.60
12. Bahary, N.	105	88	103	99	110	$8.65	_____
13. Shea, D.	98	92	102	96	106	$8.80	_____
14. Ward, M.	98	104	95	110	108	$9.10	_____

⚠ indicates an exercise that is related to the Case in Point feature.

PIECEWORK WITH OVERTIME   *Find the gross earnings for each employee. Overtime is 1.5 times the normal rate per piece. (See Example 4.)*

QUICK START

	UNITS PRODUCED			
EMPLOYEE	REG.	O.T.	RATE PER UNIT	GROSS EARNINGS
15. Shannon, B.	430	62	$.76	$397.48
16. Mc Donald, M.	530	58	$.74	
17. Jennings, A.	470	70	$.82	
18. O'Brien, K.	504	52	$.85	

COMMISSION WITH RETURNS   *Find the gross earnings for each of the following salespeople. (See Examples 5 and 6.)*

QUICK START

	Employee	Total Sales	Returns and Allowances	Rate of Commission	Gross Earnings
19.	Mares, E.	$6210	$129	10%	$608.10

($6210 − $129) × 10% = $6081 × .1 = $608.10

	Employee	Total Sales	Returns and Allowances	Rate of Commission	Gross Earnings
20.	Peterson, J.	$5734	$415	7%	
21.	Remington, J.	$2875	$64	15%	
22.	Kling, J.	$3806	$108	20%	

VARIABLE-COMMISSION PAYMENT   *Find the gross earnings for each of the following employees. (See Example 7.) Livingston's Concrete pays its salespeople the following commissions.*

   6% on first $7500 in sales
   8% on next $7500 in sales
   10% on any sales over $15,000

QUICK START

	Employee	Total Sales	Gross Earnings		Employee	Total Sales	Gross Earnings
23.	Christensen, C.	$18,550	$1405	**24.**	Hubbard, P.	$11,225	

($7500 × .06) + ($7500 × .08) + ($3550 × .10) = $1405

	Employee	Total Sales	Gross Earnings		Employee	Total Sales	Gross Earnings
25.	Steed, F.	$10,480		**26.**	Goldstein, S.	$25,860	

SALARY PLUS COMMISSION   *Stockdale Marine pays salespeople as follows: $452 per week plus a commission of .9% on sales between $15,000 and $25,000, with 1.1% paid on sales in excess of $25,000. Find the gross earnings for each of the following salespeople. (No commission is paid on the first $15,000 of sales.) (See Example 8.)*

QUICK START

	Employee	Total Sales	Gross Earnings		Employee	Total Sales	Gross Earnings
27.	West, S.	$17,900	$478.10	**28.**	Barnes, A.	$36,300	

$452 + $2900 × .009 = $478.10

	Employee	Total Sales	Gross Earnings		Employee	Total Sales	Gross Earnings
29.	Feathers, C.	$32,874		**30.**	Maguire, J.	$28,400	

QUICK CHECK ANSWERS

1. $668.38   **2.** $857.90   **3.** $631.55   **4.** $509.88   **5.** $473.68   **6.** $8085.24   **7.** $902

6.3 Social Security, Medicare, and Other Taxes

OBJECTIVES

1 Understand FICA.
2 Find the maximum FICA tax paid by an employee in one year.
3 Understand Medicare tax.
4 Find FICA tax and Medicare tax.
5 Determine the FICA tax and the Medicare tax paid by a self-employed person.
6 Find state disability insurance deductions.

case IN point ►

Sarah Brynski does the payroll at her Starbucks store. For each employee, she must find total hours worked before calculating gross income. Then she must carefully subtract all appropriate deductions from the gross income, including FICA (Social Security) and Medicare.

Finding gross earnings is only the first step in preparing a payroll. The employer must then subtract all required deductions from gross earnings. For most employees, these deductions include Social Security tax, Medicare tax, federal income tax withholding, and state income tax withholding. Other deductions may include state disability insurance, union dues, retirement, vacation pay, credit union savings or loan payments, purchase of bonds, uniform expenses, group insurance plans, and charitable contributions. Subtracting these deductions from gross earnings results in **net pay**, the amount the employee receives.

SOCIAL SECURITY ADMINISTRATION

OBJECTIVE 1 Understand FICA. The **Federal Insurance Contributions Act (FICA)** was passed into law in the 1930s in the middle of the Great Depression. This plan, now called **Social Security**, was originally designed to give monthly benefits to retired workers and their survivors. As the number of people receiving benefits has increased along with the individual benefit amounts, people paying into Social Security have had to pay a larger amount of earnings into this fund each year. From 1937 through 1950, an employee paid 1% of income into Social Security, up to a maximum of $30 per year. This amount has increased over the years until an employee in 2010 paid 6.2% of income to FICA and 1.45% to **Medicare**, which together can total more than $8000 per year.

	SOCIAL SECURITY TAX		MEDICARE TAX	
YEAR	SOCIAL SECURITY TAX RATE	EMPLOYEE EARNINGS SUBJECT TO THE TAX	MEDICARE TAX RATE	EMPLOYEE EARNINGS SUBJECT TO THE TAX
1990	6.2%	$51,300	1.45%	all
1995	6.2%	$61,200	1.45%	all
2000	6.2%	$76,200	1.45%	all
2005	6.2%	$90,000	1.45%	all
2010	6.2%	$106,800	1.45%	all

Note: The Health Care Act of 2010 will result in a somewhat higher Medicare tax for single people making more than $200,000 per year and married couples making more than $250,000 per year. Since these changes do not take effect until 2013 and they apply only to high-income individuals, they are not discussed in this book.

For many years both the Social Security tax rate and the Medicare tax rate were combined. However, since 1991 these tax rates have been expressed individually. The table above shows the tax rates and the maximum earnings on which Social Security and Medicare taxes are paid by the employee. The employer pays the same rate as the employee, *matching dollar for dollar* all employee contributions. Self-employed people pay almost double the amount paid by those who are employees, since they are paying for both employee and employer.

Each employee, whether a U.S. citizen or not, must have a Social Security card. Most post offices have applications for the cards. All money set aside for an individual is credited to his or her account according to the Social Security number. Each year, the Social Security Administration sends out a Social Security statement that shows workers how Social Security fits into their future. The statements are sent three months before the employee's birthday, but only to workers who are 25 years of age and older. However, anyone may submit a **Request for Earnings and Benefit Estimate Statement** like the one shown here. Since mistakes do occur, it is important to check the statements very carefully. There is a limit of about three years, after which errors may not be corrected. To obtain one of the forms and other information about Social Security, you may phone 800-772-1213 or go on the World Wide Web to www.socialsecurity.gov.

Form SSA-7004-SM

Congress sets the tax rates and the maximum employee earnings subject to the Social Security tax each year. Since the maximum employee earnings change each year, we will use 6.2% of the first $110,000 that an employee earns in a year for Social Security. For Medicare, we will use 1.45% of all earnings. These figures are used in all examples and exercises.

> Use the following for all examples and exercises:
> Social Security tax = 6.2% × earnings up to $110,000
> Medicare tax = 1.45% × total earnings

You might wonder where the money paid into Social Security and Medicare goes. In fact, Social Security provides more than one-half of the total income for about two-thirds of older Americans. It also makes monthly payments to many disabled individuals and to the survivors of insured workers. Medicare pays medical bills for more than 45 million people. Without Social Security and Medicare, there would be a lot more poverty among the elderly and the disabled.

OBJECTIVE 2 Find the maximum FICA tax paid by an employee in one year. Remember that Social Security tax is paid on only the first $110,000 of gross earnings in our examples. An employee earning $110,000 during the first 10 months of a year pays no more Social Security tax on any additional earnings that year.

The maximum Social Security tax payable by an employed person in one year is found as follows.

Maximum Social Security tax = .062 × $110,000 = $6820 per year

Any income above $110,000 would not be subject to the Social Security tax. Only 7% of all wage earners are affected by the Social Security maximum.

OBJECTIVE 3 Understand Medicare tax. Medicare tax is paid on all earnings. The total earnings are multiplied by 1.45%.

OBJECTIVE 4 Find FICA tax and Medicare tax. When finding the amounts to be withheld for Social Security tax and Medicare tax, the employer must use the current rates and the current maximum earnings amount.

Finding FICA Tax and Medicare Tax   **EXAMPLE 1**

Imagine that you are Sarah Brynski, the manager of a Starbucks. Find the Social Security tax and the Medicare tax that must be withheld from the gross earnings of Kelleher and Kimbrel.

(a) Kelleher: $362.40 gross earnings   **(b)** Kimbrel: $468.02 gross earnings

SOLUTION

In each case, the tax is rounded to the nearest cent.

(a)   Wage × Tax rate = Tax
$362.40 × .062   = $22.47   **Social Security tax**
$362.40 × .0145 = $5.25   **Medicare tax**

(b)   Wage × Tax rate = Tax
$468.02 × .062   = $29.02   **Social Security tax**
$468.02 × .0145 = $6.79   **Medicare tax**

> **QUICK CHECK 1**
>
> Find **(a)** the Social Security tax and **(b)** the Medicare tax that must be withheld from gross earnings of $418.50.

Finding FICA Tax **EXAMPLE 2**

Shannon Woolums has earned $107,634.05 so far this year. Her gross earnings for the current pay period are $5224.03. Find her Social Security tax.

SOLUTION

The Social Security tax is paid only on the first $110,000 in earnings. First, subtract earnings to date from $110,000 to find the amount subject to Social Security tax during the current pay period.

$110,000.00   **Maximum earnings subject to Social Security tax**
$-\ 107,634.05$ **Earnings to date**
$2,365.95   **Amount subject to Social Security tax**

Social Security tax = $2365.95 × .062 = **$146.69**

No additional Social Security tax will be withheld for the remainder of the year.

> **QUICK CHECK 2**
>
> Mary Single has earned $108,750.10 so far this year. If her gross earnings are $3080 this week, find the Social Security tax to be withheld.

The following table compares the contributions to social programs (Social Security and Medicare) in selected countries around the world. How do U.S. workers' (employee) contributions compare with those of other countries?

Numbers in the News

Social Insurance Contributions As a Percent of Total Gross Earnings

Country	Employee	Employer
Italy	10.26%	48.00%
France	20.66%	42.57%
Sweden	33.00%	7.00%
Mexico	22.00%	3.00%
Germany	21.12%	21.12%
Japan	11.00%	12.00%
U.K.	7.08%	10.00%
Canada	5.00%	8.00%
U.S.A	7.65%	7.65%

DATA: *Benefits Report* Europe, USA, and Canada;
Watson Wyatt Worldwide, and
Knight Ridder Tribune.

OBJECTIVE 5 Determine the FICA tax and the Medicare tax paid by a self-employed person. People who are self-employed pay higher Social Security tax and higher Medicare tax than people who work for others. There is no employer to match the employee contribution, so the self-employed person pays a rate that is double that of an employee. The gross earnings of the self-employed person are first multiplied by 92.35% (.9235) to find the adjusted earnings. These adjusted earnings are then multiplied by the current rates. In our examples, the self-employed person pays 12.4% of adjusted earnings for Social Security tax and 2.9% of adjusted earnings for Medicare tax.

Finding FICA and Medicare Tax for the Self-Employed **EXAMPLE 3**

Find the Social Security tax and the Medicare tax paid by Ta Shon Williams, a self-employed Web designer who had adjusted earnings of $53,820 this year.

SOLUTION

$$\text{Social Security tax} = \$53,820 \times \textbf{12.4\%} = \$53,820 \times .124 = \$6673.68$$
$$\text{Medicare tax} = \$53,820 \times \textbf{2.9\%} = \$53,820 \times .029 = \$1560.78$$

QUICK CHECK 3

Find **(a)** the Social Security tax and **(b)** the Medicare tax for a self-employed accountant who had adjusted earnings of $73,875 this year.

OBJECTIVE 6 Find state disability insurance deductions. Many states have a state disability insurance (SDI) program. Qualifying employees must pay a portion of their earnings to the program. If an employee is injured and unable to work, the program pays the employee during the period of disability. The tax rate and amount subject to tax vary widely by state, but we will use an SDI deduction of 1% of gross earnings on the first $31,800 earned in a year. We assume no SDI deductions on earnings above this amount.

Finding State Disability Insurance Deductions **EXAMPLE 4**

Find the state disability insurance deduction for an employee at Comet Auto Parts with gross earnings of $418 this pay period. The SDI rate is 1%, and the employee has not earned $31,800 this year.

SOLUTION

The state disability insurance deduction is $4.18 ($418 × **.01**).

QUICK CHECK 4

An employee has gross earnings of $525.80 this week. The employee has not earned $31,800 this year and the SDI rate is 1%. What is the state disability insurance deduction?

Knowing SDI Maximum Deductions **EXAMPLE 5**

Jenoa Perkins has earned $29,960 so far this year. Find the SDI deduction if gross earnings this pay period are $2872. Use an SDI rate of 1% on the first $31,800.

SOLUTION

The SDI deduction will be taken on $1840 of the current gross earnings.

$31,800	maximum earnings subject to SDI
−$29,960	earnings this year
$1,840	earnings subject to SDI

The SDI deduction is $18.40 ($1840 × .01).

QUICK CHECK 5

Linda Shirley has earned $30,780 so far this year. Her earnings this pay period are $3289. Find the SDI deduction using an SDI rate of 1% on the first $31,800.

6.3 Exercises

  MyMathLab Math XL PRACTICE   WATCH   DOWNLOAD READ

The **QUICK START** exercises in each section contain solutions to help you get started.

Find the Social Security tax and the Medicare tax for each of the following amounts of gross earnings. Assume a 6.2% FICA rate and a 1.45% Medicare tax rate. (See Example 1.)

QUICK START

1. $420	$26.04	$6.09	2. $942.50	$58.44	$13.67	3. $463.24	___	___
4. $606.35	___	___	5. $854.71	___	___	6. $683.65	___	___

SOCIAL SECURITY TAX Find the Social Security tax for each employee for the current pay period. Assume a 6.2% FICA rate up to a maximum of $110,000. (See Example 2.)

QUICK START

Employee	Gross Earnings This Year (So Far)	Earnings Current Pay Period	Social Security Tax
7. Dandridge, T.	$106,945.32	$6218.48	$189.39
8. Hale, R.	$107,438.75	$5200.00	$158.80
9. Hall, T.	$105,016.22	$7260.00	___
10. Maurin, J.	$108,971.95	$4487.52	___
11. Saraniti, S.	$109,329.75	$3053.73	___
12. De Bouchel, V.	$108,974.08	$6160.86	___

PAYROLL DEDUCTIONS Find the regular earnings, overtime earnings, gross earnings, Social Security tax (6.2%), Medicare tax (1.45%), and state disability insurance deduction (1%) for each employee. Assume that no employee will have earned more than the FICA or SDI maximum at the end of the current pay period. Assume that time and a half is paid for any overtime in a 40-hour week. (See Examples 1–4.)

QUICK START

Employee	Hours Worked	Regular Rate	Regular Earnings	Overtime Earnings	Gross Earnings	Social Security Tax	Medicare Tax	SDI Deduction
13. Garrett, R.	45.5	$9.22	$368.80	$76.07	$444.87	$27.58	$6.45	$4.45
14. Harcos, W.	47.75	$8.50	___	___	___	___	___	___
15. Plescia, P.	45	$14.20	___	___	___	___	___	___
16. Eckern, G.	45	$10.20	___	___	___	___	___	___
17. McIntosh, R.	47	$11.68	___	___	___	___	___	___
18. Wright, R.	46.75	$8.24	___	___	___	___	___	___

Solve the following application problems. Round to the nearest cent.

QUICK START

 19. SOCIAL SECURITY AND MEDICARE Maria Ortega worked 43.5 hours last week at Starbucks. She is paid $8.58 per hour, plus time and a half for all hours over 40 per week. Find her **(a)** Social Security tax and **(b)** Medicare tax for the week.

(a) $24.07

(b) $5.63

Gross income is $(40 \times \$8.58) + \left(3.5 \times 1\frac{1}{2}\right) \times \$8.58 = \$388.25$

(a) Social Security tax is $.062 \times \$388.25 = \$24.07$

(b) Medicare tax is $.0145 \times \$388.25 = \$5.63$

 indicates an exercise that is related to the Case in Point feature.

20. **SOCIAL SECURITY AND MEDICARE** Chriscelle Merquillo receives 7% commission on all sales. Her sales on Monday of last week were $1412.20, with $1928.42 on Tuesday, $598.14 on Wednesday, $1051.12 on Thursday, and $958.72 on Friday. Find her **(a)** Social Security tax and **(b)** Medicare tax for the week.

(a) _____

(b) _____

21. **PAYROLL DEDUCTIONS** Donna Laughman is paid an 8% commission on sales. During a recent pay period, she had sales of $19,482 and returns and allowances of $193. Find the amount of **(a)** her Social Security tax, **(b)** her Medicare tax, and **(c)** her state disability insurance deduction for this pay period. (The FICA rate is 6.2%, the Medicare rate is 1.45%, the SDI rate is 1%, and earnings will not exceed $31,800.)

(a) _____

(b) _____

(c) _____

22. **PAYROLL DEDUCTIONS** Peter Phelps is a representative for Delta International Machinery and is paid $675 per week plus a commission of 2% on sales. His sales last week were $17,240. Find the amount of **(a)** his Social Security tax, **(b)** his Medicare tax, and **(c)** his state disability insurance deduction for the pay period. (The FICA rate is 6.2%, the Medicare rate is 1.45%, the SDI rate is 1%, and earnings will not exceed $31,800.)

(a) _____

(b) _____

(c) _____

SELF-EMPLOYMENT DEDUCTIONS *The following problems refer to self-employed individuals. These people pay a Social Security tax of 12.4% and Medicare tax of 2.9%. Find both of the taxes on the following annual adjusted earnings. (See Example 3.)*

23. Tony Romano, owner of The Cutlery, earned $58,238.74.

23. _____

24. Rachel Leach, an interior designer, earned $36,724.72.

24. _____

25. Krystal McClellan, cosmetics consultant, earned $29,104.80.

25. _____

26. Ron Morris, a Chic-Filet franchise owner, earned $78,007.14.

26. _____

27. Peggy Kelleher, shop owner, earned $26,843.60.

27. _____

28. Sadie Chambers, senior account executive, earned $92,748.32.

28. _____

29. A young person who has just received her first paycheck is puzzled by the amounts that have been deducted from gross earnings. Briefly explain both the FICA and Medicare deductions to this person. (See Objectives 1–4.)

30. Describe the difference between the FICA paid by an employee and FICA paid by a self-employed person. (See Objective 5.)

QUICK CHECK ANSWERS

1. (a) $25.95 (rounded) **(b)** $6.07 (rounded) **3. (a)** $9160.50 **(b)** $2142.38 (rounded)
2. $77.49 (rounded) **4.** $5.26 (rounded) **5.** $10.20

6.4 Income Tax Withholding

OBJECTIVES

1 Understand the Employee's Withholding Allowance Certificate.

2 Find the federal withholding tax using the wage bracket method.

3 Find the federal withholding tax using the percentage method.

4 Find the state withholding tax using the state income tax rate.

5 Find net pay when given gross wages, taxes, and other deductions.

6 Find the quarterly amount owed to the Internal Revenue Service.

7 Understand additional employer responsibilities and employee benefits.

case IN point ▶

After completing the payroll at Starbucks, Sarah Brynski must be certain that all FICA taxes, Medicare taxes, and federal withholding taxes withheld from employees are sent to the Internal Revenue Service. Additionally, it's essential that Brynski keeps current with all of the changes in the tax codes that affect withholding.

The **personal income tax** is the largest single source of money for the federal government. The law requires that the bulk of the tax owed by an individual be paid as the income is earned. For this reason, employers must deduct money from the gross earnings of almost every employee. These deductions, called **income tax withholdings**, are sent periodically to the Internal Revenue Service. The IRS has an electronic funds transfer payment system called EFTPS that allows employers to transfer these funds electronically. The amount of money withheld from each employee depends on several factors, including marital status, number of withholding allowances, and income.

Marital status. Generally, the withholding tax for a married person is less than the withholding tax for a single person making the same income.

OBJECTIVE 1 Understand the Employee's Withholding Allowance Certificate. Each employee must file a W-4 form, as shown, with his or her employer. On this form, the employee states the number of **withholding allowances** being claimed along with additional information so that the employer can withhold the proper amount for income tax.

-------------------- Cut here and give Form W-4 to your employer. Keep the top part for your records. --------------------

Form **W-4**	**Employee's Withholding Allowance Certificate**	OMB No. 1545-0074
Department of the Treasury Internal Revenue Service	▶ Whether you are entitled to claim a certain number of allowances or exemption from withholding is subject to review by the IRS. Your employer may be required to send a copy of this form to the IRS.	201_

1 Type or print your first name and middle initial.	Last name	**2 Your social security number**

Home address (number and street or rural route)	**3** ☐ Single ☐ Married ☐ Married, but withhold at higher Single rate. Note. If married, but legally separated, or spouse is a nonresident alien, check the "Single" box.
City or town, state, and ZIP code	**4 If your last name differs from that shown on your social security card,** check here. You must call 1-800-772-1213 for a replacement card. ▶ ☐

5 Total number of allowances you are claiming (from line **H** above **or** from the applicable worksheet on page 2)   **5** __

6 Additional amount, if any, you want withheld from each paycheck . . . .   **6** $ __

7 I claim exemption from withholding for 201_, and I certify that I meet **both** of the following conditions for exemption.
- Last year I had a right to a refund of **all** federal income tax withheld because I had **no** tax liability **and**
- This year I expect a refund of **all** federal income tax withheld because I expect to have **no** tax liability.

If you meet both conditions, write "Exempt" here . . . . ▶ **7** __

Under penalties of perjury, I declare that I have examined this certificate and to the best of my knowledge and belief, it is true, correct, and complete.

Employee's signature
(Form is not valid unless you sign it.) ▶ _____   Date ▶ _____

8 Employer's name and address (Employer: Complete lines 8 and 10 only if sending to the IRS.)	**9** Office code (optional)	**10** Employer identification number (EIN)

For Privacy Act and Paperwork Reduction Act Notice, see page 2.   Cat. No. 10220Q   Form **W-4** (201_)

SINGLE Persons—WEEKLY Payroll Period
(For Wages Paid Through December 201_)

If the wages are –		And the number of withholding allowances claimed is —							
At least	But less than	0	1	2	3	4	5	6	7
		The amount of income tax to be withheld is —							
230	240	11	3	0	0	0	0	0	0
240	250	13	4	0	0	0	0	0	0
250	260	14	5	0	0	0	0	0	0
260	270	16	6	0	0	0	0	0	0
270	280	17	7	0	0	0	0	0	0
280	290	19	8	1	0	0	0	0	0
290	300	20	10	2	0	0	0	0	0
300	310	22	11	3	0	0	0	0	0
310	320	23	13	4	0	0	0	0	0
320	330	25	14	5	0	0	0	0	0
330	340	26	16	6	0	0	0	0	0
340	350	28	17	7	0	0	0	0	0
350	360	29	19	8	1	0	0	0	0
360	370	31	20	10	2	0	0	0	0
370	380	32	22	11	3	0	0	0	0
380	390	34	23	13	4	0	0	0	0
390	400	35	25	14	5	0	0	0	0
400	410	37	26	16	6	0	0	0	0
410	420	38	28	17	7	0	0	0	0
420	430	40	29	19	8	1	0	0	0
430	440	41	31	20	10	2	0	0	0
440	450	43	32	22	11	3	0	0	0
450	460	44	34	23	13	4	0	0	0
460	470	46	35	25	14	5	0	0	0
470	480	47	37	26	16	6	0	0	0
480	490	49	38	28	17	7	0	0	0
490	500	50	40	29	19	8	1	0	0
500	510	52	41	31	20	10	2	0	0
510	520	53	43	32	22	11	3	0	0
520	530	55	44	34	23	13	4	0	0

MARRIED Persons—WEEKLY Payroll Period
(For Wages Paid Through December 201_)

If the wages are –		And the number of withholding allowances claimed is —							
At least	But less than	0	1	2	3	4	5	6	7
		The amount of income tax to be withheld is —							
450	460	15	8	1	0	0	0	0	0
460	470	16	9	2	0	0	0	0	0
470	480	17	10	3	0	0	0	0	0
480	490	19	11	4	0	0	0	0	0
490	500	20	12	5	0	0	0	0	0
500	510	22	13	6	0	0	0	0	0
510	520	23	14	7	0	0	0	0	0
520	530	25	15	8	1	0	0	0	0
530	540	26	16	9	2	0	0	0	0
540	550	28	17	10	3	0	0	0	0
550	560	29	19	11	4	0	0	0	0
560	570	31	20	12	5	0	0	0	0
570	580	32	22	13	6	0	0	0	0
580	590	34	23	14	7	0	0	0	0
590	600	35	25	15	8	1	0	0	0
600	610	37	26	16	9	2	0	0	0
610	620	38	28	17	10	3	0	0	0
620	630	40	29	19	11	4	0	0	0
630	640	41	31	20	12	5	0	0	0
640	650	43	32	22	13	6	0	0	0
650	660	44	34	23	14	7	0	0	0
660	670	46	35	25	15	8	1	0	0
670	680	47	37	26	16	9	2	0	0
680	690	49	38	28	17	10	3	0	0
690	700	50	40	29	19	11	4	0	0
700	710	52	41	31	20	12	5	0	0
710	720	53	43	32	22	13	6	0	0
720	730	55	44	34	23	14	7	0	0
730	740	56	46	35	25	15	8	1	0
740	750	58	47	37	26	16	9	2	0

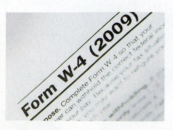

A W-4 form is usually completed when a person starts a new job. A married person with three children normally claims five allowances (one each for the employee and spouse and one for each child). However, if both spouses are employed, each may claim himself or herself. The number of allowances may be raised if an employee has been receiving a refund of income taxes, or the number may be lowered if the employee has had a balance due in previous tax years. The W-4 form has instructions to help determine the proper number of allowances. Some people enjoy receiving a tax refund when filing their income tax return, so they claim fewer allowances,

SINGLE Persons—MONTHLY Payroll Period
(For Wages Paid Through December 201_)

If the wages are –		And the number of withholding allowances claimed is —							
At least	But less than	0	1	2	3	4	5	6	7
		The amount of income tax to be withheld is —							
1,360	1,400	104	58	17	0	0	0	0	0
1,400	1,440	110	64	21	0	0	0	0	0
1,440	1,480	116	70	25	0	0	0	0	0
1,480	1,520	122	76	31	0	0	0	0	0
1,520	1,560	128	82	37	3	0	0	0	0
1,560	1,600	134	88	43	7	0	0	0	0
1,600	1,640	140	94	49	11	0	0	0	0
1,640	1,680	146	100	55	15	0	0	0	0
1,680	1,720	152	106	61	19	0	0	0	0
1,720	1,760	158	112	67	23	0	0	0	0
1,760	1,800	164	118	73	27	0	0	0	0
1,800	1,840	170	124	79	33	1	0	0	0
1,840	1,880	176	130	85	39	5	0	0	0
1,880	1,920	182	136	91	45	9	0	0	0
1,920	1,960	188	142	97	51	13	0	0	0
1,960	2,000	194	148	103	57	17	0	0	0
2,000	2,040	200	154	109	63	21	0	0	0
2,040	2,080	206	160	115	69	25	0	0	0
2,080	2,120	212	166	121	75	29	0	0	0
2,120	2,160	218	172	127	81	35	2	0	0
2,160	2,200	224	178	133	87	41	6	0	0
2,200	2,240	230	184	139	93	47	10	0	0
2,240	2,280	236	190	145	99	53	14	0	0
2,280	2,320	242	196	151	105	59	18	0	0
2,320	2,360	248	202	157	111	65	22	0	0
2,360	2,400	254	208	163	117	71	26	0	0
2,400	2,440	260	214	169	123	77	32	0	0
2,440	2,480	266	220	175	129	83	38	4	0
2,480	2,520	272	226	181	135	89	44	8	0
2,520	2,560	278	232	187	141	95	50	12	0

MARRIED Persons—MONTHLY Payroll Period
(For Wages Paid Through December 201_)

If the wages are –		And the number of withholding allowances claimed is —							
At least	But less than	0	1	2	3	4	5	6	7
		The amount of income tax to be withheld is —							
2,080	2,120	82	48	18	0	0	0	0	0
2,120	2,160	88	52	22	0	0	0	0	0
2,160	2,200	94	56	26	0	0	0	0	0
2,200	2,240	100	60	30	0	0	0	0	0
2,240	2,280	106	64	34	4	0	0	0	0
2,280	2,320	112	68	38	8	0	0	0	0
2,320	2,360	118	72	42	12	0	0	0	0
2,360	2,400	124	78	46	16	0	0	0	0
2,400	2,440	130	84	50	20	0	0	0	0
2,440	2,480	136	90	54	24	0	0	0	0
2,480	2,520	142	96	58	28	0	0	0	0
2,520	2,560	148	102	62	32	1	0	0	0
2,560	2,600	154	108	66	36	5	0	0	0
2,600	2,640	160	114	70	40	9	0	0	0
2,640	2,680	166	120	75	44	13	0	0	0
2,680	2,720	172	126	81	48	17	0	0	0
2,720	2,760	178	132	87	52	21	0	0	0
2,760	2,800	184	138	93	56	25	0	0	0
2,800	2,840	190	144	99	60	29	0	0	0
2,840	2,880	196	150	105	64	33	3	0	0
2,880	2,920	202	156	111	68	37	7	0	0
2,920	2,960	208	162	117	72	41	11	0	0
2,960	3,000	214	168	123	77	45	15	0	0
3,000	3,040	220	174	129	83	49	19	0	0
3,040	3,080	226	180	135	89	53	23	0	0
3,080	3,120	232	186	141	95	57	27	0	0
3,120	3,160	238	192	147	101	61	31	0	0
3,160	3,200	244	198	153	107	65	35	4	0
3,200	3,240	250	204	159	113	69	39	8	0
3,240	3,280	256	210	165	119	73	43	12	0

having more withheld from each check. Other individuals prefer to receive more of their income each pay period, so they claim the maximum number of allowances to which they are entitled. The exact number of allowances *must* be claimed when the income tax return is filed.

Amount of gross earnings. The withholding tax is found on the basis of the gross earnings per pay period. Income tax withholding is applied to all earnings—not just earnings up to a certain amount as with Social Security. Generally, the higher a person's gross earnings, the more withholding tax paid.

There are two methods that employers use to determine the amount of federal withholding tax to deduct from paychecks: the **wage bracket method** and the **percentage method**.

OBJECTIVE 2 Find the federal withholding tax using the wage bracket method. The Internal Revenue Service supplies withholding tax tables to be used with the wage bracket method. These tables are extensive, covering weekly, biweekly, semimonthly, monthly, and daily pay periods. The preceding pages show samples of the withholding tables. Two of the tables are for people who are paid weekly, both single and married. The other two tables are for both single and married people who are paid monthly.

Finding Federal Withholding Using the Wage Bracket Method

EXAMPLE 1

Benito Flores works for Best Buy. He is single and claims no withholding allowances since he prefers to get money back from the government when filing his income tax return. This choice will increase the amount withheld from his paycheck every week. Use the wage bracket method to find his withholding tax for a 30-hour workweek in which his gross earnings were $338.

SOLUTION

Use the table for single person, weekly payroll period. The earnings of $338 are found in the row for at least $330 but less than $340 and the column for 0 withholding allowances. The amount to be withheld for federal income taxes is $26. So, Flores's gross income for the week will be reduced by $26.

> **Quick TIP** ▼
>
> It is important to use the correct table when finding the amount to withhold.

QUICK CHECK 1

Rachel Leach is single and claims two withholding allowances. Use the wage bracket method to find her withholding tax if her weekly gross earnings are $358.

Using the Wage Bracket Method for Federal Withholding

EXAMPLE 2

Pat Rowell is married, claims three withholding allowances, and has monthly gross earnings of $3016.47. Find her withholding tax using the wage bracket method.

SOLUTION

Use the table for married persons—monthly payroll period. Look down the two left columns, and find the range that includes Rowell's gross earnings: "at least $3000 but less than $3040." Read across the table to the column headed "3" (for the three withholding allowances). The withholding tax is $83. Had Rowell claimed five withholding allowances, her withholding tax would have been only $19.

QUICK CHECK 2

Bob Martinez has monthly earnings of $2839.78. He is married and claims four withholding allowances. Find his withholding tax using the wage bracket method.

OBJECTIVE 3 Find the federal withholding tax using the percentage method. Many companies today prefer to use the *percentage method* to determine federal withholding tax. The percentage method does not require the several pages of tables needed with the wage bracket method and is more easily adapted to computer applications in the processing of payrolls.

Percentage Method: Amount for One Withholding Allowance

PAYROLL PERIOD	ONE WITHHOLDING ALLOWANCE
Weekly	$70.19
Biweekly	$140.38
Semimonthly	$152.08
Monthly	$304.17
Quarterly	$912.50
Semiannually	$1,825.00
Annually	$3,650.00

Tables for Percentage Method of Withholding
(For Wages Paid Through December 201_)

TABLE 1—WEEKLY Payroll Period

(a) SINGLE person (including head of household)—

If the amount of wages (after subtracting withholding allowances) is:　The amount of income tax to withhold is:

Not over $138 . . . . $0

Over—	But not over—		of excess over—
$138	—$200	. . .10%	—$138
$200	—$696	. . .$6.20 plus 15%	—$200
$696	—$1,279	. . .$80.60 plus 25%	—$696
$1,279	—$3,338	. . .$226.35 plus 28%	—$1,279
$3,338	—$7,212	. . .$802.87 plus 33%	—$3,338
$7,212	. . . .	. . .$2,081.29 plus 35%	—$7,212

(b) MARRIED person—

If the amount of wages (after subtracting withholding allowances) is:　The amount of income tax to withhold is:

Not over $303 . . . . $0

Over—	But not over—		of excess over—
$303	—$470	. . .10%	—$303
$470	—$1,455	. . .$16.70 plus 15%	—$470
$1,455	—$2,272	. . .$164.45 plus 25%	—$1,455
$2,272	—$4,165	. . .$368.70 plus 28%	—$2,272
$4,165	—$7,321	. . .$898.74 plus 33%	—$4,165
$7,321	. . . .	. . .$1,940.22 plus 35%	—$7,321

TABLE 2—BIWEEKLY Payroll Period

(a) SINGLE person (including head of household)—

If the amount of wages (after subtracting withholding allowances) is:　The amount of income tax to withhold is:

Not over $276 . . . . $0

Over—	But not over—		of excess over—
$276	—$400	. . .10%	—$276
$400	—$1,392	. . .$12.40 plus 15%	—$400
$1,392	—$2,559	. . .$161.20 plus 25%	—$1,392
$2,559	—$6,677	. . .$452.95 plus 28%	—$2,559
$6,677	—$14,423	. . .$1,605.99 plus 33%	—$6,677
$14,423	. . . .	. . .$4,162.17 plus 35%	—$14,423

(b) MARRIED person—

If the amount of wages (after subtracting withholding allowances) is:　The amount of income tax to withhold is:

Not over $606 . . . . $0

Over—	But not over—		of excess over—
$606	—$940	. . .10%	—$606
$940	—$2,910	. . .$33.40 plus 15%	—$940
$2,910	—$4,543	. . .$328.90 plus 25%	—$2,910
$4,543	—$8,331	. . .$737.15 plus 28%	—$4,543
$8,331	—$14,642	. . .$1,797.79 plus 33%	—$8,331
$14,642	. . . .	. . .$3,880.42 plus 35%	—$14,642

TABLE 3—SEMIMONTHLY Payroll Period

(a) SINGLE person (including head of household)—

If the amount of wages (after subtracting withholding allowances) is:　The amount of income tax to withhold is:

Not over $299 . . . . $0

Over—	But not over—		of excess over—
$299	—$433	. . .10%	—$299
$433	—$1,508	. . .$13.40 plus 15%	—$433
$1,508	—$2,772	. . .$174.65 plus 25%	—$1,508
$2,772	—$7,233	. . .$490.65 plus 28%	—$2,772
$7,233	—$15,625	. . .$1,739.73 plus 33%	—$7,233
$15,625	. . . .	. . .$4,509.09 plus 35%	—$15,625

(b) MARRIED person—

If the amount of wages (after subtracting withholding allowances) is:　The amount of income tax to withhold is:

Not over $656 . . . . $0

Over—	But not over—		of excess over—
$656	—$1,019	. . .10%	—$656
$1,019	—$3,152	. . .$36.30 plus 15%	—$1,019
$3,152	—$4,922	. . .$356.25 plus 25%	—$3,152
$4,922	—$9,025	. . .$798.75 plus 28%	—$4,922
$9,025	—$15,863	. . .$1,947.59 plus 33%	—$9,025
$15,863	. . . .	. . .$4,204.13 plus 35%	—$15,863

TABLE 4—MONTHLY Payroll Period

(a) SINGLE person (including head of household)—

If the amount of wages (after subtracting withholding allowances) is:　The amount of income tax to withhold is:

Not over $598 . . . . $0

Over—	But not over—		of excess over—
$598	—$867	. . .10%	—$598
$867	—$3,017	. . .$26.90 plus 15%	—$867
$3,017	—$5,544	. . .$349.40 plus 25%	—$3,017
$5,544	—$14,467	. . .$981.15 plus 28%	—$5,544
$14,467	—$31,250	. . .$3,479.59 plus 33%	—$14,467
$31,250	. . . .	. . .$9,017.98 plus 35%	—$31,250

(b) MARRIED person—

If the amount of wages (after subtracting withholding allowances) is:　The amount of income tax to withhold is:

Not over $1,313 . . . . $0

Over—	But not over—		of excess over—
$1,313	—$2,038	. . .10%	—$1,313
$2,038	—$6,304	. . .$72.50 plus 15%	—$2,038
$6,304	—$9,844	. . .$712.40 plus 25%	—$6,304
$9,844	—$18,050	. . .$1,597.40 plus 28%	—$9,844
$18,050	—$31,725	. . .$3,895.08 plus 33%	—$18,050
$31,725	. . . .	. . .$8,407.83 plus 35%	—$31,725

Finding the amount of withholding using the percentage method

Step 1　Multiply the number of withholding allowances by the amount for one withholding allowance from the table.

Step 2　Subtract the amount found in step 1 from gross earnings.

Step 3　Find the appropriate table for percentage method of withholding and then the row.

Step 4　Follow the directions in the table to find the tax to be withheld.

Finding Federal Withholding Using the Percentage Method

EXAMPLE 3

case **IN** point

Sarah Brynski at Starbucks is married, claims two withholding allowances, and had weekly gross earnings of $690 one week. Use the percentage method to find the withholding tax.

SOLUTION

Step 1　From the table at the bottom of the previous page, the amount for one withholding allowance, weekly payroll is $70.19.

Number of allowances × Amount for one allowance = 2 × $70.19 = **$140.38**

Step 2　Gross earnings − Amount from step 1 = $690 − **$140.38** = **$549.62**

Step 3　Use Table 1(b) above for weekly payroll period, married person.

Step 4　Go to the row of **over $470 but not over $1455**.

Withholding = $16.70 plus **15% of excess over $470**

= $16.70 + **.15 × ($549.62 − $470)**

= $16.70 + $11.94

= $28.64

The calculator solution to this example is

$$690 \;\boxed{-}\; 2 \;\boxed{\times}\; 70.19 \;\boxed{=}\; \boxed{\text{STO}}$$

$$16.7 \;\boxed{+}\; .15 \;\boxed{\times}\; \boxed{(}\; \text{RCL} \;\boxed{-}\; \$470 \;\boxed{)}\; \boxed{=}\; 28.64$$

> **QUICK CHECK 3**
>
> Sadie Simms is married and claims three withholding allowances. Use the percentage method to find her withholding tax in a week when she has earnings of $1263.

Finding Federal Withholding Using the Percentage Method **EXAMPLE 4**

Dac Kien is married, claims three withholding allowances, and receives $7850 a month working as a chemical engineer for Dupont. Use the percentage method to find his withholding tax.

SOLUTION

Step 1   The amount of one withholding allowance for monthly is $304.17.

Number of allowances × Amount for one allowance = 3 × $304.17 = **$912.51**

Step 2   Gross earnings − Amount from step 1 = $7850 − **$912.51** = $6937.49

Step 3   Use Table 4(b) for monthly payroll and married person.

Step 4   Go to the row of over $6304 but not over $9844.

$$
\begin{aligned}
\text{Withholding} &= \$712.40 + \textbf{25\% of the excess over \$6304} \\
&= \$712.40 + .25 \times (\$6937.49 - \$6304) \\
&= \$712.40 + \$158.37 \\
&= \$870.77
\end{aligned}
$$

> **QUICK CHECK 4**
>
> Howard Martin has earnings of $5735 for the month. He is married and claims four withholding allowances. Use the percentage method to find his withholding tax.

Finding Federal Withholding Using the Percentage Method **EXAMPLE 5**

Andy Herrebout is single, claims two withholding allowances, and has weekly gross earnings of $1838. Use the percentage method to find the withholding tax.

SOLUTION

One withholding allowance for weekly is $70.19.

Number of allowances × Amount for one allowance = 2 × $70.19 = **$140.38**

Gross earnings − Amount above = $1838 − **$140.38** = $1697.62

Go to the row of over $1279 but not over $3338 on Table 1(a) for single person, weekly.

$$
\begin{aligned}
\text{Withholding} &= \$226.35 + \textbf{28\% of excess over \$1279} \\
&= \$226.35 + .28(\$1697.62 - \$1279) \\
&= \$343.56
\end{aligned}
$$

> **QUICK CHECK 5**
>
> Carol Dixon has biweekly earnings of $4350, is single, and claims two withholding allowances. Use the percentage method to find her withholding tax.

The amount of withholding tax found using the wage bracket method can vary slightly from the amount of withholding tax found using the percentage method. Any differences would be eliminated when the income tax return is filed.

OBJECTIVE 4 Find the state withholding tax using the state income tax rate. Many states and cities also have an income tax collected by withholding. Income taxes vary from state to state, with no state income tax in Alaska, Florida, Nevada, South Dakota, Texas, Washington, and Wyoming. A few states have a flat tax rate (percent of income) as a **state income tax**, while the majority of the states issue tax tables with taxes going as high as 9% and 10%. A few of the states' income tax rates are shown in the following figure.

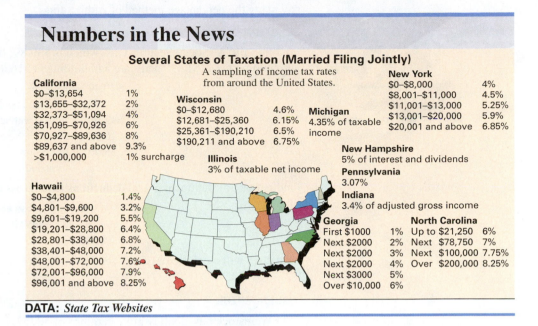

Numbers in the News

Several States of Taxation (Married Filing Jointly)

A sampling of income tax rates from around the United States.

California
$0–$13,654	1%
$13,655–$32,372	2%
$32,373–$51,094	4%
$51,095–$70,926	6%
$70,927–$89,636	8%
$89,637 and above	9.3%
>$1,000,000	1% surcharge

Hawaii
$0–$4,800	1.4%
$4,801–$9,600	3.2%
$9,601–$19,200	5.5%
$19,201–$28,800	6.4%
$28,801–$38,400	6.8%
$38,401–$48,000	7.2%
$48,001–$72,000	7.6%
$72,001–$96,000	7.9%
$96,001 and above	8.25%

Wisconsin
$0–$12,680	4.6%
$12,681–$25,360	6.15%
$25,361–$190,210	6.5%
$190,211 and above	6.75%

Michigan
4.35% of taxable income

Illinois
3% of taxable net income

New York
$0–$8,000	4%
$8,001–$11,000	4.5%
$11,001–$13,000	5.25%
$13,001–$20,000	5.9%
$20,001 and above	6.85%

New Hampshire
5% of interest and dividends

Pennsylvania
3.07%

Indiana
3.4% of adjusted gross income

Georgia
First $1000	1%
Next $2000	2%
Next $2000	3%
Next $2000	4%
Next $3000	5%
Over $10,000	6%

North Carolina
Up to $21,250	6%
Next $78,750	7%
Next $100,000	7.75%
Over $200,000	8.25%

DATA: *State Tax Websites*

Finding the State Withholding Tax

 EXAMPLE 6

Hilda Worthington works as a nurse in Indiana and earns $4250 for the month. Find the tax rate for Indiana from the chart on the previous page and calculate the state withholding tax.

SOLUTION

Indiana has a flat tax rate of 3.4%.

$$\text{Tax} = \$4250 \times .034 = \$144.50$$

QUICK CHECK 6

An optometrist assistant lives in Michigan and earns $3225 one month. Find the tax rate for Michigan from the chart on the previous page and calculate the state withholding tax.

OBJECTIVE 5 Find net pay when given gross wages, taxes, and other deductions. It is common for employees to request additional deductions, such as union dues and credit union payments. The final amount of pay received by the employee equals gross earnings minus deductions. This final amount is called net pay and is given by the following formula.

Finding Net Pay

Gross earnings

  − FICA tax (Social Security)
  − Medicare tax
  − Federal withholding tax
  − State withholding tax
  − Other deductions

Net pay

You may be thinking that is a lot of deductions, and it is. However, the category "other deductions" may include payments for medical care, life insurance, disability insurance, vision insurance, and retirement contributions. So there can be many deductions and they differ widely from employee to employee. It is important that employers calculate these numbers carefully and correctly.

Determining Net Pay After Deductions EXAMPLE 7

Kizzy Johnstone is married and claims three withholding allowances. Her weekly gross earnings are $643.35. Her state withholding is 2.5% and her union dues are $25. Find her net pay using the percentage method of withholding.

SOLUTION

First find FICA (Social Security) tax, which is $39.89; then Medicare, which is $9.33. Federal withholding tax is $12.98 and state withholding is $16.08. Total deductions are

$39.89	FICA tax (6.2%)
9.33	Medicare tax (1.45%)
$12.98	federal withholding
16.08	state withholding (2.5%)
+ 25.00	union dues
$103.28	total deductions

Find net pay by subtracting total deductions from gross earnings.

$643.35	gross earnings
− **$103.28**	total deductions
$540.07	net pay

Johnstone will receive a paycheck for $540.07.

QUICK CHECK 7

Al Weinstock has monthly gross earnings of $8762, is married, and claims three withholding allowances. His state withholding is 3% and his union dues are $58. Find his *net pay* using the percentage method of withholding.

OBJECTIVE 6 Find the quarterly amount owed to the Internal Revenue Service. An employee's contribution to Social Security and Medicare must be matched by the employer.

Finding the Amount of FICA and Medicare Tax Due EXAMPLE 8

If the employees at Fair Oaks Automotive Repair pay a total of $789.10 in Social Security tax and $182.10 in Medicare tax, how much must the employer send to the Internal Revenue Service?

SOLUTION

The employer must match this amount and send a total of $971.20 ($789.10 + $182.10 from employees) + $971.20 (from employer) = $1942.40 to the government.

QUICK CHECK 8

Payless Dry Cleaners withheld $461.90 in Social Security tax and $108.03 in Medicare tax from employees. How much must the employer send to the Internal Revenue Service?

In addition to withholding the employee's Social Security tax and a matching amount paid by the employer, the employer must also send the amount withheld for income tax to the Internal Revenue Service on a quarterly basis.

Finding the Employer's Amount Due the IRS EXAMPLE 9

During a certain quarter one movie theater collected $2765.42 from its employees for FICA tax, $646.75 for Medicare tax, and $3572.86 in federal withholding tax. Compute the total amount due to the government.

SOLUTION

$2765.42	collected from *employees* for FICA tax
2765.42	equal amount paid by *employer* for FICA tax
646.75	collected from *employees* for Medicare tax
646.75	equal amount paid by *employer* for Medicare tax
3572.86	federal withholding tax
$10,397.20	total due to government

The movie theater must send $10,397.20 to the Internal Revenue Service.

QUICK CHECK 9

In one quarter, City Electronics collected $1953.82 in Social Security tax, $456.75 in Medicare tax, and $3780.47 in federal withholding tax from its employees. Find the total amount due to the government by the employer.

OBJECTIVE 7 Understand additional employer responsibilities and employee benefits. Each quarter, employers must file **Form 941, the Employer's Quarterly Federal Tax Return.** The form itemizes total employee wages and earnings, the income taxes withheld from employees, the FICA taxes withheld from employees, and the FICA taxes paid by the employer. In addition, Form 941 divides the quarter into its three months, and the amounts of the tax liability (employee and employer) are entered on the line of the proper month in that quarter.

The **Federal Unemployment Tax Act (FUTA)** requires employers to pay an additional tax. This **unemployment insurance tax**, paid entirely by employers, is used to pay unemployment benefits to an individual who has become unemployed and is unable to find work. In general, all employers who paid wages of $1500 or more in a calendar quarter, or had one or more employees for some part of a day in any 20 or more different weeks, must file an employer's annual Federal Unemployment Tax (FUTA) return.

Although rates vary, the employer must pay up to 6.2% of the first $7000 in earnings for that year for each employee. Since most states have unemployment taxes, the employer is given credit for these when filing the FUTA return. As soon as the employee reaches earnings of $7000, no additional unemployment tax must be paid.

The **fringe benefits** offered today are very important to employees. These are the extras offered by the employer that go beyond the paycheck and include health care, dental care, retirement plan contributions, day care, housing, life insurance, tuition reimbursement, sick leave, vacation, profit sharing, and other benefits.

6.4 Exercises

The **QUICK START** *exercises in each section contain solutions to help you get started.*

FEDERAL WITHHOLDING TAX   *Find the federal withholding tax for the following employees. Use the wage bracket method. (See Examples 1 and 2.)*

QUICK START

	Employee	Gross Earnings	Married?	Withholding Allowances	Federal Withholding Tax
1.	Safron, I.	$3128.51 monthly	yes	3	$101
2.	Stanger, J.	$425.76 weekly	no	2	$19
3.	Costa, P.	$507.52 weekly	yes	0	_____
4.	Elle, M.	$2416.88 monthly	yes	1	_____
5.	Alexander, L.	$1868.29 monthly	no	2	_____
6.	Schaller, M.	$1953.35 monthly	no	1	_____
7.	Moss, L.	$3212.50 monthly	yes	5	_____
8.	Zagmon, B.	$391.18 weekly	no	1	_____
9.	Mehta, S.	$1622.41 monthly	no	3	_____
10.	Sommerfield, K.	$465.92 weekly	yes	0	_____
11.	Weisner, W.	$1834.57 monthly	no	3	_____
12.	NgauTibbits, C.	$748.30 weekly	yes	2	_____

STATE WITHHOLDING TAX   *Use the state income tax rate given to find the state withholding tax for the following employees. Round to the nearest cent. (See Example 6.)*

QUICK START

	Employee	Gross Weekly Earnings	State Income Tax Rate	State Withholding
13.	Azzaro, J.	$245.18	2.8%	$6.87
14.	Burner, P.	$368.53	3.5%	$12.90
15.	Davis, L.	$466.71	6%	_____
16.	Lundborg, J.	$541.45	5%	_____
17.	Fox, D.	$1607.23	4.3%	_____
18.	Ticarro, C.	$2802.58	4.95%	_____

indicates an exercise that is related to the Case in Point feature.

EMPLOYEE NET PAY   *Use the percentage method of withholding to find federal withholding tax, a 6.2% FICA rate to find FICA tax, and 1.45% to find Medicare tax for the following employees. Then find the net pay for each employee. The number of withholding allowances and the marital status are listed after each employee's name. Assume that no employee has earned over $110,000 so far this year. (See Examples 3 and 5.)*

QUICK START

Employee	Gross Earnings	FICA	Medicare Tax	Federal Withholding Tax	Net Pay
19. Hamel; 4, M	$576.28 weekly	$35.73	$8.36	$0	$532.19
20. Guardino; 3, S	$2878.12 monthly	$178.44	$41.73	$191.69	$2466.26
21. Foster; 1, S	$3512.53 monthly				
22. Erb; 2, M	$625 weekly				
23. Terry; 3, M	$2276.83 semimonthly				
24. Galluccio; 1, S	$420.17 weekly				
25. Derma; 6, M	$2971.06 semimonthly				
26. Eddy; 2, M	$1020 weekly				
27. Wann; 3, S	$3753.18 biweekly				
28. Zamost; 2, S	$6625.24 monthly				
29. Reilly; 1, S	$1786.44 weekly				
30. Gertz; 4, M	$2618.50 biweekly				

31. Write an explanation of how to determine the federal withholding tax using the wage bracket (tax tables) method. (See Objective 2.)

32. Write an explanation of how to find the federal withholding tax using the percentage method. (See Objective 3.)

33. In your present or past job, which deductions were subtracted from gross earnings to arrive at net pay? Which was the largest deduction?

34. If you were an employer, would you prefer to use the wage bracket method or the percentage method to determine federal withholding tax? Why? (See Objectives 2 and 3.)

AMOUNT OWED THE IRS *Calculate the total amount owed to the Internal Revenue Service from each of the following firms. (See Example 9.)*

QUICK START

Firm	FICA Tax Collected from Employees	Medicare Tax Collected from Employees	Total Federal Withholding Tax	Amount Due IRS
35. Starbucks	$1483.59	$342.37	$5096.13	$8748.05
36. Atlasta Ranch	$265.36	$61.24	$4111.68	_____
37. Tony Balony's	$8212.18	$1895.37	$33,117.42	_____
38. Plescia Produce	$212.78	$49.10	$958.68	_____
39. Todd Consultants	$7271.39	$1678.24	$26,423.84	_____
40. Hartmann Shoes	$6538.42	$1508.87	$22,738.57	_____

Use the percentage method of withholding, a FICA rate of 6.2%, a Medicare rate of 1.45%, an SDI rate of %, and a state withholding tax of 3.4% in the following problems.

QUICK START

41. MARKETING REPRESENTATIVE David Horwitz, an industrial salesperson, has weekly earnings of $975. He is married and claims four withholding allowances. His deductions include FICA, Medicare, federal withholding, state disability insurance, state withholding, union dues of $15.50, and credit union savings of $100. Find his net pay for a week in February.

41. $691.67

Net pay = $975 − $60.45 − $14.14 − $50.34 − $9.75 − $33.15 − $15.50 − $100 = $691.67

42. STARBUCKS DISTRICT MANAGER Awanata Jackson, district manager for Starbucks, has earnings of $1147 in one week of March. She is single and claims four withholding allowances. Her deductions include FICA, Medicare, federal withholding, state disability insurance, state withholding, a United Way contribution of $15, and a savings bond of $100. Find her net pay for the week.

42. _____

43. EDUCATIONAL SALES Karen Jordon, a salesperson for Weber Scientific, is paid a salary of $410 per week plus 7% of all sales over $5000. She is single and claims two withholding allowances. Her deductions include FICA, Medicare, federal withholding, state disability insurance, state withholding, credit union savings of $50, a Salvation Army contribution of $10, and dues of $15 to the National Association of Professional Saleswomen. Find her net pay for a week in April during which she had sales of $11,284 with returns and allowances of $424.50.

43. _____

44. TRAVEL-AGENCY SALES Scott Salman, a travel agent, is paid on a variable commission, is married, and claims four withholding allowances. He receives 3% of the first $20,000 in sales, 4% of the next $10,000 in sales, and 6% of all sales over $30,000. This week he has sales of $45,550 and the following deductions: FICA, Medicare, federal withholding, state disability insurance, state withholding, a retirement contribution of $45, a savings bond of $50, and charitable contributions of $20. Find his net pay after subtracting all of his deductions.

44. _____

45. HEATING-COMPANY REPRESENTATIVE   Evelyn Beaton, a commission sales representative for Alternative Heating Company, is paid a monthly salary of $4200 plus a bonus of 1.5% on monthly sales. She is married and claims three withholding allowances. Her deductions include FICA, Medicare, federal withholding, state disability insurance, no state withholding, credit union savings of $150, charitable contributions of $25, and a savings bond of $50. Find her net pay for a month in which her sales were $42,618. The state in which Beaton works has no state income tax.

45. _____

46. RIVER RAFT MANAGER   River Raft Adventures pays its manager, Kathryn Speers, a monthly salary of $2880 plus a commission of .8% based on total monthly sales volume. In May, River Raft Adventures has total sales of $86,280. Speers is married and claims five withholding allowances. Her deductions include FICA, Medicare, federal withholding, state disability insurance, state withholding of $159.30, credit union payment of $300, March of Dimes contribution of $20, and savings bonds of $250. Find her net pay for May.

46. _____

QUICK CHECK ANSWERS

1. $8

2. $29

3. $104.06

4. $444.55

5. $875.82

6. $140.29 (rounded)

7. $6672.08

8. $1139.86

9. $8601.61

Chapter 6   Quick Review

Chapter Terms   *Review the following terms to test your understanding of the chapter. For each term you do not know, refer to the page number found next to that term.*

allowances [p. 230]
commission rate [p. 229]
compensatory (comp) time [p. 220]
daily overtime [p. 219]
deductions [p. 216]
differential piece rate [p. 228]
double time [p. 220]
draw [p. 231]
Fair Labor Standards Act [p. 218]
Federal Insurance Contributions Act (FICA) [p. 235]
Federal Unemployment Tax Act (FUTA) [p. 249]

Form 941 [p. 249]
fringe benefits [p. 249]
gross earnings [p. 216]
hourly wage [p. 217]
incentive rates [p. 227]
income tax withholdings [p. 241]
marital status [p. 241]
Medicare [p. 235]
net pay [p. 235]
overtime [p. 218]
overtime premium method [p. 219]
pay period [p. 220]
payroll ledger [p. 217]

percentage method [p. 244]
personal income tax [p. 241]
piecework rate [p. 227]
premium payment plans [p. 220]
quotas [p. 228]
rate of commission [p. 230]
Request for Earnings and Benefit Estimate Statement [p. 236]
returns [p. 230]
salary [p. 220]
salary plus commission [p. 231]
SDI deduction [p. 238]
shift differential [p. 220]

sliding scale [p. 231]
Social Security [p. 235]
split-shift premium [p. 220]
state income tax [p. 246]
straight commission [p. 229]
time-and-a-half rate [p. 218]
time card [p. 216]
time rates [p. 227]
unemployment insurance tax [p. 249]
variable commission [p. 231]
wage bracket method [p. 244]
withholding allowances [p. 241]

CONCEPTS

EXAMPLES

6.1 Gross earnings

Gross earnings = Hours worked × Rate per hour

40 hours worked at $8.40 per hour
Gross earnings = **40** × $8.40 = $336

6.1 Gross earnings with overtime

First, find the regular earnings. Then, determine overtime pay at overtime rate. Finally, add regular and overtime earnings.

Gross earnings =
Earnings at regular rate + Earnings at time-and-half rate

40 regular hours at $8.40 per hour
10 overtime hours at time and a half

$$\text{Gross earnings} = (40 \times \$8.40) + (\textbf{10} \times \textbf{\$8.40} \times \textbf{1.5})$$
$$= \$336 + \$126$$
$$= \$462$$

6.1 Common pay periods

PAY PERIOD	PAYCHECKS PER YEAR
Monthly	12
Semimonthly	24
Biweekly	26
Weekly	52

Find the earnings equivalent of $2800 per month for other pay periods.

$$\text{Semimonthly} = \frac{\$2800}{2} = \$1400$$

$$\text{Biweekly} = \frac{\$2800 \times 12}{26} = \$1292.31$$

$$\text{Weekly} = \frac{\$2800 \times 12}{52} = \$646.15$$

6.1 Overtime for salaried employees

First, find the hourly equivalent. Next, multiply the hourly equivalent rate by the overtime hours by 1.5. Finally, add overtime earnings to the salary.

Salary is $648 per week for 40 hours. Find the earnings for 46 hours.

$$\$648 \div \textbf{40} = \$16.20 \text{ per hour}$$
$$\$16.20 \times \textbf{6} \times \textbf{1.5} = \$145.80 \text{ overtime}$$
$$\$648 + \$145.80 = \$793.80$$

6.2 Gross earnings for piecework

Gross earnings = Pay per item × Number of items

Items produced, 175; pay per item, $.65; find the gross earnings.

$$\textbf{\$.65} \times 175 = \$113.75$$

CONCEPTS	EXAMPLES
6.2 Gross earnings for differential piecework The rate paid per item produced varies with level of production.	1–100 items, $1.35 each 101–150 items, $1.45 each 151 or more items, $1.60 each Find the gross earnings for producing 214 items. $100 \times \mathbf{\$1.35} = \$135.00$ first 100 units $50 \times \mathbf{\$1.45} = \$72.50$ next 50 units $\underline{64 \times \mathbf{\$1.60} = \$102.40}$ number over 150 214 total items $309.90 total earnings
6.2 Overtime earnings on piecework Gross earnings = Earnings at regular rate + Earnings at overtime rate	Items produced on regular time, 530; items produced on over-time, 110; piece rate $.60; find the gross earnings. Gross earnings = $(530 \times \mathbf{\$.60}) + \mathbf{110(1.5 \times \$.60)} = \mathbf{\$318} + \mathbf{\$99}$ $= \$417$
6.2 Straight commission Gross earnings = Commission rate × Amount of sales	Sales of $25,800; commission rate is 5%. $\mathbf{.05} \times \$25,800 = \$1290$
6.2 Variable commission Commission rate varies at different sales levels.	Up to $10,000, 6% $10,001–$20,000, 8% $20,001 and up, 9% Find the commission on sales of $32,768. $\mathbf{.06} \times \$10,000 = \$600.00$ first $10,000 $\mathbf{.08} \times \$10,000 = \$800.00$ next $10,000 $\underline{\mathbf{.09} \times \$12,768 = \$1149.12}$ amount over $20,000 $32,768 $2549.12 total commission
6.2 Salary and commission Gross earnings = Fixed earnings + Commission	Salary, $450 per week; commission rate, 3%; find the gross earnings on sales of $6848. Gross earnings = $\$450 + (\mathbf{.03 \times \$6848}) = \$450 + \mathbf{\$205.44}$ $= \$655.44$
6.2 Commission with a drawing account Gross earnings = Commission − Draw	Sales for month, $38,560; commission rate, 7%; draw, $750 for month; find the gross earnings. Gross earnings = $(\mathbf{.07 \times \$38,560}) - \$750 = \mathbf{\$2699.20} - \$750$ $= \$1949.20$
6.3 FICA; Social Security tax The gross earnings are multiplied by the tax rate. When the maximum earnings are reached, no additional FICA is withheld that year.	Gross earnings, $458; Social Security tax rate, 6.2%; find the Social Security tax. $\$458 \times \mathbf{.062} = \$28.40$
6.3 Medicare tax The gross earnings are multiplied by the Medicare tax rate. Medicare tax is paid on all earnings.	Gross earnings, $458; Medicare tax rate, 1.45%; find the Medicare tax. $\$458 \times \mathbf{.0145} = \$6.64$
6.3 State disability insurance deductions Multiply the gross earnings by the SDI tax rate. When the maximum earnings are reached, no additional taxes are paid in that year.	Gross earnings, $2880; SDI tax rate, 1%; find SDI tax. $\$2880 \times \mathbf{.01} = \$28.80$

CONCEPTS	EXAMPLES
6.4 Federal withholding tax—wage bracket A tax must be paid on the total earnings. Look up the amount in the wage bracket table.	Single employee, 3 allowances, weekly earnings of $468. Find withholding amount. Wage bracket table for single, weekly, row with at least $460 but less than $470, 3 allowances. Withholding = **$14**

6.4 Federal withholding tax—percentage
 	
A tax must be paid on the total earnings.
  1. Multiply number of withholding allowances by the amount for one allowance from table.
  2. Find gross earnings – amount in step 1.
  3. Use the appropriate table and row.
  4. Follow the directions in the table.
	Single employee, 3 allowances, weekly earnings of $468. Find withholding amount.
	  1. 3 allowances $\times$ $70.19 = **$210.57**
	  2. $468 − **$210.57** = **$257.43**
	  3. Table for single, weekly, row for over $200 but not over $696
	  4. $6.20 + 15% of excess over $200
	    = $6.20 + .15 $\times$ (**$257.43** − $200)
	    = $14.81

6.4 State withholding tax Tax is paid on total earnings. No maximum as with FICA.	Married employee with weekly earnings of $692; find the state withholding tax given a state withholding tax rate of 4.5%. **4.5%** $\times$ $692 = .045 $\times$ $692 = $31.14

6.4 Quarterly report, Form 941
 	
Filed each quarter and calculated as follows:
 	
  FICA paid by employees
  FICA paid by employer
  Medicare paid by employees
  Medicare paid by employer
  + Federal withholding tax paid by employees
  <u>Total to be sent to the IRS</u>
	If quarterly FICA withheld from employees is $5269, Medicare tax is $1581, and federal withholding tax is $14,780, find the total owed to the IRS by the employer.
	
	  (**$5269 + $1581**) $\times$ **2** + $14,780 = $28,480

case study

PAYROLL: FINDING YOUR TAKE-HOME PAY

Janice Wong receives an annual salary of $42,536, which is paid weekly. Her normal workweek is 40 hours, and she is paid time and a half for all overtime. She is single and claims one withholding allowance. Her deductions include FICA, Medicare, federal withholding, state disability insurance, state withholding, credit union payments of $125, retirement deductions of $75, association dues of $12, and a Diabetes Association contribution of $25. Find each of the following for a week in which she works 52 hours.

1. Regular weekly earnings

2. Overtime earnings

3. Total gross earnings

4. FICA

5. Medicare

6. Federal withholding using the percentage method

7. State disability insurance deduction

8. State withholding (Assume that the state income tax rate is 4.4%.)

9. Net pay

1. _____

2. _____

3. _____

4. _____

5. _____

6. _____

7. _____

8. _____

9. _____

INVESTIGATE

Look at the statement that you received with your last paycheck. Be certain that your gross earnings are correct. Understand and check all of the deductions made by your employer. Subtract all deductions from your gross earnings to be certain that your net pay is accurate.

case _{IN} point summary exercise

PAYROLL AT STARBUCKS

www.SSA.GOV

Facts:

- 1935: Social Security Act passed
- 1937: First Social Security taxes collected
- 1965: Medicare established
- 2010: More than 50 million receive Social Security payments
- 2011: More than 43 million receive Medicare benefits

Sarah Brynski is busy running a Starbucks and thinking about inventory, making sure the store looks great, ensuring good service, hiring good people, motivating employees, maintaining inventories, calculating wages, deducting correct amounts for the various taxes, and getting the payroll done on time every week. She is also interested in finding ways to increase sales since part of her income is based on sales. Overtime is paid for more than 40 hours a week, the state tax rate is 3.07%, and the state disability income rate (SDI) is 1%.

1. Use the percentage method and help her calculate the weekly payroll for the employees listed.

Employee	Hourly Wage	Hours Worked	Total Pay	FICA	Medicare	Federal Tax	State Tax	SDI	Other	Net Pay
Betinez, S., 1	$8.75	28	___	___	___	___	___	___	$0	___
Parton, M., 2	$12.25	45	___	___	___	___	___	___	$25	___
Dickens, S., 0	$9.35	30	___	___	___	___	___	___	$10	___

2. Assume Brynski receives a base salary of $450 per week plus a commission of 6% of sales over $5000. Do her weekly payroll for a week with $8432 in sales.

Employee	Base Salary	Comm.	Total Pay	FICA	Medicare	Federal Tax	State Tax	SDI	Other	Net Pay
Brynski, M., 2	___	___	___	___	___	___	___	___	$65	___

3. Find the amount Brynski must send to the Internal Revenue Service for these employees.

4. Find the amount Brynski must send to the state including income tax and disability insurance.

Discussion Question: Why would the regional manager at Starbucks oversee Byrnski and the other store managers when they do payroll? Can you think of advantages if the main corporate office took over payroll calculations, payments to the IRS, and payments to the various states? Explain.

Chapter 6 Test

To help you review, the numbers in brackets show the section in which the topic was discussed.

Complete the following payroll ledger. Find the total gross earnings for each employee.
Time and a half is paid on all hours over 40 in one week. **[6.1]**

EMPLOYEE	HOURS WORKED	REG. HRS.	O.T. HRS.	REG. RATE	GROSS EARNINGS
1. Bianchi	46.5	____	____	$10.80	_____
2. Hanna	47.5	____	____	$8.60	_____

Solve the following application problems.

3. Judy Martinez is paid $34,060 annually. Find the equivalent earnings if this amount is paid **(a)** weekly, **(b)** biweekly, **(c)** semimonthly, and **(d)** monthly. **[6.2]**

(a) _____

(b) _____

(c) _____

(d) _____

4. At Jalisco Electronics, assemblers are paid according to the following differential piece rate scale: 1–20 units in a day, $4.50 each; 21–30 units, $5.50 each; and $7 each for every unit over 30. Adrian Ortega assembled 70 units in one week. Find his gross pay. **[6.2]**

4. _____

5. Rheonna Winston receives a commission of 6% for selling a $235,500 house. One-half of the commission goes to the broker and one-half of the remainder to another salesperson. Winston gets the rest. Find the amount she receives. **[6.2]**

5. _____

An employee is paid a salary of $9300 per month. If the current FICA rate is 6.2% on the first $110,000 of earnings, and the Medicare tax rate is 1.45% of all earnings, how much should be withheld for (a) FICA tax and (b) Medicare tax during the following months? **[6.3]**

6. March: **(a)** _____   **(b)** _____   7. December: **(a)** _____   **(b)** _____

Find the federal withholding tax using the wage bracket method for each of the following employees. **[6.4]**

8. Ahearn: 2 withholding allowances, single, $415.82 weekly earnings

8. _____

9. Zanotti: 2 withholding allowances, married, $675.25 weekly earnings

9. _____

10. Allgier: 3 withholding allowances, married, $3210.55 monthly earnings

10. _____

11. Yeoman: 4 withholding allowances, single, $2046.75 monthly earnings

11. _____

12. Benner: 5 withholding allowances, married, $2864.47 monthly earnings

12. _____

Find the net pay for each of the following employees after FICA, Medicare, federal withholding tax, state disability insurance, and other deductions have been taken out. Assume that none has earned over $110,000 so far this year. Assume a FICA rate of 6.2%, Medicare rate of 1.45%, and a state disability insurance rate of 1%. Use the percentage method of withholding. **[6.3 and 6.4]**

13. Tran: $1852.75 monthly earnings, 1 withholding allowance, single, $37.80 in other deductions

13. _____

14. Pupek: $1028 weekly earnings, 3 withholding allowances, married, state withholding of $50.50, credit union savings of $50, contribution of $20

14. _____

15. Comar: $677.92 weekly earnings, 6 withholding allowances, married, state withholding of $22.18, union dues of $14, charitable contribution of $15

15. _____

Solve the following application problems.

16. Joseph Flores is paid $452 per week plus a commission of 2% on all sales. Flores sold $712 worth of goods on Monday, $523 on Tuesday, $1002 on Wednesday, $391 on Thursday, and $609 on Friday. Returns and allowances for the week were $114. Find the employee's **(a)** Social Security tax (6.2%), **(b)** Medicare tax (1.45%), and **(c)** state disability insurance deduction (1%) for the week. **[6.3 and 6.4]**

(a) _____
(b) _____
(c) _____

17. Neta Fitzgerald earned $107,375.60 so far this year. This week she earned $2649.78. Find her **(a)** FICA tax and **(b)** Medicare tax for this week's earnings. **[6.3]**

(a) _____
(b) _____

For Exercises 18 and 19, find (a) the Social Security tax and (b) the Medicare tax for each of the following self-employed people. Use a FICA tax rate of 12.4% and a Medicare tax rate of 2.9%. **[6.3]**

18. Kirby: $36,714.12

(a) _____
(b) _____

19. Biondi: $42,380.62

(a) _____
(b) _____

20. The employees of Quick-Lube paid a total of $418.12 in Social Security tax last month, $96.48 in Medicare tax, and $1217.34 in federal withholding tax. Find the total amount that the employer must send to the Internal Revenue Service.

20. _____

Mathematics of Buying

7

case in point ▶

BED BATH & BEYOND INC. owns and operates a chain of home-furnishing specialty stores selling items such as bed linens, bath accessories, cookware, dinnerware, kitchen utensils, and small electric appliances. Customer service in a family-style atmosphere is an essential part of the firm's marketing strategy. The firm gives more authority to store managers than most other chains. The store managers even decide which of the firm's 30,000+ products to carry in their stores.

Jack Williams works in the main offices of Bed Bath & Beyond in the purchasing department. He works with some of the many firms that supply Bed Bath & Beyond with products. His job requires that he remain in close contact with marketing to make sure he knows what is selling and what is not selling. He also needs to understand consumer trends since products are often ordered months before they are available for sale in the stores. The last thing he wants to do is order products that no one will want to buy.

Williams works every day with suppliers to get the biggest discount possible. He knows that controlling costs is very important in maintaining profits. Besides, part of his salary is based on a bonus. The better the firm does, the more he makes. So, he has every incentive to help keep costs low and the right products flowing smoothly to the company stores.

Retail businesses make a profit by buying items and then selling them for more than they cost. As shown by the following **supply chain**, or **distribution chain**, many companies are involved in the process of building and supplying products so that they are on shelves in stores and available to customers. Of course, not every supply chain has all these firms since some use the Internet to bypass some of the steps in the traditional supply chain. For example, Dell Computer does most of its business on the Internet, thereby avoiding wholesalers and retailers.

Raw Materials ⟶ Suppliers ⟶ Manufacturing ⟶ Wholesale ⟶ Retail

Businesses use **invoices** to keep track of sales. An invoice describes the seller and buyer, the items purchased, and the number of items purchased and provides detailed cost information. Today, many firms send and receive invoices electronically over the Internet. Some simply work digitally with the invoices; others print out paper copies of the invoices. This chapter covers the mathematics needed for working with invoices and discounts.

7.1 Invoices and Trade Discounts

OBJECTIVES

1 Complete an invoice.
2 Understand common shipping terms.
3 Identify invoice abbreviations.
4 Calculate trade discounts and understand why they are given.
5 Differentiate between single and series discounts.
6 Calculate each series discount separately.
7 Use complements to calculate series discounts.
8 Use a table to find the net cost equivalent of series discounts.

case IN point ▶

Since he works with invoices every day in his job in purchasing at Bed Bath & Beyond, Jack Williams must have a good understanding of trade discounts, cash discounts, and shipping terms.

OBJECTIVE 1 Complete an invoice. An invoice from J. B. Sherr is found on the next page. It is a **sales invoice** for J. B. Sherr but a **purchase invoice** for Bed Bath & Beyond. Among other things, it shows the quantity ordered, the number shipped, the **unit price**, and the **extension total** (column labeled **Amount**), which is the number of an item shipped multiplied by the unit price. The **invoice total** is the sum of the extension totals.

Trade and cash discounts, discussed later in this chapter, *are never applied to shipping and insurance charges*. For this reason, shipping and insurance charges are often not included in the invoice total, so the purchaser must add them to the invoice total to find the total amount due. In the J. B. Sherr Company invoice, the freight (shipping) charges of $38.90 are included in the INVOICE TOTAL space.

OBJECTIVE 2 Understand common shipping terms. Some common terms found on invoices are defined.

Free on board (FOB) shipping point	Buyer pays for shipping costs. Ownership of goods passes to the purchaser prior to the shipment.
FOB destination	Seller pays the shipping charge and retains ownership until goods reach the destination.
Cash on delivery (COD)	Payment for goods is made at the time of delivery.
Free alongside ship (FAS)	Goods are delivered to the dock with all freight charges to that point paid by the seller.

Since goods can be damaged, lost, or stolen during shipment, it is important for everyone to know which firms own products that are in shipment. That is the only way it will be clear which firm must pay for goods lost or damaged while in shipment.

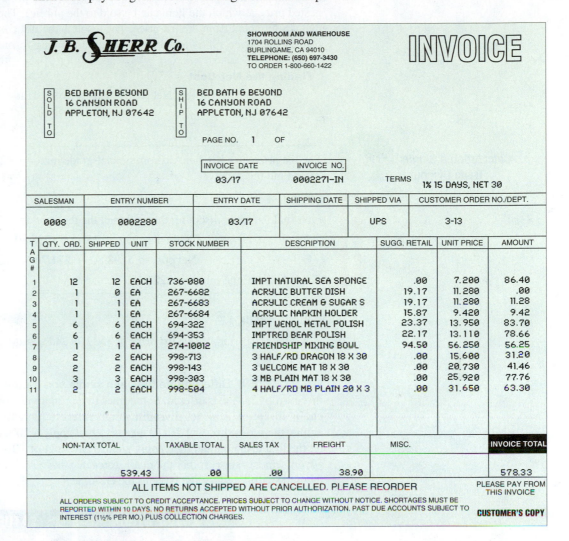

OBJECTIVE 3 Identify invoice abbreviations. Some abbreviations commonly used on invoices to identify measurements, quantities, shipping terms, and discounts are shown in the table.

Invoice Abbreviations

ea.	each	drm.	drum
doz.	dozen	cs.	case
gro.	gross (144 items)	pr.	pair
gr gro.	great gross (12 gross)	C	Roman numeral for 100
qt.	quart	M	Roman numeral for 1000
gal.	gallon (4 quarts)	cwt.	per hundredweight
bbl.	barrel	cpm.	cost per thousand
cL	centiliter	lb.	pound
L	liter	oz.	ounce
in.	inch	g	gram
ft.	foot	kg	kilogram
yd.	yard	ROG	receipt of goods
mm	millimeter	ex. or x	extra dating
cm	centimeter	FOB	free on board
m	meter	EOM	end of month
km	kilometer	COD	cash on delivery
ct.	crate	FAS	free alongside ship

OBJECTIVE 4 Calculate trade discounts and understand why they are given. **Trade discounts** are often given to businesses or individuals who buy an item for resale or produce an item that will then be sold. The seller usually gives the price of an item as its **list price** (the suggested price at which the item can be sold to the public). Then the seller gives a trade discount that is subtracted from the list price. The result is the **net cost** or **net price**, which is the amount paid by the buyer. Find the net cost with the following formula.

> **Finding the Net Cost**
>
> $$\text{Net cost} = \text{List price} - \text{Trade Discount}$$

Calculating a Single Trade Discount

 EXAMPLE 1

The list price of a KitchenAid commercial-grade mixer is $298.80, and the trade discount is 25%. Find the net cost.

SOLUTION

First find the trade discount; then subtract the discount from the list price of $298.80.

$$\text{Trade discount} = 25\% \text{ of } \$298.80 = \textbf{\$74.70}$$
$$\text{Net cost} = \$298.80 - \textbf{\$74.70} = \$224.10$$

The net cost of the mixer is $224.10.

> **QUICK CHECK 1**
>
> A wine refrigerator has a list price of $589.99 and a trade discount of 35%. Find the net cost.

OBJECTIVE 5 Differentiate between single and series discounts. In Example 1, a **single discount** of 25% was offered. Sometimes two or more discounts are combined into a **series**, or **chain**, **discount**. A **series discount** simply refers to more than one discount in a series. For example, the series discount 20/10 means to first apply a 20% discount. Start with the amount after the first discount and then apply another discount of 10%. This is shown in Example 2. The advertisements suggest that the retail stores may have received a large trade discount, allowing them to sharply reduce the price to the customers.

Trade discounts change often due to all the following.

1. Price changes
2. Size of orders placed with suppliers
3. Geographic location
4. Seasonal fluctuations
5. Level of competition

OBJECTIVE 6 Calculate each series discount separately. Three methods can be used to calculate a series discount and net cost. The first of these is **calculating discounts separately**.

Calculating Series Trade Discounts

EXAMPLE 2

case **IN** point

Bed Bath & Beyond is offered a series discount of 20/10 on a Cooking with Calphalon stainless steel cookware set with a list price of $150. Find the net cost after the series discount.

SOLUTION

Apply the first discount in 20/10, which is 20%.

$$\text{Discount} = \textbf{20\% of list price of \$150}$$
$$= \textbf{\$30}$$

$$\text{Amount after first discount} = \$150 - \textbf{\$30} = \$120$$

Now apply the second discount in 20/10, which is 10%. Importantly, apply the discount to the amount after the first discount, or $120.

$$\text{Discount} = 10\% \text{ of discounted price of } \$120$$
$$= \textbf{\$12}$$

$$\text{Net cost} = \$120 - \textbf{\$12} = \$108$$

The net cost is $108.

QUICK CHECK 2

A 12-place setting of stainless steel flatware is list priced at $249.99. If a series discount of 10/15 is offered, what is the net cost after the series discount is taken?

It is important to *never add series discounts together*. For example, a 20/10 discount is not the same as a 30% discount (20% + 10% = 30%). Apply the discounts sequentially, or one after the other.

OBJECTIVE 7 Use complements to calculate series discounts. To find the **complement** of a discount with respect to one, subtract the decimal form of the discount from 1. Here are some examples.

DISCOUNT	DECIMAL EQUIVALENT	FINDING THE COMPLEMENT		COMPLEMENT
10%	.1	1 − .1	=	.90
20%	.20	1 − .2	=	.80
25%	.25	1 − .25	=	.75
30%	.30	1 − .3	=	.70
62%	.62	1 − .62	=	.38

The complement of the discount is the portion actually paid. For example, a 10% discount means that 90% must be paid, and a 25% discount means that 75% must be paid. The complements can be used to find **the net cost equivalent**, which is then used to find the net cost after the discount.

Finding the Discount Using Net Cost Equivalent

1. Find the complement of each discount in the series discount.
2. Find the net cost equivalent by multiplying the complements from step 1.
3. The net cost after the discount is the list price times the net cost equivalent 3.

Using Complements to Find the Net Cost

EXAMPLE 3

Kitchen Crafters is offered a series discount of 20/10 on a George Foreman Grilling Machine with a list price of $180. Find the net cost after the series discount.

SOLUTION

Apply the preceding steps to find the net cost after the discount.

	Discount	Decimal Equivalent	Finding the Complement		Complement
Step 1	20%	.2	1 − .2	=	**.8**
	10%	.1	1 − .1	=	**.9**

Step 2   Net cost equivalent $= .8 \times .9 = \textbf{.72}$

Step 3　Net cost after discount = List price × Net cost equivalent
$$= \$180 \quad \times \quad .72$$
$$= \$129.60$$

To find the actual discount, subtract the net cost after discount from the original price.

$$\text{Discount} = \text{Original price} - \text{Net cost after discount}$$
$$= \quad \$180 \quad - \quad \$129.60$$
$$= \$50.40$$

 On many calculators, you can subtract the discount percents from the list price in a series calculation.

$$180 \boxed{-} 20 \boxed{\%} \boxed{-} 10 \boxed{\%} \boxed{=} 129.6$$

Note: Refer to Appendix B for calculator basics.

> **QUICK CHECK 3**
>
> A supplier offers a series discount of 25/15 on a waffle iron. If the list price of the waffle iron is $135, use the complements with respect to 1 of each of the single discounts to find **(a)** the net cost and **(b)** the amount of the discount.

Using Complements to Solve Series Discounts

EXAMPLE 4

The list price of a Heartland 30-inch combination gas and electric stove is $3095. Find the net cost after a series discount of 20/10/10.

SOLUTION

Start by finding the complements with respect to 1 of each discount.

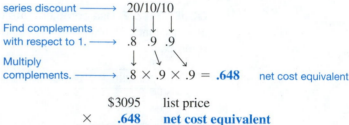

series discount ⟶ 20/10/10
Find complements with respect to 1. ⟶ .8　.9　.9
Multiply complements. ⟶ .8 × .9 × .9 = **.648**　net cost equivalent

$$
\begin{array}{rl}
\$3095 & \text{list price} \\
\times \quad \textbf{.648} & \textbf{net cost equivalent} \\
\hline
\$2005.56 & \text{net cost}
\end{array}
$$

> **QUICK CHECK 4**
>
> A 25-cubic-foot bottom-freezer refrigerator is list priced at $2249.99. What is the net cost after a series discount of 15/20/5?

It is important *not to round* the net cost equivalent. Doing so will often result in a net cost that is not correct.

OBJECTIVE 8 Use a table to find the net cost equivalent of series discounts. Finally, a table such as the following one can be used to find the net cost equivalents for common series discounts. Look in the left column for the first one or two discounts in the series discount. Then, look across the top of the table for the last discount in the series discount. For example, a 10/10/20 series discount has a net cost equivalent of .648.

NET COST EQUIVALENTS OF SERIES DISCOUNTS

	5%	10%	15%	20%	25%	30%	35%	40%
5	.9025	.855	.8075	.76	.7125	.665	.6175	.57
10	.855	.81	.765	.72	.675	.63	.585	.54
10/5	.81225	.7695	.72675	.684	.64125	.5985	.55575	.513
10/10	.7695	.729	.6885	.648	.6075	.567	.5265	.486
15	.8075	.765	.7225	.68	.6375	.595	.5525	.51
15/10	.72675	.6885	.65025	.612	.57375	.5355	.49725	.459
20	.76	.72	.68	.64	.6	.56	.52	.48
20/15	.646	.612	.578	.544	.51	.476	.442	.408
25	.7125	.675	.6375	.6	.5625	.525	.4875	.45
25/20	.57	.54	.51	.48	.45	.42	.39	.36
25/25	.534375	.50625	.478125	.45	.421875	.39375	.365625	.3375
30	.665	.63	.595	.56	.525	.49	.455	.42
40	.57	.54	.51	.48	.45	.42	.39	.36

It does not matter which discount is listed first, since the complements are simply being multiplied. So a 15/20/5 discount is the same as a 20/15/5 discount, whose net cost equivalent can be found in the table.

Using a Table of Net Cost Equivalents

 EXAMPLE 5

Use the previous table to find the net cost equivalents of the following series discounts.

(a) 10/10   **(b)** 20/10   **(c)** 25/25/5   **(d)** 35/20/15

SOLUTION

First find the row and column needed to read the net cost equivalent from the table, then get the net cost equivalent.

(a) Row 10, Column 10%:   Net cost equivalent = .81
(b) Row 20, Column 10%:   Net cost equivalent = .72
(c) Row 25/25, Column 5%:   Net cost equivalent = .534375
(d) There is no row 35/20 corresponding to the first two numbers in 35/20/15. But 35/20/15 is the same thing as 15/20/35 or as 20/15/35. Using the last of these, go to Row 20/15 and Column 35%:   Net cost equivalent = .442

QUICK CHECK 5

Use the table of net cost equivalents to find the net cost equivalents of the following series discounts: **(a)** 30/5, **(b)** 10/40, **(c)** 20/15/10, **(d)** 10/5/5.

The **QUICK START** exercises in each section contain solutions to help you get started.

USING INVOICES *Compute the extension totals and the invoice total for the following invoices.*

QUICK START

HOME ACCESSORIES WHOLESALERS

Sold to: Kitchen Crafters
10100 Fair Oaks Blvd.
Fair Oaks, CA 95628

Date: June 10
Order. No.: 796152
Shipped by: UPS
Terms: Net

	Quantity	Order No./Description	Unit Price	Extension Total
1.	6 doz.	pastry brush, wide	$37.80 doz.	$226.80
2.	3 gro.	napkins, cotton	$12.60 gro.	$37.80
3.	9 doz.	cherry pitters	$14.04 doz.	
4.	8	food processors (3 qt.)	$106.12 ea.	
5.	53 pr.	stainless tongs	$68.12 pr.	
6.			Invoice Total	
			Shipping and Insurance	$85.60
7.			Total Amount Due	

J & K'S MUSTANG PARTS
New and Used

Sold to: Dave's Auto Body & Paint
4443-B Auburn Blvd.
York, PA 17402

Date: July 17
Order. No.: 100603
Shipped by: Emery
Terms: Net

	Quantity	Order No./Description	Unit Price	Extension Total
8.	24	filler tube gaskets	$2.25 ea.	
9.	12 pr.	taillight lens gaskets	$4.75 pr.	
10.	6 pr.	taillight bezels to body	$10.80 pr.	
11.	2 gr.	door panel fasteners	$14.20 gr.	
12.	18	bumper bolt kits	$16.50 ea.	
13.			Invoice Total	
			Shipping and Insurance	$139.40
14.			Total Amount Due	

ABBREVIATIONS ON INVOICES *What does each of the following abbreviations represent?*

QUICK START

15. ft. _foot_

16. sk. _sack_

17. pr. _____

18. gr. gro. _____

19. kg _____

20. qt. _____

21. cs. _____

22. gro. _____

23. drm. _____

24. yd. _____

25. L _____

26. cpm. _____

27. gal. _____

28. cwt. _____

29. COD _____

30. FOB _____

 indicates an exercise that is related to the Case in Point feature.

31. Name six items that appear on an invoice. Try to do this without looking at an invoice. (See Objective 1.)

32. Explain in your own words the difference between *FOB shipping point* and *FOB destination*. In each case, who pays for shipping? When does ownership of the merchandise transfer? (See Objective 2.)

Using complements (with respect to 1) of the single discounts, find the net cost equivalents for each of the following discounts. Do not round. (See Examples 3 and 4.)

QUICK START

33. 10/20 $.9 \times .8 = .72$	**34.** 20/20 $.8 \times .8 = .64$
35. 10/10/10 $.9 \times .9 \times .9 = .729$	**36.** 15/20/25 $.85 \times .8 \times .75 = .51$
37. 25/5 _____	**38.** 5/15 _____
39. 40/30/20 _____	**40.** 20/20/10 _____
41. 50/10/20/5 _____	**42.** 25/10/20/10 _____

Find the net cost of each of the following list prices. Round to the nearest cent. (See Examples 1–4.)

QUICK START

43. $418 less 20/20 **$267.52**	**44.** $148 less 25/10 **$99.90**
45. $16.40 less 5/10 _____	**46.** $860 less 20/40 _____
47. $1260 less 15/25/10 _____	**48.** $8.80 less 40/10/20 _____
49. $380 less 20/10/20 _____	**50.** $2008 less 10/5/20 _____
51. $22 less 10/15 _____	**52.** $25 less 30/20 _____
53. $980 less 10/10/10 _____	**54.** $8220 less 30/5/10 _____
55. $2000 less 10/40/10 _____	**56.** $1630 less 10/5/10 _____
57. $1250 less 20/20/20 _____	**58.** $1410 less 10/20/5 _____

59. Identify and explain four reasons that might cause series trade discounts to change. (See Objective 5.)

60. Explain the difference between a single trade discount and a series or chain trade discount.

61. Explain what a complement (with respect to 1 or 100%) is. Give an example. (See Objective 7.)

62. Using complements, explain how to find the net cost equivalent of a 25/20 series discount. Explain why a 25/10/10 series discount is not the same as a 25/20 discount. (See Objective 7.)

Solve the following application problems in trade discount. Round to the nearest cent.

QUICK START

63. **VIDEO PLAYER**   The list price of a Zune 120 GB MP3/Video
    Player is $299.99. If the series discount offered is 10/10/25, what
    is the net cost after trade discounts?

    .9 × .9 × .75 = .6075
    $299.99 × .6075 = $182.243 = $182.24

63. __$182.24_____

64. **NURSING-CARE PURCHASES**   Roger Wheatley, a restorative
    nursing assistant (RNA), finds that the list price of one dozen
    adjustable walkers is $1680. Find the cost per walker if a series
    discount of 40/25 is offered.

64. _____

65. **KITCHEN ISLAND**   Kitchen Crafters purchases a tile-topped wooden kitchen island list
    priced at $480. It is available at either a 10/15/10 discount or a 20/15 discount.
    (a) Which discount gives the lower price? **(b)** Find the difference in net cost.

    (a) _____
    (b) _____

66. **HARDWARE PURCHASE**   Oaks Hardware purchases an extension ladder list priced at
    $120. It is available at either a 10/10/10 discount or a 15/15 discount. **(a)** Which discount
    gives the lower price? **(b)** Find the difference.

    (a) _____
    (b) _____

67. **TRIPOD PURCHASE**   The list price of an aluminum tripod is $65. It is available at either a
    15/10/10 discount or a 15/20 discount. **(a)** Which discount gives the lower price?
    (b) Find the difference.

    (a) _____
    (b) _____

68. **LIQUID FERTILIZER**   Continental Fertilizer Supply offers a series discount of 10/20/20
    on major purchases. If a 58,000-gallon tank (bulk) of liquid fertilizer is list priced at
    $27,200, what is the net cost after trade discounts?

    68. _____

69. **HOME BEVERAGE FOUNTAINS**   Bed Bath & Beyond
    receives a 10/5/20 series trade discount from a supplier. If
    they purchase 4 dozen Bella Home beverage fountains list
    priced at $468 per dozen, find the net cost.

69. _____

70. **WHOLESALE AUTO PARTS**   Kimara Swenson, an automotive mechanics instructor, is offered mechanics' net prices on all purchases at Foothill Auto Supply. If mechanics' net prices mean a 10/20 discount, how much will Swenson spend on a dozen sets of metallic brake pads that are list priced at $648 per dozen?

70. _____

71. **BULK CHEMICALS**   Brazilian Chemical Supply offers a series discount of 5/20/5 on all bulk purchases. A tank (bulk) of industrial solvent is list priced at $78,500. What is the net cost after trade discounts?

71. _____

72. **DANCE SHOES**   How much will Giselle, a dance instructor, pay for three dozen pairs of dance shoes if the list price is $144 per dozen and a series discount of 10/25/30 is offered?

72. _____

73. **TRADE-DISCOUNT COMPARISON**   The Door Store offers a series trade discount of 30/20 to its builder customers. Robert Gonzalez, a new employee in the billing department, understood the 30/20 terms to mean 50% and computed this trade discount on a list price of $5440. How much difference did this error make in the amount of the invoice?

73. _____

74. **FIBER OPTICS**   Pam Gondola has a choice of two suppliers of fiber optics for her business. Tyler Suppliers offers a 20/10/25 discount on a list price of $5.70 per unit. Irving Optics offers a 30/20 discount on a list price of $5.40 per unit. **(a)** Which supplier gives her the lower price? **(b)** Find the amount saved if she buys 12,500 units from the lower-priced supplier. (*Hint:* Do not round.)

(a) _____

(b) _____

7.2 Series Discounts and Single Discount Equivalents

OBJECTIVES

1 Express a series discount as an equivalent single discount.

2 Find the list price given the series discount and the net cost.

At Bed Bath & Beyond, Jack Williams pays close attention to all invoices received from suppliers. He knows that the invoices sometimes have mistakes on them, and he wants to minimize mistakes, particularly overpayments to suppliers.

OBJECTIVE 1 **Express a series discount as an equivalent single discount.** Series or chain discounts are often expressed as a single discount rate. Find a **single discount equivalent** to a series discount by subtracting the net cost equivalent from 1. This discount is equivalent to the series discount and is always written as a percent.

Finding the Single Discount Equivalent

Single discount equivalent = 1 − Net cost equivalent

Finding a Single Discount Equivalent **EXAMPLE 1**

If the Optimum Energy Company offered a 20/10 discount to wholesale accounts on all heating, ventilation, and cooling systems, what was the single discount equivalent?

SOLUTION

series discount ⟶ 20/10

Find complements ⟶ .8   .9
with respect to 1.

Multiply complements. ⟶ .8 × .9 = **.72**   net cost equivalent

$$
\begin{array}{ll}
1.00 & \text{base (100\%)} \\
-\ .72 & \textbf{net cost equivalent (remains)} \\
\hline
.28 & \text{or 28\% was discounted}
\end{array}
$$

The single discount equivalent of a 20/10 series discount is 28%.

QUICK CHECK 1

Baltimore Wholesale Electric offers a 30/20 discount on wholesale purchases of all small appliances. What is the single discount equivalent?

OBJECTIVE 2 **Find the list price given the series discount and the net cost.** Sometimes the net cost after trade discounts is given, along with the series discount, and the list price must be found.

Solving for the List Price **EXAMPLE 2**

Find the list price of a Kohler kitchen sink that has a net cost of $243.20 after trade discounts of 20/20.

SOLUTION

Use a net cost equivalent. Start by finding the percent paid, using complements.

series discount ⟶ 20/20

complements   .8 × .8 = **.64**   remains (net cost equivalent)
with respect to 1

As the work shows, **.64** or **64%**, of the list price was paid. Find the list price with the standard percent formula.

$$R \quad \times \quad B \quad = \quad P$$
64% of list price = $243.20

or

$$B = \frac{P}{R} = \frac{243.2}{.64} = \$380 \text{ list price}$$

The list price of the sink is $380.

QUICK CHECK 2

After trade discounts of 10/30, the net cost of a 10-quart crock pot is $62.36. Find the list price.

Solving for the List Price

EXAMPLE 3

case IN point ▶

Find the list price of a Bunn 10-cup Generation home brewer having a series discount of 10/30/20 and a net cost of $60.48.

SOLUTION

Use complements to find the percent paid.

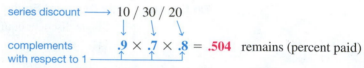

series discount ⟶ 10 / 30 / 20

complements
with respect to 1 ⟶ **.9** × **.7** × **.8** = **.504** remains (percent paid)

Therefore, **.504** of the list price is $60.48. Use the formula for base.

$$B = \frac{P}{R} = \frac{\$60.48}{.504} = \$120 \text{ list price}$$

The list price of the Bunn home brewer is $120. Check this answer as in Example 3.

QUICK CHECK 3

Find the list price of an Oster Toaster Oven having a series discount of 10/10/10 and a net cost of $43.73.

Notice that Examples 2 and 3 are decrease problems similar to those shown in **Section 3.5** in **Chapter 3**. They are still base problems but may look different because the discount is now shown as a series of two or more discounts rather than a single percent decrease as in **Chapter 3**. If you need help, refer to **Section 3.5**.

7.2 Exercises

The **QUICK START** *exercises in each section contain solutions to help you get started.*

Find the net cost equivalent and the single discount equivalent of each of the following series discounts. Do not round net cost equivalents or single discount equivalents. (See Example 1.)

QUICK START

	Series Discount	Net Cost Equivalent	Single Discount Equivalent
1.	10/20	.72	28%
	$.9 \times .8 = .72; 1.00 - .72 = 28\%$		
2.	10/10	.81	19%
	$.9 \times .9 = .81; 1.00 - .81 = 19\%$		
3.	20/15	_____	_____
4.	25/25	_____	_____
5.	10/30/20	_____	_____
6.	5/10/15	_____	_____
7.	20/10/10/20	_____	_____
8.	25/10/5/20	_____	_____

9. Using complements, show that the single discount equivalent of a 25/20/10 series discount is 46%. (See Objective 1.)

10. Suppose that you own a business and are offered a choice of a 10/20 trade discount or a 20/10 trade discount. Which do you prefer? Why? (See Objective 1.)

Find the list price, given the net cost and the series discount. (See Examples 3 and 4.)

QUICK START

11. Net cost $518.40; trade discount 20/10

    $.8 \times .9 = .72; \$518.40 \div .72 = \$720$

11. $720

12. Net cost $813.75; trade discount 30/25

12. _____

13. Net cost $1559.52; trade discount 5/10/20

13. _____

14. Net cost $2697.30; trade discount 10/10/10

14. _____

15. Net cost $265.39; trade discount 10/20/5

15. _____

16. Net cost $613.60; trade discount 25/25

16. _____

17. Net cost $4312.40; trade discount 5/10/15

17. _____

18. Net cost $43.17; trade discount 5/40

18. _____

Solve the following application problems. Round to the nearest cent.

QUICK START

19. **BRACELET** A bracelet had a net cost to a jeweler of $68.72 after a series trade discount of 10/10/5. Find the list price to the jeweler.

    .9 × .9 × .95 = .7695; $68.72 ÷ .7695 = $89.30

19. **$89.30**

20. **CALCULATOR** A programmable financial calculator had a net cost of $72.34 after a series trade discount of 10/20. Find the list price.

20. _____

21. **GPS** After a series trade discount of 20/20, a GPS had a net cost of $132.54. Find the list price.

21. _____

22. **NINTENDO** After a series trade discount of 10/5, a new Nintendo game had a net cost of $18.69. Find the list price.

22. _____

Solve the following two review application exercises on trade discounts.

23. **COMPARING DISCOUNTS** A S'mores Maker Kit has a list price of $39.95 and is offered to wholesalers with a series discount of 20/10/10. The same appliance is offered to Kitchen Crafters (a retailer) with a series discount of 20/10. **(a)** Find the wholesaler's price. **(b)** Find Kitchen Crafters' price. **(c)** Find the difference between the two prices.

    (a) _____
    (b) _____
    (c) _____

24. **STAINLESS STEEL GRILL** A stainless steel gas grill is list priced at $495. The manufacturer offers a series discount of 25/20/10 to wholesalers and a 25/20 series discount to retailers. **(a)** What is the wholesaler's price? **(b)** What is the retailer's price? **(c)** What is the difference between the prices?

    (a) _____
    (b) _____
    (c) _____

QUICK CHECK ANSWERS

1. 44%

2. $98.98 (rounded)

3. $59.99 (rounded)

7.3 Cash Discounts: Ordinary Dating Methods

OBJECTIVES

1 Calculate net cost after discounts.

2 Use the ordinary dating method.

3 Determine whether cash discounts are earned.

4 Use postdating when calculating cash discounts.

OBJECTIVE 1 Calculate net cost after discounts. Cash discounts are offered by sellers to encourage prompt payment by customers. In effect, the seller is saying, "Pay me quickly and receive a discount." Businesses often borrow money for their day-to-day operation. Immediate cash payments from customers decrease the need for borrowed money. To find the net cost, subtract any trade and cash discounts from the list price.

> **Finding the Net Cost**
>
> Net cost = (List price − Trade discount) − Cash discount

The cash discount on the Hershey invoice below is shown at the bottom right corner following TERMS. Many companies state the exact amount of the cash discount on the invoice. Others require a calculation to find the discount.

OBJECTIVE 2 Use the ordinary dating method. There are many methods for finding cash discounts, but nearly all of these are based on the **ordinary dating method**. The methods discussed here and in the next section are the most common in use today. The ordinary dating method of cash discount is expressed on an invoice as

2/10, n/30   or   **2/10, net 30**

which is read as "two ten, net thirty." Interpret this as follows: A 2% discount applies if the invoice is paid within 10 days of the invoice date. If no payment is made within 10 days, then the full invoice amount must be paid within 30 days of the invoice date. If no payment is made by the end of 30 days from the invoice date, then a penalty may apply.

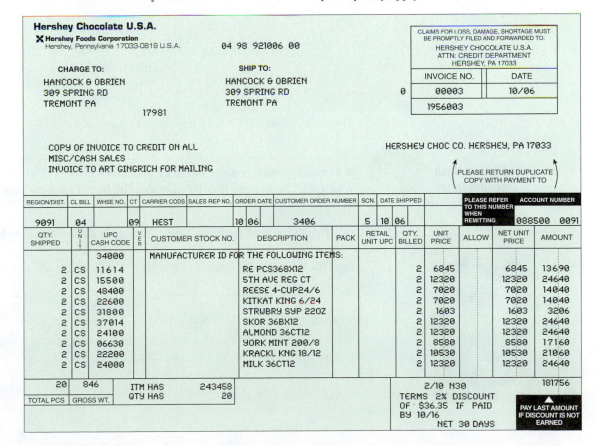

To find the due date of an invoice, use the number of days in each month, given in the following chart.

THE NUMBER OF DAYS IN EACH MONTH

30-DAY MONTHS	31-DAY MONTHS		EXCEPTION
April	January	August	February
June	March	October	(28 days normally;
September	May	December	29 days in leap year)
November	July		

The number of days in each month of the year can also be remembered using the following rhyme and "knuckle" methods:

Rhyme Method:
30 days hath September,
April, June, and November.
All the rest have 31, except
February, which has 28 and
in a leap year 29.

Knuckle Method:

Leap years occur every four years: 2008, 2012, 2016, and so on.

OBJECTIVE 3 **Determine whether cash discounts are earned.** Find the date that an invoice is due by counting from the next day after the date of the invoice. The date of the invoice is never counted. Another way to determine due dates is to add the given number of days to the starting date. For example, to determine 10 days from April 7, add the number of days to the date ($7 + 10 = 17$). The due date, or 10 days from April 7, is April 17.

When the discount date or net payment date falls in the next month, the number of days remaining in the current month is found by subtracting the invoice date from the number of days in the month. Then find the number of days in the next month needed to equal the discount period or net payment period. For example, determine the date that is 15 days from October 20.

$$
\begin{array}{rl}
31 & \text{days in October} \\
-\ 20 & \text{the beginning date is October 20} \\
\hline
11 & \text{days remaining in October} \\
\\
15 & \text{total number of days} \\
-\ 11 & \text{days remaining in October} \\
\hline
4 & \text{November (future date)}
\end{array}
$$

Therefore, November 4 is 15 days from October 20.

Finding Cash Discount Dates **EXAMPLE 1** A Hershey invoice is dated January 2 and offers terms of 2/10, net 30. Find **(a)** the last date on which the 2% discount may be taken and **(b)** the net payment date.

SOLUTION

(a) Beginning with the invoice date, January 2, the last date for taking the discount is January 12 (**2 + 10**).

(b) The net payment date is February 1 (**31 − 2** = 29 days remaining in January plus 1 day in February.)

> **QUICK CHECK 1**
>
> An invoice is dated June 8 and offers terms of 3/15, net 30. Find **(a)** the last date on which the 3% discount may be taken and **(b)** the net payment date.

Finding the Amount Due on the Invoice   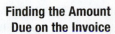 **EXAMPLE 2**

An invoice received by Bed Bath & Beyond for $840 is dated July 1 and offers terms of 2/10, n/30. If the invoice is paid on July 8 and the shipping and insurance charges, which were FOB shipping point, are $35.60, find the total amount due.

SOLUTION

Since the invoice was paid in 7 days (8 − 1 = 7), which is less than the 10-day requirement identified by 2/10, the 2% cash discount applies.

$$\text{Cash discount} = 2\% \text{ of } \$840 = \mathbf{\$16.80}$$

$$\begin{aligned}\text{Amount due} &= \text{Invoice amount} - \text{Cash discount} \\ &= \quad\$840 \quad - \quad\mathbf{\$16.80} \\ &= \$823.20\end{aligned}$$

However, the shipping and insurance charges must be added to the amount due.

$$\begin{aligned}\text{Total to be paid} &= \mathbf{\text{Amount due} + \text{Shipping and insurance charges}} \\ &= \quad\$823.20 \quad + \quad\quad\$35.60 \\ &= \$858.80\end{aligned}$$

The total amount due is $858.80.

> **QUICK CHECK 2**
>
> An invoice is received for $2830.15, is dated March 21, and offers 3/15, n/30. If the invoice is paid on April 4 and the shipping and insurance charges are $124.96, find the amount due.

In the previous example, the cash discount was not applied to the shipping and insurance charges. This is true in general. Shipping and insurance charges are not eligible for cash discounts. First, deduct applicable trade and cash discounts. Then, add the shipping and insurance charges to find the total amount due.

OBJECTIVE 4 **Use postdating when calculating cash discounts.** In the ordinary dating method, the cash discount date and net payment date are both counted from the date of the invoice. Occasionally, an invoice is **postdated**. This may be done to give the purchaser more time to take the cash discount on the invoice or may be to more closely fit the accounting practices of the seller. The seller places a date that is after the actual invoice date, sometimes labeling it **AS OF**. For example, the following Levi Strauss invoice is dated 07/25 AS OF 08/01. Both the cash discount period and the net payment date are counted from 08/01 (August 1). This results in giving additional time for the purchaser to pay the invoice and receive the discount.

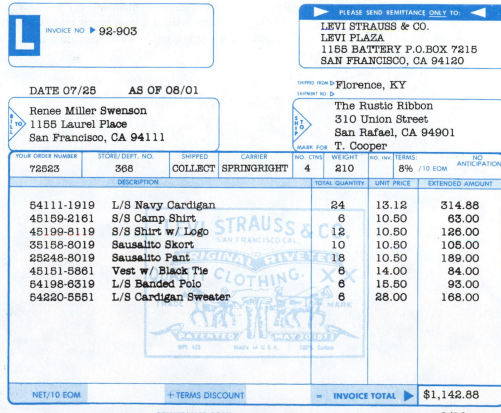

Using Postdating AS OF with Invoices   **EXAMPLE 3**

ONLY 199.99
HENKELS PREMIER CLASSIC 15-PIECE SET
Includes five kitchen knives, six steak knives, fork, shears, steel, and block

An invoice for a shipment of Henkels cutlery from Germany is dated October 21 AS OF November 1 with terms of 3/15, n/30. Find **(a)** the last date on which the cash discount may be taken and **(b)** the net payment date.

SOLUTION

(a) Beginning with the postdate (AS OF) of November 1, the last date for taking the discount is November 16 (**1 + 15**).

(b) The net payment date is December 1 **(29 days remaining in November and 1 day in December)**.

> **QUICK CHECK 3**
>
> An invoice for Waterford Crystal from Ireland is dated August 24 AS OF September 1 with terms of 1/10, n/30. Find **(a)** the last date on which the cash discount may be taken and **(b)** the net payment date.

Determining Cash Discount Due Dates for a Sliding Scale   **EXAMPLE 4**

An invoice from Cellular Products is dated May 18 and offers terms of 4/10, 3/25, 1/40, n/60. Find **(a)** the three final dates for each cash discount and **(b)** the net payment date.

SOLUTION

(a) The three final cash discount dates are

4% if paid by May 28	10 days from May 18
3% if paid by June 12	25 days from May 18
1% if paid by June 27	40 days from May 18

(b) The net payment date is July 17 (20 days beyond the cash discount period).

> **QUICK CHECK 4**
>
> An invoice is dated April 14 and offers terms of 3/10, 2/30, 1/40, n/60. Find **(a)** the three final dates for each cash discount and **(b)** the net payment date.

Never take more than one of the cash discounts. *With all methods of giving cash discounts, if the net payment period is not given, the net payment due date is assumed to be 20 days beyond the cash discount period.* After that date, the invoice is considered overdue. If either the final discount date or the net payment date is on a Sunday or holiday, the next business day is used. Many companies insist that payment is made when the payment is received. In non-retail transactions, payment is considered to be made when it is mailed.

7.3 Exercises

The **QUICK START** exercises in each section contain solutions to help you get started.

Find the final discount date and the net payment date for each of the following.
(See Examples 1 and 3.)

QUICK START

	Invoice Date	AS OF	Terms	Final Discount Date	Net Payment Date
1.	May 4		2/10, n/30	May 14	June 3
2.	Apr. 12		3/10, net 30	April 22	May 12
3.	June 30	July 10	3/15, n/60	_____	_____
4.	Nov. 7	Nov. 18	3/10, n/40	_____	_____
5.	Sept. 11		4/20, n/30	_____	_____
6.	July 31		2/15, net 20	_____	_____

Solve for the amount of discount and the total amount due on each of the following invoices.
Add shipping and insurance charges if given. (See Examples 2 and 4.)

QUICK START

	Invoice Amount	Invoice Date	Terms	Date Invoice Paid	Shipping and Insurance	Amount of Discount	Total Amount Due
7.	$85.18	Nov. 2	2/10, net 30	Nov. 11	$8.72	$1.70	$92.20
	$85.18 − $1.70 + $8.72 = $92.20						
8.	$66.10	Mar. 8	6/10, n/30	Mar. 14	$4.39	$3.97	$66.52
	$66.10 − $3.97 + $4.39 = $66.52						
9.	$78.07	May 5	net 30	June 1	$3.18	_____	_____
10.	$294	Apr. 5	net 30	May 2	$16.20	_____	_____
11.	$1080	July 8	5/10, 2/20, n/30	July 26	$62.15	_____	_____
12.	$1282	July 1	4/15, net 40	July 7	$21.40	_____	_____

13. Describe the difference between a trade discount and a cash discount. Why are cash discounts offered? (See Objective 1.)

14. Using 2/10, n/30 as an example, explain what an ordinary dating cash discount means. (See Objective 2.)

 indicates an exercise that is related to the Case in Point feature.

Solve the following application problems. Round to the nearest cent.

QUICK START

⚠ **15. CATERING COMPANY** Bed Bath & Beyond offers cash discounts of 4/10, 2/20, net 30 to all catering companies. An invoice is dated June 18 amounting to $4635.40 and is paid on July 7. Find the amount needed to pay the invoice.

  June 18 to July 7 = (30 − 18) + 7 = 19 days

  Discount is 2%; $4635.40 × .98 = $4542.69

15. $4542.69

16. RUSSIAN ELECTRICAL SUPPLIES A shipment of electrical supplies is received from the Lyskovo Electrotechnical Works. The invoice is dated March 8, amounts to $6824.58, and has terms of 2/15, 1/20 AS OF March 20. Find the amount needed to pay the invoice on April 2.

16. _____

17. PETROCHEMICAL PRODUCTS Century Petrochemical Products offers customers a trade discount of 10/20/5 on all products, with terms of net 30. Find the customer's price for products with a total list price of $2630 if the invoice was paid within 30 days.

17. _____

18. GEORGE FOREMAN GRILL A George Foreman Rotisserie Grill is list priced at $59.99 with a trade discount of 20/5/10 and terms of 4/10, n/30. Find the cost to Kitchen Crafters assuming that both discounts are earned.

18. _____

19. FINDING DISCOUNT DATES An invoice is dated January 18 and offers terms of 6/10, 4/20, 1/30, n/50. Find **(a)** the three final discount dates and **(b)** the net payment date.

(a) _____
(b) _____

20. FINDING DISCOUNT DATES An invoice with terms of 4/15, 3/20, 1/30, n/60 is dated September 4. Find **(a)** the three final discount dates and **(b)** the net payment date.

(a) _____
(b) _____

21. AS OF DATING An invoice is dated March 28 AS OF April 5 with terms of 4/20, n/30. Find **(a)** the final discount date and **(b)** the net payment date.

(a) _____
(b) _____

22. AS OF DATING An invoice is dated May 20 AS OF June 5 with terms of 2/10, n/30. Find **(a)** the final discount date and **(b)** the net payment date.

(a) _____
(b) _____

23. How do you remember the number of days in each month of the year? List the months and the number of days in each. (See Objective 2.)

24. Explain in your own words how AS OF dating (postdating) works. Why is it used? (See Objective 4.)

──────────── **QUICK CHECK ANSWERS** ────────────

1. (a) June 23   **(b)** July 8   **3. (a)** September 11   **(b)** October 1

2. $2870.21   (rounded)   **4. (a)** April 24; May 14; May 24   **(b)** June 13

7.4 Cash Discounts: Other Dating Methods

OBJECTIVES

1 Solve cash discount problems with end-of-month dating.
2 Use receipt-of-goods dating to solve cash discount problems.
3 Use extra dating to solve cash discount problems.
4 Determine credit given for partial payment of an invoice.

In addition to the ordinary dating method of cash discounts, several other cash discount methods are in common use. Jack Williams at Bed Bath & Beyond must be able to understand and use each of these. He works with many invoices everyday and sees a wide variety of discounts.

OBJECTIVE 1 Solve cash discount problems with end-of-month dating. This section discusses several other methods of finding cash discounts. **End-of-month** and **proximo** dating, abbreviated **EOM** and **prox.**, are treated the same. For example, both

3/10 EOM and 3/10 prox.

mean that 3% may be taken as a cash discount if payment is made by the 10th of the month that follows the sale. The 10 days are counted from the *end of the month* in which the invoice is dated. For example, an invoice dated July 14 with terms of 3/10 EOM would have a discount date 10 days from the end of the month, or the 10th of August (August 10).

Since this is a method of increasing the length of time during which a discount may be taken, it has become common business practice to add an extra month when the date of an invoice is the 26th of the month or later. For example, if an invoice is dated March 25 and the discount offered is 3/10 EOM, the last date on which the discount may be taken is April 10. *However, if the invoice is dated March 26 (or any later date in March) and the cash discount offered is 3/10 EOM, then the last date on which the discount may be taken is May 10.*

The practice of adding an extra month when the invoice is dated the 26th of a month or after is used *only* with the end-of-month (proximo) dating cash discount. It does *not* apply to any of the other cash discount methods.

SALE 59.99
OSTER TOASTER OVEN/BROILER
6-slice capacity, four heat settings and continuous-clean interior, #6232. Reg. 69.99

Muffins not included.

Using End-of-Month Dating **EXAMPLE 1**

If an invoice from Oster is dated June 10 with terms of 3/20 EOM, find **(a)** the final date on which the cash discount may be taken and **(b)** the net payment date.

SOLUTION

(a) The discount date is July 20 (20 days after the end of June).

(b) When no net payment due date is given, common business practice is to allow 20 days after the last discount date. The net payment date is August 9, which is **20 days** after the last discount date (July 20), since no net payment date is given.

> **QUICK CHECK 1**
>
> An invoice from Pearson Education, Inc., is dated February 15 with terms of 2/10 EOM. Find **(a)** the final date on which the discount may be taken and **(b)** the net payment date.

Using Proximo Dating **EXAMPLE 2**

Find the amount due on an invoice of $782 for some Black and Decker Belgian waffle makers dated August 3, if terms are 1/10 prox. and the invoice is paid on September 4.

SOLUTION

The last date on which the discount may be taken is September 10 (**10 days** after the end of August). September 4 is within the discount period, so the discount is earned. The 1% cash discount is computed on $782, the amount of the invoice. Subtract the discount ($782 × .01 = $7.82) from the invoice amount to find the amount due.

$782.00	invoice amount
− 7.82	cash discount (1%)
$774.18	amount due

QUICK CHECK 2

An invoice for some gourmet cookbooks is for $1475 and dated October 17. Find the amount due if the invoice terms are 3/20 proximo and the invoice is paid on November 18.

Note: With all methods of cash discounts, if the net payment period is not given, the net payment due date is assumed to be **20 days beyond the cash discount date**.

OBJECTIVE 2 Use receipt-of-goods dating to solve cash discount problems. **Receipt-of-goods dating**, abbreviated **ROG**, offers cash discounts determined from the date on which goods are actually received. This method is often used when shipping time is long. The invoice might arrive immediately over the Internet, but the goods may take several weeks. Under the ROG method of cash discount, the buyer is given the time to receive and inspect the merchandise and then is allowed to benefit from a cash discount. For example, the discount

3/15 ROG

allows a 3% cash discount if the invoice is paid within 15 days from receipt of goods. The date that goods are received is determined by the delivery date. If the invoice was dated March 5 and goods were received on April 7, the last date to take the 3% cash discount would be April 22 (April 7 plus 15 days). The net payment date, since it is not stated, is 20 days after the last discount date, or May 12 (April 22 plus 20 days).

Using Receipt-of-Goods Dating

EXAMPLE 3

Best Buy received an invoice dated December 12, with terms of 2/10 ROG. The goods were received on January 2. Find **(a)** the final date on which the cash discount may be taken and **(b)** the net payment date.

SOLUTION

(a) The discount date is January 12 (**10 days** after receipt of goods, January 2 plus **10 days**).

(b) The net payment date is February 1 (**20 days** after the last discount date).

QUICK CHECK 3

An invoice from Silver Specialties is dated June 4, with terms of 4/15 ROG. The merchandise was received on July 25. Find **(a)** the final date on which the cash discount may be taken and **(b)** the net payment date.

Working with ROG Dating

EXAMPLE 4

Find the amount due to Sir Speedy on an invoice of $285 for some printing services, with terms of 3/10 ROG, if the invoice is dated June 8, the goods are received June 18, and the invoice is paid June 30.

SOLUTION

The last date to take the 3% cash discount is June 28, 10 days after June 18. Since the invoice is paid on June 30, 2 days after the last discount date, **no cash discount may be taken**. The entire amount of the invoice must be paid.

$285	invoice amount
− 0	**no cash discount**
$285	amount due

QUICK CHECK 4

Find the amount due on an invoice of $896, with terms of 4/20 ROG, if the invoice is dated March 10, the goods are received April 28, and the invoice is paid on May 15.

OBJECTIVE 3 Use extra dating to solve cash discount problems. **Extra dating (extra, ex., or x)** gives the buyer additional time to take advantage of a cash discount. For example, the discount

2/10−50 extra   or   **2/10−50 ex.**   or   **2/10−50 x**

allows a 2% cash discount if the invoice is paid within 10 + 50 = 60 days from the date of the invoice. The discount is expressed as 2/10–50 ex. (rather than 2/60) to show that the 50 days are *extra*, or in addition to the normal 10 days offered.

There are several reasons for using extra dating. A supplier might extend the discount period during a slow sales season to generate more sales or to gain a competitive advantage. For example, the seller might offer Christmas merchandise with extra dating to allow the buyer to take the cash discount after the holiday selling period.

Using Extra Dating **EXAMPLE 5**

An invoice for Oster blenders is dated November 23 with terms of 2/10–50 ex. Find **(a)** the final date on which the cash discount may be taken and **(b)** the net payment date.

SOLUTION

(a) The discount date is January 22 (**7 days** remaining in November + 31 days in December = 38; thus, **22 more days** are needed in January to total 60).

(b) The net payment date is February 11 (**20 days** after the last discount date).

> **QUICK CHECK 5**
>
> An invoice is dated July 7 with terms of 1/10–60 ex. Find **(a)** the final date on which the cash discount may be taken and **(b)** the net payment date.

Understanding Extra Dating **EXAMPLE 6**

An invoice from Wind Turbines & Solar, Inc., is dated August 5, amounts to $8180, offers terms of 3/10–30 x, and is paid on September 12. Find the net payment.

SOLUTION

Step 1   The last day to take the 3% cash discount is September 14 (**August 5 + 40 days = September 14**). Since the invoice is paid on September 12, the **3%** discount may be taken.

Step 2   The **3%** cash discount is computed on $8180, the amount of the invoice. The discount to be taken is $245.40.

Step 3   Subtract the cash discount from the invoice amount to determine the amount of payment.

$$
\begin{array}{ll}
\$8180.00 & \text{invoice amount} \\
-\ \ \$245.40 & \textbf{3\% cash discount} \\
\hline
\$7934.60 & \text{amount of payment}
\end{array}
$$

> **QUICK CHECK 6**
>
> An invoice for $5412 is dated May 22 and offers terms of 2/20–40 x. If the invoice is paid on July 15, what is the amount of payment due?

> **Quick TIP ▼**
>
> In Example 6, the amount of payment may be found by multiplying the invoice amount by 100% − 3%, or 97%. Here, $8180 × .97 = $7934.60 is the amount of payment.

OBJECTIVE 4   Determine credit given for partial payment of an invoice. Occasionally, a customer may pay only a portion of the total amount due on an invoice. If this **partial payment** is made within a discount period, the customer is entitled to a discount on the portion of the invoice that is paid.

If the terms of an invoice are 3%, 10 days, then only 97% (100% − 3%) of the invoice amount must be paid during the first 10 days. So, for each $.97 paid, the customer is entitled to $1.00 of credit. When a partial payment is made, the credit given for the partial payment (base) is found by dividing the partial payment by the complement of the cash discount percent. Then, to find the balance due, subtract the credit given from the invoice amount. The cash discount is found by subtracting the partial payment from the credit given.

Finding Credit for Partial Payment   **EXAMPLE 7**

Dave's Body and Paint receives an invoice for $1140 dated March 8 that offers terms of 2/10 prox. A partial payment of $450 is made on April 5. Find **(a)** the amount credited for the partial payment, **(b)** the balance due on the invoice, and **(c)** the cash discount earned.

SOLUTION

(a) The cash discount is earned on the $450 partial payment made on April 5 (April 10 was the last discount date). The amount paid ($450) is part of the base (amount for which credit is given).

$$100\% - 2\% = 98\%$$

The rate 98% is used to solve for base using the formula $Base = \dfrac{Part}{Rate}$.

$$B = \frac{P}{R}$$
$$B = \frac{450}{98\%} = \frac{450}{.98} = \$459.18 \text{ (rounded)}$$

The amount credited for partial payment is $459.18.

(b) Balance due = Invoice amount − Credit given
Balance due = $1140 − **$459.18** = $680.82

(c) Cash discount = Credit given − Partial payment
Cash discount = **$459.18** − $450 = $9.18

A calculator solution to this example includes these three steps.
First, find the amount of credit given.

450 ÷ .98 = 459.18   (rounded) STO

Then, store the amount of credit and subtract this amount from the invoice amount to find the balance due.

1140 − RCL = 680.82   (rounded)

Finally, subtract the partial payment from the amount of credit given to find the cash discount.

RCL − 450 = 9.18   (rounded)

QUICK CHECK 7

Central Parts receives an invoice for $1082 dated September 14 that offers terms of 2/20 prox. A partial payment of $590 is paid on October 15. Find **(a)** the amount credited for the partial payment, **(b)** the balance due on the invoice, and **(c)** the cash discount earned.

Cash discounts are important, and a business should make the effort to pay invoices early to earn the cash discounts. In many cases, the money saved through cash discounts has a great effect on the profitability of a business. Often, companies will borrow money to enable them to take advantage of cash discounts. The mathematics of this type of loan is discussed in **Section 8.1**, Simple Interest.

The **QUICK START** exercises in each section contain solutions to help you get started.

Find the discount date and net payment date for each of the following. (The net payment date is 20 days after the final discount date. See Examples 1, 3, and 5.)

QUICK START

	Invoice Date	Terms	Date Goods Received	Final Discount Date	Net Payment Date
1.	Feb. 8	3/10 EOM		Mar. 10	Mar. 30
2.	July 14	2/15 ROG	Sept. 3	Sept. 18	Oct. 8
3.	Nov. 22	1/10–20 x		_____	_____
4.	July 6	2/10 EOM		_____	_____
5.	Apr. 12	3/15–50 ex.		_____	_____
6.	Jan. 15	3/15 ROG	Feb. 5	_____	_____

Solve for the amount of discount and the amount due on each of the following invoices. Round to the nearest cent. (See Examples 2, 4, and 6.)

QUICK START

	Invoice Amount	Invoice Date	Terms	Date Goods Received	Date Invoice Paid	Amount of Discount	Amount Due
7.	$682.28	June 4	3/20 ROG	July 25	Aug. 10	$20.47	$661.81
	$20.47 discount; $682.28 − $20.47 = $661.81 due						
8.	$356.20	May 17	3/15 prox.		June 12	$10.69	$345.51
	10.686 = $10.69 discount; $356.20 − $10.69 = $345.51 due						
9.	$785.64	Sept. 8	2/10–20 x		Oct. 14	_____	_____
10.	$12.38	Mar. 29	2/15 ROG	Apr. 15	Apr. 30	_____	_____
11.	$11,480	Apr. 6	2/15 prox.		Apr. 30	_____	_____
12.	$1380	May 28	1/15 EOM		June 10	_____	_____
13.	$23.95	Aug. 2	3/10–20 extra		Sept. 1	_____	_____
14.	$3250.60	Oct. 17	3/15–20 ex.		Oct. 20	_____	_____

15. Quite often there is no mention of a net payment date on an invoice. Explain the common business practice when no net payment date is given. (See Objective 1.)

16. Describe why ROG dating is offered to customers. Use an example in your description. (See Objective 2.)

▲ indicates an exercise that is related to the Case in Point feature.

Solve the following application problems. Round to the nearest cent.

QUICK START

17. **NOSTALGIC KITCHEN APPLIANCES** Nostalgia Electronics, a manufacturer of Nostalgic Kitchen appliances, offers terms of 2/10–30 ex. to stimulate slow sales in the winter months. Bed Bath & Beyond purchased $2382.58 worth of appliances and was offered the above terms. If the invoice was dated November 3, find **(a)** the final date on which the cash discount may be taken and **(b)** the amount paid if the discount was earned.

    (a)   Dec. 13

    (b) $2334.93

    (a)   27   days remain in November

        + 13   days in December

           40   days is December 13

    (b) $2382.58 × .02 = 47.651 = $47.65 discount

         $2382.58 − $47.65 = $2334.93 paid

18. **CANADIAN FOOD PRODUCTS** Vanitha Evans, a wholesaler of Canadian food products, offers terms of 4/15–40 ex. to encourage the sales of her products. In a recent order, a retailer purchased $9864.18 worth of Canadian foods and was offered the above terms. If the invoice was dated March 10, find **(a)** the final date on which the cash discount may be taken and **(b)** the amount paid if the discount was earned.

    (a) _____

    (b) _____

19. **GLOBAL POSITIONING SYSTEMS** A recent invoice for 24 Garmin nuvi 1490T GPS systems amounting to $6720.50 was dated February 20 and offered terms of 2/20 ROG. If the equipment was received on March 20 and the invoice was paid on April 8, find the amount due.

    19. _____

20. **WHEELS WITH BLING** Scott Ryder purchased some 21-inch and 23-inch custom wheels for his performance auto parts store and was offered a cash discount of 2/10 EOM. The invoice amounted to $7218.80 and was dated June 2. The wheels were received 7 days later, and the invoice was paid on July 7. Find the amount necessary to pay the invoice in full.

    20. _____

21. **ENGLISH SOCCER EQUIPMENT** An invoice dated December 8 is received with a shipment of soccer equipment from England on April 18 of the following year. The list price of the equipment is $2538, with allowed series discounts of 25/10/10. If cash terms of sale are 3/15 ROG, find the amount necessary to pay in full on April 21.

    21. _____

22. **CRYSTAL FROM IRELAND** Bed Bath & Beyond receives an invoice for Waterford crystal from Ireland amounting to $5382.40 and dated May 17. The terms of the invoice are 5/20–90 x and the invoice is paid on September 2. Find the amount necessary to pay the invoice in full.

    22. _____

23. **PARTIAL INVOICE PAYMENT** PetSmart receives an invoice amounting to $2016.90 with terms of 8/10, net 30 and dated August 20 AS OF September 1. If a partial payment of $1350 is made on September 8, find **(a)** the credit given for the partial payment and **(b)** the balance due on the invoice.

    (a) _____

    (b) _____

24. **FROZEN YOGURT** Yogurt for You receives an invoice amounting to $263.40 with terms of 2/20 EOM and dated September 6. If a partial payment of $150 is made on October 15, find **(a)** the credit given for the partial payment and **(b)** the balance due on the invoice.

(a) _____

(b) _____

25. **DISCOUNT DATES** An invoice received by Kitchen Crafters is dated May 12 with terms of 2/10 prox. Find **(a)** the final date on which the discount may be taken and **(b)** the net payment date.

(a) _____

(b) _____

26. **DISCOUNT DATES** An invoice from Dollar Distributors is dated November 11 with terms of 3/20 ROG, and the goods are received on December 3. Find **(a)** the final date on which the cash discount may be taken and **(b)** the net payment date.

(a) _____

(b) _____

27. **INVOICE AMOUNT DUE** Find the amount due on an invoice of $1525 with terms of 1/20 ROG. The invoice is dated October 20, goods are received December 1, and the invoice is paid on December 20.

27. _____

28. **PAYMENT DUE** Find the payment that should be made on an invoice dated September 28, amounting to $4680, offering terms of 2/10–50 x and paid on November 25.

28. _____

29. **PARTIAL INVOICE PAYMENT** An invoice received for Spode china has terms of 3/15–30 x and is dated May 20. The amount of the invoice is $4402.58, and a partial payment of $3250 is made on July 1. Find **(a)** the credit given for the partial payment and **(b)** the balance due on the invoice.

(a) _____

(b) _____

30. **AUTOMOTIVE** Orange County Choppers makes a partial payment of $8726 on an invoice of $17,680.38. If the invoice is dated April 14 with terms of 4/20 prox. and the partial payment is made on May 13, find **(a)** the credit given for the partial payment and **(b)** the balance due on the invoice.

(a) _____

(b) _____

31. Write a short explanation of partial payment. Why would a company accept a partial payment? Why would a customer make a partial payment? (See Objective 4.)

32. Of all the different types of cash discounts presented in this section, which type seemed most interesting to you? Explain your reasons.

QUICK CHECK ANSWERS

1. **(a)** March 10 **(b)** March 30
2. $1430.75
3. **(a)** August 9 **(b)** August 29
4. $860.16
5. **(a)** September 15 **(b)** October 5
6. $5303.76
7. **(a)** $602.04 (rounded) **(b)** $479.96 **(c)** $12.04

Chapter 7   Quick Review

Chapter Terms   *Review the following terms to test your understanding of the chapter. For each term you do not know, refer to the page number found next to that term.*

amount [**p. 264**]
AS OF [**p. 281**]
cash discount [**p. 279**]
chain discount [**p. 266**]
COD (cash on delivery) [**p. 264**]
complement [**p. 267**]
distribution chain [**p. 264**]
end of month (EOM) [**p. 285**]
extension total [**p. 264**]

extra dating (extra, ex., x) [**p. 286**]
FAS (free alongside ship) [**p. 264**]
FOB (free on board) [**p. 264**]
FOB destination [**p. 264**]
invoice [**p. 264**]
invoice total [**p. 264**]
list price [**p. 266**]
manufacturing [**p. 264**]
net cost [**p. 266**]

net cost equivalent [**p. 267**]
net price [**p. 266**]
ordinary dating method [**p. 279**]
partial payment [**p. 287**]
postdated "AS OF" [**p. 281**]
prox. [**p. 285**]
proximo [**p. 285**]
purchase invoice [**p. 264**]
receipt-of-goods dating [**p. 286**]

retail [**p. 264**]
ROG [**p. 286**]
sales invoice [**p. 264**]
series discount [**p. 266**]
single discount [**p. 266**]
single discount equivalent [**p. 275**]
supply chain [**p. 264**]
trade discounts [**p. 266**]
unit price [**p. 264**]
wholesale [**p. 264**]

CONCEPTS

EXAMPLES

7.1 Trade discount and net cost

First find the amount of the trade discount. Then use the formula for net cost.

Net cost = List price − Trade discount

List price, $28; trade discount, 25%; find the net cost.

$$\text{Discount} = \$28 \times \mathbf{.25} = \mathbf{\$7}$$
$$\text{Net cost} = \$28 - \mathbf{\$7} = \$21$$

7.1 Complements with respect to 1 (100%)

The complement is the number that must be added to a given discount to get 1 or 100%.

Find the complement of each with respect to 1.

DISCOUNT	DECIMAL EQUIVALENT	FINDING THE COMPLEMENT		COMPLEMENT
20%	.2	1 − .2	=	.8
32%	.32	1 − .32	=	.68

7.1 Complements and series discounts

The complement of a discount is the percent paid. Multiply the complements of the series discounts to get the *net cost equivalent*.

Series discount, 10/20/10; find the net cost equivalent.

$$\begin{array}{ccc} 10/ & 20/ & 10 \\ \downarrow & \downarrow & \downarrow \end{array}$$
$$.9 \times .8 \times .9 = \mathbf{.648}$$

7.1 Net cost equivalent (percent paid) and net cost

Multiply the net cost equivalent (percent paid) by the list price to get the net cost.

List price, $280; series discount, 10/30/20; find the net cost.

$$\begin{array}{ccc} 10/ & 30/ & 20 \\ \downarrow & \downarrow & \downarrow \end{array}$$
$$.9 \times .7 \times .8 = \mathbf{.504} \text{ percent paid}$$
$$\text{Net cost} = \mathbf{.504} \times \$280 = \$141.12$$

7.2 Single discount equivalent to a series discount

Often needed to compare one series discount to another, the single discount equivalent is found by multiplying the complements of the individual discounts to get the net cost equivalent, then subtracting from 1.

$$1 - \frac{\textbf{Net cost}}{\textbf{equivalent}} = \frac{\textbf{Single discount}}{\textbf{equivalent}}$$

What single discount is equivalent to a 10/20/20 series discount?

$$\begin{array}{ccc} 10/ & 20/ & 20 \\ \downarrow & \downarrow & \downarrow \end{array}$$
$$.9 \times .8 \times .8 = \mathbf{.576}$$
$$1 - \mathbf{.576} = .424 = 42.4\%$$

7.2 Finding list price, given the series discount and the net cost

First, find the net cost equivalent, percent paid. Then use the standard percent formula to find the list price (base).

$$B = \frac{P}{R}$$

New cost, $224; series discount, 20/20; find list price.

$$\begin{array}{cc} 20/ & 20 \\ \downarrow & \downarrow \end{array}$$
$$.8 \times .8 = \mathbf{.64}$$
$$B = \frac{P}{R} = \frac{224}{\mathbf{.64}} = \$350 \text{ list price}$$

CONCEPTS	EXAMPLES

7.3 Number of days and dates

30-DAY MONTHS	31-DAY MONTHS
April	All the rest
June	except February with
September	28 days (29 days in leap year)
November	

Date, July 24; find 10 days from date.

July 31 − 24 = 7 days remaining in July

$$\begin{array}{r} 10 \quad \text{total number of days} \\ - \ 7 \quad \text{days remaining in July} \\ \hline \text{August 3} \quad \text{(future date)} \end{array}$$

7.3 Ordinary dating and cash discounts

With ordinary dating, count days from the date of the invoice. Remember:

$$\underset{\text{\% days, net days}}{\underset{\downarrow \quad \downarrow \quad \downarrow \quad \downarrow}{2/ \ 10, \ n/ \ 30}}$$

Invoice amount $182; terms 2/10, n/30; find the cash discount and amount due.

Cash discount: $182 × **.02** = $3.64

Amount due: $182 − **$3.64** = $178.36

7.4 Cash discounts with end-of-month dating (EOM or proximo dating)

The final discount date and the net date are counted from the end of the month. If the invoice is dated the 26th or after, add the entire following month when determining the dates. If not stated, the net date is 20 days beyond the discount date.

Terms, 2/10 EOM; invoice date, Oct. 18; find the final discount date and the net payment date.

Final discount date:
November 10, which is 10 days from the end of October

Net payment date:
November 30, which is 20 days beyond the discount date

7.4 Receipt-of-goods (ROG) dating and cash discounts

Time is counted from the date goods are received to determine the final cash discount date and the net payment date. If not stated, the net date is 20 days beyond the discount date.

Terms, 3/10 ROG; invoice date, March 8; goods received, May 10; find the final discount date and the net payment date.

Final discount date:
May 20 (May 10 + 10 days)

Net payment date:
June 9 (May 20 + 20 days)

7.4 Extra dating and cash discounts

Extra dating adds extra days to the usual cash discount period, so 3/10–20 x means 3/30. If not stated, the net date is 20 days beyond the discount date.

Terms, 3/10–20 x, invoice date, January 8; find the final discount date and the net payment date.

Final discount date:
February 7 (23 days in January + 7 days in February = 30)

Net payment date:
February 27 (February 7 + 20 days)

7.4 Partial payment credit

When only a portion of an invoice amount is paid within the cash discount period, credit will be given for the partial payment. Use the standard percent formula

$$B = \frac{P}{R}$$

where the credit given is the base, the partial payment is the part, and (100% − cash discount) is the rate.

Invoice, $4000; terms, 2/10, n/30; invoice date, Oct. 10; partial payment of $2000 on Oct. 15; find credit given for partial payment and the balance due on the invoice.

$$B = \frac{P}{R} = \frac{\$2000}{\mathbf{100\% - 2\%}} = \frac{\$2000}{\mathbf{.98}}$$

Credit = $2040.82
Balance due = $4000 − $2040.82 = $1959.18

case study

GEORGE FOREMAN

George E. Foreman was born on January 10, 1949, in Marshal, Texas. He grew up on the tough streets of Houston's Fifth Ward area, and as a young kid he was always getting into trouble. He joined the Job Corps and his life changed. One of the counselors noticed that he was always into fights, so he decided that George should put all of his energy into something positive. This started his boxing career. Since 1995 Foreman has been a partner with Salton in promoting the George Foreman cooking grills and other barbecue products. Today, "if there is one thing George Foreman knows, it's good cooking."

1. Kitchen Crafters purchased George Foreman Super Searing Grills that were list priced at $149.99. If the supplier offered a trade discount of 20/20, find the cost of one dozen grilling machines.

2. The list price of a George Foreman Next Grilleration Contact Grill is $119.99. The manufacturer gives a 25/10 trade discount and offers a cash discount of 3/15, net/30. Find the cost to Kitchen Crafters if both discounts are earned and taken.

3. The list price of a *George Foreman Knock-Out-the-Fat Barbecue and Grilling Cookbook* is $16.95. If the cookbook is offered at a reduced price of $13.95 when purchased on the Internet, what is the percent of markdown? Round to the nearest tenth of a percent.

 **INVESTIGATE**

Talk with one or two business owners or store managers. Ask what kinds of trade and cash discounts are standard in their particular line of business. Do they take their earned discounts? Are these discounts important to them? Who is responsible for making sure that discounts are taken? Do they do any of their purchasing electronically? How does their electronic purchasing work?

case _{in} point summary exercise

DISCOUNTS AT BED BATH & BEYOND

www.bedbathandbeyond.com

Facts:

- 1971: First formed
- 1985: Open first superstore
- 1992: Listed on public stock exchange
- 2010: More than 1000 stores and $7 billion in revenue

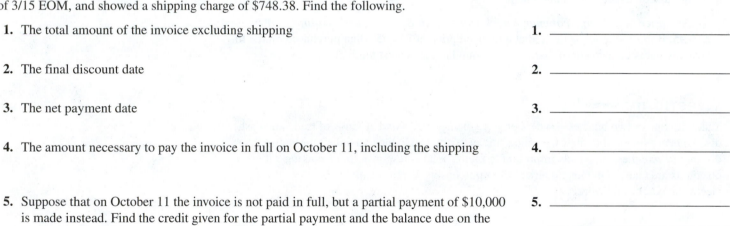

Jack Williams works in a very active department called purchasing. He works with store managers, marketing, and supply companies. His job is to have the right product, in the right amount, at the lowest cost, where and when it's needed. With more than 1000 stores, that is a very tough job! Of course, there are others that work with him in the department.

In early September, Williams placed an order with one vendor for products having a combined list price of $27,393. The vendor offered trade discounts of 20/10/10. The invoice arrived through the computer system the next day. It was dated September 4, had terms of 3/15 EOM, and showed a shipping charge of $748.38. Find the following.

1. The total amount of the invoice excluding shipping

   1. _____

2. The final discount date

   2. _____

3. The net payment date

   3. _____

4. The amount necessary to pay the invoice in full on October 11, including the shipping

   4. _____

5. Suppose that on October 11 the invoice is not paid in full, but a partial payment of $10,000 is made instead. Find the credit given for the partial payment and the balance due on the invoice including shipping.

   5. _____
   _____

Discussion Question: Have you thought about a career in purchasing? All firms that carry inventory have purchasing departments that work with people inside their own company and suppliers to keep the right products on the shelves. See what you can find out about this career on the Web. You may wish to search for the American Purchasing Society.

Chapter 7 Test

To help you review, the numbers in brackets show the section in which the topic was discussed.

Find the net cost (invoice amount) for the following. Round to the nearest cent. **[7.1]**

1. List price: $348.22 less 10/20/10

1. _____

2. List price: $1308 less 20/25

2. _____

Find (a) the net cost equivalent and (b) the single discount equivalent for the following series discounts. **[7.2]**

3. 30/10

(a) _____

(b) _____

4. 20/10/20

(a) _____

(b) _____

Find the final discount date for the following. **[7.4]**

Invoice Date	Terms	Date Goods Received	Final Discount Date
5. Feb. 10	4/15 EOM	Feb. 16	_____
6. May 8	2/10 ROG	May 20	_____
7. Dec. 8	4/15 prox.	Jan. 5	_____
8. Oct. 20	2/20 – 40 extra	Oct. 31	_____

9. The following invoice was paid on November 15. Find **(a)** the invoice total, **(b)** the amount that should be paid after the cash discount, and **(c)** the total amount due, including shipping and insurance. **[7.1–7.4]**

(a) _____

(b) _____

(c) _____

GOURMET KITCHEN WHOLESALER			
Terms: 2/10, 1/15, n/60			November 6
Quantity	**Description**	**Unit Price**	**Extension Total**
16	tablecloths, linen	@ 35.00 ea.	
8	rings, napkin	@ 6.50 ea.	
4 cases	cups, ceramic	@ 25.30 ea.	
12	bowls, 1 qt. stainless	@ 6.30 ea.	
		(a) Invoice Total	
		Cash Discount	
		(b) Due after Cash Discount	
		Shipping and Insurance	$38.75
		(c) Total Amount Due	

Solve the following application problems involving cash and trade discounts. Round to the nearest cent.

10. The Toy Train Store made purchases at a net cost of $46,746 after a series discount of 20/20/20. Find the list price. **[7.2]**

10. _____

11. An invoice of $3168 from Scottish Importers has cash terms of 4/20 EOM and is dated June 5. Find (a) the final date on which the cash discount may be taken and (b) the amount necessary to pay the invoice in full if the cash discount is earned. **[7.4]**

(a) _____

(b) _____

12. Mel's Diner purchased paper products list priced at $696 less series discounts of 10/20/10, with terms of 3/10–50 extra. If the retailer paid the invoice within 60 days, find the amount paid. **[7.4]**

12. _____

13. The Fireside Shop offers chimney caps for $120 less 25/10. The same chimney cap is offered by Builders Supply for $111 less 25/5. Find (a) the firm that offers the lower price and (b) the difference in price. **[7.1]**

(a) _____

(b) _____

14. The amount of an invoice from Cloverdale Creamery is $1780 with terms of 2/10, 1/15, net 30 with shipping charges of $120.39. The invoice is dated March 8. (a) What amount should be paid on March 20? (b) What amount should be paid on April 3? **[7.3]**

(a) _____

(b) _____

15. Diamond Consulting receives an invoice dated November 23 for $2514 with terms of 3/15 EOM with shipping and insurance charges of $88.50. If the invoice is paid on December 14, find the amount necessary to pay the invoice in full. **[7.4]**

15. _____

16. Jim Havey receives an invoice amounting to $2916 with cash terms of 3/10 prox. and dated June 7. If a partial payment of $1666 is made on July 8, find (a) the credit given for the partial payment and (b) the balance due on the invoice. **[7.4]**

(a) _____

(b) _____

Mathematics of Selling

8

case IN point

JAMES SMELTER works in inventory management at REI, one of the great retail companies totally devoted to outdoor activities. The firm was started by 23 experts in mountain climbing and, today, employees still design many of the products. It carries products for many types of outdoor activities, including camping, hiking, mountain climbing, skiing, paddling, snowboarding, snowshoeing, and kayaking.

REI's easy-to-navigate Internet store offers more than 40,000 products. The firm allocates 3% of operating income for donations that support the outdoors. If you are interested in trekking in Nepal, check the REI Web site since they organize trips to many wild places in the world. REI has been on Fortune's list of the 100 Best Companies to Work for in America for 11 years in a row.

REI is now the largest consumer cooperative in the nation, with more than three million members and 80 stores. As a cooperative, REI is owned by its members. If you become a member and buy products from REI, you will receive a refund check at the end of the year based on company profits and the amount of your purchases.

The success of a retailer depends on many things, including knowing the customers, controlling costs, and hiring great people. It also depends on the price at which products are offered to consumers. In this chapter, we use the language that people working in retail use, including cost, markup, and selling price.

8.1 Markup on Cost

OBJECTIVES

1. Recognize the terms used in selling.
2. Use the basic formula for markup.
3. Calculate markup based on cost.
4. Apply percent to markup problems.

case in point ▶

James Smelter must determine the appropriate selling price for a shipment of backpacks he just received at REI. He must be careful since a price that is too high results in backpacks that cannot be sold and customers that shop elsewhere. A price that is too low may result in a loss on the backpacks for REI.

OBJECTIVE 1

Recognize the terms used in selling

The terms used in markup are summarized here.

Cost is the amount paid to the manufacturer or supplier after trade and cash discounts have been taken. Shipping and insurance charges are included in cost.

Selling price is the price at which merchandise is offered for sale to the public.

Markup, margin, or **gross profit** is the difference between the cost and the selling price. These three terms are often used interchangeably.

Operating expenses, or **overhead,** include the expenses of operating the business, such as wages and salaries of employees, rent for buildings and equipment, utilities, insurance, and advertising. Even an expense like postage can add up when making thousands or millions of shipments.

Net profit (net earnings) is the amount (if any) remaining for the business after operating expenses and the cost of goods have been paid. (Income tax is computed on net profit.)

OBJECTIVE 2 Use the basic formula for markup. Managers mark up the cost of an item before selling it. For example, assume a backpack costs REI $176.92 and that it is marked up by $53.07 before putting it up for sale. The basic **markup formula** that follows shows that the selling price is the sum of the cost and the markup.

$$\text{Selling price} = \text{Cost} + \text{Markup}$$
$$S = C + M$$
$$= \$176.92 + \$53.07$$
$$= \$229.99$$

In general, the markup should be large enough to cover all associated operating expenses, such as wages and rent, and to have some left over for profit. However, smaller markups are sometimes used during a storewide sale to encourage customers to shop at the store or when trying to quickly move outdated products out of the store. Look at the following related to the backpack.

Cost	$176.92			C	$176.92
+ Markup	$53.07	**or**		+ M	$53.07
Selling price	$229.99			S	$229.99

Cost is the amount paid to supplier and includes shipping costs. Any markup remaining after paying operating expenses is profit.

Markup problems often give two of the values in the basic formula ($S = C + M$) and ask you to find the unknown value, as shown in Example 1.

Using the Basic Markup Formula

EXAMPLE 1

REI received three different types of snowshoes in one shipment. Use the basic markup formula to find the unknown for each of the following.

(a) C \$34.48
+M \$13.40
S \$

(b) C \$83.82
+M \$
S \$124.99

(c) C \$
+M \$ 68.17
S \$227.24

SOLUTION

(a) C \$34.48
+M \$13.40
S **\$47.88**

(b) C \$ 83.82
+M **\$ 41.17**
S \$124.99

(c) C **\$159.07**
+M \$ 68.17
S \$227.24

QUICK CHECK 1

Find the selling price in part (a), the markup in (b), and the cost in (c).

(a) C \$25
+ M \$ 8
S \$

(b) C \$72
+ M \$
S \$98

(c) C \$
+ M \$ 35
S \$118

$$R = \frac{P}{B}$$

OBJECTIVE 3 Calculate markup based on cost. Since manufacturers often talk about inventories in terms of cost, they often use the phrase **markup on cost**, in which markup is stated as a percent of cost. This is an application of the basic percent equation introduced in Chapter 3 with the base being cost, or 100%.

Finding Markup on Cost

$$\text{Markup on cost} = \frac{\text{Amount of markup}}{\text{Cost}} \quad \textbf{State as a percent.}$$

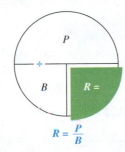

Assume an iPod that costs a retailer \$90 sells for \$126. Since the markup is on cost, cost is the base, or 100%. The unknown values indicated in the table are found just below the table by referencing 1, 2, and 3.

100%	C	\$ 90
② → %	M	\$ ← ①
③ → %	S	\$126

The three missing values in the table are found as follows.

1. Selling price = Cost + Markup   or

    Markup = Selling price − Cost
    = \$126 − \$90 = \$36

2. **Markup as a percent of Cost = Markup ÷ Cost**
    = \$36 ÷ 90 = 40%

3. **Selling price as a percent of Cost = Selling price ÷ Cost**
    = \$126 ÷ \$90 = 140%

The completed table looks as follows.

100%	C	\$ 90
40%	M	\$ 36
140%	S	\$126

Notice that the percents in the left column add to 140%, just as the amounts in the right column add to \$126. Also notice that all percents are given in terms of cost, which is the base, or 100%.

OBJECTIVE 4 Apply percent to markup problems.

Solving for Percent of Markup on Cost | **EXAMPLE 2**

The manager of a discount store bought hiking boots manufactured in Mexico for $60 and plans to sell them for $81 a pair. Find the percent of markup based on cost.

SOLUTION

Set up the problem using the table form given earlier. Since this problem is related to markup based on cost, cost is the base, or 100%. All other percents *must be in terms of cost*.

100%	C	$60	base
? %	M	$?	
? %	S	$81	

Find the unknown values as follows.

$$\text{Markup} = \text{Selling price} - \text{Cost}$$
$$= \quad \$81 \quad - \$60 = \$21$$

$$\text{Markup percent} = \text{Markup} \div \text{Cost}$$
$$= \quad \$21 \quad \div \$60 = 35\%$$

$$\text{Selling price percent} = 100\% + \text{Markup percent}$$
$$= 100\% + \quad 35\% \quad = 135\%$$

The following table shows that the markup based on cost is 35% and that the selling price is 135% of cost.

100%	C	$60	base
35%	M	$21	
135%	S	$81	

The calculator solution to this example is as follows.

$$(\boxed{81} \; \boxed{-} \; \boxed{60} \;) \; \boxed{\div} \; \boxed{60} \; \boxed{=} \; .35$$

Note: Refer to Appendix B for calculator basics.

QUICK CHECK 2

A retail buyer purchased some pedometers at a cost of $12 and will sell them for $16. What is the percent of markup based on cost?

Now we try a different type of example using markup on cost.

Finding Cost When Cost Is Base | **EXAMPLE 3**

Olympic Sports places a markup on a 50-lb iron barbell set of $16, which is 50% based on cost. Find the cost and the selling price.

SOLUTION

Set up the table using the fact that the markup of 50% based on cost is $16. Cost is the base, or 100%. Cost is not known.

100%	C	$?	base
50%	M	$16	
? %	S	$?	

Find the cost using the fact that markup of $16 is 50% of cost.

$$\text{Markup} = 50\% \times \text{Cost}$$
$$\$16 \quad = \quad .5 \times \quad C$$

Divide both sides of the equation by .5 to find

$$C = \$16 \div .5 = \$32$$

Quick TIP ▼

It is important to first find the base (the cost in this problem) and then find the other values in the table.

Complete the table by adding the percent and dollar columns to find the totals.

100%	C	$32	base
+ 50%	M	+$16	
150%	S	$48	

The weight set costs the retailer $32 and is marked up by $16. The selling price of $48 is 150% of the cost of $32.

Finding the Markup and the Selling Price   EXAMPLE 4

Find the markup and the selling price for an Adidas hooded sweatshirt if the cost is $23.60 and the markup is 45% of cost.

SOLUTION

Use the information given to set up the problem.

100%	C	**$23.60**	base
45%	M	$?	
?%	S	$?	

The percent column totals to 145%. Use the basic percent equation to find the following.

$$M = 45\% \text{ of Cost} = .45 \times \$23.60 = \$10.62$$

The selling price can be found either by adding the cost of $23.60 to the markup of $10.62, or as follows:

$$S = 145\% \text{ of Cost} = 1.45 \times \$23.60 = \$34.22$$

The table shows that the selling price of the hooded sweatshirt is $34.22.

100%	C	**$23.60**	base
45%	M	$10.62	
145%	S	$34.22	

This calculator solution uses the percent add-on feature found on many calculators.

23.6 ⊞ 45 ☒ ⊟ 34.22

Finding Cost When Cost Is Base EXAMPLE 5

case IN point

REI sells a lightweight down sleeping bag for very cold weather for $308. If the markup on cost is 40%, find the amount that REI pays for one sleeping bag.

SOLUTION

The cost is 100% and the markup is 40%, so the selling price is 140% of cost.

100%	C	$?	base
40%	M	$?	
140%	S	$308	

It is important to notice that *the base is not known* in this example. So, use the basic percent equation to find the base or think through it as follows:

$$\textbf{140\% of Cost} = \textbf{Selling price}$$
$$1.40 \times C = S$$
$$1.40 \times C = \$308 \quad \textbf{Substitute \$308 for } S.$$
$$C = \frac{\$308}{1.40} \quad \textbf{Divide both sides by 1.40.}$$
$$C = \$220$$

So, the sleeping bag cost $220. Finally, markup = selling price − cost.

$$M = S - C$$
$$= \$308 - \$220 = \$88$$

All values are given in the table.

100%	C	**$220**	base
40%	M	$ 88	
140%	S	$308	

Check the answer by making sure that both column totals are correct.

Finding the Cost and the Markup **EXAMPLE 6**

The retail price of a 50-inch portable basketball system is $549.99. The retailer has operating expenses of 29.5% and wants a 5.5% profit, both based on cost, on this item. First find the total markup on cost; then find cost and markup.

SOLUTION

Add operating expense and profit percents to find the percent markup on cost required by the retailer.

$$\textbf{Markup on cost} = \textbf{operating expense} + \textbf{profit}$$
$$= \quad 29.5\% \quad + 5.5\%$$
$$= 35\%$$

Now set the problem up in the table form.

100%	C	$?	base
35%	M	$?	
? %	S	$549.99	

The percent column total is 135%. Find the base (cost) as follows.

$$\text{Cost} = \frac{\text{Base}}{\text{Rate}} = \frac{\$549.99}{1.35}$$
$$= \mathbf{\$407.40}$$

$$\text{Markup} = \text{Selling price} - \text{Cost}$$
$$= \$549.99 \quad - \mathbf{\$407.40}$$
$$= \$142.59$$

The final table is shown.

100%	C	**$407.40**	base
35%	M	$142.59	
135%	S	$549.99	

The cost is $407.40 and the markup is $142.59.

Quick TIP ▼

Remember, when calculating markup on cost, *cost is always the base* and 100% always goes next to cost.

The QUICK START exercises in each section contain solutions to help you get started.

Solve for the missing numbers. Markup is based on cost. Round dollar amounts to the nearest cent. (See Examples 1–6.)

QUICK START

1. 100% C $12.40
    40% M $ 4.96
    140% S $ 17.36

2. 100% C $5.40
    25% M $1.35
    125% S $6.75

3. % C $
    % M $
    120% S $32.60

4. % C $
    50% M $ 50.00
    % S $

5. % C $
    30% M $ 50.40
    % S $

6. 100% C $78.00
    % M $17.94
    % S $

Find the missing numbers. Round rates to the nearest tenth of a percent and dollar amounts to the nearest cent. (See Examples 1–6.)

QUICK START

	Cost Price	Markup	% Markup on Cost	Selling Price
7.	$9.00	$2.70	30%	$11.70
8.	$36.00	$7.20	20%	$43.20
9.	$12.00	$7.20	___	___
10.	___	___	100%	$68.98
11.	$153.60	___	___	$215.04
12.	___	$54.38	50%	___
13.	___	$8.45	___	$42.25
14.	$7.75	___	28%	___

15. Markup may be calculated on cost or on selling price. Explain why most manufacturers use cost as base when calculating markup. (See Objective 1.)

16. Write the markup formula in vertical form. Define each term. (See Objective 2.)

Solve the following application problems, using cost as a base. Round rates to the nearest tenth of a percent and dollar amounts to the nearest cent.

QUICK START

 17. EXERCYCLE REI pays $330.30 for a ProForm Exercycle, and the markup is 45% of cost. Find the markup.

100% C $330.30 base
  45% M $?
145% S $

$P = B \times R = \$330.30 \times .45 = 148.635 = \$148.64$

17. $148.64 _____

18. **SKI JACKETS**   REI offers ski jackets, sizes S, M, and L, for $138. If the markup is 35% of cost, find the cost.

18. _____

19. **TAIWAN TOOL PRODUCTS**   The cost of some socket-wrench sets from Taiwan is $10.36 per set. Harbor Tool decides to use a markup of 25% on cost. Find the selling price of the socket wrench set.

19. _____

20. **WEIGHT-TRAINING BOOKS**   Gold's Gym sells weight-training books for $15.60 per copy. If this includes a markup of 50% on cost, find the cost.

20. _____

21. **TABLE-TENNIS TABLES**   Target purchases TIGA table-tennis tables at a cost of $180 each. If the company's operating expenses are 16% of cost, and a net profit of 7% of cost is desired, find the selling price of one table-tennis table.

21. _____

22. **TEXTBOOKS**   A college bookstore pays $128.50 for the business math textbook you are currently reading. The bookstore is small and has a fairly high operating expense of 25.4%. The manager of the bookstore also wants a profit of 8.1%. Find the selling price per book and total selling price for 50 books.

22. _____

23. **OUTDOOR LIGHTING**   Patios Plus sold an outdoor lighting set for $119.95. The markup on the set was $23.99. Find **(a)** the cost, **(b)** the markup percent on cost, and **(c)** the selling price as a percent of cost.

(a) _____
(b) _____
(c) _____

24. **GOLF CLUBS**   Olympic Sports had a markup of $46.64 on golf clubs sold for $222.64. Find **(a)** the cost, **(b)** the markup percent on cost, and **(c)** the selling price as a percent of cost.

(a) _____
(b) _____
(c) _____

25. **TRACTOR PARTS**   Bismark Tractor put a markup of 26% on cost on a part for which it paid $450. Find **(a)** the selling price as a percent of cost, **(b)** the selling price, and **(c)** the markup.

(a) _____
(b) _____
(c) _____

26. **CUSTOM-MADE JEWELRY**   A jewelry dealer sold custom-made necklaces at a selling price that was 250% of his cost. If the markup is $135, find **(a)** the markup percent on cost, **(b)** the cost, and **(c)** the selling price.

(a) _____
(b) _____
(c) _____

QUICK CHECK ANSWERS

1. (a) $33   (b) $26   (c) $83
2. 33.3%   (rounded)
3. $240 cost; $324 selling price
4. $9.90 markup; $54.90 selling price
5. $3.84   (rounded)
6. $46.42 cost   (rounded); $18.57 markup (rounded)

8.2 Markup on Selling Price

OBJECTIVES

1 Understand the phrase *markup based on selling price*.
2 Solve markup problems when selling price is the base.
3 Use the markup formula to solve variations of markup problems.
4 Determine the percent markup on cost and the equivalent percent markup on selling price.
5 Convert markup percent on cost to selling price.
6 Convert markup percent on selling price to cost.
7 Find the selling price for perishables.

case IN point

REI faces stiff competition across a range of products from large retailers such as Academy Sports + Outdoors. It also faces serious competition from smaller specialty ski stores when selling items such as skis. In fact, competition is usually very severe in business.

OBJECTIVE 1 Understand the phrase *markup based on selling price*. Markup on cost, discussed in the previous section, is often used by manufacturers. However, retailers often compare business operations to sales revenue and therefore often prefer to use **markup on selling price**. In this case, markup is stated as a percent of selling price.

> **Finding Markup on Selling Price**
>
> $$\text{Markup on selling price} = \frac{\text{Amount of markup}}{\text{Selling price}}$$

The same basic markup formula is used when using markup on selling price: $C + M = S$.

OBJECTIVE 2 Solve markup problems when selling price is the base. The table form used for these problems is identical to that of the previous section. However, *selling price is now the base* rather than cost. Since selling price is the base, put 100% adjacent to selling price, as shown.

? %	C	$	?
%	M	$	
100%	S	**$**	**base**

Solving for Markup on Selling Price   **EXAMPLE 1**

To remain competitive, REI sells Body Glove Sunglasses for only $39.99. They pay $35 for each pair and calculate markup on selling price. Find the amount of markup, the percent of markup on selling price, and the percent of cost on selling price.

SOLUTION

Set up the problem.

?%	C	$35.00
?%	M	$?
100%	S	$39.99 **base**

Markup = Selling price − Cost
$$= \quad \$39.99 \quad - \quad \$35 = \$4.99$$

Solve for either of the rates and subtract the result from 100% to find the other. For example, here we solve for the markup rate using the basic percent formula at the lower left.

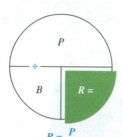

$$R = \frac{P}{B}$$

$$\textbf{Rate} = \frac{\textbf{Part}}{\textbf{Base}}$$
$$= \frac{\$4.99}{\$39.99}$$
$$= 12.5\% \quad \textbf{(rounded)}$$

Cost as a percent of selling price can be found either by subtracting 100% − 12.5%, or by dividing the cost of $35 by the selling price of $39.99. Notice that percents are rounded to the nearest tenth of a percent.

87.5%	C	$35.00
12.5%	M	$4.99
100.0%	S	**$39.99** **base**

Here, selling price is the base and is associated with 100%. The markup in this example is very low—REI will probably take a loss on these sunglasses, but managers hope the low price will bring customers into the store.

QUICK CHECK 1

The cost of a two-piece exercise suit is $13.50 and the selling price is $19.99. Find **(a)** the amount of markup, **(b)** the percent of markup on selling price, and **(c)** the percent of cost on selling price.

Markups vary widely from industry to industry and from business to business. This variation is a result of different costs of merchandise, operating costs, levels of profit margin, and local competition. The next table shows average markups for different types of retail stores.

Average Markups for Retail Stores (Markup on Selling Price)

TYPE OF STORE	MARKUP	TYPE OF STORE	MARKUP
General merchandise stores	29.97%	Furniture and home furnishings	35.75%
Grocery stores	22.05%	Bars	52.49%
Other food stores	27.31%	Restaurants	56.35%
Motor vehicle dealers (new)	12.83%	Drug and proprietary stores	30.81%
Gasoline service stations	14.47%	Liquor stores	20.19%
Other automotive dealers	29.57%	Sporting goods and bicycle shops	29.72%
Apparel and accessories	37.64%	Gift, novelty, and souvenir shops	41.86%

(*Source:* Sole-proprietorship income tax returns, U.S. Treasury Dept., Internal Revenue Service, Statistics Division.)

OBJECTIVE 3 Use the markup formula to solve variations of markup problems. As with problems where markup is based on cost, this basic formula may be used for all markup problems in which selling price is the base. In each of these examples, the selling price has a percent value of 100%.

Finding Cost When Selling Price Is Base   **EXAMPLE 2**

A Kmart® employee needs a 35% markup on selling price in order to have a markup of $5.16 on a pair of "PRO CLASSIC" Batting Gloves. How much can Kmart afford to pay for each pair of gloves?

SOLUTION

Cost as a percent of selling price is found by subtracting 35% from 100% to find 65%.

65%	C	$?
35%	M	$5.16
100%	S	$? base

Find the selling price as follows.

$$\text{Markup} = \textbf{35\% of selling price}$$
$$\$5.16 = .35 \times S$$

Divide both sides by .35 to find the selling price.

$$S = \$5.16 \div .35 = \$14.74 \quad \textbf{base} \quad \textbf{(rounded)}$$

Finally, find cost by subtracting.

$$C = S - M = \$14.74 - \$5.16 = \$9.58$$

The final table is shown here.

65%	C	$ 9.58
35%	M	$ 5.16
100%	S	$14.74

QUICK CHECK 2

The manager of a golf pro shop wants a 15% markup on selling price so that she can have a markup of $13.50 on a "Tiger Lies" fairway wood golf club. How much can she afford to pay for each club?

Finding Markup When Selling Price Is Given   **EXAMPLE 3**

Marilyn Westby must calculate the markup on a Wilson youth tennis racket. The selling price of the tennis racket is $15.99, and the markup is 20% of selling price. Find the markup.

SOLUTION

Cost as a percent of selling price is found by subtracting 20% from 100% to find 80%.

80%	C	$?
20%	M	$?
100%	S	$15.99 base

Solve for the missing values using $P = R \times B$:

$$\text{Cost} = \$15.99 \times .8 = \$12.79 \quad \textbf{(rounded)}$$
$$\text{Markup} = \text{Selling price} - \text{Cost}$$
$$= \$15.99 - \$12.79 = \$3.20$$

The markup is $3.20.

Quick TIP ▼

If the rate for cost, 80%, had been used in the formula, the result would have been the cost.

QUICK CHECK 3

The selling price of a three-pack of tennis balls is $3.95, and the markup is 25% of selling price. Find the markup.

Finding Markup When Cost Is Given   **EXAMPLE 4**

Find the markup on a dartboard made in England if the cost is $27.45 and the markup is 25% of selling price.

SOLUTION

Subtract 25% from 100% to find that cost is 75% of selling price.

75%	C	$27.45?
25%	M	$?
100%	S	$? base

Solve for cost as follows.

$$Cost = 75\% \text{ of Selling price}$$
$$\$27.45 = .75 \times S$$
$$S = \$27.45 \div .75 \qquad \textbf{Divide both sides by .75.}$$
$$S = \$36.60$$

Finally:

$$Selling\ price - Cost = \$36.60 - \$27.45$$
$$= \$9.15$$

Here is the completed table.

75%	C	$27.45	
25%	M	$ 9.15	
100%	S	**$36.60**	**base**

Quick TIP ▼

Remember, when calculating markup on selling price, *selling price* is *always the base* and 100% always goes next to selling price.

QUICK CHECK 4

What is the markup on a sleeping bag if the cost is $40.80 and the markup is 32% of selling price?

OBJECTIVE 4 **Determine the percent markup on cost and the equivalent percent markup on selling price.** Sometimes a markup based on cost must be compared with a markup based on selling price. For example, a salesperson who sells to both manufacturers which use markup on cost and to retailers which use markup on selling price might have to make conversions from one markup method to the other. Make these comparisons by first computing the markup on cost and then the markup on selling price.

Determining Equivalent Markups **EXAMPLE 5**

Benito's Fishing Lures, Inc., makes and sells a lot of fishing lures and struggles to keep costs very low. One particular lure has a cost of $2.10 and is sold to distributors and wholesalers for $3.20. Find the percent markup on cost and also the percent markup on selling price.

SOLUTION

First set up the problem using *cost as the base*, or 100%.

100%	**C**	**$2.10**	**base**
? %	M	$?	
? %	S	$3.20	

Markup = $S - C = \$3.20 - \$2.10 = \$1.10$
Markup as a percent of cost = $\$1.10 \div \$2.10 = 52.4\%$ **(rounded)**
Selling price as a percent of cost = $100\% + 52.4\% = 152.4\%$

Next, set up the table with *selling price as the base*, or 100%. The markup of $1.10 remains the same and can be entered in the table.

? %	C	$2.10	
? %	M	$1.10	
100%	**S**	**$3.20**	**base**

Cost as a percent of selling price = $\$2.10 \div \$3.20 = 65.6\%$ **(rounded)**
Markup as a percent of selling price = $100\% - 65.6\% = 34.4\%$

This example shows that a 52.4% markup on cost results in the same dollar markup as a 34.4% markup on selling price. In other words, a 52.4% markup on cost is equivalent to a 34.4% markup on selling price.

QUICK CHECK 5

The cost of a Razor A-3 Kick Scooter is $45 and it sells for $59.99. Find **(a)** the percent of markup on cost and **(b)** the percent of markup on selling price.

Some people in the retail business use markup on cost and others use markup on selling price. Neither is better than the other—the two just represent different ways to talk about the same thing. Some companies and managers tend to use one of them, and other companies and managers tend to use the other.

OBJECTIVE 5 Convert markup percent on cost to selling price. Another method for markup comparisons is to use **conversion formulas**.

> **Converting Markup Percent on Cost to Markup Percent on Selling Price**
>
> $$\frac{\% \text{ markup on cost}}{100\% + \% \text{ markup on cost}} = \% \text{ markup on selling price}$$

Converting Markup on Cost to Markup on Selling Price

 EXAMPLE 6

Convert a markup of 25% on cost to its equivalent markup on selling price.

SOLUTION

Use the formula for converting markup on cost to markup on selling price.

$$\frac{\% \text{ markup on cost}}{100\% + \% \text{ markup on cost}} = \% \text{ markup on selling price}$$

$$\frac{25\%}{100\% + 25\%} = \frac{25\%}{125\%} = \frac{.25}{1.25} = .20 = 20\%$$

As shown, a markup of 25% on cost is equivalent to a markup of 20% on selling price.

The markup on cost (25%) is divided by 100% plus the markup on cost.

25 % ÷ (100 % + 25 %) = 0.2

> **QUICK CHECK 6**
>
> Convert a markup of 100% on cost to a markup on selling price.

OBJECTIVE 6 Convert markup percent on selling price to cost.

> **Converting Markup Percent on Selling Price to Markup Percent on Cost**
>
> $$\frac{\% \text{ markup on selling price}}{100\% - \% \text{ markup on selling price}} = \% \text{ markup on cost}$$

Converting Markup on Selling Price to Markup on Cost

 EXAMPLE 7

Convert a markup of 20% on selling price to its equivalent markup on cost.

SOLUTION

Use the formula for converting markup on selling price to markup on cost.

$$\frac{\% \text{ markup on selling price}}{100\% - \% \text{ markup on selling price}} = \% \text{ markup on cost}$$

$$\frac{20\%}{100\% - 20\%} = \frac{20\%}{80\%} = \frac{.2}{.8} = .25 = 25\%$$

A markup of 20% on selling price is equivalent to a markup of 25% on cost.

> **QUICK CHECK 7**
>
> Convert a markup of 40% on selling price to a markup on cost.

The following table shows common markups expressed as percent on cost and as percent on selling price. A table like this is helpful to anyone using markup equivalents on a regular basis.

Markup Equivalents

MARKUP ON COST	MARKUP ON SELLING PRICE
20%	$16\frac{2}{3}\%$
25%	20%
$33\frac{1}{3}\%$	25%
50%	$33\frac{1}{3}\%$
$66\frac{2}{3}\%$	40%
75%	$42\frac{6}{7}\%$
100%	50%

OBJECTIVE 7 Find the selling price for perishables. When a business sells items that are perishable (such as baked goods, fruits, or vegetables), the fact that some items will spoil and cannot be sold must be considered when determining the selling price of each item that is sold.

The bar graph below shows the top 10 retailers in the United States. Which of these companies do you think considers perishables as part of their business operations? It appears that half of them sell groceries as part of the product line.

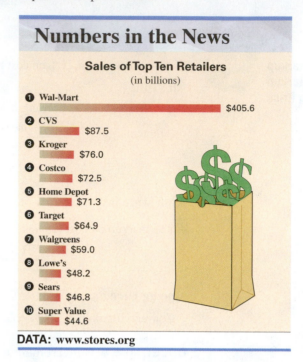

Numbers in the News

Sales of Top Ten Retailers
(in billions)

- ❶ **Wal-Mart** — $405.6
- ❷ **CVS** — $87.5
- ❸ **Kroger** — $76.0
- ❹ **Costco** — $72.5
- ❺ **Home Depot** — $71.3
- ❻ **Target** — $64.9
- ❼ **Walgreens** — $59.0
- ❽ **Lowe's** — $48.2
- ❾ **Sears** — $46.8
- ❿ **Super Value** — $44.6

DATA: www.stores.org

Finding Selling Price for Perishables   **EXAMPLE 8**

The Bagel Boy bakes 60 dozen bagels at a cost of $2.16 per dozen. If a markup of 50% on selling price is needed and 5% of the bagels remain unsold and will be donated to a shelter, find the selling price per dozen bagels.

SOLUTION

Step 1   Find the total cost of the bagels.

$$\text{Cost} = 60 \text{ dozen} \times \$2.16 = \$129.60$$

Step 2   Find the selling price, using a markup of 50% of selling price.

50%	C	$129.60
50%	M	$
100%	S	$? **base**

$$\text{Base} = \frac{\text{Part}}{\text{Rate}} = \frac{\mathbf{\$129.60}}{.5} = \$259.20$$

The total selling price is $259.20.

Step 3   Find the number of dozen bagels that will be sold. Since 5% will not be sold, 95%(100% − 5%) will be sold.

$$95\% \times 60 \text{ dozen} = \mathbf{57} \text{ dozen bagels sold}$$

The selling price of $259.20 must be received from the sale of **57** dozen bagels.

Step 4   Find the selling price per dozen bagels by dividing the total selling price by the number of bagels sold.

$$\frac{\$259.20}{57} = \$4.55 \text{ selling price per dozen}   \text{(rounded)}$$

A selling price of $4.55 per dozen gives the desired markup of 50% on selling price while allowing for 5% of the bagels to be unsold.

QUICK CHECK 8

The Cookie Jar bakes 80 dozen cookies at a cost of $1.08 per dozen. If a markup of 60% on selling price is needed and 10% of the cookies remain unsold and will be donated, find the selling price per dozen cookies.

8.2 Exercises

The **QUICK START** exercises in each section contain solutions to help you get started.

Solve for the missing numbers. Markup is based on selling price. Round dollar amounts to the nearest cent. (See Examples 1–4.)

QUICK START

1.	75%	C	$21.00	2.	60%	C	$18.60	3.		C	$145.00
	25%	M	$ 7.00		40%	M	$12.40			M	
	100%	S	**$28.00**		100%	S	**$31.00**		100%	S	$250.00

4.	$66\frac{2}{3}\%$	C		5.	50%	C	$2025	6.	65%	C	
		M	$ 89.00			M				M	$ 527.80
		S				S				S	

Find the missing quantities by first computing the markup on one base and then computing the markup on the other. Round rates to the nearest tenth of a percent and dollar amounts to the nearest cent. (See Example 5.)

QUICK START

	Cost	Markup	Selling Price	% Markup on Cost	% Markup on Selling Price
7.	**$1920**	$480.00	**$2400.00**	25%	20%
8.	**$357.52**	$78.48	$436.00	**22%**	**18%**
9.	$13.80	_____	_____	_____	38%
10.	$33.75	_____	$67.50	_____	_____
11.	_____	$300.00	_____	40%	_____
12.	$5.15	_____	$15.45	_____	_____

Find the equivalent markups on either cost or selling price using the appropriate formula. Round to the nearest tenth of a percent. (See Examples 6 and 7.)

QUICK START

	Markup on Cost	Markup on Selling Price			Markup on Cost	Markup on Selling Price
13.	100%	**50%**		14.	_____	20%
	$\frac{100\%}{100\% + 100\%} = \frac{1}{2} = .5 = 50\%$					
15.	18%	_____		16.	50%	_____

17. Use the table on page 308 to find the three types of retail stores with the lowest markups. Why do markups differ so much from one type of retail store to another?

18. To have a markup of 100% or greater, the markup must be calculated on cost. Show why this is always true. (See Objective 6.)

▲ indicates an exercise that is related to the Case in Point feature.

Solve the following application problems. Round rates to the nearest tenth of a percent and dollar amounts to the nearest cent.

19. **HOME-WORKOUT EQUIPMENT**   Olympics Sports has a markup of $437.50 on an Epic Perspective 1.0 treadmill. If this is a 35% markup on selling price, find **(a)** the selling price, **(b)** the cost, and **(c)** the cost as a percent of selling price.

(a) _____

(b) _____

(c) _____

20. **SWIMMING POOL PUMP**   Leslie's Pool Supply pays $187.19 for a new pool pump. If the markup is 28% on the selling price, find **(a)** the cost as a percent of selling price, **(b)** the selling price, and **(c)** the markup.

(a) _____

(b) _____

(c) _____

21. **BLOUSES**   Jana's Boutique purchased 20 blouses for $930. It sold 12 of the blouses for $85 each, 5 blouses for $68 each, and the remaining blouses for $49 each. Find **(a)** the total amount received for the blouses, **(b)** the total markup, **(c)** the markup percent on selling price, and **(d)** the equivalent markup percent on cost.

(a) _____

(b) _____

(c) _____

(d) _____

22. **RIVER-RAFT SALES**   Olympic Sports purchased a job lot of 380 river rafts for $7600. If they sold 158 of the rafts at $45 each, 74 at $35 each, 56 at $30 each, and the remainder at $25 each, find **(a)** the total amount received for the rafts, **(b)** the total markup, **(c)** the markup percent on selling price, and **(d)** the equivalent markup percent on cost.

(a) _____

(b) _____

(c) _____

(d) _____

23. **SELLING BANANAS**   The produce manager at Tom Thumb Market knows that 10% of the bananas purchased will spoil and will have to be thrown out. If she buys 500 pounds of bananas for $.56 per pound and wants a markup of 45% on the selling price, find the selling price per pound of bananas.

23. _____

24. **POTTERY-SHOP SALES**   The Aztec Pottery Shop finds that 15% of their production cannot be sold. If they produce 100 items at a cost of $12.90 each and desire a markup of 40% on selling price, find the selling price per item.

24. _____

Supplementary Application Exercises on Markup

Solve each of the following application problems. Round rates to the nearest tenth of a percent and dollar amounts to the nearest cent.

1. **DRUMS**   Baytown Music pays $1040 for a Yamaha extreme electronic drum set. Find the markup if the markup percent on cost is 53.8%.

   1. _____

2. **BED IN A BAG**   A complete comforter and sheet set has a cost of $132 to the retailer and is marked up 45% on cost. Find the markup.

   2. _____

3. **SNOWBOARD PACKAGES**   What percent of markup on cost must be used if an Atlantis Snowboard package costing $335 is sold for $399?

   3. _____

4. **WINE**   Benjamin's Discount Wines sells a particular bottle of wine for $15.95. If it pays an average of $9.97 per bottle, find the percent markup on cost.

   4. _____

5. **AUTOMOTIVE SUPPLIES**   An auto-parts dealer pays $41.88 per dozen cans of Chevron Techron fuel-injector cleaner and the markup is 50% on selling price. Find the selling price per can.

   5. _____

6. **GIFT SHOP SALES**   Goodies Gifts pays $26.88 for one-half dozen stoneware milk jug banks. If the markup is 50% of the selling price, what is the selling price per bank?

   6. _____

7. **CEILING FANS**   The Fan Gallery's cost for a ceiling fan is $92.82 and its markup is 22% on the selling price. Find the selling price.

   7. _____

 8. **FLY-FISHING**   REI pays $62.40 for a fly rod and marks it up 35% on selling price. Find the selling price.

   8. _____

9. **GOLF CART**   A dealer pays $112.40 for an Express 180 golf cart. The markup is 24% on selling price. Find **(a)** the cost as a percent of selling price, **(b)** the selling price, and **(c)** the markup.

   (a) _____
   (b) _____
   (c) _____

10. **DOUBLE-PANE WINDOWS**   Eastern Building Supply pays $3808 for all the double-pane windows needed for the back wall of a 3-bedroom, 2-bath home. If the markup on the windows is 15% on selling price, what is **(a)** the cost as a percent of selling price, **(b)** the selling price, and **(c)** the markup?

    (a) _____
    (b) _____
    (c) _____

 indicates an exercise that is related to the Case in Point feature.

11. **COMMUNICATION EQUIPMENT**   A discount store purchased DVD players at a cost of $288 per dozen. If the store needs 20% of cost to cover operating expenses and 15% of cost for the net profit, what are **(a)** the selling price of a DVD player and **(b)** the percent of markup on selling price?

(a) _____

(b) _____

12. **BOWLING EQUIPMENT**   The Bowlers Pro-Shop determines that operating expenses are 23% of selling price and desires a net profit of 12% of selling price. If the cost of a team shirt is $29.25, what are **(a)** the selling price and **(b)** the percent of markup on cost?

(a) _____

(b) _____

13. **MOUNTAIN BIKE SALES**   REI advertises mountain bikes for $199.90. If the store's cost is $2100 per dozen, what are **(a)** the markup per bicycle, **(b)** the percent of markup on selling price, and **(c)** the percent of markup on cost?

(a) _____

(b) _____

(c) _____

14. **COMPUTER FLASH DRIVE**   Office Depot advertises 32 GB USB 2.0 flash drives for $49.99. Their cost is $449.91 per dozen. Find **(a)** the markup per flash drive, **(b)** the percent of markup on selling price, and **(c)** the percent of markup on cost.

(a) _____

(b) _____

(c) _____

15. **LONG-STEMMED ROSES**   Farmers Flowers purchased 12 gross of long-stemmed roses at a cost of $1890. If 25% of the roses cannot be sold and a markup of 100% on cost is needed, find the regular selling price per dozen roses.

15. _____

16. **SPORTSWEAR**   Olympic Sports buys 2000 baseball caps at $5.00 per hat. If a markup of 50% on selling price is needed and 5% of the caps are damaged and cannot be sold, what is the selling price of each cap?

16. _____

8.3 Markdown

OBJECTIVES

1 Define the term *markdown* when applied to selling.
2 Calculate markdown, reduced price, and percent of markdown.
3 Define the terms associated with loss.
4 Determine the break-even point and operating loss.
5 Determine the amount of a gross or absolute loss.

case IN point ▶

James Smelter keeps a close eye on inventory at the REI store in which he works. He notes some slow-moving winter parkas of odd colors and sizes and marks them down to move them out of the store. It is important to move slow-moving inventory out of stores to make room for other items that are in demand.

Markdowns are used to stimulate sales volume. The newspaper clipping shows how slashed prices have stimulated the sales of electronics items for holiday gift giving. When retailers discounted high-profile products, "men took the opportunity to stock up on their own entertainment centers."

Lower Prices Increase Sales

After distressed retailers marked down the prices on electronic items, men rushed in to buy. They bought flat–screen TVs, laptop computers, and cell phones. Men in the area spent an average of $450.67 compared with $365.20 spent by women during the weekend after Thanksgiving. Men usually don't shop just after Thanksgiving, but the markdowns on electronic items brought them out in force.

OBJECTIVE 1 Define the term *markdown* when applied to selling. When merchandise does not sell at its marked price, the price is often reduced. The difference between the original selling price and the reduced selling price is called the **markdown**, with the selling price after the markdown called the **reduced price, sale price**, or **actual selling price**. The basic **formula for markdown** is as follows.

Finding Reduced Price

$$\text{Reduced price} = \text{Original price} - \text{Markdown}$$

Finding the Reduced Price   **EXAMPLE 1**

Olympic Sports has marked down an Atlas Home Fitness Center. Find the reduced price if the original price was $2879 and the markdown is 30%.

SOLUTION

The markdown is 30% of $2879, or $.3 \times \$2879 = \$863.70$. Find the reduced price as follows.

OBJECTIVE 2 Calculate markdown, reduced price, and percent of markdown.

$2879.00	original price
− 863.70	markdown (.30 × $2879)
$2015.30	reduced price (70% of original price)

▦ The calculator solution to this example uses the complement, with respect to 1, of the discount.

$2879 ⊠ ⟮ 1 ⊟ .3 ⟯ ⊜ 2015.3

Quick TIP ▼

The original selling price is always the base or 100%, and the percent of markdown is always calculated on the original selling price.

The next example shows how to find a **percent of markdown**.

Calculating the Percent of Markdown   **EXAMPLE 2**

The total inventory of coffee mugs at the local bookstore has a retail value of $785. If the mugs were sold at reduced prices that totaled $530, what is the percent of markdown on the original price?

SOLUTION

First find the amount of the markdown.

$$\begin{array}{rl} \$785 & \text{original price} \\ - \quad 530 & \text{reduced price} \\ \hline \$255 & \text{markdown} \end{array}$$

Finding the percent of the original price that is the markdown is a rate problem. (See Chapter 3.)

$$\text{Rate} = \frac{\textbf{Part}}{\textbf{Base}} = \frac{255}{785} = .3248 = 32\% \text{ markdown rounded to the nearest whole percent}$$

The mugs were sold at a markdown of 32%.

Finding the Original Price   **EXAMPLE 3**

Bouza's Baby News offers a child's car seat at a reduced price of $63 after a 25% markdown from the original price. Find the original price.

SOLUTION

After the 25% markdown, the reduced price of $63 represents 75% of the original price. The original price, or base, must be found.

$$\text{Base} = \frac{\textbf{Part}}{\textbf{Rate}} = \frac{63}{.75} = \$84 \text{ original price}$$

The original price of the car seat was $84.

Check the answer by subtracting 25% of $84 from $84: $84 − (.25 × $84) = $63.

Quick TIP ▼

In Example 3, notice that 75% is used in the formula rather than 25%. The reduced price, $63, is represented by 75%.

OBJECTIVE 3 Define the terms associated with loss. Managers want to sell items for the full retail price to maximize profit. However, sometimes they must mark down the prices of slow-moving or discontinued items to move them out of the store. But marking prices down reduces the profit on an item, and it may even result in a loss, depending on the amount of the markdown. Here are some important terms.

The **break-even point** is a selling price that covers just the cost of the item plus the associated overhead, including operating expenses. A company neither makes nor loses money on an item sold at the break-even point.

A **reduced net profit** occurs when an item is marked down from the original price but is still sold for more than the break-even point.

An **operating loss** occurs when the selling price of an item is below the break-even point but above the cost of the item.

An **absolute loss**, or **gross loss**, occurs if the selling price is less than the actual cost paid for the item. For example, a firm that buys a pair of slacks for $38 and then sells the slacks for $25 has an absolute loss, which is the difference between the two, or $13.

The following diagram illustrates the meaning of these terms.

These formulas may help you.

Break-even point = Cost + Operating expenses

Operating loss = Break-even point − Reduced selling price

Absolute loss = Cost − Reduced selling price

Determining a Profit or a Loss

 EXAMPLE 4

Appliance Giant paid $1600 for a 52-inch LCD flat-panel HDTV. If operating expenses are 30% of cost and the television is sold for $2000, find the amount of profit or loss.

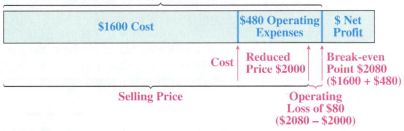

SOLUTION

Operating expenses are 30% of cost.

$$\text{Operating expenses} = .30 \times \$1600 = \$480$$

The break-even point for the LCD HDTV is

$$\text{Cost} + \text{Operating expenses} = \text{Break-even point}$$
$$\$1600 + (.3 \times \$1600) = \$1600 + \$480 = \$2080 \text{ break-even point}$$

So, the company makes a profit if the television is sold for more than the $2080 break-even point or incurs a loss if sold for less. Since the selling price is $2000, there is a loss, found as follows.

$$\$2080 - \$2000 = \$80$$

The $80 loss is an operating loss, since the selling price is less than the break-even point but greater than the cost.

⊞ The calculator solution to this example follows.

1600 ⊞ ⦅ .3 ⊠ 1600 ⦆ ⊟ 2000 ▣ 80

QUICK CHECK 4

Big Chime Electronics paid $480 for a flat-screen television set. If operating expenses are 35% of cost and the television is sold for $600, find the amount of the operating loss.

Determining the **Operating Loss and the Absolute Loss**

EXAMPLE 5

A game table normally selling for $360 at Dick's Sporting Goods is marked down 30%. If the cost of the game table is $260 and the operating expenses are 20% of cost, find **(a)** the operating loss and **(b)** the absolute loss.

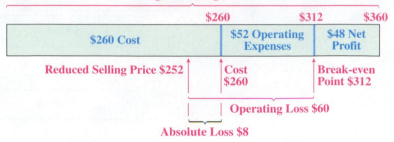

Original Selling Price

$260		$312	$360
$260 Cost		$52 Operating Expenses	$48 Net Profit

Reduced Selling Price $252 ↑   Cost $260 ↑   Break-even Point $312 ↑

Operating Loss $60

Absolute Loss $8

SOLUTION

(a) Break-even point = Cost + Operating expenses
$$= \$260 + \quad 20\% \text{ of } \$260$$
$$= \$312$$

Reduced price $= \$360 - (.3 \times \$360) = \$360 - \$108 = \$252$

Operating loss $= \$312 \text{ break-even point} - \$252 \text{ reduced price} = \$60$

(b) The absolute or gross loss is the difference between the cost and the reduced price.

$$\$260 \text{ cost} - \$252 \text{ reduced price} = \$8 \text{ absolute loss}$$

QUICK CHECK 5

A propane forced-air heater normally selling for $290 is marked down 25%. If the cost of the heater is $220 and the operating expenses are 15% of cost, find **(a)** the operating loss and **(b)** the absolute loss.

The following bar graph shows the percent of adults who get an emotional high from making certain purchases. Customers love buying things—especially when they are on sale. This is valuable information to manufacturers, retailers, and all merchandisers.

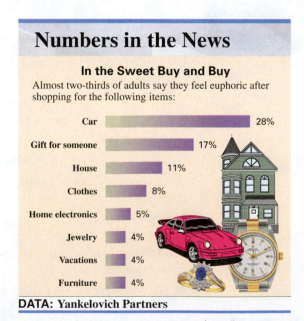

Numbers in the News

In the Sweet Buy and Buy

Almost two-thirds of adults say they feel euphoric after shopping for the following items:

Car	28%
Gift for someone	17%
House	11%
Clothes	8%
Home electronics	5%
Jewelry	4%
Vacations	4%
Furniture	4%

DATA: Yankelovich Partners

8.3 Exercises

The **QUICK START** exercises in each section contain solutions to help you get started.

Find the missing quantities. Round rates to the nearest whole percent and dollar amounts to the nearest cent. (See Examples 1–3.)

QUICK START

	Original Price	% Markdown	$ Markdown	Reduced Price
1.	$860	<u>25%</u>	$215	<u>$645</u>

$$R = \frac{P}{B} = \frac{215}{860} = .25 = 25\%; \quad \$860 - \$215 = \$645$$

	Original Price	% Markdown	$ Markdown	Reduced Price
2.	<u>$240</u>	40%	<u>$96</u>	$144

$$B = \frac{P}{R} = \frac{144}{.6} = \$240; \quad \$240 - \$144 = \$96$$

	Original Price	% Markdown	$ Markdown	Reduced Price
3.	$61.60	____	____	$43.12
4.	____	$66\frac{2}{3}\%$	____	$3.10
5.	$6.50	____	$1.30	____
6.	____	50%	$65.25	____

Complete the following. If there is no operating loss or absolute loss, write "none."
(See Examples 4 and 5.)

QUICK START

	Cost	Operating Expense	Break-even Point	Reduced Price	Operating Loss	Absolute Loss
7.	$96	$24	<u>$120</u>	$100	<u>$20</u>	<u>none</u>

$$\$96 + \$24 = \$120; \quad \$120 - \$100 = \$20$$

	Cost	Operating Expense	Break-even Point	Reduced Price	Operating Loss	Absolute Loss
8.	$25	$8	<u>$33</u>	$22	<u>$11</u>	<u>$3</u>

$$\$25 + \$8 = \$33; \quad \$33 - \$22 = \$11; \quad \$25 - \$22 = \$3$$

	Cost	Operating Expense	Break-even Point	Reduced Price	Operating Loss	Absolute Loss
9.	$50	____	$66	$44	____	____
10.	$12.50	____	$16.50	$11	____	____
11.	$310	$75	____	____	$135	____
12.	$156	$44	____	____	$60	____

13. Give five reasons a store will mark down the price of merchandise to get it sold.

14. As a result of a markdown, there are three possible results: reduced net profit, operating loss, and absolute loss. As a business owner, which would concern you the most? Explain. (See Objectives 4 and 5.)

Solve the following application problems. Round rates to the nearest whole percent and dollar amounts to the nearest cent.

QUICK START

15. **GPS SYSTEMS**   Best Buy prices its entire inventory of Tom Tom portable in-car Global Positioning Systems at $133,509. If the original price of the inventory was $226,284, find the percent of markdown on the original price.

$226,284 - $133,509 = $92,775;

$R = \frac{P}{B} = \frac{92,775}{226,284} = .409 = 41\%$

15. _41%_____

16. **OAK DESK**   An oak desk originally priced at $837.50 is reduced to $686.75. Find the percent of markdown on the original price.

16. _____

17. **ELLIPTICAL TRAINER**   Olympic Sports paid $360 for a ProForm 850 elliptical trainer. The operating expenses are $33\frac{1}{3}\%$ of cost. If they sell the elliptical trainer at a clearance price of $449.99, find the amount of profit or loss.

17. _____

18. **KAYAK**   REI has an end-of-season sale, during which it sells an ocean kayak for two people for $865. If the cost was $641 and operating expenses are 28% of cost, find the amount of profit or loss.

18. _____

19. **TRUCK ACCESSORIES**   Pep Boys Automotive paid $208.50 for a pickup truck bedliner. The original selling price was $291.90, but this was marked down 35%. If operating expenses are 28% of the cost, find **(a)** the operating loss and **(b)** the absolute loss.

(a) _____

(b) _____

20. **ANTIQUES**   American Antiques paid $153.49 for a fern stand. The original selling price was $208.78, but this was marked down 46% in order to make room for incoming merchandise. If operating expenses are 14.9% of cost, find **(a)** the operating loss and **(b)** the absolute loss.

(a) _____

(b) _____

QUICK CHECK ANSWERS

1. $173.99   (rounded)

2. 75%

3. $29.98   (rounded)

4. $48 operating loss

5. (a) $35.50 operating loss

  (b) $2.50 absolute loss

8.4 Turnover and Valuation of Inventory

OBJECTIVES

1 Determine average inventory.

2 Calculate inventory turnover.

3 Methods for tracking inventory.

4 Use the specific identification method to value inventory.

5 Determine inventory value using the weighted-average method.

6 Use the FIFO method to value inventory.

7 Use the LIFO method to value inventory.

8 Estimate inventory value using the retail method.

case in point ▶

The marketing and inventory managers at REI work together to make sure they order only products that will sell. The last thing either wants is for inventory to build up needlessly in the company stores and warehouses.

OBJECTIVE 1 Determine average inventory. Several measures of the financial performance of a company are based on **average inventory**. Find average inventory by finding the average (mean) of all inventories taken during a specific interval of time, such as a month or a quarter. For example, some firms take a physical inventory only once a quarter. In that event, the average inventory for the quarter is the average of the beginning and ending inventory for the quarter.

Determining Average Inventory   **EXAMPLE 1**

Inventory at Dick's Sporting Goods was $285,672 on April 1 and $198,560 on April 30. What was the average inventory?

SOLUTION

First add the inventory values.

$$\begin{array}{ll} \$285,672 & \textbf{April 1} \\ +\ \ 198,560 & \textbf{April 30} \\ \hline \$484,232 & \end{array}$$

Then divide by the number of times inventory was taken.

$$\frac{\$484,232}{2} = \$242,116$$

The average inventory was $242,116.

QUICK CHECK 1

Inventory on September 1 was $176,840 and on September 30 it was $153,210. Find the average inventory.

Management must carefully monitor and control the inventory of each item. Inventories can become too large due to a business recession or simply because a particular product is not popular among consumers. To reduce the inventories of slow-moving products, it may be necessary to mark prices down, increase advertising, or do both at the same time. The following ad is evidence of a sale designed to reduce inventory.

OBJECTIVE 2 Calculate inventory turnover. One measure of how well a company is doing financially is based on how fast inventory is moving, as measured by **inventory turnover**, also called **inventory turns** and **stock turnover**. Inventory turnover varies widely from one business to the next. For example, a flower shop must turn inventory over rapidly to avoid the costly waste of wilting flowers. On the other hand, a furniture store will have a lower inventory turnover since furniture often sits in a store before being sold.

Inventory turnover refers to the number of times the average inventory is turned over, or sold, during a period of time, such as a year. Businesses value inventory either at retail or at cost. For this reason, inventory turnover can be found using either of these formulas. Both are used in business.

Measuring Inventory Turnover

$$\text{Turnover at retail} = \frac{\text{Retail sales}}{\text{Average inventory at retail}}$$

$$\text{Turnover at cost} = \frac{\text{Cost of goods sold}}{\text{Average inventory at cost}}$$

The turnover ratio may be identical by using either method. The variation that often exists is caused by stolen merchandise (called *inventory shrinkage*) or merchandise that has been marked down or has become unsellable. Normally, turnover at retail is slightly lower than turnover at cost. For this reason, many businesses prefer this more conservative figure.

Finding Stock Turnover at Retail — **EXAMPLE 2**

During May, Red Lolly Pop Children's Apparel had retail sales of $55,194 and an average retail inventory of $19,712. Find the stock turnover at retail.

SOLUTION

$$\text{Turnover at retail} = \frac{\text{Retail sales}}{\text{Average inventory at retail}} = \frac{\$55,194}{\$19,712} = \textbf{2.8 at retail} \quad \textbf{(rounded)}$$

On average, the store turned over or sold the value of its entire inventory 2.8 times during the month.

QUICK CHECK 2

In July, Painters Supply had an average retail inventory of $112,040 and retail sales of $183,308. Find the stock turnover at retail.

Finding Stock Turnover at Cost — **EXAMPLE 3**

If the average inventory value at cost for Red Lolly Pop Children's Apparel in Example 2 was $11,826 and the cost of goods sold was $34,134, find the stock turnover at cost.

SOLUTION

$$\text{Turnover at cost} = \frac{\text{Cost of goods sold}}{\text{Average inventory at cost}} = \frac{\$34,134}{\$11,826} = \textbf{2.9 at cost} \quad \textbf{(rounded)}$$

Notice that the two turnover values from Examples 2 and 3 are similar, as expected.

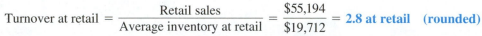

QUICK CHECK 3

If the cost of goods sold by Painters Supply in Quick Check 2 was $150,348 and the average inventory at cost was $91,644, find the stock turnover at cost.

The stock turnover is useful for comparison purposes only. Many trade organizations publish such operating statistics to permit businesses to compare their operation with the industry as a whole. In addition to this, management uses these rates to compare turnover from period to period and from department to department.

OBJECTIVE 3 Methods for tracking inventory. It is important for managers to track inventory moving along the supply chain, sitting in warehouses, and on shelves in stores. Only by tracking inventory can they cut down on theft, figure out what is selling and what is not selling, prevent the waste of a buildup in unneeded inventory, and move inventory quickly to locations where it is needed. Years ago, managers used **periodic inventory** systems, which required a

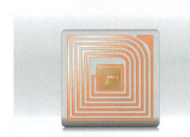

physical inventory at specific intervals, such as the end of each quarter. However, today, most firms have moved to **perpetual inventory** systems, also called **continuous inventory** systems. These inventory systems continually track the quantity and availability of inventory.

A number of technologies have been developed to help track inventory in perpetual inventory systems. One of the first techniques and one that is still used today is the **universal product code (UPC)**. This technique requires a tag with black stripes, called a **barcode**, to be imprinted on each item in inventory. The tag can be scanned at cash registers or other readers. A disadvantage of the UPC technique is the requirement that it be scanned with light rays. As a result, the UPC code has to be visible and directed toward the machine reading the code. You may have watched cashiers as they repeatedly scan an item at the cash register trying to get the machine to read the code.

Many firms use **radio frequency identification (RFID)** chips, which are read using **electronic product code (EPC)** devices. The giant retailer Walmart was one of the first to adopt this technology when it required all suppliers to put RFID chips on pallets and cases by the end of 2006. Although some RFID chips have tiny batteries, most use energy emitted from the machine reading them to respond with an electronic signal. One advantage of RFID chips is that they do not have to be pointed at the machine reading the information on the chip. Another advantage is that they can be very small and cheap—scientists have even glued RFID chips on tiny ants to study their movements.

RFID chips can also be read quickly, as evidenced by new toll-booth technologies, which read the information stored on RFID chips on the windshields of automobiles driving through the booth at 50 miles per hour. In the future, the same RFID chips that allow managers to monitor inventory may be used to electronically provide cooking instructions to a stove or microwave. Amazing, isn't it?

There are four major methods used for inventory valuation: the specific identification method; the weighted-average method; the first-in, first-out method; and the last-in, first-out method.

OBJECTIVE 4 Use the specific identification method to value inventory. The **specific identification method** is useful when items are easily identified and costs do not fluctuate. Each item is cost coded with either numerals or letters. These costs are then added to find ending inventory.

Since the cost of many items changes with time, there may be several of the same item in stock that were purchased at different costs. For this reason, many businesses prefer taking inventory at retail. The retail value of all identical items is the same.

OBJECTIVE 5 Determine inventory value using the weighted-average method. The **weighted average (average cost)** of inventory involves finding the average cost of an item and then multiplying the number of items remaining by the average cost per item.

Using Weighted Average (Average Cost) Inventory Valuation | **EXAMPLE 4**

Suppose REI made the following purchases of the Explorer internal frame backpack during the year.

Beginning inventory	20 backpacks at $70
January	50 backpacks at $80
March	100 backpacks at $90
July	60 backpacks at $85
October	40 backpacks at $75

At the end of the year, there are 75 backpacks in inventory. Use the weighted-average method to find the inventory value.

SOLUTION

Find the total cost of all the backpacks.

Beginning inventory	**20** × $70 = $1400
January	**50** × $80 = $4000
March	**100** × $90 = $9000
July	**60** × $85 = $5100
October	**40** × $75 = $3000
Total	**270** **$22,500**

Find the average cost per backpack by dividing this total cost by the number purchased.

$$\frac{\$22{,}500}{270} = \$83.33 \text{ (rounded)}$$

Since the average cost is $83.33 and 75 backpacks remain in inventory, the weighted-average method gives the inventory value of the remaining backpacks as $83.33 × 75 = $6249.75.

⊞ The calculator solution to this example has several steps. First, find the total number of backpacks purchased and place the total in memory.

20 $\boxed{+}$ 50 $\boxed{+}$ 100 $\boxed{+}$ 60 $\boxed{+}$ 40 $\boxed{=}$ 270 $\boxed{\text{STO}}$

Next, find the total cost of all the backpacks purchased and divide by the number stored in memory. This gives the average cost per backpack.

20 $\boxed{\times}$ 70 $\boxed{+}$ 50 $\boxed{\times}$ 80 $\boxed{+}$ 100 $\boxed{\times}$ 90 $\boxed{+}$ 60 $\boxed{\times}$ 85 $\boxed{+}$

40 $\boxed{\times}$ 75 $\boxed{=}$ $\boxed{\div}$ $\boxed{\text{RCL}}$ $\boxed{=}$ 83.3333

Finally, round the average cost to the nearest cent and multiply by the number of backpacks in inventory to get the weighted average inventory value.

83.33 $\boxed{\times}$ 75 $\boxed{=}$ 6249.75

QUICK CHECK 4

Dick's Sporting Goods made the following purchases of the Iron Horse BMX bicycle during the year.

Beginning inventory	20 bicycles at $115
February	30 bicycles at $95
April	50 bicycles at $100
June	40 bicycles at $110
August	80 bicycles at $105
November	60 bicycles at $130

At the end of the year, there are 85 bicycles in inventory. Use the weighted-average method to find the inventory value.

The cost of items purchased by the retailer is one of the greatest influences on the final retail price. The factors affecting cost include the quality of the product, the quantity purchased, and the geographic location of the purchaser. The following graphic shows the average price paid for a tennis racket in various countries around the world.

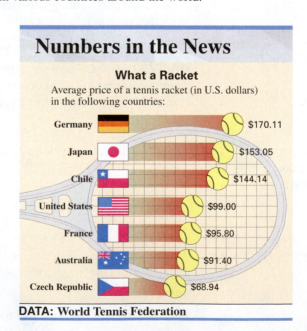

OBJECTIVE 6 Use the FIFO method to value inventory. The **first-in, first-out (FIFO) method** of inventory valuation assumes a natural flow of goods through the inventory. The first goods to arrive are the first goods to be sold, so the last items purchased are the items remaining in inventory.

Using FIFO to Determine Inventory Valuation

EXAMPLE 5

Use the FIFO method to find the inventory value of the 75 backpacks from REI in Example 4.

SOLUTION

With the FIFO method, the 75 remaining backpacks are assumed to consist of the 40 backpacks bought in October and 35 (75 − 40 = 35) backpacks from the previous purchase in July. The value of the inventory is:

October	**40** backpacks at $75 = $3000	value of last 40
July	**35** backpacks at $85 = $2975	value of previous 35
	75 valued at $5975	

The value of the backpack inventory is $5975 using the FIFO method.

QUICK CHECK 5

Use the FIFO method to find the inventory value of the 85 bicycles from Dick's Sporting Goods in Quick Check 4.

OBJECTIVE 7 Use the LIFO method to value inventory. The **last-in, first-out (LIFO) method** of inventory valuation assumes a flow of goods through the inventory that is just the opposite of the FIFO flow. With LIFO, the goods remaining in inventory are those goods that were first purchased.

Using LIFO to Determine Inventory Valuation

EXAMPLE 6

Use the LIFO method to value the 75 backpacks in inventory at REI in Example 4.

SOLUTION

The calculation starts with the beginning inventory and moves through the year's purchases, resulting in 75 backpacks still in stock. The beginning inventory and January purchases come to 70 backpacks, so the cost of 5 more (75 − 70 = 5) backpacks from the March purchase is needed.

Beginning inventory	**20** backpacks at $70 = $1400	value of first 20
January	**50** backpacks at $80 = $4000	value of next 50
March	**5** backpacks at $90 = $ 450	value of last 5
Total	**75** valued at $5850	

The value of the backpack inventory is $5850 using the LIFO method.

QUICK CHECK 6

Use the LIFO method to value the 85 bicycles in inventory at Dick's Sporting Goods in Quick Check 4.

Depending on the method of valuing inventories that is used, REI may show the inventory value of the 75 backpacks as follows.

Average cost method	$6249.75
FIFO	$5975
LIFO	$5850

The preferred inventory valuation method is determined by management on the advice of an accountant.

OBJECTIVE 8 Estimate inventory value using the retail method. An estimate of the value of inventory may be found using the **retail method of estimating inventory**. With this method, the cost of goods available for sale is found as a percent of the retail value of the goods available for sale during the same period. This percent is then multiplied by the retail value of inventory at the end of the period. The result is an estimate of the inventory at cost.

Estimating Inventory Value Using the Retail Method

EXAMPLE 7

The inventory on December 31 at one Apple Store in the mall was $129,200 at cost and $171,000 at retail. Purchases during the next three months were $165,400 at cost, $221,800 at retail, and net sales were $168,800. Use the retail method to estimate the value of inventory at cost on March 31.

SOLUTION

Step 1   Find the value of goods available for sale (inventory) at cost and at retail.

	At cost		At retail	
	$129,200		$171,000	beginning inventory
	+ 165,400		+ 221,800	purchases
	$294,600		$392,800	goods available for sale
			− 168,800	net sales
			$224,000	March 31 inventory at retail

Step 2   Find the retail value of current inventory.

Step 3   Now find the percent of the value of goods available for sale at cost to goods available for sale at retail (cost ratio).

$$\frac{\$294,600 \quad \text{goods available for sale at cost}}{\$392,800 \quad \text{goods available for sale at retail}} = .75 = 75\% \text{ (cost ratio)}$$

Step 4   Finally, the estimated inventory value at cost on March 31 is found by multiplying inventory at retail on March 31 by 75% (cost ratio).

Ending inventory at retail × % (cost ratio) = Inventory at cost

$224,000 × **.75** = $168,000 March 31 inventory at cost

QUICK CHECK 7

At the end of June, Solar Solutions had an inventory of $87,500 at cost and $125,000 at retail. During the next three months, there were purchases of $103,200 at cost, $147,600 at retail, and net sales were $185,000. Use the retail method to estimate the value of inventory at cost at the end of September.

The World Wide Web first became widely available in 1993. From the very beginning, businesses were looking for ways to make retail sales directly to the consumer without any company or retail store in the middle. Online retail sales took off and continue to grow rapidly, as shown in the following figure. Direct sales to consumers reduce cost to businesses since such sales allow a firm to hold inventory at one central warehouse rather than in several retail stores. Companies such as Amazon.com sell only on the Internet, whereas many large retail firms such as Target sell both through retail outlets and on the Internet.

Numbers in the News

Online Retail Sales with a Forecast
(in billions of dollars)

2006	2007	2008	2009	2010	2011	2012
$145	$174	$204	$235	$268	$301 (estimated)	$335 (estimated)

DATA: Census Bureau

The QUICK START exercises in each section contain solutions to help you get started.

Find the average inventory in each of the following. (See Example 1.)

QUICK START

Date	Inventory Amount at Retail	Average Inventory	Date	Inventory Amount at Retail	Average Inventory
1. July 1	$18,300		**2.** January 1	$42,312	
October 1	$26,580		July 1	$38,514	
December 31	$23,139	$22,673	December 31	$30,219	$37,015
$68,019 total of inv. ÷ 3 = $22,673			$111,045 total of inv. ÷ 3 = $37,015		
3. January 1	$65,430		**4.** January 31	$69,480	
April 1	$58,710		April 30	$55,860	
July 1	$53,410		July 31	$80,715	
October 1	$78,950		October 31	$88,050	
December 31	$46,340	_____	January 31	$63,975	_____

Find the stock turnover at cost and at retail in each of the following. Round to the nearest hundredth. (See Examples 2 and 3.)

QUICK START

	Average Inventory at Cost	Average Inventory at Retail	Cost of Goods	Retail Sales	Turnover at Cost	Turnover at Retail
5.	$17,830	$35,390	$50,394	$99,450	2.83	2.81
	$50,394 ÷ $17,830 = 2.83 at cost; $99,450 ÷ $35,390 = 2.81 at retail					
6.	$15,140	$24,080	$67,408	$106,193	4.45	4.41
	$67,408 ÷ $15,140 = 4.45 at cost; $106,193 ÷ $24,080 = 4.41 at retail					
7.	$72,120	$138,460	$259,123	$487,379	_____	_____
8.	$38,074	$48,550	$260,420	$330,060	_____	_____
9.	$180,600	$256,700	$846,336	$1,196,222	_____	_____
10.	$411,580	$780,600	$1,905,668	$3,559,536	_____	_____

◢ indicates an exercise that is related to the Case in Point feature.

Find the inventory values using (a) the weighted-average method, (b) the FIFO method,
and (c) the LIFO method for each of the following. Round to the nearest cent if necessary.
(See Examples 4–6.)

QUICK START

Purchases	Now in Inventory	Weighted-Average Method	FIFO Method	LIFO Method
11. Beginning inventory: 10 units at $8 June: 25 units at $9 August: 15 units at $10	20 units	$182	$195	$170

($455 purchases ÷ 50) × 20 = $9.10 × 20 = $182 average cost method

$$15 \times \$10 = \$150$$
$$\underline{+ \ 5 \times \$ 9 = \$ \ 45}$$
$$20 \qquad \$195 \ \text{FIFO}$$

$$10 \times \$8 = \$ \ 80$$
$$\underline{+ \ 10 \times \$9 = \$ \ 90}$$
$$20 \qquad \$170 \ \text{LIFO}$$

Purchases	Now in Inventory	Weighted-Average Method	FIFO Method	LIFO Method
12. Beginning inventory: 80 units at $14.50 July: 50 units at $15.80 October: 70 units at $13.90	90 units	_____	_____	_____
13. Beginning inventory: 50 units at $30.50 March: 70 units at $31.50 June: 30 units at $33.25 August: 40 units at $30.75	75 units	_____	_____	_____
14. Beginning inventory: 700 units at $1.25 May: 400 units at $1.75 August: 500 units at $2.25 October: 600 units at $3.00	720 units	_____	_____	_____

15. Identify three types of businesses that you think would have a high turnover. Identify three types of businesses that you think would have a low turnover.

16. Which departments in a grocery store do you think have the highest turnover? Which ones have the lowest turnover? Why do you think this is true?

Solve the following application problems. Round stock turnover to the nearest hundredth.

17. STOCK TURNOVER AT COST The Glass Works has an average inventory at cost of $15,730, and cost of goods sold for the same period is $85,412. Find the stock turnover at cost.

$\frac{\$85,412}{\$15,730} = $ **5.43 turnover at cost**

17. **5.43 turnover at cost**

18. STOCK TURNOVER AT RETAIL Jumbo Market has an average canned-fruit inventory of $2320 at retail. Retail sales of canned fruit for the year were $98,669. Find the stock turnover at retail.

18. _____

19. SPRAY-PAINT INVENTORY The Graphic Hobby House made purchases of assorted colors of spray paint during the year as follows.

(a) _____

(b) _____

(c) _____

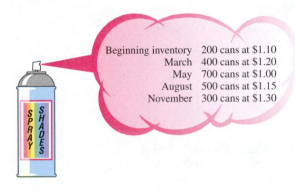

Beginning inventory	200 cans at $1.10
March	400 cans at $1.20
May	700 cans at $1.00
August	500 cans at $1.15
November	300 cans at $1.30

At the end of the year, they had 450 cans of spray paint in stock.

(a) Find the inventory value using the weighted-average method.
(b) Find the inventory value using the FIFO method.
(c) Find the inventory value using the LIFO method.

20. SPORT T-SHIRTS REI made the following purchases of sport T-shirts made in Taiwan: beginning inventory was 650 shirts at $3.80 each; June, 500 shirts at $4.20 each; September, 450 shirts at $3.95 each; and December, 600 shirts at $4.05 each. An inventory at the end of the year shows that 775 T-shirts remain. **(a)** Find the inventory value using the weighted-average method. **(b)** Find the inventory value using the FIFO method. **(c)** Find the inventory value using the LIFO method.

(a) _____

(b) _____

(c) _____

21. ATHLETIC SOCKS REI made the following purchases of 3-pair packages of wool socks.

(a) _____

(b) _____

(c) _____

Beginning inventory	200 packages at $3.10
May	250 packages at $3.50
August	300 packages at $4.25
October	280 packages at $4.50

An inventory at the end of October shows that 320 packages remain. **(a)** Find the inventory value using the weighted-average method. **(b)** Find the inventory value using the FIFO method. **(c)** Find the inventory value using the LIFO method.

22. **ATHLETIC SHOES**   The beginning inventory and purchases of shoes made by The Sports Authority this year are as shown.

(a) _____

(b) _____

(c) _____

Beginning inventory	300 pairs at $21.60
March	400 pairs at $24.00
August	450 pairs at $24.30
November	350 pairs at $22.50

An inventory at the end of December shows that 530 pairs of shoes remain. **(a)** Find the inventory value using the weighted-average method. **(b)** Find the inventory value using the FIFO method. **(c)** Find the inventory value using the LIFO method.

23. **PIANO REPAIR**   The September 30 inventory at Liverpool Piano Repair was $43,750 at cost and $62,500 at retail. Purchases during the next three months were $51,600 at cost, $73,800 at retail, and net sales were $92,500. Use the retail method to estimate the value of the inventory at cost on December 31.

23. _____

24. **EVALUATING INVENTORY**   Cell Phones Plus had an inventory of $27,000 at cost and $45,000 at retail on March 31. During the next three months, they made purchases of $108,000 at cost and $180,000 at retail and had net sales of $162,000. Use the retail method to estimate the value of inventory at cost on June 30.

24. _____

25. In your opinion, what are the benefits to a merchant which is using RFID chips to electronically track inventory?

26. Which of the three inventory valuation methods discussed in this section is most interesting to you? Explain how this method determines inventory value.

QUICK CHECK ANSWERS

1. $165,025

2. 1.64 at retail   (rounded)

3. 1.64 at cost   (rounded)

4. $9334.70 weighted average   (rounded)

5. $10,425 FIFO

6. $8650 LIFO

7. $61,320 inventory at cost

Chapter 8 Quick Review

Chapter Terms *Review the following terms to test your understanding of the chapter. For each term you do not know, refer to the page number found next to that term.*

absolute loss [**p. 319**]

actual selling price [**p. 317**]

average inventory [**p. 323**]

barcode [**p. 325**]

break-even point [**p. 318**]

continuous inventory systems [**p. 325**]

conversion formulas [**p. 311**]

cost [**p. 300**]

electronic product code (EPC) [**p. 325**]

first-in, first-out (FIFO) method [**p. 326**]

formula for markdown [**p. 317**]

gross loss [**p. 319**]

gross profit [**p. 300**]

inventory turns [**p. 324**]

inventory turnover [**p. 324**]

last-in, first-out (LIFO) method [**p. 327**]

margin [**p. 300**]

markdown [**p. 317**]

markup [**p. 300**]

markup on cost [**p. 301**]

markup formula [**p. 300**]

markup on cost [**p. 301**]

markup on selling price [**p. 307**]

net earnings [**p. 300**]

net profit [**p. 300**]

operating expenses [**p. 300**]

operating loss [**p. 318**]

overhead [**p. 300**]

percent of markdown [**p. 318**]

periodic inventory [**p. 324**]

perpetual inventory [**p. 325**]

physical inventory [**p. 325**]

radio frequency identification (RFID) [**p. 325**]

reduced net profit [**p. 318**]

reduced price [**p. 317**]

retail method of estimating inventory [**p. 327**]

sale price [**p. 317**]

selling price [**p. 300**]

specific identification method [**p. 325**]

stock turnover [**p. 324**]

universal product code (UPC) [**p. 325**]

weighted-average (average cost) method [**p. 325**]

CONCEPTS

8.1 Finding the markup on cost

100%	Cost	base
% +	**Markup** **?**	
%	Selling price	

Cost is base. Use the basic percent formula.

$$P = B \times R$$

8.1 Calculating the percent of markup

	100%	C	$	base
rate	**?%**	M	$
	%	S	$

Solve for rate.

8.1 Finding the cost and the selling price

100%	C	$? **base**
%	M	$
%	S	$?

Solve for base.

8.2 Finding the markup on selling price

%	C	$
%	M	$? **part**
100%	S	$ **base**

Solve for part.

EXAMPLES

	100%	C	$160 base
rate	25%	M	**$?**
	%	S	$

$$P = B \times R$$
$$P = \$160 \times .25$$
$$P = \$40 \text{ markup}$$

	100%	C	$420 base
rate	**?%**	M	$
	%	S	$546

$$\$546 - \$420 = \$126 \text{ markup}$$
$$R = \frac{P}{B} = \frac{126}{420}$$
$$R = 30\%$$

	100%	C	$? base
rate	50%	M	$56
	%	S	$?

$$B = \frac{P}{R} = \frac{56}{.5}$$
$$B = \$112 \text{ cost}$$
$$\$112 + \$56 = \$168 \text{ selling price}$$

	%	C	$
rate	25%	M	$? **part**
	100%	S	$6.00 base

$$P = B \times R$$
$$P = \$6.00 \times .25$$
$$P = \$1.50$$

CONCEPTS	EXAMPLES
8.2 Finding the cost % C \$? part % M \$ 100% S \$ base	% C \$? part rate 35% M \$87.50 100% S \$ base $B = \frac{P}{R} = \frac{87.5}{.35} =$ \$250 selling price \$250 − \$87.50 = \$162.50 cost
8.2 Calculating the selling price and the markup % C \$ % M \$? 100% S \$? base	% C \$150 rate 25% M \$? 100% S \$? base 100% − 25% = 75% cost $B = \frac{P}{R} = \frac{150}{.75} =$ \$200 selling price \$200 − \$150 = \$50 markup
8.2 Converting markup on cost to markup on selling price Use the formula $\%\text{ markup on selling price} = \frac{\%\text{ markup on cost}}{100\% + \%\text{ markup on cost}}$	Convert 25% markup on cost to markup on selling price. $\%\text{ markup on selling price} = \frac{25\%}{100\% + 25\%}$ $= \frac{.25}{1.25} = .2 = 20\%$
8.2 Converting markup on selling price to markup on cost Use the formula $\%\text{ markup on cost} = \frac{\%\text{ markup on selling price}}{100\% - \%\text{ markup on selling price}}$	Convert 20% markup on selling price to markup on cost. $\%\text{ markup on cost} = \frac{20\%}{100\% - 20\%}$ $= \frac{.2}{.8} = .25 = 25\%$
8.1 Finding the selling price for perishables 1. Find total cost and selling price. 2. Subtract the quantity not sold to find the number that are sold. 3. Divide the remaining sales by the number of sellable units to get selling price per unit.	60 doughnuts cost 25¢ each; 10 are not sold; 50% markup on selling price; find selling price per doughnut. Cost = 60 × \$.25 = \$15 (rate) 50% C \$15 part 50% M \$ 100% S \$? base $B = \frac{P}{R} = \frac{15}{.5} =$ \$30 60 − 10 = 50 doughnuts sold \$30 ÷ 50 = \$.60 per doughnut
8.3 Finding the percent of markdown Markdown is always a percent of the original price. Use the formula $R = \frac{P}{B}$ $\text{Markdown percent} = \frac{\text{Markdown amount}}{\text{Original price}}$	Original price, \$76; markdown, \$19; find the percent of markdown. $R = \frac{P}{B} = \frac{19}{76} = .25$ R = 25% markdown
8.3 Calculating the break-even point The cost plus operating expenses equals the break-even point.	Cost, \$54; operating expenses, \$16; find the break-even point. \$54 cost + **\$16 operating expenses** = \$70 break-even point

CONCEPTS	EXAMPLES
8.3 Finding operating loss	Break-even point, $70; reduced price, $58; find the operating loss.
The difference between the break-even point and the reduced price (when below the break-even point) is the operating loss.	$$\begin{array}{rl} \$70 & \text{break-even point} \\ -\$58 & \textbf{reduced price} \\ \hline \$12 & \text{operating loss} \end{array}$$
8.3 Finding absolute loss (gross loss)	Cost, $54; reduced price, $48; find the absolute loss.
When the reduced price is below cost, the difference between the cost and reduced price is the absolute loss.	$54 cost − **$48 reduced price** = $6 absolute loss
8.4 Determining average inventory	Inventories, $22,635, $24,692, and $18,796; find the average inventory.
Inventory is taken two or more times. Totals are added together, then divided by the number of inventories taken to get the average.	$$\frac{\$22,635 + \$24,692 + \$18,796}{3}$$ $$= \frac{\$66,123}{3} = \$22,041 \text{ average inventory}$$
8.4 Finding turnover at retail	Quarterly retail sales, $78,496; average inventory at retail, $18,076; find turnover at retail.
Use the formula $$\text{Turnover} = \frac{\text{Retail sales}}{\text{Average inventory at retail}}$$	$$\frac{\$78,496}{\$18,076} = 4.34 \text{ at retail} \quad \text{(rounded)}$$
8.4 Finding turnover at cost	Quarterly cost of goods sold, $26,542; average inventory at cost, $6592; find turnover at cost.
Use the formula $$\text{Turnover} = \frac{\text{Cost of goods sold}}{\text{Average inventory at cost}}$$	$$\frac{\$26,542}{\$6592} = 4.03 \text{ at cost} \quad \text{(rounded)}$$
8.4 Using specific identification to value inventory	Individual cost of each item in inventory is: item 1, $593; item 2, $614; item 3, $498; find total value of inventory.
Each item is cost coded, and the cost of each of the items is added to find total inventory.	**$593 + $614 + $498** = $1705 total value of inventory
8.4 Using weighted-average (average cost) method of inventory valuation	Beginning inventory of 20 at $75; purchases of 15 at $80; 25 at $65; 18 at $70; 22 remain in inventory. Find the inventory value.
This method values items in an inventory at the average cost of buying them.	$$\begin{array}{l} \mathbf{20} \times \$75 = \$1500 \\ \mathbf{15} \times \$80 = \$1200 \\ \mathbf{25} \times \$65 = \$1625 \\ \mathbf{18} \times \$70 = \$1260 \\ \hline \text{Total } \mathbf{78} \qquad \$5585 \end{array}$$ $$\frac{5585}{78} = \$71.60 \text{ average cost} \quad \text{(rounded)}$$ $71.60 × 22 = $1575.20 weighted-average method inventory value
8.4 Using first-in, first-out (FIFO) method of inventory valuation	Beginning inventory of 25 items at $40; purchased on August 7, 30 items at $35; 35 remain in inventory. Find the inventory.
The first items in are the first sold. Inventory is based on cost of last items purchased.	$$\begin{array}{ll} \mathbf{30} \times \$35 = \$1050 & \text{value of last 30} \\ \mathbf{5} \times \$40 = \$\ 200 & \text{value of previous 5} \\ \hline \mathbf{35} \qquad \$1250 & \text{value of inventory FIFO method} \end{array}$$

CONCEPTS   **EXAMPLES**

8.4 Using last-in, first-out (LIFO) method of inventory valuation

The items remaining in inventory are those items that were first purchased.

Beginning inventory of 48 items at $20 each; purchase on May 9, 40 items at $25 each; 55 remain in inventory. Find the inventory value.

$$
\begin{array}{ll}
48 \times \$20 = \$\ 960 & \text{value of first 48} \\
\underline{\ 7 \times \$25 = \$\ 175} & \text{value of last 7} \\
55 \qquad\qquad \$1135 & \text{value of inventory LIFO method}
\end{array}
$$

8.4 Estimating inventory value using the retail method

$$\frac{\text{Goods available for sale at cost}}{\text{Goods available for sale at retail}} = \%\ (\text{cost ratio})$$

$$\begin{array}{c}\text{Ending inventory}\\ \text{at retail}\end{array} \times \%\ (\text{cost ratio}) = \begin{array}{c}\text{Inventory}\\ \text{at cost}\end{array}$$

Use the retail method to estimate the inventory value at cost.

	Cost	Retail
beginning inventory	$9,000	$15,000
purchases	+ 36,000	+ 60,000
goods available for sale	**$45,000**	**$75,000**
net sales		− 54,000
ending inventory		$21,000

$$\frac{\$45,000}{\$75,000}\quad \begin{array}{l}\text{goods available for sale at cost}\\ \text{goods available for sale at retail}\end{array} = .6 = 60\%$$

$$\$21,000 \times .6 = \$12,600 \text{ inventory value at cost}$$

case study

MARKDOWN: REDUCING PRICES TO MOVE MERCHANDISE

Olympic Sports purchased two dozen pairs of 5th Element Adult Aggresive in-line skates at a cost of $1950. Operating expenses for the store are 25% of cost, while total markup on this type of product is 35% of selling price. Only 6 pairs of the skates sell at the original price, and the manager decides to mark down the remaining skates. The price is reduced 25% and 6 more pairs sell. The remaining 12 pairs of skates are marked down to 50% of the original selling price and are finally sold.

1. Find the original selling price of each pair of skates.

1. _____

2. Find the total of the selling prices of all the skates.

2. _____

3. Find the operating loss.

3. _____

4. Find the absolute loss.

4. _____

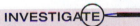 **INVESTIGATE**

Talk with the manager of a retail store. Does the store calculate markup based on cost or retail? Does the store use markdowns to promote the sale or liquidation of merchandise? How does the management decide how much to mark down merchandise? Ask the manager for an example of a product that had to be marked down so much that a gross loss resulted.

case ⟂ point summary exercise

RECREATIONAL EQUIPMENT INC. (REI)

www.REI.com

Facts:

- 1938: Established by 23 mountaineers
- 2001: Exceeded 2 million members
- 2005: Annual sales passed $1 billion
- 2010: More than 100 stores, 8000 employees, and 3.7 million members

REI has always had a focus on the great outdoors. The firm is a cooperative—anyone can shop there but membership is based on those who pay a one-time fee of $15 to join. Members are the owners of the company and each shares in profits by receiving annual dividends based on profits and amount of his or her purchases.

The marketing manager at REI was interested in a new line of skis developed by Shaman Industries. These skis are designed for off-piste skiing, which means skiing over rugged terrain and even jumping off of cliffs. Since REI prides itself on having the best in outdoor gear, the manager works with James Smelter in inventory to place an order for 15 pairs of the new skis to test the quality. Shortly thereafter, they order an additional 22 pairs of a different model of ski also manufactured by Shaman Industries.

	Model Name	Number	Total Cost
1st order	Steep Alpine	15 pairs	$4395
2nd order	Cliff Hoppers	22 pairs	$7194

1. Find the cost per pair of skis for both models.

    1. _____

2. If management marks up the cost of each pair of skis by 38%, find the list price for each pair of skis.

    2. _____

3. Assume the skis were received on January 1 and that a physical inventory at the end of January showed that 7 pairs of Steep Alpine and 14 pairs of Cliff Hoppers remained in the store. Find the average inventory at cost.

    3. _____

4. Use the data for these skis to find the turnover at cost for the month of January.

    4. _____

5. The two managers are not happy with how well the Shaman Industries skis are selling or with the quality of the skis and sell the remaining skis at a markdown of 40%. Find the price per ski after being marked down.

    5. _____

6. Assume that operating expenses at REI are 22% of cost and determine the amount of any profit on these skis. If there was no profit, find the amount of the operating loss or the absolute loss.

6. _____

7. Should REI use markup on cost or markup on selling price? Or, is either of these suitable for the firm?

7. _____

Discussion Question: Do you think firms often lose money on new products? What do you think would happen to a company that often loses money on new products? Explain.

Chapter 8 Test

To help you review, the numbers in brackets show the section in which the topic was discussed.

Solve for (a), (b), and (c). **[8.1 and 8.2]**

1.	100%	*C*	$64.00	**2.**	100%	*C*	$(b)
	(a)%	*M*	$12.80		38%	*M*	$(c)
	(b)%	*S*	$(c)		(a)%	*S*	$504.39

3.	(a)%	*C*	$134.40	**4.**	(a)%	*C*	$(c)
	(b)%	*M*	$(c)		(b)%	*M*	$ 6.15
	100%	*S*	$168.00		100%	*S*	$24.60

Find the equivalent markup on either cost or selling price, using the appropriate formula. Round to the nearest tenth of a percent. **[8.2]**

Markup on Cost	Markup on Selling Price		Markup on Cost	Markup on Selling Price
5. 25%	_____	**6.**	100%	_____

Complete the following. If there is no operating loss or absolute loss, write "none." **[8.3]**

Cost	Operating Expense	Break-even Point	Reduced Price	Operating Loss	Absolute Loss
7. $160	$40	_____	$186	_____	_____
8. $225	_____	$297	$198	_____	_____

Find the stock turnover at cost and at retail in the following. Round to the nearest hundredth. **[8.4]**

Average Inventory at Cost	Average Inventory at Retail	Cost of Goods Sold	Retail Sales	Turnover at Cost	Turnover at Retail
9. $14,120	$25,572	$81,312	$146,528	_____	_____

Solve the following application problems.

 10. REI buys jogging shorts manufactured in Indonesia for $195.00 per dozen pair. Find the selling price per pair if the retailer maintains a markup of 35% on selling price. **[8.2]**

10. _____

11. Restaurant Supply sells a walk-in refrigerator for $5250 while using a markup of 25% on cost. Find the cost. **[8.1]**

11. _____

12. The Computer Service Center sells a DeskJet print cartridge for $37.50. If the print cartridge costs the store $22.50, find the markup as a percent of selling price. **[8.2]**

12. _____

13. REI offers a men's soft-shell waterproof jacket for $199.95. If the jackets cost $1943.52 per dozen, find **(a)** the markup, **(b)** the percent of markup on selling price, and **(c)** the percent of markup on cost. Round to the nearest tenth of a percent. **[8.1 and 8.2]**

(a) _____

(b) _____

(c) _____

 indicates an exercise that is related to the Case in Point feature.

14. A motorcycle originally priced at $13,875 is marked down to $9990. Find the percent of markdown on the original price. **[8.3]**

14. _____

15. Leslie's Pool Supply, a retailer, pays $285 for a diving board. The original selling price was $399, but it was marked down 40%. If operating expenses are 30% of cost, find (a) the operating loss and (b) the absolute loss. **[8.3]**

(a) _____

(b) _____

16. Carpets Plus had an inventory of $117,328 on January 1, $147,630 on July 1, and $125,876 on December 31. Find the average inventory. **[8.4]**

16. _____

Round to the nearest dollar amount.

17. Craighead Products made the following purchases of fuel tanks during the year: 25 at $270 each, 40 at $330 each, 15 at $217 each, and 30 at $284 each. An inventory shows that 45 fuel tanks remain. Find the inventory value using the weighted-average method. **[8.4]**

17. _____

18. Find the value of the inventory listed in Exercise 17 using (a) the FIFO method and (b) the LIFO method. **[8.4]**

(a) _____

(b) _____

Chapters 5–8   Cumulative Review

CHAPTERS 5–8

The following credit-card transactions were made at the Patio Store. Answer Exercises 1–5 using this information. Round to the nearest cent.   **[5.2]**

SALES			CREDITS
$428.80	$733.18	$22.51	$76.15
$316.25	$38.00	$162.15	$118.44
$68.95	$188.36		$13.86

1. Find the total amount of the sales slips.

1. _____

2. What is the total amount of the credit slips?

2. _____

3. Find the total amount of the deposit.

3. _____

4. Assuming that the bank charges the retailer a $1\frac{1}{4}$% discount charge, find the amount of the discount charge at the statement date.

4. _____

5. Find the amount of the credit given to the retailer after the fee is subtracted.

5. _____

Solve the following application problems.

6. Shaundra Brown worked 7 hours on Monday, 10 hours on Tuesday, 8 hours on Wednesday, 9 hours on Thursday, and 10 hours on Friday. Her regular hourly pay is $12.80. Find her gross earnings for the week if Brown is paid time and a half for all hours over 8 worked in a day.   **[6.1]**

6. _____

7. The employees of Feather Farms paid a total of $968.50 in Social Security tax last month, $223.50 in Medicare tax, and $1975.38 in federal withholding tax. Find the total amount the employer must send to the Internal Revenue Service.   **[6.4]**

7. _____

Find the net cost (invoice amount) for each of the following. Round to the nearest cent.   **[7.1]**

8. List price $475.50, less 20/20 _____

9. List price $375, less 25/10/5 _____

Find the single discount equivalent for each of the following series discounts.   **[7.2]**

10. 10/20 _____

11. 30/40/10 _____

Find the discount date and the net payment date for each of the following. The net payment date is 20 days after the final discount date. **[7.4]**

	Invoice Date	Terms	Date Goods Received	Final Discount Date	Net Payment Date
12.	May 27	2/10 ROG	June 5	_____	_____
13.	Oct. 9	3/15 EOM		_____	_____
14.	June 24	4/10–30 ex.		_____	_____

Complete the following. If there is no operating loss or absolute loss, write "none."   **[8.3]**

	Cost	Operating Expense	Break-even Point	Reduced Price	Operating Loss	Absolute Loss
15.	$312	$88	_____	_____	$120	_____
16.	_____	_____	_____	$220	$112	$32

Solve the following application problems.

17. The list price of an Iron Horse BMX bike at Olympic Sports is $149.99. Find the dealer's cost if given a 20/20 trade discount and a 3/20, n/30 cash discount. Assume that the dealer earns the maximum cash discount.   **[7.1 and 7.3]**

17. _____

18. Computer Towne purchases mouse pads for $43.20 per box of 3 dozen. If the store wants a markup of 52% on the selling price, find the selling price per mouse pad.   **[8.2]**

18. _____

19. The Retro-Fit Window Company has an average inventory of $18,784 at cost. If the cost of goods sold for the year was $241,938, find the stock turnover at cost. Round to hundredths.   **[8.4]**

19. _____

20. Inventory at a local store was taken at retail value four times and was found to be $53,820; $49,510; $60,820; and $56,380. Sales during the same period were $252,077. Find the stock turnover at retail. Round to hundredths.   **[8.4]**

20. _____

21. Thunder Manufacturing made the following purchases of rivet drums during the year: 25 at $135 each, 40 at $165 each, 15 at $108.50 each, and 30 at $142 each. An inventory shows that 45 rivet drums remain. Find the inventory value, using the weighted-average method.   **[8.4]**

21. _____

22. Refer to Exercise 21. Find the inventory value using **(a)** the FIFO method and **(b)** the LIFO method.   **[8.4]**

(a) _____

(b) _____

Simple Interest

case in point ▶

APPLE INC. was founded by Steven Wozniak and Steven Jobs in 1976. Its early success was based on the Apple II and Macintosh computers. However, it revolutionized the music, phone, and book worlds with the introduction of the iPod, iPhone, and—finally—the iPad in 2010. In a recent quarter, Apple sold more than 3 million Macintoshes, 10 million iPods, and 7 million iPhones.

While completing her degree in Computer Information Systems at a local community college, Jessica Hernandez worked part time in one of Apple's retail stores in a local mall. She continued to work at the store for 3 years after graduating and receiving a promotion to assistant manager. However, she had always wanted to own her own business and finally had the opportunity to do so. Although at first Hernandez felt she needed to do computer repairs to help increase her income, her long-range goal was to design and build Web pages for individuals and businesses and offer training classes for various software packages. Since she planned to work with businesses, Hernandez also wanted to develop some expertise in accounting software.

Interest is a fee charged to borrow money. Ancient clay tablets show that interest was being charged 5000 years ago. Banks, corporations, states, cities, countries, partnerships, and individuals borrow money. Large, financially strong corporations such as Microsoft and McDonald's borrow at the most favorable interest rate called the **prime rate**. The remainder of us must pay higher rates when we borrow to buy a car, a house, or to charge items to our charge cards.

Simple interest applies only to the **principal**, or the original amount borrowed, and it is usually used for loans lasting less than 1 year. Simple interest is discussed in this chapter. **Compound interest** requires interest to be paid on the principal and *also* on previously earned interest. Compound interest is covered in Chapter 10.

9.1 Basics of Simple Interest

OBJECTIVES

1 Solve for simple interest.
2 Calculate maturity value.
3 Use a table to find the number of days from one date to another.
4 Use the actual number of days in a month to find the number of days from one date to another.
5 Find exact and ordinary interest.
6 Define the basic terms used with notes.
7 Find the due date of a note.

case IN ▶ point

Jessica Hernandez knew that expenses on a new business would begin immediately, yet revenues would be slow coming in at first. So she realized that she would need to borrow money to start her company. Fortunately, her uncle, a successful businessperson, helped her obtain the loan she needed.

Interest rates affect the costs of many things. For example, the following graph shows the number of new houses on which construction has started and the prime rate of interest. High interest costs make it more expensive to own a home and lower interest rates make it less expensive to own a home. As a result, high interest rates should slow the number of new houses under construction, as happened during 1980–82. Similarly, lower interest rates should result in increased housing starts as happened in 1983 and 2002–05.

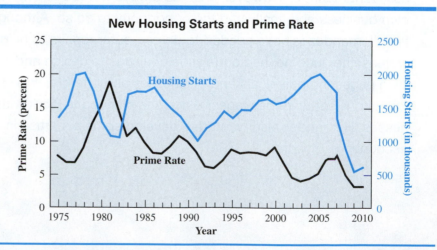

Notice that new house starts fell to a historically low level in 2009 even though the prime interest rate fell to a historical low of 3.25%. Why? Very low interest rates result in low cost of home ownership, which should result in large numbers of new house starts. Both interest rates and new house starts fell sharply due to the financial crisis that began in 2008. Banks lost a lot of money, unemployment soared, home prices fell, and many who still had incomes became very cautious and saved, rather than spent, their money. The federal government lowered various interest rates as business activity slowed—so the prime rate fell. Banks would lend only to individuals with excellent credit and a large down payment, and new home purchases slowed markedly. The government used the tool of very low interest rates during 2008–2011 to try and stimulate new housing starts in the midst of the financial crisis.

OBJECTIVE 1 Solve for simple interest. Simple interest is interest charged on the entire principal for the entire length of the loan. It is found using the formula shown in the following box. **Principal** is the loan amount, **rate** is the interest rate, and **time** is the length of the loan *in years*.

Finding Simple Interest

$$\text{Simple interest} = \text{Principal} \times \text{Rate} \times \text{Time}$$
$$I \quad\quad = \quad P \quad \times \quad R \quad \times \quad T$$

When using the formula $I = PRT$:

1. Rate (R) must first be changed to a decimal or fraction.

2. Time (T) must first be converted to years.

So, for example, a rate of 7.5% should be changed to .075 and a time of 6 months should be changed to $\frac{6}{12} = 0.5$ year before using $I = PRT$.

Finding Simple Interest **EXAMPLE 1**

case IN point

Jessica Hernandez needed to borrow $85,000 for 9 months to start a small computer business. Since her bank would not lend her the funds, Jessica went to an individual who offered to lend her the funds at 18.5% per year. She then went to her uncle, who agreed to **cosign** her loan. This means that he would have to pay the loan in full if Jessica failed to do so. With the cosigner, the bank agreed to lend Jessica $85,000 at a rate of 10% simple interest per year. Find the interest **(a)** at 18.5% and **(b)** at 10%. **(c)** Then find the amount saved using the second loan.

SOLUTION

(a) First, convert 18.5% to .185 and 9 months to $\frac{9}{12}$ year. Then substitute values into $I = PRT$ to find the interest. The principal (P) is the amount of the loan.

$$I = PRT$$
$$I = \$85,000 \times .185 \times \tfrac{9}{12}$$
$$I = \$11,793.75 \qquad \text{simple interest}$$

(b)
$$I = PRT$$
$$I = \$85,000 \times .10 \times \tfrac{9}{12} \qquad \textbf{Convert 10\% to .10 (or .1).}$$
$$I = \$6375 \qquad\qquad\qquad \text{simple interest}$$

(c) Difference = $11,793.75 − $6375 = $5418.75

Hernandez quickly learned an important lesson: Interest costs can be very high. She was delighted that her uncle had agreed to cosign for her. It saved her nearly $5500 in interest charges in only 9 months. Now she had to figure out how to make her business profitable!

⊞ The calculator solution for part **(a)** follows:
$$85000 \;\boxed{\times}\; 18.5 \;\boxed{\%}\; \boxed{\times}\; 9 \;\boxed{\div}\; 12 \;\boxed{=}\; 11793.75$$

Note: Refer to Appendix B for calculator basics.

QUICK CHECK 1

Find the interest on a loan of $14,680 for 6 months at 9%.

OBJECTIVE 2 Calculate maturity value. The amount that must be repaid when the loan is due is the **maturity value** of the loan. Find this value by adding principal and interest.

Finding Maturity Value

$$\text{Maturity value} = \text{Principal} + \text{Interest}$$
$$M \quad\quad = \quad P \quad + \quad I$$

Quick TIP ▼
You can think of interest as rent. A person must pay rent to live in an apartment or house. Interest is "the rent," or the cost, of borrowing money.

Finding Maturity Value

EXAMPLE 2

Tom Swift needs to borrow $28,300 to remodel his bookstore so that he can serve coffee to customers as they browse or sit and read. He borrows the funds for 10 months at an interest rate of 9.25%. Find the interest due on the loan and the maturity value at the end of 10 months.

SOLUTION

Interest due is found using $I = PRT$, where T must be in years $\left(10 \text{ months} = \frac{10}{12} \text{ year}\right)$.

$$\textit{Interest} = \textit{PRT}$$

$$I = \$28,300 \times .0925 \times \frac{10}{12} = \$2181.46 \quad (\text{rounded})$$

$$\textit{Maturity value} = P + I$$

$$M = \$28,300 + \$2181.46 = \$30,481.46$$

QUICK CHECK 2

Find the maturity value of a loan of $48,600 at 9% for 8 months.

OBJECTIVE 3 Use a table to find the number of days from one date to another. Up to this point, the period of the loan was given in months, but it can also be given in days. Or a loan may be due at a fixed date, such as April 17, and we may have to figure out the number of days until the loan must be paid off. One way to do this is to number the days of the year as in the table on the next page. Note that this table is also on the inside of the back cover of the book.

For example, suppose it is June 11 and you want to know how many days until Christmas. In the table, June 11 is day 162 of the year and December 25 is day 359 of the year. Subtract to find the number of days until Christmas.

December 25 is day	359
June 11 is day	−162
	197 days from June 11 to December 25

There are 197 days from June 11 to December 25.

Leap years are years with one additional day in February. If it is a leap year, June 11 is day 163 and December 25 is day 360. There are still 197 days from June 11 to December 25.

Finding the Number of Days from One Date to Another, Using a Table

EXAMPLE 3

Use the table on the next page to find the number of days from **(a)** March 24 to July 22, **(b)** April 4 to October 10, **(c)** November 8 to February 17 of the following year, and **(d)** December 2 to January 17 of the following year. Assume that it is not a leap year.

SOLUTION

(a)

July 22 is day	203
March 24 is day	− 83
	120 days from March 24 to July 22

(b)

October 10 is day	283
April 4 is day	− 94
	189 days from April 4 to October 10

(c) November 8 is day 312, so there are $365 - 312 = 53$ days from November 8 to the end of the year. Add days until the end of the year plus days into the next year to find the total.

November 8 to end of year	**53**
February 17 is day	+ **48**
	101 days from November 8 to February 17 of next year

(d) December 2 is day 336, so there are $365 - 336 = 29$ days to the end of the year. Add days until the end of the year plus days into the next year to find the total.

December 2 to end of year	**29**
January 17 is day	+ **17**
	46 days from December 2 to January 17 of the next year

QUICK CHECK 3

Find the number of days from **(a)** July 7 to November 7 and **(b)** August 25 to January 20 of the following year.

The Number of Each of the Days of the Year*

DAY OF MONTH	JAN.	FEB.	MAR.	APR.	MAY	JUNE	JULY	AUG.	SEPT.	OCT.	NOV.	DEC.	DAY OF MONTH
1	1	32	60	91	121	152	182	213	244	274	305	335	1
2	2	33	61	92	122	153	183	214	245	275	306	336	2
3	3	34	62	93	123	154	184	215	246	276	307	337	3
4	4	35	63	94	124	155	185	216	247	277	308	338	4
5	5	36	64	95	125	156	186	217	248	278	309	339	5
6	6	37	65	96	126	157	187	218	249	279	310	340	6
7	7	38	66	97	127	158	188	219	250	280	311	341	7
8	8	39	67	98	128	159	189	220	251	281	312	342	8
9	9	40	68	99	129	160	190	221	252	282	313	343	9
10	10	41	69	100	130	161	191	222	253	283	314	344	10
11	11	42	70	101	131	162	192	223	254	284	315	345	11
12	12	43	71	102	132	163	193	224	255	285	316	346	12
13	13	44	72	103	133	164	194	225	256	286	317	347	13
14	14	45	73	104	134	165	195	226	257	287	318	348	14
15	15	46	74	105	135	166	196	227	258	288	319	349	15
16	16	47	75	106	136	167	197	228	259	289	320	350	16
17	17	48	76	107	137	168	198	229	260	290	321	351	17
18	18	49	77	108	138	169	199	230	261	291	322	352	18
19	19	50	78	109	139	170	200	231	262	292	323	353	19
20	20	51	79	110	140	171	201	232	263	293	324	354	20
21	21	52	80	111	141	172	202	233	264	294	325	355	21
22	22	53	81	112	142	173	203	234	265	295	326	356	22
23	23	54	82	113	143	174	204	235	266	296	327	357	23
24	24	55	83	114	144	175	205	236	267	297	328	358	24
25	25	56	84	115	145	176	206	237	268	298	329	359	25
26	26	57	85	116	146	177	207	238	269	299	330	360	26
27	27	58	86	117	147	178	208	239	270	300	331	361	27
28	28	59	87	118	148	179	209	240	271	301	332	362	28
29	29		88	119	149	180	210	241	272	302	333	363	29
30	30		89	120	150	181	211	242	273	303	334	364	30
31	31		90		151		212	243		304		365	31

*Add 1 to each date after February 29 for a leap year.

OBJECTIVE 4 Use the actual number of days in a month to find the number of days from one date to another. The number of days between specific dates can be found using the number of days in each month of the year as shown in the table.

Number of Days in Each Month

31 DAYS		30 DAYS	28 DAYS
January	August	April	February
March	October	June	(29 days in leap year)
May	December	September	
July		November	

Two other ways of remembering the number of days in each month are the rhyme method and the knuckle method, as seen below.

Rhyme Method:

30 days hath September
April, June, and November.
All the rest have 31, except
February, which has 28 and
in a leap year 29.

Knuckle Method:

Jan. Mar. May July 31 days Aug. Oct. Dec.

Feb. Apr. June   Sept. Nov.

30 days (28 in Feb.)

Finding the Number of Days from One Date to Another, Using Actual Days

EXAMPLE 4

Find the number of days from **(a)** June 3 to August 14 and **(b)** November 4 to February 21.

SOLUTION

(a) June has 30 days, so there are $30 - 3 = 27$ days from June 3 to the end of June.

June 3 to the end of June	27
31 days in July	31
14 days in August	+ 14
	72 days from June 3 to August 14

(b) November has 30 days, so there are $30 - 4 = 26$ days from November 4 to the end of November.

November 4 to end of November	26
31 days in December	31
31 days in January	31
21 days in February	+ 21
	109 days from November 4 to February 21

> **Quick TIP ▼**
>
> To find the number of days from one date to another, do not count the day the loan was made, but do count the day the loan is paid.

QUICK CHECK 4

Find the number of days from March 14 to September 9.

OBJECTIVE 5 Find exact and ordinary interest. A simple interest rate is given as an annual rate, such as 7% per year. Since the rate is per year, time must also be given in years or fraction of a year when using $I = PRT$. If time is given in number of days, first change it to a fraction of a year.

> **Finding Time in Fraction of a Year**
>
> $$T = \frac{\text{Number of days in the loan period}}{\text{Number of days in a year}}$$

Exact interest calculations require the use of the exact number of days in the year, 365 or 366 if a leap year. **Ordinary interest**, or **banker's interest**, calculations require the use of 360 days. Banks commonly used 360 days in a year for interest calculations before calculators and computers became widely available. Today, many institutions, the government, and the Federal Reserve Bank use the exact number of days in a year in interest calculations. However, some banks and financial institutions still use 360 days. You need to be able to use both.

> **Finding Exact and Ordinary Interest**
>
> **For exact interest:** Use 365 days (or 366 days if a leap year).
>
> $$T = \frac{\text{Number of days in a loan period}}{365}$$
>
> **For ordinary, or banker's, interest:** Use 360 days for the number of days.
>
> $$T = \frac{\text{Number of days in a loan period}}{360}$$

Example 5 shows that **ordinary interest produces more interest** for the lending institution than does exact interest.

Finding Exact and Ordinary Interest — **EXAMPLE 5**

KOMA

Radio station KOMA borrowed $148,500 on May 12 with interest due on August 27. If the interest rate is 10%, find the interest on the loan using **(a)** exact interest and **(b)** ordinary interest.

SOLUTION

Either the table method or the method of the number of days in a month can be used to find that there are 107 days from May 12 to August 27.

(a) The exact interest is found from $I = PRT$ with $P = \$148{,}500$, $R = .1$, and $T = \frac{107}{365}$.

$$I = PRT$$

$$I = \$148{,}500 \times .1 \times \frac{107}{365} \quad \text{Use 365 days.}$$

$$I = \$4353.29 \quad \text{(rounded)}$$

(b) Find ordinary interest with the same formula and values, except $T = \frac{107}{360}$.

$$I = PRT$$

$$I = \$148{,}500 \times .1 \times \frac{107}{360} \quad \text{Use 360 days.}$$

$$I = \$4413.75 \quad \text{(rounded)}$$

In this example, the ordinary interest is $\$4413.75 - \$4353.29 = \$60.46$ more than the exact interest.

> **Quick TIP** ▼
>
> Ordinary interest results in slightly more interest than exact interest. Thus ordinary interest favors those banks that use it when calculating loans.

QUICK CHECK 5

Find the exact and ordinary interest for a 200-day loan of $19,500 at 9% to the nearest cent. Then find the difference between the two interest amounts.

> **Use ordinary or banker's interest throughout the remainder of the book unless stated otherwise.**

OBJECTIVE 6 Define the basic terms used with notes. A **promissory note** is a *legal document* in which one person or firm agrees to pay a certain amount of money, on a specific day in the future, to another person or firm. An example of a promissory note follows.

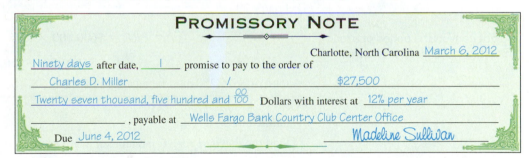

PROMISSORY NOTE

Charlotte, North Carolina March 6, 2012

Ninety days after date, __I__ promise to pay to the order of

Charles D. Miller / $27,500

Twenty seven thousand, five hundred and 00/100 Dollars with interest at 12% per year

_____, payable at Wells Fargo Bank Country Club Center Office

Due June 4, 2012 Madeline Sullivan

This type of promissory note is called a **simple interest note**, since simple interest calculations involving $I = PRT$ are used. Here is the language of a simple interest promissory note.

Maker or **payer:** The person borrowing the money. (Madeline Sullivan in the sample note)

Payee: The person who loaned the money and who will receive the payment (Charles D. Miller in the sample note)

Term: The length of time until the note is due (90 days in the sample note)

Face value or **principal:** The amount being borrowed ($27,500 in the sample note)

Maturity value: The face value plus interest, also the amount due at maturity

Maturity date or **due date:** The date the loan must be paid off with interest (June 4 in the sample note)

Find the interest and the maturity value on the loan in the sample note above.

$$\textbf{Interest} = \textbf{Face value} \times \textbf{Rate} \times \textbf{Time}$$

$$\text{Interest} = \$27{,}500 \times .12 \times \frac{90}{360} = \textbf{\$825}$$

$$\textbf{Maturity value} = \textbf{Face value} + \textbf{Interest}$$

$$\text{Maturity value} = \$27{,}500 + \textbf{\$825} = \$28{,}325$$

Madeline Sullivan must pay $28,325 to Charles D. Miller on June 4, the maturity date of the note.

Banks and financial institutions lend money only to individuals and firms they believe will repay the loan with interest. Even then, banks often require **collateral** or assets such as an automobile or stock in order to make a loan. If the loan is not repaid, the bank **forecloses** on the collateral, takes ownership, and sells or liquidates it. Funds from the sale of the collateral are first used to pay off the note and the expenses of the foreclosure. Any excess is returned to the maker of the note.

OBJECTIVE 7 Find the due date of a note. Time is in months in some promissory notes. When this occurs, the loan is due after the given number of months has passed but on the same day of the month as the original loan was made. For example, a 4-month note made on May 25 is due 4 months later on the 25th of September. Other examples follow.

DATE MADE	LENGTH OF LOAN	DATE DUE
March 12	5 months	August 12
April 24	7 months	November 24
October 7	9 months	July 7
January 31	3 months	April 30

A loan made on January 31 for 3 months would normally be due on April 31. However, there are only 30 days in April, so the loan is due on April 30. Whenever a due date does not exist, such as February 30 or November 31, use the last day of the month (February 28 or November 30 in these examples).

Finding Due Date, Interest, and Maturity Value

EXAMPLE 6

Find the due date, interest, and maturity value for a $600,000 loan made to Benson Automotive on July 31 for 7 months at 7.5% interest.

SOLUTION

Interest and principal are due 7 months from July 31 or February 31, which *does not* exist. Since February has only 28 days (unless it is a leap year), interest and principal are due on the last day of February, or February 28. If it were a leap year, the maturity value would be due on February 29.

$$I = PRT = \$600,000 \times .075 \times \frac{7}{12} = \mathbf{\$26,250}$$

$$M = P + I = \$600,000 + \mathbf{\$26,250} = \$626,250$$

A total of $626,250 must be repaid on February 28.

> **Quick TIP ▼**
> Do not convert the period of a loan from months to days to find the due date.

QUICK CHECK 6

Find the due date for a 6-month loan made on March 31.

9.1 Exercises

The **QUICK START** exercises in each section contain solutions to help you get started.

Find simple interest and maturity value to the nearest cent. (See Examples 1 and 2.)

QUICK START

	Interest	Maturity Value
1. $3800 at 11% for 6 months	$209	$4009

$I = \$3800 \times .11 \times \frac{6}{12} = \$209$

$M = \$3800 + \$209 = \$4009$

2. $10,200 at 9.5% for 10 months   _____   _____

3. $5500 at 8% for 1 year   _____   _____

4. $18,500 at 7.5% for $1\frac{1}{4}$ years   _____   _____

Find the exact number of days from the first date to the second. (See Examples 3 and 4.)

QUICK START

5. February 15 to April 24   **5. 68**

   From the table, February 15 is day 46; April 24 is day 114
   Number of days = 114 − 46 = 68 days

6. May 22 to August 30   6. _____

7. December 1 to March 10 of the following year   7. _____

8. October 12 to February 22 of the following year   8. _____

Find (a) the exact interest and (b) the ordinary interest for each of the following to the nearest cent. Then find (c) the amount by which the ordinary interest is larger. (See Example 5.)

QUICK START

9. $52,000 at $8\frac{3}{4}$% for 200 days   (a) $2493.15

   (a) Exact interest = $52,000 \times .0875 \times \frac{200}{365} = \$2493.15$ (b) $2527.78

   (b) Ordinary interest = $52,000 \times .0875 \times \frac{200}{360} = \$2527.78$ (c) $34.63

   (c) Ordinary is larger by $2527.78 − $2493.15 = $34.63

△ indicates an exercise that is related to the Case in Point feature.

10. $185,000 at 7.5% for 180 days

(a) _____

(b) _____

(c) _____

11. $29,500 at $11\frac{1}{4}$% for 120 days

(a) _____

(b) _____

(c) _____

12. $52,610 at $8\frac{1}{2}$% for 82 days

(a) _____

(b) _____

(c) _____

Identify each of the following from the promissory note shown. (See Objective 6.)

PROMISSORY NOTE

Jackson, Mississippi _October 27, 2012_

Ninety days after date, ___I___ promise to pay to the order of

Donna Sharp   / $8750.00

Eight thousand, seven hundred fifty and $\frac{00}{100}$ Dollars with interest at _12% per year_

_____ , payable at __Crocker–Citizens Bank, Oak Park Branch__

Due _January 25, 2012_   _Helen Spence_

13. Maker _____   **14.** Payer _____

15. Payee _____   **16.** Face value _____

17. Term of loan _____   **18.** Date loan was made _____

19. Date loan is due _____   **20.** Maturity value _____

Find the date due, the amount of interest (rounded to the nearest cent if necessary), and the maturity value. (See Example 6.)

QUICK START

Date Loan Was Made	Face Value	Term of Loan	Rate	Date Loan Is Due	Maturity Value
21. Mar. 12	$4800	220 days	9%	Oct. 18	$5064
$I = \$4800 \times .09 \times \frac{220}{360} = \$264; \ M = \$4800 + \$264 = \$5064$					
22. Jan. 3	$12,000	100 days	9.8%	_____	_____
23. Nov. 10	$6300	180 days	$9\frac{1}{4}$%	_____	_____
24. July 14	$20,400	90 days	$11\frac{3}{4}$%	_____	_____

Solve the following application problems. Round dollar amounts to the nearest cent.

QUICK START

25. INVENTORY   Benson Automotive borrows $2,000,000 at $9\frac{1}{4}$% from a bank to buy land to build a building for a new dealership. Given that the loan is for 9 months, find **(a)** the interest and **(b)** the maturity value.

(a) $I = \$2,000,000 \times .0925 \times \frac{9}{12} = \$138,750$

(b) $M = \$2,000,000 + \$138,750 = \$2,138,750$

(a) $138,750

(b) $2,138,750

26. **LOANS BETWEEN BANKS** A bank in New York City borrows $25,000,000 at 9% for 90 days from a bank in Chicago. Find **(a)** the interest and **(b)** the maturity value.

(a) _____

(b) _____

27. **ROAD PAVING** Gilbert Construction Company needs to borrow $280,000 to build a short, paved road and install all utilities in a subdivision. The company decides to borrow the funds at 10% for 180 days. In 1980, the same note would have been at a rate of 22%. Find the difference in the interest charges based on the two rates.

27. _____

28. **INTERNATIONAL BUSINESS** Lesly Pacas borrows 300,000 pesos for 90 days at 18% per year to remodel her hair salon. She lives in Guadalajara, Mexico, where the rate would have been 35% a few years earlier. Find the difference in the interest charges based on the different rates.

28. _____

29. **CAPITAL IMPROVEMENT** Elizabeth Barton borrowed $6850 to install a small rock fountain and fish pond in front of her flower shop. She signed a 90-day note on July 5 at $9\frac{1}{4}\%$ interest. Find **(a)** the due date and **(b)** the maturity value of the note.

(a) _____

(b) _____

30. **WEB DESIGN** On September 10, Jessica Hernandez signed a promissory note with a face value of $32,500 to help her pay the salaries of employees during the season of slow sales at her Web design firm. The 90-day note is at 11% interest. Find **(a)** the due date and **(b)** maturity value of the note.

(a) _____

(b) _____

31. **HEALTH FOOD** On March 10, the owner of The Granary borrowed $80,000 on a 180-day promissory note at 10.5% interest. Find **(a)** the due date and **(b)** the maturity value of the note.

(a) _____

(b) _____

32. **CORPORATE FINANCE** On October 15, IBM borrows $45,000,000 at 8% from a bank in San Francisco and agrees to repay the loan in 120 days using ordinary interest. Find **(a)** the due date and **(b)** the maturity value.

(a) _____

(b) _____

33. **PENALTY ON UNPAID PROPERTY TAX** Joe Simpson's property tax is $3416.05 and is due on April 15. He does not pay until July 23. The county adds a penalty of 9.3% simple interest on his unpaid tax. Find the penalty using exact interest.

33. _____

34. PENALTY ON UNPAID INCOME TAX   On January 5, Helen Terry made an income tax payment that was due on September 15. The penalty was 11% simple interest on the unpaid tax of $2100. Find the penalty using exact interest.

34. _____

35. PAINT STORE   On January 31, Jackson Paints & Supplies borrowed $128,000 to build a metal building for use as a warehouse. The 8-month loan has a rate of 9.5%. Find **(a)** the due date and **(b)** the maturity value of the loan.

(a) _____

(b) _____

36. LOAN TO EMPLOYEE   On the last day in November, Terry Thompson loaned one of his employees $1600 for 3 months at 10% interest. Find **(a)** the due date and **(b)** the maturity value.

(a) _____

(b) _____

37. Explain the difference between exact interest and ordinary, or banker's, interest. (See Objective 5.)

38. List three companies that you have purchased products or services from in the past. List two reasons each of the companies may have needed to borrow money in the past.

9.2 Finding Principal, Rate, and Time

OBJECTIVES

1   Find the principal.

2   Find the rate.

3   Find the time.

Principal (P), rate (R), and time (T) were given for all problems in **Section 9.1**, and we calculated interest. In this section, interest is given, and we solve for principal, rate, or time.

OBJECTIVE 1   Find the principal. The principal (P) is found by dividing both sides of the simple interest equation $I = PRT$ by RT. See Chapter 4 for a review of algebra if needed.

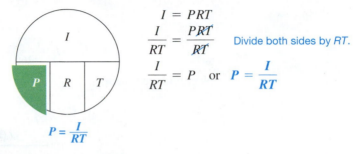

$$I = PRT$$

$$\frac{I}{RT} = \frac{PRT}{RT} \qquad \text{Divide both sides by } RT.$$

$$\frac{I}{RT} = P \quad \text{or} \quad P = \frac{I}{RT}$$

$$P = \frac{I}{RT}$$

The various forms of the simple interest equation can be remembered using the circle sketch shown above. In the sketch, I (interest) is in the top half of the circle, with P (principal), R (rate), and T (time) in the bottom half of the circle. Find the formula for any one variable by covering than letter in the circle and then read the remaining letters, noticing their position. For example, cover P and you are left with $\frac{I}{RT}$.

> $$\text{Principal} = \frac{\text{Interest}}{\text{Rate} \times \text{Time (in years)}} \quad \text{or} \quad P = \frac{I}{RT}$$

Note: Use banker's interest with 360 days for all problems in this section.

Finding Principal Given Interest in Days

EXAMPLE 1

Gilbert Construction Company borrows funds at 10% for 54 days to finish building a home. Find the principal that results in interest of $780.

SOLUTION

Write the rate as .10, the time as $\frac{54}{360}$, and then use the formula for principal.

$$P = \frac{I}{RT}$$

$$P = \frac{\$780}{.10 \times \dfrac{54}{360}}$$

$$.10 \times \frac{54}{360} = .015 \qquad \text{Simplify the denominator.}$$

$$P = \frac{\$780}{.015} = \$52,000 \quad \text{Divide.}$$

The principal is $52,000.

    Check the answer using $I = PRT$. The principal is $52,000, the rate is 10%, and the time is $\frac{54}{360}$ year. The interest should be, and is, $780.

$$I = \$52,000 \times .10 \times \frac{54}{360} = \mathbf{\$780}$$

▦ The calculator approach to finding the principal uses parentheses so that the numerator is divided by the entire denominator.

780 [÷] [(] .10 [×] 54 [÷] 360 [)] [=] 52000

Quick TIP ▼

Remember that time must be in years or fraction of a year.

Finding Principal **Given Length of Loan**

Frank Thomas took out a loan to pay his college tuition on February 2. The loan is due to be repaid on April 15 when Thomas expects to receive an income tax refund. The interest on the loan is $75.60 at a rate of 10.5%. Find the principal.

SOLUTION

First find the number of days.

$$
\begin{array}{rl}
26 & \text{days remaining in February} \\
31 & \text{March} \\
+\ 15 & \text{April} \\
\hline
72 & \text{days from February 2 to April 15}
\end{array}
$$

$$T = \frac{72}{360}$$

Next find the principal.

$$P = \frac{I}{RT}$$

$$P = \frac{\$75.60}{.105 \times \dfrac{72}{360}} \qquad \text{Substitute values into the formula.}$$

$$.105 \times \frac{72}{360} = .021 \qquad \text{Simplify the denominator.}$$

$$P = \frac{\$75.60}{.021} = \$3600 \qquad \text{Divide.}$$

The principal is $3600. Check the answer using the formula for simple interest.

$$I = \$3600 \times .105 \times \frac{72}{360} = \textbf{\$75.60}$$

OBJECTIVE 2 Find the rate. Solve the formula $I = PRT$ for rate (R) by dividing both sides of the equation by PT. The rate found in this manner will be the annual interest rate. See Chapter 4 for a review of algebra if needed.

$$I = PRT$$

$$\frac{I}{PT} = \frac{PRT}{PT} \qquad \text{Divide both sides by } PT.$$

$$\frac{I}{PT} = R \quad \text{or} \quad R = \frac{I}{PT}$$

$$R = \frac{I}{PT}$$

$$\text{Rate} = \frac{\text{Interest}}{\text{Principal} \times \text{Time (in years)}} \quad \text{or} \quad R = \frac{I}{PT}$$

Finding Rate Given Length of Loan **EXAMPLE 3**

An exchange student from the United States living in Brazil deposits $2500 in U.S. currency in a Brazilian bank for 45 days. Find the rate if the interest is $37.50 in U.S. currency.

SOLUTION

$$\text{Rate} = \frac{I}{PT}$$

$$R = \frac{\$37.50}{\$2500 \times \dfrac{45}{360}}$$

$$\$2500 \times \frac{45}{360} = \$312.50 \qquad \text{Simplify the denominator.}$$

$$R = \frac{\$37.50}{\$312.50} = .12 \qquad \text{Divide.}$$

Convert .12 to a percent to get 12%. Check the answer using the simple interest formula.

▦ Solve using a calculator as follows. Notice that parentheses set off the denominator.

37.50 ÷ (2500 × 45 ÷ 360) = .12

QUICK CHECK 3

A 120-day loan for $15,000 has interest of $412.50. Find the rate to the nearest tenth of a percent.

Finding Rate Given Length of Loan **EXAMPLE 4**

Blaine Plumbing kept extra cash of $86,500 in an account from June 1 to August 16. Find the rate if the company earned $365.22 in interest during this period of time.

SOLUTION

Find the number of days using the table on page 349.

$$\begin{aligned} \text{August 16 is day} &\quad 228 \\ \text{June 1 is day} &\quad -\ 152 \\ \hline &\quad \textbf{76 days} \end{aligned}$$

There are 76 days from June 1 to August 16.

$$T = \frac{76}{360}$$

$$\text{Rate} = \frac{I}{PT}$$

$$R = \frac{\$365.22}{\$86,500 \times \dfrac{76}{360}} = .02 \text{ (rounded)}$$

The rate of interest is 2%.

QUICK CHECK 4

A loan of $37,000 made on February 4 results in interest of $770.83. If the loan is due on May 15, find the rate to the nearest tenth of a percent.

OBJECTIVE 3 **Find the time.** The time (T) is found by dividing both sides of the simple interest equation $I = PRT$ by PR. Note that time will be in years or fraction of a year. See Chapter 4 for a review of algebra if needed.

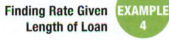

$$T = \frac{I}{PR}$$

$$I = PRT$$

$$\frac{I}{PR} = \frac{\cancel{PR}T}{\cancel{PR}} \qquad \text{Divide both sides by } PR.$$

$$\frac{I}{PR} = T \quad \text{or} \quad T = \frac{I}{PR}$$

> **Finding Time**
>
> $$\text{Time (in years)} = \frac{\text{Interest}}{\text{Principal} \times \text{Rate}} \quad \text{or} \quad T = \frac{I}{PR}$$

The preceding formula gives time in years, but we often need time in days or months. Find these as follows.

> **Finding Time**
>
> $$\text{Time in days} = \frac{I}{PR} \times 360$$
>
> $$\text{Time in months} = \frac{I}{PR} \times 12$$

Finding Time in Days Given Principal and Rate **EXAMPLE 5**

Roberta Sanchez deposited $6200 in an account paying 3% and she earned $72.33 in interest. Find the number of days that the deposit earned interest. Round to a whole number of days.

SOLUTION

$$T \text{ in days} = \frac{I}{PR} \times \textbf{360}$$

$$T = \frac{\$72.33}{\$6200 \times .03} \times \textbf{360} = 140 \text{ days} \quad \text{(rounded)}$$

The money was on deposit for 140 days.

Use parentheses around the denominator of the fraction to make sure that the calculations are done in the correct order. Round to the nearest day.

72.33 ÷ (6200 × .03) × 360 = 140

QUICK CHECK 5

A loan for $22,000 results in interest of $1283.33 at 10.5%. Find the time to the nearest day.

> **Summary**
>
> | | | |
> |---|---|---|
> | **Interest** | $I = PRT$ | |
> | **Principal** | $P = \dfrac{I}{RT}$ | |
> | **Rate** | $R = \dfrac{I}{PT}$ | |
> | **Time** | $T \text{ (in years)} = \dfrac{I}{PR}$ | All of these are modifications of the formula $I = PRT$. |
> | | $T \text{ (in months)} = \dfrac{I}{PR} \times 12$ | |
> | | $T \text{ (in days)} = \dfrac{I}{PR} \times 360$ | |

9.2 Exercises

The **QUICK START** *exercises in each section contain solutions to help you get started.*

Find the principal in each of the following. Round to the nearest cent. (See Example 1.)

QUICK START

	Rate	Time (in days)	Interest	Principal
1.	$7\frac{3}{4}\%$	90	$271.25	**$14,000**

$$P = \frac{\$271.25}{.0775 \times \frac{90}{360}} = \$14{,}000$$

	Rate	Time (in days)	Interest	Principal
2.	9.5%	120	$63.79	**$2014.42**

$$P = \frac{\$63.79}{.095 \times \frac{120}{360}} = \$2014.42$$

	Rate	Time (in days)	Interest	Principal
3.	10%	80	$112.00	_____
4.	6%	24	$62.40	_____
5.	$8\frac{1}{2}\%$	120	$306	_____
6.	10.5%	140	$87.20	_____

Find the rate in each of the following. Round to the nearest tenth of a percent. (See Example 3.)

QUICK START

	Principal	Time	Interest	Rate
7.	$7600	200 days	$498.22	**11.8%**

$$R = \frac{\$498.22}{\$7600 \times \frac{200}{360}} = 11.8\%$$

	Principal	Time	Interest	Rate
8.	$15,600	90 days	$312	_____
9.	$42,800	60 days	$677.67	_____
10.	$20,000	90 days	$625	_____
11.	$8000	4 months	$200	_____
12.	$4800	5 months	$197.60	_____

 indicates an exercise that is related to the Case in Point feature.

Find the time in each of the following. In Exercises 13–16, round to the nearest day;
in Exercises 17 and 18, round to the nearest month. (See Example 5.)

QUICK START

	Principal	Rate	Interest	Time
13.	$74,000	9.5%	$2343.33	120 days

$$T = \frac{\$2343.33}{\$74,000 \times .095} \times 360 = 119.9998 \text{ or } 120 \text{ days}$$

	Principal	Rate	Interest	Time
14.	$36,000	9%	$585.00	_____
15.	$24,000	11%	$454.70	_____
16.	$20,000	8%	$1200	_____
17.	$3500	$10\frac{1}{4}$%	$143.50	_____
18.	$8400	$7\frac{1}{4}$%	$357	_____

In each of the following application problems, find principal to the nearest cent,
rate to the nearest tenth of a percent, or time to the nearest day.

QUICK START

19. SHORT-TERM SAVINGS Hoyt Axton earned $244.80 interest in 9 months in a short-term savings account that paid 3.2% per year. Use the simple interest formula to estimate the amount initially invested.

19. $10,200 _____

$$P = \frac{\$244.80}{.032 \times \frac{9}{12}} = \$10,200$$

20. BANK LOAN Citizens Bank earned $12,250 interest in 45 days from a short-term investment that paid 5.6% interest per year. Find the amount initially invested.

20. _____

21. INVESTING IN BONDS Joan Gretz invested $3600 in a mutual fund containing bonds. Find the rate if she earned $237.50 in interest in 250 days.

21. _____

22. LAW ENFORCEMENT The Smith County Police Department borrowed $120,000 for 135 days to purchase new radar-detection equipment to detect speeders. Find the rate if the interest was $4050.

22. _____

23. PAYROLL Jessica Hernandez borrowed $45,000 so that she could meet payroll for the quarter. She agreed to pay interest of $1881.25 in 140 days. Find the rate.

23. _____

24. **SAVING FOR RETIREMENT** Mike Jordan deposited $2000 into a Roth Individual Retirement Account (IRA) investing in a mutual fund containing corporate bonds. Find the rate if he has $2192.50 in the account 15 months later.

24. _____

25. **RETIREMENT ACCOUNT** Over a period of 300 days, Shawna Johnson earned $450 interest in a retirement account paying interest at a rate of 5%. Find **(a)** the principal at the beginning of the 300 days and **(b)** the amount in the account at the end of 300 days.

(a) _____
(b) _____

26. **INTEREST EARNINGS** Patterson Plumbing had an account that earned $214.67 interest in 280 days. If the interest rate was 4%, find **(a)** the principal at the beginning of the 280 days and **(b)** the amount in the account at the end of the 280 days.

(a) _____
(b) _____

27. **TIME OF DEPOSIT** Benson Automotive earned $69.46 interest on a $9400 deposit in an account paying 3.5%. Find the number of days that the funds were on deposit.

27. _____

28. **TIME OF DEPOSIT** Find how long Quinlan Enterprises must deposit $7500 at 6% in order to earn $243.75 interest.

28. _____

29. **RATE OF INTEREST** Ti Lee earns $223.03 in interest in 320 days after making a deposit of $6272.73. Find the interest rate.

29. _____

30. **PENALTY ON LATE PAYMENT** Smithville Used Toyota lets an $1800 mortgage payment go 70 days overdue and is charged a penalty of $59.50. Find the rate of interest that was charged as a penalty. (*Note:* Penalty rates are frequently quite high.)

30. _____

31. **COMPUTER PURCHASE** Shanghai Computers purchased 10 computers from a Chinese computer manufacturer. Shanghai paid the bill after 45 days, paying a finance charge of $150. If the Chinese company charges 10% interest, find **(a)** the cost of the 10 computers excluding the interest and **(b)** the cost per computer.

(a) _____
(b) _____

32. **LAWN-MOWER PURCHASE** Yard Mowers, Inc., bought 15 self-propelled, 22-inch lawn mowers from Green Lawns, Ltd. The company paid after 90 days and was charged an annual finance charge of 12% or $126. Find **(a)** the cost of the 15 lawn mowers excluding the interest and **(b)** the cost per mower.

(a) _____
(b) _____

33. **PROMISSORY NOTE**   Jan Rice signed a promissory note for $6400 at $11\frac{1}{2}$% interest with interest charges of $425.24. Find the term of the note to the nearest day.

33. _____

34. **TIME OF DEPOSIT**   The Frampton Chamber of Commerce earns $682.71 interest on a $16,385 investment at 5.5%. Find the length of time of the investment to the nearest day.

34. _____

35. **HOME CONSTRUCTION**   Gilbert Construction Company needs to borrow $220,000 for 1 year for materials needed to build three homes. They can borrow from either of two banks. Interest charges from Bank One would amount to $23,650, whereas interest charges from First National Bank would amount to $25,000. Find the interest rates associated with a loan from **(a)** Bank One and **(b)** First National Bank.

(a) _____
(b) _____

36. **INVENTORY PURCHASE**   Forest Nursery needs to borrow $9500 on February 1 to buy additional inventory and will repay the loan on July 15. Interest charges for State Bank and First National Bank are $480 and $443.60, respectively. Find the rate for **(a)** the State Bank loan and **(b)** the First National Bank loan.

(a) _____
(b) _____

37. A retired couple receives $14,000 per year from Social Security and an additional $18,000 in interest from retirement plans and lifetime savings. They need all of their income to pay expenses including medical bills. What will happen if the interest rate on their retirement plans and lifetime savings decreases significantly?

38. How would the formula for calculating time in days (given principal, interest, and rate) change if exact interest were used rather than ordinary interest?

QUICK CHECK ANSWERS

1. $9500
2. $28,200
3. 8.3%
4. 7.5%
5. 200 days

9.3 Simple Discount Notes

OBJECTIVES

1 Define the basic terms used with simple discount notes.
2 Find the bank discount and proceeds.
3 Find the face value.
4 Find the effective interest rate.
5 Understand U.S. Treasury bills.

case IN point ▶ Jessica Hernandez does not like to borrow money, but sometimes she must. For example, she recently had to borrow to pay her expenses when a large firm delayed its payment to her company. She had expenses that had to be paid in a timely way, but her revenue was delayed.

The following clipping shows that the federal government has the power to change interest rates somewhat. Higher interest rates make it more expensive to borrow and often slow economic growth. Lower interest rates make it cheaper to borrow and often increase economic growth. The federal government uses interest rates as a tool to control the growth rate of the economy. The goal is to keep the economy growing fast enough to generate jobs but not so fast as to cause inflation, which is discussed in the next chapter. So, interest rates are set in a complex way in a market and by the federal government.

Economists Differ

All eyes are on the Fed chairman while economists wait for the outcome of the next meeting. Economists differ in the direction they expect interest rates to go from here. Some expect the Fed to increase interest rates slightly next year, but others think rates will remain the same or decrease slightly.

In this section, we discuss **simple discount notes**, which are simply a different way to set up a promissory note based on simple interest calculations. Any note that uses simple interest calculations with a lump-sum payment can be set up *either* as a simple interest note or as a simple discount note. One type of note is *not* better than the other type of note. They merely represent two different ways to discuss the same thing. We study both because some banks use simple interest notes while others use simple discount notes.

OBJECTIVE 1 Define the basic terms used with simple discount notes. As we saw in **Section 9.2**, simple interest notes involve principal (face value or loan amount), interest rate, time, interest, and maturity value. Simple discount notes involve the same ideas but are called **proceeds (loan amount), discount rate, time, bank discount (interest),** and **face value** (or **maturity value**). Face value in a simple interest note is the amount loaned to the borrower, but it is the maturity value in a simple discount note. Simple discount notes are also called **interest-in-advance notes**, since interest is subtracted before funds are given to the borrower. A basic difference between the two types of notes is that simple interest is calculated based on principal, whereas simple discount is calculated based on maturity value, as shown in the table. College students sometimes borrow money from the government using **Stafford loans**, which are simple discount notes.

Simple Interest versus Simple Discount Notes

Type of Note	Loan Amount		Interest		Repayment Amount
Simple interest	Face value (Principal)	+	Interest	=	Maturity value
Simple discount	Proceeds	+	Discount (Interest)	=	Face value (Maturity value)

Note: Simple interest is calculated on the *principal*, while simple discount is calculated on the *maturity value*.

OBJECTIVE 2 Find the bank discount and proceeds. The formula for finding the bank discount is a form of the basic percent equation of Chapter 3. The formula is similar to the one used to calculate simple interest, but different letters are used since the ideas differ slightly.

Calculating Bank Discount

Bank discount = Face value × Discount rate × Time   or $B = MDT$

where

B = Bank discount D = Discount rate
M = Face value (maturity value) T = Time (in years)

Then, if P is the proceeds,

Proceeds (loan amount) = Face value − Bank discount   or $P = M - B$

Stated in another way,

Face value = Proceeds (loan amount) + Bank discount   or $M = P + B$

Finding Discount and Proceeds

Jim Peterson signs a simple discount note with a face or maturity value of $35,000 so that he can purchase a truck with plow for his snow removal business. The banker discounts the 10-month note at 9%. Find the amount of the discount and the proceeds.

SOLUTION

Peterson *does not* receive $35,000 from the bank—that is the amount he must repay when the loan matures. Use $M = \$35,000$, $D = 9\%$, and $T = \frac{10}{12}$ in the formula $B = MDT$ to find the discount, which is the interest that must be paid at maturity.

$$\text{Bank discount} = \quad M \quad \times D \times T$$
$$B = \$35,000 \times .09 \times \tfrac{10}{12} = \$2625$$

The discount of **$2625** is the interest charge on the loan. The proceeds that Peterson actually receives when making the loan is found using $P = M - B$.

$$P = \quad M \quad - \quad B$$
$$P = \$35,000 - \$2625 = \$32,375$$

Peterson signs the discount note with a face value of $35,000, but receives $32,375. Ten months later he must pay $35,000 to the bank.

QUICK CHECK 1

A simple discount loan has a maturity value of $15,800, discount rate of 9%, and time of 180 days. Find the bank discount and proceeds.

Finding the Proceeds

To finance a new electronic sign to put in front of its retail store, Mustang Auto Sales signs a 6-month, simple discount note with a face value of $4500. Find the proceeds if the discount rate is 10.5%.

SOLUTION

The bank discount (B) is not known, but we do know that $B = MDT$. Therefore, we can substitute MDT in place of B.

$$P = M - B$$
$$P = M - MDT \qquad \text{Substitute } MDT \text{ in place of } B.$$
$$P = \$4500 - \left(\$4500 \times .105 \times \frac{6}{12} \right) \qquad \text{Substitute values.}$$
$$P = \$4263.75$$

Mustang Auto Sales receives $4263.75 but must pay back $4500 in 6 months.

OBJECTIVE 3 Find the face value. If the loan amount (proceeds) of a simple discount note is known, use the following formula to find the corresponding face value.

> **Calculating Face Value to Achieve Desired Proceeds**
>
> $$M = \frac{P}{1 - DT}$$
>
> where
>
> M = Face value of the simple discount note
> P = Proceeds received by the borrower
> D = Discount rate used by the bank   *Note:* The symbol D is the discount *rate*,
> T = Time of the loan (in years)   not the bank discount.

Finding the Face Value **EXAMPLE 3**   Tina Watson purchased a classic 1961 Corvette and plans to rebuild it. She estimates that she will need to borrow $18,000 for 180 days. Find the face value of the 10% simple discount note that would result in proceeds of $18,000 to Watson.

SOLUTION

Use the formula.

$$M = \frac{P}{1 - DT}$$

Replace P with $18,000, D with .10, and T with $\frac{180}{360}$.

$$M = \frac{\$18{,}000}{1 - \left(.10 \times \dfrac{180}{360}\right)} = \$18{,}947.37 \quad \text{(rounded)}$$

The face value of the note is $18,947.37. However, Watson receives only $18,000 from the bank when the note is signed. She must repay $18,947.37 to the bank in 180 days.

 The problem

$$\frac{\$18{,}000}{1 - \left(.10 \times \dfrac{180}{360}\right)}$$

can be solved using a calculator by first thinking of the problem as shown here, with brackets to set off the denominator.

$$\$18{,}000 \div \left[1 - \left(.10 \times \frac{180}{360}\right)\right]$$

The parentheses inside the brackets are not really needed due to order of operations. The problem is then solved as follows.

18000 [÷] [(] 1 [−] .10 [×] 180 [÷] 360 [)] [=] 18947.37   (rounded)

Comparing Discount Notes and Simple Interest Notes

 EXAMPLE 4

Jane Benson of Benson Automotive has been offered loans from two different banks. Each note has a face value of $75,000 and a time of 90 days. One note has a simple interest rate of 10%, and the other a simple discount rate of 10%. Benson wants to know which is the better deal.

SOLUTION

Find the interest owed on each.

SIMPLE INTEREST NOTE	SIMPLE DISCOUNT NOTE
$I = PRT$	$B = MDT$
$I = \$75{,}000 \times .10 \times \dfrac{90}{360}$	$B = \$75{,}000 \times .10 \times \dfrac{90}{360}$
$I = \$1875$	$B = \$1875$

The amount of interest is the same in both notes. Now find the amount the borrower would receive.

SIMPLE INTEREST NOTE	SIMPLE DISCOUNT NOTE
Face value = $75,000	Proceeds = $M - B$
	= $75,000 - $1875
	= $73,125

The borrower has the use of $75,000 with the simple interest note, but only $73,125 with the simple discount note. Yet the amount of interest is identical. Therefore, the simple interest note is the better loan for Benson Automotive. However, it is not true that a simple interest note is necessarily better than a simple discount note. You must look at each note individually to understand the terms. Find the maturity value for each note.

SIMPLE INTEREST NOTE	SIMPLE DISCOUNT NOTE
$M = P + I$	Maturity = Face value
= $75,000 + $1875	= $75,000
= $76,875	

The differences between these two notes can be summarized as follows.

	SIMPLE INTEREST NOTE	SIMPLE DISCOUNT NOTE
Face value	$75,000	$75,000
Interest	$1875	$1875
Amount available to borrower	$75,000	$73,125
Maturity value	$76,875	$75,000

Quick TIP ▼

This example shows that a simple discount rate of 10% is not equivalent to a simple interest rate of 10%.

QUICK CHECK 4

Two notes both have face values of $24,000 and a time of 180 days. The first note has a simple interest rate of 9%, and the second has a simple discount rate of 9%. Find the maturity value of each.

OBJECTIVE 4 Find the effective interest rate. The federal **Truth in Lending Act** was passed in 1969 because the different ways of calculating interest were confusing. This law does not regulate interest rates, but it does require that interest rates be given in a form that can easily be compared.

The **effective rate of interest** is also called the **annual percentage rate**, the **APR**, and the **true rate**. It is the interest rate that is calculated based on the actual amount received by the borrower. The discount rate of 10% stated in Example 4 is called the **stated rate**, or **nominal rate**, since it is the rate written on the note. It is not the effective rate, since the 10% applies to the maturity value of $75,000 and *not* to the proceeds of $73,125 actually received by the borrower. The next example shows how to find the effective rate for Example 4.

Finding the Effective Interest Rate   **EXAMPLE 5**

Find the effective rate of interest (APR) for the simple discount note of Example 4.

SOLUTION

Find the effective rate (APR) by using the formula for simple interest: $I = PRT$. In this case, $I = \$1875$ (the discount), $P = \$73,125$ (the proceeds), and $T = \frac{90}{360}$. Use the following formula from **Section 9.2.**

$$R = \frac{I}{PT}$$

$$R = \frac{\$1875}{\$73,125 \times \dfrac{90}{360}} = .1026 = 10.26\% \text{ (rounded)}$$

> **Quick TIP ▼**
>
> The discount rate is not an interest rate to be applied to proceeds (loan amount)—rather it is applied to face value.

> **QUICK CHECK 5**
>
> Find the effective rate (APR) for a loan with a loan amount of \$31,000, a time of 90 days, and interest of \$891.25.

The interest rate 10.26% in Example 5 is the **effective**, or **true**, **rate of interest**. Federal regulations require that rates be rounded to the nearest quarter of a percent when communicated to a borrower. Note that 10.26% is closer to 10.25% than to 10.50%. Therefore, an annual percentage rate (APR) of 10.25% must be reported to someone signing a discount note with a face value of \$75,000 for 90 days at a discount rate of 10%.

The table below shows two identical loans, one a simple interest loan and the other a simple discount loan. Proceeds, interest charges, terms of the loans, and maturity values are all identical.

	SIMPLE INTEREST LOAN	SIMPLE DISCOUNT LOAN
Proceeds	\$11,100	\$11,100
Interest	\$900	\$900
Maturity Value	\$12,000	\$12,000
Face Value	\$11,100	\$12,000
Time	10 months	10 months
Interest Rate	9.73%	—
Discount Rate	—	9%

Since the loans are identical, a 9.73% simple interest loan for 10 months is equivalent to a 9% simple discount note for 10 months. In both situations, the borrower receives \$11,100 and must repay \$12,000 ten months later. Therefore, the two loans have the *same effective rate*.

OBJECTIVE 5 Understand U.S. Treasury bills. The United States government borrows very large amounts of money from banks, various financial institutions, pension funds, wealthy individuals, and even foreign governments. In fact, the U.S. national debt is projected to pass \$14 trillion in 2011, much of it owed to Japan and China. Do you know how many digits are needed to write the number \$14 trillion?

$$\$14 \text{ trillion} = \$14,\underset{\text{billions}}{\underbrace{000}},000,000,000$$

$\overset{\text{trillions}}{}$

If 14 trillion \$1 bills could be stacked on top of one another, the stack would rise from the surface of the earth far past the moon. However, debt is not really in \$1 bills. It is more useful to think of debt as numbers written on contracts of one form or another and stored in computers. Our monetary system is not really based on paper currency. Instead, it is based on the government's backing of the dollar and (effectively) the many contractual promises to repay loans that are everywhere in our society.

The U.S. government uses **U.S. Treasury bills**, or **T-bills**, to borrow for less than one year. An individual can buy a T-bill directly from the government or indirectly through a broker such as Merrill Lynch. T-bills use discount interest.

Finding Facts About T-Bills　 **EXAMPLE 6**　The owner of a construction company in Mexico is worried that the peso is going to devalue, or fall in value. As a result, he purchases $1,000,000 in U.S. T-bills in order to place cash in a safe place for a short period of time. The T-bills are at a 4% discount rate for 26 weeks. Find **(a)** the total purchase price, **(b)** the total maturity value, **(c)** the interest earned, and **(d)** the effective rate of interest.

SOLUTION

$M = \$1,000,000; D = .04; T = \frac{26}{52}$

(a) **Bank discount** = *Face value* × *Discount rate* × *Time*
$$= \$1,000,000 \times .04 \times \tfrac{26}{52} = \$20,000$$

　　Purchase price = *Face value* − *Bank discount*
$$= \$1,000,000 - \$20,000 = \$980,000$$

(b) **Maturity value** = **Face value**
$$= \$1,000,000$$

(c) **Interest** = **Bank discount**
$$= \$20,000$$

(d) **Effective rate** = $\dfrac{\textbf{Interest earned}}{\textbf{Purchase price (proceeds)} \times \textbf{Time}}$

$$= \frac{\$20,000}{\$980,000 \times \frac{26}{52}} = .04081 = 4.08\%$$

QUICK CHECK 6

Find **(a)** the purchase price, **(b)** the maturity value, **(c)** the interest, and **(d)** the effective rate of interest (to the nearest hundredth) for a $1,000,000, 13-week T-bill with a discount rate of 5.2%. Round to the nearest hundredth of a percent.

9.3 Exercises

The **QUICK START** exercises in each section contain solutions to help you get started.

Find the discount to the nearest cent, then find the proceeds. (See Example 1.)

QUICK START

	Face Value	Discount Rate	Time (Days)	Discount	Proceeds or Loan Amount
1.	$7800	9%	120	$234	$7566

$B = \$7800 \times .09 \times \frac{120}{360} = \$234; \; P = \$7800 - \$234 = \$7566$

	Face Value	Discount Rate	Time (Days)	Discount	Proceeds or Loan Amount
2.	$15,000	10.25%	90	_____	_____
3.	$19,000	10%	180	_____	_____
4.	$12,500	11%	150	_____	_____
5.	$22,400	$8\frac{3}{4}\%$	75	_____	_____
6.	$18,050	8%	80	_____	_____

Find the maturity date and the proceeds for the following. Round to the nearest cent. (See Examples 1 and 2.)

QUICK START

	Face Value	Discount Rate	Date Made	Time (Days)	Maturity Date	Proceeds or Loan Amount
7.	$6400	9.5%	Mar. 22	90	Jun. 20	$6248

$P = \$6400 - \left(\$6400 \times .095 \times \frac{90}{360}\right) = \$6248$

	Face Value	Discount Rate	Date Made	Time (Days)	Maturity Date	Proceeds or Loan Amount
8.	$9500	12%	Oct. 12	100	_____	_____
9.	$10,000	$10\frac{1}{4}\%$	July 12	150	_____	_____
10.	$18,500	$9\frac{1}{4}\%$	May 1	220	_____	_____
11.	$24,000	10%	Dec. 10	60	_____	_____
12.	$8000	10.5%	Nov. 4	165	_____	_____

C indicates an exercise that is related to the Case in Point feature.

Solve each of the following application problems. Round rate to the nearest tenth of a percent, time to the nearest day, and money to the nearest cent.

QUICK START

13. **BOAT PURCHASE**   An ExxonMobil employee borrowed $6000 from First National Bank to purchase a boat. He plans to repay the loan with a Christmas bonus he is to receive in 120 days. If he borrowed the money at a discount rate of 11%, find **(a)** the discount and **(b)** the proceeds.

(a) $B = \$6000 \times .11 \times \frac{120}{360} = \$220;$
(b) $P = \$6000 - \$220 = \$5780$

(a) $220

(b) $5780

14. **INCOME TAX PAYMENT**   Managers at Benson Automotive sign a $48,000 simple discount note for six months for funds to pay corporate income taxes. If the discount rate is 8.5%, find **(a)** the discount and **(b)** the proceeds.

(a) _____

(b) _____

15. **CHRISTMAS TREE FARM**   To plant Christmas trees in another field, Tom Parsons signed a note with a face value of $25,000 at an 11% discount rate. Find the length of the loan in days if the discount is $1527.78.

15. _____

 16. **WEB-PAGE DESIGN**   Jessica Hernandez was unable to collect funds owed her from a customer that declared bankruptcy. The shortage of cash forced Hernandez to sign a $12,200 note at a discount rate of 11% to pay her bills. She was told the interest would be $931.94. Find the length of the loan in days.

16. _____

17. **CASINO**   Wyatt Construction borrowed $157.25 million during the construction phase of adding a wing to a casino in Las Vegas. Management signed a 270-day note with a face value of $170 million. Find the discount rate.

17. _____

18. **CELL PHONES**   Ben Dayton needed funds to open a cell phone store and his uncle agreed to put up collateral for the loan. Dayton signed a 130-day simple discount note with a face value of $12,000 and proceeds of $11,523.33. Find the discount rate.

18. _____

19. **NEW ROOF**   Roy Gerard needs $7260 to pay for a new roof on his house. His bank loans him money at a discount rate of 12%, and the loan is for 240 days. Find the face value of the loan so he will have $7260.

19. _____

20. **AUTO REPAIR**   Lane Engineering needs $120,000 to install computers and a new network. The simple discount note has a 9.5% rate and matures in 80 days. Find the face value of the loan needed.

20. _____

21. **POOR CREDIT**   Cathy Cox has poor credit but she found a bank that will lend her $4200 when she uses some collateral. Still, the bank charges a 12% discount rate. Find **(a)** the proceeds if the note is for 10 months and **(b)** the effective interest rate charged by the bank.

(a) _____

(b) _____

22. BAD CREDIT HISTORY Tim Garcia has a bad credit history partly due to a divorce. The bank agrees to lend him funds based on a note with a face value of $9400, but it requires him to use his truck as collateral. Even then, the bank charges him a high 16% discount rate. Find **(a)** the proceeds and **(b)** the effective rate if the note is for 7 months.

(a) _____

(b) _____

23. INTERNATIONAL FINANCE A business owner in England signs a 10% discount note for 40,000 English pounds (£40,000) with a bank in London. If the proceeds are £38,833.33, find the time of the note in days.

23. _____

24. SIMPLE DISCOUNT RATE A plumbing contractor receives proceeds of $4713.54 on a 12.5% simple discount note with a face value of $5000. Find the time of the note in days.

24. _____

25. EARTHQUAKE DAMAGE A bridge in Japan was damaged by an earthquake. The firm repairing the bridge needs proceeds of 165 million Japanese yen (¥165,000,000) for 30 days to pay wages and buy supplies. A bank lends the funds at an 8% discount rate. Find **(a)** the face value and **(b)** the effective rate.

(a) _____

(b) _____

26. INTERNATIONAL FINANCE A Malaysian electric company requires proceeds of $720,000 (local currency) and borrows from a bank in Thailand at a 12% discount rate for 45 days. Find **(a)** the face value of the note and **(b)** the effective interest rate.

(a) _____

(b) _____

27. RACE HORSES Robert Johnson owns a farm and breeds race horses. To purchase three thoroughbreds, he signs a 180-day note with a maturity value of $265,000 and proceeds of $253,737.50. Find **(a)** the discount and **(b)** the true rate.

(a) _____

(b) _____

28. PIZZA To remodel a restaurant, Two Brothers Pizza signs a 250-day note with proceeds of $63,159.72 and a maturity value of $68,000. Find **(a)** the discount and **(b)** the APR.

(a) _____

(b) _____

The following exercises apply to U.S. Treasury bills, discussed at the end of this section. (Assume 52 weeks per year for each exercise, and round to the nearest hundredth of a percent.) (See Example 6.)

29. **PURCHASE OF T-BILLS**   A large British investment firm purchases $25,000,000 in U.S. T-bills at a 6% discount rate for 13 weeks. Find **(a)** the purchase price of the T-bills, **(b)** the maturity value of the T-bills, **(c)** the interest earned, and **(d)** the effective rate.

(a) _____

(b) _____

(c) _____

(d) _____

30. **T-BILLS**   Nina Horn buys a $50,000 T-bill at a 5.8% discount rate for 26 weeks. Find **(a)** the purchase price of the T-bill, **(b)** the maturity value, **(c)** the interest earned, and **(d)** the effective rate of interest.

(a) _____

(b) _____

(c) _____

(d) _____

31. Explain the main differences between simple interest notes and simple discount notes. (See Objective 1.)

32. As a borrower, would you prefer a simple interest note with a rate of 11% or a simple discount note at a rate of 11%? Explain using an example. (See Example 4.)

QUICK CHECK ANSWERS

1. $711; $15,089
2. $37,066.67
3. $51,798.56
4. $25,080; $24,000
5. 11.5%

6. **(a)** $987,000
   (b) $1,000,000
   (c) $13,000
   (d) 5.27%

9.4 Discounting a Note Before Maturity

OBJECTIVES

1. Understand the concept of discounting a note.
2. Find the proceeds when discounting simple interest notes.
3. Find the proceeds when discounting simple discount notes.

A note is a *legal responsibility* for one individual or firm to pay a specific amount on a specific date to another individual or firm. Notes can be bought and sold just as an automobile can be bought and sold. The clipping taken from a newspaper shows firms that buy notes. This section shows how to find the value of a note that is sold before its maturity date.

OBJECTIVE 1 Understand the concept of discounting a note. Businesses sometimes help their customers purchase products or services by accepting a promissory note rather than requiring an immediate cash payment. For example, a company that manufactures boats, a retailer that sells the boats, and a bank may do business as follows:

1. Boat manufacturer sells boats to a retailer and accepts a promissory note instead of cash.
2. Boat manufacturer needs cash and sells the note to a bank before it matures.
3. Retailer pays the maturity value of the note to the bank when due.

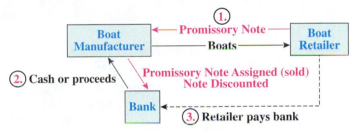

The bank deducts a fee from the maturity value of the note when it buys the note from the manufacturer. The fee is interest for the number of days, called the **discount period,** that the bank will hold the note until it is due. The fee charged by the bank is the **bank discount** or just **discount.** The **discount rate** is the percent used by the bank to find the discount. The process of finding the value of the note on a specific date before it matures is **discounting the note.** Both simple interest notes and simple discount notes can be discounted before they mature.

OBJECTIVE 2 Find the proceeds when discounting simple interest notes. The amount of cash actually received by the boat manufacturer on the sale of a promissory note is the **proceeds.** The bank then collects the maturity value from the maker of the note, the retailer, when it is due. These notes are usually sold with **recourse.** This means that the bank receives reimbursement from the manufacturer if the retailer does not pay the bank when the note matures. Thus the bank is protected against loss. Many banks refuse to buy these types of notes unless they have recourse.

The figure below shows the Federal discount rate that is set by the government. It is used to influence economic activity by changing the cost of borrowing money. The figure shows

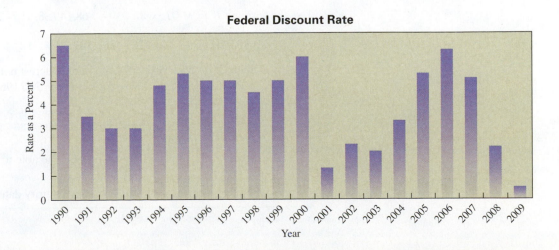

Federal Discount Rate

that interest rates change frequently. As a result, it is common for the rate at which a note is discounted to differ from the original rate of the loan.

Calculate the Proceeds When Discounting a Simple Interest Note

1. First, understand the simple interest note by finding:
   (a) the **due date** of the original note and
   (b) the **maturity value** of the original note ($M = P + I$, where $I = PRT$).
2. Then discount the simple interest note.
   (a) Find the **discount period**, which is the time (e.g., number of days) from the sale of the note to the maturity date of the note.
   (b) Find the **discount** using the formula
$$B = M \times D \times T$$
$$= \text{Maturity value} \times \text{Discount rate} \times \text{Discount period}$$
   (c) Find the **proceeds** after discounting the original note using $P = M - B$.

Finding Proceeds

Jameson Plumbing takes a simple interest, 180-day note from a contractor with a face value of $64,750 and a rate of 10.5%. The company sells the note to a bank 50 days later at a discount rate of 12%. Find the proceeds to the plumbing company.

$$\text{Contractor} \xrightarrow{\text{Note}} \text{Jameson Plumbing}$$
$$\downarrow \text{\textbf{Sells note}}$$
$$\text{Bank}$$

SOLUTION

Step 1 **Find the maturity value.** The face value equals the proceeds, since this is a simple interest note.

Maturity value = Principal + Interest on the simple interest note
Maturity value = $64,750 + **PRT**   Since $I = PRT$

Maturity value = $64,750 + **$64,750 \times .105 \times \dfrac{180}{360}** = \$68,149.38$ (rounded)

Step 2 The note is discounted after 50 days, so the discount period is $180 - 50 = 130$ days. This means that the buyer of the note will own it for 130 days before the note is paid off.

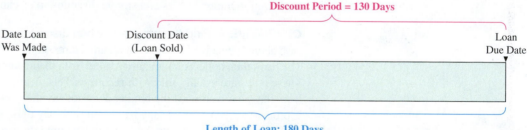

Use the formula $B = MDT$, with $M = \$68,149.38$, $D = .12$, and $T = \frac{130}{360}$ to find the discount.

$$\text{Bank discount} = \textbf{MDT} = \textbf{\$68,149.38} \times \textbf{.12} \times \frac{130}{360} = \$2953.14$$

Proceeds = Maturity value of simple interest note − Bank discount
Proceeds = $68,149.38 − $2953.14 = $65,196.24

So, the following occurs:

1. A contractor signs a 180-day simple interest note with a face value of $64,750 to Jameson Plumbing.
2. After 50 days, Jameson Plumbing sells the note to a bank and receives $65,196.24 in cash.
3. The bank receives $68,149.38 on the maturity date of the loan.

QUICK CHECK 1

A simple interest note has a face value of $14,000, a rate of 9%, and a time to maturity of 240 days. It is discounted after 80 days at a rate of 11%. Find the maturity value of the simple interest note and the proceeds at the time of the discount.

Finding Proceeds **EXAMPLE 2**

Blues Recording holds a 200-day simple interest note from a rock group that agreed to pay them to record an album and produce 1000 CDs. The 12% simple interest note is dated March 24 and has a face value of $4800. Blues Recording wishes to convert the note to cash, so they sell it to a bank on August 15. If the bank requires a discount rate of 12.5%, find the proceeds to the recording studio.

SOLUTION

Go through the two steps of discounting a note.

Step 1   *Find the maturity value.* The note is dated March 24 and is due in 200 days. The due date is found as follows.

$$\text{day } 83 \text{ (March 24)} + 200 \text{ days} = \text{day } 283 \text{ (October 10)}$$

Since this is a simple interest note, the proceeds are given but the maturity value must be found. First find the **interest** on the note if held until maturity.

$$I = \mathbf{PRT} = \$4800 \times .12 \times \frac{200}{360} = \$320$$

The **maturity value** is $4800 + $320 = $5120.

Step 2   Now discount this simple interest note.

(a) *Find the discount period.* The **discount period** is the number of days from August 15, which is the date the note is discounted (sold) to the bank, to the due date of the note (October 10).

Discount Period = 56 Days

Date Loan Was Made	Discount Date (Loan Sold)	Loan Due Date
March 24	August 15	October 10

Length of Loan: 200 Days

October 10 is day	283
August 15 is day	− 227
Discount period	**56 days**

Blues Recording holds the 200-day note for 200 − 56 = 144 days before they sell it. The buyer of the note holds it for 56 days before the rock group must pay off the note.

> **Quick TIP ▼**
>
> When finding the bank discount, be sure to use the maturity value of the original note.

(b) *Find the bank discount.* Find the **discount** by using the formula $B = MDT$, where $M = \$5120$, $D = 12.5\%$, and T is $\frac{56}{360}$.

$$B = \mathbf{MDT} = \$5120 \times .125 \times \frac{56}{360} = \$99.56 \text{ (rounded)}$$

The bank discount is $99.56.

(c) *Find the proceeds.* **Proceeds** are found by subtracting the bank discount from the maturity value.

$$P = \mathbf{M} - \mathbf{B}$$
$$P = \$5120 - \$99.56 = \$5020.44$$

Date	Transaction
March 24	Rock group signs 200-day simple interest note for $4800.
August 15	Blues Recording sells note to bank for $5020.44.
October 10	Bank receives $5120 from payer (rock group).

QUICK CHECK 2

On March 27, Dayton Finance loans Jorge Rivera $9200 for 150 days at 11% simple interest. The finance company sells the note to a private investor on April 24. Find the maturity value of the simple interest note and the proceeds to Dayton Finance if the note is sold at a discount rate of 12%.

It is also common for a business needing cash to sell part of its accounts receivable (money owed to the company) before it is due. The process is called **factoring**, and those who buy the accounts receivable are called **factors**. The calculations involved in factoring are the same as those for finding the discount discussed in this section.

OBJECTIVE 3 Find the proceeds when discounting simple discount notes.

Calculate the Proceeds When Discounting a Simple Discount Note

1. First, understand the simple discount note by finding:
   (a) the **due date** of the original note,
   (b) the **discount** of the original note using $B = MDT$, and
   (c) the **proceeds** from the original note using $P = M - B$.
   The **maturity value (face value)** of the note is written on the note itself and is the value needed in step 2(b) below.

2. Then discount the simple discount note.
   (a) Find the **discount period**, which is the time (e.g., number of days) from the sale of the note to the maturity date of the note.
   (b) Find the **discount** using the formula $B = MDT$.
   (c) Find the **proceeds** after discounting the original note using $P = M - B$.

> **Quick TIP ▼**
>
> There are two different discounts in problems of this type. The first occurs when the original note is signed. The second discount occurs when this note is sold before maturity.

The steps for finding the proceeds at the time of sale are shown for a U.S. Treasury bill in Example 3. The calculations to find the proceeds are the same for any simple discount note.

Finding the Proceeds   **EXAMPLE 3**   Benson Automotive used excess cash to purchase a $100,000 Treasury bill with a term of 26 weeks at a 6.5% simple discount rate. However, the firm needs cash exactly 8 weeks later and sells the T-bill. During the 8 weeks, market interest rates moved up slightly so that the bill was sold at a 7% discount rate. Find **(a)** the initial purchase price of the T-bill, **(b)** the proceeds received by the firm at the subsequent sale of the T-bill, and **(c)** the effective interest rate received by Benson Automotive.

SOLUTION

(a) *Find the discount and proceeds.* The discount that Benson Automotive receives when buying the T-bill is found as follows.

$$B = \mathbf{MDT} = \$100{,}000 \times .065 \times \frac{26}{52} = \$3250$$

The cost to the company is the maturity value minus the discount.

$$P = \mathbf{M} - \mathbf{B} = \$100{,}000 - \$3250 = \$96{,}750$$

Therefore, the U.S. government receives $96,750 from the sale of the T-bill.

(b) *Find the discount period, discount, and proceeds.* Now follow the steps in the table on the previous page to find the proceeds Benson Automotive receives for selling the T-bill 8 weeks later. The discount period is 18 weeks, since the T-bill is sold $26 - 8 = 18$ weeks before its due date.

8 weeks   Discount Period = 18 weeks

| Note Purchased | → | Benson Automotive sells note | → | U.S. Government pays off note |

Length of Note: 26 weeks

The discount at the time of the sale is as follows.

$$B = MDT = \$100,000 \times .07 \times \frac{18}{52} = \$2423.08$$

Finally, the proceeds equal the maturity value of the T-bill ($100,000) less the discount at the time of the sale.

$$P = M - B = \$100,000 - \$2423.08 = \$97,576.92$$

(c) Benson Automotive paid $96,750 to buy the T-bill and received $97,576.92 for it 8 weeks later.

$$\text{Interest received} = \$97,576.92 - \$96,750 = \mathbf{\$826.92}$$

$$R = \frac{\mathbf{\$826.92}}{\$96,750 \times \frac{8}{52}} = 5.56\% \text{ (rounded)}$$

The company would have earned 6.5% on the T-bill had it left the Treasury bill invested until maturity. Instead, the company sold it after market interest rates rose, but before the T-bill matured. This caused the company to end up with an effective interest rate somewhat less than 6.5%.

QUICK CHECK 3

A 240-day discount note has a maturity value of $24,000 and a discount rate of 8%. It is sold after 100 days at a discount rate of 10.5%. Find the maturity value of the original discount note and the proceeds at the time of the sale.

9.4 Exercises

The QUICK START exercises in each section contain solutions to help you get started.

Find the discount period for each of the following. (See Examples 2 and 3, Step 2.)

QUICK START

	Date Loan Was Made	Length of Loan	Date of Discount	Discount Period
1.	Apr. 29	200 days	July 31	107 days
2.	July 28	120 days	Sept. 20	_____
3.	May 28	74 days	June 18	_____
4.	Sept. 17	130 days	Jan. 13	_____

Find the proceeds to the nearest cent when each of the following is discounted.
(Hint: The maturity value is given.) (See Examples 1 and 2.)

QUICK START

	Maturity Value	Discount Rate	Discount Period	Proceeds
5.	$10,400	8.5%	90 days	$10,179

$B = \$10,400 \times .085 \times \frac{90}{360} = \$221; P = \$10,400 - \$221 = \$10,179$

	Maturity Value	Discount Rate	Discount Period	Proceeds
6.	$4800	10.3%	200 days	_____
7.	$25,000	9%	30 days	_____
8.	$3000	11%	60 days	_____

Find the maturity value of each of the following simple interest notes. Each note is then discounted at 12%. Find the discount period, the discount, and the proceeds after discounting. (See Examples 1 and 2.)

QUICK START

	Date Loan Was Made	Face Value	Length of Loan	Rate	Maturity Value	Date of Discount	Discount Period	Discount	Proceeds
9.	Feb. 7	$6200	90 days	$10\frac{1}{2}$%	$6362.75	Apr. 1	37 days	$78.47	$6284.28

$I = \$6200 \times .105 \times \frac{90}{360} = \$162.75; M = \$6200 + \$162.75 = \$6362.75$
Feb. 7 is day 38; Apr. 1 is day 91; 91 − 38 = 53
Discount period = 90 − 53 = 37 days
$B = \$6362.75 \times .12 \times \frac{37}{360} = \$78.47$
Proceeds = $6362.75 − $78.47 = $6284.28

	Date Loan Was Made	Face Value	Length of Loan	Rate	Maturity Value	Date of Discount	Discount Period	Discount	Proceeds
10.	June 15	$9200	140 days	12%	_____	Oct. 22	_____	_____	_____

Date Loan Was Made	Face Value	Length of Loan	Rate	Maturity Value	Date of Discount	Discount Period	Discount	Proceeds
11. July 10	$2000	72 days	11%	_____	Aug. 2	_____	_____	_____
12. May 29	$5500	80 days	10%	_____	July 8	_____	_____	_____

First, find the initial proceeds of each of the following simple discount notes. Each note is then discounted at 11%. Find the discount period, the discount, and the proceeds after discounting. (See Example 3.)

QUICK START

Date Loan Was Made	Maturity Value	Length of Loan	Rate	Initial Proceeds	Date of Discount	Discount Period	Discount	Proceeds at Time of Sale
13. Jan. 12	$17,800	90 days	10%	$17,355	Mar. 1	42 days	$228.43	$17,571.57

$B = MDT = \$17,800 \times .10 \times \frac{90}{360} = \$445; P = M - B = \$17,800 - \$445 = \$17,355$
Jan. 12 is day 12; Due date is 12 + 90 = 102 or Apr. 12
Mar. 1 is day 60; Discount period is 102 − 60 = 42 days
$B = MDT = \$17,800 \times .11 \times \frac{42}{360} = \$228.43$
$P = M - B = \$17,800 - \$228.43 = \$17,571.57$

14. Aug. 4	$24,000	120 days	10.5%	_____	Oct. 8	_____	_____	_____
15. May 4	$32,100	150 days	9.5%	_____	July 10	_____	_____	_____
16. Apr. 30	$22,000	200 days	9%	_____	July 12	_____	_____	_____

Solve the following application problems. Round interest and discount to the nearest cent.

QUICK START

17. ROCK CRUSHER First Bank loaned $360,000 for 180 days to a company purchasing a rock-crushing machine. The bank sold the 7% simple interest note 120 days later at an 8% discount rate. Find **(a)** the bank discount and **(b)** the proceeds.

(a) $4968

(b) $367,632

(a) $M = \$360,000 + \left(\$360,000 \times .07 \times \frac{180}{360}\right) = \$372,600$ **(b)** $P = \$372,600 - \$4968 = \$367,632$
Discount period = 180 days − 120 days = 60 days
$B = \$372,600 \times .08 \times \frac{60}{360} = \$4968$

18. **TRACTOR PURCHASE** Cook and Daughters Farm Equipment accepts a $5800 simple interest note at 12% for 100 days, for a small used tractor. The note is dated May 12. On June 17, the firm discounts the note at the bank, at a 13% discount rate. Find **(a)** the bank discount and **(b)** the proceeds.

(a) _____

(b) _____

19. **AUTOMOBILE DEALERSHIP** Benson Automotive signed a 180-day simple discount note with a face value of $250,000 and a rate of 9% on March 19. The lender sells the note at an 8% discount rate on June 14. Find **(a)** the proceeds of the original note to the dealership, **(b)** the discount period, **(c)** the discount, and **(d)** the proceeds at the sale of the note on June 14.

(a) _____

(b) _____

(c) _____

(d) _____

20. **SEWING CENTER** Kathy Bates, owner of Marie's Sewing Center, agreed to a 10% simple discount note with a maturity value of $18,500 on July 30. She planned to add to her inventory of sewing machines with the funds. The 120-day note is sold by the lender at a 12% discount rate on September 2. Find **(a)** the proceeds of the original note to Bates, **(b)** the discount period, **(c)** the discount, and **(d)** the proceeds at the sale of the note on September 2.

(a) _____

(b) _____

(c) _____

(d) _____

21. **FINANCING CONSTRUCTION** To build a new warehouse, ALDI International signed a $300,000 simple interest note at 9% for 150 days with National Bank on November 20. On February 6, National Bank sold all of its notes to Bank One. Find **(a)** the maturity value of the note and **(b)** the proceeds to National Bank given a discount rate of 10.5%.

(a) _____

(b) _____

22. **BATTERY STORE** A National Tire and Battery outlet borrowed $48,500 on a 200-day simple interest note to expand the battery store. The note was signed on December 28 and carried an interest rate of 9.8%. The note was then sold on March 17 at a discount rate of 10%. Find **(a)** the maturity value of the note and **(b)** the proceeds to the seller of the note on May 17.

(a) _____

(b) _____

23. **PURCHASE OF A T-BILL**   Elizabeth Barton bought a $25,000, 26-week T-bill at a discount rate of 6.8% on August 7. She sold it 10 weeks later at a discount rate of 7%. Find **(a)** Barton's purchase price, **(b)** the discount 10 weeks later when she sold it, **(c)** the proceeds to Barton, and **(d)** the effective interest rate rounded to the nearest hundredth of a percent for the time Barton held the note.

(a) _____

(b) _____

(c) _____

(d) _____

24. **PURCHASE OF A T-BILL**   Tina Klein bought a $10,000, 7.5%, 52-week T-bill on June 29 and sold it 26 weeks later at a discount rate of 8%. Find Klein's **(a)** purchase price for the T-bill, **(b)** the discount at time of sale, **(c)** the proceeds to Klein, and **(d)** the effective interest rate rounded to the nearest hundredth of a percent.

(a) _____

(b) _____

(c) _____

(d) _____

25. Explain the procedure used to determine the bank discount and the proceeds for a note. (See Objective 2.)

26. Explain the effect of a rise in general market interest rates on an investor who is holding notes. Give an example. (See Example 3.)

Supplementary Application Exercises on Simple Interest and Simple Discount

The QUICK START *exercises in each section contain solutions to help you get started.*

There are similarities and differences between simple interest and simple discount calculations. This exercise set compares these two important concepts. First, the key similarities between the two are as follows.

1. Both types of notes involve lump sums repaid with a single payment at the end of a stated period of time.
2. The length of time is generally 1 year or less.

The following table compares simple interest and simple discount notes.

	SIMPLE INTEREST NOTE	SIMPLE DISCOUNT NOTE
Variables	I = Interest	B = Discount
	P = Principal (face value)	P = Proceeds
	R = Rate of interest	D = Discount rate
	T = Time, in years or fraction of a year	T = Time, in years or fraction of a year
	M = Maturity value	M = Maturity value (face value)
Face value	Stated on note	Same as maturity value
Interest charge	$I = PRT$	$B = MDT$
Maturity value	$M = P + I$	Same as face value
Amount received by borrower	Face value or principal	Proceeds: $P = M - B$
Identifying phrases	Interest at a certain rate	Discount at a certain rate
	Maturity value greater than face value	Proceeds
		Maturity value equal to face value
Effective interest rate	Same as stated rate, R	Greater than stated rate, D

Quick TIP ▼

The variable P is used for *principal or face value* in simple interest notes, but P is used for *proceeds* in simple discount notes. P represents the amount received by the borrower.

Solve the following application problems. Round rates to the nearest tenth of a percent, time to the nearest day, and money to the nearest cent.

QUICK START

1. The owner of Redwood Furniture, Inc., signed a 120-day note for $18,000 at 11% simple interest. Find (a) the interest and (b) the maturity value.

   (a) $I = PRT = \$18,000 \times .11 \times \frac{120}{360} = \$660$
   (b) $M = \$18,000 + \$660 = \$18,660$

   (a) $\underline{\$660}$
   (b) $\underline{\$18,660}$

2. Bill Travis signed a note for $18,500 with his uncle to start an auto repair shop on Commerce Street. The note is due in 300 days and has a discount rate of 14%. Travis hopes that a bank will refinance the note for him at a lower rate after he has been in business for 300 days. Find the proceeds.

   $B = \$18,500 \times .14 \times \frac{300}{360} = \$2158.33; P = \$18,500 - \$2158.33 = \$16,341.67$

   2. $\underline{\$16,341.67}$

△ indicates an exercise that is related to the Case in Point feature.

3. Jessica Hernandez borrowed money to remodel a retail space she had leased for her computer training and Web-design business. She signed a note with a 10% simple interest rate, interest of $4800, and time of 180 days. Find the principal.

3. _____

4. Bill Abel signed a simple interest note at a rate of only 6% because he had excellent collateral—a $200,000 CD at the same bank. If the loan matures in 300 days and the interest is $9000, find the principal.

4. _____

5. Benson Automotive signed a $150,000 note at a simple discount rate of 10.5% and a discount of $8750. Find the length of the loan in days.

5. _____

6. A loan to a German bank was for $1,290,000 with a maturity value of $1,327,410 and a rate of 6%. Find the time.

6. _____

7. Jane Barber loaned her nephew $20,000 for 150 days at 9% simple interest. Find **(a)** the interest and **(b)** the maturity value.

(a) _____
(b) _____

8. John O'Neill borrowed $24,000 for 250 days at 7% simple interest. Find **(a)** the interest and **(b)** the maturity value.

(a) _____
(b) _____

9. BlueWater Pools signed a 5-month, $145,000 note at an 11.5% discount rate. Find the effective rate of interest.

9. _____

10. First Bank signed an 80-day, $82,000 note at a 12% discount rate. Find the effective rate of interest.

10. _____

11. On October 14, Citibank loaned $10,000,000 to Fleet Mortgage Company for 180 days at a 10.5% discount rate. Find **(a)** the due date and **(b)** the proceeds.

(a) _____
(b) _____

12. On December 24, Junella Martin signed a 100-day note for $80,000 for a new Jaguar. Given a discount rate of 11%, find **(a)** the due date and **(b)** the proceeds.

(a) _____
(b) _____

13. Lupe Galvez has a serious problem: two of her more energetic preschoolers keep getting out of the yard of her child-care center. She signs a note with interest charges of $670.83 to reinforce the fence around the entire yard. The simple interest note is for 140 days at 11.5%. Find the principal to the nearest dollar.

13. _____

14. Quality Furnishings accepted a 270-day, $8000 note on May 25. The interest rate on the note is 12% simple interest. The note was then discounted at 14% on August 7. Find the proceeds.

14. _____

15. On November 19, a firm accepts an $18,000, 150-day note with a simple interest rate of 9%. The firm discounts the note at 12% on February 2. Find the proceeds.

15. _____

16. Barton's Flowers accepted a $16,000, 150-day note from Wedded Bliss Catering. The note had a simple interest rate of 11% and was accepted on May 12. The note was then discounted at 13% on July 20. Find the proceeds to Barton's Flowers.

16. _____

17. Leon Herbert signed a 220-day, 10% simple interest note with a face value of $28,000. In turn, the bank he borrowed the money from sold the note 90 days later at an 11% discount rate. Find (a) the interest, (b) the maturity value, (c) the discount period, (d) the discount, and (e) the proceeds to the bank.

(a) _____

(b) _____

(c) _____

(d) _____

(e) _____

18. Janice Dart signed a 140-day simple discount note at a rate of 9.9% with a maturity value of $82,000. The bank she borrowed the funds from sold the note 40 days later at a 10% discount rate. Find (a) the discount on the original note, (b) the proceeds of the original note, (c) the discount period, (d) the discount at the time of sale, and (e) the proceeds to the bank at the time of sale.

(a) _____

(b) _____

(c) _____

(d) _____

(e) _____

19. James and Tiffany Paterson need a 220-day loan for $68,000 to open Adventure Sports Unlimited. Bank One agrees to a simple interest note with a loan amount of $68,000 at $9\frac{1}{4}$% interest. Union Bank agrees to a simple discount note with proceeds of $68,000 and a 9.5% simple discount rate. Find (a) the interest for the simple interest note, (b) the maturity value of the discount note, (c) the interest for the discount note, and (d) the savings in interest charges of the simple interest note over the discount note.

(a) _____

(b) _____

(c) _____

(d) _____

20. Gilbert Construction Company needs to borrow $380,000 for $1\frac{1}{2}$ years to purchase some land to subdivide. One bank offers the firm a simple interest note with a principal of $380,000 and a rate of 12%. A second bank offers the company a discount note with proceeds of $380,000 and an 11% discount rate. **(a)** Which note produces the lower interest charges? **(b)** What is the difference in interest?

(a) _____

(b) _____

21. Show with an example that the effective interest rate is higher than the discount rate stated on a note.

22. Explain the difference in the meaning of the variable P (principal) in a simple interest note and the variable P (proceeds) in a simple discount note.

23. What is interest? Why is interest used?

24. Why might a bank use ordinary interest rather than exact interest?

Chapter 9 Quick Review

Chapter Terms *Review the following terms to test your understanding of the chapter. For each term you do not know, refer to the page number found next to that term.*

annual percentage rate (APR) **[p. 368]**
bank discount **[p. 375]**
banker's interest **[p. 350]**
collateral **[p. 352]**
compound interest **[p. 346]**
cosign **[p. 347]**
discount **[p. 375]**
discounting the note **[p. 375]**
discount period **[p. 375]**
discount rate **[p. 375]**
due date **[p. 376]**

effective rate of interest **[p. 368]**
exact interest **[p. 350]**
face value **[p. 351]**
factoring **[p. 378]**
factors **[p. 378]**
foreclose **[p. 352]**
interest **[p. 346]**
interest-in-advance notes **[p. 365]**
loan amount **[p. 365]**
maker of a note **[p. 351]**

maturity date **[p. 351]**
maturity value **[p. 351]**
nominal rate **[p. 368]**
ordinary interest **[p. 350]**
payee of a note **[p. 351]**
payer of a note **[p. 351]**
prime rate **[p. 346]**
principal **[p. 346]**
proceeds of a note **[p. 365]**
promissory note **[p. 351]**
rate **[p. 347]**
recourse **[p. 375]**

simple discount note **[p. 365]**
simple interest **[p. 346]**
simple interest note **[p. 351]**
Stafford loan **[p. 365]**
stated rate **[p. 368]**
T-bills **[p. 369]**
term of a note **[p. 351]**
time **[p. 347]**
true rate of interest **[p. 369]**
Truth in Lending Act **[p. 368]**
U.S. Treasury bills **[p. 369]**

CONCEPTS

EXAMPLES

9.1 Finding the simple interest when time is expressed in years

1. Use the formula $I = PRT$.
2. Express R in decimal form.
3. Express time in years.
4. Substitute values for P, R, and T and multiply.

A loan of $9800 is made for $1\frac{1}{4}$ years at 10% per year. Find the simple interest.

$$I = PRT$$
$$I = \$9800 \times .10 \times 1.25 = \$1225$$

The simple interest is $1225.

9.1 Finding the simple interest when time is expressed in months

1. Use the formula $I = PRT$.
2. Express R in decimal form.
3. Express time in years by dividing the number of months by 12.
4. Substitute values for P, R, and T and multiply.

Find the simple interest on $24,000 for 8 months at 10%.

$$I = PRT$$
$$I = \$24,000 \times .10 \times \frac{8}{12} = \$1600$$

The simple interest is $1600.

9.1 Finding the maturity value of a loan

1. Find I using the formula $I = PRT$.
2. Find the maturity value using the formula $M = P + I$.

A loan of $8500 is made for 1 year at 9%. Find the maturity value of the loan.

$$I = PRT$$
$$I = \$8500 \times .09 \times 1 = \$765$$
$$M = P + I$$
$$M = \$8500 + \$765 = \$9265$$

The maturity value is $9265.

9.1 Finding the number of days from one date to another using a table

1. Find the day corresponding to the final date using the table.
2. Find the day corresponding to the initial date.
3. Subtract the smaller number from the larger number.

Find the number of days from February 15 to July 28.
1. July 28 is day 209.
2. Feb. 15 is day 46.
3. Number of days is

$$\begin{array}{r} 209 \\ - 46 \\ \hline 163 \end{array}$$

There are 163 days from February 15 to July 28.

CONCEPTS	EXAMPLES
9.1 Finding the number of days from one date to another using actual number of days in a month Add the actual number of days in each month or partial month from initial date to final date.	Find the number of days from April 20 to June 27. April 20 to April 30 **10 days** May **31 days** June **27 days** **68 days**
9.1 Finding the exact interest Use the formula $$I = PRT$$ $$\text{with } T = \frac{\text{Number of days of loan}}{365}$$	Find the exact interest on a $9000 loan at 8% for 140 days. $$I = PRT$$ $$I = \$9000 \times .08 \times \frac{140}{365} = \$276.16$$ The exact interest is $276.16.
9.1 Finding the ordinary, or banker's, interest Use the formula $$I = PRT$$ $$\text{with } T = \frac{\text{Number of days of loan}}{360}$$	Find the ordinary interest on a loan of $14,000 at 7% for 120 days. $$I = PRT$$ $$I = \$14,000 \times .07 \times \frac{120}{360} = \$326.67$$ The ordinary, or banker's, interest is $326.67.

9.1 Finding the due date, interest, and maturity value of a simple interest promissory note when the term of the loan is in months
 	
   1. Add the number of months in the term of the note to the initial date of note.
   2. Use the formula $I = PRT$ to find interest.
   3. Find the maturity value as follows.
 	
   Maturity value = Principal + Interest
	Find the due date, the interest, and the maturity value of a loan made on February 15 for 7 months at 8% with a face value of $9400.
	
	September 15 is 7 months from February 15, so note is due on September 15.
	
	$$I = PRT$$
	$$I = \$9400 \times .08 \times \frac{7}{12} = \$438.67$$
	
	M = Principal + Interest
	M = $9400 + $438.67 = $9838.67

9.1 Finding the due date of a promissory note when the term of the loan is expressed in days Use either a table or the actual number of days in each month.	A loan is made on August 14 and is due in 80 days. Find the due date. August 14 to August 31 17 days September 30 days October 31 days 78 days The loan is for 80 days, which is 2 days more than 78. Therefore, the loan is due on November 2.
9.2 Finding the principal given the interest, interest rate, and time Use the formula $$P = \frac{I}{RT}$$ $$P = \frac{I}{RT}$$	Find the principal that produces interest of $240 at 9% for 60 days. $$P = \frac{I}{RT}$$ $$P = \frac{\$240}{.09 \times \dfrac{60}{360}} = \$16,000$$ The principal is $16,000.

CONCEPTS	EXAMPLES

9.2 Finding the rate of interest given the principal, interest, and time

Use the formula

$$R = \frac{I}{PT}$$

$$R = \frac{I}{PT}$$

A principal of $8000 deposited for 45 days earns interest of $75. Find the rate of interest.

$$R = \frac{I}{PT}$$

$$R = \frac{\$75}{\$8000 \times \dfrac{45}{360}} = .075$$

Rate of interest = 7.5%.

9.2 Finding the time given the principal, rate of interest, and interest

To find the time in days, use the formula

$$T \text{ (in days)} = \frac{I}{PR} \times 360$$

To find the time in months, use the formula

$$T \text{ (in months)} = \frac{I}{PR} \times 12$$

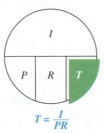

$$T = \frac{I}{PR}$$

Tom Jones invested $8000 at 8% and earned interest of $320. Find the time of the loan in days.

$$T = \frac{I}{PR} \times 360$$

$$T = \frac{\$320}{\$8000 \times .08} \times 360 = 180 \text{ days}$$

The loan was for 180 days.

9.3 Finding the proceeds of a simple discount note

Calculate the bank discount using the formula $B = MDT$. Then calculate the proceeds or loan amount using the formula $P = M - B$.

Karen Pattern borrows $12,000 for 120 days at a discount rate of 9%. Find the proceeds.

$$B = MDT$$

$$B = \$12,000 \times .09 \times \frac{120}{360} = \$360$$

$$P = M - B$$

$$P = \$12,000 - \$360 = \$11,640$$

9.3 Finding the face value of a simple discount note

Use the formula

$$M = \frac{P}{1 - DT}$$

Sam Spade needs $15,000 for new equipment for his restaurant. Find the face value of a note that will provide the $15,000 in proceeds if he plans to repay the note in 180 days and the bank charges an 11% discount rate.

$$M = \frac{P}{1 - DT}$$

$$M = \frac{\$15,000}{1 - \left(.11 \times \dfrac{180}{360}\right)} = \$15,873.02 \text{ (rounded)}$$

9.3 Finding the effective interest rate

Find the interest (B) from the formula

$$B = MDT$$

Find proceeds from the formula

$$P = M - B$$

Then use the formula

$$R = \frac{I}{PT}$$

A 150-day, 11% simple discount note has a face value of $12,400. Find the effective rate to the nearest tenth of a percent.

$$B = \$12,400 \times .11 \times \frac{150}{360} = \$568.33$$

$$P = \$12,400 - \$568.33 = \$11,831.67$$

$$R = \frac{\$568.33}{\$11,831.67 \times \dfrac{150}{360}} = 11.5\% \text{ (rounded)}$$

CONCEPTS	EXAMPLES

9.4 Finding the proceeds to an individual or firm

1. If necessary, find
   (a) the **due date** of the original note and
   (b) the **maturity value** of the original note ($M = P + I$, where $I = PRT$).

Moe's Ice Cream holds a 150-day note dated March 1 with a face value of $15,000 and a simple interest rate of 9%. Moe sells the note at a discount on June 1. Assume a discount rate of 11%. Find the proceeds.

1. Due date = day 60 (March 1) + 150 days = day 210 or July 29

$$I = PRT = \$15{,}000 \times .09 \times \frac{150}{360} = \mathbf{\$562.50}$$

$$M = P + I = \$15{,}000 + \mathbf{\$562.50} = \mathbf{\$15{,}562.50}$$

2. (a) Find the **discount period**, which is the time (e.g., number of days) from the sale of the note to the maturity date of the note.
   (b) Find the **discount** using the formula $B = MDT$.
   (c) Find the **proceeds** using $P = M - B$.

2. (a) The discount period is 58 days.

Discount Period = 58 Days

Date Loan Was Made	Discount Date	Loan Due Date
March 1	June 1	July 29

Length of Loan: 150 Days

(b) Bank discount = MDT

$$B = \mathbf{\$15{,}562.50} \times .11 \times \frac{58}{360} = \$275.80$$

(c) Proceeds = $M - B$

$$D = \mathbf{\$15{,}562.50} - \$275.80 = \$15{,}286.70$$

9.4. Finding the proceeds to an individual or firm that discounts a simple interest note

1. If necessary, find
   (a) the **due date** of the original note,
   (b) the **discount** of the original note using $B = MDT$, and
   (c) the **proceeds** from the original note using $P = M - B$.
   The **maturity value (face value)** of the note is written on the note itself.

2. (a) Find the **discount period**, which is the time (e.g., number of days) from the sale of the note to the maturity date of the note.
   (b) Find the **discount** using the formula $B = MDT$.
   (c) Find the **proceeds** using $P = M - B$.

On May 10, Applecrest Farm Orchards signed a 120-day note for $22,000 at a simple discount rate of 10%. The note was sold on June 30 at a discount rate of 10.5%. Find **(a)** the proceeds from the original note and **(b)** the proceeds at the time of sale.

(a) Due date is day 130 (May 10) + 120 days = day 250 or Sept. 7

$$B = MDT = \$22{,}000 \times .10 \times \frac{120}{360} = \mathbf{\$733.33}$$

$$P = M - B = \$22{,}000 - \mathbf{\$733.33} = \$21{,}266.67$$

(b) June 30 is day 181
Discount period is $250 - 181 = 69$ days

$$B = MDT = \$22{,}000 \times .105 \times \frac{69}{360} = \mathbf{\$442.75}$$

(c) $P = M - B = \$22{,}000 - \mathbf{\$442.75} = \$21{,}557.25$

case *study*

BANKING IN A GLOBAL WORLD: HOW DO LARGE BANKS MAKE MONEY?

Bank of America borrowed $80,000,000 at 5% interest for 180 days from a Japanese investment house. At the same time, the bank made the following loans, each for the exact same 180-day period:

1. A 7% *simple interest note* for $38,000,000 to a Canadian firm that extracts oil from Canadian tar sands;

2. An 8.2% *simple discount note* for $27,500,000 to a European contractor building a factory in South Africa; and

3. An 8% *simple discount note* for $14,500,000 to a Louisiana company building mine-sweepers in New Orleans for the British government.

    (a) Find the difference between interest received and interest paid by the bank on these funds.

    (a) _____

    (b) The bank did not loan out all $80,000,000. Find the amount it actually loaned out.

    (b) _____

    (c) Find the effective rate of interest to the nearest hundredth of a percent.

    (c) _____

This seems like a low rate; however, this is the amount the bank earned over and above that paid out to the Japanese investment house on the same funds.

INVESTIGATE

The very idea of interest is not acceptable in some third-world countries where a bank often takes partial ownership of a company when it lends to a company, at least until funds are repaid. Even in countries that do allow interest, interest rates vary considerably. Use financial newspapers, magazines, or the World Wide Web to find interest rates in three different countries and compare them to similar rates in the United States.

case ɴ point summary exercise

APPLE, INC.

www.apple.com

Facts:

- 1976: Founded
- 1984: Introduced Macintosh
- 2001: Introduced iPod
- 2003: Opened iTunes Music Store
- 2007: Introduced iPhone
- 2010: More than 3 billion iPhone apps downloaded

After opening her own computer and Web-design business, Jessica Hernandez checked into selling Apple's popular iPhones. But she was not able to sell them since Apple only allowed a few large companies to sell them. So, Hernandez focused on computer training classes as she built her reputation designing Web pages for small firms. She knew that she needed to borrow some money as her business grew and wondered how to go about it.

1. Hernandez decided to borrow $85,000 for 10 months. She found that banks would lend to her only if she had a cosigner on the note—fortunately her uncle was a successful business owner and he agreed to cosign. Bank One offered the funds at a 10% simple discount. Find the maturity value of the loan and the discount.

    1. _____

2. Union Bank offered to lend Hernandez $85,000 at 10.5% simple interest. Find the interest and maturity value.

    2. _____

3. Find the loan with the lower interest and find the difference in interest.

    3. _____

4. Find the effective interest rate for both loans to the nearest hundredth of a percent.

    4. _____

Bank	Interest	Loan Amount	Effective Rate
Bank One	$7727.27	$85,000	
Union Bank	$7437.50	$85,000	

Discussion Question: Assume Hernandez has successfully managed her business for several years. List five reasons she may still need to borrow from time to time.

Chapter 9 Test

To help you review, the numbers in brackets show the section in which the topic was discussed.

Find the simple interest for each of the following. Round to the nearest cent. **[9.1]**

1. $12,500 at $10\frac{1}{2}$% simple interest for 280 days

   1. _____

2. $8250 at $9\frac{1}{4}$% simple interest for 8 months

   2. _____

3. A loan of $6000 at 11% simple interest made on June 8 and due August 22

   3. _____

4. A promissory note for $4500 at 10.3% simple interest made on November 13 and due March 8

   4. _____

5. Joan Davies signed a 140-day simple interest note for $12,500 with a bank that uses *exact* interest. If the rate is 10.7%, find the maturity value. **[9.1]**

   5. _____

6. Chez Bazan Bakery borrowed $24,300 for a new commercial oven. The simple interest loan was repaid in 6 months at $10\frac{1}{2}$%. Find the amount of the repayment. **[9.1]**

   6. _____

7. Glenda Pierce plans to borrow $14,000 for a new hot tub and deck for her home. She has decided on a term of 200 days at 10.5% simple interest. However, she has a choice of two lenders. One calculates interest using a 360-day year and the other uses a 365-day year. Find the amount of interest Pierce will save by using the lender with the 365-day year. **[9.1]**

   7. _____

8. Lupe Gonzalez has $6500 in her retirement account. Find the interest rate required for the fund to grow to $7247.50 in 15 months. **[9.2]**

   8. _____

9. Hilda Heinz lends $1200 to her sister Olga at a rate of 9%. Find how long it will take for her investment to earn $100 in interest. (Round to the nearest day.) **[9.2]**

   9. _____

10. A woman invested money received from an insurance settlement for 7 months at 5% simple interest. If she received $1254.17 interest on her investment during this time, find the amount that she invested. (Round to the nearest dollar.) **[9.2]**

    10. _____

11. Mike Fagan needs $25,000 to expand his flower shop. Find the face value of a simple discount note that will provide the $25,000 in proceeds if he plans to repay the note in 240 days and the bank charges a 9% discount rate. **[9.3]**

    11. _____

Find the discount and the proceeds for the following simple discount notes. **[9.3]**

Face Value	Discount Rate	Time (Days)	Discount	Proceeds
12. $9800	11%	120	_____	_____
13. $10,250	9.5%	60	_____	_____

14. Barbara Waters signed a simple discount note for $15,000 for 120 days at a rate of 9%. Find **(a)** the proceeds and **(b)** the effective interest rate based on the proceeds received by Waters. **[9.3]**

(a) _____

(b) _____

15. Lizabeth Neault needed funds to open a law office. She borrowed $28,400 at 8.5% simple interest for 150 days on July 7. The bank she borrowed from sold the note at a 9% discount on August 20. Find the proceeds to the bank. **[9.4]**

15. _____

16. A 90-day simple discount promissory note for $9200 with a simple discount rate of 11% was signed on January 25. It was discounted on March 2 at 12%. Find the proceeds at the time of the sale. **[9.4]**

16. _____

17. A $20,000 T-bill is purchased at a 3.75% discount rate for 13 weeks. Find **(a)** the purchase price of the T-bill, **(b)** the maturity value, **(c)** the interest earned, and **(d)** the effective rate of interest to the nearest hundredth of a percent. **[9.3]**

(a) _____

(b) _____

(c) _____

(d) _____

The following note was discounted at $12\frac{1}{2}$%. Find the discount period, the discount, and the proceeds. **[9.4]**

Date Loan Was Made	Face Value	Length of Loan	Rate	Date of Discount	Discount Period	Discount	Proceeds
18. Jan. 25	$9200	90 days	10%	Mar. 12	_____	_____	_____

19. Jan Guerra lends $9000 to her second cousin using a 180-day 10% simple interest note that was signed on October 30. Guerra subsequently has a car accident and desperately needs money, so she sells the note at a discount of 15% on January 3 to an investor. Find **(a)** the discount, **(b)** the proceeds, and **(c)** the amount of money Guerra gains or loses. **[9.4]**

(a) _____

(b) _____

(c) _____

Compound Interest and Inflation

10

BY 2007, Bank of America was already one of the largest banks in the world. However, it greatly expanded operations in the aftermath of the 2008–09 financial crises when it took over two large firms: Countrywide Financial (home loans) and Merrill Lynch (investments). In fact, the U.S. government helped and (strongly) encouraged Bank of America to take over these two large companies to help keep the banking system working in the worst financial crisis since the Great Depression of the 1930s. Today, Bank of America is truly a giant in the global financial services world.

*case **IN** point* ▶

As we saw in Chapter 9, interest is calculated only once on **simple interest** loans. These short-term loans are typically for one year or less. Bank loans to businesses are often simple interest loans.

In contrast, **compound interest** loans require interest to be calculated more than once during the life of the loan. Every time compound interest is calculated, it is added to the principal before interest is calculated again. Thus, compound interest is found based on principal plus any interest previously credited. Compound interest is used to find interest for savings accounts, money market accounts, certificates of deposits, and retirement accounts.

10.1 Compound Interest

OBJECTIVES

1 Use the simple interest formula $I = PRT$ to calculate compound interest.
2 Identify interest rate per compounding period and number of compounding periods.
3 Use the formula $M = P(1 + i)^n$ to find compound amount.
4 Use the table to find compound amount.

case IN point ▶

Regina Foster worked overtime as a nurse and earned an extra $2000. She banks at Bank of America and wonders what the difference would be between a 6-year investment earning 5% offered by her bank and one earning 8% that the bank paid her father some years ago.

Present value is the value of an investment today, right now. Money left in an investment usually grows over time. The amount in an investment at a specific future date is called the **future amount**, **compound amount**, or **future value**. The future value depends not only on the amount initially invested, it also depends on the following:

"The most powerful force in the universe is compound interest."—Albert Einstein

1. **Compound interest—Compound interest results in a greater future value than simple interest.**

2. **Interest rate—A higher rate results in a greater future value.**

3. **Length of investment—An investment held longer usually results in a greater future value.**

To see this, compare the future values of a $10,000 investment using the following table:

Investments A and B show the value of compound interest over simple interest.
Investments B and C show the value of a higher interest rate.
Investments C and D show the value of a longer investment period.

Investment	Term	Annual Rate	Interest	Future Value
A. Simple interest	6 years	5%	$3,000	$13,000
B. Compound interest	6 years	5%	$3,401	$13,401
C. Compound interest	6 years	8%	$5,869	$15,869
D. Compound interest	10 years	8%	$11,589	$21,589

It is no coincidence that most wealthy people tend to be older. It takes time to build wealth, and it also requires compound interest. You can use this idea to build wealth for yourself if you choose to do so. The following figure shows the power of compound interest. A one-time investment of $10,000 earning 8% per year in a retirement account results in more than $100,000 in 30 years.

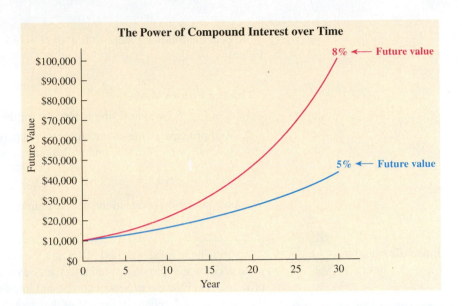

The Power of Compound Interest over Time

OBJECTIVE 1 Use the simple interest formula $I = PRT$ **to calculate compound interest.** **Compound interest** is interest calculated on previously credited interest in addition to the original principal. Compound interest calculations require that interest be calculated and credited to an account more than once each year. Examples 1 and 2 show how the simple interest formula can be used to find compound interest. Later in this section, we show easier methods for finding compound interest.

Comparing Simple to Compound Interest   **EXAMPLE 1**

Regina Foster wants to compare simple interest to compound interest on a $2000 investment.

(a) Find the interest if funds earn 6% simple interest for 1 year.

(b) Find the interest if funds earn 6% interest compounded every 6 months for 1 year.

(c) Find the difference between the two.

SOLUTION

(a) Simple interest on $2000 at 6% *for 1 year* is found as follows.
$$I = PRT = \$2000 \times .06 \times 1 = \$120$$

(b) Interest compounded every 6 months means that interest must be calculated at the end of each 6-months using $I = PRT$. Interest must then be added to principal before going on to the next 6-month interval.

> **Quick TIP ▼**
> Round interest amounts to the nearest cent each time interest is calculated.

$$\text{Interest for first 6 months} = PRT = \$2000 \times .06 \times \tfrac{1}{2} = \$60$$
$$\text{Principal at end of first 6 months} = \text{Original principal} + \text{Interest}$$
$$= \$2000 + \$60 = \$2060$$

The new principal of $2060 earns interest for the second 6 months.

$$\text{Interest for second 6 months} = PRT = \$2060 \times .06 \times \tfrac{1}{2} = \$61.80$$
$$\text{Principal at end of 1 year} = \$2060 + \$61.80 = \$2121.80$$

The interest earned in the second 6 months ($61.80) is greater than that earned in the first 6 months ($60). This occurs because the interest earned in the first 6 months becomes principal and it also earns interest during the second 6 months.

$$\text{Total compound interest} = \$60 + \$61.80 = \$121.80$$

(c) Difference in interest = $121.80 − $120 = $1.80.

More interest is earned using compound interest. The difference of $1.80 over a year does not seem like much, but *compound interest leads to huge differences* when applied to larger sums of money over long time periods.

QUICK CHECK 1

$15,000 is invested for 1 year. Find the future value based on (a) simple interest of 8% and (b) 8% interest compounded every 6 months. (c) Then find the difference between the future values.

Repeat the following steps to find the future value of an investment involving compound interest.

Finding Future Value

1. Use $I = PRT$ to find simple interest for the period.

2. Add principal at the end of the previous period to the interest for the current period to find the principal at the end of the current period.

We show how this is done in the next example.

Finding Compound Interest

EXAMPLE 2

The Peters hope to have $5000 in 4 years for a down payment on a new car. They invest $3800 in an account that pays 6% interest at the end of each year, on previous interest in addition to principal. **(a)** Find the excess of compound interest over simple interest after 4 years. **(b)** Will they have enough money at the end of 4 years to meet their goal of a down payment?

SOLUTION

For each year, first calculate interest using $I = PRT$ and round to the nearest cent. Then find the new principal by adding the interest earned to the preceding principal.

(a)

Year	$P \times R \times T$	Interest	$P + I$	Compound Amount
1	$3800.00 × .06 × 1 =	$228.00	$3800.00 + **$228.00** =	$4028.00
2	$4028.00 × .06 × 1 =	$241.68	$4028.00 + **$241.68** =	$4269.68
3	$4269.68 × .06 × 1 =	$256.18	$4269.68 + **$256.18** =	$4525.86
4	$4525.86 × .06 × 1 =	$271.55	$4525.86 + **$271.55** =	$4797.41

$$\text{Compound interest} = \$4797.41 - \$3800 = \$997.41$$
$$\text{Simple interest} = \$3800 \times .06 \times 4 = \$912$$
$$\text{Difference} = \$997.41 - \$912 = \$85.41$$

(b) No, but almost! They will be short of their goal by $5000 − $4797.41 = **$202.59**.

QUICK CHECK 2

Find the future amount at the end of 2 years for an $80,000 investment that earns 7% at the end of each year.

OBJECTIVE 2 Identify interest rate per compounding period and number of compounding periods. The **compounding period** is the time period over which interest is calculated and added to principal. It is stated alongside the interest. So, 6% compounded quarterly means that interest will be calculated and added to principal *at the end of each quarter.* Compound interest often results in more than one interest rate calculation each year. For example, compounding quarterly means that interest must be found at the end of each quarter and added to the principal. This requires four interest-rate calculations in one year.

INTEREST COMPOUNDED	COMPOUND AT THE END OF EVERY	NUMBER OF COMPOUNDING PERIODS IN 1 YEAR
Semiannually	6 months	2
Quarterly	3 months	4
Monthly	1 month	12
Daily	1 day	365*

*Leap year has 366 compounding periods.

The interest rate applied at the end of each compounding period is called **the interest rate per compounding period**. To find this rate, divide the annual interest rate by the number of compounding periods in one year. Then, the *total number of compounding periods* in the investment is the product of the number of years in the term of the investment and the number of compounding periods per year, as shown here.

RATE	COMPOUNDED	NUMBER OF COMPOUNDING PERIODS PER YEAR	TERM	RATE PER COMPOUNDING PERIOD	TOTAL NUMBER OF COMPOUNDING PERIODS
8%	semiannually	2	3 years	$\frac{8\%}{2} = 4\%$	3 years $\times$ 2 per year = 6
12%	monthly	12	$2\frac{1}{2}$ years	$\frac{12\%}{12} = 1\%$	$2\frac{1}{2}$ years $\times$ 12 per year = 30
9%	quarterly	4	5 years	$\frac{9\%}{4} = 2.25\%$	5 years $\times$ 4 per year = 20

Finding the Interest Rate per Compounding Period and the Number of Compounding Periods

 EXAMPLE 3

Find the interest rate per compounding period and the number of compounding periods over the life of each loan.

(a) 8% compounded semiannually, 3 years

(b) 12% per year, compounded monthly, $2\frac{1}{2}$ years

(c) 9% per year, compounded quarterly, 5 years

SOLUTION

(a) 8% compounded semiannually is $\frac{8\%}{2} = 4\%$ credited at the end of each 6 months. There are 3 years $\times$ 2 periods per year = 6 compounding periods in 3 years.

(b) 12% per year, compounded monthly, results in $\frac{12\%}{12} = 1\%$ credited at the end of each month. There are 2.5 years $\times$ 12 periods per year = 30 compounding periods in 2.5 years.

(c) 9% per year, compounded quarterly, results in $\frac{9\%}{4} = 2.25\%$ credited at the end of each quarter. There are 5 years $\times$ 4 periods per year = 20 compounding periods in 5 years.

QUICK CHECK 3

A loan requires that the 8% interest be compounded quarterly for 6 years. Find the interest rate per compounding period and the number of compounding periods.

OBJECTIVE 3 Use the formula $M = P(1 + i)^n$ to find compound amount. The **formula for compound interest** uses **exponents**, which is a short way of writing repeated products. For example,

Exponent: 3 tells how many times the base 2 is multiplied by itself.

$$2 \times 2 \times 2 = 2^3$$

base

Also, $4^2 = 4 \times 4 = 16$, and $5^4 = 5 \times 5 \times 5 \times 5 = 625$.

Assume that P dollars are deposited at a rate of interest i per compounding period for n periods. Then the compound amount and the interest are found as follows.

Formulas for Compounding Interest

Maturity value $= M = P(1 + i)^n$ where $P =$ initial investment

Interest $= I = M - P$ $n =$ total number of compounding periods

                                     $i =$ interest rate per compounding period

It is important to keep in mind that i is the interest rate *per compounding period*, not per year. Also, n is *the total number of compounding periods*.

Finding Compound Interest

 EXAMPLE 4

An investment at Bank of America pays 7% interest per year compounded semiannually. Given an initial deposit of $4500, **(a)** use the formula to find the compound amount after 5 years, and **(b)** find the compound interest.

SOLUTION

(a) Interest is compounded at $\frac{7\%}{2} = 3.5\%$ every 6 months for 5 years $\times$ 2 periods per year $=$ 10 periods. Therefore, 3.5% is the interest rate per compounding period (i) and 6 is the number of compounding periods (n).

$$M = P(1 + i)^n$$
$$= \$4500 \times (1 + .035)^{10}$$
$$= \$4500 \times (1.035)^{10}$$
$$= \$6347.69 \quad \text{(rounded)}$$

The compound amount is $6347.69.

(b) $$I = M - P$$
$$= \$6347.69 - \$4500 = \$1847.69$$

The interest is $1847.69.

The calculator solution for part (a) is as follows.

4500 $\boxed{\times}$ $\boxed{(}$ 1 $\boxed{+}$ .035 $\boxed{)}$ $\boxed{y^x}$ 10 $\boxed{=}$ $6347.69 (rounded)

Note: Refer to Appendix B for calculator basics.

QUICK CHECK 4

Use the formula for maturity value to find the compound amount and interest on a $9000 investment at 6% compounded semiannually for 5 years.

Compound Interest Table

PERIOD	1%	$1\frac{1}{2}$%	2%	$2\frac{1}{2}$%	3%	4%	5%	6%	8%	10%	PERIOD
1	1.01000	1.01500	1.02000	1.02500	1.03000	1.04000	1.05000	1.06000	1.08000	1.10000	1
2	1.02010	1.03023	1.04040	1.05063	1.06090	1.08160	1.10250	1.12360	1.16640	1.21000	2
3	1.03030	1.04568	1.06121	1.07689	1.09273	1.12486	1.15763	1.19102	1.25971	1.33100	3
4	1.04060	1.06136	1.08243	1.10381	1.12551	1.16986	1.21551	1.26248	1.36049	1.46410	4
5	1.05101	1.07728	1.10408	1.13141	1.15927	1.21665	1.27628	1.33823	1.46933	1.61051	5
6	1.06152	1.09344	1.12616	1.15969	1.19405	1.26532	1.34010	1.41852	1.58687	1.77156	6
7	1.07214	1.10984	1.14869	1.18869	1.22987	1.31593	1.40710	1.50363	1.71382	1.94872	7
8	1.08286	1.12649	1.17166	1.21840	1.26677	1.36857	1.47746	1.59385	1.85093	2.14359	8
9	1.09369	1.14339	1.19509	1.24886	1.30477	1.42331	1.55133	1.68948	1.99900	2.35795	9
10	1.10462	1.16054	1.21899	1.28008	1.34392	1.48024	1.62889	1.79085	2.15892	2.59374	10
11	1.11567	1.17795	1.24337	1.31209	1.38423	1.53945	1.71034	1.89830	2.33164	2.85312	11
12	1.12683	1.19562	1.26824	1.34489	1.42576	1.60103	1.79586	2.01220	2.51817	3.13843	12
13	1.13809	1.21355	1.29361	1.37851	1.46853	1.66507	1.88565	2.13293	2.71962	3.45227	13
14	1.14947	1.23176	1.31948	1.41297	1.51259	1.73168	1.97993	2.26090	2.93719	3.79750	14
15	1.16097	1.25023	1.34587	1.44830	1.55797	1.80094	2.07893	2.39656	3.17217	4.17725	15
16	1.17258	1.26899	1.37279	1.48451	1.60471	1.87298	2.18287	2.54035	3.42594	4.59497	16
17	1.18430	1.28802	1.40024	1.52162	1.65285	1.94790	2.29202	2.69277	3.70002	5.05447	17
18	1.19615	1.30734	1.42825	1.55966	1.70243	2.02582	2.40662	2.85434	3.99602	5.55992	18
19	1.20811	1.32695	1.45681	1.59865	1.75351	2.10685	2.52695	3.02560	4.31570	6.11591	19
20	1.22019	1.34686	1.48595	1.63862	1.80611	2.19112	2.65330	3.20714	4.66096	6.72750	20
21	1.23239	1.36706	1.51567	1.67958	1.86029	2.27877	2.78596	3.39956	5.03383	7.40025	21
22	1.24472	1.38756	1.54598	1.72157	1.91610	2.36992	2.92526	3.60354	5.43654	8.14027	22
23	1.25716	1.40838	1.57690	1.76461	1.97359	2.46472	3.07152	3.81975	5.87146	8.95430	23
24	1.26973	1.42950	1.60844	1.80873	2.03279	2.56330	3.22510	4.04893	6.34118	9.84973	24
25	1.28243	1.45095	1.64061	1.85394	2.09378	2.66584	3.38635	4.29187	6.84848	10.83471	25
26	1.29526	1.47271	1.67342	1.90029	2.15659	2.77247	3.55567	4.54938	7.39635	11.91818	26
27	1.30821	1.49480	1.70689	1.94780	2.22129	2.88337	3.73346	4.82235	7.98806	13.10999	27
28	1.32129	1.51722	1.74102	1.99650	2.28793	2.99870	3.92013	5.11169	8.62711	14.42099	28
29	1.33450	1.53998	1.77584	2.04641	2.35657	3.11865	4.11614	5.41839	9.31727	15.86309	29
30	1.34785	1.56308	1.81136	2.09757	2.42726	3.24340	4.32194	5.74349	10.06266	17.44940	30

INTEREST RATE PER COMPOUNDING PERIOD

Parents believe that their children should study personal finance. The following pie chart indicates when parents believe this education should begin.

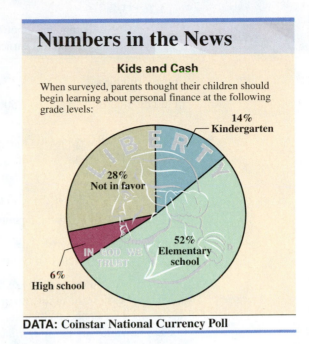

Numbers in the News

Kids and Cash

When surveyed, parents thought their children should begin learning about personal finance at the following grade levels:

- 14% Kindergarten
- 28% Not in favor
- 52% Elementary school
- 6% High school

DATA: Coinstar National Currency Poll

OBJECTIVE 4 Use the table to find compound amount. The value of $(1 + i)^n$ in the formula $M = P(1 + i)^n$ can be calculated using a calculator, or it can be found in the compound interest table. The interest rate i at the top of the table is the interest rate *per compounding period*. The value of n down the far left (or far right) column of the table is *the total number of compounding periods*. The value in the body of the table is the compound amount, or maturity value, for each $1 in principal.

Finding Compound Amount

Compound amount = Principal × Number from compound interest table

Finding Compound Interest **EXAMPLE 5**

In each case, find the interest earned on a $2000 deposit.

(a) For 3 years, compounded annually at 4%

(b) For 5 years, compounded semiannually at 6%

(c) For 6 years, compounded quarterly at 8%

(d) For 2 years, compounded monthly at 12%

SOLUTION

(a) In 3 years, there are $3 \times 1 = 3$ compounding periods. The interest rate per compounding period is $4\% \div 1 = 4\%$. Look across the top of the compound interest table above for 4% and down the side for 3 periods to find **1.12486**.

$$\text{Compound amount} = M = \$2000 \times 1.12486 = \$2249.72$$
$$\text{Interest earned} = I = \$2249.72 - \$2000 = \$249.72$$

(b) In 5 years, there are $5 \times 2 = 10$ semiannual compounding periods. The interest rate per compounding period is $6\% \div 2 = 3\%$. In the compound interest table, look at 3% at the top and 10 periods down the side to find **1.34392**.

$$\text{Compound amount} = M = \$2000 \times 1.34392 = \$2687.84$$
$$\text{Interest earned} = I = \$2687.84 - \$2000 = \$687.84$$

(c) Interest compounded quarterly is compounded 4 times a year. In 6 years, there are $4 \times 6 = 24$ quarters, or 24 periods. Interest of 8% per year is $\frac{8\%}{4} = 2\%$ per quarter. In the compound interest table, locate 2% across the top and 24 periods at the left, finding the number **1.60844**.

$$\text{Compound amount} = M = \$2000 \times 1.60844 = \$3216.88$$
$$\text{Interest earned} = I = \$3216.88 - \$2000 = \$1216.88$$

(d) In 2 years, there are $2 \times 12 = 24$ monthly periods. Interest of 12% per year is $\frac{12\%}{12} = 1\%$ per month. Look in the compound interest table for 1% and 24 periods, finding the number **1.26973**.

$$\text{Compound amount} = M = \$2000 \times \mathbf{1.26973} = \mathbf{\$2539.46}$$
$$\text{Interest earned} = I = \mathbf{\$2539.46} - \$2000 = \$539.46$$

> **QUICK CHECK 5**
>
> Find the interest earned on a $5000 deposit for 4 years at 6% compounded semiannually.

We now show how to work Example 5(d) using a financial calculator. See Appendix C for a more detailed discussion of financial calculators and the notation used with them. But here are a few important things to keep in mind:

1. Present value (PV) is the amount of money today.
2. Future value (FV) is the amount of money at a specific date in the future.
3. The interest rate i refers to the interest rate per compounding period.
4. The symbol n refers to the number of compounding periods in the term of the investment.

Most financial calculators use the following convention: A negative number is used for an outflow of cash from an investor, and a positive number is used for an inflow of cash to an investor. Use a financial calculator by entering the three known values; then press the key for the unknown to find its value. Since financial calculators differ greatly, you should look at the instruction booklet that comes with your calculator.

Financial Calculator Solution Example 5(d) involves a $2000 deposit, which is the present value (PV). The unknown is the future value (FV). Since the original $2000 investment is an outflow to the investor, enter -2000 for PV. Then enter 24 (compounding periods) for n and 1% (per month) for the interest rate per compounding period. Finally, press FV to find the unknown future value.

-2000 PV 24 n 1 i FV 2539.47 (rounded)

This answer differs by 1¢ from that found in Example 5(d) due to rounding.

The more often interest is compounded, the greater the amount of interest earned. Using a financial calculator, a compound interest table more complete than the compound interest table on page 402, or the compound interest formula will give the results of interest on $1000 shown in the following table. (Leap years were ignored in finding daily interest.)

Compounding makes a BIG difference!

COMPOUNDED	INTEREST
Not at all (simple interest)	$ 800.00
Annually	$1158.92
Semiannually	$1191.12
Quarterly	$1208.04
Monthly	$1219.64
Daily	$1225.35

Interest on $1000 at 8% per Year for 10 Years

Finding Compound Interest **EXAMPLE 6** John Smith sold his truck and boat for $15,000, which he deposited in a retirement account that pays interest compounded semiannually. How much will he have after 15 years if the funds grow at

(a) 6%?   **(b)** 8%?   **(c)** 10%?

SOLUTION

In 15 years, there are $15 \times 2 = 30$ semiannual periods. The semiannual interest rates are

(a) $\frac{6\%}{2} = 3\%$ **(b)** $\frac{8\%}{2} = 4\%$ **(c)** $\frac{10\%}{2} = 5\%$

Using factors from the table:

(a) $15,000 × **2.42726** = $36,408.90

(b) $15,000 × **3.24340** = $48,651

(c) $15,000 × **4.32194** = $64,829.10

The graph shows the growth in compound amount at different interest rates over time. It is amazing that an investment of $15,000 can grow to over $36,000 in 15 years! Interestingly, annual interest earned becomes larger as the amount invested grows.

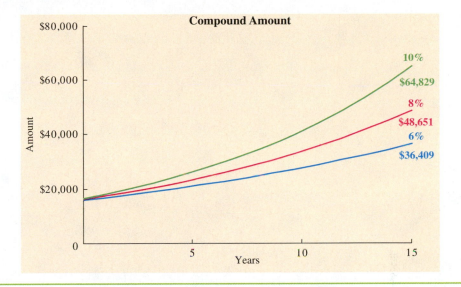

QUICK CHECK 6

A bank offers a certificate of deposit that earns 6% compounded quarterly for 3 years. Find the compound amount for an investment of $3500.

The **QUICK START** *exercises in each section contain solutions to help you get started.*

Use the formula for compound amount, not the table, to find the compound amount and interest. Round to the nearest cent. (See Examples 3 and 4.)

QUICK START

	Compound Amount	Interest
1. $12,000 at 8% compounded annually for 4 years	**$16,325.87**	**$4325.87**

Compound interest is 8% per year for 4 years.
$M = \$12,000 \times (1 + .08)^4 = \$12,000 \times 1.08 \times 1.08 \times 1.08 \times 1.08 = \$16,325.87$
$I = \$16,325.87 - \$12,000 = \$4325.87$

2. $14,800 at 6% compounded semiannually for 4 years _____ _____

3. $28,000 at 10% compounded quarterly for 1 year _____ _____

4. $20,000 at 5% compounded quarterly for $\frac{3}{4}$ year _____ _____

Use values from the compound interest table on page 402 to find both the compound amount and the compound interest. Round the compound amount to the nearest cent. (See Examples 3–6.)

QUICK START

	Compound Amount	Interest
5. $32,350 at 6% compounded annually for 4 years	**$40,841.23**	**$8491.23**

Compound interest is 6% per year for 4 years.
$M = \$32,350 \times 1.26248 = \$40,841.23; I = \$40,841.23 - \$32,350 = \$8491.23$

6. $19,400 at 8% compounded quarterly for 3 years _____ _____

7. $14,500 at 10% compounded quarterly for 7 years _____ _____

8. $12,500 at 8% compounded quarterly for 5 years _____ _____

9. $45,000 at 6% compounded semiannually for 5 years _____ _____

10. $82,000 at 8% compounded semiannually for 4 years _____ _____

 indicates an exercise that is related to the Case in Point feature.

Find the simple interest for the period indicated. Then use table values to find the compound interest. Finally, find the difference between compound interest and simple interest. Round each to the nearest cent. (Interest is compounded annually.)

QUICK START

	Principal	Rate	Number of Years	Simple Interest	Compound Interest	Difference
11.	$5400	6%	4	$1296	$1417.39	$121.39
12.	$9200	5%	6	_____	_____	_____
13.	$1200	8%	15	_____	_____	_____
14.	$4625	4%	12	_____	_____	_____

Use the table to solve the following application problems. Round to the nearest cent.

QUICK START

15. CREDIT UNION Bill Jensen deposits $8500 with Bank of America in an investment paying 5% compounded semiannually. Find **(a)** the compound amount and **(b)** the interest in 6 years.

Compound interest is $\frac{5\%}{2}$ = 2.5% and there are 2 × 6 = 12 compounding periods.
(a) M = $8500 × 1.34489 = $11,431.57; **(b)** I = $11,431.57 − $8500 = $2931.57

(a) $11,431.57
(b) $2931.57

16. SAVINGS Vickie Ewing deposits her savings of $2800 in an account paying 6% compounded quarterly and she leaves it there for 7 years. Find **(a)** the compound amount and **(b)** the interest.

(a) _____
(b) _____

17. SAVINGS Tom Blasting invested $4500 in an investment paying 8% compounded quarterly for 3 years. Find **(a)** the compound amount and **(b)** the interest.

(a) _____
(b) _____

18. INVESTMENT John Crandall deposited $6000 in an account at a bank that pays 5% compounded semiannually for 4 years. Find **(a)** the compound amount and **(b)** the interest.

(a) _____
(b) _____

19. INTERNATIONAL FINANCE Chi Tang, a businessperson from Taiwan, deposits 25,000 yuan in a Hong Kong branch of Bank of America that pays 6% compounded semiannually. Find **(a)** the balance in the account after 4 years and **(b)** the interest.

(a) _____
(b) _____

20. UNITED KINGDOM A firm in the UK places £42,000 (forty-two thousand pounds) in an account paying 6% compounded quarterly and leaves it there as collateral for a loan. Find **(a)** the balance in the account after 1 year and **(b)** the interest.

(a) _____
(b) _____

21. INVESTMENT DECISION Bill Baxter has $25,000 to invest for a year. He can lend it to his sister, who has agreed to pay 10% simple interest for the year. Or, he can invest it with a bank at 6% compounded quarterly for a year. How much additional interest would the simple interest loan to his sister generate?

21. _____

22. **MAXIMIZING INTEREST**   Bank of America has $850,000 to lend for 9 months. It can lend it to a local contractor at a simple interest rate of 12%, or it can lend it to a small business that will pay 12% compounded monthly. How much additional interest would the compound interest loan to the small business generate?

22. _____

23. **INTERNATIONAL FINANCE**   Barton's Ltd. lends $1,400,000 for 2 years at 12% compounded monthly to an Egyptian company that manufactures tug boats. Find (**a**) the future value and (**b**) the interest.

(a) _____

(b) _____

24. **CORPORATE FINANCE**   Key Bank lends $4,500,000 for $1\frac{1}{2}$ years at 8% compounded quarterly to Rengen Biomedical to fund a clinical trial on a new cancer drug. Find (**a**) the future value and (**b**) the interest.

(a) _____

(b) _____

25. **INVESTING**   William Jones has $25,000 to invest and believes that he will earn 6% compounded semiannually. Find the compound amount if he invests (**a**) for 2 years and (**b**) for 12 years. (**c**) Then find the additional amount earned due to the longer period.

(a) _____

(b) _____

(c) _____

26. **WHICH INVESTMENT?**   Jan Reus sold her home and has $18,000 to invest. She believes she can earn 8% compounded quarterly. Find the compound amount if she invests for (**a**) 3 years and (**b**) 6 years. (**c**) Then find the additional amount earned due to the longer time period.

(a) _____

(b) _____

(c) _____

27. **TIME OR RATE?**   Becky Hilton has a choice for her investment of $7500. She can invest it in funds she believes will earn either (**a**) 8% compounded quarterly for 2 years or (**b**) 6% compounded semiannually for 5 years. Find the future value of both. (**c**) Which is larger?

(a) _____

(b) _____

(c) _____

28. **TIME OR RATE?**   Manager Isat Riyadh has a choice to make regarding short-term, excess corporate cash of $330,000. He can invest it (**a**) at 6% compounded quarterly for 6 months or (**b**) at 5% compounded semiannually for 1 year. Find the future amount of both. (**c**) Which is larger?

(a) _____

(b) _____

(c) _____

29. Explain the difference between simple interest and compound interest. (See Objectives 1 and 3.)

30. Explain the difference between 8% compounded monthly for 1 year and 8% simple interest for 1 year. If you were lending money, which type of interest would you specify? Why?

31. Show the effect of both the interest rate and the period on an original investment of $2500. Decide on your own rates and time periods.

32. List five companies that you think borrow money and state why they might need the funds.

QUICK CHECK ANSWERS

1. (a) $16,200   (b) $16,224   (c) $24   4. $12,095.25; $3095.25
2. $91,592   5. $1333.85
3. 2%; 24 periods   6. $4184.67

10.2 Interest-Bearing Bank Accounts and Inflation

OBJECTIVES

1 Define passbook, savings, and other interest-bearing accounts.
2 Find interest compounded daily.
3 Define time deposit accounts.
4 Define inflation and the consumer price index.
5 Examine the effect of inflation on spendable income.
6 Understand the role of the government related to inflation.

case IN point

Individuals, businesses, states, and even countries have money on deposit at Bank of America. These deposits can be in many forms, including checking accounts, savings accounts, money market accounts, and time deposits, such as certificates of deposits.

People sometimes think that banks have huge vaults of stored cash, but that is rarely the case. Banks usually have only enough cash to meet customers' needs for cash during the next few days. Most bank assets are in the loans to their many customers, rather than in cash.

OBJECTIVE 1 Define passbook, savings, and other interest-bearing accounts. **Savings accounts, passbook accounts, money market accounts,** and other interest-bearing accounts are offered by banks and credit unions and can be a safe place to deposit money. These accounts are commonly insured by the Federal Deposit Insurance Corporation (FDIC) on deposits up to $250,000. Many of these accounts require a minimum balance. Interest rates paid on these accounts have varied from less than 1% per year to more than 5% per year and is often compounded daily. The Truth in Savings Act of 1991 resulted in Regulation DD, which requires that interest on savings accounts be paid based on the *exact* number of days.

Interest-bearing checking accounts are also offered by many banks and credit unions. These accounts often have a minimum balance, such as $1500, that must be maintained, but they have the advantage that checks can be written on the account. They can be a good way to earn interest on your money as long as your balance does not fall too low, in which case the bank commonly charges a fee. People do this because they want to maximize interest by leaving money in an interest-paying account as long as possible.

OBJECTIVE 2 Find interest compounded daily. Interest on savings accounts, passbook accounts, and other interest-bearing checking accounts is found using compound interest. It is common for banks to pay interest **compounded daily** so that interest is credited for every day that the money is on deposit.

The formula for daily compounding is *exactly* the same as the formula given in **Section 10.1**. However, because the annual interest rate must be divided by 365 (for daily compounding), the arithmetic is tedious. To avoid this, use the following special tables that give the necessary numbers for 1 to 90 days, as well as for 1 to 4 ninety-day quarters, assuming $3\frac{1}{2}\%$[*] interest compounded daily. Even with daily compounding, interest is often credited to an account *only at the end of each quarter* to make record keeping easier for the bank.

The four quarters in a year begin on January 1, April 1, July 1, and October 1. Although some quarters have 91 or 92 days in them, we assume 90-day quarters for convenience in calculation. Assuming daily compounding and a compounding period expressed in days or quarters, compound amount and interest are found as follows.

Interest by Quarter for $3\frac{1}{2}\%$ Compounded Daily Assuming 90-Day Quarters

NUMBER OF QUARTERS	VALUE OF $(1 + i)^n$
1	1.008667067
2	1.017409251
3	1.026227205
4	1.035121585

Finding Compound Amount and Interest

$$\text{Compound amount} = \text{Principal} \times \text{Number from table}$$
$$\text{Interest} = \text{Compound amount} - \text{Principal}$$

[*]*Note:* Interest rates vary widely. No one, including the authors of this textbook, knows what interest rates will be in the future. Thus, the interest rate in this section is $3\frac{1}{2}\%$, or close to the historical average for accounts of this type.

Find the value from the table below if the number of days of the deposit is 90 days or less. Use the smaller table at the side if time is given in number of quarters.

Values of $(1 + i)^n$ for $3\frac{1}{2}$% Compounded Daily

NUMBER OF DAYS n	VALUE OF $(1 + i)^n$	n	VALUE OF $(1 + i)^n$	n	VALUE OF $(1 + i)^n$	n	VALUE OF $(1 + i)^n$	n	VALUE OF $(1 + i)^n$
1	1.000095890	19	1.001823491	37	1.003554076	55	1.005287650	73	1.007024219
2	1.000191790	20	1.001919556	38	1.003650307	56	1.005384048	74	1.007120783
3	1.000287699	21	1.002015631	39	1.003746548	57	1.005480454	75	1.007217357
4	1.000383617	22	1.002111714	40	1.003842797	58	1.005576870	76	1.007313939
5	1.000479544	23	1.002207807	41	1.003939056	59	1.005673296	77	1.007410531
6	1.000575480	24	1.002303909	42	1.004035324	60	1.005769730	78	1.007507132
7	1.000671426	25	1.002400021	43	1.004131602	61	1.005866174	79	1.007603742
8	1.000767381	26	1.002496141	44	1.004227888	62	1.005962627	80	1.007700362
9	1.000863345	27	1.002592271	45	1.004324184	63	1.006059089	81	1.007796990
10	1.000959318	28	1.002688410	46	1.004420489	64	1.006155560	82	1.007893628
11	1.001055300	29	1.002784558	47	1.004516803	65	1.006252041	83	1.007990276
12	1.001151292	30	1.002880716	48	1.004613127	66	1.006348531	84	1.008086932
13	1.001247293	31	1.002976882	49	1.004709460	67	1.006445030	85	1.008183598
14	1.001343303	32	1.003073058	50	1.004805802	68	1.006541538	86	1.008280273
15	1.001439322	33	1.003169243	51	1.004902153	69	1.006638056	87	1.008376958
16	1.001535350	34	1.003265438	52	1.004998513	70	1.006734583	88	1.008473651
17	1.001631388	35	1.003361641	53	1.005094883	71	1.006831119	89	1.008570354
18	1.001727435	36	1.003457854	54	1.005191262	72	1.006927665	90	1.008667067

Note: The value of $(1 + i)^n$ for $3\frac{1}{2}$% compounded daily for a quarter with 91 days is 1.008763788 and for a quarter with 92 days is 1.008860519.

Finding Daily Interest **EXAMPLE 1**

Becky Gonzales received $12,500 from a divorce settlement. She plans to use the money for a down payment on a new Toyota Camry but decides to wait 60 days until the new models are out. She puts her money in a savings account earning $3\frac{1}{2}$% interest compounded daily for the 60 days. Find the amount of interest she will earn.

SOLUTION

The table value for 60 days is **1.005769730**.

$$\text{Compound amount} = \$12,500 \times \mathbf{1.005769730} = \mathbf{\$12,572.12}$$
$$\text{Interest} = \mathbf{\$12,572.12} - \$12,500 = \$72.12$$

The additional $72.12 isn't much money to Gonzales, but she is happy to earn some interest.

QUICK CHECK 1

Find the interest if $1200 is invested in a money market account earning 3.5% compounded daily for 90 days.

The next two examples show how interest is calculated when there are several deposits and/or withdrawals within a short period of time.

Finding Interest on Multiple Deposits **EXAMPLE 2**

Tom Blackmore is a private investigator who keeps his extra cash in a savings account to earn interest. On January 10, he deposited $2463 in a savings account paying $3\frac{1}{2}$% compounded daily. He deposited an additional $1320 on February 18 and $840 on March 3. Find the interest earned through April 10.

SOLUTION

Treat each deposit separately. The $2463 was in the account for 90 days (21 days in January, 28 days in February, 31 days in March, and 10 days in April). The value for 90 days from the table is **1.008667067**.

Compound amount = $2463 × **1.008667067** = **$2484.35**   first deposit plus interest

The $1320 deposited on February 18 was in the account for 51 days (10 days in February, 31 days in March, and 10 days in April).

Compound amount = $1320 × **1.004902153** = **$1326.47**   second deposit plus interest

The $840 was in the account for 38 days (28 days in March and 10 days in April).

Compound amount = $840 × **1.003650307** = **$843.07**   final deposit plus interest

The total amount in the account on April 10 is found by adding the three compound amounts.

Total in account = **$2484.35** + **$1326.47** + **$843.07** = **$4653.89**

The preceding information is summarized in this table.

AMOUNT	NUMBER OF DAYS LEFT IN ACCOUNT	COMPOUND AMOUNT
$2463	90	$2484.35
$1320	51	$1326.47
$ 840	38	$ 843.07
		$4653.89

Total in account at end of quarter.

The interest earned is the total amount in the account less the deposits.

Interest earned = **$4653.89** − ($2463 + $1320 + $840) = $30.89

> **QUICK CHECK 2**
>
> A money market account is opened with an $8500 deposit on April 10, and another $1500 is deposited on May 5. Find the total in the account on June 30 if funds earn $3\frac{1}{2}\%$ compounded daily. Also find the interest earned.

Finding Interest for the Quarter **EXAMPLE 3**

Beth Gardner owns Blacktop Paving, Inc. She needs a place to keep extra cash, a place that will earn interest but that will allow her to get funds when needed. She opened a money market account on July 20 with a $24,800 deposit. She then withdrew $3800 on August 29 for an unexpected truck repair, and she made another withdrawal of $8200 on September 29 for payroll. Find the interest earned through October 1, given interest at $3\frac{1}{2}\%$ compounded daily.

Quick TIP ▼

See **Appendix C** for financial calculator solutions that do not require the use of a table.

SOLUTION

Of the original $24,800, a total of $24,800 − $3800 − $8200 = $12,800 earned interest from July 20 to October 1 or for 274 − 201 = 73 days. Find the factor **1.007024219** from the table.

Compound amount = $12,800 × **1.007024219** = $12,889.91
Interest = $12,889.91 − $12,800 = **$89.91**

The withdrawn $3800 earned interest from July 20 to August 29 or for 241 − 201 = 40 days.

Compound amount = $3800 × **1.003842797** = $3814.60
Interest = $3814.60 − $3800 = **$14.60**

Finally, the withdrawn $8200 earned interest from July 20 to September 29 or for 272 − 201 = 71 days.

Compound amount = $8200 × **1.006831119** = $8256.02
Interest = $8256.02 − $8200 = **$56.02**

The total interest earned is ($89.91 + $14.60 + $56.02) = **$160.53.** The total in the account on October 1 is found as follows.

Deposits + Interest −   Withdrawals   = Balance on October 1
$24,800 + **$160.53** − ($3800 + $8200) = $12,960.53

The following information assumes that all interest is credited on the last day of the quarter.

DATE	DEPOSIT		WITHDRAWAL	BALANCE
July 20	$24,800		—	$24,800
Aug. 29	—		$3800	$21,000
Sept. 29	—		$8200	$12,800
Oct. 1	$160.53	(Int.)	—	$12,960.53

QUICK CHECK 3

An account is opened with a deposit of $4000, but $3000 is withdrawn 40 days later. Find the amount in the account and the interest earned at the end of 90 days from the original deposit if interest is $3\frac{1}{2}\%$ compounded daily.

OBJECTIVE 3 Define time deposit accounts. Banks pay higher interest rates on funds left on deposit for *longer time periods* in **time deposits.** A **certificate of deposit (CD)** requires a minimum amount of money, such as $1000, to be on deposit for a minimum period of time, such as 1 year. Find the compound amount of a time deposit as follows.

Finding Compound Amount and Interest

Compound amount = Principal × Number from the table

Interest = Compound amount − Principal

Compound Interest for Time Deposit Accounts Compounded Daily

NUMBER OF YEARS	3%	4%	5%	6%	7%	NUMBER OF YEARS
1	1.03045326	1.04080849	1.05126750	1.06183131	1.07250098	1
2	1.06183393	1.08328232	1.10516335	1.12748573	1.15025836	2
3	1.09417024	1.12748944	1.16182231	1.19719965	1.23365322	3
4	1.12749129	1.17350058	1.22138603	1.27122408	1.32309429	4
5	1.16182708	1.22138937	1.28400343	1.34982553	1.41901993	5
10	1.34984217	1.49179200	1.64866481	1.82202895	2.01361756	10

Note: This compound interest table assumes daily compounding. The compound interest table on page 402 of Section 10.1 *does not.*

Finding Interest and Compound Amount for Time Deposits **EXAMPLE 4**

Tony Sanchez plans to purchase three machines for his auto-repair shop. Bank of America requires $20,000 in collateral before making the loan. Therefore, Tony deposits $20,000 with the bank in a 2-year certificate of deposit yielding 4% compounded daily. Find the compound amount and interest.

SOLUTION

Look at the table for 4% and 2 years, finding **1.08328232**.

Compound amount = $20,000 × **1.08328232** = **$21,665.65** rounded

Interest = **$21,665.65** − $20,000 = $1665.65

QUICK CHECK 4

Find the compound amount and interest on $10,000 invested in a 4-year CD earning 6% compounded daily.

OBJECTIVE 4 Define inflation and the consumer price index. Inflation results in a continual rise in the price of goods and services. A better way to think about inflation is that a dollar is worth less each year. Either way you think about it, the end result is that inflation means you have to earn more each year to buy the same goods and services.

For example, if inflation averages 3% per year, an automobile costing $25,000 today will cost about $45,000 in 20 years. The following graph shows the increase in the average annual cost of college tuition. Is it that college costs are increasing or that the dollar is going down in value requiring more dollars to buy the same thing? The answer is both in this case, since annual tuition costs have increased at such a rapid rate.

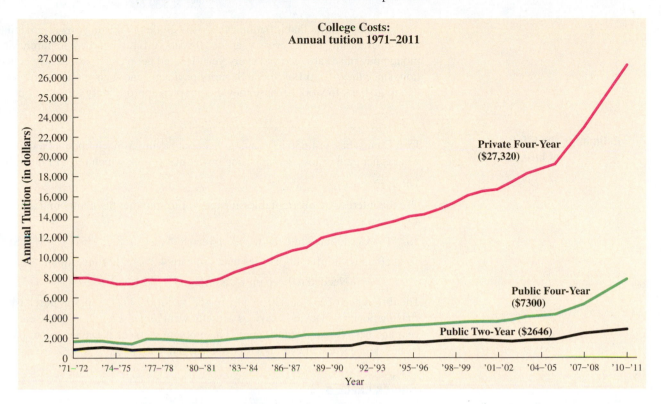

Many people use an index called the **consumer price index (CPI)**, or **cost of living index**, to track inflation. This index is calculated by the government. It measures the average change in prices from one year to the next for a common select group of goods and services, including food, housing, fuel, utilities, apparel, transportation, insurance, health care, and even pet care. Go to the Bureau of Labor Statistics Web site (http://www.bls.gov/) to see the effect of inflation over time.

OBJECTIVE 5 Examine the effect of inflation on spendable income. Inflation reduces the buying power of a family. Example 5 shows what happens to purchasing power when a 2% pay raise is received in a year with 4.8% inflation. It isn't pretty!

Estimating the Effects of Inflation

EXAMPLE 5

Inflation from one year to the next was 4.8% as measured by the CPI.

(a) Find the effect of the increase on a family with an after-tax annual income and budget of $39,600 (after taxes).

(b) What is the overall effect if the family members receive only a 2% (after tax) increase in pay for the year?

SOLUTION

(a) This is a percent problem. The cost of the goods and services that this family buys, if they buy the common bundle of goods and services, went up by 4.8% as measured by the CPI.

$$.048 \times \$39,600 = \mathbf{\$1900.80}$$

Therefore next year these same goods and services will cost the family

$$\$39,600 + \mathbf{\$1900.80} = \mathbf{\$41,500.80}$$

(b) The family's income went up 2% after taxes, or by

$$.02 \times \$39,600 = \mathbf{\$792}$$

Thus, their new income is $39,600 + $792 = $40,392. In effect, the family loses $41,500.80 − $40,392 = **$1108.80** in purchasing power.

QUICK CHECK 5

A family with an income of $32,000 receives a raise of 1.5% in a year when inflation is 3.5%. Find the decrease in purchasing power.

Example 5 can also be solved as follows.

$$
\begin{array}{ll}
\text{Inflation rate} & 4.8\% \\
-\ \text{Raise} & 2.0\% \\
\hline
\text{Loss} & 2.8\% \\
\end{array}
$$

$$2.8\% \times \$39{,}600 = \mathbf{\$1108.80}$$

Example 5 shows that inflation can slowly erode purchasing power. Imagine the effect of losing purchasing power every year for 10 years. Inflation can erode purchasing power even though pay raises are received every year. Retired people are particularly concerned with inflation, since they live off of Social Security payments and their estate. Some retired people have had to go back to work because they did not plan appropriately for inflation.

Estimating the Effects of Inflation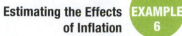

Joan Davies has $14,650 in a savings account paying $3\frac{1}{2}\%$ compounded daily. Ignoring taxes, what is her gain or loss in purchasing power in a year in which the CPI index increases by 4.2%?

SOLUTION

Use the interest-by-quarter table on page 411 to find that the compound amount factor for 4 quarters is **1.035121585**.

$$\text{Compound amount at end of year} = \$14{,}650 \times \mathbf{1.035121585} = \mathbf{\$15{,}164.53}$$

To keep up with inflation, Davies needs to earn 4.2% on her investment.

$$\text{Needed to keep up with inflation} = \$14{,}650 \times 1.042 = \mathbf{\$15{,}265.30}$$

The difference of $15,265.30 − $15,164.53 = $100.77 is the loss in purchasing power. The purchasing power of Davies's savings actually went *down*, even though she earned interest for the year and her account balance grew. The problem worsens if Davies has to pay taxes on interest earned, since she will end up with even less interest.

> **QUICK CHECK 6**
>
> Tador Roofing deposits $50,000 in an account earning $3\frac{1}{2}\%$ compounded daily for 1 year. Find the loss in purchasing power in a year with an increase in the CPI of 4%.

The opposite of inflation is **deflation**, which is a decrease in the general prices of goods and services. Deflation is relatively rare but potentially very serious. During the Great Depression of the 1930s, the prices of goods and services fell sharply in a deflationary spiral. People became worried about their savings and jobs. They also believed they could buy items more cheaply if they waited, since companies were marking down inventory to sell it. So, people postponed purchases, demand fell, and sales at firms plummeted. In turn, managers responded by laying off even more workers, causing higher unemployment and even more fear. It was a vicious cycle. In 1933, unemployment grew to (a horrible) 25% of the workforce.

OBJECTIVE 6 Understand the role of the government related to inflation. Both inflation that is too high (prices increasing rapidly) and deflation (prices falling) can be very harmful to families and businesses. As a result, the federal government works to control inflation using tools such as interest rates, which they control.

When the economy is too "hot" and inflation is too high, the government increases interest rates, making it more expensive to borrow, thereby slowing lending and growth. When economic growth is too slow or there is a threat of deflation, the government decreases interest rates to encourage borrowing and, therefore, encourage business activity. Controlling inflation and deflation is very difficult to do, but it is an important issue for the leaders of every country.

10.2 Exercises

  PRACTICE WATCH DOWNLOAD READ

The QUICK START *exercises in each section contain solutions to help you get started.*

Find the interest earned by the following. Assume $3\frac{1}{2}\%$ interest compounded daily.
(See Examples 1–3.)

QUICK START

	Amount	Date Deposited	Date Withdrawn	Interest Earned
1.	$4800	July 6	September 30	**$39.75**

There are $(31 - 6) + 31 + 30 = 86$ days.
Interest is $4800 \times 1.008280273 - \$4800 = \$39.75$.

	Amount	Date Deposited	Date Withdrawn	Interest Earned
2.	$3850	January 5	February 9	**$12.94**

There are $(31 - 5) + 9 = 35$ days.
Interest is $3850 \times 1.003361641 - \$3850 = \$12.94$.

	Amount	Date Deposited	Date Withdrawn	Interest Earned
3.	$8200	October 4	December 7	_____
4.	$2830	May 4	June 23	_____
5.	$17,958	September 9	November 7	_____
6.	$12,000	December 3	February 20	_____

Find the compound amount for each of the following certificates of deposit. Assume daily compounding. (See Example 4.)

QUICK START

	Amount Deposited	Interest Rate	Time in Years	Compound Amount
7.	$3900	5%	4	**$4763.41**

$3900 \times 1.22138603 = \$4763.41$

	Amount Deposited	Interest Rate	Time in Years	Compound Amount
8.	$8000	4%	1	_____
9.	$12,900	3%	10	_____
10.	$3600.40	6%	10	_____

11. Explain how you can use a time deposit to your advantage. Use an example. (See Objective 3.)

12. List five ways in which inflation affects your family. (See Objective 4.)

⚠ indicates an exercise that is related to the Case in Point feature.

Solve the following application problems. If no interest rate is given, assume $3\frac{1}{2}\%$ interest compounded daily. Round to the nearest cent.

QUICK START

13. **SAVINGS ACCOUNT** Hilda Worth opened a savings account at Bank of America on April 1 with a $2530 deposit. She then deposited $150 on May 8 and $580 on May 24. Find **(a)** the balance on June 30 and **(b)** the interest earned through that date.

(a) $3284.75

(b) $24.75

(a) The $2530 (for 90 days) becomes $2530 × 1.008667067 = $2551.93
    The $150 (for 53 days) becomes $150 × 1.005094883   = $ 150.76
    The $580 (for 37 days) becomes $580 × 1.003554076   = $ 582.06
                                          Total is $3284.75

(b) Interest earned is $3284.75 − ($2530 + $150 + $580) = $24.75

14. **PRINT SHOP** The manager of Quick Printing, Inc., is trying to get the most out of his assets including cash that has been sitting in a checking account that does not pay interest. He opened a savings account with a deposit of $8765 on January 4. On February 11, he deposited $936. Then, on March 21, he deposited a tax refund check for $650. Find **(a)** the balance on March 31 and **(b)** the interest earned through that date.

(a) _____

(b) _____

15. **SAVINGS ACCOUNT FOR EXTRA CASH** On April 1, MVP Sports opened a savings account at Bank of America with a deposit of $17,500. A withdrawal of $5000 was made 21 days later, another withdrawal of $980 was made 12 days before July 1. Find **(a)** the balance on July 1 and **(b)** the interest earned through that date. (*Hint:* See the table footnote for 91 days.)

(a) _____

(b) _____

16. **SAVINGS ACCOUNT** The owner of International Magic opened a savings account at Bank of America for the extra cash in the firm. The initial deposit of $7800 was made on July 7. A withdrawal of $1500 was made 46 days later, and an additional withdrawal of $1000 was made 30 days before October 1. Find **(a)** the balance on October 1 and **(b)** the interest earned through that date.

(a) _____

(b) _____

17. **TIME DEPOSIT** Wes Cockrell has $4000 to deposit in a certificate of deposit, but he is debating whether to leave it there for 2 years or for 3 years. Assume 5% compounded daily in both situations, and find the compound amount in each case.

17. _____

18. **COMPOUNDING** Georgia Pastel Fabric has $15,000 to deposit in a certificate of deposit for either 3 or 5 years. Assume 6% compounded daily in both situations, and find the compound amount in each case.

18. _____

19. **LOAN COLLATERAL** An Italian firm deposited $800,000 in a 2-year time deposit earning 6% compounded daily with a New York bank as partial collateral for a loan. Find **(a)** the compound amount and **(b)** the interest earned.

(a) _____

(b) _____

20. PUTTING UP COLLATERAL   Joni Perez needs to borrow $20,000 to open a welding shop, but the bank will not lend her the money. Joni's uncle agrees to put up collateral for the loan with a $20,000, 4-year certificate of deposit paying 4% compounded daily. This means that the bank will take all or part of his deposit if Perez should fail to repay the loan. Find **(a)** the compound amount earned by her uncle and **(b)** the interest earned by her uncle.

(a) _____

(b) _____

21. RETIREMENT INCOME   The Walters accumulated $235,000 during more than 40 years of work. They originally deposited this money in a 5-year time deposit earning 6% and used the income for living expenses. On renewing the time deposit, they found that interest rates on a 5-year time deposit had fallen and that they were going to receive only 4%. Find the difference in their *annual income* due to the decline in interest rates. (*Hint:* Don't use the compound interest table.)

21. _____

22. INHERITANCE   Jessica Thompson inherited $80,000 and decided to put the money in one of two 4-year time deposits. The first time deposit yielded 5%, but the second yielded only 4%. Find the difference in the annual income. (*Hint:* Don't use the compound interest table.)

22. _____

23. DETERMINING PURCHASING POWER   A family with a spending budget of $26,500 receives an increase in wages of 3% in a year in which inflation was 4.5%. Find the net gain or loss in their purchasing power.

23. _____

24. INFLATION AND RETIREMENT   Ben and Martha Wheeler are retired and they have $184,500 in a savings account at Bank of America paying $3\frac{1}{2}$% compounded daily. What is their gain or loss in purchasing power from interest in a year in which inflation is 5%?

24. _____

25. CORPORATE SAVINGS   Dayton Tires has $180,000 to invest for 1 year. Find the future value if it earns **(a)** 4% per year compounded daily and **(b)** 6% per year compounded daily. **(c)** Then find the difference between the two.

(a) _____

(b) _____

(c) _____

26. EMERGENCY CASH   After working long days in her small business for years, Kaitlyn Plank was finally making money. Since she was still worried about emergencies, she decided to put $85,000 in an investment for 4 years. Find the future value if it earns **(a)** 4% per year compounded daily and **(b)** 7% per year compounded daily. **(c)** Then find the difference between the two.

(a) _____

(b) _____

(c) _____

27. Define inflation and discuss the government's role in controlling inflation. (See Objectives 5 and 6.)

28. Define deflation and discuss how it can lead to severe problems. (See Objective 6.)

29. Point out several differences between inflation and deflation. (See Objective 5.)

30. Describe the advantages to a family of having money in a savings account or certificate of deposit. (See Objectives 1–6.)

10.3   Present Value and Future Value

OBJECTIVES

1   Define the terms *future value* and *present value*.

2   Use tables to calculate present value.

3   Use future value and present value to estimate the value of a business.

OBJECTIVE 1   Define the terms *future value* and *present value*. Future value is the amount available at a specific date in the future. It is the amount available after an investment has earned interest. All of the values found in Sections 10.1 and 10.2 were future values.

In contrast, **present value** is the amount needed today so that the desired future value will be available when needed. For example, an individual may need to know the present value that must be invested today in order to have a down payment for a new car in 3 years. Or a firm may need to know the present value that must be invested today in order to have enough money to purchase a new computer system in 20 months. The bar chart shows present value as the value today and future value as the value at a future date.

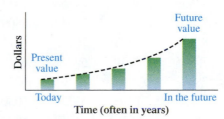

In this section, the future value, interest rate, and term are given and the present value that must be invested today to reach the future value is calculated.

OBJECTIVE 2   Use tables to calculate present value. First, find the interest rate per compounding period (*i*) and the total number of compounding periods (*n*) of the investment. Then use these values to find the appropriate value in the Present Value of a Dollar Table. Finally, use the formula to find present value.

Finding Present Value

$$\text{Present value } (PV) = \text{Future value} \times \text{Table value}$$

Finding Present Value   **EXAMPLE 1**

Betty Clark needs to replace two pumps at her gas station in 3 years at an estimated cost of $12,000. What lump sum deposited today at 5% compounded annually must she invest to have the needed funds? How much interest will she earn?

SOLUTION

Step 1   The interest rate is 5% per compounding period for 3 compounding periods (years in this case). Look across the top of the table for 5% and down the left column for 3 to find **.86384**.

$$\text{Present value} = \$12,000 \times \textbf{.86384} = \textbf{\$10,366.08}$$

Step 2   Interest earned = $12,000 − **$10,366.08** = $1633.92.

Step 3   Check the answer by finding the future value of an investment of $10,366.08 in an account earning 5% compounded annually for 3 years. Use the table on page 402 to find **1.15763**.

$$\text{Future value} = \$10,366.08 \times \textbf{1.15763} = \$12,000.09$$

The reason it is not exactly $12,000 is rounding in the table value.

QUICK CHECK 1

Find the lump sum that must be deposited today to have a future value of $25,000 in 5 years if funds earn 6% compounded annually.

Present Value of a Dollar Table

PERIOD	1%	1½%	2%	2½%	3%	4%	5%	6%	8%	10%	PERIOD
1	.99010	.98522	.98039	.97561	.97087	.96154	.95238	.94340	.92593	.90909	1
2	.98030	.97066	.96117	.95181	.94260	.92456	.90703	.89000	.85734	.82645	2
3	.97059	.95632	.94232	.92860	.91514	.88900	.86384	.83962	.79383	.75131	3
4	.96098	.94218	.92385	.90595	.88849	.85480	.82270	.79209	.73503	.68301	4
5	.95147	.92826	.90573	.88385	.86261	.82193	.78353	.74726	.68058	.62092	5
6	.94205	.91454	.88797	.86230	.83748	.79031	.74622	.70496	.63017	.56447	6
7	.93272	.90103	.87056	.84127	.81309	.75992	.71068	.66506	.58349	.51316	7
8	.92348	.88771	.85349	.82075	.78941	.73069	.67684	.62741	.54027	.46651	8
9	.91434	.87459	.83676	.80073	.76642	.70259	.64461	.59190	.50025	.42410	9
10	.90529	.86167	.82035	.78120	.74409	.67556	.61391	.55839	.46319	.38554	10
11	.89632	.84893	.80426	.76214	.72242	.64958	.58468	.52679	.42888	.35049	11
12	.88745	.83639	.78849	.74356	.70138	.62460	.55684	.49697	.39711	.31863	12
13	.87866	.82403	.77303	.72542	.68095	.60057	.52032	.46884	.36770	.28966	13
14	.86996	.81185	.75788	.70773	.66112	.57748	.50507	.44230	.34036	.26333	14
15	.86135	.79985	.74301	.69047	.64186	.55526	.48102	.41727	.31524	.23939	15
16	.85282	.78803	.72845	.67362	.62317	.53391	.45811	.39365	.29189	.21763	16
17	.84438	.77639	.71416	.65720	.60502	.51337	.43630	.37136	.27027	.19784	17
18	.83602	.76491	.70016	.64117	.58739	.49363	.41552	.35034	.25025	.17986	18
19	.82774	.75361	.68643	.62553	.57029	.47464	.39573	.33051	.23171	.16351	19
20	.81954	.74247	.67297	.61027	.55368	.45639	.37689	.31180	.21455	.14864	20
21	.81143	.73150	.65978	.59539	.53755	.43883	.35894	.29416	.19866	.13513	21
22	.80340	.72069	.64684	.58086	.52189	.42196	.34185	.27751	.18394	.12285	22
23	.79544	.71004	.63416	.56670	.50669	.40573	.32557	.26180	.17032	.11168	23
24	.78757	.69954	.62172	.55288	.49193	.39012	.31007	.24698	.15770	.10153	24
25	.77977	.68921	.60953	.53939	.47761	.37512	.29530	.23300	.14602	.09230	25
26	.77205	.67902	.59758	.52623	.46369	.36069	.28124	.21981	.13520	.08391	26
27	.76440	.66899	.58586	.51340	.45019	.34682	.26785	.20737	.12519	.07628	27
28	.75684	.65910	.57437	.50088	.43708	.33348	.25509	.19563	.11591	.06934	28
29	.74934	.64936	.56311	.48866	.42435	.32065	.24295	.18456	.10733	.06304	29
30	.74192	.63976	.55207	.47674	.41199	.30832	.23138	.17411	.09938	.05731	30
31	.73458	.63031	.54125	.46511	.39999	.29646	.22036	.16425	.09202	.05210	31
32	.72730	.62099	.53063	.45377	.38834	.28506	.20987	.15496	.08520	.04736	32
33	.72010	.61182	.52023	.44270	.37703	.27409	.19987	.14619	.07889	.04306	33
34	.71297	.60277	.51003	.43191	.36604	.26355	.19035	.13791	.07305	.03914	34
35	.70591	.59387	.50003	.42137	.35538	.25342	.18129	.13011	.06763	.03558	35
36	.69892	.58509	.49022	.41109	.34503	.24367	.17266	.12274	.06262	.03235	36
37	.69200	.57644	.48061	.40107	.33498	.23430	.16444	.11579	.05799	.02941	37
38	.68515	.56792	.47119	.39128	.32523	.22529	.15661	.10924	.05369	.02673	38
39	.67837	.55953	.46195	.38174	.31575	.21662	.14915	.10306	.04971	.02430	39
40	.67165	.55126	.45289	.37243	.30656	.20829	.14205	.09722	.04603	.02209	40
41	.66500	.54312	.44401	.36335	.29763	.20028	.13528	.09172	.04262	.02009	41
42	.65842	.53509	.43530	.35448	.28896	.19257	.12884	.08653	.03946	.01826	42
43	.65190	.52718	.42677	.34584	.28054	.18517	.12270	.08163	.03654	.01660	43
44	.64545	.51939	.41840	.33740	.27237	.17805	.11686	.07701	.03383	.01509	44
45	.63905	.51171	.41020	.32917	.26444	.17120	.11130	.07265	.03133	.01372	45
46	.63273	.50415	.40215	.32115	.25674	.16461	.10600	.06854	.02901	.01247	46
47	.62646	.49670	.39427	.31331	.24926	.15828	.10095	.06466	.02686	.01134	47
48	.62026	.48936	.38654	.30567	.24200	.15219	.09614	.06100	.02487	.01031	48
49	.61412	.48213	.37896	.29822	.23495	.14634	.09156	.05755	.02303	.00937	49

Finding Present Value **EXAMPLE 2**

The local Harley-Davidson shop has seen business grow rapidly. The owners plan to increase the size of their 6000-square-foot shop in one year at a cost of $280,000. How much should be invested in an account paying 6% compounded semiannually to have the funds needed?

SOLUTION

The interest rate per compounding period is $\frac{6\%}{2} = 3\%$, and the number of compounding periods is 1 year $\times$ 2 periods per year = 2. Use the table to find **.94260**.

$$\text{Present value} = \$280,000 \times .94260 = \$263,928$$

A deposit of $263,928 today at 6% compounded semiannually will provide $280,001.22 in one year. The difference is due to rounding.

> **QUICK CHECK 2**
>
> In 5 years, Great Lakes Dairy estimates it will need $350,000 for a down payment to purchase a nearby farm. Find the amount that should be invested today to meet the down payment if funds earn 8% compounded quarterly.

Applying Present Value **EXAMPLE 3**

Radiux Inc. wishes to partner with a Korean company to purchase a satellite in 3 years. Radiux plans to make a cash down payment of 40% of its anticipated $8,000,000 cost and borrow the remaining funds from a bank. Find the amount Radiux should invest today in an account earning 6% compounded annually to have the down payment needed in 3 years.

SOLUTION

First find the down payment to be paid in 3 years.

$$\text{Down payment} = .40 \times \$8,000,000 = \$3,200,000$$

This is the future value needed exactly 3 years from now. Using the present value of a dollar table on page 422 with 3 periods and 6% per period gives

$$\$3,200,000 \times .83962 = \$2,686,784$$

Radiux must invest $2,686,784 today at 6% interest compounded annually to have the required down payment of $3,200,000 in 3 years.

> **Financial Calculator Solution** Using data from Example 3, the future value is $3,200,000. The number of periods is 3 and the interest rate per period is 6%. Enter these values into the financial calculator with the future value being a positive number. Then press PV for the present value. It will be a negative number, indicating the outflows from Radiux.
>
>   3200000 FV 3 $\boxed{n}$ 6 $\boxed{i}$ PV $\boxed{-}$ −2686782 (rounded to the nearest dollar)

The difference from the value found in the example is due to rounding.

> **QUICK CHECK 3**
>
> Mom and Pop Jenkins plan to buy a new car in 2 years and want to make a down payment of 25% of the estimated purchase price of $32,000. Find the amount they need to invest to make the down payment if funds earn 6% compounded quarterly.

OBJECTIVE 3 Use future value and present value to estimate the value of a business. Sometimes a business has such a strong growth opportunity that it is valued at more than it would be if it had normal growth. In this case, the strong growth opportunity increases the market price of the business. To estimate the value of a business with strong growth, first estimate the future value of the business 2 to 5 years in the future. Then find the present value of this amount using the appropriate discount rate.

Evaluating a Business   **EXAMPLE 4**

Brianna McGruder and Tanya Zoban own Extreme Sports, Inc., whose value is $120,000 today assuming normal growth. However, the partners believe the value will grow at 15% per year for the next four years. They want to take this rapid growth into consideration when valuing the business for a potential sale.

(a) Find the future value of the business in 4 years.

(b) Estimate the value of the retail store by finding the present value of the amount found in part **(a)** at 6% compounded quarterly.

SOLUTION

(a) The partners expect the business to grow at 15% per year for the next 4 years. There is no 15% column in the compound interest table of Section 10.1, so we use the formula $(1 + i)^n$, where $i = .15$ and $n = 4$.

$$\text{Future value} = \$120{,}000 \times (1 + i)^n$$
$$= \$120{,}000 \times (1 + .15)^4 = \textbf{\$209{,}881 (rounded)}$$

This is an estimate of the value of the store in 4 years.

(b) Now find the present value of $209,881 assuming 6% compounded quarterly for 4 years or at $\frac{6\%}{4} = 1.5\%$ per quarter for $4 \times 4 = 16$ compounding periods. The value from the present value of a dollar table on page 422 is **.78803**.

$$\text{Present value} = \$209{,}881 \times \textbf{.78803} = \$165{,}393 \text{ (rounded)}$$

Thus, the partners should ask $165,400 for their business. The rapid growth rate adds about $165,400 - $120,000 = $45,400 to the value of the business.

QUICK CHECK 4

Assuming normal growth, a clothing store is worth $100,000. But the owners believe it will grow at 9% per year for the next three years. Estimate a reasonable selling price for the business by finding the present value at 5% per year compounded semiannually.

10.3 Exercises

The QUICK START exercises in each section contain solutions to help you get started.

Find the present value of the following. Round to the nearest cent. Also, find the amount of interest earned. (See Examples 1 and 2.)

QUICK START

	Amount Needed	Time (Years)	Interest	Compounded	Present Value	Interest Earned
1.	$12,300	3	6%	annually	$10,327.33	$1972.67

$P = \$12,300 \times .83962 = \$10,327.33; I = \$12,300 - \$10,327.33 = \$1972.67$

	Amount Needed	Time (Years)	Interest	Compounded	Present Value	Interest Earned
2.	$14,500	$2\frac{1}{2}$	8%	quarterly	$11,895.08	$2604.92

$P = \$14,500 \times .82035 = \$11,895.08; I = \$14,500 - \$11,895.08 = \$2604.92$

	Amount Needed	Time (Years)	Interest	Compounded	Present Value	Interest Earned
3.	$9350	4	5%	semiannually	_____	_____
4.	$850	10	8%	semiannually	_____	_____
5.	$18,853	11	6%	quarterly	_____	_____
6.	$20,984	9	10%	quarterly	_____	_____

Solve the following application problems.

QUICK START

7. DIVORCE SETTLEMENT The Prestons are getting a divorce, and part of the divorce settlement involves setting aside money today for college tuition for their daughter who enters college in 7 years. They estimate that the cost of four years' tuition, food, and lodging at the state university their daughter will attend will be $40,000. Find **(a)** the lump sum that must be invested at 6% compounded semiannually and **(b)** the amount of interest earned.

(a) $26,444.80
(b) $13,555.20

(a) Lump sum $= P = \$40,000 \times .66112 = \$26,444.80$
(b) $I = \$40,000 - \$26,444.80 = \$13,555.20$

8. SELF-EMPLOYMENT Janet Becker wishes to start her own day-care business in her home in 4 years and estimates that she will need $25,000 to do so. **(a)** What lump sum should be invested today at 5%, compounded semiannually, to produce the needed amount? **(b)** How much interest will be earned?

(a) _____
(b) _____

9. FINANCING COLLEGE EXPENSES Mrs. Lorez wants all of her grandchildren to go to college and decides to help financially. How much must she give to each child at birth if they are to have $10,000 on entering college 18 years later, assuming 6% interest compounded annually?

9. _____

10. BAKERY Carlos Mora recently immigrated to the United States from Central America. His family has agreed to help him set aside the cash needed to open a small bakery in 2 years once he completes a program at a culinary institute. Find the amount they must deposit today in an investment account expected to yield 4% compounded quarterly if he needs $95,000 to open the shop in 2 years.

10. _____

11. **EXPANDING MANUFACTURING OPERATIONS**   Quantum Logic recently expanded its computer-chip assembly operations at a cost of $450,000. Management expects that the value of the investment will grow at a rate of 12% per year compounded annually for the next 5 years. **(a)** Find the future value of the investment. **(b)** Find the present value of the amount found in part **(a)** at a rate of 6% compounded annually. Round to the nearest dollar at each step.

(a) _____

(b) _____

12. **BUSINESS EXPANSION**   Village Hardware expands its business at a cost of $20,000. They expect that the investment will grow at a rate of 10% per year compounded annually for the next 4 years. **(a)** Find the future value of the investment. **(b)** Find the present value of the amount found in part **(a)** at a rate of 6% compounded annually. Round to the nearest dollar at each step.

(a) _____

(b) _____

13. **VALUE OF A BUSINESS**   Jessie Marquette believes her hair salon is worth $20,000 and estimates that its value will grow at 10% per year compounded annually for the next 3 years. If she sells the business, the funds will be invested at 8% compounded quarterly. **(a)** Find the future value if she holds onto the business. **(b)** What price should she insist on now if she sells the business?

(a) _____

(b) _____

14. **VALUE OF A BUSINESS**   John Fernandez figures his bike shop is worth $88,000 if sold today and that it will grow in value at 8% per year compounded annually for the next 6 years. If he sells the business, the funds will be invested at 5% compounded semiannually. **(a)** Find the future value of the shop. **(b)** What price should he insist on at this time if he sells the business?

(a) _____

(b) _____

15. Explain the difference between future value and present value. (See Objective 1.)

16. Explain how and when to use both the compound interest table in Section 10.1 and the present value table in this section.

QUICK CHECK ANSWERS

1. $18,681.50   **3.** $7101.68
2. $235,539.50   **4.** $111,670.35

Chapter 10 Quick Review

Chapter Terms *Review the following terms to test your understanding of the chapter. For each term you do not know, refer to the page number found next to that term.*

CD [**p. 414**]

CPI [**p. 415**]

certificate of deposit [**p. 414**]

compound amount [**p. 398**]

compound interest [**p. 398**]

compounded daily [**p. 411**]

compounding period [**p. 400**]

consumer price index [**p. 415**]

cost of living index [**p. 415**]

deflation [**p. 416**]

exponents [**p. 401**]

formula for compounding interest [**p. 401**]

future amount [**p. 398**]

future value [**p. 398**]

inflation [**p. 414**]

interest-bearing checking accounts [**p. 411**]

interest rate per compounding period [**p. 401**]

money market accounts [**p. 411**]

passbook accounts [**p. 411**]

present value [**p. 421**]

savings accounts [**p. 411**]

simple interest [**p. 398**]

time deposit [**p. 414**]

CONCEPTS

EXAMPLES

10.1 Finding compound amount and compound interest

Find the number of compounding periods (n) and the interest rate per period (i).

Use the compound interest table to find the interest on $1. Multiply the table value by the principal to obtain the compound amount.

Subtract principal from compound amount to obtain the interest.

Tom Jones invested $3000 at 6% compounded quarterly for 7 years.

There are $7 \times 4 = 28$ quarters or compounding periods in 7 years.

Interest of 6% per year $= \frac{6\%}{4} = 1\frac{1}{2}\%$ per period.

Find $1\frac{1}{2}\%$ across the top of the compound interest table and 28 down the left side to find **1.51722**.

Compound amount $= \$3000 \times$ **1.51722** $= \$4551.66$

Interest $= \$4551.66 - \$3000 = \$1551.66$

10.2 Finding the interest earned when the interest is compounded daily

Find the number of days that the deposit earns interest. Use the 90-day or 1-quarter table to calculate interest on $1.

Find compound amount using the formula

Compound amount = Principal × Table value

Find interest earned using the formula

Interest = Compound amount − Principal

Mary Carver deposits $1000 at $3\frac{1}{2}\%$ compounded daily on May 15. She withdraws the money on July 17. Find the compounded amount and interest earned.

May 15–May 31	16 days
June	30 days
July 1–July 17	17 days
	63 days

Table value = **1.006059089**

Compound amount $= \$1000 \times$ **1.006059089** $=$ **$1006.06**

Interest $=$ **$1006.06** $- \$1000 = \$6.06$

10.2 Finding the interest on time deposits

Use the compound interest for time deposit accounts table to find the interest on $1 compounded daily.

Find the compound amount using the formula

Compound amount = Principal × Table value

Find interest using the formula

Interest = Compound amount − Principal

Susan Barbee invests $50,000 in a certificate of deposit paying 5% compounded daily. Find the amount after 4 years.

Table value for 4 years at 5% = **1.22138603**

Compound amount $= \$50,000 \times$ **1.22138603** $= \$61,069.30$

Interest $= \$61,069.30 - \$50,000 = \$11,069.30$

10.2 Finding the effect of inflation on a pay raise

Find the new salary by multiplying the old salary by $(1 + \text{percent increase})$.

Find the salary needed to offset inflation by multiplying the old salary by $(1 + \text{inflation rate})$.

Find the gain or loss by subtracting.

Leticia Jaramillo earns $45,000 per year as a computer programmer. She gets a raise of 3.5% in a year in which inflation is 5%. Ignoring taxes, find the effect on her purchasing power.

New salary $= \$45,000 \times 1.035 =$ **$46,575**

Salary needed to offset
inflation $= \$45,000 \times 1.05 =$ **$47,250**

Loss in purchasing power $= \$47,250 - \$46,575 = \$675$

CONCEPTS	EXAMPLES
10.3 Finding the present value of a future amount	Sue York must pay a lump sum of $4500 in 6 years. What lump sum deposited today at 6% compounded quarterly will amount to $4500 in 6 years?

10.3 Finding the present value of a future amount

Determine the number of compounding periods (n).
Determine the interest per compounding period (i).
Use the values of n and i to determine the table value from the present value table.

Find present value from the following formula.

$$\text{Present value} = \text{Future value} \times \text{Table value}$$

Sue York must pay a lump sum of $4500 in 6 years. What lump sum deposited today at 6% compounded quarterly will amount to $4500 in 6 years?

$$\text{Number of compounding periods} = 6 \times 4 = 24$$

$$\text{Interest per compounding period} = \frac{6\%}{4} = 1\frac{1}{2}\% \text{ per period}$$

$$\text{Table value} = .69954$$

$$\text{Present value} = \$4500 \times .69954 = \$3147.93$$

case study

VALUING A CHAIN OF MCDONALD'S RESTAURANTS

James and Mary Watson own a small chain of McDonald's restaurants that is valued at $2,300,000. They believe that the chain will grow in value at 12% per year compounded annually for the next 5 years. If they sell the chain, the funds will be invested at a rate of 6% compounded semiannually. They expect inflation to be 4% per year for the next 5 years. Ignore taxes, and answer the following, rounding answers to the nearest dollar at each step.

1. Find the future value of the chain after 5 years. Then find the price they should sell the chain for if they wish to have the same future value at the end of 5 years.

1. _____

2. Find the future value of the chain if it grows at only 2% per year for 5 years. Then find the price they should ask for the chain given a 2% growth rate per year.

2. _____

3. What future value would the chain be worth if it grew at their expected rate of inflation? Find the price they should ask for the chain if it grows at the rate of inflation.

3. _____

4. Complete the following table.

Growth Rate	Future Value	Market Value Today
2%	_____	_____
4% (inflation)	_____	_____
12%	_____	_____

The value of the chain varies by more than one million dollars, depending on the rate of growth assumed for the business for the next 5 years.

INVESTIGATE

The interest rates that a bank pays depend on whether the money is in a checking account, money market account, savings account, or time deposit. Visit a local bank, and find the different interest rates that the bank will pay. Identify the conditions such as the minimum amount in an account, the minimum deposit, and the length of time the money must be on deposit to earn each interest rate.

case ▷ point summary exercise

BANK OF AMERICA

www.bankofamerica.com

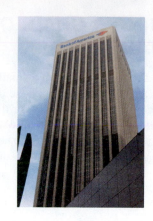

Facts:

- 1904: Founded by son of Italian immigrants
- 1930s: Survived the Great Depression
- 2008: Acquired Countrywide Financial (home loans)
- 2009: Acquired Merrill Lynch (investments)

The 2008–2010 financial crisis was caused by a speculative bubble in home prices amidst far too much debt. As home prices fell, the excessive debt of families, banks, and other financial institutions became obvious. People spent less and tried to save or simply survive for those who had lost their jobs and homes. Corporations cut costs by laying off workers and rapidly slowing the inventory flowing in global supply chains. Home builders built far fewer homes and tried to quickly reduce debt. Banks lent less and credit became very difficult to obtain. As the losses mounted, stock markets fell sharply. By the end of 2008, many governments around the world reacted to prevent another Great Depression like the one that occurred in the 1930s.

To keep the economic systems working, the U.S. government spent more than $1 trillion ($1,000,000,000,000) to support failing financial institutions and banks, extend unemployment benefits, increase employment, and support the sales of cars and homes. When it appeared that Countrywide Financial (home loans) and Merrill Lynch (investments) were in serious trouble, the U.S. government helped broker deals in which Bank of America took over both firms with the help of government loans and guarantees. However, Bank of America repaid the $45 billion in debt to the government at the end of 2009.

To demonstrate the effect of the recent financial crisis, we will use a small custom home builder called Horizon Homes which used Bank of America. As you can see, this firm first showed losses in 2007 since home builders were hit before many other types of firms in this financial crisis.

1. Find the gross profit for each year by multiplying gross sales by the profit margin.

Year	Gross Sales	Profit Margin	Profit or Loss	
2006	$92,080,000	4.6%	_____	
2007	$64,160,000	−12.3%	_____	Financial crisis begins
2008	$28,034,000	−30.5%	_____	Firm struggles to survive
2009	$15,509,000	−11.4%	_____	
2010 (projected)	$24,000,000	2.0%	_____	Assumes modest recovery

2. In 1995, managers at Horizon Homes had anticipated eventual financial problems and they invested $2,500,000 earning 6% per year (ignore taxes). Find the future value of this investment in 2007 when the firm had its first big loss. Was the value of the investment enough to offset the 2007 loss?

2. _____

3. **(a)** Add the losses for 2007, 2008, and 2009 together. **(b)** Find the present value that needed to be set aside in 1995 at 6% per year to offset the total losses for the three years. *Hint:* For simplicity, assume that the total of the 3 years' losses occurred in the middle year of 2008.

(a) _____

(b) _____

4. Business entails risk, which is the possibility that unexpected bad things happen. For example, two bad things that can happen in business are that the principal manager may be injured in a car accident and unable to work or a financial crisis may occur. Discuss what managers can do to better prepare for risk.

Discussion: Do families also face risk? Explain using examples. If so, discuss what parents can do to prepare for risk.

Chapter 10 Test

To help you review, the numbers in brackets show the section in which the topic was discussed.

In each of these problems, round to the nearest cent. Find the compound amount and the interest earned for the following. [10.1]

	Amount	Rate	Compounded	Time (Years)	Compound Amount	Interest Earned
1.	$8700	10%	annually	8	_____	_____
2.	$12,000	6%	semiannually	5	_____	_____
3.	$9800	6%	semiannually	5	_____	_____
4.	$12,500	10%	quarterly	4	_____	_____

Find the interest earned by the following. Assume $3\frac{1}{2}$% interest compounded daily. [10.2]

5. $6400 deposited September 24 and withdrawn December 15 ·

5. _____

6. $63,340 deposited December 5 and withdrawn March 2

6. _____

7. $37,650 deposited December 12 and withdrawn on February 29 (leap year)

7. _____

Find the present value of the following. [10.3]

	Amount Needed	Time (Years)	Rate	Compounded	Present Value
8.	$35,000	20	8%	annually	_____
9.	$15,750	7	6%	quarterly	_____
10.	$56,900	10	4%	semiannually	_____

Solve the following application problems.

11. A local branch of Gamestop, Inc., deposited $12,500 in a savings account on July 3 and then deposited an additional $3450 in the account on August 5. Find the balance on October 1 assuming an interest rate of $3\frac{1}{2}$% compounded daily. [10.2]

11. _____

12. Discount Auto Insurance deposited $1800 in a savings account paying $3\frac{1}{2}$% compounded daily on January 1 and deposited an additional $2300 in the account on March 12. Find the balance on April 1. [10.2]

12. _____

13. Mike George deposits $4000 in a certificate of deposit for 5 years. Find the compound amount if the interest rate is 6% compounded daily. [10.2]

13. _____

14. Benton Signs places $35,000 in a 2-year certificate of deposit yielding 5% compounded daily and uses it for collateral for a loan. Find the compound amount. [10.2]

14. _____

15. Liz Mulig earns $52,000 per year as a philosophy professor. She receives a raise of 2.5% in a year in which the CPI increases by 3.8%. Ignoring taxes, find the effect of the two increases on her purchasing power. [10.2]

15. _____

16. James Arnosti makes $65,000 per year as an editor for a publisher. He was notified of a 1.5% raise in a year in which the CPI increased by 4%. Find the gain or loss in his purchasing power. [10.2]

16. _____

17. A note for $3500 was made at 8% per year compounded annually for 3 years. Find **(a)** the maturity value and **(b)** the present value of the note assuming 5% per year compounded semiannually. **[10.3]**

(a) _____

(b) _____

18. Computers, Inc., accepted a 2-year note for $12,540 in lieu of immediate payment for computer equipment sold to a local firm. Find **(a)** the maturity value given a 10% rate compounded annually and **(b)** the present value of the note at 6% per year compounded semiannually. **[10.3]**

(a) _____

(b) _____

19. A business worth $180,000 is expected to grow at 12% per year compounded annually for the next 4 years. **(a)** Find the expected future value. **(b)** If funds from the sale of the business today would be placed in an account yielding 8% compounded semiannually, what would be the minimum acceptable price for the business at this time? **[10.3]**

(a) _____

(b) _____

20. A corporation worth $40 million is expected to grow at 8% per year compounded annually for 5 years. **(a)** Find the future value to the nearest million. **(b)** The owners then propose to sell the firm and invest the proceeds in a new venture that should grow at 12% compounded annually for 4 years. Beginning with the future value from part **(a)** rounded to the nearest million, find the expected future value to the nearest million at the end of 4 additional years. **[10.1]**

(a) _____

(b) _____

Chapters 9–10 / Cumulative Review

CHAPTERS 9 AND 10

Round money amounts to the nearest cent, time to the nearest day, and rates to the nearest tenth of a percent.

Find the value of the unknown quantity using simple interest. Use banker's interest. **[9.1–9.2]**

	Interest	Principal	Rate	Time	
1.	_____	$6800	8%	6 months	1. _____
2.	_____	$6200	9.7%	250 days	2. _____
3.	$165.28	_____	7%	100 days	3. _____
4.	$475	_____	9.5%	180 days	4. _____
5.	$249.38	$10,500	_____	90 days	5. _____
6.	$733.33	$12,000	_____	200 days	6. _____
7.	$202.22	$9100	10%	_____	7. _____
8.	$915	$18,300	12%	_____	8. _____

Find the discount and the proceeds. **[9.3]**

	Face Value	Discount Rate	Time (Days)	Discount	Proceeds
9.	$9000	12%	90	_____	_____
10.	$875	$6\frac{1}{2}\%$	210	_____	_____

Find the net proceeds when each of the following is discounted. **[9.4]**

	Maturity Value	Discount Rate	Discount Period	Net Proceeds
11.	$5000	10%	90 days	_____
12.	$12,000	12%	150 days	_____

Find the compound amounts for the following. **[10.1]**

13. $1000 at 4% compounded annually for 17 years

13. _____

14. $3520 at 8% compounded annually for 10 years

14. _____

Find the interest earned and compound amounts for each of the following. Assume $3\frac{1}{2}\%$ interest compounded daily. **[10.2]**

	Amount	Date Deposited	Date Withdrawn	Interest Earned	Compound Amount
15.	$12,600	March 24	June 3	_____	_____
16.	$7500	Nov. 20	Feb. 14	_____	_____

Find the present value and the amount of interest earned for the following. Round to the nearest cent. **[10.3]**

	Amount Needed	Time (Years)	Interest	Compounded	Present Value	Interest
17.	$1000	7	8%	annually	_____	_____
18.	$19,000	9	5%	semiannually	_____	_____

Solve the following application problems. Use a 360-day year where applicable.

19. Cathy Cockrell signed a 180-day simple discount note with a rate of 10% and a face value of $25,000. Find **(a)** the interest and **(b)** the proceeds. **[9.3]**

(a) _____

(b) _____

20. As a project manager, Regina Foster received a bonus of $18,000 for completing a difficult project on time. She invests it at 6% compounded quarterly for 5 years. Find the future value. **[10.1]**

20. _____

21. A divorce settlement requires Samantha James to pay her ex-spouse $12,000 in 2 years. What lump sum can be invested today at 5% compounded semiannually so that enough will be available for the payment? **[10.3]**

21. _____

22. Tom Davis owes $7850 to a relative. He has agreed to repay the money in 5 months, at an interest rate of 6%. One month before the loan is due, the relative discounts the loan at the bank. The bank charges a 7.92% discount rate. How much money does the relative receive? **[9.4]**

22. _____

23. The owner of Jessica's Cookies has an extra $3200 that she puts into a savings account paying $3\frac{1}{2}\%$ per year compounded daily. Find the interest if the funds are left there for 65 days. **[10.2]**

23. _____

Annuities, Stocks, and Bonds

case IN point

ROMAN RODRIGUEZ received his associate of arts degree in computer information systems at American River College and then received a bachelor's degree in the same field of study at a 4-year university. He worked in various computer labs at the community college when he was a student and was very pleased when he was offered a full-time job after graduation.

The director of the Human Resources Department explained health insurance and retirement plan benefits to Rodriguez. Roman already knew that contributions he made into the retirement plan would be tax deductible, thereby reducing his current taxes. However, he was surprised to learn that the community college would match any contributions he made into the retirement plan up to 5% of his annual salary.

Roman wrote down his thoughts about the retirement plan:

1. He can put up to 5% of his income into the plan.
2. The contribution is tax deductible, thereby reducing his current income taxes.
3. The college will contribute an equal amount to his plan.
4. Funds in the plan grow income-tax free until taken out.

Roman happily signed up to contribute 5% of his salary to his retirement plan.

11.1 Annuities and Retirement Accounts

OBJECTIVES

1 Define the basic terms involved with annuities.
2 Find the amount of an annuity.
3 Find the amount of an annuity due.
4 Understand different retirement accounts and find the amount of a retirement account.

case IN point

The benefits coordinator at the college asked Roman Rodriguez if he preferred an annuity paying a guaranteed interest or one invested in a mutual fund containing stocks. Rodriguez knew that he needed to be careful, since it was his financial future they were discussing.

OBJECTIVE 1 Define the basic terms involved with annuities. In Chapter 10, we discussed lump sums that were invested for periods of time. In this chapter, we talk about an **annuity**, or a series of equal payments made at regular intervals. Monthly mortgage payments, quarterly payments by a company into an employee retirement account, and monthly checks paid by Social Security to a retired couple are examples of annuities. The following graph shows why people buy annuities.

Numbers in the News

Top Reasons People Buy Annuities:

Guaranteed income for life	80%
Safe retirement investment	72%
Suggested by an advisor/broker	64%
No need to make investment decisions	64%
Offered through employer	46%

Note: Multiple responses allowed

DATA: Mintel annuities study

The two basic purposes of an annuity are to

1. accumulate money for a future need such as a cash payment for a new factory, or
2. make regular monthly payments from an accumulated sum of money such as monthly benefits from a retirement plan.

In the second type of annuity, the amount of money in the annuity decreases as payments are made. Here are some other important definitions you need to know.

Ordinary annuity: one in which payments are made at the end of each period
Payment period: time between payments
Term of the annuity: time needed for all payments to be made

Interest calculations for annuities are done using compound interest. The total amount in an annuity on a future date is the **amount, compound amount, or future value of the annuity**. These terms are used interchangeably.

Suppose that a company uses an annuity to save money to purchase a new vehicle. Assume the company makes deposits of $3000 *at the end of each year* for 6 years into an account earning 8% compounded annually. The first deposit is made at the end of year 1 and earns interest for 5 years. Use the compound interest table in Section 10.1 (page 402) for 5 years and 8% to find the future value of the first payment.

$$\$3000 \times \mathbf{1.46933} = \$4407.99$$

The future value of the annuity is *the sum* of the compound amounts of all six payments. The annuity ends on the day of the last payment. Therefore, the last payment, which is made at the end of year 6, earns no interest.

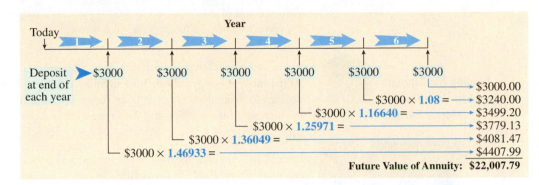

The future value of the annuity is $22,007.79. Find the total amount deposited in the annuity and interest earned as follows:

$$\text{Total deposits} = 6 \text{ years} \times \$3000 \text{ per year} = \$18,000$$

$$\begin{aligned}
\text{Interest earned} &= \text{Future value of annuity} - \text{Total deposits} \\
&= \qquad \$22,007.79 \qquad - \qquad \$18,000 \\
&= \$4007.79
\end{aligned}$$

OBJECTIVE 2 Find the amount of an annuity. The amount of an annuity can also be found using the amount of an annuity table on page 439. The number from the table is the amount or future value of an annuity with a payment of $1. The amount of an annuity with any payment is found as follows.

> **Finding Amount of an Annuity**
>
> Amount = Payment × Number from amount of an annuity table

As a check, reconsider the annuity of $3000 at the end of each year for 6 years at 8% compounded annually. Locate 8% at the top of the table on page 439 and 6 periods in the far left (or far right) column to find **7.33593.**

$$\text{Amount} = \$3000 \times \mathbf{7.33593} = \$22,007.79$$

This amount is identical to the amount calculated earlier.

Finding the Value of an Annuity and Interest Earned

EXAMPLE 1

The community college will match Roman Rodriguez's contribution into his retirement plan, but only up to 5% of his salary. In other words, the college will put $1 into his retirement plan for every $1 that Rodriguez puts into it, but they will not contribute more than 5% of his $32,000 yearly salary. Rodriguez decides to put 5% of his salary into the retirement plan. Using quarterly calculations, find the future value in 8 years **(a)** if the account earns 4% compounded quarterly and **(b)** if the account earns 8% compounded quarterly. **(c)** Then find the difference between the two future values.

SOLUTION

$$\text{Salary per quarter} = \$32,000 \div 4 = \$8000$$

$$\begin{aligned}
\text{Total contributions} &= \text{Rodriguez's contributions} + \textbf{Employer's matching contributions} \\
&= \qquad .05 \times \$8000 \qquad + \qquad \mathbf{.05 \times \$8000} \\
&= \qquad\quad \$400 \qquad\qquad + \qquad\quad \mathbf{\$400} \\
&= \$800 \text{ invested per quarter}
\end{aligned}$$

(a) Interest of $\frac{4\%}{4} = 1\%$ is earned per quarter for $8 \times 4 = 32$ quarters. Look across the top of the table for 1% and down the side for 32 periods to find **37.86901.**

$$\text{Amount} = \$800 \times \mathbf{37.86901} = \mathbf{\$30,295.21} \text{ (rounded)}$$

(b) Interest of $\frac{8\%}{4} = 2\%$ is earned per quarter for $8 \times 4 = 32$ quarters. Look across the top of the table for 2% and down the side for 32 periods to find **44.22703**.

$$\text{Amount} = \$800 \times \textbf{44.22703} = \textbf{\$35,381.62} \text{ (rounded)}$$

(c) Difference $= \$35,381.62 - \$30,295.21 = \textbf{\$5086.41}$

QUICK CHECK 1

At the end of every quarter, $2000 is put into a retirement plan that earns 6% compounded quarterly. Find the future value in 5 years.

Finding the Amount of an Annuity and Interest Earned

EXAMPLE 2

At the birth of her grandson, Junella Smith commits to help pay for his college education. She decides to make deposits of $600 at the end of each 6 months into an account for 17 years. Find the amount of the annuity and the interest earned, assuming 6% compounded semiannually.

SOLUTION

Interest of $\frac{6\%}{2} = 3\%$ is earned each semiannual period. There are $2 \times 17 = 34$ semiannual periods in 17 years. Find 3% across the top and 34 periods down the side of the table for **57.73018**.

$$\text{Amount} = \$600 \times \textbf{57.73018} = \$34,638.11$$

$$\text{Interest} = \$34,638.11 - (\textbf{34} \times \textbf{\$600}) = \textbf{\$14,238.11} \text{ (rounded)}$$

Smith knows that a college education will cost a lot more in 17 years than it does now, but she also knows that $34,638.11 will be of great help to her grandson.

Financial Calculator Solution   In this example, payment ($600), interest rate per compounding period (3%), and number of compounding periods (34) are known. Future value is the unknown. Enter the payment as a negative number since it is an outflow of cash that Junella Smith pays each month. Finally, press the [FV] key to find the future value, which is a positive value since it will be an inflow of cash to her grandson.

 $\quad -600$ [PMT] 3 [i] 34 [n] [FV] 34638.11 (rounded)

QUICK CHECK 2

Bob Nelson deposits $250 into a retirement account at the end of every month for 30 months. The fund holds international stocks and Nelson optimistically thinks it may yield 12% compounded monthly. Find the future amount.

OBJECTIVE 3 Find the amount of an annuity due. Payments were made at the *end of each period* in the ordinary annuities discussed previously. In contrast, an annuity in which payments are made at the *beginning of each time period* is called an **annuity due**.

Finding the Amount of an Annuity Due

Step 1   Add 1 to the number of periods.

Step 2   Find: Amount = Payment × Number from amount of an annuity table.

Step 3   Subtract 1 payment.

Finding the Amount of an Annuity Due

EXAMPLE 3

Mr. and Mrs. Thompson set up an investment program using an *annuity due* with payments of $500 at the *beginning of each quarter*. Find **(a)** the amount of the annuity and **(b)** the interest if they make payments for 7 years into an investment account expected to pay 8% compounded quarterly.

SOLUTION

> **Quick TIP ▼**
>
> For an annuity due, be sure to add 1 period to the number of compounding periods and subtract 1 payment from the amount calculated.

(a) Step 1 Interest of $\frac{8\%}{4} = 2\%$ is earned each quarter. There are $4 \times 7 = 28$ periods in 7 years. Since it is an annuity due, add 1 period to 28, making 29 periods.

Step 2 Look across the top of the table for 2% and down the side for 29 periods to find **38.79223**.

$$\$500 \times \textbf{38.79223} = \textbf{\$19,396.12} \text{ (rounded)}$$

Step 3 Now subtract one payment to find the amount of the annuity due.

$$\text{Amount of annuity due} = \textbf{\$19,396.12} - \$500 = \$18,896.12$$

(b) Subtract the 28 payments (7 years × 4 payments per year) of $500 each to find the interest.

Interest = $18,896.12 − (**28** × **$500**) = $4896.12

The calculator solution to finding the interest in part **(b)** follows.

18896.12 [−] 28 [×] 500 [=] 4896.12

Note: Refer to Appendix B for calculator basics.

QUICK CHECK 3

If $1000 is deposited at the beginning of every six months into an account that earns 5% compounded semiannually, find the amount after 8 years.

Amount of an Annuity Table

PERIOD				INTEREST RATE PER PERIOD								PERIOD
n	1%	1½%	2%	2½%	3%	4%	5%	6%	8%	10%	12%	*n*
1	1.00000	1.00000	1.00000	1.00000	1.00000	1.00000	1.00000	1.00000	1.00000	1.00000	1.00000	1
2	2.01000	2.01500	2.02000	2.02500	2.03000	2.04000	2.05000	2.06000	2.08000	2.10000	2.12000	2
3	3.03010	3.04522	3.06040	3.07562	3.09090	3.12160	3.15250	3.18360	3.24640	3.31000	3.37440	3
4	4.06040	4.09090	4.12161	4.15252	4.18363	4.24646	4.31013	4.37462	4.50611	4.64100	4.77933	4
5	5.10101	5.15227	5.20404	5.25633	5.30914	5.41632	5.52563	5.63709	5.86660	6.10510	6.35285	5
6	6.15202	6.22955	6.30812	6.38774	6.46841	6.63298	6.80191	6.97532	7.33593	7.71561	8.11519	6
7	7.21354	7.32299	7.43428	7.54743	7.66246	7.89829	8.14201	8.39384	8.92280	9.48717	10.08901	7
8	8.28567	8.43284	8.58297	8.73612	8.89234	9.21423	9.54911	9.89747	10.63663	11.43589	12.29969	8
9	9.36853	9.55933	9.75463	9.95452	10.15911	10.58280	11.02656	11.49132	12.48756	13.57948	14.77566	9
10	10.46221	10.70272	10.94972	11.20338	11.46388	12.00611	12.57789	13.18079	14.48656	15.93742	17.54874	10
11	11.56683	11.86326	12.16872	12.48347	12.80780	13.48635	14.20679	14.97164	16.64549	18.53117	20.65458	11
12	12.68250	13.04121	13.41209	13.79555	14.19203	15.02581	15.91713	16.86994	18.97713	21.38428	24.13313	12
13	13.80933	14.23683	14.68033	15.14044	15.61779	16.62684	17.71298	18.88214	21.49530	24.52271	28.02911	13
14	14.94742	15.45038	15.97394	16.51895	17.08632	18.29191	19.59863	21.01507	24.21492	27.97498	32.39260	14
15	16.09690	16.68214	17.29342	17.93193	18.59891	20.02359	21.57856	23.27597	27.15211	31.77248	37.27971	15
16	17.25786	17.93237	18.63929	19.38022	20.15688	21.82453	23.65749	25.67253	30.32428	35.94973	42.75328	16
17	18.43044	19.20136	20.01207	20.86473	21.76159	23.69751	25.84037	28.21288	33.75023	40.54470	48.88367	17
18	19.61475	20.48938	21.41231	22.38635	23.41444	25.64541	28.13238	30.90565	37.45024	45.59917	55.74971	18
19	20.81090	21.79672	22.84056	23.94601	25.11687	27.67123	30.53900	33.75999	41.44626	51.15909	63.43968	19
20	22.01900	23.12367	24.29737	25.54466	26.87037	29.77808	33.06595	36.78559	45.76196	57.27500	72.05244	20
21	23.23919	24.47052	25.78332	27.18327	28.67649	31.96920	35.71925	39.99273	50.42292	64.00250	81.69874	21
22	24.47159	25.83758	27.29898	28.86286	30.53678	34.24797	38.50521	43.39229	55.45676	71.40275	92.50258	22
23	25.71630	27.22514	28.84496	30.58443	32.45288	36.61789	41.43048	46.99583	60.89330	79.54302	104.60289	23
24	26.97346	28.63352	30.42186	32.34904	34.42647	39.08260	44.50200	50.81558	66.76476	88.49733	118.15524	24
25	28.24320	30.06302	32.03030	34.15776	36.45926	41.64591	47.72710	54.86451	73.10594	98.34706	133.33387	25
26	29.52563	31.51397	33.67091	36.01171	38.55304	44.31174	51.11345	59.15638	79.95442	109.18177	150.33393	26
27	30.82089	32.98668	35.34432	37.91200	40.70963	47.08421	54.66913	63.70577	87.35077	121.09994	169.37401	27
28	32.12910	34.48148	37.05121	39.85980	42.93092	49.96758	58.40258	68.52811	95.33883	134.20994	190.69889	28
29	33.45039	35.99870	38.79223	41.85630	45.21885	52.96629	62.32271	73.63980	103.96594	148.63093	214.58275	29
30	34.78489	37.53868	40.56808	43.90270	47.57542	56.08494	66.43885	79.05819	113.28321	164.49402	241.33268	30
31	36.13274	39.10176	42.37944	46.00027	50.00268	59.32834	70.76079	84.80168	123.34587	181.94342	271.29261	31
32	37.86901	40.68829	44.22703	48.15028	52.50276	62.70147	75.29883	90.88978	134.21354	201.13777	304.84772	32
33	38.86901	42.29861	46.11157	50.35403	55.07784	66.20953	80.06377	97.34316	145.95062	222.25154	342.42945	33
34	40.25770	43.93309	48.03380	52.61289	57.73018	69.85791	85.06696	104.18375	158.62667	245.47670	384.52098	34
35	41.66028	45.59209	49.99448	54.92821	60.46208	73.65222	90.32031	111.43478	172.31680	271.02437	431.66350	35

OBJECTIVE 4 Understand different retirement accounts and find the amount of a retirement account. Many students see retirement as something very far away and mistakenly think they can or should wait until they are much older (say 50—ouch, that's old!) to worry about it. However, it takes a long time to save enough to retire comfortably. The clipping shows what can happen to someone who has not saved enough.

Retired Without Enough Assets...

In 2011, Tom Wheat found out that his Social Security retirement check would be $1247 per month. Given that he had his home paid for and had saved up some money, he retired. However, he has since developed diabetes and needs more money each month than he thought. Tom is almost 70 now, can no longer work, and is barely getting by on his fixed income from the government. He may need to sell his home, but where would he live?

In Chapter 10, we saw that it takes time to accumulate a large amount of money. So, the idea is to start saving for retirement as soon as possible. Thankfully, you have help. Many employers make contributions into a retirement plan for their employees. The government allows you to deduct your own contributions into a retirement plan and allows funds in the plan to grow free of income taxes until you retire. This type of savings reduces current income taxes and grows tax free. Try to work for an employer which contributes to your retirement plan and begin saving your own money as soon as possible. Retirement plans are for everyone, *especially* recent college graduates.

Even if your employer does not sponsor a retirement plan, an employee can set up an **individual retirement account (IRA)** at a bank or brokerage firm such as Merrill Lynch or Schwab. Each person in a married couple can contribute to an IRA even if only one of them works. Deposits to a **regular IRA** are usually tax deductible and grow income-tax free in the account until retirement. For example, putting $5000 into a regular IRA could reduce your combined federal and state income taxes by $1000 or more. The government is trying to encourage you to save for retirement. There is a penalty for taking money out of an IRA before age 59½ unless the withdrawal is related to disability, death, or expensive medical treatments or is used to pay for a first home or college expenses.

Another type of IRA is a **Roth IRA**. Deposits to a Roth IRA *are not excluded from federal taxes in the year paid*, so they do not reduce current income taxes. However, the deposits and interest grow tax-free. In addition, withdrawals from a Roth IRA at retirement **are not subject to income taxes** when withdrawn. This offers you a great opportunity to save money for retirement without having to pay taxes as you withdraw the funds. The following table may help you.

Roth IRA

WHICH IRA IS BEST FOR YOU?*		
	DEDUCTIBLE IRA	**ROTH IRA**
Tax deductible?	If you qualify	No
Taxable at withdrawal?	Yes	No
Penalty for early withdrawal?	Yes, prior to age 59.5	Yes
Mandatory withdrawal age?	70.5	None
Penalty-free withdrawals?	$10,000 for first-time home buyers; unlimited for education	$10,000 for first-time home buyers, after five-year wait; unlimited for education

*There are numerous rules related to each type of IRA. Research carefully before deciding which is best for you.

Allowable IRA Contribution

YEAR	AGE	
	UNDER 50	50 AND OVER
2010	$5000	$6000

The following figure shows some of the many reasons companies offer retirement plans to full-time employees. There are several different types of company-sponsored retirement plans. Two common plans are the **401(k)** plan for individuals working for private-sector companies and the **403(b)** plan for employees of public schools and certain tax-exempt organizations. The names 401(k) and 403(b) refer to sections of the Internal Revenue Service code that define these plans. Each of these plans allows an employer to deduct money from your paycheck *before* taxes are calculated and to invest those funds in the plan.

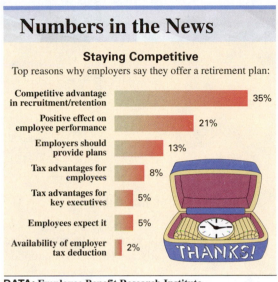

Numbers in the News

Staying Competitive
Top reasons why employers say they offer a retirement plan:

Competitive advantage in recruitment/retention	35%
Positive effect on employee performance	21%
Employers should provide plans	13%
Tax advantages for employees	8%
Tax advantages for key executives	5%
Employees expect it	5%
Availability of employer tax deduction	2%

DATA: Employee Benefit Research Institute

Quick TIP ▼

Individuals who pay FICA (Social Security) taxes are eligible for monthly payments from the Social Security system at retirement. Social Security benefits are in addition to any income from IRAs or company retirement plans.

Regular contributions into either an IRA or a company-sponsored retirement plan are an annuity. The amount of the annuity is found using the same methods discussed earlier in this section. Payments are at the end of each period in an ordinary annuity, and payments are at the beginning of each period in an annuity due.

Finding the Value of an IRA

EXAMPLE 4

At 27, Joann Gretz sets up an IRA with online broker Charles Schwab, where she plans to deposit $2000 at the end of each year until age 60. Find the amount of the annuity if she invests in **(a)** a bond fund that has historically yielded 6% compounded annually versus **(b)** a stock fund that has historically yielded 10% compounded annually. Assume that future yields equal historical yields.

SOLUTION

Age 60 is 60 − 27 = **33 years away**, so she will make deposits at the end of each year for 33 years.

(a) Bond fund: Look down the left column of the amount of an annuity table on page 439 at 33 years and across the top for 6% to find **97.34316**.

$$\text{Amount} = \$2000 \times 97.34316 = \$194{,}686.32 \text{ (rounded)}$$

(b) Stock fund: Look down the left column of the table for 33 years and across the top for 10% to find **222.25154**.

$$\text{Amount} = \$2000 \times 222.25154 = \$444{,}503.08$$

The differences in the two investments are shown in the figure. Gretz wants the larger amount, but she is worried she might lose money in the stock fund. See *Exercise 20* at the end of this section to find her investment choice.

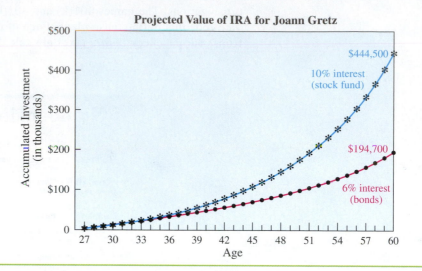

Projected Value of IRA for Joann Gretz

QUICK CHECK 4

Bill James plans to deposit $2500 in a regular IRA at the end of six months for the next 17 years until he retires. Find the future value if funds earn **(a)** 5% compounded semiannually and **(b)** 8% compounded semiannually.

Currently, more than 50 million people receive regular payments from Social Security. Workers can retire as early as age 62 and get reduced benefits, or they can wait until full retirement age and receive full benefits. The full retirement age will increase gradually until it reaches age 67 for people born after 1959. The bar graph shows the importance of Social Security to Americans.

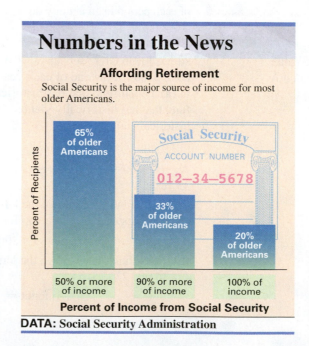

Numbers in the News

Affording Retirement

Social Security is the major source of income for most older Americans.

DATA: Social Security Administration

11.1 Exercises

The QUICK START *exercises in each section contain solutions to help you get started.*

Find the amount of the following ordinary annuities rounded to the nearest cent. Find the total interest earned. (See Examples 1 and 2.)

QUICK START

	Amount of Each Deposit	Deposited	Rate	Time (Years)	Amount of Annuity	Interest Earned
1.	$900	annually	5%	18	$25,319.14	$9119.14

$900 × 28.13238 = $25,319.14; *I* = $25,319.14 − (18 × $900) = $9119.14

2.	$2900	annually	8%	5	$17,013.14	$2513.14

$2900 × 5.86660 = $17,013.14; *I* = $17,013.14 − (5 × $2900) = $2513.14

3.	$7500	semiannually	6%	10	_____	_____
4.	$9200	semiannually	8%	5	_____	_____
5.	$3500	quarterly	10%	7	_____	_____
6.	$6900	quarterly	8%	4	_____	_____

Find the amount of the following annuities due rounded to the nearest cent. Find the total interest earned. (See Example 3.)

QUICK START

	Amount of Each Deposit	Deposited	Rate	Time (Years)	Amount of Annuity	Interest Earned
7.	$1200	annually	8%	5	$7603.12	$1603.12

Look up 8%, 5 + 1 = 6 periods, finding 7.33593. $1200 × 7.33593 − $1200 = $7603.12
Interest = $7603.12 − 5 × $1200 = $1603.12

8.	$400	annually	6%	6	$2957.54	$557.54

Look up 6%, 6 + 1 = 7 periods, finding 8.39384. $400 × 8.39384 − $400 = $2957.54
Interest = $2957.54 − 6 × $400 = $557.54

9.	$9500	semiannually	4%	9	_____	_____
10.	$1800	semiannually	5%	6	_____	_____
11.	$3800	quarterly	8%	3	_____	_____
12.	$10,200	quarterly	10%	5	_____	_____

ⓒ indicates an exercise that is related to the Case in Point feature.

13. Explain the difference between an annuity and an annuity due. (See Objectives 2 and 3.)

14. Describe the differences between an IRA, a 401(k), and a 403(b). (See Objective 4.)

Solve the following application problems.

QUICK START

15. RETIREMENT PLANNING Roman Rodriguez would like to know if he can retire in 35 years at age 60, when he plans to fish a lot. Assume the total deposit into his retirement account at the community college is $3800 at the end of each year and that the fund earns 6% per year. Find **(a)** the amount of the annuity and **(b)** the interest earned.

(a) Amount = $3800 × 111.43478 = $423,452.16 (rounded)
(b) Interest = $423,452.16 − 35 × $3800 = $290,452.16

(a) $423,452.16

(b) $290,452.16

16. SAVING FOR A HOME Jim and Betty Collins need an additional $6500 for a down payment on a home they hope to buy in 2 years. They invest $800 at the end of each quarter in an account earning 6% compounded quarterly. Find **(a)** the amount of the annuity and **(b)** the interest earned.

(a) _____

(b) _____

17. CHILD-CARE PAYMENTS Monique Chaney places $250 of her quarterly child support check into an annuity for the education of her child. She does this at the beginning of each quarter for 8 years into an account paying 8% per year, compounded quarterly. Find **(a)** the amount of the annuity and **(b)** the interest earned.

(a) _____

(b) _____

18. RETIREMENT Jason Horton works for Chevron as a welder on offshore drilling rigs. His retirement plan contributions are $3800 at the beginning of each 6-month period. Assume that the account grows at 6% compounded semiannually for 15 years. Find the **(a)** future value of the annuity and **(b)** the interest earned.

(a) _____

(b) _____

19. MUTUAL FUND INVESTING Sandra Gonzales deposits $1000 into a mutual fund containing international stocks at the end of each semiannual period for 12 years. Assume the fund earns 10% interest compounded semiannually and find the future value.

19. _____

20. T-BILL AND STOCK INVESTING Joann Gretz (see Example 4, page 441) decides to place half of her $2000 deposit at the end of each year into the bond fund and half into the stock fund. Assume the bond fund earns 6% compounded annually and the stock fund earns 10% compounded annually. Find the amount available in 33 years.

20. _____

QUICK CHECK ANSWERS

1. $46,247.34

2. $8696.22

3. $19,864.73

4. (a) $131,532.23 **(b)** $174,644.78

11.2 Present Value of an Ordinary Annuity

OBJECTIVES

1. Define the present value of an ordinary annuity.
2. Use the formula to find the present value of an ordinary annuity.
3. Find the equivalent cash price of an ordinary annuity.

OBJECTIVE 1 Define the present value of an ordinary annuity. Chapter 10 was about lump sums of money. In that chapter, present value was defined as the lump sum that must be deposited in an account today so that it will grow to the required future value by a certain date. Those calculations required the interest rate per compounding period (i) and the number of compounding periods (n), as do the calculations in this chapter.

Chapter 11 is about annuities that involve periodic payments. In Section 11.1, you learned how to find the future value of an annuity. In this section, you will learn how to find the present value of an annuity. The **present value of an annuity** can be thought of in two ways. The first way, described next, is an annuity that accumulates funds. The second uses up funds that have already been accumulated to make a series of payments.

> **Present Value of an Annuity**
>
> 1. Assume a firm needs $100,000 exactly 3 years from today. It can achieve that goal by making a single, lump-sum deposit today, or it can accumulate the $100,000 by making regular payments into an investment. Since both accumulate exactly the same future amount of $100,000 at the end of 3 years, the two methods can be thought of as equivalent to one another. (See Example 1.)
>
> 2. A divorced man must make a $1500 payment at the end of each quarter for child support until his daughter turns 18. The present value of this annuity is the amount that must be deposited today that will generate the needed payments. (See Example 2.)

OBJECTIVE 2 Use the formula to find the present value of an ordinary annuity. The present value of an annuity with periodic payments at the end of each period is found using values from the table.

> **Finding Present Value of an Annuity**
>
> $$\text{Present value of annuity} = \text{Payment} \times \frac{\text{Number from the present value}}{\text{of an annuity table}}$$

Finding the Present Value of an Annuity **EXAMPLE 1**

At the end of each quarter for 5 years, the Daily News deposits $4325 in an account paying 6% compounded quarterly. The goal is to accumulate funds for a new printing press. (**a**) Use the concepts of Section 11.1 to find the future value of the annuity. (**b**) Then find the lump sum (present value) that must be deposited today to accumulate the same future value.

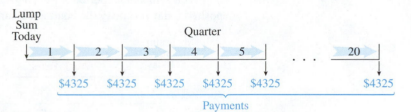

SOLUTION

(**a**) $\frac{6\%}{4} = 1.5\%$ per quarter; 5 years $\times 4 = 20$ quarters. Use the amount of an annuity table in Section 11.1 to find **23.12367**.

$$\text{Future value} = \$4325 \times \mathbf{23.12367} = \$100,009.87 \text{ (rounded)}$$

(**b**) It is not necessary to use this future value to find the present value of the annuity. Instead, use the present value of an annuity table with 1.5% per period and 20 periods to find **17.16864**.

$$\text{Present value} = \$4325 \times \mathbf{17.16864} = \$74,254.37$$

Thus, a deposit of $4325 at the end of every quarter for 5 years has a present value today of $74,254.37. If we assume 6% compounded quarterly and ignore income taxes, each of the following has exactly the same value:

1. 20 end-of-quarter deposits of $4325
2. A future value at the end of 5 years of $100,009.87
3. A present value on hand today of $74,254.37

QUICK CHECK 1

Walter and Beth Bates save $1200 at the end of each quarter for 7 years. Assume 8% compounded quarterly and find both **(a)** the future value and **(b)** the present value.

The three items listed at the end of the solution to Example 1 reinforce a very important idea in finance. The value of money depends on when it is available. Generally, money available today is worth more than money available in (say) 10 years. Lenders and investors use this idea every day to create profit. Suppose a bank lends you money today. It expects the interest on the debt to be enough to pay all bank expenses, make up for bad loans, and also make a profit. So, you have to pay the bank back more than you borrowed.

Finding the Present Value **EXAMPLE 2**

Tom and Brandy Barrett recently divorced. The judge gave custody of their 4-year-old son to Brandy and ruled that Tom must pay $900 in child support to Brandy at the end of each quarter until the son turns 16. Find the lump sum that Tom must put into an account earning 6% compounded quarterly to cover the periodic payments. Find the interest earned.

SOLUTION

> **Quick TIP** ▼
>
> Although the $900 withdrawals to Brandy are at the end of each quarter, the original lump sum must be deposited at the beginning of the first year.

Payments must be made for $16 - 4 = 12$ years, or for $12 \times 4 = 48$ quarters. The interest rate per quarter is $\frac{6\%}{4} = 1.5\%$ per quarter. Look across the top of the present value of an annuity table for 1.5% and down the side for 48 payments to find **34.04255**.

$$\text{Present value of annuity} = \$900 \times \textbf{34.04255} = \$30,638.30 \text{ (rounded)}$$

A deposit of $30,638.30 today will make 48 end-of-quarter payments of $900 each. Interest earned during the 12 years is the sum of all payments less the original lump sum.

$$\text{Interest} = (48 \times \$900) - \$30,638.30 = \textbf{\$12,561.70}$$

QUICK CHECK 2

Find the lump sum that must be set aside today to make end-of-month payments of $1000 for 2 years, assuming 12% compounded monthly. Then find the interest earned.

Finding the Present Value **EXAMPLE 3**

An American company hires a project manager to work in Saudi Arabia. The contract states that if the manager works there for 5 years, he will receive an extra benefit of $15,000 at the end of each semiannual period for the 8 years that follow. Find the lump sum that can be deposited today to satisfy the contract, assuming 6% compounded semiannually.

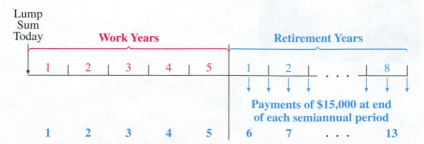

SOLUTION

The project manager works from years 1 to 5. He then receives two $15,000 annuity payments each year during years 6 through 13. Solve this problem in two steps.

1. _Find the present value **at the beginning of year 6** of the annuity with $15,000 payments._

   Use $\frac{6\%}{2} = 3\%$ per compounding period and $2 \times 8 = 16$ compounding periods to find **12.56110** in the present value of an annuity table.

   Present value of annuity = $15,000 × **12.56110** = $188,416.50

   This is the _present value_ of the annuity needed at the beginning of year 6 to fund payments in years 6 through 13. But it is also the _future value_ needed for the investment made today that will fund the eventual payments.

2. _Find the future value **needed today** to accumulate the $188,416.50 by the end of year 5._

   Use the table showing present value of a dollar in Section 10.3 (page 422) with $\frac{6\%}{2} = 3\%$ per compounding period and $5 \times 2 = 10$ compounding periods to find **.74409**.

   Present value needed today = $188,416.50 × **.74409** = $140,198.83

   A lump sum of $140,198.83 today will grow to $188,416.50 in 5 years. The $188,416.50 at the end of year 5 is enough to make 16 semiannual payments of $15,000 each during years 6 through 13.

Present Value of an Annuity Table

PERIOD	1%	1½%	2%	2½%	3%	4%	5%	6%	8%	10%	PERIOD
					INTEREST RATE PER PERIOD						
1	.99010	.98522	.98039	.97561	.97087	.96154	.95238	.94340	.92593	.90909	1
2	1.97040	1.95588	1.94156	1.92742	1.91347	1.88609	1.85941	1.83339	1.78326	1.73554	2
3	2.94099	2.91220	2.88388	2.85602	2.82861	2.77509	2.72325	2.67301	2.57710	2.48685	3
4	3.90197	3.85438	3.80773	3.76197	3.71710	3.62990	3.54595	3.46511	3.31213	3.16987	4
5	4.85343	4.78264	4.71346	4.64583	4.57971	4.45182	4.32948	4.21236	3.99271	3.79079	5
6	5.79548	5.69719	5.60143	5.50813	5.41719	5.24214	5.07569	4.91732	4.62288	4.35526	6
7	6.72819	6.59821	6.47199	6.34939	6.23028	6.00205	5.78637	5.58238	5.20637	4.86842	7
8	7.65168	7.48593	7.32548	7.17014	7.01969	6.73274	6.46321	6.20979	5.74664	5.33493	8
9	8.56602	8.36052	8.16224	7.97087	7.78611	7.43533	7.10782	6.80169	6.24689	5.75902	9
10	9.47130	9.22218	8.98259	8.75206	8.53020	8.11090	7.72173	7.36009	6.71008	6.14457	10
11	10.36763	10.07112	9.78685	9.51421	9.25262	8.76048	8.30641	7.88687	7.13896	6.49506	11
12	11.25508	10.90751	10.57534	10.25776	9.95400	9.38507	8.86325	8.38384	7.53608	6.81369	12
13	12.13374	11.73153	11.34837	10.98318	10.63496	9.98565	9.39357	8.85268	7.90378	7.10336	13
14	13.00370	12.54338	12.10625	11.69091	11.29607	10.56312	9.89864	9.29498	8.24424	7.36669	14
15	13.86505	13.34323	12.84926	12.38138	11.93794	11.11839	10.37966	9.71225	8.55948	7.60608	15
16	14.71787	14.13126	13.57771	13.05500	12.56110	11.65230	10.83777	10.10590	8.85137	7.82371	16
17	15.56225	14.90765	14.29187	13.71220	13.16612	12.16567	11.27407	10.47726	9.12164	8.02155	17
18	16.39827	15.67256	14.99203	14.35336	13.75351	12.65930	11.68959	10.82760	9.37189	8.20141	18
19	17.22601	16.42617	15.67846	14.97889	14.32380	13.13394	12.08532	11.15812	9.60360	8.36492	19
20	18.04555	17.16864	16.35143	15.58916	14.87747	13.59033	12.46221	11.46992	9.81815	8.51356	20
21	18.85698	17.90014	17.01121	16.18455	15.41502	14.02916	12.82115	11.76408	10.01680	8.64869	21
22	19.66038	18.62082	17.65805	16.76541	15.93692	14.45112	13.16300	12.04158	10.20074	8.77154	22
23	20.45582	19.33086	18.29220	17.33211	16.44361	14.85684	13.48857	12.30338	10.37106	8.88322	23
24	21.24339	20.03041	18.91393	17.88499	16.93554	15.24696	13.79864	12.55036	10.52876	8.98474	24
25	22.02316	20.71961	19.52346	18.42438	17.41315	15.62208	14.09394	12.78336	10.67478	9.07704	25
26	22.79520	21.39863	20.12104	18.95061	17.87684	15.98277	14.37519	13.00317	10.80998	9.16095	26
27	23.55961	22.06762	20.70690	19.46401	18.32703	16.32959	14.64303	13.21053	10.93516	9.23722	27
28	24.31644	22.72672	21.28127	19.96489	18.76411	16.66306	14.89813	13.40616	11.05108	9.30657	28

(continued)

Present Value of an Annuity Table (continued)

PERIOD	1%	1½%	2%	2½%	3%	4%	5%	6%	8%	10%	PERIOD
						Interest Rate per Period					
29	25.06579	23.37608	21.84438	20.45355	19.18845	16.98371	15.14107	13.59072	11.15841	9.36961	29
30	25.80771	24.01584	22.39646	20.93029	19.60044	17.29203	15.37245	13.76483	11.25778	9.42691	30
31	26.54229	24.64615	22.93770	21.39541	20.00043	17.58849	15.59281	13.92909	11.34980	9.47901	31
32	27.26959	25.26714	23.46833	21.84918	20.38877	17.87355	15.80268	14.08404	11.43500	9.52638	32
33	27.98969	25.87895	23.98856	22.29188	20.76579	18.14765	16.00255	14.23023	11.51389	9.56943	33
34	28.70267	26.48173	24.49859	22.72379	21.13184	18.41120	16.19290	14.36814	11.58693	9.60857	34
35	29.40858	27.07559	24.99862	23.14516	21.48722	18.66461	16.37419	14.49825	11.65457	9.64416	35
36	30.10751	27.66068	25.48884	23.55625	21.83225	18.90828	16.54685	14.62099	11.71719	9.67651	36
37	30.79951	28.23713	25.96945	23.95732	22.16724	19.14258	16.71129	14.73678	11.77518	9.70592	37
38	31.48466	28.80505	26.44064	24.34860	22.49246	19.36786	16.86789	14.84602	11.82887	9.73265	38
39	32.16303	29.36458	26.90259	24.73034	22.80822	19.58448	17.01704	14.94907	11.87858	9.75696	39
40	32.83469	29.91585	27.35548	25.10278	23.11477	19.79277	17.15909	15.04630	11.92461	9.77905	40
41	33.49969	30.45896	27.79949	25.46612	23.41240	19.99305	17.29437	15.13802	11.96723	9.79914	41
42	34.15811	30.99405	28.23479	25.82061	23.70136	20.18563	17.42321	15.22454	12.00670	9.81740	42
43	34.81001	31.52123	28.66156	26.16645	23.98190	20.37079	17.54591	15.30617	12.04324	9.83400	43
44	35.45545	32.04062	29.07996	26.50385	24.25427	20.54884	17.66277	15.38318	12.07707	9.84909	44
45	36.09451	32.55234	29.49016	26.83302	24.51871	20.72004	17.77407	15.45583	12.10840	9.86281	45
46	36.72724	33.05649	29.89231	27.15417	24.77545	20.88465	17.88007	15.52437	12.13741	9.87528	46
47	37.35370	33.55319	30.28658	27.46748	25.02471	21.04294	17.98102	15.58903	12.16427	9.88662	47
48	37.97396	34.04255	30.67312	27.77315	25.26671	21.19513	18.07716	15.65003	12.18914	9.89693	48
49	38.58808	34.52468	31.05208	28.07137	25.50166	21.34147	18.16872	15.70757	12.21216	9.90630	49
50	39.19612	34.99969	31.42361	28.36231	25.72976	21.48218	18.25593	15.76186	12.23348	9.91481	50

> **QUICK CHECK 3**
>
> A project manager signs a contract that will pay him a bonus of $20,000 at the end of each year for 5 years, beginning in 4 years. Assuming 4% per year, find the amount that must be set aside today to fund this benefit.

Planning for Retirement **EXAMPLE 4**

Tish Baker plans to retire from nursing at age 65 and hopes to withdraw $25,000 per year until she is 90. **(a)** If money earns 8% per year compounded annually, how much will she need at age 65? **(b)** If she deposits $2000 per year into her retirement plan beginning at age 32, and if the retirement plan earns 8% per year compounded annually, will her retirement account have enough for her to meet her goals?

SOLUTION

(a) The amount needed at age 65 is the present value of an annuity of $25,000 per year for $90 - 65 = 25$ years with interest of 8% compounded annually. The present value of an annuity table is used to find the following.

$$\text{Present value} = \$25,000 \times \mathbf{10.67478} = \$266,869.50$$

Baker will need $266,869.50 at age 65. This sum, at 8% compounded annually, will permit withdrawals of $25,000 per year until age 90.

(b) Baker makes payments of $2000 at the end of each year for $65 - 32 = 33$ years, at 8% compounded annually. These payments form a regular annuity. The amount of an annuity table in Section 11.1 is used to find the following.

$$\text{Future value} = \$2000 \times \mathbf{145.95062} = \$291,901.24$$

The value in the retirement account at 65 (**$291,901.24**) exceeds the amount needed to fund 25 yearly withdrawals of $25,000 each (**$266,869.50**). Therefore, Tish Baker should have enough, but she will need to earn an average of 8% on her money to do so. It is very unlikely that she would earn 8% at a bank, so she will need to use stocks and bonds.

Quick TIP ▼

Example 7 in Appendix C shows how a financial calculator can be used to solve a problem similar to Example 4.

Financial Calculator Solution This problem can readily be solved using a financial calculator, although the numbers differ very slightly from those above due to rounding errors.

(a) The present value (PV) is unknown. The interest rate (i) is 8%; the payment (PMT) is $25,000; and the number of years (n) is 25. Enter the payment as a positive number since it is an inflow of cash to Tish Baker.

 25000 PMT 8 i 25 n PV −266,869.40 (rounded)

(b) The unknown is the future value (FV). The interest rate (i) is 8%; the payment (PMT) is $2000; and the number of years (n) is 33. Enter the payment as a negative number since it is a cash outflow to be paid by Tish Baker.

−2000 PMT 8 i 33 n FV $291,901.24

Since the projected future value of $291,901.24 is more than the needed amount of $266,869.40, Baker should have enough.

QUICK CHECK 4

The Smiths want to plan for retirement using an annual income of $35,000 at the end of each year for 25 years based on a rate of 5% per year. (a) Find the present value needed when they retire to generate this income. (b) If they save $20,000 at the end of each year for 15 years, will they have enough?

OBJECTIVE 3 Find the equivalent cash price of an ordinary annuity. Payments made at different times cannot be compared directly to one another to see which is better. Rather, it is necessary to first find the present value of each payment (or series of payments) and compare these. The one that results in the larger present value is *the better of the two*. The present value that is equivalent to a payment (or series of payments) is called the **equivalent cash price**. Thus, the way to find the better deal is to compare the equivalent cash prices, which are the present values.

Comparing Methods of Investment **EXAMPLE 5**

Jean Braddock offers some land to two different real estate developers. Kapton Homes offers $200,000 in cash today for the land. RealProperty offers $80,000 now as a down payment and payments of $10,000 at the end of each quarter for 4 years. Assume that money can be invested at 8% per year compounded quarterly. Which offer is better?

SOLUTION

Since payments from the two real estate developers occur over different time periods, the present value of each offer must be found to determine which is better.

The present value of Kapton Homes' offer is **$200,000**, since that payment is made now.

The present value of RealProperty's offer is the sum of the down payment plus the present value of the series of payments. Use $\frac{8\%}{4}$ = 2% per compounding period for 4 years × 4 quarters per year = 16 compounding periods. Use the present value of an annuity table to find **13.57771**.

Present value of payments = $10,000 × **13.57771** = $135,777.10
Down payment   + $80,000.00
              Present value of RealProperty's offer   **$215,777.10**

Therefore, $215,777.10 is the equivalent cash price to $80,000 down plus 16 quarterly payments of $10,000 each.

RealProperty's offer is the better of the two by the following amount.

$$\textbf{\$215,777.10} - \textbf{\$200,000} = \textbf{\$15,777.10}$$

QUICK CHECK 5

Ben James has two different offers for a lot: (1) $48,000 cash and (2) $12,000 down and $2659 per quarter for 12 quarters. Assuming 6% compounded quarterly, find the present value of both and determine the better of the two.

As shown in the next example, we can use the concepts in this section to estimate the present value of Social Security payments at the time of retirement. To do so, first simplify the problem by assuming that payments are made at the end of each year and that the payments remain constant. Note that increases in Social Security payments are due to inflation, so Social Security payments effectively do remain constant in terms of buying power.

Finding the Present Value of Social Security Payments **EXAMPLE 6**

Debra Shorter expects to receive $20,940 per year in Social Security payments. Assume that she receives these payments for 28 years and use a rate of 6% per year. Find the present value of her retirement payments.

SOLUTION

Use the present value of an annuity table with 28 years and 6% per year to find **13.40616**.

$$\text{Present value} = \$20{,}940 \times \mathbf{13.40616} = \$280{,}724.99$$

Her Social Security retirement payments have a present value of $280,724.99. In other words, the Social Security payments equate to having cash of $280,724.99 at the time of retirement.

> **QUICK CHECK 6**
>
> Benjamin Thomason decides to wait until age 70 to begin receiving Social Security benefits, since it will result in higher payments. Find the present value of his estimated $26,000 per year in payments assuming 5% per year and payments until his 85th birthday.

Social Security was enacted during the 1930s during the Great Depression. Benefits include monthly payments to disabled workers, the children of deceased workers, and retired workers. Today, it is common to read and hear statements that Social Security is going broke and may not be there in the future. However, most experts believe that the financial problems of Social Security can readily be fixed and that the system will be around for decades to come. Today, many elderly people depend on the monthly payments from Social Security to pay for necessities such as food and housing.

11.2 Exercises

The QUICK START *exercises in each section contain solutions to help you get started.*

Find the present value of the following annuities. Round to the nearest cent. (See Examples 1–3.)

QUICK START

	Amount per Payment	Payment at End of Each	Time (Years)	Rate of Investment	Compounded	Present Value
1.	$1800	year	18	10%	annually	$14,762.54
	Present value = $1800 × 8.20141 = $14,762.54					
2.	$4100	year	7	6%	annually	$22,887.76
	Present value = $4100 × 5.58238 = $22,887.76					
3.	$2000	6 months	12	8%	semiannually	_____
4.	$1700	6 months	14	5%	semiannually	_____
5.	$894	quarter	6	4%	quarterly	_____
6.	$7500	quarter	5	10%	quarterly	_____

7. Explain the difference between the two ways to think of the present value of an annuity. (See Objective 1.)

8. Explain the meaning of equivalent cash price. (See Objective 3.)

Solve the following application problems. Round to the nearest cent.

QUICK START

9. **INJURY LAWSUIT** The court ruled that Bakon Corporation was liable in the death of an employee. The settlement called for the company to pay the employee's widow $65,000 at the end of each year for 20 years. Find the amount the company must set aside today, assuming 5% compounded annually.

   Present value of annuity = $65,000 × 12.46221 = $810,043.65

9. $810,043.65

 10. **COMPUTER REPLACEMENT** The community college where Roman Rodriguez works sets aside an annual payment of $35,000 per year for 5 years so it will have funds to replace the personal computers, servers, and printers in the computer labs when needed. Assuming 5% compounded annually, what lump sum deposited today would result in the same future value?

10. _____

11. **COLLEGE EXPENSES** In addition to his scholarship, Benjamin Wink needs $8000 every 6 months for living expenses and tuition at the university. As an engineering major, it will take 5 years to complete his degree. Assume funds earn 5% per year and find (**a**) the lump sum that must be deposited to meet this need and (**b**) the interest earned.

(a) _____

(b) _____

 indicates an exercise that is related to the Case in Point feature.

12. **DISASTER RELIEF**   After a terrible cyclone in Bangladesh, an international disaster relief organization agreed to help support families in a small city who lost everything with a payment of $25,000 every quarter for 5 years. Find **(a)** the lump sum that must be deposited to meet this need and **(b)** the interest earned assuming 6% per year, compounded quarterly.

(a) _____

(b) _____

13. **PAYING FOR COLLEGE**   Tom Potter estimates that his daughter's college needs, beginning in 8 years, will be $3600 at the end of each quarter for 4 years. **(a)** Find the total amount needed in 8 years assuming 8% compounded quarterly. **(b)** Will he have enough money available in 8 years if he invests $700 at the end of each quarter for the next 8 years at 8% compounded quarterly?

(a) _____

(b) _____

14. **VAN PURCHASE**   In 4 years, Jennifer Videtto will need a delivery van that will require a down payment of $10,000 with payments of $1200 per month for 36 months. **(a)** Find the total amount needed in 4 years assuming 12% compounded monthly. **(b)** Will she have enough money available if she invests $1000 at the end of each month for the next 4 years at 12% compounded monthly?

(a) _____

(b) _____

15. **SELLING A RESTAURANT**   Anna Stanley has two offers for her pizza business. The first offer is a cash payment of $85,000, and the second is a down payment of $25,000 with payments of $3500 at the end of each quarter for 5 years. **(a)** Identify the better offer assuming 8% compounded quarterly. **(b)** Find the difference in the present values.

(a) _____

(b) _____

16. **GROCERY STORE**   Adolf Hegman has two offers for his Canadian grocery company. The first offer is a cash payment of $540,000, and the second is a down payment of $240,000 with payments of $65,000 at the end of each semiannual period for 4 years. **(a)** Identify the better offer assuming 10% compounded semiannually. **(b)** Find the difference in the present values.

(a) _____

(b) _____

17. **SOCIAL SECURITY**   Jessica Thames expects to receive $18,400 per year based on her deceased husband's contributions to Social Security. Assume that she receives payments for 14 years and a rate of 8% per year, and find the present value of this annuity.

17. _____

18. **SOCIAL SECURITY**   Warren and Bernice White's combined Social Security payments add up to $35,400 per year. Assume payments for 20 years and a rate of 6% per year, and find the present value.

18. _____

QUICK CHECK ANSWERS

1. **(a)** $44,461.45   **(b)** 25,537.52
2. $21,243.39; $2756.61
3. $76,108.31
4. **(a)** $493,287.90
   (b) no, short by $61,716.70

5. $48,000; $41,003.07; $48,000 cash is the better offer.
6. $269,871.16

11.3   Sinking Funds (Finding Annuity Payments)

OBJECTIVES

1   Understand the basics of a sinking fund.

2   Set up a sinking fund table.

case IN point

Roman Rodriguez is excited! The president of the college has decided to set up a sinking fund to accumulate funds needed in 5 years for a new building that will include a gymnasium and an indoor 50-meter swimming pool, which Rodriguez plans to use.

OBJECTIVE 1   Understand the basics of a sinking fund.   Individuals and businesses often need to raise a certain amount of money for use *at some fixed time in the future*. For example, Paul Pence needs $28,000 to purchase a truck in 3 years. Using 6% compounded quarterly and the amount of an annuity table in Section 11.1, one can guess the required payment at the end of each quarter needed to accumulate the $28,000. The interest rate is $\frac{6\%}{5} = 1.5\%$ per quarter, and the number of compounding periods is 3 years $\times$ 4 quarters per year $= 12$.

Guess of quarterly payment	From table	Future value	The guess is
$1500	$1500 × **13.04121** =	$19,561.82	*too low*
$2800	$2800 × **13.04121** =	$36,515.39	*too high*

Clearly, the method of guessing and then checking to see if it is correct works very poorly. No telling how many guesses it would take. The exact payment in this example can be found by dividing the future value of $28,000 by **13.41209**, or by using the table and methods provided in this section. In fact, this section shows how to find the periodic payment needed to achieve a specific future value at a specific date.

A fund set up to receive periodic payments is called a **sinking fund**. Sinking funds are used to provide money *to pay off a loan* in one lump sum *or to accumulate money* to build new factories, buy equipment, and so on. Large corporations and some government agencies use a form of debt called a **bond**, which is a promise to pay a fixed amount of money at some stated time in the future. Bonds are discussed in detail in Section 11.5. This section covers only the use of a sinking fund to pay off a bond when it is due.

The amount of the periodic payment needed, at the end of each period, to accumulate a fixed amount at a future date is found as follows.

> **Finding Payment Needed to Accumulate a Specific Amount**
>
> Payment = Future value × Number from sinking fund table

Finding Periodic Payments   **EXAMPLE 1**

case IN point

Administrators at a community college have decided to build, in 5 years, a new sports complex with two indoor 50-meter swimming pools and a large gymnasium. The cost estimate is $16,500,000. They decide to make end-of-quarter deposits into a fund expected to earn 6% compounded quarterly. Find (**a**) the amount of each quarterly payment and (**b**) the interest earned.

SOLUTION

(**a**)   Use $\frac{6\%}{4} = 1.5\%$ per compounding period for 4 × 5 years = 20 compounding periods in the sinking fund table on page 455 to find **.04325**.

Quarterly payment = $16,500,000 × **.04325** = **$713,625**

Twenty end-of-quarter payments of $713,625 at 6% compounded quarterly will grow to $16,501,629 using the table in Section 11.1.

(**b**)   Interest is the future value minus the payments.

Interest = $16,501,629 − (20 × **$713,625**) = $2,229,129 (rounded)

Finding the Periodic Payments **EXAMPLE 2**

First Christian Church sold $100,000 worth of bonds that must be paid off in 8 years. It now must set up a sinking fund to accumulate the necessary $100,000 to pay off the debt. Find the amount of each payment into a sinking fund if the payments are made at the end of each year and the fund earns 10% compounded annually. Find the amount of interest earned.

SOLUTION

Look along the top of the sinking fund table for 10% and down the side for 8 periods to find **.08744**.

$$\text{Payment} = \$100,000 \times \textbf{.08744} = \$8744$$

The church must deposit $8744 at the end of each year for 8 years into an account paying 10% compounded annually to accumulate $100,000. The interest earned is the future value less all payments.

$$\text{Interest} = \$100,000 - (\textbf{8} \times \textbf{\$8744}) = \$30,048$$

OBJECTIVE 2 Set up a sinking fund table. A **sinking fund table** is used to show the interest earned and the accumulated amount of a sinking fund at the end of each period.

Setting up a Sinking Fund Table **EXAMPLE 3**

First Christian Church in Example 2 deposited $8744 at the end of each year for 8 years into a sinking fund that earned 10% compounded annually. Set up a sinking fund table for these deposits. After each calculation, round each answer to the nearest cent before proceeding.

SOLUTION

The sinking fund account contains no money until the end of the first year, when a single deposit of $8744 is made. Since the deposit is made at the end of the year, no interest is earned.

At the end of the second year, the account contains the original $8744 plus the interest earned by this money. This interest is found by the formula for simple interest.

$$I = \$8744 \times .10 \times 1 = \textbf{\$874.40}$$

An additional deposit is also made at the end of the second year, so that the sinking fund then contains the following total.

$$\$8744 + \textbf{\$874.40} + \$8744 = \textbf{\$18,362.40}$$

Continue this work to get the following sinking fund table.

> **Quick TIP ▼**
>
> Normally the last payment is adjusted as needed so that the future value exactly equals the desired amount. We assume this is true from this point forward.

	BEGINNING OF PERIOD		END OF PERIOD	
PERIOD	ACCUMULATED AMOUNT	PERIODIC DEPOSIT	INTEREST EARNED	ACCUMULATED AMOUNT
1	$0	$8744.00	$0	$8,744.00
2	$8,744.00	$8744.00	$874.40	$18,362.40
3	$18,362.40	$8744.00	$1836.24	$28,942.64
4	$28,942.64	$8744.00	$2894.26	$40,580.90
5	$40,580.90	$8744.00	$4058.09	$53,382.99
6	$53,382.99	$8744.00	$5338.30	$67,465.29
7	$67,465.29	$8744.00	$6746.53	$82,955.82
8	$82,955.82	$8748.60	$8295.58	$100,000.00

The last payment differs from the earlier payments by $4.60, since the final amount needs to be exactly $100,000 to pay off the bonds.

Sinking Fund Table

INTEREST RATE PER COMPOUNDING PERIOD

PERIOD	1%	1½%	2%	2½%	3%	4%	5%	6%	8%	10%	PERIOD
1	1.00000	1.00000	1.00000	1.00000	1.00000	1.00000	1.00000	1.00000	1.00000	1.00000	1
2	.49751	.49628	.49505	.49383	.49261	.49020	.48780	.48544	.48077	.47619	2
3	.33002	.32838	.32675	.32514	.32353	.32035	.31721	.31411	.30803	.30211	3
4	.24628	.24444	.24262	.24082	.23903	.23549	.23201	.22859	.22192	.21547	4
5	.19604	.19409	.19216	.19025	.18835	.18463	.18097	.17740	.17046	.16380	5
6	.16255	.16053	.15853	.15655	.15460	.15076	.14702	.14336	.13632	.12961	6
7	.13863	.13656	.13451	.13250	.13051	.12661	.12282	.11914	.11207	.10541	7
8	.12069	.11858	.11651	.11447	.11246	.10853	.10472	.10104	.09401	.08744	8
9	.10674	.10461	.10252	.10046	.09843	.09449	.09069	.08702	.08008	.07364	9
10	.09558	.09343	.09133	.08926	.08723	.08329	.07950	.07587	.06903	.06275	10
11	.08645	.08429	.08218	.08011	.07808	.07415	.07039	.06679	.06608	.05396	11
12	.07885	.07668	.07456	.07249	.07046	.06655	.06283	.05928	.05270	.04676	12
13	.07241	.07024	.06812	.06605	.06403	.06014	.05646	.05296	.04652	.04078	13
14	.06690	.06472	.06260	.06054	.05853	.05467	.05102	.04758	.04130	.03575	14
15	.06212	.05994	.05783	.05577	.05377	.04994	.04634	.04296	.03683	.03147	15
16	.05794	.05577	.05365	.05160	.04961	.04582	.04227	.03895	.03298	.02782	16
17	.05426	.05208	.04997	.04793	.04595	.04220	.03870	.03544	.02963	.02466	17
18	.05098	.04881	.04670	.04467	.04271	.03899	.03555	.03236	.02670	.02193	18
19	.04805	.04588	.04378	.04176	.03981	.03614	.03275	.02962	.02413	.01955	19
20	.04542	.04325	.04116	.03915	.03722	.03358	.03024	.02718	.02185	.01746	20
21	.04303	.04087	.03878	.03679	.03487	.03128	.02800	.02500	.01983	.01562	21
22	.04086	.03870	.03663	.03465	.03275	.02920	.02597	.02305	.01803	.01401	22
23	.03889	.03673	.03467	.03270	.03081	.02731	.02414	.02128	.01642	.01257	23
24	.03707	.03492	.03287	.03091	.02905	.02559	.02247	.01968	.01498	.01130	24
25	.03541	.03326	.03122	.02928	.02743	.02401	.02095	.01823	.01368	.01017	25
26	.03387	.03173	.02970	.02777	.02594	.02257	.01956	.01690	.01251	.00916	26
27	.03245	.03032	.02829	.02638	.02456	.02124	.01829	.01570	.01145	.00826	27
28	.03112	.02900	.02699	.02509	.02329	.02001	.01712	.01459	.01049	.00745	28
29	.02990	.02778	.02578	.02389	.02211	.01888	.01605	.01358	.00962	.00673	29
30	.02875	.02664	.02465	.02278	.02102	.01783	.01505	.01265	.00883	.00608	30
31	.02768	.02557	.02360	.02174	.02000	.01686	.01413	.01179	.00811	.00550	31
32	.02667	.02458	.02261	.02077	.01905	.01595	.01328	.01100	.00745	.00497	32
33	.02573	.02364	.02169	.01986	.01816	.01510	.01249	.01027	.00685	.00450	33
34	.02484	.02276	.02082	.01901	.01732	.01431	.01176	.00960	.00630	.00407	34
35	.02400	.02193	.02000	.01821	.01654	.01358	.01107	.00897	.00580	.00369	35
36	.02321	.02115	.01923	.01745	.01580	.01289	.01043	.00839	.00534	.00334	36
37	.02247	.02041	.01851	.01674	.01511	.01224	.00984	.00786	.00492	.00303	37
38	.02176	.01972	.01782	.01607	.01446	.01163	.00928	.00736	.00454	.00275	38
39	.02109	.01905	.01717	.01544	.01384	.01106	.00876	.00689	.00419	.00249	39
40	.02046	.01843	.01656	.01484	.01326	.01052	.00828	.00646	.00386	.00226	40
41	.01985	.01783	.01597	.01427	.01271	.01002	.00782	.00606	.00356	.00205	41
42	.01928	.01726	.01542	.01373	.01219	.00954	.00739	.00568	.00329	.00186	42
43	.01873	.01672	.01489	.01322	.01170	.00909	.00699	.00533	.00303	.00169	43
44	.01820	.01621	.01439	.01273	.01123	.00866	.00662	.00501	.00280	.00153	44
45	.01771	.01572	.01391	.01227	.01079	.00826	.00626	.00470	.00259	.00139	45
46	.01723	.01525	.01345	.01183	.01036	.00788	.00593	.00441	.00239	.00126	46
47	.01677	.01480	.01302	.01141	.00996	.00752	.00561	.00415	.00221	.00115	47
48	.01633	.01437	.01260	.01101	.00958	.00718	.00532	.00390	.00204	.00104	48
49	.01591	.01396	.01220	.01062	.00921	.00686	.00504	.00366	.00189	.00095	49
50	.01551	.01357	.01182	.01026	.00887	.00655	.00478	.00344	.00174	.00086	50

Frequently, an item costs more if its purchase is delayed a few years. The next example shows how to estimate the cost of a large purchase at a future date. It then shows how to find the payment needed to accumulate the necessary funds.

Finding Periodic Payments and Interest Earned   **EXAMPLE 4**

Managers at Baton Chemicals frequently travel between the corporate offices in the United States and manufacturing plants and mines in South America. The chief financial officer has decided that the firm should purchase a private jet in 4 years. The jet costs $14,800,000 today, and its cost is expected to grow at 5% per year. Find the quarterly payments needed to accumulate the necessary funds in a sinking fund in 4 years if the firm earns 6% compounded quarterly.

SOLUTION

First, find the cost (future value) of the jet in 4 years:

Use a rate of 5% per year and four compounding periods (years) in the compound interest table on page 402 to find **1.21551**.

$$\text{Future cost of jet} = \$14,800,000 \times 1.21551 = \$17,989,548$$

Next, find the quarterly payment needed to accumulate $17,989,548 in 4 years:

Use a rate of $\frac{6\%}{4} = 1.5\%$ per quarter and $4 \times 4 = 16$ compounding periods in the sinking fund table to find **.05577**.

$$\text{Quarterly payment} = \$17,989,548 \times .05577 = \$1,003,277.09 \quad \text{(rounded)}$$

Payments of $1,003,277.09 at the end of each quarter for 4 years into a sinking fund earning 6% compounded quarterly will result in the funds needed to purchase the jet.

Two different interest rates are involved in Example 4. The price is increasing at 5% per year compounded annually, but deposits in the sinking fund earn 6% compounded quarterly. **Interest rate spreads** such as this are common in business. For example, banks use an interest rate spread between what they pay for funds on deposit and what they charge on loans to customers.

11.3 Exercises

The QUICK START *exercises in each section contain solutions to help you get started.*

Find the amount of each payment needed to accumulate the indicated amount in a sinking fund. Round to the nearest cent. (See Examples 1–3.)

QUICK START

1. $12,000, money earns 5% compounded annually, 4 years
   Payment = $12,000 × .23201 = $2784.12

   1. $2784.12 _____

2. $125,000, money earns 6% compounded annually, 25 years
   Payment = $125,000 × .01823 = $2278.75

   2. $2278.75 _____

3. $8200, money earns 6% compounded semiannually, 5 years

   3. _____

4. $12,000, money earns 10% compounded semiannually, 3 years

   4. _____

5. $50,000, money earns 4% compounded quarterly, 5 years

   5. _____

6. $32,000, money earns 6% compounded quarterly, 3 years

   6. _____

7. $7894, money earns 12% compounded monthly, 3 years

   7. _____

8. $29,804, money earns 12% compounded monthly, 2 years

   8. _____

9. Explain the difference between a sinking fund (see Objective 1) and the present value of an annuity discussed in Section 11.2.

10. What is a sinking fund table? Who would use one? (See Objective 2.)

Solve each application problem. Round to the nearest cent.

QUICK START

11. **STUDENT UNION**   A college needs $920,000 in 3 years to remodel the student union. It decides to make payments into a sinking fund at the end of each semiannual period. **(a)** Find the amount of each payment assuming 5% per year compounded semiannually. **(b)** Find the total interest earned.

    (a) Payment = $920,000 × .15655 = $144,026
    (b) Interest = $920,000 − (6 × $144,026) = $55,844

    (a) $144,026 _____
    (b) $55,844 _____

 ▲ indicates an exercise that is related to the Case in Point feature.

12. SCUBA DIVING   The owner of Emerald Diving plans to buy all new scuba diving equipment to rent to divers in 5 years at a cost of $34,000. He believes that he can earn 8% compounded quarterly. Find **(a)** the amount of each of the quarterly payments needed and **(b)** the total interest earned.

(a) _____

(b) _____

13. ACCUMULATING $1,000,000   Kyle Anderson is 20 years old and wants to accumulate $1,000,000 by the time he is 60. He believes he can earn 8% per year by investing in stocks and bonds. Find **(a)** the amount of the annual payment needed and **(b)** the total interest earned.

(a) _____

(b) _____

14. ALLIGATOR HUNTING   Cajun Jack needs $45,000 in 4 years for boats used to hunt alligators. **(a)** Find the amount of each payment if payments are made at the end of each quarter with interest at 6% compounded quarterly. **(b)** Find the total amount of interest earned.

(a) _____

(b) _____

15. NEW MACHINERY   Smith Dry Cleaning must buy new cleaning machines in 7 years for $120,000. The firm sets up a sinking fund for this purpose. Find the payment into the fund at the end of each year if money in the fund earns 10% compounded annually.

15. _____

16. NEW AUDITORIUM   The membership of the Green Fields Baptist Church is large and growing rapidly. The leaders of the church are planning to build a new auditorium with special features for their televised broadcasts at a cost of $2,800,000 in 5 years. The membership has set up a sinking fund with the idea of making a payment at the end of each quarter. Find the payment needed if money earns 8% compounded quarterly.

16. _____

17. A NEW SHOWROOM   A Ford dealership wants to build a new showroom costing $2,300,000. It set up a sinking fund with end-of-the-month payments in an account earning 12% compounded monthly. Find the amount that should be deposited in this fund each month if the dealership wishes to build the showroom in **(a)** 3 years and **(b)** 4 years.

(a) _____

(b) _____

18. AIRPORT IMPROVEMENTS   A city near Chicago sold $9,000,000 in bonds to pay for improvements to an airport. It sets up a sinking fund with end-of-the-quarter payments in an account earning 8% compounded quarterly. Find the amount that should be deposited in this fund each quarter if the city wishes to pay off the bonds in **(a)** 7 years and **(b)** 12 years.

(a) _____

(b) _____

19. **LAND SALE** Helen Spence sells a lot in Nevada. She will be paid a lump sum of $60,000 in 4 years. Until then, the buyer pays 8% simple interest every quarter. (a) Find the amount of each quarterly interest payment. (b) The buyer sets up a sinking fund so that enough money will be present to pay off the $60,000. The buyer wants to make semiannual payments into the sinking fund. The account pays 8% compounded semiannually. Find the amount of each payment into the fund. (c) Prepare a table showing the amount in the sinking fund after each deposit.

(a) _____

(b) _____

PAYMENT NUMBER	AMOUNT OF DEPOSIT	INTEREST EARNED	TOTAL IN ACCOUNT

20. **RARE STAMPS** Jeff Reschke bought a rare stamp for his collection. He agreed to pay a lump sum of $4000 after 5 years. Until then, he pays 6% simple interest every 6 months. (a) Find the amount of each semiannual interest payment. (b) Reschke sets up a sinking fund so that money will be available to pay off the $4000. He wants to make annual payments into the fund. The account pays 8% compounded annually. Find the amount of each payment into the fund. (c) Prepare a table showing the amount in the sinking fund after each deposit.

(a) _____

(b) _____

PAYMENT NUMBER	AMOUNT OF DEPOSIT	INTEREST EARNED	TOTAL IN ACCOUNT

21. **SPORTS COMPLEX** Prepare a sinking fund table for the first four payments for the community college sports complex described in Example 1.

PAYMENT NUMBER	AMOUNT OF DEPOSIT	INTEREST EARNED	TOTAL IN ACCOUNT

22. **COMMERCIAL BUILDING**   John Bangstrom plans to make a down payment of $70,000 on a commercial building for his plumbing company in 5 years. Construct a sinking fund table given semiannual payments of $6106.10 at the end of each period and an interest rate of 6% compounded semiannually.

PAYMENT NUMBER	AMOUNT OF DEPOSIT	INTEREST EARNED	TOTAL IN ACCOUNT

23. **SAVING FOR COLLEGE**   Barbara Funicello hopes to go to a private college where tuition is $22,500 per year. She believes that tuition will increase at 8% for the 4 years until she plans to enter college. Find the end-of-quarter payments needed to accumulate funds to pay the first year's tuition if funds earn 6% compounded quarterly. Round to the nearest dollar.

23. _____

24. **FIRE TRUCK**   A volunteer fire department anticipates purchasing a fire truck in 3 years. Today it would cost $175,000, but the cost is increasing at 10% per year. Find the semiannual payments needed to accumulate funds to purchase the truck if funds earn 8% compounded semiannually. Round to the nearest dollar.

24. _____

25. **NEW ROOF**   The manager of an apartment complex estimates she will need a new roof on one of the buildings in 5 years. Today it would cost $52,000 to reroof the building, but the cost is increasing at 8% per year. Find the semiannual payments needed to accumulate the necessary funds at 5% compounded semiannually.

25. _____

26. **NEW KITCHEN**   A restaurant manager believes he will need all new kitchen appliances in 2 years. The cost today is $48,800, but costs are going up at 10% per year. Find the semiannual payments needed if funds earn 5% compounded semiannually.

26. _____

QUICK CHECK ANSWERS

1. $9,861,000

2. (a) $114,470   (b) $84,240

3.

	BEGINNING OF PERIOD		END OF PERIOD	
PERIOD	ACCUMULATED AMOUNT	PERIODIC DEPOSIT	INTEREST EARNED	ACCUMULATED AMOUNT
1	$0.00	$2400.00	$0.00	$2400.00
2	$2400.00	$2400.00	$36.00	$4836.00
3	$4836.00	$2400.00	$72.54	$7308.54
4	$7308.54	$2400.00	$109.63	$9818.17

4. $21,994.97; $3233.70

Supplementary Application Exercises on Annuities and Sinking Funds

Solve the following application problems. Round to the nearest cent.

QUICK START

1. Bill Carter deposits $500 at the end of each quarter for 6 years into a mutual fund that he believes will grow at 8% compounded quarterly. Find **(a)** the future value and **(b)** the interest.

   (a) Future value = $500 × 30.42186 = $15,210.93
   (b) Interest = $15,210.93 − (24 × $500) = $3210.93

   (a) $15,210.93
   (b) $3210.93

2. For 6 years, Jessica Savage deposits $1000 at the end of each quarter into an account earning 8% per year compounded quarterly. Find **(a)** the future value and **(b)** the interest.

   (a) _____
   (b) _____

3. Mr. and Mrs. Thompson deposit $2000 at the beginning of each year for 20 years into a retirement account earning 6% compounded annually. Find **(a)** the future value and **(b)** the interest.

   (a) _____
   (b) _____

4. Jaime Navarro deposits $1000 at the end of every 6 months into a Roth IRA for 8 years at 10% compounded semiannually. Find **(a)** the future value and **(b)** the interest.

   (a) _____
   (b) _____

5. Solectron needs to purchase new equipment for its production line in 3 years. The company has been advised to deposit $135,000 at the end of each quarter into an account that managers believe will yield 10% per year compounded quarterly. Find the lump sum that could be deposited today that will grow to the same future value.

   5. _____

6. Abel Plumbing saves $12,000 at the end of every semiannual period in an account earning 6% compounded semiannually to replace several of its trucks in 5 years. Find the lump sum that could be deposited today that will grow to the same future value.

   6. _____

7. Katherine Wysong was injured when she fell on ice at work. Her employer's workers compensation insurance paid for her medical bills and must also pay her $5000 per quarter for the next 6 years. Find the lump sum that must be deposited into an investment earning 4% per year compounded quarterly needed to make the payments.

   7. _____

8. Carl and Amy Glaser recently divorced. As part of the divorce settlement, Carl must pay Amy $1000 at the end of every quarter for 8 years. Find the lump sum he must deposit into an account earning 8% per year compounded quarterly to make the payments.

   8. _____

9. Ajax Coal sets up a sinking fund to purchase a new coal extractor in 3 years at a price of $870,000. Find the annual payment the firm must make if funds are deposited into an account earning 8% compounded annually. Then set up a sinking fund table.

PAYMENT NUMBER	AMOUNT OF DEPOSIT	INTEREST EARNED	TOTAL IN ACCOUNT

10. Swift Petrochemicals wishes to purchase a new distillation tower costing $3,200,000 in 2 years. Find the semiannual payment the company must make into a sinking fund account earning 6% compounded semiannually. Then set up a sinking fund table.

PAYMENT NUMBER	AMOUNT OF DEPOSIT	INTEREST EARNED	TOTAL IN ACCOUNT

11. Ben Jamison is 45. He wants to retire at age 65 and draw $25,000 per year until he turns 85. He assumes that he can earn 8% per year *before* retiring but that he would invest more conservatively and earn 6% per year *after retiring*. **(a)** Find the amount needed at 65 to fund his retirement. **(b)** Then find the end-of-the-year payment into a sinking fund needed to accumulate this amount.

(a) _____

(b) _____

12. An engineer agrees to work in Hong Kong and signs a contract to work there for 5 years. The contract also specifies that at the end of his 5 years of service, he will receive $90,000 at the end of the following 3 years. Assume funds earn 6% compounded annually. **(a)** Find the amount needed at the end of his 5 years of service to fund the payments. **(b)** Find the end-of-year payment into a sinking fund needed to accumulate this amount.

(a) _____

(b) _____

11.4 Stocks and Mutual Funds

OBJECTIVES

1 Define the types of stock.
2 Read stock tables.
3 Find the current yield on a stock.
4 Find the stock's PE ratio.
5 Define the Dow Jones Industrial Average and the NASDAQ Composite Index.
6 Define a mutual fund.

case IN point ▶

When Roman Rodriguez began his new job, he was given the choice of investing his retirement funds in a fixed interest fund or in a fund containing stocks and/or bonds. Which should he choose? Which would you choose? Why?

Almost all large businesses and also many smaller ones are set up as **corporations**. For example, companies that we commonly refer to as Microsoft, Apple, Nike, McDonald's, and Toyota are actually corporations. **Publicly held corporations** are those owned by the public; their stocks are traded daily in markets called stock markets. **Privately held corporations** are owned by one or a few individuals, and their stock is not traded on a market. For example, your medical doctor or plumber may have organized her small business as a privately held corporation.

A corporation is a form of business that gives the owners (the stockholders) **limited liability**. You do not have to worry that lawsuits will be filed against you or your family just because you own stock in General Motors, Inc. The owners of corporations have protection through the limited-liability laws and will never lose more than they have invested in the corporation.

A corporation is set up with money, or **capital**, raised through the sale of shares of **stock**. A share of stock represents partial ownership of a corporation. If one million shares of stock are sold to establish a new firm, the owner of one share will own one-millionth of the corporation. In the past, stock ownership was indicated by **stock certificates** such as the one shown here. However, very few people hold stock certificates anymore. Rather, proof of ownership of stock is simply the regular statements and records maintained by brokerage firms.

In most states, corporations are required to have an **annual meeting**. At this meeting, open to all **stockholders** (owners of stock), the management of the firm is open to questions from stockholders. The stockholders also elect a **board of directors**—a group of people who represent the stockholders. The board of directors hires the **executive officers** of the corporation, such as the president, vice-presidents, and so on. The board of directors also distributes a portion of any profits in the form of **dividends**, which are regular payments to stockholders.

OBJECTIVE 1 Define the types of stock. The two types of stock normally issued are **preferred stock** and **common stock**. As the name suggests, preferred stockholders *have certain rights* over common stockholders. For example, owners of preferred stock must be paid dividends *before* any dividends can be paid to owners of common stock. Also, corporate debt and preferred shareholders must be paid *before* common shareholders receive anything in the event that a corporation declares bankruptcy.

The shares of **publicly held corporations** are typically owned by many different individuals and institutions. Share prices of these firms are determined by supply and demand in public markets called **stock exchanges**. The New York Stock Exchange (NYSE) is the largest of the several exchanges in the United States. This exchange is located on Wall Street in New York City. Many foreign countries, including Japan, Taiwan, Germany, England, Canada, and Mexico, have their own stock exchanges.

OBJECTIVE 2 Read stock tables. Daily stock prices are readily found in many places on the World Wide Web, such as finance.yahoo.com or wsj.com. Information on the stock of many widely held companies such as Apple or Nike is also found in the weekly financial magazine *Barron's*. In this section, we will use data as presented in *Barron's*.

Reading the Stock Table **EXAMPLE 1**

After receiving his first paycheck from the college, Roman Rodriguez went to Best Buy to look at iPods and MP3 players. He liked the company so well that he decided to do some research on it. Analyze the information about Best Buy stock given in the table.

case IN point

52-WEEK			TICK	VOL.				WEEK'S		EARNINGS			DIV
										LATEST	THIS	NEXT	
High	Low	Name	Sym.	100s	Yld.	P/E	Last	Chg.		Year	Year	Year	Amt
45.55	23.97	BestBuy	BBY	884920	1.4	15.6	39.50	−4.84		2.88	3.08	3.30	.14

SOLUTION

(a) The highest price the stock sold for during the year was $45.55 per share.

(b) The lowest price the stock sold for during the year was $23.97 per share.

(c) The ticker symbol under which the stock trades on the market is BBY.

(d) The volume of shares sold during the day was $100 \times 884920 = 88,492,000$ shares.

(e) The annual dividend yield is 1.4% of the current price.

(f) The ratio of stock price to annual earnings is 15.6.

(g) The stock closed at $39.50 at the end of the week.

(h) The price of the stock was down $4.84 this week.

(i) Best Buy earned $2.88 per share last year, and it is forecast to earn $3.08 this year and $3.30 next year.

(j) The most recent quarterly dividend was $.14 per share.

> **QUICK CHECK 1**
>
> Find the information in the stock table about Revlon A.

Individuals must use **stockbrokers** to trade publicly held stocks. Regular stockbrokers charge more, but they offer financial advice. Some people trade stocks using **discount brokers**, who offer less advice and a lower cost. Yet others trade stock over the Internet using E*Trade, Schwab, or Ameritrade, for example, where the costs of trading are very low. Some firms on the Internet will let you play a game of buying and selling stock to help you learn about trading stocks.

Finding the Cost of Stocks **EXAMPLE 2**

Ignoring commissions, find Roman Rodriguez's cost for the following purchases.

(a) 100 shares of BankAm (BAC) at the close for the week

(b) 200 shares of Radio Shack (RSH) at the low for the year

(c) Then find the combined *annual dividend* from this investment.

Mkt Sym	52-Wk High	52-Wk Low	Name	Tick Sym	Vol. 100s	Yld	P/E	Week's Last	Week's Chg.	Latest Year	This Year	Next Year	Div Amt
	30.82	10.21 ♣	BaldorElec	BEZ	14980	2.4	17	27.81	+0.62	2.15	.98	1.43	.17
	52.46	36.50	Ball Cp	BLL	36562	.8	14	51.26	−0.23	3.61	3.92	4.39	.10
	45.32	12.91	BallyTch	BYI	30524	...	19	41.49	+0.09	2.22	2.44	2.78	...
s	19.78	5.59	BcoBilViz	BBVA	17104	3.5	10	17.69	−0.08	1.96	2.14	1.92	.1306
	22.70	7.81	BncoBrdsco	BBD	408689	3.7	16	20.37	−1.86	1.40	1.34	1.69	.0084
	54.00	30.39	BcoDeChli	BCH	z68451	4.5	15	51.25	−2.19	3.62	3.43	4.39	2.3281
	15.10	6.83	BcoLatin	BLX	9536	4.3	13	13.93	+0.01	1.51	1.57	1.73	.15
	33.85	8.71	BancoMacro	BMA	4147	2.2	10	29.13	+0.74	3.34	3.10	3.17	.6504
n	14.58	11.50	BancSantandBr	BSBR	281204	...	...	13.43	−0.28	NA	.70	1.24	...
▲	64.55	30.56 ♣	BcoSantChile ADS	SAN	11029	3.3	16	61.05	−1.70	3.41	3.74	4.35	2.0206
	17.89	4.87	BcoSantdr	STD	133671	5.3	10	16.12	−0.23	1.78	1.55	1.85	.1749
▲	48.00	15.90	Bancol ADS	CIB	21069	2.5	23	45.16	−0.34	2.92	2.86	3.56	.3107
	25.30	15.60	Bncpsouth	BXS	29665	3.7	19	23.56	+0.55	1.45	1.31	1.30	.22
	19.10	2.53	BankAm	BAC	f92442	.3	cc	15.03	−0.60	.55	−.12	.84	.01
	46.75	25.33	Bk Hawaii	BOH	13405	3.9	16	46.17	+0.60	3.99	2.90	3.10	.45
	20.18	0.66	Bklrlnd ADS	IRE	45379	...	...	7.19	−1.29	...	...	...	...
	52.50	19.32	BkMntrl g	BMO	17193	...	18g	50.69	+0.75	3.97	4.04	4.99	.70
	33.62	15.44	BankNY Mellon	BK	404122	1.3	dd	26.77	−0.17	2.39	2.06	2.42	.09
	47.79	19.24	BKNovaScotia g	BNS	16681	...	15g	45.40	+0.61	3.31	3.29	4.19	.49
	6.68	0.66	BkAtlBcp A	BBX	15150	...	dd	1.32	−0.08	−19.78	−9.74	−1.85	...
	25.68	2.75	Barclays ADS	BCS	119921	.4	9	17.41	−1.36	...	...	...	.0669
	88.43	68.94	Bard CR	BCR	105869	.9	16	78.49	−4.56	4.44	5.06	5.70	.17
	28.78	12.64	BarnesNoble	BKS	81096	5.4	15	18.39	−1.22	NA	.63	1.11	.25
	19.11	7.69 ♣	BarnesGp	B	13060	2.0	31	15.92	−0.14	1.91	.83	1.08	.08
	48.02	25.54 ♣	BarckGld	ABX	783689	1.0	dd	39.52	−0.06	1.84	1.90	2.43	.20
	15.18	5.30	BscEngySvs	BAS	17905	...	dd	9.06	+1.69	2.00	−2.08	−1.53	...
	60.99	45.46	Baxterlnt	BAX	242439	2.0	16	57.60	−1.90	3.38	3.80	4.29	.29
	27.95	7.84 ♣	BaytexEngyTr g	BTE	11051	...	27	27.40	+1.14	2.59	1.07	1.43	.18
	6.93	0.24	BeazerHm	BZH	161411	...	dd	4.88	+0.81	−4.90	−2.57	−.80	...
	71.57	40.04	BeckmnCoultr	BEC	40866	1.1	25	64.28	−3.08	3.63	3.81	4.56	.18
	78.81	60.40	BectonDksn	BDX	80908	2.0	15	74.86	−2.59	4.95	5.09	5.57	.37
	26.88	8.18	Belden	BDC	15483	.9	dd	22.10	−0.96	2.68	1.08	1.59	.05
	6.18	0.47 ♣	Belo	BLC	35659	...	dd	5.57	−0.31	.78	.32	.54	...
	31.41	16.85 ♣	Bemis	BMS	43949	3.0	20	29.92	−0.57	1.65	1.68	2.06	.225
	19.81	8.60	BenchmkElec	BHE	17318	...	dd	18.69	−0.19	1.25	.86	1.07	...
	31.21	18.59	Berkley	WRB	60751	1.0	17	23.36	−1.39	2.96	2.36	2.73	.06
	108450	70050.01	BerkHathwy A	BRKA	z4939	...	33	100899	+1899	...	...	...	...
	3569	2241	BerkHathwy B	BRKB	1894	...	dd	3303.63	+16.63	...	...	...	...
	31.37	5.50 ♣	BerryPete A	BRY	26477	1.0	28	29.94	+3.43	3.40	1.42	2.27	.075
▲	45.55	23.97	BestBuy	BBY	884920	1.4	15.6	39.50	−4.84	2.88	3.08	3.30	.14
▲	29.55	12.62	BigLots	BIG	97624	...	14	29.36	+0.61	1.89	2.18	2.43	...
	37.81	17.08	BillBarrett	BBG	32825	...	31	31.12	+2.69	2.39	1.66	1.32	...
▲	15.92	6.02	BiomdRltyTr	BMR	54025	3.6	27	15.73	+1.08	.67	.47	.17	.14
h	100.99	51.33	BioRadLab A	BIO	2687	...	27	95.99	−1.08	4.76	4.96	5.41	...
h	100.00	52.04	BioRadLab B	BIOB	z2159	...	...	96.23	−0.90	...	...	...	...
	15.50	8.56	Biovail	BVF	44568	2.6	dd	13.90	−0.10	1.44	1.36	1.41	.09
▲	65.90	20.10	BlackDeck	BDK	74515	.8	27	63.44	+1.23	5.47	2.53	2.89	.12
	27.84	14.54	BlackHills	BKH	20486	5.4	dd	26.50	+0.50	−1.30	1.64	1.84	.355
	240.50	88.91	BlackRock	BLK	17071	1.3	47	238.81	+12.80	6.45	6.76	10.36	.78

(continued)

SOLUTION

(a) 100 shares × $15.03 = $1503

(b) 200 shares × $6.47 = $1294

(c) Quarterly dividend from Bank America = .01 × 100 = $1.00

Quarterly dividend from Radio Shack = .25 × 200 = $50.00

Total quarterly dividend = $51.00

Total annual dividend = $51.00 × 4 = $204.00

QUICK CHECK 2

Ignore commissions and find the cost of 300 shares of Berkshire Hathaway (BRKB) at the low for the year. Then find the *annual* dividend these shares will pay.

OBJECTIVE 3 Find the current yield on a stock. There is no certain way of choosing stocks that will go up in price. However, two **stock ratios** that people commonly look at before buying shares of a company are the **current yield** and the **price–earnings ratio**. Although current yield is shown in the stock tables as Yld, we show how to find it here since you may not always have the tables available. It is used to compare the dividends paid by stocks selling at different prices. The result is commonly rounded to the nearest tenth of a percent.

Finding Current Yield

$$\text{Current yield} = \frac{\text{Annual dividend per share}}{\text{Closing price per share}}$$

Mkt Sym	52-Wk High	52-Wk Low	Name	Tick Sym	Vol. 100s	Yld	P/E	Week's Last	Week's Chg.	EARNINGS Latest Year	EARNINGS This Year	EARNINGS Next Year	Div Amt
	3.45	0.45	RAIT FnclTr	RAS	32788	...	dd	1.41	−0.02	1.84	.34	−.30	...
	62.00	42.51	RLI Cp	RLI	4588	2.1	17	53.40	+0.01	4.99	4.50	3.82	.28
	11.97	5.17	RPC	RES	9213	1.5	cc	10.90	+1.16	.85	−.26	.08	.04
	20.83	9.09 ♣	RPM	RPM	36635	4.1	21	19.88	−0.27	1.05	1.29	1.55	.205
	9.05	4.00	RSC Hldg	RRR	23428	...	dd	7.08	+0.21	1.18	−.61	−.19	...
	26.19	8.99	RTI IntMtls	RTI	39012	...	dd	23.80	+2.51	2.44	−.18	.31	...
	22.61	4.00	RackspaceHstng	RAX	86383	...	cc	22.55	+2.65	.19	.23	.37	...
	12.48	0.95	RadianGrp	RDN	91516	.2	dd	6.16	−0.14	−9.51	−1.79	−1.85	.0025
	20.57	6.47	RadioShack	RSH	140582	1.3	13	19.59	+0.11	1.54	1.60	1.64	.25
	14.78	10.91	RailAmerica	RA	14968	...	...	13.15	−0.47	NA	.38	.50	...
	64.90	52.01	RalcpHldg	RAH	16120	...	11	57.88	−0.45	4.46	4.77	5.30	...
▲	11.97	3.56 ♣	RmcoGrshn	RPT	12843	6.5	26	9.93	+0.57	1.27	.72	.53	.1633
	60.13	30.06 ♣	RangeRes	RRC	212924	.3	cc	51.12	+7.74	1.94	.99	.87	.04
	5.24	1.05	RaserTech	RZ	28625	...	dd	1.05	−0.08	−.79	−.34	−.46	...
	26.65	10.77	RayJamFnl	RJF	32913	1.8	19	23.94	+0.91	1.29	1.64	2.05	.11
	45.00	22.28	RayonierReit	RYN	42638	4.8	12	41.68	−0.27	2.01	1.50	1.80	.50
	53.84	33.20	Raytheon	RTN	119057	2.4	11	52.45	−0.29	3.95	4.83	4.98	.31
	17.02	4.44	Raytheon wt		112	...	...	14.81	−0.72	...	...	...	...
	28.23	14.25	RltyIncoCp	O	59535	6.3	29	27.40	+1.37	1.06	.99	.97	.143
	29.68	11.54	RedHat	RHT	122318	...	67	29.27	+1.05	.86	.67	.75	...
	6.43	1.49	RedLionHtls	RLH	4758	...	dd	4.59	−0.21	.11	−.05	−.13	...
	6.30	1.04	ReddyIceHldg	FRZ	6061	...	dd	3.70	−0.11	−5.47	.03	.38	...
	19.45	10.10	RedwdTr	RWT	23626	7.1	dd	14.10	−0.33	−13.46	.30	1.82	.25
	25.30	19.59	ReedElsvr NV	ENL	11617	4.2	33	24.24	+0.27	...	...	...	.3032
	33.56	26.09	ReedElsvr ADS	RUK	1662	3.8	25	31.85	+0.51	...	...	...	.3573
	14.83	8.83	Regal A	RGC	42044	5.3	23	13.62	−0.48	.73	.61	.82	.18
	52.50	25.64	RgalBeloit	RBC	17470	1.3	21	51.16	+1.28	3.87	2.35	2.82	.16
	47.13	20.72	RegencyCtrs	REG	73020	5.5	dd	33.65	−0.39	1.90	−.86	.43	.4625
	9.07	2.35	RegionsFin	RF	962105	.7	dd	5.45	−0.13	−8.09	−.98	−.64	.01
	24.50	9.65	Regions TrTruPS		2953	10.1	...	22.05	−1.16	...	...	...	.5547
	20.36	9.81	RegisCp	RGS	35714	1.0	dd	15.48	+0.08	1.84	1.37	1.56	.04
▲	31.75	12.44	RehabCrGp	RHB	19148	...	19	30.28	+1.18	1.14	1.78	2.55	...
	49.85	21.27	ReinsGA	RGA	21685	.8	11	46.70	−0.22	6.12	5.86	6.77	.09
	64.56	27.00	Relns Gp Amer		2446	4.8	...	59.73	−0.59	...	...	...	.7188
	45.00	18.25 ♣	RelianceStl	RS	44550	.9	26	42.96	+0.73	6.56	1.13	3.12	.10
	57.37	39.37 ♣	RensHldg	RNR	25839	1.9	dd	51.85	−1.35	3.04	11.72	7.97	.24
	7.90	2.02	ReneSola	SOL	161833	...	dd	4.82	+0.66	−.84	−.69	.40	...
	28.65	14.19	RepsIYPF ADS	REP	13332	5.3	10	25.82	−1.17	3.29	1.88	2.57	.6404
	29.82	15.05	RepSvcs	RSG	150340	2.7	61	27.83	−1.74	1.73	1.48	1.66	.19
	53.18	31.49	ResMed	RMD	21283	...	27	51.04	−1.81	1.97	2.29	2.61	...
h	11.52	9.72	ResoluteEnrg	REN	10929	...	...	11.00	...	NA	−.48	.48	...
h	2.35	1.00	ResolEnrgWt		1127	...	...	2.17	−0.02	...	...	...	...
	6.37	1.43	ResourceCap	RSO	44343	23.4	dd	4.91	+0.27	...	...	...	.25
	8.70	1.45	RetailVent	RVI	18512	...	dd	8.50	+0.79	...	...	...	...
	19.87	2.30	Revlon A	REV	13738	...	20	17.83	−1.07	.26	1.05	2.26	...
	15.00	5.52	RexStores	RSC	1787	...	dd	13.06	−1.52	...	...	...	...

Finding the Current Yield   **EXAMPLE 3**   Use data in the stock table to estimate the current yield for Barnes and Noble (BKS) and Red Hat (RHT) rounded to the nearest tenth of a percent.

SOLUTION

$$\text{Current yield for Barnes and Noble} = \frac{\text{Annual dividend}}{\text{Closing price}} = \frac{4 \times \$.25}{\$18.39} = 5.4\%$$

$$\text{Current yield for Red Hat} = \frac{\text{Annual dividend}}{\text{Closing price}} = \frac{4 \times \$0}{\$29.27} = 0.0\%$$

QUICK CHECK 3

Find the current yield for ExxonMobil to the nearest tenth of a percent if the closing price is $68.26 and the annual dividend is $1.68.

Note that a company such as Red Hat in Example 3 may not pay a dividend since it may be having financial problems and needs to keep its cash or because it may be growing rapidly and needs the cash to finance its future growth.

OBJECTIVE 4   Find the stock's PE ratio. One number that some people use to help decide which stock to buy is the **price–earnings ratio**, also called the **PE ratio**. It is often rounded to the nearest whole number.

Finding PE Ratio

$$\text{Finding PE Ratio} \quad \text{PE ratio} = \frac{\text{Closing price per share}}{\text{Annual net income per share}}$$

Finding the PE Ratio EXAMPLE 4

Find the PE ratio for each of the following corporations and round to the nearest whole number.

(a) Chevron (CVX) with a closing price of $70.28 and earnings of $7.91

(b) Target (TGT) with a closing price of $57.59 and earnings of $2.98

SOLUTION

(a) PE ratio for Chevron $= \dfrac{\$70.28}{\$7.91} = 9$

(b) PE ratio for Target $= \dfrac{\$57.59}{\$2.98} = 19$

QUICK CHECK 4

Pfizer Inc (PFE) has a closing price of $26.38 and earnings of $1.72. Find the PE ratio to the nearest whole number.

Investors are often willing to pay more for rapidly growing companies because these companies may generate even higher profits in the near future. As a result, the PE ratios of rapidly growing companies are often higher than those of slow-growing companies.

A low PE ratio may indicate that a company is growing slowly or that it is having financial problems. It is best to compare the PE ratios of similar companies, such as oil giants Exxon Mobil and Chevron. It usually is not worthwhile to compare the PE ratios of very different companies such as Wal-Mart and Exxon Mobil, since they have very different business environments.

OBJECTIVE 5 Define the Dow Jones Industrial Average and the NASDAQ Composite Index. Both the **Dow Jones Industrial Average** and the **NASDAQ Composite Index** are used as indicators of trends in stock prices. The Dow Jones Industrial Average refers to an average of 30 specific, large industrial companies. The NASDAQ Composite Index includes price information on over 5000 companies, many of which are involved with technology. Both of these indexes are commonly quoted by television and radio, in newsprint, and on the Internet.

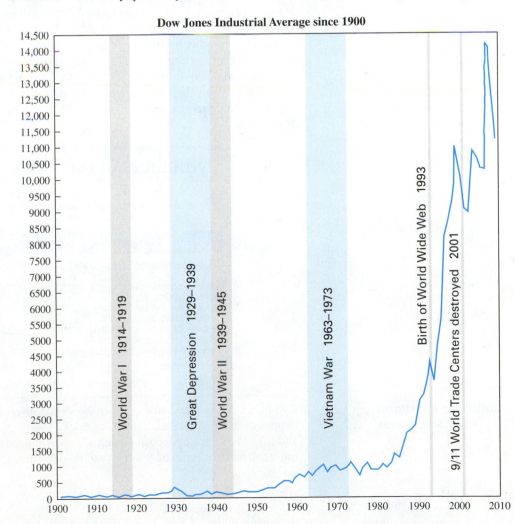

Dow Jones Industrial Average since 1900

The Dow Jones Industrial Average has been widely available for over 100 years, as you can see on the graph. The Great Depression of the 1930s devastated many investors, businesses, and families. Stock prices collapsed during the early years of the depression followed by many companies, including banks, going bankrupt. Many people were out of work and were unable to find a job. The entire world was mired in the depression until World War II, when war-related activity brought us out of the depression. However, stock prices did not recover to pre-depression levels until the 1950s.

In spite of the Great Depression and the many smaller recessions in the United States, you can clearly see that the trend of stock prices has been up over the past 100 years or so. Historically, stocks have usually had a greater return on investment than savings accounts, certificates of deposit, or bonds. Most financial planners agree that stocks should be a part of any long-range investment plan.

OBJECTIVE 6 **Define a mutual fund.** Ownership of shares in a single company *can be risky*—the company may suffer poor financial results causing the stock price to fall. The **risk** of losing money in the stock of a single company *can be reduced* by simultaneously investing in the stocks of several different companies, especially when they are in different industries.

One way to participate in the profits of successful corporations but to reduce risk is to purchase shares in a mutual fund that invests in stocks. A **mutual fund** receives money from many different investors and uses the money to purchase stocks or bonds in many different companies. For example, a $1000 investment in a typical mutual fund that owns stock means that you own a very small piece of perhaps 100 different companies.

Most mutual funds are actively managed, meaning that managers are paid to buy and sell stock as they think best for investors in the fund. **Exchange-traded funds (ETFs)** are similar to mutual funds except that they tend not to be actively managed. They attempt to match the performance of an index such as the Dow Jones Averages, a market sector such as energy, or a commodity such as petroleum. Essentially, ETFs are a low-cost way to purchase a portfolio with some diversification.

The next table shows that some funds *specialize* by investing in the stocks *of different types* of publicly held companies. For example, mutual funds or exchange-traded funds may specialize in large-cap (large companies), small-cap (small companies), overseas (global), or specialty (real estate, oil, banking, etc.) stocks. Many financial planners say that *the first fund* you should invest in is an **index fund** that tracks a broad index such as Standard & Poors 500, which includes 500 of the largest and best-managed companies in the world. Funds that specialize in companies in one industry, such as biotechnology, or funds that specialize in international stock are usually more volatile and can be risky. However, most financial planners recommend investing in international stock since the growth of emerging economies, including China and India, is so rapid.

Numbers in the News

Going Global

By mixing just two or three of these low-priced exchange-traded funds, you can create a globally diversified portfolio

Exchange-traded fund (Ticker)	Invests in
Vanguard Total Stock Market VIPERs (VTI)	U.S. stocks, all sizes
iShares S&P 500 (IVV)	Large-cap U.S. stocks
iShares S&P Midcap 400 (IJH)	Mid-cap U.S. stocks
Midcap SPDRs (MDY)	Mid-cap U.S. stocks
iShares Russell 2000 (IWM)	Small-cap U.S. stocks
iShares MSCI Japan (EWJ)	Japanese stocks
iShares MSCI Pacific Ex-Japan (EPP)	Pacific Rim, but not Japan
iShares MSCI EAFE (EFA)	Europe and Pacific Rim
iShares MSCI Emerging Markets (EEM)	Emerging markets

Comparing Investment Alternatives **EXAMPLE 5**

Cynthia Peck wants to know whether she should invest her retirement monies in certificates of deposit or in a mutual fund containing stock. Assume payments of $2000 per year for 30 years and **(a)** a certificate of deposit paying 4% compounded annually or **(b)** a mutual fund containing stock that has returned 8% per year. Find the future value for both and **(c)** compare the two investments.

SOLUTION

(a) Use 4% per year and 30 years in the table in Section 11.1 to find **56.08494**.

$$\text{Future value} = \$2000 \times \mathbf{56.08494} = \$112{,}169.88$$

(b) Use 8% per year and 30 years in the table in Section 11.1 to find **113.28321**.

$$\text{Future value} = \$2000 \times \mathbf{113.28321} = \$226{,}566.42$$

(c) Difference = $\$226{,}566.42 - \$112{,}169.88 = \$114{,}396.54$

Stocks yield more but have higher risk. Cynthia Peck will need to decide how much risk she will accept before making a decision.

Note: Neither the 4% on the certificate of deposit nor the 8% on the mutual fund is guaranteed for 30 years. Stocks may do better or worse than bank deposits in any year, but stocks tend to have higher returns over the long time periods required for retirement planning.

QUICK CHECK 5

The owner of Termites Inc. plans to deposit $15,000 at the end of each year for 10 years into an investment account. A bank deposit would pay 5% per year, and he assumes a stock fund would continue to yield 10% per year. Find the future value of both.

11.4 Exercises

The QUICK START *exercises in each section contain solutions to help you get started.*

Find the following from the stock table on pages 465 and 466. (See Example 1.)

QUICK START

1. Low for the year for RSC Holding (RRR) **1.** $\underline{\$4.00}$
2. High for the year for Bard Cr (BCR) **2.** $\underline{\$88.43}$
3. Most recent quarterly dividend for Big Lots (BIG) **3.** _____
4. Most recent quarterly dividend for RPM (RPM) **4.** _____
5. Volume for Rex Stores (RSC) **5.** _____
6. Volume for Ball Corporation (BLL) **6.** _____
7. PE ratio for BlackRock (BLK) **7.** _____
8. PE ratio for Baytex Energy Trust (BTE) **8.** _____
9. Estimated earnings per share for this year for Barck Gold (ABX) **9.** _____
10. Estimated earnings per share for this year for Bank Hawaii (BOH) **10.** _____
11. Dividend yield for Realty Inco (O) **11.** _____
12. Dividend yield for Regel A (RGC) **12.** _____
13. Estimated earnings next year for ReneSola (SOL) **13.** _____
14. Estimated earnings next year for RailAmerica (RA) **14.** _____
15. Change from previous week for BankNY Mellon (BK) **15.** _____
16. Change from previous week for Benchmark Electric (BHE) **16.** _____
17. Closing price for the week for ResMed (RMD) **17.** _____
18. Closing price for the week for Ratheon (RTN) **18.** _____

Ignore commissions and find the cost for the following stock purchases at the closing price for the week. Then find the annual dividend that will be paid on those shares.

QUICK START

Stock	Number of Shares	Cost	Dividend
19. Regis Corp. (RGS)	800	$12,384	$128
$800 \times \$15.48 = \$12,384; 800 \times (4 \times \$.04) = \$128$			
20. Barnes and Noble (BKS)	200	_____	_____
21. Best Buy (BBY)	100	_____	_____
22. Barclays ADS (BCS)	1200	_____	_____
23. Red Lions Hotels (RLH)	600	_____	_____
24. Regal A (RGC)	350	_____	_____

25. Define and explain (**a**) current yield and (**b**) PE ratio. (See Objectives 3 and 4.)

26. Use the chart of the Dow Jones Industrial Average and estimate the years in which stocks fell by more than 10%. (See Objective 5.)

Find the current yield for each of the following stocks. Round to the nearest tenth of a percent.
(See Example 3.)

QUICK START

	Stock	Current Price per Share	Annual Dividend	Current Yield
27.	Coca-Cola (KO)	$50.06	$1.24	<u>2.5%</u>
	$1.24 ÷ $50.06 = 2.5%			
28.	Microsoft (MSFT)	$29.81	$.40	_____
29.	McDonalds (MCD)	$63.36	$2.20	_____
30.	Apple Inc. (AAPL)	$202.10	$0	_____
31.	Nike (NKE)	$65.44	$1.08	_____
32.	Wal-Mart (WMT)	$53.32	$1.09	_____

Find the PE ratio for each of the following. Round all answers to the nearest whole number.
(See Example 4.)

QUICK START

	Stock	Current Price per Share	Annual Net Earnings per Share	PE Ratio
33.	Pepsi (PBG)	$37.51	$1.16	<u>32</u>
	$37.51 ÷ $1.16 = 32			
34.	Target (TGT)	$48.85	$2.87	_____
35.	General Electric (GE)	$15.41	$1.09	_____
36.	Exxon Mobil (XOM)	$72.72	$6.59	_____
37.	Abercrombie & Fitch (ANF)	$22.29	$.54	_____
38.	Intel (INTC)	$21.19	$1.01	_____

Stock prices on consecutive days for a stock are shown next. Find the increase (decrease) in the price of each stock as a number and the percent increase (decrease) rounded to the nearest tenth of a percent.

39. 34.35, 35.20   **40.** 46.50, 45.90

Solve the following application problems.

41. STOCK PURCHASE   Patsy Bonner buys 200 shares of Target at $56.30 and 100 shares of Pepsi at $38.60. Find the total cost ignoring commissions.

200 × $56.30 + 100 × $38.60 = $15,120

41. $\underline{\$15,120}$

42. WRITING A WILL   In her will, Barbara Bains stated that the trustee should purchase 300 shares of McDonalds and 200 shares of Wal-Mart and give the stock to her grandson on his 25th birthday. If the stocks are selling for $58.70 per share and $52.20 per share, respectively, find the total amount paid, ignoring broker's commissions.

42. _____

43. CDS OR GLOBAL STOCKS   Stan Walker is comparing treasury bills currently yielding 5% compounded semiannually to a mutual fund with stocks that he believes will yield 8% compounded semiannually. Find the future value of an annuity with deposits of $600 every 6 months for 10 years for **(a)** the CDs and **(b)** the mutual fund. **(c)** Find the difference.

(a) _____

(b) _____

(c) _____

44. FIXED RATE OR STOCKS   Jesica Tate plans to contribute $2500 per year to a retirement plan and is debating the use of a certificate of deposit that pays 4% per year versus an Asian stock fund that she believes will yield 10% per year. Find the future value after 12 years for **(a)** the certificate of deposit and **(b)** the stock fund. **(c)** Find the difference.

(a) _____

(b) _____

(c) _____

QUICK CHECK ANSWERS

1. High for the year = $19.87; low for the year = $2.30; ticker symbol is REV; volume was 1,373,800 shares; no dividend yield; price to earnings ratio is 20; stock closed at $17.83; stock price fell by $1.07 during the week; last year's earnings were $.26; this year's earnings are forecast to be $1.05; next year's earnings are forecast to be $2.26; no dividend

2. $672,300; $0

3. 2.5%

4. 15

5. $188,668.35; $239,061.30

11.5 Bonds

OBJECTIVES

1 Define the basics of bonds.
2 Read bond tables.
3 Find the commission charge on bonds and the cost of bonds.
4 Understand how mutual funds containing bonds are used for monthly income.

case IN point ▶

Roman Rodriguez has decided to include mutual funds holding stocks in his retirement plan, but he doesn't know about bonds. What are bonds? Should he invest in them?

OBJECTIVE 1 Define the basics of bonds. Corporations can sell shares of stock to raise funds. Shares represent ownership in the corporation. However, managers sometimes prefer to borrow money rather than issue stock. They borrow money for short-term needs from banks or insurance companies. Managers can also make long-term loans with banks, but they often prefer to borrow for the long term by issuing bonds. **Bonds** are legally binding promises (contracts) to repay borrowed money at a specific date in the future. Corporations commonly pay interest on each bond each year. Unlike shareholders, bondholders do not own part of the corporation. Other entities, including countries, cities, and even churches, also borrow money by using bonds.

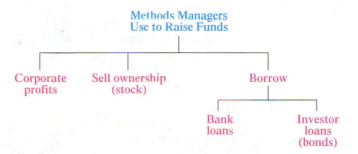

A company is said to go **bankrupt** if it can no longer meet its financial obligations to suppliers, banks, bondholders, and others. Bankruptcy is a complex process involving management, creditors, lawyers, and courts. Generally bankruptcy lawyers are paid first. Remaining assets are then used to pay off debt, including bonds. Shareholders *do not receive anything* unless there are assets remaining after all debts have been paid. Shareholders often receive very little or nothing from a bankruptcy, and bondholders often receive only a few cents on every dollar originally loaned.

Corporations frequently use substantial amounts of debt to build factories, expand operations, or buy other companies. The interest that must be paid on that debt is the *cost of having debt*. The larger the debt, the greater the amount of revenue the company must set aside to pay interest. As interest rates go higher, companies must set aside additional money to pay interest, leaving less for other purposes including profits. On the other hand, interest costs go down when interest rates go down. The article on the next page describes the increasing problems with government debt in the United States and suggests that Republicans and Democrats need to work together to solve the problems.

OBJECTIVE 2 Read bond tables. The **face value**, or **par value**, of a bond is *the original amount of money* borrowed by a company. Most public corporations issue bonds with a par value of $1000. Principal and any interest due must be paid when a bond **matures**. Suppose that a bond's owner needs money before the **maturity date** of the bond. In that event, the bond can be quickly sold through a bond dealer, such as Merrill Lynch. However, the price of the bond is determined, not by its initial price, but instead *by market conditions at the time of the sale* and the credit history of the firm. As you might expect, the bonds of a firm with poor credit history trade at much lower prices since investors worry the firm may not be able to repay its debt with interest.

Market *interest rates fluctuate widely* from year to year, yet each bond pays exactly the same dollar amount of interest each year. If interest rates rise, investors will pay less for a bond because they want the new, higher interest yield. If interest rates fall, investors will pay more for a bond because they are satisfied with the lower yield. As a result, the price of a bond fluctuates in the opposite direction of interest rates. A bond may have a face value of $1000, but it often trades at a different value than $1000, as shown in Example 1.

To Solve Budget Deficit Problems, Parties Need to Take Risks Jointly

By Richard Wolf
USA TODAY

WASHINGTON—Divided government has been good for the federal budget deficit in the past, but both sides would have to compromise on core issues if budget problems are to be solved during the next few years.

That's the conclusion of budget experts and veterans of past deficit reduction efforts, most of which succeeded because Democrats and Republicans took political risks together.

As the nation faces a huge budget deficit and the prospect of paying out more and more in Medicare and Social Security benefits, everything—including tax increases—needs to be on the table, some experts say.

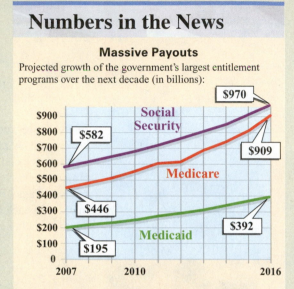

Numbers in the News

Massive Payouts

Projected growth of the government's largest entitlement programs over the next decade (in billions):

DATA: Congressional Budget Office

Working with the Bond Table

EXAMPLE 1

Brandy Barrett was in an automobile accident that put her in the hospital for 3 weeks and required months of rehabilitation. The other driver was at fault, and his insurance company paid Barrett the liability limits on his policy of $50,000. Barrett needs monthly income and is thinking about investing the funds in Merrill Lynch Inc (BAC) bonds that mature in 2018. Analyze the data in the table.

COMPANY (TICKER)	COUPON	MATURITY	LAST PRICE	LAST YIELD	EST VOL (000S)
Merrill Lynch Inc (BAC)	6.875	Apr 25, 2018	108.767	5.546	446,025

SOLUTION

(a) The ticker symbol for Merrill Lynch is BAC.

(b) Annual interest paid per bond = 6.875% of $1000 = $68.75

(c) The bond matures on April 25, 2018, at which time Merrill Lynch must pay it off.

(d) The last price at which the bond traded was 108.767% of $1000.

$$\text{Last price} = 1.08767 \times \$1000 = \$1087.67$$

(e) An investor holding the bond until its maturity date would earn 5.546% per year on his investment. This is often called the **yield to maturity**.

(f) The estimated volume of this bond that sold during the week is

$$446{,}025 \times 1000 = \$446{,}025{,}000$$

QUICK CHECK 1

Analyze the data in the bond table for Pfizer (PFE) that matures in 2019.

Corporate Bonds

Company (Ticker)	Coupon	Maturity	Last Price	Last Yield	Est $ Vol (000's)
Cit Group (CIT)	7.000	May 01, 2017	86.094	9.692	529,364
Merrill Lynch Inc (BAC)	6.875	Apr 25, 2018	108.767	5.546	446,025
Time Warner Cable (TWC)	5.000	Feb 01, 2020	98.569	5.182	418,636
Dow Chemical Co (DOW)	8.550	May 15, 2019	120.785	5.665	327,315
Cisco Systems (CSCO)	4.450	Jan 15, 2020	100.380	4.403	299,927
Aflac (AFL)	6.900	Dec 17, 2039	99.885	6.909	266,846
Morgan Stanley (MS)	5.625	Sep 23, 2019	102.120	5.342	239,476
Citigroup (C)	8.500	May 22, 2019	116.582	6.152	238,600
Pfizer (PFE)	6.200	Mar 15, 2019	112.932	4.473	237,408
Lorillard Tobacco Co (LO)	8.125	Jun 23, 2019	111.527	6.481	233,029
Petrobras International Finance Co (PETBRA)	7.875	Mar 15, 2019	116.000	5.627	228,545
Cit Group (CIT)	7.000	May 01, 2016	86.000	10.004	215,862
Goldman Sachs Group (GS)	6.750	Oct 01, 2037	103.300	6.491	213,189
International Paper Co (IP)	7.950	Jun 15, 2018	117.389	5.369	209,183
Time Warner Cable (TWC)	8.250	Apr 01, 2019	121.487	5.287	206,192
Petrobras International Finance Co (PETBRA)	5.750	Jan 20, 2020	101.650	5.534	204,632
Boston Scientific * (BSX)	6.000	Jan 15, 2020	103.729	5.511	201,800
Goldman Sachs Group (GS)	7.500	Feb 15, 2019	118.889	4.910	199,127
General Electric Capital (GE)	6.000	Aug 07, 2019	105.571	5.254	196,039
Cvs Caremark (CVS)	5.750	Jun 01, 2017	106.660	4.679	185,247
E I Du Pont De Nemours And Co (DD)	4.625	Jan 15, 2020	100.331	4.581	182,131
Altria Group (MO)	9.250	Aug 06, 2019	123.249	6.028	178,915
Bank Of America (BAC)	7.625	Jun 01, 2019	116.894	5.324	161,370
Anadarko Petroleum (APC)	5.950	Sep 15, 2016	110.508	4.143	152,929
Allied Waste North America (RSG)	7.125	May 15, 2016	106.500	4.749	152,221
International Paper Co* (IP)	7.500	Aug 15, 2021	113.729	5.856	150,951
Novartis Securities Investment Ltd (NOVART)	5.125	Feb 10, 2019	106.661	4.237	149,852

Using the Bond Table

EXAMPLE 2

Find the estimated volume sold and the last sale price of the following bonds.

(a) International Paper Co (IP) maturing in 2021
(b) CVS Caremark (CVS) maturing in 2017
(c) Time Warner Cable (TWC) maturing in 2020

SOLUTION

	Company	Volume Sold	Last Sale Price per Bond
(a)	International Paper Co	$150,951,000	$1137.29
(b)	CVS Caremark	$185,247,000	$1066.60
(c)	Time Warner Cable	$418,636,000	$ 985.69

QUICK CHECK 2

Find the volume sold and the last sale price for General Electric Capital (GE) bonds maturing in 2019.

OBJECTIVE 3 Find the commission charge on bonds and the cost of bonds. Commissions charged on bond sales vary among brokers. A common charge is $10 per bond, either to buy or to sell. However, commissions are lower for large volumes.

It is important to know that the effective interest rate is not the same as the last yield. The last yield takes into consideration the cost of the bond, the maturity value of the bond, the time to maturity, and all interest payments. See Example 3.

Finding the Cost to Buy Bonds   **EXAMPLE 3**

Assume that the sales charge is $10 per bond, and find the following for Aflac (AFL) bonds maturing in 2039.

(a) The total cost of purchasing 20 bonds

(b) The total annual interest paid on these bonds

(c) The effective interest rate to the buyer including the cost of buying the bonds

SOLUTION

(a) Total cost = (Price per bond + Sales charge per bond) × Number of bonds
$$= (\$998.85 + \$10) \times 20 = \$20{,}177$$

(b) Annual interest = Coupon rate × Par value of bond × Number of bonds
$$= (.069 \times \$1000) \times 20 = \$1380$$

(c) Effective rate $= \dfrac{\text{Total interest}}{\text{Total cost of bonds}} = \dfrac{\$1380}{\$20{,}177} = 6.8\%$ (rounded)

> **QUICK CHECK 3**
>
> Find the total cost, annual interest, and effective rate for 10 Boston Scientific (BSX) bonds maturing in 2020.

Finding the Net Amount from the Sale of Bonds   **EXAMPLE 4**

Find the amount received from the sale of 50 General Electric Capital (GE) bonds maturing in 2019.

SOLUTION

Amount received = (Sales price of a bond − Sales charge per bond) × Number of bonds
$$= (\$1055.71 - \$10) \times 50 = \$52{,}285.50$$

> **QUICK CHECK 4**
>
> Find the amount received from the sale of 200 Morgan Stanley (MS) bonds maturing in 2019.

OBJECTIVE 4 Understand how mutual funds containing bonds are used for monthly income. A mutual fund can invest everything in stocks, everything in bonds, or part in stocks and part in bonds. Stock prices can be quite volatile, so financial planners recommend stock investments for people *who have a longer time horizon* over which to accumulate funds. Many planners recommend that *people invest in both stocks and bonds* during their lifetimes. Stocks may be a better investment *when investors are young*, since stocks have tended to have a higher return. Bonds may be a better investment *for investors close to retirement*, since there is less risk of losing principal in bonds and bonds pay regular interest.

Using a Bond Fund for Income **EXAMPLE 5**

Brandy Barrett from Example 1 is undergoing rehabilitation and needs safety of principal. She also needs regular interest payments to help with medical expenses. She decides to place the $50,000 received from the insurance company in a mutual fund containing bonds. **(a)** Find her annual income if the fund yields 6.5% per year. **(b)** How much would Barrett need to invest in the fund to earn $10,000 per year?

SOLUTION

(a) Use the formula for simple interest: $I = PRT$.

$$\text{Interest} = \$50,000 \times .065 = \$3250$$

(b) Again use the formula for simple interest, but now the principal (P) is unknown. Divide both sides of $I = PRT$ by RT to find the following form of the equation.

$$\text{Principal} = P = \frac{I}{RT} = \frac{\$10,000}{.065 \times 1} = \$153,846.15$$

QUICK CHECK 5

James Corporation wants $80,000 per year in interest. Find the amount the firm must invest in a bond fund yielding 6.125% to attain this annual income.

11.5 Exercises

The QUICK START *exercises in each section contain solutions to help you get started.*

Use the bond table in this section to find the following for Allied Waste of North America (RSG) maturing in 2016. (See Examples 1 and 2.)

QUICK START

1. Price per bond   1. **$1065.00**

2. Volume of bonds sold during the week   2. _____

3. Date when bonds must be paid off by Kraft Foods   3. _____

4. Annual interest paid   4. _____

5. Last yield or yield to maturity   5. _____

6. Price to buy 50 of these bonds including sales charge of $10 per bond   6. _____

Find the cost, including sales charges of $10 per bond, for each of the following purchases. (See Example 3.)

QUICK START

Bond	Maturity	Number Purchased	Cost
7. Petrobras Int. Finance (PETBRA) ($1016.50 + 10) × 50 = $51,325	Jan 20, 2020	50	**$51,325**
8. Altria Group (MO)	Aug 06, 2019	100	_____
9. International Paper Co (IP)	Aug 15, 2021	80	_____
10. Cit Group (CIT)	May 01, 2017	350	_____
11. Goldman Sachs Group (GS)	Oct 01, 2037	250	_____
12. Cisco Systems (CSCO)	Jan 15, 2020	1000	_____

13. Explain the purpose of bonds. (See Objective 1.)

14. Explain how a bondholder can estimate the effective interest rate return on the total cost of the investment, including commissions. (See Example 3.)

Solve each application problem. Assume a sales commission of $10 per bond, unless indicated otherwise, and use the table in this section. Round the rate to the nearest tenth of a percent.

QUICK START

15. **BOND FUND** Pete Chong manages bonds for a fund company. He purchases 4000 Goldman Sachs Group (GS) bonds that mature in 2037. Since this is a large purchase, the commission is only $.80 per bond. Find **(a)** the total cost of the purchase including commissions, **(b)** the annual interest payment, and **(c)** the effective interest rate based on total cost including commissions.

    (a) Total cost = (1.033 × $1000 + $.80) × 4000 = $4,135,200
    (b) Annual interest = (.0675 × $1000) × 4000 = $270,000
    (c) Effective interest rate = $270,000 ÷ $4,135,200 = 6.5%

(a) <u>$4,135,200</u>

(b) <u>$270,000</u>

(c) <u>6.5%</u>

16. **BOND PURCHASE** New York City purchased 10,000 General Electric Capital (GE) bonds maturing in 2019. **(a)** Find the total cost of the purchase, including commissions (assume commissions of $1 per bond based on the large purchase). Then find **(b)** the annual interest payment and **(c)** the effective interest rate to total cost, including commissions.

(a) _____

(b) _____

(c) _____

17. **BOND PURCHASE** An investor bought 15 Altria Group (MO) bonds maturing in 2019. Find **(a)** the total cost of the purchase including commissions, **(b)** the annual interest payment, and **(c)** the effective interest rate using total cost including commissions.

(a) _____

(b) _____

(c) _____

18. **RETIREMENT FUNDS** The manager of a retirement account for United Pensions of America purchased 300 Anadarko Petroleum (APC) bonds maturing in 2016. Find **(a)** the total cost of the purchase including commissions, **(b)** the annual interest payment, and **(c)** the effective interest rate using total cost including commissions.

(a) _____

(b) _____

(c) _____

19. **BOND FUND** Bernice Clarence places $45,000 in a bond fund that is currently yielding 8% compounded annually. **(a)** Find interest for the first year. **(b)** She decides to let all interest payments remain in the account. Find the amount in the account after 10 years if the fund continues to earn 8% compounded annually.

(a) _____

(b) _____

20. **BOND FUND** The community college where Roman Rodriguez works has an endowment funded by alumni and business owners in the community. The manager of the endowment invested $500,000 in a bond fund yielding 6% compounded semiannually. Find **(a)** the interest for the first year and **(b)** the future value of the account in 8 years.

(a) _____

(b) _____

QUICK CHECK ANSWERS

1. Ticker symbol (PFE); annual interest = $62.00; matures on March 15, 2019; last price = $1129.32; yield to maturity = 4.473%; estimated volume sold during the week = $237,408,000.

2. estimated volume $196,039,000; last sale price = $1055.71

3. $10,472.90; $600; 5.7%

4. $202,240

5. $1,306,122.45

Chapter 11 | Quick Review

Chapter Terms *Review the following terms to test your understanding of the chapter. For each term you do not know, refer to the page number found next to that term.*

401(k) [**p. 441**]
403(b) [**p. 441**]
amount of the annuity [**p. 437**]
annual meeting [**p. 463**]
annuity [**p. 436**]
annuity due [**p. 438**]
bankrupt [**p. 475**]
board of directors [**p. 463**]
bond [**p. 453**]
capital [**p. 463**]
common stock [**p. 464**]
compound amount of the
   annuity [**p. 436**]
corporation [**p. 463**]
current yield [**p. 465**]
discount brokers [**p. 464**]

dividends [**p. 463**]
Dow Jones Industrial Average
   [**p. 467**]
equivalent cash price [**p. 449**]
ETF [**p. 468**]
exchange-traded funds (ETFs)
   [**p. 468**]
executive officers [**p. 463**]
face value [**p. 475**]
future value of the annuity
   [**p. 436**]
index fund [**p. 468**]
individual retirement account
   (IRA) [**p. 440**]
interest rate spreads [**p. 456**]
IRA [**p. 440**]

limited liability [**p. 463**]
mature [**p. 475**]
maturity date [**p. 475**]
mutual fund [**p. 468**]
NASDAQ Composite Index
   [**p. 467**]
ordinary annuity [**p. 436**]
par value [**p. 475**]
payment period [**p. 436**]
PE ratio [**p. 466**]
preferred stock [**p. 464**]
present value of an annuity
   [**p. 445**]
price–earnings (PE) ratio [**p. 465**]
privately held corporation
   [**p. 463**]

publicly held corporation
   [**p. 463**]
regular IRA [**p. 440**]
risk [**p. 468**]
Roth IRA [**p. 440**]
sinking fund [**p. 453**]
sinking fund table [**p. 454**]
stock [**p. 463**]
stockbrokers [**p. 464**]
stock certificates [**p. 463**]
stock exchanges [**p. 464**]
stockholders [**p. 463**]
stock ratios [**p. 465**]
term of the annuity [**p. 436**]
yield to maturity [**p. 476**]

CONCEPTS

EXAMPLES

11.1 Finding the amount of an ordinary annuity

Determine the number of periods in the annuity (n) and the interest rate per annuity period (i).
Use n and i in the annuity table to find the value of $1 at the term of annuity.

Find the value of an annuity using the formula.

   Amount = Payment × Number from table

Ed Navarro deposits $800 at the end of each quarter for 7 years into an IRA. Given interest of 8% compounded quarterly, find the future value.

$$n = 7 \times 4 = 28 \text{ periods}; \quad i = \tfrac{8\%}{4} = 2\% \text{ per period}$$

Number from table is **37.05121**.

Amount = $800 × **37.05121** = **$29,640.97** (rounded)

11.1 Finding the amount of an annuity due

Determine the number of periods in the annuity. Add 1 to the value and use this as the value of n.
Determine the interest rate per annuity period, and use the table to find the value of $1 at term of annuity.

The amount of the annuity is

Payment × Number from table − 1 payment

Find the amount of an annuity due if payments of $700 are made at the beginning of each quarter for 3 years in an account paying 8% compounded quarterly.

$$n = 3 \times 4 + 1 = 13; \quad i = \tfrac{8\%}{4} = 2\%$$

Number from table is **14.68033**.

Amount = $700 × **14.68033** − **$700** = $9576.23

11.2 Finding the present value of an annuity

Determine the payment per period.
Determine the number of periods in the annuity (n).
Determine the interest rate per period (i).
Use the values of n and i to find the number in the present value of an annuity table.

The present value of an annuity is

Present value = Payment × Number from table

What lump sum deposited today at 8% compounded annually will yield the same total as payments of $600 at the end of each year for 10 years?

Payment = $600; n = 10

Interest = 8%

Number from table is **6.71008**.

Present value = $600 × **6.71008** = **$4026.05**

CONCEPTS	EXAMPLES

11.2 Finding the equivalent cash price

Determine the amount of the annuity payment. Determine the number of periods in the annuity (n). Determine the interest rate per annuity period (i). Use n and i in the present value of an annuity table. Add the present value of the annuity to the down payment to obtain today's equivalent cash price.

A buyer offers to purchase a business for $75,000 down and payments of $4000 at the end of each quarter for 5 years. Money is worth 8% compounded quarterly. How much is the buyer actually offering for the business?

Payment = $4000; $n = 20$

Interest = $\frac{8\%}{4} = 2\%$

Number from table is **16.35143**.

Present value = $4000 × **16.35143** = **$65,405.72**

Equivalent cash value = $75,000 + **$65,405.72**

= $140,405.72

11.3 Determining the payment into a sinking fund

Determine the number of payments (n). Determine the interest rate per period (i). Find the value of the payment needed to accumulate $1 from the sinking fund table.

Calculate the payment using

Payment = Future value × Number from table

No-Leak Plumbing plans to accumulate $500,000 in 4 years in a sinking fund for a new building. Find the amount of each semiannual payment if the fund earns 10% compounded semiannually.

$$n = 4 × 2 = 8 \text{ periods}; \quad i = \frac{10\%}{2} = 5\% \text{ per period}$$

Number from table is **.10472**.

Payment = $500,000 × **.10472** = $52,360

11.3 Setting up a sinking fund table

Determine the required payment into the sinking fund. Calculate the interest at the end of each period. Add the previous total, next payment, and interest to determine the total. Repeat these steps for each period.

A company wants to set up a sinking fund to accumulate $10,000 in 4 years. It wishes to make semiannual payments into the account, which pays 8% compounded semiannually. Set up a sinking fund table.

$$n = 8; \quad i = 4\%$$

Number from table is **.10853**.

Payment = $10,000 × **.10853** = $1085.30

PAYMENT	AMOUNT OF DEPOSIT	INTEREST EARNED	TOTAL
1	$1085.30	$0	$1085.30
2	$1085.30	$43.41	$2214.01
3	$1085.30	$88.56	$3387.87
4	$1085.30	$135.51	$4608.68
5	$1085.30	$184.35	$5878.33
6	$1085.30	$235.13	$7198.76
7	$1085.30	$287.95	$8572.01
8	$1085.11	$342.88	$10,000.00

11.4 Reading the stock table

Use the stock table in Section 11.4 to find the following information for Regal A (RFC).

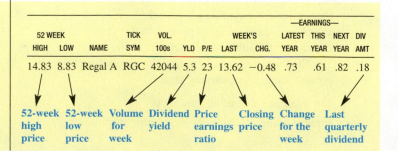

52 WEEK			TICK	VOL.			WEEK'S		—EARNINGS—			DIV
HIGH	LOW	NAME	SYM	100s	YLD	P/E	LAST	CHG.	LATEST YEAR	THIS YEAR	NEXT YEAR	AMT
14.83	8.83	Regal A	RGC	42044	5.3	23	13.62	−0.48	.73	.61	.82	.18

52-week high price → 52-week low price → Volume for week → Dividend yield → Price earnings ratio → Closing price → Change for the week → Last quarterly dividend

CONCEPTS	EXAMPLES

11.4 Finding the current yield on a stock

To determine the current yield, use the formula

$$\text{Current yield} = \frac{\text{Annual dividend}}{\text{Closing price}}$$

Find the current yield for a stock if the purchase price is $35 and the annual dividend is $.64.

$$\text{Current yield} = \frac{\$.64}{\$35} = 1.8\% \text{ (rounded)}$$

11.4 Finding the price–earnings (PE) ratio

To find the PE ratio, use the formula

$$\text{PE ratio} = \frac{\text{Price per share}}{\text{Annual net income per share}}$$

Find the PE ratio for a stock priced at $42.50 with earnings of $2.11.

$$\text{PE Ratio} = \frac{\$42.50}{\$2.11} = 20 \text{ (rounded)}$$

11.5 Reading the bond table

Use the bond table in Section 11.5 to find the following information for EI DuPont De Nemours and Co (DD) maturing in 2020.

COMPANY (TICKER)	COUPON	MATURITY	LAST PRICE	LAST YIELD	EST VOL (000s)
EI DuPont De Nemours (DD)	4.625	Jan 15, 2020	100.331	4.581	182,131

Pays 4.625% of $1000 per year
Matures Jan. 15, 2020
Closed at $1003.31 per bond
Yield to maturity of 4.581%
Estimated volume of $182,131,000 traded for week

11.5 Determining the cost of purchasing bonds

First locate the bond in the table. Then determine the price of the bond and multiply this value by $1000 and the number of bonds purchased. Finally, add $10 per bond to the total cost of bonds purchased.

Including sales charges of $10 per bond, find the cost of 50 Dow Chemical Co (DOW) bonds maturing in 2019.

$$(1.20785 \times \$1000 + \$10) \times 50 = \$60,892.50$$

11.5 Determining the amount received from the sale of bonds

First locate the bond in the table. Then determine the price of the bond and multiply this value by 1000 and the number of bonds sold. Finally, subtract $10 per bond from the total selling price.

Find the amount received after the sales charge from the sale of 20 Time Warner Cable (TWC) bonds maturing in 2020.

$$(.98569 \times \$1000 - \$10) \times 20 = \$19,513.80$$

11.5 Finding the effective yield of a bond

Find the cost of the bond after commission. Find the interest paid on the bond using the coupon rate. Finally, divide the interest by the cost of the bond.

Find the effective interest rate, to the nearest tenth, for a bond with a coupon rate of 3.8% and selling at 98.25.

Price of bond $= .9825 \times \$1000 + \$10 = $ **$992.50**
Interest $= .038 \times \$1000 = \$38$

$$\text{Effective rate} = \frac{\$38}{\$992.50} = 3.8\% \text{ (rounded)}$$

case study

LONG-TERM FINANCIAL PLANNING

At age 37, Paul Li decides to plan for his retirement at age 67. He currently has a net worth of about $45,000 including the equity in his home. He assumes that his employer will contribute $3500 to his retirement plan at the end of each year for the next 30 years. He plans to put one-half of his money in a mutual fund containing stocks and the other one-half in a mutual fund containing bonds.

1. Estimate Li's future accumulation if his net worth grows at 5% and the mutual funds with stocks and bonds grow at 10% and 6%, respectively.

    1. _____

2. Li is amazed that he will be able to accumulate over $600,000. However, he knows that inflation will increase his cost of living significantly in 30 years. He assumes 3% inflation and wants to find the income he needs at age 67 to have the same purchasing power as $40,000 today. (*Hint:* Look at inflation in Section 10.2 and use the compound interest table in Section 10.1.)

    2. _____

3. Li has read newspaper articles stating that Social Security benefits will be reduced in the years ahead. After some thought, he decides to be conservative and assume that Social Security will pay only the first $30,000 of the annual income he needs at age 67. Find the remaining income he will need beginning at age 67.

    3. _____

4. Li decides to plan funding for his retirement for 20 years, from ages 67 to 87. If funds earn 8% compounded annually, find the present value of the annual income that he needs at 67 based on the income from part (c).

    4. _____

5. Will his expected savings fund his retirement?

    5. _____

6. What could go wrong with his plans?

    6. _____

> **INVESTIGATE**
>
> There is some discussion about the ability of Social Security to pay retirement benefits. Do you think Social Security will be around to help you during your retirement? What percent of your retirement needs do you think Social Security will pay? Try to support your views with recent articles from newspapers, magazines, or the World Wide Web.

case ⫫ point summary exercise

AMERICAN RIVER COLLEGE

www.arc.losrios.edu

Facts:

- 1955: Founded
- 2010: About 35,000 students
- 2011: 58% of the students are under 30
- 2011: 50.3% of students are women

American River offers students a choice of more than 70 different majors of study, including biology, engineering, hospitality management, mortuary science, collision repair, business, and even fire technology. College personnel work closely with students to help them find financial aid. Amazingly, about one-half of the students at American River College receive some kind of financial aid.

Roman Rodriguez had 3 years of experience when he went to work in Human Resources at American River College at a salary of $42,000. He began work on his 30th birthday. The college matches his contributions to his retirement plan up to 8% of his salary.

1. Rodriguez decides to contribute a total of 10% of his salary to his retirement plan. So, American River contributes 8% and he contributes a full 10% of his salary. Find the total annual contribution into the retirement plan.

   1. _____

2. For planning purposes, Rodriguez assumes he will work at American River until he is 60 and believes he can earn 8% per year in a global stock fund. Assume the contributions continue at the same level as in Exercise 1 and estimate the future value.

   2. _____

3. Assume that there are 422 full-time faculty at American River College and that their average income is $48,500 per year. Find the annual payroll for the faculty.

   3. _____

4. Based on the annual payroll in Exercise 3, estimate the annual contributions American River must make into retirement plans if all faculty contribute at least 8% of their salary into their own plans.

   4. _____

5. Assume that a wealthy donor has agreed to give American River College $250,000 per year for the next 5 years. Find the present value of these gifts, assuming 6% per year.

   5. _____

6. American River has decided to build a new classroom building and will need $8,250,000 in 7 years. They decide to make contributions into a sinking fund at the end of each 6-month period. Find the payment needed if funds earn 5% per year.

   6. _____

Chapter 11 Test

To help you review, the numbers in brackets show the section in which the topic was discussed.

Find the amounts of the following annuities. **[11.1]**

	Amount of Each Deposit	Deposited	Rate per Year	Number of Years	Type of Annuity	Amount of Annuity
1.	$1000	annually	6%	8	ordinary	_____
2.	$4500	semiannually	10%	9	ordinary	_____
3.	$30,000	quarterly	8%	6	due	_____
4.	$2600	semiannually	5%	12	due	_____

5. James Rivera earned his degree in drafting at a community college and recently began his new career. He was happy to learn that his new employer will deposit $2500 into his 401(k) retirement account at the end of each year. Find the amount he will have accumulated in 15 years if funds earn 8% per year. **[11.1]**

5. _____

6. James Rivera from Exercise 5 has also decided to invest $1000 at the end of each 6 months in an IRA that grows tax deferred. Find the amount he will have accumulated if he does this for 15 years and earns 6% compounded semiannually. **[11.1]**

6. _____

Find the present value of the following annuities. **[11.2]**

	Amount per Payment	Payment at End of Each	Number of Years	Interest Rate	Compounded	Present Value
7.	$1000	year	9	6%	annually	_____
8.	$4500	6 months	6	10%	semiannually	_____
9.	$708	month	3	12%	monthly	_____
10.	$14,000	quarter	6	8%	quarterly	_____

11. Betty Yowski borrows money for a new swimming pool and hot tub. She agrees to repay the note with a payment of $1200 per quarter for 6 years. Find the amount she must set aside today to satisfy this capital requirement in an account earning 8% compounded quarterly. **[11.2]**

11. _____

12. Dan and Mary Foster just divorced. The divorce settlement included $650 a month payment to Dan for the 4 years until their son turns 18. Find the amount Mary must set aside today in an account earning 12% per year compounded monthly to satisfy this financial obligation. **[11.2]**

12. _____

Find the amount of each payment into a sinking fund for the following. **[11.3]**

	Amount Needed	Years Until Needed	Interest Rate	Interest Compounded	Amount of Payment
13.	$100,000	9	6%	annually	_____
14.	$250,000	10	8%	semiannually	_____
15.	$360,000	11	6%	quarterly	_____
16.	$800,000	12	10%	semiannually	_____

Solve the following application problems.

17. The owner of Hickory Bar-B-Que plans to open a new restaurant in 4 years at a cost of $200,000. Find the required semiannual payment into a sinking fund if funds are invested in an account earning 6% per year compounded semiannually. **[11.3]**

17. _____

18. Lupe Martinez will owe her retired mother $45,000 for a piece of land. Find the required quarterly payment into a sinking fund if Lupe pays it off in 4 years and the interest rate is 10% per year compounded quarterly. **[11.3]**

18. _____

19. George Jones purchases 200 shares of Merck stock at $45.60 per share. Find **(a)** the total cost and **(b)** the annual dividend if the dividend per share is $1.52. **[11.4]**

(a) _____

(b) _____

20. Belinda Deal purchases 25 IBM bonds that mature in 2021 at 95.1. They have a coupon rate of 4.2%. Find **(a)** the total cost if commissions are $10 per bond, **(b)** the annual interest, and **(c)** the effective interest rate rounded to the nearest tenth. **[11.5]**

(a) _____

(b) _____

(c) _____

21. Explain the following from the stock table. **[11.4]**

| 52-WK | | NAME | TICK SYM. | VOL. 100s | YLD. | P/E | WEEK'S | | EARNINGS | | | DIV AMT |
HIGH	LOW						LAST	CHG.	LATEST YEAR	THIS YEAR	NEXT YEAR	
65.90	20.10	BlackDeck	BDK	74515	.8	27	63.44	+1.23	5.47	2.53	2.89	.12

22. Explain the following from the bond table. **[11.5]**

COMPANY (TICKER)	COUPON	MATURITY	LAST PRICE	LAST YIELD	EST $ VOL (000s)
International Paper Co (IP)	7.950	Jun 15, 2018	117.389	5.369	209,183

Business and Consumer Loans

12

case IN ▶ point

AFTER JACKIE WATERTON received her degree in business, she went to work for Citigroup, Inc. Citi which is one of the largest banks in the world. Since she is interested in computers and the Internet, she went to work in the department that manages electronic banking. After working there for 3 years, Waterton moved to the department that manages consumer credit. Recently, she was promoted, and she now manages a small group that works with bank customers who have major credit problems.

In this important chapter, we look at debt and the associated interest charges. Both individuals and companies borrow and pay resulting interest charges. People borrow for purchases at department stores, gas stations, furniture stores, automobile dealerships, or even when using cell phones. Companies borrow to fund large projects or to cover payroll while waiting for payments from customers. Sometimes, individuals or companies end up with more debt than they can handle, resulting in a lot of stress and even bankruptcy.

12.1 Open-End Credit and Charge Cards

OBJECTIVES

1 Define open-end credit.
2 Define revolving charge accounts.
3 Use the unpaid balance method.
4 Use the average daily balance method.
5 Define loan consolidation.

case in point

Jackie Waterton has worked with many families who have serious debt problems. She often helps these families set up budgets and then tries to reduce their monthly debt payments by refinancing loans when possible.

The newspaper clipping shows that young adults commonly struggle with debt because they are often trying to start a household and pay for college at the same time.

Students use of Credit-card Debt Grows

In a recent study done by the lender Sallie Mae, the following was discovered:

- 84% of undergraduates have at least one credit card, with an average of 4.6 credit cards per student.
- The average credit-card debt of graduating seniors has increased by 41% in 4 years to $4100.
- 20% of graduating seniors owe more than $7000 on credit cards.

Average Credit Card Debt by Grade Level

	2004	2009
Freshmen	$1601	$2038
Sophomore	$1575	$2362
Junior	$2000	$2912
Senior	$2864	$4138

(*Source:* Sallie Mae, 2009.)

OBJECTIVE 1 Define open-end credit. A common way of buying on credit, called **open-end credit**, has no fixed payments. The customer continues making payments until no outstanding balance is owed. With open-end credit, additional credit is often extended before the initial amount is paid off. Examples of open-end credit include most department-store charge accounts and charge cards, including MasterCard and Visa. Individuals are given a **credit limit**, or a maximum amount that may be charged on these accounts. The lender determines the credit limit for each person based on income, assets, other debts, and credit history.

A sale paid for with a **debit card** authorizes the retailer's bank to debit the purchaser's checking account immediately upon receipt. Debit cards do not involve credit since their use results in an immediate debit, or withdrawal of funds, from an account. Debit cards are being used more and more. A Visa or MasterCard can be either a charge card or a debit card, depending on the bank and the card holder's preference.

OBJECTIVE 2 Define revolving charge accounts. With a typical department-store account or bank card, a customer might make several small purchases during a month. Such accounts are often *never paid off*, although a minimum amount must be paid each month, since new purchases are continually being made. Since the account may never be paid off, it is called a **revolving charge account**. Visa, MasterCard, Discover, and some oil-company cards use this method of extending credit. Sometimes there is an annual membership fee or a minimum monthly charge for the use of this service.

A sample copy of a credit card receipt is shown on the left. The graph shows the percent of families in the United States who have a credit card and also the percent who have a balance after paying the previous month's bill. Notice that both credit-card use and loan balances have increased markedly since 1989.

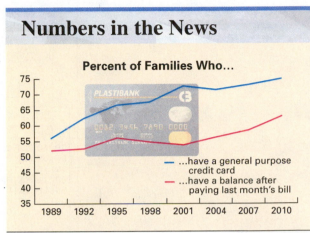

DATA: Federal Reserve, Survey of Consumer Finances; 2010.

At the end of each billing period, the customer receives a statement of payments and purchases made. An example of such an **itemized billing** is shown on page 494. Notice that it shows a variety of transactions, including new charges, refunds and payments (shown as credits), and any finance charges. The statement also shows bank fees related to exchanging currency in the event that charges were made in a foreign country.

Finance charges are interest charges beyond the cash price of an item and may include interest, credit life insurance, a time-payment differential, and carrying charges. Interest charges can be avoided if the total balance is paid by the end of the **grace period**. Grace periods range between 15 and 30 days depending on the company. Often, there is no grace period on cash advances, so that finance charges are assessed beginning immediately. Many lenders also charge **late fees** for payments that are received after the due date. **Over-the-limit fees** are charged by the lender when the borrower charges more than an approved maximum amount of debt.

> **Quick TIP** ▼
>
> Both late fees and over-the-limit fees are high. Avoid them!

OBJECTIVE 3 Use the unpaid balance method. Finance charges on open-end credit accounts may be calculated using the **unpaid balance method**. This method calculates finance charges based on the unpaid balance at *the end of the previous month*. Any purchases or returns during the current month are not used in calculating the finance charge, as you can see in the next example.

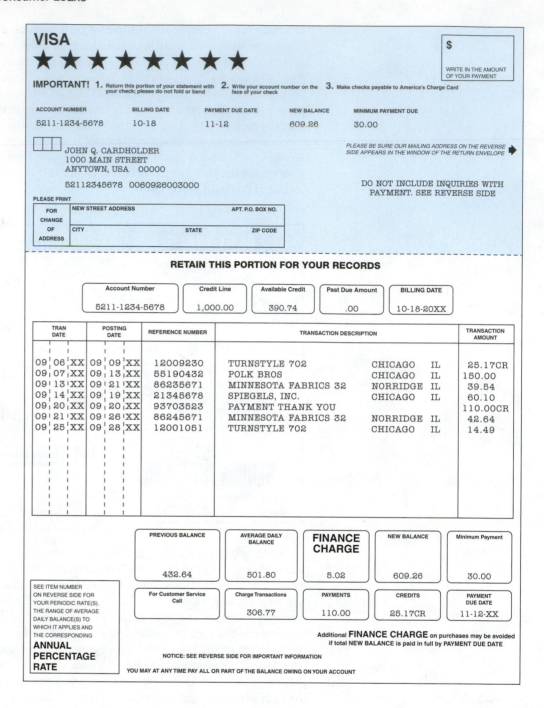

VISA

★ ★ ★ ★ ★ ★ ★ ★ ★ ★

$

WRITE IN THE AMOUNT
OF YOUR PAYMENT

IMPORTANT! 1. Return this portion of your statement with your check; please do not fold or bend   2. Write your account number on the face of your check   3. Make checks payable to America's Charge Card

ACCOUNT NUMBER	BILLING DATE	PAYMENT DUE DATE	NEW BALANCE	MINIMUM PAYMENT DUE
5211-1234-5678	10-18	11-12	609.26	30.00

JOHN Q. CARDHOLDER
1000 MAIN STREET
ANYTOWN, USA 00000

52112345678 0060926003000

PLEASE BE SURE OUR MAILING ADDRESS ON THE REVERSE
SIDE APPEARS IN THE WINDOW OF THE RETURN ENVELOPE ➤

DO NOT INCLUDE INQUIRIES WITH
PAYMENT. SEE REVERSE SIDE

PLEASE PRINT

FOR CHANGE OF ADDRESS	NEW STREET ADDRESS		APT. P.O. BOX NO.
	CITY	STATE	ZIP CODE

RETAIN THIS PORTION FOR YOUR RECORDS

Account Number	Credit Line	Available Credit	Past Due Amount	BILLING DATE
5211-1234-5678	1,000.00	390.74	.00	10-18-20XX

TRAN DATE	POSTING DATE	REFERENCE NUMBER	TRANSACTION DESCRIPTION			TRANSACTION AMOUNT
09 06 XX	09 09 XX	12009230	TURNSTYLE 702	CHICAGO	IL	25.17CR
09 07 XX	09 13 XX	55190432	POLK BROS	CHICAGO	IL	150.00
09 13 XX	09 21 XX	86235671	MINNESOTA FABRICS 32	NORRIDGE	IL	39.54
09 14 XX	09 19 XX	21345678	SPIEGELS, INC.	CHICAGO	IL	60.10
09 20 XX	09 20 XX	93703523	PAYMENT THANK YOU			110.00CR
09 21 XX	09 26 XX	86245671	MINNESOTA FABRICS 32	NORRIDGE	IL	42.64
09 25 XX	09 28 XX	12001051	TURNSTYLE 702	CHICAGO	IL	14.49

PREVIOUS BALANCE	AVERAGE DAILY BALANCE	FINANCE CHARGE	NEW BALANCE	Minimum Payment
432.64	501.80	5.02	609.26	30.00

SEE ITEM NUMBER ON REVERSE SIDE FOR YOUR PERIODIC RATE(S). THE RANGE OF AVERAGE DAILY BALANCE(S) TO WHICH IT APPLIES AND THE CORRESPONDING **ANNUAL PERCENTAGE RATE**

For Customer Service Call	Charge Transactions	PAYMENTS	CREDITS	PAYMENT DUE DATE
	306.77	110.00	25.17CR	11-12-XX

Additional **FINANCE CHARGE** on purchases may be avoided
if total NEW BALANCE is paid in full by PAYMENT DUE DATE

NOTICE: SEE REVERSE SIDE FOR IMPORTANT INFORMATION

YOU MAY AT ANY TIME PAY ALL OR PART OF THE BALANCE OWING ON YOUR ACCOUNT

Finding Finance Charge Using the Unpaid Balance Method

EXAMPLE 1

(a) Peter Brinkman's MasterCard account had an unpaid balance of $870.40 on November 1. During November, he made a payment of $100 and used the card to purchase a yellow Lab costing $150 for his son. Find the finance charge and the unpaid balance on December 1 if the bank charges 1.5% per month on the unpaid balance.

A finance charge of 1.5% per month on the unpaid balance would be

$$\$870.40 \times .015 = \$13.06 \text{ for the month}$$

Find the unpaid balance on December 1 as follows.

$$\underset{\substack{\text{previous} \\ \text{balance}}}{\$870.40} + \underset{\substack{\text{finance} \\ \text{charge}}}{\$13.06} + \underset{\substack{\text{purchases} \\ \text{during} \\ \text{month}}}{\$150} - \underset{\text{payment}}{\$100} = \underset{\substack{\text{new} \\ \text{balance}}}{\$933.46}$$

(b) During December, Brinkman made a payment of $50, charged $240.56 for Christmas presents, returned $35.45 worth of items, and took his family to dinner with charges of $92.45. Find his unpaid balance on January 1.

The finance charge calculated on the unpaid balance is $933.46 \times .015 = 14.00. The unpaid balance on January 1 follows.

$$933.46 + \textbf{\$14.00} + \textbf{\$240.56} + \textbf{\$92.45} - \textbf{\$35.45} - \textbf{\$50} = \$1195.02$$

MONTH	UNPAID BALANCE AT BEGINNING OF MONTH	FINANCE CHARGE	PURCHASES DURING MONTH	RETURNS	PAYMENT	UNPAID BALANCE AT END OF MONTH
November	$870.40	$13.06	$150.00	—	$100	$ 933.46
December	$933.46	$14.00	$333.01	$35.45	$ 50	$1195.02

The total finance charge during the 2-month period was $13.06 + $14.00 = 27.06.

(c) Brinkman knows that his debt is increasing. He moves the balance to another charge card that charges only .8% per month. Find his savings in finance charges for January.

$$\text{Savings} = (\$1195.02 \times \textbf{.015}) - (\$1195.02 \times \textbf{.008}) = \$8.37$$

old charge card   new charge card

QUICK CHECK 1

The unpaid balance on a Visa card was $284.37. During the month, a payment of $200 was made and charges of $357.54 were added. If the finance charge is 1.2% per month on the unpaid balance, find **(a)** the finance charge for the month and **(b)** the new balance at the end of the month.

Suppose you decide to purchase a $1000 digital television set and charge it to a Visa card with finance charges of 1.5% per month on the unpaid balance. Further suppose that you make payments of $50 every month and don't charge anything else on the card. As shown in the table, it will take 24 months to pay off the television set. The $1000 television set will cost you an extra $197.83 in finance charges for a total cost of $1197.83, or nearly $1200.

MONTH	UNPAID BALANCE AT BEGINNING OF MONTH	FINANCE CHARGE	PAYMENT	UNPAID BALANCE AT END OF MONTH
1	$1,000.00	$15.00	$50.00	$965.00
2	$965.00	$14.48	$50.00	$929.48
3	$929.48	$13.94	$50.00	$893.42
⋮	⋮	⋮	⋮	⋮
22	$143.53	$ 2.15	$50.00	$95.68
23	$ 95.68	$ 1.44	$50.00	$47.12
24	$ 47.12	$ 0.71	$47.83	$ 0.00
Totals		$197.83	$1197.83	

The cost of technology items often falls rapidly. If you had waited eight months and saved your money before buying, you might have been able to purchase the same television set for $750 cash rather than paying nearly $1200. This would have saved you 37.5%!

OBJECTIVE 4 Use the average daily balance method. Most revolving charge plans now calculate finance charges using the **average daily balance method.** First, the balance owed on the account is found at the end of each day during a month or billing period. All of these amounts are added, and the total is divided by the number of days in the month or billing period. The result is the average daily balance of the account, which is then used to calculate the finance charge.

Finding the Average Daily Balance **EXAMPLE 2**

Beth Hogan's balance on a Visa card was $209.46 on March 3. Her activity for the next 30 days is shown in the table. **(a)** Find the average daily balance on April 3. Given finance charges based on $1\frac{1}{2}\%$ on the average daily balance, find **(b)** the finance charge for the month and **(c)** the balance owed on April 3.

TRANSACTION DESCRIPTION		TRANSACTION AMOUNT
Previous balance $209.46		
March 3	Billing date	
March 12	Payment	$50.00 CR*
March 17	Walmart	$28.46
March 20	Mail order	$31.22
April 1	Auto parts	$59.10

*CR represents *credit.*

SOLUTION

(a)

DATE	UNPAID BALANCE	NUMBER OF DAYS UNTIL BALANCE CHANGES
March 3	$209.46	9
March 12	$159.46 = $209.46 − **March 12 payment of $50**	5
March 17	$187.92 = $159.46 + **March 17 charge of $28.46**	3
March 20	$219.14 = $187.92 + **March 20 charge of $31.22**	12
April 1	$278.24 = $219.14 + **April 1 charge of $59.10**	2
April 3	end of billing cycle . . .	31 total number of days in billing period

It is 9 days from March 3 to March 12, so the unpaid balance remains at $209.46 for 9 days.

Quick TIP ▼

The billing period in Example 2 is 31 days. Some billing periods are 30 days (or 28 or 29 days in February). Be sure to use the correct number of days for the month of the billing period.

There are 31 days in the billing period (March has 31 days). Find the average daily balance as follows:

Step 1 Multiply each unpaid balance by the number of days for that balance.

Step 2 Total these amounts.

Step 3 Divide by the number of days in that particular billing cycle (month).

Step 1

UNPAID BALANCE		DAYS		TOTAL BALANCE
$209.46	×	9	=	$1885.14
$159.46	×	5	=	797.30
$187.92	×	3	=	563.76
$219.14	×	12	=	2629.68
$278.24	×	2	=	556.48
				$6432.36

← **Step 2**

Step 3

$$\frac{\$6432.36}{31} = \$207.50 \text{ average daily balance}$$

Hogan will pay a finance charge based on the average daily balance of $207.50.

(b) The finance charge is $.015 × \$207.50 = \$3.11$ (rounded).

(c) The amount owed on April 3 is the beginning unpaid balance less any returns or payments, plus new charges and the finance charge.

$$\underset{\substack{\text{previous} \\ \text{balance}}}{\$209.46} - \underset{\text{payment}}{\$50} + \underset{\text{new charges}}{(\$28.46 + \$31.22 + \$59.10)} + \underset{\substack{\text{finance} \\ \text{charge}}}{\$3.11} = \$281.35$$

QUICK CHECK 2

The July 5 balance on a credit card was $494. A payment of $400 was made on July 22, and a charge of $258.67 was made on July 25. If the finance charge is based on $1\frac{1}{2}\%$, find **(a)** the average daily balance on August 5, **(b)** the finance charge for the month, and **(c)** the unpaid balance on August 5.

The finance charge in the previous example was small, only $3.11. Have you ever wondered how banks make money on charge cards? Let's explore this issue. Citigroup recently had a balance of just over $148 billion outstanding on credit cards. Many of these people will pay off their balances at the end of the month, resulting in no finance charges to the bank. However, assume the bank earns an average of 1.2% on credit outstanding of $105 billion and find the interest earned for a month as follows:

$$\text{Interest} = \$105,000,000,000 \times .012 = \$1,260,000,000$$

At this rate, the bank earned about $1.2 billion in 1 month from finance charges on credit cards. That is a lot of money!

If the finance charges are expressed on a per-month basis, find the **annual percentage rate** by multiplying the monthly rate by 12, the number of months in a year. For example, $1\frac{1}{2}\%$ per month is the same as:

$$1\tfrac{1}{2}\% \times 12 = 1.5\% \times 12 = 18\% \text{ per year}$$

OBJECTIVE 5 Define loan consolidation. Credit is *very easy to get* for individuals who have a good credit history and a stable job. The clipping shows that too much spending and borrowing often creates problems.

Easy Credit–Big Worry

James Machler has a degree in nursing and a great job. In the past, he has been careful with his money, even paying off an extra $80 each month on his student loans and saving a little each month. Then he decided he needed a new Lexus. Now his cash flow is tight and the clinic where he works just announced there will be some layoffs in the near future. James is suddenly very worried about his future.

Too many people get caught in a credit trap. They effectively spend more than they can afford by borrowing. They then end up with problems that can last for months or years. Below are some tips to gain control of your finances. We warn you—it takes discipline.

Gaining Control of Your Finances

1. Increase your income by investing in yourself. Choose a career you enjoy, and get training and education.

2. Make a budget and stick to it.

3. Spend less. Here are some suggestions.

   (a) Make sure you can afford your rent or mortgage payment.

   (b) Eat out less often.

   (c) Drive that old automobile one or two more years.

   (d) Purchase a less expensive automobile or reduce the number of automobiles in your family by one.

   (e) Be careful with the amount you spend on entertainment, hobbies, and travel.

   (f) Don't buy on impulse. If you want something, write it down on a piece of paper and stick it on your refrigerator for 30 days. After 30 days, ask yourself if you actually need the item.

4. Try to pay cash for things the day you buy them rather than using credit.

5. Save more by paying yourself first. Do this by saving a certain amount every month before you spend money on other things.

6. Set some money aside for emergencies.

7. Contribute to a long-range retirement plan.

Have you ever found yourself in a position where you cannot make all of your monthly payments? If so, you may be able to **consolidate your loans** into a single loan with one lower monthly payment. The new loan may have a lower interest rate and also a longer term, meaning that payments must be made for a longer period of time. This process can help you afford your monthly payments rather than defaulting on debt. **Defaulting on your debt**, or not making your payments, can mean repossession of your automobile or furniture, eviction from your apartment or house, and/or court appearances. Defaulting on your debt also ruins your credit history and can make it difficult to borrow money to buy a car or a home for years into the future.

Consolidating Loans **EXAMPLE 3**

Bill and Jane Smith were married two years ago. Both were happy when they had their first child, but they needed to buy several things on credit. They now have the monthly payments shown below. The Smiths are having difficulties making the payments and they sometimes argue over money. They bank online at Citibank Direct and ask Jackie Waterton for help.

REVOLVING ACCOUNTS	DEBT	ANNUAL PERCENTAGE RATE	MINIMUM MONTHLY PAYMENT
Sears	$3880.54	18%	$150
Home Depot	$1620.13	16%	$ 60
MasterCard	$3140.65	14%	$100
Visa	$4920.98	18%	$200
Total	$13,562.30	Total	$510

OTHER PAYMENTS	MONTHLY PAYMENT
Rent	$800
Jane's car payment	$315
Bill's truck payment	$268
Total	$1383

SOLUTION

case IN point

Jackie Waterton:

1. Put the Smiths on a **strict monthly budget**.

2. Consolidated their revolving account debts into one longer-term, low-interest loan (this required a loan guarantee from Bill's father).

3. Decreased one automobile payment by refinancing the loan over a longer term.

Here are their new monthly payments.

ACCOUNT	MONTHLY PAYMENT	NEW STATUS
Credit union loan for $13,562.30	$337.50	Revolving loans were consolidated
Rent	$800.00	Unchanged
Jane's car payment	$247.50	Refinanced using a longer term
Bill's truck payment	$268.00	Unchanged
Total	$1653.00	

Reduction in payments = ($510 + $1383) − $1653 = **$240 per month**

The Smiths should be all right as long as they do the following.

1. **Stay on their monthly budget.**
2. **Do not make additional credit purchases.**
3. **Continue to make all payments.**

The Smiths may end up with severe debt problems if they borrow more before the existing loan balances are significantly reduced. Borrowing more could force them to declare bankruptcy.

Quick TIP ▼

Individuals who consolidate their loans and then borrow even more can get into very serious financial difficulties.

> **QUICK CHECK 3**
>
> A family refinanced the mortgage on their home, reducing the payment from $1269.45 to $1093.12. They also sold a car that had a monthly payment of $385.65 and negotiated a $50-per-month payment reduction on their second car. Find the decrease in monthly payments.

12.1 Exercises

The **QUICK START** exercises in each section contain solutions to help you get started.

Find the finance charge on each of the following revolving charge accounts. Assume interest is calculated on the unpaid balance of the account. Round to the nearest cent. (See Example 1.)

QUICK START

	Unpaid Balance	Monthly Interest Rate	Finance Charge
1.	$6425.40	0.8%	$51.40
	$6425.40 × .008 = $51.40		
2.	$595.35	$1\frac{1}{2}\%$	_____
3.	$1201.43	$1\frac{1}{4}\%$	_____
4.	$2540.33	1.2%	_____

Complete the following tables, showing the unpaid balance at the end of each month. Assume an interest rate of 1.4% on the unpaid balance. (See Example 1.)

	Month	Unpaid Balance at Beginning of Month	Finance Charge	Purchases During Month	Returns	Payment	Unpaid Balance at End of Month
5.	October	$437.18	_____	$128.72	$27.85	$125	_____
	November	_____	_____	$291.64	—	$175	_____
	December	_____	_____	$147.11	$17.15	$150	_____
	January	_____	_____	$27.84	$127.76	$225	_____
6.	October	$255.40	_____	$27.50	—	$50	_____
	November	_____	_____	$59.60	$22.15	$45.50	_____
	December	_____	_____	$85.45	$32.00	$125	_____
	January	_____	_____	$325.68	—	$100	_____

7. Compare the unpaid balance method and the average daily balance method for calculating interest on open-end credit accounts. (See Objectives 3 and 4.)

8. Explain how consolidating loans may be of some advantage to the borrower. What disadvantages can you think of? (See Objective 5.)

⚠ indicates an exercise that is related to the Case in Point feature.

Find the finance charge for the following revolving charge accounts. Assume that interest is calculated on the average daily balance of the account. (See Example 2.)

	Average Daily Balance	Monthly Interest Rate	Finance Charge
9.	$1458.25	1.4%	**$20.42**
	$1458.25 × .014 = $20.42		
10.	$841.60	$1\frac{1}{2}$%	**$12.62**
	$841.60 × .015 = $12.62		
11.	$389.95	$1\frac{1}{4}$%	_____
12.	$6320.10	0.9%	_____
13.	$1235.68	1.4%	_____
14.	$4235.47	$1\frac{3}{4}$%	_____

Solve the following application problems.

15. HOT TUB PURCHASE Betty Thomas borrowed $6500 on her Visa card to install a hot tub with landscaping around it. The interest charges are 1.6% per month on the unpaid balance. **(a)** Find the interest charges. **(b)** Find the interest charges if she moves the debt to a credit card charging 1% per month on the unpaid balance. **(c)** Find the monthly savings.

(a) _____

(b) _____

(c) _____

16. CREDIT CARD BALANCE Alphy Jurarim used a credit card from Citibank Direct to help pay for tuition expenses while in college and now owes $5232.25. The interest charges are 1.75% per month. **(a)** Find the interest charges. **(b)** Find the interest charges if he moves the debt to a credit card charging .8% per month on the unpaid balance. **(c)** Find the savings.

(a) _____

(b) _____

(c) _____

(a) *Find the average daily balance for the following credit card accounts. Assume one month between billing dates using the proper number of days in the month.* (b) *Then find the finance charge if interest is 1.5% per month on the average daily balance.* (c) *Finally, find the new balance. (See Example 2.)*

QUICK START

17. Previous balance $2340.52

November 12	Billing date	
November 20	Payment	$1000
November 21	Road bicycle & equipment	$1440.30
November 30	Flowers	$65.40

Nov. 12 to Nov. 20 = 8 days at $2340.52 gives $18,724.16
Nov. 20 to Nov. 21 = 1 day at $1340.52 gives $1340.52
Nov. 21 to Nov. 30 = 9 days at $2780.82 gives $25,027.38
Nov. 30 to Dec. 12 = 12 days at $2846.22 gives $34,154.64
8 + 1 + 9 + 12 = 30 days
$18,724.16 + $1340.52 + $25,027.38 + $34,154.64 = $79,246.70

(a) Average daily balance = $\dfrac{\$79{,}246.70}{30}$ = $2641.56

(b) Finance charge = $2641.56 × .015 = $39.62
(c) New balance = $2340.52 + $39.62 − $1000 + $1440.30 + $65.40 = $2885.84

(a) $2641.56

(b) $39.62

(c) $2885.84

18. Previous balance $228.95

January 27	Billing date	
February 9	Tennis-balls	$11.08
February 13	Returns	$26.54
February 20	Payment	$29
February 25	Restaurant	$71.19

(a) _____

(b) _____

(c) _____

19. Previous balance $312.78

June 11	Billing date	
June 15	Returns	$106.45
June 20	Watch	$115.73
June 24	Car rental	$74.19
July 3	Payment	$115

(a) _____

(b) _____

(c) _____

20. Previous balance $714.58

August 17	Billing date	
August 21	Mail order	$26.94
August 23	Returns	$25.41
August 27	Beverages	$31.82
August 31	Payment	$128.00
September 9	Returns	$71.14
September 11	Groceries	$110.00
September 14	Cash advance	$100.00

(a) _____

(b) _____

(c) _____

21. Previous balance $355.72

March 29	Billing date	
March 31	Returns	$209.53
April 2	Auto parts	$28.76
April 10	Pharmacy	$14.80
April 12	Returns	$63.54
April 13	Returns	$11.71
April 20	Payment	$72.00
April 21	Flowers	$29.72

(a) _____

(b) _____

(c) _____

12.2 Installment Loans

OBJECTIVES

1 Define installment loan.
2 Find the total installment cost and the finance charge.
3 Use the formula for approximate APR.
4 Use the table to find APR.

OBJECTIVE 1 Define installment loan. A loan is **amortized** if both principal and interest are paid off by a sequence of equal periodic payments. This type of loan is called an **installment loan**. Installment loans are used for cars, boats, home improvements, and even for consolidating several smaller loans into one affordable payment. The graphic below shows the interest you might have to pay to finance a new automobile. Look on the World Wide Web to find competitive interest rates for car loans. Incidentally, you can also check the market value of an automobile on the Web.

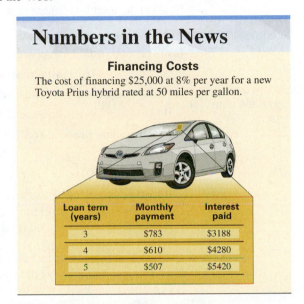

Numbers in the News

Financing Costs

The cost of financing $25,000 at 8% per year for a new Toyota Prius hybrid rated at 50 miles per gallon.

Loan term (years)	Monthly payment	Interest paid
3	$783	$3188
4	$610	$4280
5	$507	$5420

Notice that the total interest paid is much higher the longer the term of the loan. It may be harder to handle the higher payments of a short-term loan, but it results in less total interest!

The federal **Truth in Lending Act** (Regulation Z) of 1969 requires lenders to disclose their **finance charge** (the charge for credit) and **annual percentage rate (APR)** on installment loans. The federal government *does not* regulate rates. Each individual state sets the maximum allowable rates and charges.

The interest rate that is **stated** (in the newspaper, a marketing brochure, or a problem in a textbook) is also called the **nominal rate**. The nominal or stated rate can differ from the annual percentage rate or APR, which is based on the actual amount received by the borrower. The APR is the true effective annual interest rate for a loan. Information on two loans of $1000 each is shown below. An advertisement indicates a rate of 10% for each loan, and the actual interest is $100 for each. However, the terms differ.

	STATED RATE	INTEREST	TERM	APR
Loan 1	10%	$100	1 year	$R = \dfrac{I}{PT} = \dfrac{\$100}{\$1000 \times 1} = 10\%$
Loan 2	10%	$100	9 months	$R = \dfrac{I}{PT} = \dfrac{\$100}{\$1000 \times \frac{9}{12}} = 13.3\%$

The interest rates on these two loans are very different. In fact, interest rate charges vary a surprising amount from one lender to another, so it pays to shop around for the lowest APR. Furthermore, institutions usually charge a much higher interest rate for individuals with poor **credit history**. Thus, it is worth it to maintain a good credit history by paying all bills on time.

OBJECTIVE 2 Find the total installment cost and the finance charge. As shown next, the total **installment cost** includes the down payment and all subsequent payments. The **finance charge** is the difference between the total installment cost and the price if paid for in cash. So, the finance charge includes interest and any fees charged by the lender.

Finding the Total Installment Cost, Finance Charge, and Amount Financed

Total installment cost = Down payment + Payment amount × Number of payments

Finance charge = Total installment cost − Cash price

Amount financed = Cash price − Down payment

Finding the Total Installment Cost **EXAMPLE 1**

Frank Kimlicko recently received his master's degree and began work at a large community college as a music professor specializing in classical guitar. He purchased an exquisite-sounding classical guitar costing $3800 with $500 down and 36 monthly payments of $109.61 each. Find **(a)** the total installment cost, **(b)** the finance charge, and **(c)** the amount financed.

SOLUTION

(a) The total installment cost is the down payment plus the total of all monthly payments.

Total installment cost = $500 + ($109.61 × 36) = **$4445.96**

(b) The finance charge is the total installment cost less the cash price.

Finance charge = **$4445.96** − $3800 = $645.96

(c) The amount financed is $3800 − $500 = $3300.

> **Quick TIP ▼**
>
> To find the total installment cost, add the down payment to the sum of all monthly payments.

QUICK CHECK 1

Robert Chu purchased a new Honda Civic costing $24,200, including taxes and licensing, with $4000 down and 48 payments of $488.25 each. Find **(a)** the total installment cost, **(b)** the finance charge, and **(c)** the amount financed.

Many students use an installment loan called a **Stafford loan** to help pay costs while in college. The government pays the interest on a *subsidized* Stafford loan while the student borrower is in school on at least a half-time basis. In contrast, the student is responsible for interest on *unsubsidized* Stafford loans. Repayment of a loan begins six months after the borrower ceases at least half-time enrollment. You can find information about Stafford loans at the financial aid office at your college or at a bank.

OBJECTIVE 3 Use the formula for approximate APR. The **approximate annual percentage rate (APR)** for a loan paid off in monthly payments can be found with the following formula.

$$\text{Approximate APR} = \frac{24 \times \text{Finance charge}}{\text{Amount financed} \times (1 + \text{Total number of payments})}$$

The formula is *only an estimate* of the APR. It is not accurate enough for the purposes of the federal Truth in Lending Act, which requires the use of tables.

Finding the Annual Percentage Rate **EXAMPLE 2**

Ed Chamski decides to buy a used car for $6400. He makes a down payment of $1200 and monthly payments of $169 for 36 months. Find the approximate annual percentage rate.

SOLUTION

Use the steps outlined above.

Total installment cost = $1200 + ($169 × 36 months) = **$7284**
Finance charge = **$7284** − $6400 = $884
Amount financed = $6400 − $1200 = $5200

Quick TIP ▼

The precise APR can be found using a financial calculator as shown in examples in Appendix C.

Use the formula for approximate APR. Replace the finance charge with $884, the amount financed with $5200, and the number of payments with 36.

$$\text{Approximate APR} = \frac{24 \times \text{Finance charge}}{\text{Amount financed} \times (1 + \text{Total number of payments})}$$

$$= \frac{24 \times \$884}{\$5200 \times (1 + 36)}$$

$$= \frac{\$21,216}{\$192,400}$$

$$= .110 \ or \ 11\% \text{ approximate APR}$$

The approximate annual percentage rate on this loan is 11%. Example 3 shows how to find the actual APR for this loan.

QUICK CHECK 2

Bob Drake purchases a Harley-Davidson motorcycle costing $26,500. He financed the purchase at his bank with a $5000 down payment and payments of $693.74 for 36 months. Estimate the annual percentage rate to the nearest tenth of a percent.

OBJECTIVE 4 Use the table to find APR. Special tables must be used to find annual percentage rates *accurate enough* to satisfy federal law which requires accuracy to the nearest quarter of a percent. These tables are available from a Federal Reserve Bank or the Board of Governors of the Federal Reserve System, Washington, DC 20551. The table on page 506 shows a small portion of these tables. The APR is found from the APR table as follows.

Finding the Annual Percentage Rate (APR)

Step 1   Multiply the finance charge by $100, and divide by the amount financed.

$$\frac{\text{Finance charge} \times \$100}{\text{Amount financed}}$$

The result is the finance charge per $100 of the amount financed.

Step 2   Read down the left column of the annual percentage rate table to the proper number of payments. Go across to the number closest to the number found in Step 1. Read the number at the top of that column to find the annual percentage rate.

Finding the Annual Percentage Rate

EXAMPLE 3

In Example 2, a used car costing $6400 was financed at $169 per month for 36 months after a down payment of $1200. The total finance charge was $884, and the amount financed was $5200. Find the annual percentage rate.

SOLUTION

Step 1   Multiply the finance charge by $100, and divide by the amount financed.

$$\frac{\$884 \times \$100}{\$5200} = \$17.00 \qquad \text{Round to two decimal places for use in the table.}$$

This gives the finance charge per $100 financed.

Step 2   Read down the left column of the annual percentage rate table to the line for 36 months (the actual number of monthly payments). Follow across to the right to find the number closest to $17.00. Here, find **$17.01**. Read the number at the top of this column of figures to find the annual percentage rate, 10.50%.

In this example, 10.50% is the annual percentage rate that must be disclosed to the buyer of the car. In Example 2, the formula for the approximate annual percentage rate gave an answer of 11%, which is not accurate enough to meet the requirements of the law.

Quick TIP ▼

When using the annual percentage rate table, select the column with the table number that is closest to the finance charge per $100 of amount financed.

QUICK CHECK 3

A refrigerator costing $1450 was financed with $100 down and 20 monthly payments of $74.95 each. Find **(a)** the finance charge, **(b)** amount financed, and **(c)** the annual percentage rate.

Finding the Annual Percentage Rate   **EXAMPLE 4**

Two Brothers from Italy Pizza borrowed $48,000 to remodel their store. They agreed to a note with payments of $1565.78 per month for 36 months. They were able to do so with no down payment by putting up a CD for collateral. Find the annual percentage rate.

SOLUTION

Total installment cost = $0 down payment + $1565.78 × 36 = **$56,368.08**
Finance charge = **$56,368.08** − $48,000 = **$8368.08**
Amount financed = $48,000 − $0 down payment = **$48,000**

Now use the formula for the APR.

$$\frac{\$8368.08 \times \$100}{\$48,000} = 17.4335$$

Find the row associated with 36 payments in the annual percentage rate table. Look to the right across that row to find the number closest to 17.4335, which is 17.43. Look to the top of that column to find **10.75%**. This is the APR to the nearest quarter of a percent.

> **QUICK CHECK 4**
>
> An insurance agent borrowed $22,500 for new hardware and software for her growing business. She agreed to a note with payments of $858.10 per month for 30 months and put a CD up for collateral instead of making a down payment. Find the annual percentage rate.

Annual Percentage Rate Table for Monthly Payment Plans

NUMBER OF PAYMENTS	ANNUAL PERCENTAGE RATE (FINANCE CHARGE PER $100 OF AMOUNT FINANCED)																NUMBER OF PAYMENTS
	10.00%	10.25%	10.50%	10.75%	11.00%	11.25%	11.50%	11.75%	12.00%	12.25%	12.50%	12.75%	13.00%	13.25%	13.50%	13.75%	
12	5.50	5.64	5.78	5.92	6.06	6.20	6.34	6.48	6.62	6.76	6.90	7.04	7.18	7.32	7.46	7.60	12
14	6.36	6.52	6.69	6.85	7.01	7.17	7.34	7.50	7.66	7.82	7.99	8.15	8.31	8.48	8.64	8.81	14
16	7.23	7.41	7.60	7.78	7.97	8.15	8.34	8.53	8.71	8.90	9.08	9.27	9.46	9.64	9.83	10.02	16
18	8.10	8.31	8.52	8.73	8.93	9.14	9.35	9.56	9.77	9.98	10.19	10.40	10.61	10.82	11.03	11.24	18
20	8.98	9.21	9.44	9.67	9.90	10.13	10.37	10.60	10.83	11.06	11.30	11.53	11.76	12.00	12.23	12.46	20
22	9.86	10.12	10.37	10.62	10.88	11.13	11.39	11.64	11.90	12.16	12.41	12.67	12.93	13.19	13.44	13.70	22
24	10.75	11.02	11.30	11.58	11.86	12.14	12.42	12.70	12.98	13.26	13.54	13.82	14.10	14.38	14.66	14.95	24
26	11.64	11.94	12.24	12.54	12.85	13.15	13.45	13.75	14.06	14.36	14.67	14.97	15.28	15.59	15.89	16.20	26
28	12.53	12.86	13.18	13.51	13.84	14.16	14.49	14.82	15.15	15.48	15.81	16.14	16.47	16.80	17.13	17.46	28
30	13.43	13.78	14.13	14.48	14.83	15.19	15.54	15.89	16.24	16.60	16.95	17.31	17.66	18.02	18.38	18.74	30
32	14.34	14.71	15.09	15.46	15.84	16.21	16.59	16.97	17.35	17.73	18.11	18.49	18.87	19.25	19.63	20.02	32
34	15.25	15.65	16.05	16.44	16.85	17.25	17.65	18.05	18.46	18.86	19.27	19.67	20.08	20.49	20.90	21.31	34
36	16.16	16.58	17.01	17.43	17.86	18.29	18.71	19.14	19.57	20.00	20.43	20.87	21.30	21.73	22.17	22.60	36
38	17.08	17.53	17.98	18.43	18.88	19.33	19.78	20.24	20.69	21.15	21.61	22.07	22.52	22.99	23.45	23.91	38
40	18.00	18.48	18.95	19.43	19.90	20.38	20.86	21.34	21.82	22.30	22.79	23.27	23.76	24.25	24.73	25.22	40
42	18.93	19.43	19.93	20.43	20.93	21.44	21.94	22.45	22.96	23.47	23.98	24.49	25.00	25.51	26.03	26.55	42
44	19.86	20.39	20.91	21.44	21.97	22.50	23.03	23.57	24.10	24.64	25.17	25.71	26.25	26.79	27.33	27.88	44
46	20.80	21.35	21.90	22.46	23.01	23.57	24.13	24.69	25.25	25.81	26.37	26.94	27.51	28.08	28.65	29.22	46
48	21.74	22.32	22.90	23.48	24.06	24.64	25.23	25.81	26.40	26.99	27.58	28.18	28.77	29.37	29.97	30.57	48
50	22.69	23.29	23.89	24.50	25.11	25.72	26.33	26.95	27.56	28.18	28.80	29.42	30.04	30.67	31.29	31.92	50

12.2 Exercises

The QUICK START exercises in each section contain solutions to help you get started.

Find the finance charge (FC) and the total installment cost (TIC) for the following. *(See Example 1.)*

QUICK START

	Amount Financed	Down Payment	Cash Price	Number of Payments	Amount of Payment	Total Installment Cost	Finance Charge
1.	$1400	$400	$1800	24	$68.75	$2050	$250

TIC = $400 + (24 × $68.75) = $2050; FC = $2050 − $1800 = $250

2.	$650	$125	$775	24	$32	$893	$118

TIC = $125 + (24 × $32) = $893; FC = $893 − $775 = $118

	Amount Financed	Down Payment	Cash Price	Number of Payments	Amount of Payment	Total Installment Cost	Finance Charge
3.	$150	none	$150	12	$15	_____	_____
4.	$1200	none	$1200	20	$70	_____	_____
5.	$2525	$375	$2900	18	$176	_____	_____
6.	$6388	$380	$6768	60	$136	_____	_____

Find the approximate annual percentage rate using the approximate annual percentage rate formula. Round to the nearest tenth of a percent. *(See Example 2.)*

QUICK START

	Amount Financed	Finance Charge	No. of Monthly Payments	Approximate APR
7.	$11,500	$1200	30	8.1%

Approx. APR $= \dfrac{24 \times \$1200}{\$11{,}500 \times (1 + 30)} = 8.1\%$

	Amount Financed	Finance Charge	No. of Monthly Payments	Approximate APR
8.	$2200	$434	36	_____
9.	$7542	$1780	48	_____
10.	$4500	$650	36	_____
11.	$132	$11	12	_____
12.	$8046	$973	24	_____

Find the annual percentage rate using the annual percentage rate table. (See Example 3.)

QUICK START

	Amount Financed	Finance Charge	No. of Monthly Payments	APR
13.	$1400	$185.68	24	12.25%

$$\frac{FC \times \$100}{AF} = \frac{\$185.68 \times \$100}{\$1400} = 13.26; \text{ from 24-payment row, APR} = 12.25\%$$

14.	$345	$24.62	12	_____
15.	$442	$28.68	14	_____
16.	$4690	$1237.22	48	_____
17.	$1450	$132.50	18	_____
18.	$650	$73.45	24	_____

19. Explain the difference between open-end credit and installment loans. (See Section 12.1 and Objective 1 of this section.)

20. Make a list of all of the items that you have bought on an installment loan. Make another list of things you plan to buy in the next 2 years on an installment loan. (See Objective 1.)

Solve the following application problems. Use the formula on page 505 to estimate the APR, and round rates to the nearest tenth of a percent.

QUICK START

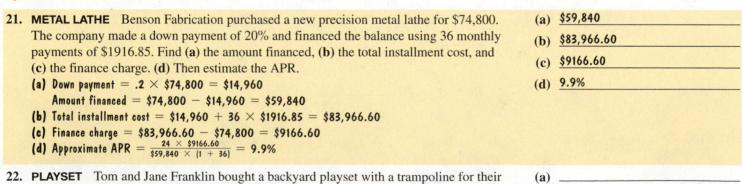

21. METAL LATHE Benson Fabrication purchased a new precision metal lathe for $74,800. The company made a down payment of 20% and financed the balance using 36 monthly payments of $1916.85. Find **(a)** the amount financed, **(b)** the total installment cost, and **(c)** the finance charge. **(d)** Then estimate the APR.

(a) Down payment = .2 × $74,800 = $14,960
    Amount financed = $74,800 − $14,960 = $59,840
(b) Total installment cost = $14,960 + 36 × $1916.85 = $83,966.60
(c) Finance charge = $83,966.60 − $74,800 = $9166.60
(d) Approximate APR = $\frac{24 \times \$9166.60}{\$59,840 \times (1 + 36)}$ = 9.9%

(a) $59,840
(b) $83,966.60
(c) $9166.60
(d) 9.9%

22. PLAYSET Tom and Jane Franklin bought a backyard playset with a trampoline for their grandchildren for $9400. They paid 10% down and financed the balance with 24 monthly payments of $398.24. Find **(a)** the amount financed, **(b)** the total installment cost, and **(c)** the finance charge. **(d)** Then estimate the APR.

(a) _____
(b) _____
(c) _____
(d) _____

23. **ELECTRIC GUITAR** Yanni Benjamin purchased a good-quality electric guitar with amplifier and financed $3600 over 12 months. The finance charge was $260. **(a)** Estimate the APR, then **(b)** find the exact APR using the table.

(a) _____

(b) _____

24. **CANNING MACHINE** Aluminum Cans Inc. purchased a new machine to press aluminum into cans and financed $385,000 over 30 months. The finance charge was $54,411. **(a)** Estimate the APR, then **(b)** find the exact APR using the table.

(a) _____

(b) _____

Solve the following application problems and use the table to find the annual percentage rate.

QUICK START

25. **CHIP FABRICATION** A Chinese computer chip manufacturer borrowed $84 million worth of Chinese yuan to purchase some sophisticated equipment. The note required 24 monthly payments of $3.88 million each. Find the annual percentage rate.

FC = 24 × $3.88 million − $84 million = $9.12 million

$$\frac{FC \times \$100}{AF} = \frac{\$9.12 \times \$100}{\$84 \text{ million}} = 10.86; \text{ from 24-payment row, APR} = 10.00\%$$

25. <u>10.00%</u>

26. **REFRIGERATOR PURCHASE** Sears offers a refrigerator for $1600 with no down payment, $294.06 in interest charges, and 30 equal payments. Find the annual percentage rate.

26. _____

27. **AUTO PURCHASE** Pat Waller bought a Toyota Corolla for $20,800 including taxes and license. She made a down payment of $2000 and agreed to make 50 payments to Citibank of $472 each. Find **(a)** the amount financed, **(b)** the total installment cost, **(c)** the total interest paid, and **(d)** the APR.

(a) _____

(b) _____

(c) _____

(d) _____

28. **SKI BOAT** James Berry purchased a ski boat costing $12,800 with $500 down and loan payments to Citibank of $399 per month for 36 months. Find **(a)** the amount financed, **(b)** the total installment cost, **(c)** the total interest paid, and **(d)** the APR.

(a) _____

(b) _____

(c) _____

(d) _____

29. **COMPUTER SYSTEM** A contractor in Mexico City purchased a computer system for 650,000 pesos. After making a down payment of 100,000 pesos, he agreed to make payments of 26,342.18 pesos per month for 24 months. Find **(a)** the total installment cost and **(b)** the annual percentage rate.

(a) _____

(b) _____

30. TRACTOR PURCHASE   An electrical contractor in Hiroshima, Japan with poor credit, purchased a tractor costing 2,700,000 yen. He made a down payment of 1,000,000 yen and agreed to monthly payments of 54,855 yen for 36 months. Find **(a)** the total installment cost and **(b)** the annual percentage rate.

(a) _____

(b) _____

31. PECAN TREES   Josefina Torres and her husband need $85,000 to plant pecan trees on their small farm. They pay $20,000 down and finance the balance with 40 payments of $1942.24. Find **(a)** the total installment cost and **(b)** the annual percentage rate.

(a) _____

(b) _____

32. GOAT CHEESE   Toni Smith wants to produce goat cheese and needs $120,000 to purchase 400 goats. He pays $30,000 down and finances the balance with 24 monthly payments of $4253.44. Find **(a)** the total installment cost and **(b)** the annual percentage rate.

(a) _____

(b) _____

33. Should businesses be able to charge interest rates of over 20% to customers with very poor credit histories? Why or why not? If not, do you think any firm would lend to these customers?

34. Explain why it is important for the government to regulate the way in which interest rates are stated.

12.3 Early Payoffs of Loans

OBJECTIVES

1 Use the United States Rule for an early payment.
2 Find the amount due on the maturity date using the United States Rule.
3 Use the Rule of 78 when prepaying a loan.

OBJECTIVE 1 Use the United States Rule for an early payment. It is common for a payment to be made on a loan *before it is due*. This may occur when a person receives extra money or refinances a debt at a lower interest rate somewhere else. Prepayments of loans are discussed in this section.

The first method for calculating early loan payment is the **United States Rule**, and it is used by the U.S. government as well as most states and financial institutions. Under the United States Rule, any payment is first applied to any interest owed. The balance of the payment is then used to reduce the principal amount of the loan. We will continue to use 360-day years in the calculations of this section.

Using the United States Rule

Step 1 Find the simple interest due from the date the loan was made until the date the partial payment is made. Use the formula $I = PRT$.

Step 2 Subtract this interest from the amount of the payment.

Step 3 Any difference is used to reduce the principal.

Step 4 Treat additional partial payments in the same way, always finding interest on *only* the unpaid balance after the last partial payment.

Step 5 The remaining principal plus interest on this unpaid principal is then due on the due date of the loan.

OBJECTIVE 2 Find the amount due on the maturity date using the United States Rule. If the partial payment is not large enough to pay the interest due, the payment is simply held until enough money is available to pay the interest due. This means that a partial payment smaller than the interest due offers no advantage to the borrower—the lender just holds the partial payment until enough money is available to pay the interest owed.

Finding the Amount Due **EXAMPLE 1**

On August 14, Dr. Jane Ficker signed a 180-day note for $28,500 for an x-ray machine for her dental office. The note has an interest rate of 10% compounded annually. On October 25, a payment of $8500 is made. **(a)** Find the balance owed on the principal after the payment. **(b)** If no additional payments are made, find the amount due at maturity of the loan.

SOLUTION

(a) Step 1 Use $I = PRT$ to find interest from August 14 to October 25 (72 days).

$$\text{Interest} = \$28{,}500 \times .10 \times \frac{72}{360} = \mathbf{\$570}$$

Step 2 Amount applied to principle = Payment − Interest
$$= \$8500 - \mathbf{\$570}$$
$$= \mathbf{\$7930}$$

Step 3 New principal = Previous principal − Amount applied to principal
$$= \$28{,}500 - \mathbf{\$7930}$$
$$= \$20{,}570$$

(b) Step 4 Go on to Step 5 since there are no additional partial payments.

Step 5 The partial payment was made on day 72 of the 180-day note. Interest on the new principal of $20,570 will be for $180 - 72 = \mathbf{108}$ days.

$$\text{Interest} = \$20{,}570 \times .10 \times \frac{108}{360} = \mathbf{\$617.10}$$

Due at maturity = $20,570 + **$617.10** = $21,187.10

Finding the Interest Paid and Amount Due **EXAMPLE 2**

On March 1, Boston Dairy signs a promissory note for $38,500 to replace milking equipment for their Holsteins. The note is for 180 days at a rate of 10%. The dairy makes the following partial payments: $6000 on June 9 and $3500 on July 11. Find the interest paid on the note and the amount due on the due date of the note.

SOLUTION

The first partial payment is on June 9 or, using the number of days in each month, after $(30 + 30 + 31 + 9) = 100$ days.

$$\text{Interest for 100 days} = \$38{,}500 \times .10 \times \frac{100}{360} = \textbf{\$1069.44} \text{ (rounded)}$$

First partial payment	$6000.00
Portion going to interest	− 1069.44
Portion going to reduce debt	**$4930.56**

Debt on June 9 *after 1st partial payment* = $38,500 − **$4930.56** = $33,569.44

The second partial payment occurs $21 + 11 = 32$ days later.

$$\text{Interest for 32 days} = \$33{,}569.44 \times .10 \times \frac{32}{360} = \textbf{\$298.40} \text{ (rounded)}$$

Second partial payment	$3500.00
Portion going to interest	−298.40
Portion going to reduce debt	**$3201.60**

Debt on July 11 *after 2nd partial payment* = $33,569.44 − **$3201.60** = $30,367.84

The first partial payment is made after 100 days, and the second partial payment is made after an additional 32 days. Thus, the due date of the note is $180 − 100 − 32 = 48$ days after the second partial payment.

$$\text{Interest for the last 48 days} = \$30{,}367.84 \times .10 \times \frac{48}{360} = \textbf{\$404.90} \text{ (rounded)}$$

Amount due *at maturity* = $30,367.84 + **$404.90** = $30,772.74

DATE PAYMENT MADE	AMOUNT OF PAYEMENT	APPLIED TO INTEREST	APPLIED TO PRINCIPAL	REMAINING BALANCE
June 9	$6,000.00	$1069.44	$4,930.56	$33,569.44
July 11	$3,500.00	$298.40	$3,201.60	$30,367.84
At maturity	$30,772.74	$404.90	$30,367.84	$0
Total $40,272.74		$1772.74	$38,500.00	

OBJECTIVE 3 Use the Rule of 78 when prepaying a loan. A variation of the United States Rule, called the **Rule of 78**, is still used by many lenders for installment loans. This rule allows a lender *to earn more of the finance charge during the early months* of the loan compared with the United States Rule. Lenders typically use this rule *to protect against* early payoffs on small loans. Effectively, the lender will earn a higher rate of interest in the event of an early payoff under the Rule of 78 than under the United States Rule.

The Rule of 78 gets its name based on a loan of 12 months—the sum of the months $1 + 2 + 3 + \cdots + 12 = 78$. The finance charge for the first month is $\frac{12}{78}$ of the total charge, with $\frac{11}{78}$ in the second month, $\frac{10}{78}$ in the third month, and so on, with $\frac{1}{78}$ in the final month. The Rule of 78 can be applied to loans *with terms other than 12 months*. For example, the sum of the months in a

6-month contract is $1 + 2 + 3 + 4 + 5 + 6 = 21$. The finance charge for the first month is $\frac{6}{21}$; $\frac{5}{21}$ for the second month; and so on. Similarly, the sum of the months in a 15-month contract is $1 + 2 + \cdots + 15 = 120$. The finance charge for the first month of a 15-month contract is $\frac{15}{120}$ or $\frac{1}{8}$, and so on.

Monthly Finance Charges

TERM OF LOAN	MONTH 1	MONTH 2	MONTH 3	MONTH 4	MONTH 5	MONTH 6	MONTH 7	MONTH 8	MONTH 9	MONTH 10	MONTH 11	MONTH 12
12 months	$\frac{12}{78}$	$\frac{11}{78}$	$\frac{10}{78}$	$\frac{9}{78}$	$\frac{8}{78}$	$\frac{7}{78}$	$\frac{6}{78}$	$\frac{5}{78}$	$\frac{4}{78}$	$\frac{3}{78}$	$\frac{2}{78}$	$\frac{1}{78}$
6 months	$\frac{6}{21}$	$\frac{5}{21}$	$\frac{4}{21}$	$\frac{3}{21}$	$\frac{2}{21}$	$\frac{1}{21}$						

The total finance charge on an installment loan is calculated when a loan is first made. Early payoff of a loan results in a lower finance charge. The portion of the finance charge that *has not yet been earned* by the lender under the Rule of 78, called **unearned interest** or **refund**, is found as follows.

Finding unearned interest

$$U = F\left(\frac{N}{P}\right)\left(\frac{1+N}{1+P}\right)$$

where

U = unearned interest $\qquad F$ = finance charge

N = number of payments remaining $\qquad P$ = original number of payments

Finding Unearned Interest and Balance Due

 EXAMPLE 3

Adrian Ortega borrowed $6000, which he is paying back in 24 monthly payments of $295 each. With 9 payments remaining, he decides to repay the loan in full. Find **(a)** the amount of unearned interest and **(b)** the amount necessary to repay the loan in full. Use the Rule of 78.

SOLUTION

(a) Total of all payments = 24 payments × $295 = **$7080**

Amount borrowed

Finance charge = **$7080** − $6000 = **$1080**

Find the amount of unearned interest as follows. The finance charge is $1080, the scheduled number of payments is 24, and the loan is paid off with 9 payments left. Solve as follows.

$$\text{Unearned interest} = \$1080 \times \frac{9}{24} \times \frac{(1+9)}{(1+24)} = \$162$$

(b) When Ortega decides to pay off the loan, he has 9 payments of $295 left.

Sum of remaining payments = 9 payments × $295 = **$2655**

Ortega saves the unearned interest of $162 by paying off the loan early. Therefore, the amount needed to pay the loan in full is the sum of the remaining payments minus the unearned interest.

Amount needed to repay the loan in full = Remaining payments − Unearned interest
= **$2655** − $162 = $2493

QUICK CHECK 3

Simplot Maps has signed a note with a face value of $24,000 that requires 20 monthly payments of $1307.76. The manager pays the debt in full after 12 payments. Find **(a)** the finance charge, **(b)** the amount of unearned interest, and **(c)** the amount needed to repay the loan in full using the Rule of 78.

Finding Unearned Interest and BalanceDue

EXAMPLE 4

The Smiths borrow $1200 for a new washer and dryer and agree to make 18 monthly payments of $74.30 each. After the 10th payment, they pay the loan in full. Find **(a)** the amount of unearned interest and **(b)** the amount needed to repay the loan in full using the Rule of 78.

SOLUTION

(a)
$$\text{Sum of payments} = 18 \text{ payments} \times \$74.30 = \$1337.40$$
$$\text{Finance charge} = \$1337.40 - \$1200 = \$137.40$$

Since there are $(18 - 10) = $ **8 payments remaining** when he pays the loan off, the unearned interest is found as follows.

$$\text{Unearned interest} = \$137.40 \times \frac{8}{18} \times \frac{(1 + 8)}{(1 + 18)} = \$28.93 \text{ (rounded)}$$

(b) The amount needed to pay the loan in full is the sum of the remaining payments less the unearned interest.

$$\text{Sum of remaining 8 payments} = 8 \text{ payments} \times \$74.30 = \$594.40$$
$$\text{Amount needed to repay the loan in full} = \$594.40 - \$28.93 = \$565.47$$

QUICK CHECK 4

Tim O'Murphy borrows $2100 to buy a riding lawn mower and agrees to make 12 monthly payments of $186.58 each. He pays the debt in full after 6 months. Find **(a)** the finance charge, **(b)** the amount of unearned interest, and **(c)** the amount needed to repay the loan in full using the Rule of 78.

12.3 Exercises

The **QUICK START** exercises in each section contain solutions to help you get started.

Find the balance due on the maturity date of the following notes. Find the total amount of interest paid on each note. Use the United States Rule. (See Examples 1 and 2.)

QUICK START

	Principal	Interest	Time (Days)	Partial Payments	Balance Due	Total Interest Paid
1.	$9800	$8\frac{1}{2}\%$	150	$1800 on day 50	**$8307.31**	**$307.31**

Interest for 50 days = $9800 \times .085 \times \frac{50}{360} = \$115.69$
Amount of 1st payment applied to reduce debt = $1800 - \$115.69 = \$1684.31$
Debt after 1st payment = $9800 - \$1684.31 = \$8115.69$
Interest due at end of 150-day note = $8115.69 \times .085 \times \frac{100}{360} = \$191.62$
Balance due on maturity date = $191.62 + \$8115.69 = \$8307.31$
Total interest paid = $115.69 + \$191.62 = \$307.31$

	Principal	Interest	Time (Days)	Partial Payments	Balance Due	Total Interest Paid
2.	$5800	12%	120	$2000 on day 45	_____	_____
3.	$15,000	10.5%	200	$6500 on day 100	_____	_____
4.	$76,900	11%	180	$31,250 on day 75	_____	_____
5.	$18,457	12%	120	$5978 on day 34 $3124 on day 55	_____	_____
6.	$39,864	9%	105	$8458 on day 43 $11,354 on day 88	_____	_____

Each of the following loans is paid in full before the date of maturity. Find the amount of unearned interest. Use the Rule of 78. (See Example 3.)

QUICK START

	Finance Charge	Total Number of Payments	Remaining Number of Payments When Paid in Full	Unearned Interest
7.	$1050	24	11	**$231**

$1050 \times \frac{11}{24} \times \frac{(1 + 11)}{(1 + 24)} = \$231$

	Finance Charge	Total Number of Payments	Remaining Number of Payments When Paid in Full	Unearned Interest
8.	$422	30	16	_____
9.	$881	36	12	_____
10.	$325	24	22	_____
11.	$900	36	6	_____
12.	$1250	60	12	_____

C indicates an exercise that is related to the Case in Point feature.

13. Explain why banks prefer the Rule of 78 to the United States Rule in the event of prepayment. (See Objective 3.)

14. Describe a situation in which a bank might prefer a loan to be prepaid.

Solve the following application problems using the United States Rule.

QUICK START

15. LANDSCAPING Andrew Raring borrowed $8900 from Citibank to landscape his yard. The 240-day note had an interest rate of 12% compounded annually. He repaid the note in 140 days with his income-tax refund. Find **(a)** the interest due and **(b)** the total amount due.

(a) Loan is for 140 days

Interest = $8900 × .12 × $\frac{140}{360}$ = $415.33

(b) Amount due = $8900 + $415.33 = $9315.33

(a) $415.33

(b) $9315.33

16. COMPUTER CONSULTANT The computer system at Genome Therapy crashed several times last year. On January 10, the company borrowed $125,000 at 11% compounded annually for 250 days to pay a consultant to work on the Novell network. However, they decide to pay the loan in full on July 1. Find **(a)** the interest due and **(b)** the total amount due.

(a) _____

(b) _____

17. PARTIAL PAYMENT Johnson Solar Technologies borrowed $92,000 on May 7, signing a note due in 90 days at 11.25% interest. On June 24, the company made a partial payment of $24,350. Find **(a)** the amount due on the maturity date of the note and **(b)** the interest paid on the note.

(a) _____

(b) _____

18. REMODELING The Second Avenue Butcher Shop financed a remodeling program by giving the builder a note for $32,500. The note was made on September 14 and is due in 120 days. Interest on the note is 9.75%. On December 9, the firm makes a partial payment of $9000. Find **(a)** the amount due on the maturity date of the note and **(b)** the interest paid on the note.

(a) _____

(b) _____

19. **INVENTORY** The Washington News orders large quantities of paper every 4 months to save on freight charges. For its last order, the firm signed a note on February 18, maturing on May 15. The face value of the note was $104,500, with interest of 11%. The firm made a partial payment of $38,000 on March 20 and a second partial payment of $27,200 on April 16. Find **(a)** the amount due on the maturity date of the note and **(b)** the amount of interest paid on the note.

(a) _____

(b) _____

20. **SURVEILLANCE CAMERAS** To help detect trespassers at night, a small security firm purchased some high-technology cameras using a note from Citibank for $32,000. The note was signed on July 26 and was due on November 20. The interest rate is 13%. The firm made a partial payment of $6000 on August 31 and a second partial payment of $11,700 on October 4. Find **(a)** the amount due on the maturity date of the note and **(b)** the interest paid on the note.

(a) _____

(b) _____

Solve the following application problems using the Rule of 78. (See Example 3.)

QUICK START

21. **ENGAGEMENT RING** Tom Stowe purchased a diamond engagement ring for $1150. He paid $100 down and agreed to 12 monthly payments of $95 each. After making 7 payments, he paid the loan in full. Find **(a)** the unearned interest and **(b)** the amount necessary to pay the loan in full.

(a) **Finance charge** = $100 + ($95 × 12) − $1150 = $90
$U = \$90 \times \frac{5}{12} \times \frac{6}{13} = \$17.31$ (rounded)

(b) (5 × $95) − $17.31 = $457.69

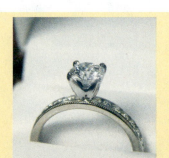

(a) $17.31

(b) $457.69

22. **GARBAGE TRUCK** Haul-it-Away, Inc., purchased a dump truck for $62,000. The owners made a down payment of $22,000 and financed the remainder with 36 payments of $1328.57 each. They paid off the note with 12 payments remaining. Find **(a)** the amount of unearned interest and **(b)** the amount necessary to pay the loan in full.

(a) _____

(b) _____

△ **23. PRINTING** BlackTop Printing made a $5000 down payment on a special copy machine costing $23,800. The loan agreement with Citibank called for 20 monthly payments of $1025 each. Find **(a)** the finance charge, **(b)** the unearned interest, and **(c)** the amount necessary to pay the loan in full after the 14th payment.

(a) _____

(b) _____

(c) _____

24. MOVIE PROJECTORS Movie 6, Inc., purchased two movie projectors at a total cost of $12,200 with a down payment of $1500. The company agreed to make 12 monthly payments of $945 each. Find **(a)** the finance charge, **(b)** the unearned interest, and **(c)** the amount necessary to pay the loan in full after the 8th payment.

(a) _____

(b) _____

(c) _____

25. WEB DESIGN Blackstone Web Design needed $76,800 to purchase computers, software, and network equipment.The owners paid $15,000 down and financed the balance with 30 monthly payments of $2423.89 each. Find **(a)** the total installment cost, **(b)** the finance charge, **(c)** the unearned interest, and **(d)** the amount needed to pay the loan in full after the 10th payment.

(a) _____

(b) _____

(c) _____

(d) _____

26. ASPHALT CRUMB Binston Asphalt borrowed $850,000 to purchase a machine that converts old tires into asphalt crumb for use as a base material under sports arenas. The company paid $200,000 of the cost up front and financed the balance with 36 monthly payments of $20,821.42 each. Find **(a)** the total installment cost, **(b)** the finance charge, **(c)** the unearned interest, and **(d)** the amount needed to pay the loan in full after the 25th payment.

(a) _____

(b) _____

(c) _____

(d) _____

QUICK CHECK ANSWERS

1. (a) $37,253.93 **(b)** $38,380.86

2. (a) $5895.83 **(b)** $6046.50

3. (a) $2155.20 **(b)** $369.46
   (c) $10,092.62

4. (a) $138.96 **(b)** $37.41
   (c) $1082.07

12.4 Personal Property Loans

OBJECTIVES

1 Define personal property and real estate.
2 Use the formula for amortization to find payment.
3 Set up an amortization schedule.
4 Find monthly payments.

Before she worked at Citibank, Jackie Waterton made personal property loans for a neighborhood bank. Every day she would receive many loan applications showing income, assets, and debt, as well as employment information. She would then carefully check the creditworthiness of each applicant.

OBJECTIVE 1 Define personal property and real estate. Items that can be moved from one location to another, such as an automobile, a boat, or a stereo, are called **personal property**. In contrast, land and homes cannot be moved and are called **real estate** or **real property**. Personal property loans are discussed in this section, and real estate loans are discussed in the next section.

Real Property

Personal Property

Banks, credit unions, finance companies, and many other types of companies make money through personal property loans. Typically, these loans are repaid, or **amortized**, using monthly payments. Sometimes, a buyer is not able to make the payments as promised. In that event, the lender must **repossess** the personal property and sell it to someone else. Financial companies charge a slightly higher interest rate to everyone to make up for loans on which they never fully recover their money. Interest rates for personal property loans vary significantly from lender to lender and from year to year. Be sure to shop carefully before borrowing.

OBJECTIVE 2 Use the formula for amortization to find payment. The periodic payment needed at the end of each period to amortize a loan with interest i per period, over n periods, is found by using the following formula.

> **Finding Periodic Payment**
>
> Payment = Loan amount × Number from amortization table

Amortizing a Loan **EXAMPLE 1**

Sven Yarborough earned his degree at a community college and is now a mechanic at a Ford dealership. He was so impressed with the quality of Fords that he purchased an SUV at a cost of $29,400, including tax, title, and license, after the rebate. He made a down payment of $3500 and was able to finance the balance at a special incentive rate of 6% per year for 4 years. Find **(a)** the monthly payment, **(b)** the portion of the first payment that is interest, **(c)** the balance due after one payment, **(d)** the interest owed for the second month, and **(e)** the balance after the second payment.

SOLUTION

(a) Amount financed = $29,400 − $3500 = $25,900.

   Use $\frac{6\%}{12}$ = .5% per month and 4 years × 12 = 48 months in the table to find **.02349**.

   Monthly payment = $25,900 × **.02349** = $608.39 (rounded)

(b) Interest for month = $I = PRT$ = $25,900 × .06 × $\frac{1}{12}$ = **$129.50**

   Amount of 1st payment applied to principal = $608.39 − **$129.50** = **$478.89**

(c) Balance after 1st payment = $25,900 − **$478.89** = $25,421.11.

(d) Interest for 2nd month = PRT = $25,421.11 × .06 × $\frac{1}{12}$ = **$127.11** (rounded)

   Amount of 2nd payment applied to principal = $608.39 − **$127.11** = $481.28

(e) Balance after 2nd payment = $25,421.11 − $481.28 = **$24,939.83**.

> **QUICK CHECK 1**
>
> Marine Ltd. paid $300,000 down on a tugboat costing $1,800,000. The firm financed the balance at 12% per year for 4 years. Find **(a)** the monthly payment and **(b)** the balance after the first payment.

OBJECTIVE 3 Set up an amortization schedule.

Creating an Amortization Table **EXAMPLE 2**

Clarence Thomas purchased new automated equipment for his car wash at a cost of $22,300. He made a down payment of $5000 and agreed to pay the balance off in quarterly payments over 2 years at 12% compounded quarterly. **(a)** Find the quarterly payment, and **(b)** show the first four payments in a table called an **amortization schedule**.

SOLUTION

(a) The amount financed is $22,300 − $5000 = $17,300. Find the factor from the table using 2 × 4 = 8 quarters and $\frac{12\%}{4}$ = 3% per quarter. Then multiply the amount financed by the factor to find the payment.

$$\text{Payment} = \$17,300 \times .14246 = \$2464.56 \text{ (rounded)}$$

(b)

Amortization Schedule

PAYMENT NUMBER	AMOUNT OF PAYMENT	INTEREST FOR PERIOD	PORTION TO PRINCIPAL	PRINCIPAL AT END OF PERIOD
0	—	—	—	$17,300.00
1	$2464.56	$519.00	$1945.56	$15,354.44
2	$2464.56	$460.63	$2003.93	$13,350.51
3	$2464.56	$400.52	$2064.04	$11,286.47
4	$2464.56	$338.59	$2125.97	$9,160.50

> ┌─ **Quick TIP** ▼
> Notice that interest is large at first when the debt is high but it decreases with every payment as the debt goes down.

> **QUICK CHECK 2**
>
> BlueLake Marina purchased a party barge costing $85,700 with a down payment of $20,000 and financed the balance at 8% for 4 quarters. Find the payment and construct an amortization schedule for the first 2 quarters.

Amortization Table

PERIOD	$\frac{1}{2}$%	1%	$1\frac{1}{2}$%	2%	$2\frac{1}{2}$%	3%	4%	6%	8%	10%	PERIOD
					INTEREST RATE PER PERIOD						
1	1.00500	1.01000	1.01500	1.02000	1.02500	1.03000	1.04000	1.06000	1.08000	1.10000	1
2	.50375	.50751	.51128	.51505	.51883	.52261	.53020	.54544	.56077	.57619	2
3	.33667	.34002	.34338	.34675	.35014	.35353	.36035	.37411	.38803	.40211	3
4	.25313	.25628	.25944	.26262	.26582	.26903	.27549	.28859	.30192	.31547	4
5	.20301	.20604	.20909	.21216	.21525	.21835	.22463	.23740	.25046	.26380	5
6	.16960	.17255	.17553	.17853	.18155	.18460	.19076	.20336	.21632	.22961	6
7	.14573	.14863	.15156	.15451	.15750	.16051	.16661	.17914	.19207	.20541	7
8	.12783	.13069	.13358	.13651	.13947	.14246	.14853	.16104	.17401	.18744	8
9	.11391	.11674	.11961	.12252	.12546	.12843	.13449	.14702	.16008	.17364	9
10	.10277	.10558	.10843	.11133	.11426	.11723	.12329	.13587	.14903	.16275	10
11	.09366	.09645	.09929	.10218	.10511	.10808	.11415	.12679	.14008	.15396	11
12	.08607	.08885	.09168	.09456	.09749	.10046	.10655	.11928	.13270	.14676	12
13	.07964	.08241	.08524	.08812	.09105	.09403	.10014	.11296	.12652	.14078	13
14	.07414	.07690	.07972	.08260	.08554	.08853	.09467	.10758	.12130	.13575	14
15	.06936	.07212	.07494	.07783	.08077	.08377	.08994	.10296	.11683	.13147	15
16	.06519	.06794	.07077	.07365	.07660	.07961	.08582	.09895	.11298	.12782	16
17	.06151	.06426	.06708	.06997	.07293	.07595	.08220	.09544	.10963	.12466	17
18	.05823	.06098	.06381	.06670	.06967	.07271	.07899	.09236	.10670	.12193	18
19	.05530	.05805	.06088	.06378	.06676	.06981	.07614	.08962	.10413	.11955	19
20	.05267	.05542	.05825	.06116	.06415	.06722	.07358	.08718	.10185	.11746	20
21	.05028	.05303	.05587	.05878	.06179	.06487	.07128	.08500	.09983	.11562	21
22	.04811	.05086	.05370	.05663	.05965	.06275	.06920	.08305	.09803	.11401	22
23	.04613	.04889	.05173	.05467	.05770	.06081	.06731	.08128	.09642	.11257	23
24	.04432	.04707	.04992	.05287	.05591	.05905	.06559	.07968	.09498	.11130	24
25	.04265	.04541	.04826	.05122	.05428	.05743	.06401	.07823	.09368	.11017	25
26	.04111	.04387	.04673	.04970	.05277	.05594	.06257	.07690	.09251	.10916	26
27	.03969	.04245	.04532	.04829	.05138	.05456	.06124	.07570	.09145	.10826	27
28	.03836	.04112	.04400	.04699	.05009	.05329	.06001	.07459	.09049	.10745	28
29	.03713	.03990	.04278	.04578	.04889	.05211	.05888	.07358	.08962	.10673	29
30	.03598	.03875	.04164	.04465	.04778	.05102	.05783	.07265	.08883	.10608	30
31	.03490	.03768	.04057	.04360	.04674	.05000	.05686	.07179	.08811	.10550	31
32	.03389	.03667	.03958	.04261	.04577	.04905	.05595	.07100	.08745	.10497	32
33	.03295	.03573	.03864	.04169	.04486	.04816	.05510	.07027	.08685	.10450	33
34	.03206	.03484	.03776	.04082	.04401	.04732	.05431	.06960	.08630	.10407	34
35	.03122	.03400	.03693	.04000	.04321	.04654	.05358	.06897	.08580	.10369	35
36	.03042	.03321	.03615	.03923	.04245	.04580	.05289	.06839	.08534	.10334	36
37	.02967	.03247	.03541	.03851	.04174	.04511	.05224	.06786	.08492	.10303	37
38	.02896	.03176	.03472	.03782	.04107	.04446	.05163	.06736	.08454	.10275	38
39	.02829	.03109	.03405	.03717	.04044	.04384	.05106	.06689	.08419	.10249	39
40	.02765	.03046	.03343	.03656	.03984	.04326	.05052	.06646	.08386	.10226	40
41	.02704	.02985	.03283	.03597	.03927	.04271	.05002	.06606	.08356	.10205	41
42	.02646	.02928	.03226	.03542	.03873	.04219	.04954	.06568	.08329	.10186	42
43	.02590	.02873	.03172	.03489	.03822	.04170	.04909	.06533	.08303	.10169	43
44	.02538	.02820	.03121	.03439	.03773	.04123	.04866	.06501	.08280	.10153	44
45	.02487	.02771	.03072	.03391	.03727	.04079	.04826	.06470	.08259	.10139	45
46	.02439	.02723	.03025	.03345	.03683	.04036	.04788	.06441	.08239	.10126	46
47	.02393	.02677	.02980	.03302	.03641	.03996	.04752	.06415	.08221	.10115	47
48	.02349	.02633	.02938	.03260	.03601	.03958	.04718	.06390	.08204	.10104	48
49	.02306	.02591	.02896	.03220	.03562	.03921	.04686	.06366	.08189	.10095	49
50	.02265	.02551	.02857	.03182	.03526	.03887	.04655	.06344	.08174	.10086	50

OBJECTIVE 4 Find monthly payments. The loan payoff table below can be used as an alternative to the amortization table on the preceding page. The table on this page shows some higher interest rates and longer terms than the previous table. Personal property loans sometimes have higher interest rates, since people are more likely to default on a loan for an expensive plasma television set than, say, on the loan on their home.

This table has a different format from the table on the preceding page. The APR is down the left column, and the number of months is across the top of this table.

> **Finding Loan Payment**
>
> Payment = Loan amount × Number from loan payoff table

Loan Payoff Table

APR	NUMBER OF MONTHS								APR
	18	24	30	36	42	48	54	60	
8%	.05914	.04523	.03688	.03134	.02738	.02441	.02211	.02028	8%
9%	.05960	.04568	.03735	.03180	.02785	.02489	.02259	.02076	9%
10%	.06006	.04615	.03781	.03227	.02832	.02536	.02307	.02125	10%
11%	.06052	.04661	.03828	.03274	.02879	.02585	.02356	.02174	11%
12%	.06098	.04707	.03875	.03321	.02928	.02633	.02406	.02225	12%
13%	.06145	.04754	.03922	.03369	.02976	.02683	.02456	.02275	13%
14%	.06192	.04801	.03970	.03418	.03025	.02733	.02507	.02327	14%
15%	.06238	.04849	.04018	.03467	.03075	.02783	.02558	.02379	15%
16%	.06286	.04896	.04066	.03516	.03125	.02834	.02610	.02432	16%
17%	.06333	.04944	.04115	.03565	.03176	.02885	.02662	.02485	17%
18%	.06381	.04993	.04164	.03615	.03226	.02937	.02715	.02539	18%
19%	.06428	.05041	.04213	.03666	.03278	.02990	.02769	.02594	19%
20%	.06476	.05090	.04263	.03716	.03330	.03043	.02823	.02649	20%

Finding Amortization Payments   **EXAMPLE 3** After a trade-in, Vickie Ewing owes $17,400 on a new Harley-Davidson motorcycle and wishes to pay the loan off in 60 months. She has found that she can finance the loan at 9% per year if she has a good credit history, but at 14% per year if she has a poor credit history.

(a) Find the monthly payment at both interest rates.

(b) Find the total finance charge at both interest rates.

(c) Find the extra cost of having poor credit.

SOLUTION

(a) Monthly payment at 9% = $17,400 × .02076 = $361.22 (rounded).
    Monthly payment at 14% = $17,400 × .02327 = $404.90 (rounded).

(b) The finance charge is the sum of all of the payments minus the amount financed.

number of payments

Finance charge at 9% = 60 × $361.22 − $17,400 = **$4273.20**
Finance charge at 14% = 60 × $404.90 − $17,400 = **$6894**

(c) Extra cost of poor credit = **$6894** − **$4273.20** = $2620.80.

Clearly, having a poor credit history can be very costly.

> **QUICK CHECK 3**
>
> After his down payment, Josh Crandall needs to borrow $12,800 for 48 months to buy a truck. He can finance it at 8% per year if he has excellent credit but, at 15% per year if he has poor credit. Find **(a)** the monthly payment at both interest rates, **(b)** the total finance charge for both rates, and **(c)** the extra cost of having poor credit.

The **QUICK START** exercises in each section contain solutions to help you get started.

Find the payment necessary to amortize the following loans using the amortization table. Round to the nearest cent if needed. (See Example 1.)

QUICK START

	Amount of Loan	Interest Rate	Payments Made	Number of Years	Payment
1.	$6800	8%	annually	5	$1703.13
	Payment = $6800 × .25046 = $1703.13				
2.	$7500	10%	annually	6	$1722.08
	Payment = $7500 × .22961 = $1722.08				
3.	$4500	8%	semiannually	$7\frac{1}{2}$	_____
4.	$12,000	6%	semiannually	8	_____
5.	$96,000	8%	quarterly	$7\frac{3}{4}$	_____
6.	$210,000	12%	quarterly	8	_____
7.	$4876	12%	monthly	3	_____
8.	$6800	6%	monthly	3	_____

Use the loan payoff table to find the monthly payment (MP) and finance charge (FC) for each of the following loans. (See Example 3.)

QUICK START

	Amount Financed	Number of Months	APR	Monthly Payment	Finance Charge
9.	$5300	42	9%	$147.61	$899.62
	MP = $5300 × .02785 = $147.61; FC = (42 × $147.61) − $5300 = $899.62				
10.	$4800	24	12%	$225.94	$622.56
	MP = $4800 × .04707 = $225.94; FC = (24 × $225.94) − $4800 = $622.56				
11.	$12,000	48	13%	_____	_____
12.	$8102	48	8%	_____	_____
13.	$11,750	60	11%	_____	_____
14.	$16,000	60	10%	_____	_____

indicates an exercise that is related to the Case in Point feature.

15. Explain the process of amortizing a loan. (See Objective 2.)

16. Explain why a loan officer at a bank might look at a credit report on someone before making a loan. What would you do if your credit report was inaccurate?

Solve the following application problems using the amortization table.

QUICK START

17. FORESTRY OPERATIONS Blackstone Logging borrowed $62,400 to purchase a used truck to haul logs. The loan has a rate of 12% per year and requires 40 monthly payments. Find **(a)** the monthly payment and **(b)** the total interest paid.

(a) Monthly payment = $62,400 × .03046 = $1900.70
(b) Total interest = (40 × $1900.70) − $62,400 = $13,628

(a) $1900.70
(b) $13,628

18. OPENING A RESTAURANT Chuck and Judy Nielson opened a restaurant at a cost of $340,000. They paid $40,000 of their own money and agreed to pay the remainder in quarterly payments over 7 years at 12%. Find **(a)** the quarterly payment and **(b)** the total amount of interest paid over 7 years.

(a) _____
(b) _____

19. PRINTER An insurance firm pays $4000 for a new high-speed color printer. It amortizes the loan for the printer in 4 annual payments at 8%. Prepare an amortization schedule for this machine.

PAYMENT NUMBER	AMOUNT OF PAYMENT	INTEREST FOR PERIOD	PORTION TO PRINCIPAL	PRINCIPAL AT END OF PERIOD

20. TRACTOR PURCHASE Long Haul Trucking purchases a used tractor for pulling 18-wheel trailers on interstate highways at a cost of $72,000. It agrees to pay for it with a loan from Citibank that will be amortized over 9 annual payments at 8% interest. Prepare an amortization schedule for the truck.

PAYMENT NUMBER	AMOUNT OF PAYMENT	INTEREST FOR PERIOD	PORTION TO PRINCIPAL	PRINCIPAL AT END OF PERIOD

Solve the following application problems. Use the loan payoff table. (See Objective 3.)

21. **ELECTRONIC EQUIPMENT**   An engineering firm purchases 7 powerful workstations with special printers for $3500 each. The firm makes a down payment of $10,000 and amortizes the balance with monthly loan payments to Citibank of 11% for 4 years. Prepare an amortization schedule showing the first 5 payments.

PAYMENT NUMBER	AMOUNT OF PAYMENT	INTEREST FOR PERIOD	PORTION TO PRINCIPAL	PRINCIPAL AT END OF PERIOD

22. **AMORTIZING A LOAN**   Rebecca Reed just graduated from dental school and borrows $120,000 from Citibank to purchase equipment for her own business. She agreed to amortize the loan with monthly payments at 10% for 4 years. Prepare an amortization schedule for the first 5 payments.

PAYMENT NUMBER	AMOUNT OF PAYMENT	INTEREST FOR PERIOD	PORTION TO PRINCIPAL	PRINCIPAL AT END OF PERIOD

23. **CELL PHONE**   Ben Watson needs $50,000 to set up his own cell phone booth at a local mall. He has $15,000 and financed the balance at a high rate of 14% for 36 months since he did not have much credit history. Prepare an amortization schedule showing the first 5 payments.

PAYMENT NUMBER	AMOUNT OF PAYMENT	INTEREST FOR PERIOD	PORTION TO PRINCIPAL	PRINCIPAL AT END OF PERIOD

24. SCUBA EQUIPMENT Jessica Chien needed $280,000 for inventory for a scuba diving shop that she was opening. She had $40,000, and the bank loaned her the balance at 11% for 30 months. Prepare an amortization schedule showing the first 5 payments.

PAYMENT NUMBER	AMOUNT OF PAYMENT	INTEREST FOR PERIOD	PORTION TO PRINCIPAL	PRINCIPAL AT END OF PERIOD

12.5   Real Estate Loans

OBJECTIVES

1. Determine monthly payments on a home.
2. Prepare a repayment schedule.
3. Define escrow accounts.
4. Define fixed and variable rate loans.
5. Understand your credit score.

case IN point ▶

Jackie Waterton's position at Citibank requires her to work with customers who have difficulty paying their bills. Since the house payment is often the largest expense for a family, she often looks to see if she can reduce the monthly payment on the mortgage.

OBJECTIVE 1   Determine monthly payments on a home.   A home is *one of the most expensive purchases* that a person makes in his or her lifetime. The monthly payment for a home **mortgage** depends on the amount borrowed, the interest rate, and the term of the loan.

The bar graph shows that home **mortgage rates** have fallen from a high of over 15% in 1981 to below 5% in 2010. Interest rates are a very important factor in determining the monthly payment and therefore the affordability of a particular home. If interest rates fall, people **refinance** their home loans at lower rates to reduce their monthly payments. The interest on a home loan may also be tax deductible, which can help people afford homes by reducing their income taxes.

Numbers in the News

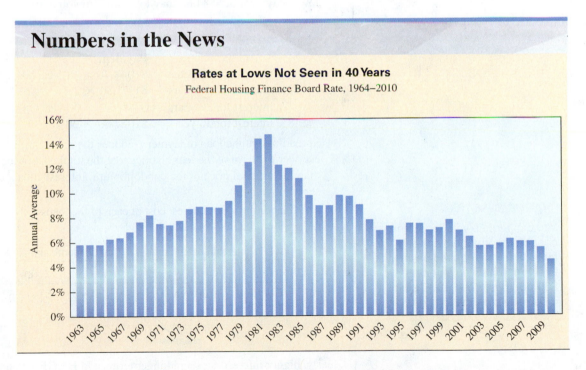

Rates at Lows Not Seen in 40 Years
Federal Housing Finance Board Rate, 1964–2010

The amount of the monthly payment is found by the methods given in Section 12.4, but different tables are used for real estate loans because of the long repayment periods. The real estate amortization table on the next page shows the monthly payment necessary to repay a $1000 loan for differing interest rates and lengths of repayment. To use the table, first find the amount to be financed in thousands by dividing the total amount to be borrowed by $1000. Then multiply this value by the appropriate number from the table.

Real Estate Amortization Table (Principal and Interest per Thousand Dollars Borrowed)

TERMS IN YEARS	6%	6¼%	6½%	6¾%	7%	7¼%	7½%	7¾%	8%	8¼%	8½%	9%	TERMS IN YEARS
10	11.10	11.23	11.35	11.48	11.62	11.75	11.88	12.01	12.14	12.27	12.40	12.67	10
15	8.44	8.57	8.71	8.85	8.99	9.13	9.28	9.42	9.56	9.71	9.85	10.15	15
20	7.16	7.31	7.46	7.60	7.76	7.91	8.06	8.21	8.37	8.53	8.68	9.00	20
25	6.44	6.60	6.75	6.91	7.07	7.23	7.39	7.56	7.72	7.89	8.06	8.40	25
30	6.00	6.16	6.32	6.49	6.65	6.83	7.00	7.17	7.34	7.52	7.69	8.05	30

Understanding the Effects of Rate and Term **EXAMPLE 1**

After making a down payment, the Stringers need to borrow $140,000 to purchase a condominium. They want to know the effect of the interest rate and term of the loan on cost. **(a)** Find the monthly payment for both 20 and 30 years at 6½% and at 8%. Then find **(b)** the total cost of the home with each loan and **(c)** the finance charge for each loan.

SOLUTION

(a) The amount to be financed in thousands = $140,000 ÷ $1000 = 140. Multiply this value by the appropriate factor from the real estate amortization table.

> **Quick TIP ▼**
>
> Be sure to divide the loan amount by $1000 before calculating the monthly payment.

	Monthly Payment
6½% interest for 20 years = 140 × **7.46** =	**$1044.40**
8% interest for 20 years = 140 × **8.37** =	**$1171.80**
6½% interest for 30 years = 140 × **6.32** =	**$ 884.80**
8% interest for 30 years = 140 × **7.34** =	**$1027.60**

Monthly payments range from $884.80 to $1171.80, depending on rate and term. The lower payment of $884.80 may look good to you at first, but look at part **(b)**.

(b) The total cost of financing the home is the sum of all payments.

	Monthly Payment		Total Cost
6½% interest for 20 years =	$1044.40 × 20 years × 12 month/yr =		**$250,656**
8% interest for 20 years =	$1171.80 × 20 years × 12 month/yr =		**$281,232**
6½% interest for 30 years =	$ 884.80 × 30 years × 12 month/yr =		**$318,528**
8% interest for 30 years =	$1027.60 × 30 years × 12 month/yr =		**$369,936**

Spreading out the loan repayment reduces the payment, BUT it results in much more interest over the term of the loan. Notice that the total cost of the condominium is much more than the original price of the condominium. Interest adds *a lot of cost* to the purchase as shown in part **(c)**.

> **Quick TIP ▼**
>
> You can reduce your long-term cost of a mortgage by paying more than the required payment every month. Even an extra $60 per month can make a big difference over the long run.

(c) The finance charge or interest cost of each of the loans is the total cost found in part **(b)** minus the amount financed of $140,000.

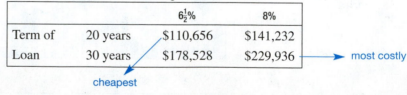

Interest Cost of Purchasing the Condominium

		6½%	8%
Term of Loan	20 years	$110,656	$141,232
	30 years	$178,528	$229,936 → most costly

cheapest

Clearly, higher interest rates and longer terms add **HUGE** amounts to the interest that must be paid to purchase a property.

> **QUICK CHECK 1**
>
> A couple plans to borrow $220,000 for 30 years to purchase a home. Find both the payment and the total 30-year cost assuming **(a)** a 6.5% rate and **(b)** a 7.25% rate.

Mortgage payoffs of 25 or 30 years have been common in the past. However, **accelerated mortgages**, with payoffs of 15 or 20 years, are becoming more common for the reason pointed out in Example 1—lower total costs. Mortgages with shorter terms also tend to have slightly lower interest rates.

OBJECTIVE 2 Prepare a repayment schedule. Many lenders use a computer to calculate an **amortization schedule**, also called a **repayment schedule**. This schedule separates each payment into the portion going to interest and the portion reducing the debt (principal payment).

Preparing a Repayment Schedule

EXAMPLE 2

The Zinks purchase a house by borrowing $195,000 at 7% for 30 years. Prepare a loan repayment schedule for this loan.

SOLUTION

First find the monthly payment, then use simple interest calculations for the first two months. Be sure to round to the nearest cent at each step.

$$\text{Monthly payment} = \$195 \times 6.65 = \$1296.75$$

First month:

$$\text{Interest} = PRT = \$195,000 \times .07 \times \tfrac{1}{12} = \$1137.50$$

monthly payment ———↓   ↓——— 1st month's interest

Amount that payment reduces principal = $1296.75 − $1137.50 = **$159.25**
Remaining debt at end of 1st month = $195,000 − **$159.25** = $194,840.75

Every time a payment is made, interest is first subtracted from the payment. As a result, only a small portion of the first payment is applied to reduce the principal.

Second month:

$$\text{Interest} = PRT = \$194,840.75 \times .07 \times \tfrac{1}{12} = \$1136.57$$
Amount that payment reduces principal = $1296.75 − $1136.57 = **$160.18**
Remaining debt at end of 2nd month = $194,840.75 − **$160.18** = $194,680.57

These and other results are shown in the table. Notice that at first the amount applied to interest is large and the amount applied to reduce principal is small. But every month, the debt goes down, resulting in lower interest the following month, and more of each payment is applied to reduce the principal. It requires 262 months (nearly 22 years) to pay off half of the debt and only 98 months (just over 8 years) to pay off the other half of the loan.

Loan Repayment Schedule

	LOAN: $195,000; TERM: 30 YEARS; RATE 7%; PAYMENT $1296.75						
PAYMENT NUMBER	INTEREST PAYMENT	PRINCIPAL PAYMENT	REMAINING BALANCE	PAYMENT NUMBER	INTEREST PAYMENT	PRINCIPAL PAYMENT	REMAINING BALANCE
0	—	—	$195,000.00	258	$586.73	$710.02	$99,872.80
1	$1137.50	$159.25	$194,840.75	259	$582.59	$714.16	$99,158.64
2	$1136.57	$160.18	$194,680.57	260	$578.43	$718.32	$98,440.32
3	$1135.64	$161.11	$194,519.46	261	$574.24	$722.51	$97,717.81
4	$1134.70	$162.05	$194,357.41	262	$570.02	$726.73	$96,991.08
5	$1133.75	$163.00	$194,194.41	·	·	·	·
6	$1132.80	$163.95	$194,030.46	·	·	·	·
7	$1131.84	$164.91	$193,865.55	·	·	·	·
8	$1130.88	$165.87	$193,699.68	359	$19.14	$1277.61	$2,004.17
9	$1129.91	$166.84	$193,532.84	360	$11.69	$2004.17*	$0.00

*Due to rounding, the last payment needs to be a little larger to bring the debt to exactly $0.

OBJECTIVE 3 Define escrow accounts. To prevent losses from unpaid taxes or uninsured damages, many lenders require **escrow accounts** (also called **impound accounts**) for people taking out a mortgage. With an escrow account, buyers pay $\frac{1}{12}$ of the total estimated property tax and insurance each month. The lender holds these funds until the taxes and insurance fall due and then *pays the bills for the borrower*. Many consumer groups oppose this practice, since the lender earns interest on the money while waiting for payments to come due. In fact, a few states require that interest be paid on escrow accounts on any homes located in those states.

Finding the Total Monthly Payment **EXAMPLE 3**

Susan Beckman received a $75,000 loan for 25 years at $7\frac{1}{4}$% to purchase a summer cabin. Annual insurance and taxes on the property are $654 and $1329, respectively. Find the total monthly payment.

SOLUTION

Use the real estate amortization table to find a factor of $7.23. Add monthly insurance and taxes to the payment amount.

$$\text{Monthly payment} = \overbrace{(75 \times \$7.23)}^{\text{principal and interest}} + \left(\frac{\overbrace{\$654}^{\text{insurance}} + \overbrace{\$1329}^{\text{taxes}}}{12}\right)$$
$$= \$542.25 + \$165.25 = \$707.50$$

OBJECTIVE 4 Define fixed and variable rate loans. Home loans with fixed, stated interest rates are called **fixed-rate loans**. Many borrowers prefer fixed-rate loans, since they know that the principal and interest portion of their monthly payments will be fixed until they either sell the house or pay off the debt. In particular, it is good for a borrower (but bad for the lender) if he or she locks in a fixed-rate loan before interest rates go up. If interest rates fall after a person has borrowed money for a home, the person can usually refinance at a lower interest rate.

Another type of home loan called an **adjustable rate mortgage, or ARM**, has a **variable interest rate.** This means that the interest rate is periodically reset by the lender to either a higher or a lower rate. Usually, there is a maximum limit to the increase in the rate during any one reset. Nonetheless, higher interest rates mean higher monthly payments for home owners.

Since ARM home loans were often offered with a very low initial interest rate, millions of people chose to finance their homes using an ARM loan. Many believed that the value of the home would continue to increase along with their income, making it easy to refinance the ARM loan as needed. However, home prices reached a speculative peak in 2008 and then fell rapidly throughout most of the country in 2009–10. This left many homeowners **underwater**, meaning that the debt on their home was higher than the market price, the price at which the home would sell. Many underwater home buyers stopped making payments and moved out of their homes, causing banks to foreclose on homes. Banks then tried to resell the homes to other buyers.

The following figure shows the number of foreclosures on homes during the recent severe recession. Notice that there were about 350,000 foreclosures per month in early 2010. This issue was viewed as a very serious economic problem and it is one that the president and his economic advisors were trying to help resolve.

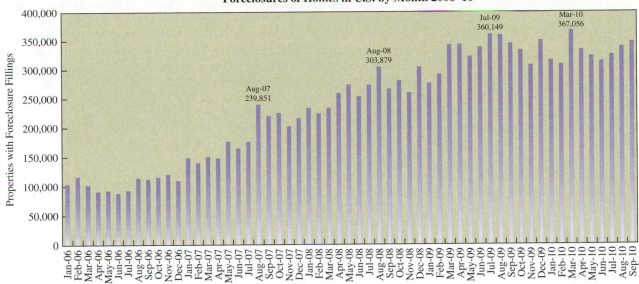

Foreclosures of Homes in U.S. by Month 2006–10

Source: RealtyTrac 2010.

OBJECTIVE 5 **Understand your credit score.** Mortgage companies, banks, and other lending institutions determine your creditworthiness using a FICO® score. This **credit score** was established by **FICO** (Fair Isaac Corporation) in 1989, and it is based on numerical values ranging from 300 to 850. The higher the score, the higher the creditworthiness; the lower the score, the more difficult it is to get a loan at a good interest rate. Three national credit-reporting agencies have databases that contain financial information about you: Equifax, TransUnion, and Experian. Each calculates a FICO score for you. The three scores may differ slightly from one agency to the next, since they do not always have the same information about you. It is a good idea to contact at least one of the three credit reporting agencies annually to examine your credit history.

Here is how one large lender uses FICO scores:

FICO Score	Creditworthiness
above 730	excellent
700–729	good
670–699	increased scrutiny
585–669	higher credit risk
below 585	high credit risk

Your FICO score is based on a weighted average of the following factors:

1. payment history,
2. amount owed,
3. length of credit history,
4. new credit, and
5. types of credit in use.

The largest weights in the FICO score are applied to the first two factors: payment history and amounts owed. You can control both of these factors, but you do not have control over the third factor (length of credit history), since that is partly based on age. New credit refers to the amount of new credit you have recently been given.

Quick TIP ▼

Higher FICO scores result in lower interest rates, whether on a personal property loan or on a home mortgage.

Quick TIP ▼

Charging rates that depend on creditworthiness helps a lender ensure that its portfolio of loans remains profitable.

The higher your FICO score, the easier it is to obtain a loan and the lower the interest rate at which you borrow. The opposite is also true. Consider what will happen if you end up with too much debt and fail to make payments or start making late payments. Your credit score will fall and it will quickly become more difficult to borrow money. If you are still able to borrow, it is likely that the interest rate will be much higher, meaning that it will cost you more to borrow. It is important to protect your credit rating.

To raise your FICO score, first make sure the credit agencies do not have any false information on your records. They handle billions of pieces of information monthly, so it is easy for them to make mistakes. Your credit rating will be hurt by late payments, too many sources of credit, and high debt compared to your income. To raise your score, correct any mistakes on your financial records at the agencies, close accounts you no longer use, pay off existing balances, and always make payments on time.

12.5 Exercises

The **QUICK START** *exercises in each section contain solutions to help you get started.*

Use the real estate amortization table to find the monthly payment for the following loans. (See Example 1.)

QUICK START

	Amount of Loan	Interest Rate	Term of Loan	Monthly Payment
1.	$310,000	$6\frac{1}{4}\%$	20 years	**$2266.10**
	Payment = 310 × $7.31 = $2266.10			
2.	$149,000	$7\frac{3}{4}\%$	20 years	**$1223.29**
	Payment = 149 × 8.21 = $1223.29			
3.	$112,800	$8\frac{1}{2}\%$	15 years	_____
4.	$132,000	$6\frac{1}{2}\%$	25 years	_____
5.	$92,400	$6\frac{3}{4}\%$	30 years	_____
6.	$280,000	6%	15 years	_____

7. Explain how different interest rates can make a large difference in interest charges over a number of years. (See Example 1.)

8. Explain how interest can result in a total cost that is over twice the original loan amount when a home is financed over 30 years. (See Example 1.)

Find the total monthly payment, including taxes and insurance, for the following loans. Round to the nearest cent. (See Example 3.)

QUICK START

	Amount of Loan	Interest Rate	Term of Loan	Annual Taxes	Annual Insurance	Monthly Payment
9.	$98,000	7%	30 years	$1250	$560	**$802.53**
	98 × $6.65 = $651.70; $651.70 + + $\frac{\$1250\ +\ \$560}{12}$ = $802.53					
10.	$150,800	$8\frac{1}{2}\%$	20 years	$3240	$602	**$1629.11**
	150.8 × $8.68 = $1308.94; $1308.94 + $\frac{\$3240\ +\ \$602}{12}$ = $1629.11					
11.	$275,800	$7\frac{1}{4}\%$	30 years	$6840	$758	_____
12.	$68,400	9%	30 years	$1256	$350	_____

🔺 indicates an exercise that is related to the Case in Point feature.

	Amount of Loan	Interest Rate	Term of Loan	Annual Taxes	Annual Insurance	Monthly Payment
13.	$91,580	$8\frac{1}{4}\%$	25 years	$1326	$489	_____
14.	$173,000	$6\frac{1}{2}\%$	30 years	$2800	$920	_____

Solve the following application problems.

QUICK START

15. HOME PURCHASE The Potters want to buy a cottage costing $127,000 with annual insurance and taxes of $720 and $2300, respectively. They have saved $10,000 for a down payment, and they can get a $7\frac{1}{2}\%$, 30-year mortgage from Citibank. They are qualified for a home loan as long as the total monthly payment does not exceed $1200. Are they qualified?

15. <u>Yes, qualified</u>

Loan amount = $127,000 − $10,000 = $117,000
Monthly payment = 117 × $7.00 = $819
Total payment = $819 + $\frac{\$720 + \$2300}{12}$ = $1070.67; **Yes, qualified**

16. CONDOMINIUM PURCHASE The Polinki family wants to buy a condominium that costs $225,000 with annual insurance and taxes of $850 and $3200, respectively. They plan to pay $20,000 down and amortize the balance at 8% per year for 25 years. They are qualified for a loan as long as the payments do not exceed $1800. Are they qualified for the loan?

16. _____

17. HOME LOAN June and Bill Able borrow $122,500 on their home at $7\frac{1}{2}\%$ for 15 years. Prepare a repayment schedule for the first two payments. (See Example 2.)

Payment Number	Total Payment	Interest Payment	Principal Payment	Remaining Balance

18. ELDERLY HOUSING Tom Ajax purchases a tiny home for his elderly mother. After a large down payment, he finances $88,600 at $7\frac{1}{4}\%$ for 10 years. Prepare a repayment schedule for the first two payments. (See Example 2.)

Payment Number	Total Payment	Interest Payment	Principal Payment	Remaining Balance

---

QUICK CHECK ANSWERS

1. (a) $1390.40; $500,544 **(b)** $1502.60; $540,936

2. Monthly payment = $1178

PAYMENT NUMBER	INTEREST PAYMENT	PRINCIPAL PAYMENT	REMAINING BALANCE
0	—	—	$155,000.00
1	$871.88	$306.12	$154,693.88
2	$870.15	$307.85	$154,386.03
3	$868.42	$309.58	$154,076.45

3. $1350.54

Chapter 12 | Quick Review

Chapter Terms *Review the following terms to test your understanding of the chapter. For each term you do not know, refer to the page number found next to that term.*

accelerated mortgages [p. 528]

adjustable rate mortgages (ARM) [p. 530]

amortization schedule [p. 520]

amortize [p. 503]

annual percentage rate [p. 503]

approximate annual percentage rate [p. 504]

APR [p. 503]

average daily balance method [p. 495]

consolidate loans [p. 498]

credit history [p. 503]

credit limit [p. 492]

credit score [p. 531]

debit cards [p. 492]

defaulting on debt [p. 498]

escrow accounts [p. 530]

FICO [p. 531]

finance charges [p. 493]

fixed-rate loans [p. 530]

grace period [p. 493]

impound accounts [p. 530]

installment cost [p. 504]

installment loan [p. 503]

itemized billing [p. 493]

late fees [p. 493]

mortgage [p. 527]

mortgage rates [p. 527]

nominal rate [p. 503]

open-end credit [p. 492]

over-the-limit fees [p. 493]

personal property [p. 519]

real estate [p. 519]

real property [p. 519]

refinance [p. 527]

refund of unearned interest [p. 513]

repayment schedule [p. 529]

repossess [p. 519]

revolving charge account [p. 493]

Rule of 78 [p. 512]

Stafford loan [p. 504]

stated rate [p. 503]

Truth in Lending Act [p. 503]

underwater [p. 530]

unearned interest [p. 513]

United States Rule [p. 511]

unpaid balance method [p. 493]

variable interest rate loans [p. 530]

CONCEPTS

EXAMPLES

12.1 Finding the finance charge on a revolving charge account, using the unpaid balance method

Start with the unpaid balance of the previous month. Then find the finance charge on the unpaid balance. Next, add the finance charge and any purchases. Finally, subtract any payments made.

Debbie Mahoney's MasterCard account had an unpaid balance of $385.65 on March 1. During March, she made a $100 payment and charged $68.92. Find the finance charge and the unpaid balance on April 1 if the bank charges 1.25% per month on the unpaid balance.

$$\text{Finance charge} = \$385.65 \times .0125 = \$4.82$$

$$\underset{\substack{\text{previous} \\ \text{balance}}}{\$385.65} + \underset{\substack{\text{finance} \\ \text{charge}}}{\$4.82} + \underset{\substack{\\ \text{purchases}}}{\$68.92} - \underset{\substack{\\ \text{payment}}}{\$100} = \underset{\substack{\text{new} \\ \text{balance}}}{\$359.39}$$

12.1 Finding the finance charge on a revolving charge account, using the average daily balance method

First find the unpaid balance on each day of the month. Then add up the daily unpaid balances.

Next divide the total of the daily unpaid balances by the number of days in the billing period.

Finally, calculate the finance charge by multiplying the average daily balance by the finance charge.

The following is a summary of a credit card account.

Previous balance		$115.45
November 1	Billing date	
November 15	Payment	$35.00
November 22	Charge	$45.00

Find the average daily balance and the finance charge if interest is 2% per month on the average daily balance.

Balance on Nov. 1 = $115.45

Nov. 1 − 15 = 14 days at $115.45

14 × $115.45 = **$1616.30**

Payment on Nov. 15 = $35.00
Balance on Nov. 15 = $115.45 − $35 = $80.45

Nov. 15 − Nov. 22 = 7 days at $80.45

7 × $80.45 = **$563.15**

Charge on Nov. 22 of $45.00
Balance on Nov. 22 = $80.45 + $45 = $125.45

Nov. 22 − Dec. 1 = 9 days at $125.45

9 × $125.45 = **$1129.05**

Daily balances
        $1616.30 + **$563.15** + **$1129.05** = **$3308.50**

$$\text{Average daily balance} = \frac{\$3308.50}{30} = \$110.28$$

Finance charges = $110.28 × .02 = $2.20

CONCEPTS	EXAMPLES

12.2 Finding the total installment cost, finance charge, and amount financed

Total installment cost
= Down payment
+ (Amount of each payment × Number of payments)

Finance charge (interest)
    = Total installment cost − Cash price

Amount financed (principal of loan)
        = Cash price − Down payment

Joan Taylor bought a leather coat for $1580. She put $350 down and then made 12 payments of $115 each. Find the total installment cost, the finance charge, and the amount financed.

Total installment cost = $350 + ($115 × 12) = $1730

Finance charge = $1730 − $1580 = $150

Amount financed = $1580 − $350 = $1230

12.2 Determining the approximate APR using a formula

First determine the finance charge. Then find the amount financed. Next calculate approximate APR using the formula.

Approximate APR
$$= \frac{24 \times \text{Finance charge}}{\text{Amt. fin.} \times (1 + \text{Total number of payments})}$$

Tom Jones buys a motorcycle for $8990. He makes a down payment of $1800 and then makes monthly payments of $230 for 36 months. Find the approximate APR.

Total installment cost = $1800 + ($230 × 36) = $10,080

Finance charge = $10,080 − $8990 = **$1090**

Amount financed = $8990 − $1800 = $7190

Approximate APR $= \dfrac{24 \times \$1090}{\$7190 \times (1 + 36)} = 9.8\%$ (rounded)

12.2 Finding the APR using a table

First determine the finance charge per $100 of amount financed, using the formula

$$\frac{\text{Finance charge} \times \$100}{\text{Amount financed}}$$

Then read down the left column of the annual percentage rate table to the proper number of payments. Go across to the number closest to the number found above. Look to the top of the column to find the annual percentage rate.

Lupe Torres buys a used car for $6500. She makes a down payment of $1000 and agrees to make 24 monthly payments of $260.83. Use the table to find the APR.

Finance charge = $1000 + ($260.83 × 24) − $6500
                = $759.92

Amount financed = $5500

Finance charge per $100

$$\frac{\$759.92 \times \$100}{\$5500} = \textbf{13.817 (rounded)}$$

Use the 24-payment row in the table to find APR = 12.75%

12.3 Finding the amount due on the maturity date using the United States Rule

First determine the simple interest due from the date the loan was made until the date of the partial payment.

Then subtract this interest from the amount of the payment and reduce the principal by the difference.

Next find the interest from the date of partial payment to the due date of the note, and add the unpaid balance and interest to find the amount due.

Sam Wiley signs a 90-day note on August 1 for $5000 at an interest rate of 12%. On September 15, he makes a payment of $1800. Find the balance owed on the principal. If no additional payments are made, find the amount due on the maturity date of the loan.

From August 1 to September 15, there are 30 + 15 = 45 days.

$$I = \$5000 \times .12 \times \frac{45}{360} = \textbf{\$75} \text{ interest due}$$

$$
\begin{array}{rl}
\$1800 & \text{payment} \\
-\ \ 75 & \text{interest due} \\
\hline
\$1725 & \text{applied to principal} \\
 & \text{reduction}
\end{array}
$$

$$
\begin{array}{rl}
\$5000 & \text{amount owed} \\
-\ 1725 & \text{principal reduction} \\
\hline
\$3275 & \textbf{balance owed}
\end{array}
$$

Note is for 90 days; a partial payment was made after 45 days. Interest on $3275 will be charged for 90 − 45 = 45 days.

$$I = \$3275 \times .12 \times \frac{45}{360} = \textbf{\$49.13}$$

$$
\begin{array}{rl}
\$3275.00 & \text{principal owed} \\
+\ \ 49.13 & \text{interest} \\
\hline
\$3324.13 & \textbf{amount due}
\end{array}
$$

CONCEPTS

EXAMPLES

12.3 Finding the unearned interest using the Rule of 78

First calculate the finance charge. Then find the unearned interest using the formula

$$U = F\left(\frac{N}{P}\right)\left(\frac{1+N}{1+P}\right)$$

where U = unearned interest
   F = finance charge
   N = number of payments remaining
   P = total number of payments

Next find the total of the remaining payments. Finally, subtract the unearned interest to find the balance remaining.

Tom Fish borrows $1500, which he is paying back in 36 monthly installments of $52.75 each. With 10 payments remaining, he decides to pay the loan in full. Find **(a)** the amount of unearned interest and **(b)** the amount necessary to pay the loan in full.

36 payments of $52.75 each for a total repayment of $36 \times \$52.75 = \$1899$.

Finance charge = $1899 − $1500 = **$399**

Unearned interest = **$399** $\times \dfrac{10}{36} \times \dfrac{(1+10)}{(1+36)}$ = **$32.95**

10 payments of $52.75 are left. These payments total

$$\$52.75 \times 10 = \$527.50$$
$$\$527.50 - \$32.95 = \$494.55$$

This is the amount needed to pay the loan in full.

12.4 Finding the periodic payment for amortizing a loan

First determine the number of periods for the loan and the interest rate per period.

The payment is found by multiplying the loan amount by the number from the amortization table.

Bob Smith agrees to pay $12,000 for a used car. The amount will be repaid in monthly payments over 3 years at an interest rate of 12%. Find the amount of each payment.

$$12 \times 3 = \textbf{36 periods (payments)}$$

$$\frac{12\%}{12} = \textbf{1\% per period}$$

Number from table is **.03321**.

Payment = $12,000 × **.03321** = **$398.52**

12.4 Setting up an amortization schedule

First find the periodic payment. Then calculate the interest owed in the first period using the formula $I = PRT$. Next subtract the value of I from the periodic payment.

This is the amount applied to the reduction of the principal. Then find the balance after the first periodic payment by subtracting the value of the debt reduction from the original amount. Now repeat the above steps until the original loan is amortized (paid off).

Terri Meyer borrows $1800. She will repay this amount in 2 years with semiannual payments at an interest rate of 8%. Set up an amortization schedule.

4 periods (payments); 4% per period

Number from table is **.27549**

Payment = $1800 × **.27549** = $495.88

$$I = PRT$$

Interest owed = $1800 \times .08 \times \dfrac{1}{2}$ = $72

Debt reduction = $495.88 − $72 = $423.88
Balance of loan = $1800 − $423.88 = $1376.12

PAYMENT NUMBER	AMOUNT OF PAYMENT	INTEREST FOR PERIOD	PORTION TO PRINCIPAL	PRINCIPAL AT END OF PERIOD
0	—	—	—	$1800.00
1	$495.88	$72.00	$423.88	$1376.12
2	$495.88	$55.04	$440.84	$ 935.28
3	$495.88	$37.41	$458.47	$ 476.81
4	$495.88	$19.07	$476.81	$ 0.00

CONCEPTS	EXAMPLES
12.4 Finding monthly payments, total amount paid, and finance charge	Ben Apostolides purchased a new Toyota Camry and owes $16,400 after the trade-in. He decides on a term with 50 monthly payments. Assume an interest rate of 12% compounded monthly and find the amount of each payment and the finance charge.
First multiply the amount to be financed by the number from the amortization table or the loan payoff table to find the periodic payment. Then find the total amount repaid by multiplying the periodic payment by the number of payments. Finally, subtract the amount financed from the total amount repaid to obtain the finance charge.	Monthly payment = $16,400 × **.02551** = **$418.36** Finance charge = 50 × **$418.36** − $16,400 = $4518

12.5 Finding the amount of monthly home loan payments and total interest charges over the life of a home loan

Using the number of years and the interest rate, find the amortization value per thousand dollars from the real estate amortization table.

Next multiply the table value by the number of thousands in the principal to obtain the monthly payment.

Then find the total amount of the payments and subtract the original amount owed from the total payments to obtain interest paid.

Lou and Rose Waters bought a house overlooking a small stream. After a large down payment, they owe $75,000. Find the monthly payment at $8\frac{1}{2}\%$ and the total interest charges over the life of a 25-year loan.

$$n = 25 \qquad i = 8\frac{1}{2}\%$$

Table value = $8.06

There are $\dfrac{\$75,000}{1000} = 75$ thousands in $75,000.

Monthly payment = 75 × $8.06 = $604.50

There are 25 × 12 = 300 payments.

Total payment = 300 × $604.50 = $181,350

Interest paid = $181,350 − $75,000 = $106,350

case study

CONSOLIDATING LOANS

Roberto and Julie Hernandez are struggling to make their monthly payments. They accumulated too much debt, which was easy to do with two young kids at home. Julie works 30 hours a week and takes care of the two kids. Their credit history had been poor, but Roberto took on a second job during the evenings and they have been making payments regularly for 8 months.

1. Find the monthly payments on each of the following purchases and the total monthly payment.

PURCHASE	ORIGINAL LOAN AMOUNT	INTEREST RATE	TERM OF LOAN	MONTHLY PAYMENT
Honda Accord	$18,800	12%	4 years	_____
Ford truck	$14,300	18%	4 years	_____
Home	$96,500	$8\frac{1}{2}$%	15 years	_____
2nd mortgage on home	$4,500	12%	3 years	_____
			Total	_____

2. These monthly expenses do not include car insurance ($215 per month), health insurance ($290 per month), or real estate taxes on their home ($3350 per year), among other expenses. Find their total monthly outlay for all of these expenses.

EXPENSE	MONTHLY OUTLAY
Payments on debt from **(a)**	_____
Car insurance	_____
Health insurance	_____
Real estate taxes on home	_____
Total	_____

3. After discussing things with Jackie Waterton at Citibank, the Hernandez's have learned that they can (1) refinance the remaining $14,900 amount on the Honda Accord at 12% over 4 years, (2) refinance the remaining $8600 loan amount on the Ford truck at 12% over 3 years, (3) refinance the remaining $94,800 loan amount on their home at 8% over 30 years, and (4) reduce their car insurance payments by $28 per month. Complete the following table.

ITEM	CURRENT LOAN AMOUNT	NEW INTEREST RATE	NEW TERM OF LOAN	NEW MONTHLY PAYMENT
Honda Accord				_____
Ford truck				_____
Home				_____
2nd mortgage on home				_____
Car insurance				_____
Health insurance				_____
Real estate taxes on home				_____
				_____

4. Find the reduction in their monthly payments.

4. _____

Part of the savings in the monthly payment came from reducing the interest rates. The remainder of the savings came from extending the loans further into the future.

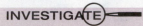

INVESTIGATE

The interest rate that you are charged for borrowing money differs depending on the bank you go to for a loan. Find current interest rates for financing a 2-year-old Toyota Camry from at least two banks in the area in which you live. Then go onto the World Wide Web and look for a lower interest rate.

case ɪɴ point summary exercise

CITIGROUP INC.—HOME FINANCING

www.citigroup.com

Facts:

- 1812: Founded in New York City
- 1914: Opened first international branch, in Argentina
- 1998: Merged with Travelers Insurance Group
- 2008: Lost $27.7 billion Took funds from government during financial crisis
- 2010: Revenue estimated to fall 40% compared to 2007

Citigroup Inc. (Citi) provides various banking, lending, insurance, and investment services to individual and corporate customers worldwide. It operates more than 7200 branches and 7000 ATMs. Citi had more than $150 billion in credit-card loans outstanding in 2010 in addition to huge volumes of home loans and business loans.

The financial crisis of 2008–10 created very serious problems for Citigroup. To illustrate the nature of some of the problems, we use the example of one family: Tom and Marie Duston purchased their first home in 2008 when home loans were still very easy to get. They bought a beautiful new 4-bedroom, $2\frac{1}{2}$-bath home with a down payment of only $8500.

1. They financed the loan balance of $306,500 using an adjustable rate mortgage (ARM). The monthly payment of $1100 did not include taxes and insurance. In fact, the monthly payment was all interest, meaning that nothing was applied against the debt each month. Find the monthly payment given taxes of $6400 per year and insurance of $980 per year.

    1. _____

2. At the time of the purchase in 2008, the Dustons were told that the interest rate on their ARM loan would reset in 2011, so they knew the payments might increase. However, they were not worried since they assumed that their incomes and also the value of the house would be higher by then. But home prices fell across much of the country in 2008–11, as did the value of their home. By 2011, an appraiser estimated that it was worth only 75% of the original loan balance of $306,500, which they still owed. They were underwater on their home! Find out what the house was worth in 2011 and the amount by which they were underwater.

    2. _____

3. The Dustons were shocked to find out that they would have to come up with $76,625 to pay off the bank loan to sell their home. They were further shocked to find out they would also need to come up with an additional $23,000 to pay various expenses, such as the real estate commission related to the sale of their home. Estimate the total amount they would have to pay to sell their home, rounded to the nearest thousand.

    3. _____

4. The Dustons did not have the funds needed, so they asked about refinancing the loan
balance of $306,500. At first, the bank wanted them to pay off the loan, but it finally agreed
to try to work to refinance it. The Dustons felt trapped! It was difficult to understand that
they were underwater by so much given that they had made every payment on time for
3 years. With the help of a government program designed to help underwater home owners
current on their mortgage payments, the bank agreed to refinance $285,000 on the home
on a 30-year fixed mortgage at $6\frac{3}{4}\%$. The difference between the debt of $306,500 and
$285,000 was essentially forgiven due to the government program. Find the new home
payment not including taxes and insurance.

4. _____

5. So the Dustons' monthly payment, not including taxes and insurance, increased from
$1100 per month up to the figure found for #4 above. Find the increase in the monthly
payment.

5. _____

From the Dustons' perspective: The Dustons were shocked about what had happened. They
had financed their home using an ARM loan and made every payment on time for 3 years.
However, the value of their home fell by 25% and they had to effectively refinance their home
in 2011 due to the nature of the ARM loan. They did not have the money needed to sell the
house and pay off the debt. After a stressful period, the bank finally agreed to help by refinancing $285,000 on their home. The monthly payment increased significantly. But, importantly, the
home was still worth quite a bit less than they owed on it! They were still underwater and might
have more losses on the house later. The good news is that they were able to stay in the house.

From the bank's perspective: In 2008, the bank lent the Dustons $306,500 on an ultra-low in-
terest ARM loan and received payments for 3 years. It was not the bank's fault that the value of
the home fell by 25%. Managers essentially believed that the loss was the homeowner's responsibility. However, they found a government program that would allow the bank to forgive part
of the Dustons' debt and refinance the remaining $285,000. This was still more than the house
was worth. The managers were worried that the Dustons might still abandon the house. In that
event, the bank would be forced to go through the lengthy and costly foreclosure process,
which would probably result in further losses for the bank.

*Discussion Quesstion: Are the Dustons' right? Is the bank right? Can you argue for each side
in the case?*

Chapter 12 Test

To help you review, the numbers in brackets show the section in which the topic was discussed.

Solve for following problems.

1. A cruise line needs to update some sonar equipment on one of its luxury ships that sails the Caribbean. The cost of the equipment is $214,500. The company makes a down payment of $20,000 and agrees to 24 monthly payments of $8975 per month. Find the total finance charge. **[12.1]**

1. _____

2. The balance on John Baker's MasterCard on November 1 is $680.45. In November, he charges an additional $337.32, has returns of $45.42, and makes a payment of $50. If the finance charges are calculated at 1.5% per month on the unpaid balance, find his balance on December 1. **[12.1]**

2. _____

Find the annual percentage rate, using the annual percentage rate table. **[12.2]**

Amount Financed	Finance Charge	Number of Payments	APR
3. $5280	$1010.59	36	_____
4. $1130	$149.84	24	_____

Solve the following application problems.

5. Barton Springs Landscaping buys a used truck for $18,700 and agrees to make 36 payments of $612.25 each. Find the annual percentage rate on the loan. **[12.2]**

5. _____

6. A note with a face value of $7000 is made on June 21. The note is for 90 days and carries interest of 13%. A partial payment of $2800 is made on July 17. Find the amount due on the maturity date of the note. **[12.3]**

6. _____

7. Mockton Construction bought a truck and financed $7400 with 48 monthly payments of $228.14 each. Suppose the firm pays the loan off with 12 payments left. Use the Rule of 78 to find **(a)** the amount of unearned interest and **(b)** the amount necessary to pay off the loan. **[12.3]**

(a) _____

(b) _____

Find the amount of each payment necessary to amortize the following loans. **[12.4]**

8. Jenson SawLogs borrows $34,500 to buy a new electric generator. The company agrees to make quarterly payments for 2 years at 10% per year. Find the amount of the quarterly payment.

8. _____

9. Scented Candles remodeled its lobby at a cost of $36,000. It pays $6000 down and pays off the balance in payments made at the end of each quarter for 5 years. Interest is 10% compounded quarterly. Find the amount of each payment so that the loan is fully amortized.

9. _____

Find the monthly payment necessary to amortize the following home mortgages. [12.5]

10. $123,500, $7\frac{1}{2}$%, 30 years

10. _____

11. $134,560, 7%, 15 years

11. _____

Work the following application problems. [12.5]

12. Mr. and Mrs. Zagorin plan to buy a $90,000 one-room cabin, paying 20% down and financing the balance at 8% for 30 years. The taxes are $960 per year, with fire insurance costing $252 per year. Find the monthly payment (including taxes and insurance).

12. _____

13. Billiards Galore purchases a commercial building for $680,000, pays 20% down, and finances the balance at $7\frac{1}{4}$% for 15 years. Taxes and insurance are $14,500 and $3200 per year, respectively. **(a)** Find the monthly payment. **(b)** Assume that insurance and taxes do not increase, and find the total cost of owning the building for 15 years, including the down payment.

(a) _____

(b) _____

14. Jerome Watson, owner of Watson Welding, purchases a storage building for his business and makes a $25,000 down payment. He finances the balance of $122,500 for 20 years at 8%. **(a)** Find the total monthly payment given taxes of $3200 per year and insurance of $1275 per year. **(b)** Assume that insurance and taxes do not increase, and find the total cost owning the building for 20 years (including the down payment).

(a) _____

(b) _____

Chapters 11-12 / Cumulative Review

CHAPTERS 11 AND 12

Round money amounts to the nearest cent and rates to the nearest tenth of a percent.

Find the amount and interest earned of each of the following ordinary annuities.   **[11.1]**

	Amount of Each Deposit	Deposited	Rate	Time (Years)	Amount of Annuity	Interest Earned
1.	$1000	annually	4%	8	_____	_____
2.	$2000	quarterly	6%	5	_____	_____

Find the amount of each annuity due and the interest earned.   **[11.1]**

	Amount of Each Deposit	Deposited	Rate	Time (Years)	Amount of Annuity	Interest Earned
3.	$2500	annually	5%	6	_____	_____
4.	$1800	semiannually	8%	5	_____	_____

Find the present value of the following annuities.   **[11.2]**

	Amount per Payment	Payment at End of Each	Time (Years)	Rate of Investment	Compounded	Present Value
5.	$925	6 months	11	8%	semiannually	_____
6.	$27,235	quarter	8	8%	quarterly	_____

Find the required payment into a sinking fund.   **[11.3]**

	Future Value	Interest Rate	Compounded	Time (Years)	Payment
7.	$3600	8%	annually	7	_____
8.	$4500	10%	quarterly	7	_____

Solve the following application problems using 360-day years where applicable.

9. At 58, Thomas Jones knows that he needs to save more. He decides to invest $300 per quarter in an account paying 10% compounded quarterly. Find the accumulated amount **(a)** at age 65 and **(b)** at age 70.   **[11.1]**

(a) _____

(b) _____

10. A public utility needs $60 million in 5 years for a major capital expansion. What annual payment must the firm place into a sinking fund earning 10% per year in order to accumulate the required funds?   **[11.3]**

10. _____

11. Jerry Walker purchased 100 shares of stock at $23.45 per share. The company had earnings of $1.56 and a yearly dividend of $.35. Find **(a)** the cost of the purchase ignoring commissions, **(b)** the price–earnings ratio to the nearest whole number, and **(c)** the dividend yield.   **[11.4]**

(a) _____

(b) _____

(c) _____

12. Martin Wicker buys 9000 GM bonds due in 2020 at 104.38 for the pension fund he manages. The coupon rate is 6.4%. Find **(a)** the cost to purchase the bonds if the commission is $1 per bond, **(b)** the annual interest from all of the bonds, and **(c)** the effective interest rate.   **[11.5]**

(a) _____

(b) _____

(c) _____

13. James Thompson purchased a large riding lawnmower costing $2800 with $500 down and payments of $108.27 per month for 24 months. Find **(a)** the total installment cost, **(b)** the finance charge, and **(c)** the amount financed. **(d)** Then use the table to find the annual percentage rate to the nearest quarter of a percent. **[12.2]**

(a) _____

(b) _____

(c) _____

(d) _____

14. Abbie Spring's unpaid balance on her Visa card on July 8 was $204.37. She made a payment of $100 on July 14 and had charges of $34.95 on July 16 and $95.12 on July 30. Assume an interest rate of 1.6% per month and find the balance on August 8 using **(a)** the unpaid balance method and **(b)** the average daily balance method. **[12.1]**

(a) _____

(b) _____

15. Mayberry Pets borrows to purchase a van to transport animals and supplies. They agree to make quarterly payments on the $22,400 debt for 3 years at a rate of 8% compounded quarterly. Find **(a)** the quarterly payment and **(b)** the total amount of interest paid.   **[12.4]**

(a) _____

(b) _____

16. The Hodges purchase an older 4-bedroom home for $195,000 with 5% down. They finance the balance at $7\frac{1}{2}$% per year for 30 years. If insurance is $720 per year and taxes are $4140 per year, find the monthly payment.   **[12.5]**

16. _____

17. On January 10, Bob Jones signed a 200-day note for $24,000 to finance some work on a roof. The note was at 9% per year simple interest. Due to an unexpected income tax refund, he was able to repay $10,000 on April 15. Use the United States Rule and **(a)** find the balance owed on the principal after the partial payment. **(b)** Then find the amount due at maturity of the loan.   **[12.3]**

(a) _____

(b) _____

18. Karoline Jacobs borrowed $2200 for new kitchen appliances. She agreed to pay the loan back with 8 payments of $290.69 each. After 3 payments, she decides to go ahead and pay off the loan in full. Use the Rule of 78 to find **(a)** the amount of unearned interest and **(b)** the amount needed to repay the loan in full.   **[12.3]**

(a) _____

(b) _____

19. Waterford Landscaping lost a lawsuit and must pay the injured party $3500 at the end of each quarter for 1 year. If funds earn 8% compounded quarterly, find the amount that needs to be set aside today to fulfill this obligation.   **[11.2]**

19. _____

20. James Booker signs an employment contract that guarantees him $35,000 at the end of each year for 3 years when he retires in 4 years. If funds earn 8% per year, find the present value needed today to meet the eventual payment stream.   **[10.3 and 11.2]**

20. _____

21. Explain the terms *present value, future value*, and *annuity*.

22. Describe stocks and bonds, explaining similarities and differences.

Taxes and Insurance

13

case in point ▶

MARTHA SPENCER OWNS The Doll House. She specializes in antique dolls from around the world and sells a lot of antique Barbie dolls. Her business was struggling to survive in 2000 when she decided to set up a Web site to try to grow her business. Not only have sales increased markedly since then, but international sales have really taken off, as shown in the following bar graph. Spencer estimates that one-third of total sales in 2012 will be to overseas clients.

Spencer owns the building in which her business is located, and she has several employees. As a result, she must keep up with all the laws related to taxes and insurance. It is not fun to work through tax and insurance issues, but Spencer knows it must be done—and done well—in order for her small business to prosper.

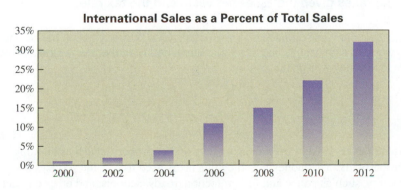

International Sales as a Percent of Total Sales

Both **taxes** and **insurance** are facts of life. In one form or another, we pay taxes to many different entities, including the federal government, states, counties, school districts, and cities. Supreme Court Justice Oliver Wendell Holmes, Jr., said, "Taxes are the price we pay to live in a civilized society." The pie chart shows the number of days per year the "average worker" works to pay various taxes. Property taxes and federal income taxes are discussed in this chapter.

Americans Work 98.5 Days to Pay All Federal, State and Local Taxes

Other Taxes: 6 Days
Corporate Income Taxes: 8 Days
Property Taxes: 12 Days
Sales & Excise Taxes: 15 Days
Estate & Gift Taxes: 12 Hours
Individual Income Taxes: 32 Days
Social Insurance Taxes: 25 Days

(*Source*: www.taxfoundation.org/)

Individuals buy insurance to protect from catastrophic losses to their homes and automobiles and also to pay medical expenses or to pay expenses at the time of death of a family member. Companies buy insurance to protect from potential losses to buildings and property, losses due to workers injured on the job, or even lawsuits from customers. Three common types of insurance are discussed in this chapter.

13.1 Property Tax

OBJECTIVES

1 Define *fair market value* and *assessed value*.
2 Find the tax rate.
3 Find the property tax.
4 Express tax rate in percent, in dollars per $100, in dollars per $1000, and in mills.
5 Find taxes given the assessed value and the tax rate.

case IN point ▶

Martha Spencer was surprised by the amount of the property tax on her business this year. Her taxes went up significantly and she was determined to find out why. She also wanted to know where the money was going.

In virtually every area of the nation, owners of real property (such as buildings and land) must pay property tax. The money raised by this tax is used to provide services needed by the local community, such as police and fire protection, roads, schools, and other city and county services. The figure on the next page shows that the average property tax per person has generally increased over the years.

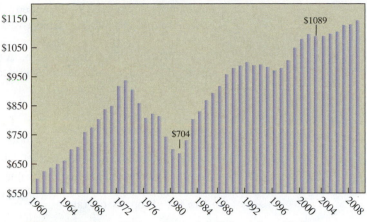

America's Rising Property Tax Burden

■ Annual Property Taxes per Person, in Inflation-Adjusted Dollars

DATA: The Tax Foundation

The following newspaper clipping shows the financial pressures some school districts faced during the recent financial crisis.

School District Battles Financial Problems

A local school district is struggling against all odds. The mission of the school district is founded on a quality education to all, but the current financial picture is grim. The board is considering closing eight schools and reducing the number of days the remaining schools are open. The head of the school board says, "Property taxes have fallen off sharply—the situation is dire, but we are hopeful."

OBJECTIVE 1 Define *fair market value* and *assessed value*. A local tax assessor estimates the market value of all the land and buildings in an area. The **fair market value** is the price at which a property can reasonably be expected to be sold. The fair market value could be used to find the amount of the property tax. However, many tax authorities first find what is called the **assessed value**, by multiplying the fair market value by a percent called the **assessment rate**. The assessed value is then used to calculate the property tax. In fact, the only purpose of the assessed value is for use in finding the property tax. The assessment rate varies widely from 25% in some states to 100% in others.

Fair Market Value $\Rightarrow$ Assessed Value $\Rightarrow$ Property Tax

Finding the Assessed Valuation of Property

EXAMPLE 1

Find the assessed value for the following pieces of property owned by Martha Spencer.

(a) Home: fair market value $185,300; assessment rate 35%

(b) Business property: fair market value $328,500; assessment rate 35%

(c) Commercial lot located in a different state: fair market value $123,800; assessment rate 60%

SOLUTION

Multiply the fair market value by the assessment rate.

(a) $185,300 \times .35 = $64,855

(b) $328,500 \times .35 = $114,975

(c) $123,800 \times .60 = $74,280

QUICK CHECK 1

A commercial building has a fair market value of $1,480,000. If the assessment rate is 70%, find the assessed value.

Just because the assessment rate is higher in one area than another does not necessarily mean that the taxes are higher. The assessed value of the property must be multiplied by the tax rate to find the tax. (See Objective 3.)

OBJECTIVE 2   Find the tax rate. A taxing authority such as a city or community college district first estimates the revenue needed and then finds the **property-tax rate** needed to generate that amount of tax as follows.

Finding the Property-Tax Rate

Step 1   Identify the amount of money needed.

Step 2   Find the total fair market value of all real properties in the area.

Step 3   Find the total assessed value of all real properties in the area.

Step 4   Property tax rate $= \dfrac{\text{Total tax amount needed}}{\text{Total assessed value}}$

Finding the Tax Rate

EXAMPLE 2

Find the tax rate for the following school districts, rounded to the nearest hundredth of a percent.

(a) Amount needed = \$14,253,000; total assessed value = \$1,575,890,000

(b) Amount needed = \$8,490,000; total assessed value = \$983,270,000

SOLUTION

(a) Tax rate $= \dfrac{\$14,253,000}{\$1,575,890,000} = .90\%$ (rounded)

(b) Tax rate $= \dfrac{\$8,490,000}{\$983,270,000} = .86\%$ (rounded)

QUICK CHECK 2

A large community college district needs \$22,350.000. The taxing authority has determined that the total assessed value of all the real estate in the district is \$3.48 billion. Find the property tax rate to the nearest hundredth of a percent.

OBJECTIVE 3   Find the property tax. The tax rate is applied to the assessed value to find the property tax due as follows.

Finding the Property Tax

Tax = Tax rate × Assessed value

OBJECTIVE 4   Express tax rate in percent, in dollars per \$100, in dollars per \$1000, and in mills. Tax rates are stated differently by different taxing entities. However, just because they are stated differently does not mean that the tax is either higher or lower in one area than in another. Here are methods that are in common use.

Percent. Some areas express tax rates as a percent of assessed value. The tax on a piece of property with an assessed value of \$174,000 at a tax rate of 2.17% follows.

$$\text{Tax} = .0217 \times \mathbf{\$174,000} = \$3775.80$$

Dollars per \$100.   In some areas, the tax rate is expressed as a number of dollars per \$100 of assessed value. In this event, find the tax on a piece of land by first finding the number of hundreds in the assessed value and then multiplying the number of hundreds by the tax rate. For example, assume an assessed value of \$56,300 and a tax rate of \$11.42 per \$100 of assessed value and find taxes as follows.

$$\$56,300 \div 100 = \mathbf{563\ hundreds} \qquad \text{Divide by 100 by moving the decimal point 2 places to the left.}$$

$$\text{Tax} = 563 \times \$11.42 = \mathbf{\$6429.46} \qquad \text{Multiply by the tax rate to find tax.}$$

Dollars per $1000. In other areas, the tax rate is expressed as a number of dollars per $1000 of assessed value. If the tax rate is $98.12 per $1000, a piece of property having an assessed value of $197,000 would be taxed as follows.

$$\$197,000 = \textbf{197 thousands}$$ Move the decimal point 3 places to the left to divide by 1000.

$$\text{Tax} = \$98.12 \times \textbf{197} = \textbf{\$19,329.64}$$

Mills. Other taxing authorities express tax rates in mills or one-thousandths of a dollar. For example, a tax rate might be expressed as 46 mills. Divide the 46 mills by 1000 to find $.046 per dollar of assessed value. Assuming a tax rate of 46 mills, the tax on a house assessed at $81,000 is found as follows.

$$\text{46 mills} = \$.046$$
$$\text{Tax} = .046 \times \$81,000 = \textbf{\$3726}$$

The following chart shows the same tax rates written in the four different systems. Although expressed differently, the rates in each row of this chart are equivalent tax rates.

PERCENT	PER $100	PER $1000	IN MILLS
1.25%	$1.25	$12.50	12.5
3.2%	$3.20	$32	32
9.87%	$9.87	$98.70	98.7

OBJECTIVE 5 Find taxes given the assessed value and the tax rate. Property taxes are found by multiplying the tax rate by the assessed value, as shown in the following example.

Finding the Property Tax

EXAMPLE 3

Find the taxes on each of the following pieces of property. Assessed values and tax rates are given.

(a) $58,975; 8.4%
(b) $875,400; $7.82 per $100
(c) $129,600; $64.21 per $1000
(d) $221,750; 94 mills

SOLUTION

Multiply the tax rate by the assessed value.

(a) 8.4% = .084

$$\text{Tax} = \text{Tax rate} \times \text{Assessed value}$$
$$\text{Tax} = .084 \times \$58,975 = \$4953.90$$

(b) $875,400 = **8754 hundreds**

$$\text{Tax} = \$7.82 \times \textbf{8754} = \$68,456.28$$

(c) $129,600 = **129.6 thousands**

$$\text{Tax} = \$64.21 \times \textbf{129.6} = \$8321.62$$

(d) 94 mills = .094

$$\text{Tax} = .094 \times \$221,750 = \$20,844.50$$

QUICK CHECK 3

A home is assessed at $65,000. Find the property tax if the tax rate is (a) 3.4%, (b) $4.50 per $100, (c) $38.40 per $1000, and (d) 48.2 mills.

Not everyone pays at the same property-tax rates. For example, churches are usually exempt from property taxes. Many states give homeowners an exemption that reduces the property tax on their home. Still other states give property-tax exemptions to the elderly.

Comparing Tax Rates **EXAMPLE 4**

As Ben Waller decides where to build a 60-unit apartment complex that he estimates will have a market value of $2,800,000, he considers property tax. In one county, property is assessed at 50% of market value with a tax rate of 3.2%. In a second county, property is assessed at 80% with a tax rate of 35 mills. **(a)** Find the county with the lower tax. **(b)** Find the amount saved by building in the county with the lower tax.

SOLUTION

(a) Property tax 1st county = $2,800,000 × .5 × .032 = **$44,800**

Property tax 2nd county = $2,800,000 × .8 × .035 = **$78,400**

The first county has the lower tax.

(b) Amount saved = **$78,400** − **$44,800** = $33,600 per year

---

QUICK CHECK 4

One county has a tax rate of $2.40 per $100, and a second county has a tax rate of $26.60 per $1000. A planned home will have an assessed value of $290,000. **(a)** Find the county with the lower tax. **(b)** Find the amount saved by building in the county with the lower tax.

The **QUICK START** *exercises in each section contain solutions to help you get started.*

Find the assessed value for each of the following pieces of property. (See Example 1.)

QUICK START

Fair Market Value	Rate of Assessment	Assessed Value		Fair Market Value	Rate of Assessment	Assessed Value
1. $85,000	40%	**$34,000**	**2.**	$68,000	60%	**$40,800**
$85,000 × .4 = $34,000				$68,000 × .6 = $40,800		
3. $142,300	50%	_____	**4.**	$98,200	42%	_____
5. $1,300,500	25%	_____	**6.**	$2,450,000	80%	_____

Find the tax rate for the following. Write the tax rate as a percent, rounded to the nearest tenth of a percent. (See Example 2.)

QUICK START

Total Tax Amount Needed	Total Assessed Value	Tax Rate		Total Tax Amount Needed	Total Assessed Value	Tax Rate
7. $18,300,000	$6,850,000,000	**.3%**	**8.**	$7,600,000	$1,752,500,000	**.4%**
$18,300,000 ÷ $6,850,000,000 = .0027 = .3% (rounded)				$7,600,000 ÷ $1,752,500,000 = .0043 = .4% (rounded)		
9. $1,580,000	$19,750,000	_____	**10.**	$2,175,000	$54,375,000	_____
11. $1,224,000	$40,800,000	_____	**12.**	$28,630,000	$12,350,000,000	_____

Write the given tax rate using the other three methods. (See Example 3.)

QUICK START

	Percent	Per $100	Per $1000	In Mills
13.	4.84%	(a) **$4.84**	(b) **$48.40**	(c) **48.4**
14.	(a) _____	$6.75	(b) _____	(c) _____
15.	(a) _____	(b) _____	$70.80	(c) _____
16.	(a) _____	(b) _____	(c) _____	28

17. What is the difference between fair market value and assessed value? How is the assessment rate used when finding the assessed value? (See Objective 1.)

18. Explain the difference between fair market value, assessed value, and property tax. (See Objectives 1, 2, and 3.)

Find the property tax for the following. (See Example 3.)

Assessed Value	Tax Rate	Tax		Assessed Value	Tax Rate	Tax
19. $86,200	$6.80 per $100	$5861.60	**20.**	$41,300	$46.40 per $1000	_____
862 × $6.80 = $5861.60						
21. $128,200	42 mills	_____	**22.**	$37,250	3.4%	_____

Solve the following application problems.

23. REAL ESTATE TAXES   Martha Spencer owns the real estate used by The Doll House. The property has a fair market value of $328,500, the assessment rate is 35%, and the local tax rate is 5.2%. Find the tax.

$328,500 × .35 = $114,975; $114,975 × .052 = $5978.70

23. $5978.70

24. APARTMENT OWNER   Chad LeCompte owns a four-unit apartment building with a fair market value of $248,000. Property in the area is assessed at 40% of market value, and the tax rate is 5.5%. Find the amount of the property tax.

24. _____

25. COMMERCIAL PROPERTY TAX   A new FM radio station broadcasts from a building having a fair market value of $334,400. The building is in an area where property is assessed at 25% of market value, and the tax rate is $75.30 per $1000 of assessed value. Find the property tax.

25. _____

26. OFFICE COMPLEX   Huron Development just purchased a modern office complex for $12,380,000. The county assesses the property at 60% of market value and has a property tax of $18.40 per $1000 of assessed value. Find the property tax.

26. _____

27. WALMART SUPERCENTER   A new Walmart Supercenter is expected to have a fair market value of $18,500,000. It will be assessed at 65% and the tax rate is $2.18 per $100 of assessed value. Estimate the annual property tax.

27. _____

28. MOTORCYCLES   Harley-Davidson of Lincoln has property with a fair market value of $518,600. The property is located in an area that is assessed at 35% of market value. The tax rate is $7.35 per $100. Find the property tax.

28. _____

29. COMPARING PROPERTY TAX RATES In one parish (county), property is assessed at 40% of market value, with a tax rate of 32.1 mills. In a second parish, property is assessed at 24% of market value, with a tax rate of 50.2 mills. A telephone company is trying to decide where to place a small storage building with a fair market value of $95,000. **(a)** Which parish would charge the lower property tax? **(b)** Find the annual amount saved.

(a) ____________________

(b) ____________________

30. TAXES ON HOME Jacque Henri plans to build a home with a fair market value of $240,000 in one of two neighboring counties. In Smith County, property is assessed at 30% of market value, with a tax rate of 45.6 mills. In Justin County, property is assessed at 58% of market value with a tax rate of 38.5 mills. Find **(a)** which county has the lower property tax and **(b)** the annual amount saved if the home is built in that county.

(a) ____________________

(b) ____________________

QUICK CHECK ANSWERS

1. $1,036,000

2. .64%

3. **(a)** $2210 **(b)** $2925 **(c)** $2496 **(d)** $3133

4. **(a)** first county **(b)** $754 per year

13.2 Personal Income Tax

OBJECTIVES

1 List the four steps that determine income-tax liability.
2 Find the adjusted gross income.
3 Know the standard deduction amounts.
4 Find the taxable income and income tax.
5 List possible deductions.
6 Determine a balance due or a refund from the Internal Revenue Service.
7 Prepare a 1040A and a Schedule 1 federal tax form.

case IN point ▶ Martha Spencer is responsible for paying all appropriate taxes related to her business as well as her personal taxes. Since she is busy and taxes are complex, she hires an accountant to help her in her business.

The following pie charts show the sources of income and expenditures for the U.S. government. Most of the government's income is from personal and corporate **income taxes**, which are taxes on income. Personal income taxes were 43% of the government's revenue, and corporate income taxes were 13% of the government's revenue. The largest outlays of money were for Social Security, Medicare, and national defense/military.

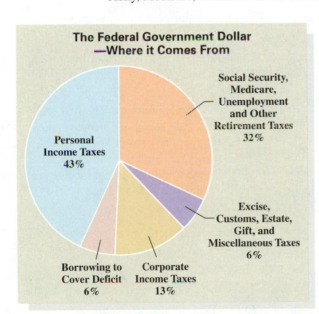

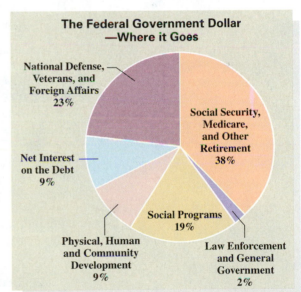

Data: Internal Revenue Service (2009)

Many are worried about the significant increase in interest payments that the government will have to pay as debt grows to record levels during 2009–11 in response to the financial crisis. Most experts agree that the U.S. government needs to either spend less and/or somehow increase tax revenue. In this environment, a debate is occurring about whether the tax cuts implemented during President George W. Bush's administration should be allowed to expire as scheduled at the end of 2010.

Some believe that those with high incomes do not pay income taxes, but that is usually not the case. According to the Tax Foundation, the top 50% of all earners in the United States pay more than 97.1% of all personal income taxes paid. Recent headlines in newspapers indicate that the lowest 47% of all earners paid no federal income taxes. Importantly, many of these lower income individuals did pay other taxes, including Medicare, Social Security, sales taxes, and property taxes.

Most working adults in the United States are required to file an income tax return each year with the **Internal Revenue Service (IRS)**. The IRS is the branch of the U.S. government responsible for collecting income taxes. In 2011, it is estimated that over 150,000,000 personal income-tax returns will be filed in the United States and most of those will be filed electronically. Since the forms and laws change frequently, check the IRS Web site (www.irs.gov) for the most recent information.

There are thousands of rules about income tax preparation and many different forms, each with its own instructions. However, many people have relatively simple income tax returns that do not require professionals to complete. No matter whether you use a professional to file your income-tax return or do it yourself, you should carefully save all records related to income and expenses. These records should be kept until the statute of limitations runs out, which is 3 years from the date the tax return was filed or 2 years from the date the tax was paid, whichever is later. The IRS can audit you during this period and it requires proof of income and deductions. Many accountants recommend that you keep records for 7 years, but you should keep records on property such as your home as long as they are needed, often longer than 3 years.

OBJECTIVE 1 List the four steps that determine income tax liability. It can be very complex to find the income tax for some people. However, the following four steps are common to all personal tax returns. They are listed here and then described in detail in the remainder of this section.

Finding Your Income Tax Liability

Step 1 Find the adjusted gross income (AGI) for the year.

Step 2 Find the taxable income.

Step 3 Find the tax.

Step 4 Check to see if a refund is due or if money is owed to the government.

Note: It can be very complex to find the income tax for some people. This section introduces only the basic concepts.

OBJECTIVE 2 Find the adjusted gross income. The first step in finding personal income tax is to find **adjusted gross income**. Adjusted gross income is the total of all income less certain adjustments. Employers are required to send out **W-2 forms** showing wages paid, federal income taxes withheld, Social Security tax withheld, and Medicare tax withheld. Other types of income such as interest, dividends, and self-employment income are shown on **1099 forms**, which are also mailed to each individual. Sample W-2 and 1099-INT forms are shown on the next page.

Finding Adjusted Gross Income

Step 1 Add amounts from all W-2 and 1099 forms along with dividends, capital gains, unemployment compensation, and tips or other employee compensation.

Step 2 From this sum, subtract adjustments such as contributions to a *regular* **individual retirement account (IRA)** or alimony payments.

Finding Adjusted Gross Income (AGI)   **EXAMPLE 1**

As an assistant manager at The Doll House, Jennifer Crum earned $24,738.41 last year and $1624.01 in interest from her credit union (see her W-2 and 1099 forms). She had $1500 in regular IRA contributions. Find her adjusted gross income.

SOLUTION

$$\text{Adjusted gross income} = \text{Wages} + \text{Interest} - \textbf{IRA contribution}$$
$$= \$24{,}738.41 + \$1624.01 - \$1500$$
$$= \$24{,}862.42$$

QUICK CHECK 1

Last year, Marelli Food Distribution paid marketing manager Beth Hogan $95,000. Hogan also earned $6450 in interest and contributed $2500 to an IRA. Find her adjusted gross income.

When you file your income tax return, a copy of all W-2 forms is sent to the Internal Revenue Service along with the completed tax forms. However, the IRS does not require copies of 1099 forms to be sent unless income tax was withheld.

22222	Void ☐	a Employee's social security number 123-45-6789	For Official Use Only ▶ OMB No. 1545-0008	

b Employer identification number (EIN) 94–1287319	1 Wages, tips, other compensation $24,738.41	2 Federal income tax withheld $3275.60

c Employer's name, address, and ZIP code The Doll House 1568 Liberty Heights Ave. Baltimore, MD 21230	3 Social security wages $24,738.41	4 Social security tax withheld $1533.78
	5 Medicare wages and tips $24,738.41	6 Medicare tax withheld $358.71
	7 Social security tips	8 Allocated tips

d Control number	9 Advance EIC payment	10 Dependent care benefits

e Employee's first name and initial Jennifer	Last name Crum	Suff.	11 Nonqualified plans	12a See instructions for box 12

13 Statutory employee ☐ Retirement plan ☐ Third-party sick pay ☐   12b

2136 old Road
Towson, MD 21285

14 Other   12c

12d

f Employee's address and ZIP code

15 State Employer's state ID number MD	600–5076	16 State wages, tips, etc.	17 State income tax	18 Local wages, tips, etc.	19 Local income tax	20 Locality name

Form **W-2** **Wage and Tax Statement**

Department of the Treasury—Internal Revenue Service

9292   ☐ VOID   ☐ CORRECTED

PAYER'S name, street address, city, state, ZIP code, and telephone no. Employees Credit Union 2572 Brookhaven Drive Dundalk, MD 21222	Payer's RTN (optional)	OMB No. 1545–0112	Interest Income
	1 Interest income $	20__	
	2 Early withdrawal penalty $	Form **1099-INT**	

PAYER'S federal identification number 94–1287319	RECIPIENT'S identification number 123-45-6789	3 Interest on U.S. Savings Bonds and Treas. obligations $1624.01	Copy A For Internal Revenue Service Center File with Form 1096.
RECIPIENT'S name Jennifer Crum		4 Federal income tax withheld $	5 Investment expenses $
Street address (including apt. no.) 2136 Old Road		6 Foreign tax paid $	7 Foreign country or U.S. possession $
City, state, and ZIP code Towson, MD 21285		8 Tax-exempt interest $	9 Specified private activity bond interest $
Account number (see instructions)	2nd TIN not. ☐	10 Tax-exempt bond CUSIP no. (see instructions)	

For Privacy Act and Paperwork Reduction Act Notice. see the **2010 General Instructions for Certain Information Returns.**

Form **1099-INT**   Cat. No. 14410K   Department of the Treasury—Internal Revenue Service

OBJECTIVE 3 Know the standard deduction amounts. Most people are almost finished at this point. A taxpayer next subtracts the larger of either the itemized deductions or the standard deduction from adjusted gross income. Itemized deductions are described in Objective 5 in this section and are associated with several limitations based on adjusted gross income. The **standard deduction** amount is based on the taxpayer's filing status as follows.

Finding Standard Deduction

- $5,700 for single taxpayers
- $11,400 for married taxpayers filing jointly
- $5,700 for married taxpayers filing separately
- $8,350 for head of household

A **head of household** is an unmarried person who provides a home for other people, such as a dependent child or even a dependent parent of the taxpayer.

Additional standard deductions are given for taxpayers and dependents who are blind or 65 years of age or older. The standard deduction amounts change from one year to the next. The most current amounts can be obtained from the IRS.

The next step is to find the number of **personal exemptions**. One exemption is allowed for yourself, another for your spouse if filing a joint return, and yet another exemption for each child or other dependent. A **dependent** is a child, spouse, parent, or certain other relative to whom the primary taxpayer contributes all or a major portion of necessary financial support. The number of exemptions does not depend on whether the filing status is single or married. The deduction for personal exemptions is $3650 times the number of exemptions. Here are some examples.

Filing Status and Exemptions	Total Deduction
Single individual (1 exemption)	$1 \times \$3650 = \$3650$
Married with 3 children (5 exemptions)	$5 \times \$3650 = \$18,250$
Single, head of household, 2 children (3 exemptions)	$3 \times \$3650 = \$10,950$

Taxable income is found by subtracting the standard deduction amount and personal exemptions from adjusted gross income. Taxes are then calculated based on taxable income as shown next.

OBJECTIVE 4 Find the taxable income and income tax. Taxable income is used along with data from the tax rate schedule shown next to find the income tax. As you can see from the tax rate schedules, individual income tax rates range from a low of 10% to a high of 35% depending on income and filing status*. Assume a single filer has a taxable income of $37,300. Use the table for single filer below to find:

$$\text{Federal income tax} = \$4675 + \textbf{25\% of excess over \$33,950}$$
$$= \$4675 + \mathbf{.25 \times (\$37,300 - \$33,950)}$$
$$= \$5512.50$$

Note that the 25% rate applies only to the excess over $33,950 and not to the entire amount of $37,300. In fact, the percent of the taxable income that goes for taxes is found as follows.

$$\frac{\text{Percent of taxable}}{\text{income paid in taxes}} = \frac{\text{Amount paid in taxes}}{\text{Taxable income}}$$

$$= \frac{\$5512.50}{\$37,300} = 14.78\% \quad \text{(rounded)}$$

Thus, this taxpayer must pay about 15% of taxable income in income taxes, not considering taxes related to Medicare and Social Security. The tax rates increase as income increases.

---

*The highest tax rate will go from 35% to 39.6% if the Bush tax cuts expire.

2009 Tax Rate Schedules

Schedule X—If your filing status is **Single**

If your taxable income is:		The tax is:	of the amount
Over—	But not over—		over—
$0	$8,350	·········· 10%	$0
8,350	33,950	$835.00 + 15%	8,350
33,950	82,250	4,675.00 + 25%	33,950
82,250	171,550	16,750.00 + 28%	82,250
171,550	372,950	41,754.00 + 33%	171,550
372,950	·········	108,216.00 + 35%	372,950

Schedule Y-1—If your filing status is **Married filing jointly** or **Qualifying widow(er)**

If your taxable income is:		The tax is:	of the amount
Over—	But not over—		over—
$0	$16,700	·········· 10%	$0
16,700	67,900	$1,670.00 + 15%	16,700
67,900	137,050	9,350.00 + 25%	67,900
137,050	208,850	26,637.50 + 28%	137,050
208,850	372,950	46,741.50 + 33%	208,850
372,950	·········	100,894.50 + 35%	372,950

Schedule Y-2—If your filing status is **Married filing separately**

If your taxable income is:		The tax is:	of the amount
Over—	But not over—		over—
$0	$8,350	·········· 10%	$0
8,350	33,950	$835.00 + 15%	8,350
33,950	68,525	4,675.00 + 25%	33,950
68,525	104,425	13,318.75 + 28%	68,525
104,425	186,475	23,370.75 + 33%	104,425
186,475	·········	50,447.25 + 35%	186,475

Schedule Z—If your filing status is **Head of household**

If your taxable income is:		The tax is:	of the amount
Over—	But not over—		over—
$0	$11,950	·········· 10%	$0
11,950	45,500	$1,195.00 + 15%	11,950
45,500	117,450	6,227.50 + 25%	45,500
117,450	190,200	24,215.00 + 28%	117,450
190,200	372,950	44,585.00 + 33%	190,200
372,950	·········	104,892.50 + 35%	372,950

Note: The figures in the tax-rate schedule change each year, so always look for the current tables. Many believe that marginal tax rates will increase, at least for high-income individuals, as the tax cuts that were implemented during President George W. Bush's administration expire. Expect these numbers to change each year as the United States wrestles with its massive budgetary problems.

Find Taxable Income and the Income Tax Amount

 EXAMPLE 2

Find the taxable income and income tax for each of the following.

(a) Herbert White, married filing jointly, 5 daughters, adjusted gross income $48,300

(b) Onita Fields, single, no dependents, adjusted gross income $28,400

(c) Imogene Griffin, single, head of household, 2 children, adjusted gross income $74,500

(d) Jeffy Norwood, married filing separately, 1 child, adjusted gross income $145,000

SOLUTION

(a) Herbert White + spouse + 5 daughters = 7 exemptions

$$\underset{\text{deduction}}{\text{standard}} \quad \underset{\text{for exemptions}}{\text{deduction}} \quad \underset{\text{income}}{\text{taxable}}$$

Taxable income = $48,300 − $11,400 − (7 × $3650) = **$11,350**

The tax rate for married filing jointly with less than $15,100 in taxable income is 10%.

Income tax = .10 × **$11,350** = $1135

(b) Onita Fields = 1 exemption

$$\underset{\text{deduction}}{\text{standard}} \quad \underset{\text{for exemptions}}{\text{deduction}} \quad \underset{\text{income}}{\text{taxable}}$$

Taxable income = $28,400 − $5700 − (1 × $3650) = **$19,050**

Income tax = $835 + **15% of excess over $8350**
= $835 + .15 × (**$19,050** − **$8350**)
= **$2440**

(c) Imogene Griffin + 2 children = 3 exemptions

$$\underset{\text{deduction}}{\text{standard}} \quad \underset{\text{for exemptions}}{\text{deduction}} \quad \underset{\text{income}}{\text{taxable}}$$

Taxable income = $74,500 − $8350 − (3 × $3650) = **$55,200**

Income tax = $6227.50 + **25% of excess over $45,500**
= $6227.50 + .25 × (**$55,200** − $45,500)
= **$8652.50**

(d) Jeffy Norwood + 1 child = 2 exemptions

$$\underset{\text{deduction}}{\text{standard}} \quad \underset{\text{for exemptions}}{\text{deduction}} \quad \underset{\text{income}}{\text{taxable}}$$

Taxable income = $145,000 − $5700 − (2 × $3650) = **$132,000**

Income tax = $23,370.75 + **33% of excess over $104,425**
= $23,370.75 + .33 × (**$132,000** − $104,425)
= **$32,470.50**

QUICK CHECK 2

John O'Neill files jointly with his wife. They have 1 child and an adjusted gross income of $62,300. Find their taxable income and income tax.

OBJECTIVE 5 List possible deductions. Actually, taxpayers may deduct *the larger of* **itemized deductions** *or* the standard deduction from their adjusted gross income *before* finding taxable income. This is particularly applicable to individuals who are paying interest on a home loan, but sometimes others can use this to their advantage. The most common **tax deductions** are listed next.

Medical and dental expenses: Only medical and dental expenses exceeding 7.5% of adjusted gross income may be deducted. This deduction is effectively limited to catastrophic illnesses for most taxpayers. Expenses reimbursed by an insurance company are not deductible.

Taxes: State and local income taxes, real estate taxes, and personal property taxes may be deducted (but not federal income or gasoline taxes).

Interest: Deductible interest includes interest on a home morgage and qualified interest on other real estate. Other personal interest is not deductible.

Gifts to charity: Gifts to an eligible charity (such as a church) are deductible.

Casualty or theft losses: Losses due to a casualty (e.g., fire) or theft are deductible if not reimbursed by insurance.

Unreimbursed job expenses, tax preparation, and **miscellaneous deductions:** These expenses are deductible only if the total exceeds 2% of the taxpayer's adjusted gross income.

Using Itemized Deductions to Find Taxable Income and Income Tax

EXAMPLE 3

Kristina Kelly is single, has 1 child, and had an adjusted gross income of $58,700 last year. She paid $3240 in real estate taxes, $7280 in home mortgage interest, and donated $1200 to her church. Find her taxable income and her income tax if she files as head of household.

SOLUTION

$$\text{Itemized deductions} = \$3240 + \$7280 + \$1200 = \mathbf{\$11,720}$$

Her itemized deductions of $11,720 exceed the standard deduction of $5700 for a single person, so she uses the itemized deduction amount.

$$\text{Taxable income} = \$58,700 - \underset{\substack{\text{itemized}\\\text{deductions}}}{\mathbf{\$11,720}} - \underset{\substack{\text{personal}\\\text{exemptions}}}{(2 \times \$3650)} = \mathbf{\$39,680}$$

$$\begin{aligned}\text{Income tax} &= \$1195 + \mathbf{15\% \text{ of the excess over } \$11,950}\\ &= \$1195 + .15 \times (\$39,680 - \$11,950)\\ &= \$5354.50\end{aligned}$$

QUICK CHECK 3

Tom Garcia and his wife file jointly. They have no children, earned an adjusted gross income of $48,200, and paid the following: $2350 in other taxes, $6807.45 in home mortgage interest, and $500 to the Red Cross. Find their taxable income and income tax.

OBJECTIVE 6 Determine a balance due or a refund from the Internal Revenue Service.
A taxpayer may have paid more to the IRS than is due. Add up the total amount of income tax paid using the W-2 forms. Usually, no taxes are withheld on 1099 forms. If the amount withheld is greater than the tax owed, the taxpayer is entitled to a refund. If the amount withheld is less than the tax owed, then the taxpayer must send the difference along with the tax return to the IRS.

Determining Tax Due or Refund

EXAMPLE 4

At age 29, Jim Clark works as a petroleum engineer for ExxonMobil, where he helps design deep, complex wells being drilled offshore Africa. His wife stays at home and takes care of their toddler. His salary last year was $123,500, and $1210 was withheld from each monthly paycheck. They file a joint return and use the standard deduction. Find the amount of income tax due to the IRS or the amount overpaid, as applicable.

SOLUTION

Adjusted gross income	$123,500	
Standard deduction	− 11,400	**married filing jointly**
Personal exemptions	− 10,950	**3 exemptions × $3650**
Taxable income	$101,150	

$$\begin{aligned}\text{Income tax} &= \$9350 + \mathbf{25\% \text{ of the excess over } \$67,900}\\ &= \$9350 + .25 \times (\$101,150 - \$67,900)\\ &= \$17,662.50\end{aligned}$$

$$\text{Amount withheld last year} = \$1210 \times 12 = \mathbf{\$14,520}$$
$$\text{Amount owed to IRS} = \$17,662.50 - \mathbf{\$14,520} = \$3142.50$$

The Clarks must send an additional $3142.50 in income taxes to the IRS with their income-tax return. Depending on the state in which they live, they may also owe some state income taxes. Although a few states do not have income taxes, most states do have them.

QUICK CHECK 4

James Benson files as head of household and has 2 children. His adjusted gross income is $59,200, and he uses the standard deduction. Last year, his employer held $280 out of every bimonthly paycheck. Find **(a)** his taxable income, **(b)** tax due, **(c)** amount withheld by his employer last year, and **(d)** either the additional amount of income taxes he owes or the amount he overpaid.

Note: Every year, many of the rules related to the calculation of income taxes change. Always use the most current information and forms from the Internal Revenue Service when preparing your taxes.

Use the simplest IRS form possible when filing your income taxes. Here are basic guidelines starting with the simplest form. Be sure to check with the IRS before choosing the tax form—the rules change often!

1040EZ (general guidelines)

1. Single or married filing jointly with no dependents
2. No adjustments to income
3. Cannot itemize
4. Limited sources of income and use of tax credits
5. Under age 65 with taxable income less than $100,000

1040A (general guidelines)

1. Sources of income limited to wages, interest, capital gains, and other categories
2. Limited adjustments to income and use of tax credits
3. Cannot itemize
4. Taxable income less than $100,000

If neither the 1040EZ nor the 1040A form applies, then you must use the 1040 form. Partnerships and corporations require a completely different set of forms.

OBJECTIVE 7   Prepare a 1040A and a Schedule 1 federal tax form. The next example shows how to complete an income tax return using **Form 1040A** and **Schedule 1 (Form 1040A)**.

Preparing a 1040A and a Schedule 1   **EXAMPLE 5**

Jennifer Crum is single and claims one exemption. Her income appears on the W-2 and 1099 forms on page 561. She contributes $1500 to a regular IRA. Crum satisfies the requirements to use Form 1040A, but she must also fill out Schedule 1 (Form 1040A), since she has more than $1500 in interest. Round figures to the nearest dollar.

Form **1040A**	Department of the Treasury—Internal Revenue Service **U.S. Individual Income Tax Return** (99)		IRS Use Only—Do not write or staple in this space.

Label
(See page 17.)

Use the IRS label.

Otherwise, please print or type.

Presidential Election Campaign ▶

	L A B E L — H E R E	Your first name and initial **Jennifer**	Last name **Crum**		OMB No. 1545-0074

Your social security number 123456789

Spouse's social security number

If a joint return, spouse's first name and initial | Last name

Home address (number and street). If you have a P.O. box, see page 17. **2136 Old Road** | Apt. no.

▲ You **must** enter your SSN(s) above. ▲

City, town or post office, state, and ZIP code. If you have a foreign address, see page 17. **Towson, MD 21285**

Checking a box below will not change your tax or refund.

Check here if you, or your spouse if filing jointly, want $3 to go to this fund (see page 17) ▶ [X] **You**   [ ] **Spouse**

Filing status
Check only one box.

1 [✓] Single
2 [ ] Married filing jointly (even if only one had income)
3 [ ] Married filing separately. Enter spouse's SSN above and full name here. ▶
4 [ ] Head of household (with qualifying person). (See page 18.) If the qualifying person is a child but not your dependent, enter this child's name here. ▶
5 [ ] Qualifying widow(er) with dependent child (see page 19)

Exemptions

6a [✓] **Yourself.** If someone can claim you as a dependent, **do not** check box 6a.

b [ ] **Spouse**

c **Dependents:**

(1) First name Last name	(2) Dependent's social security number	(3) Dependent's relationship to you	(4) ✓ if qualifying child for child tax credit (see page 20)
			[ ]
			[ ]
			[ ]
			[ ]
			[ ]
			[ ]

If more than six dependents, see page 20.

Boxes checked on 6a and 6b — **1**

No. of children on 6c who:
• lived with you
• did not live with you due to divorce or separation (see page 21)

Dependents on 6c not entered above

Add numbers on lines above ▶ **1**

d Total number of exemptions claimed.

Income

Attach Form(s) W-2 here. Also attach Form(s) 1099-R if tax was withheld.

If you did not get a W-2, see page 24.

Enclose, but do not attach, any payment. Also, please use **Form 1040-V.**

7	Wages, salaries, tips, etc. Attach Form(s) W-2.	7	$24,738
8a	**Taxable** interest. Attach Schedule B if required.	8a	$1,624
b	**Tax-exempt** interest. **Do not** include on line 8a.	8b	
9a	Ordinary dividends. Attach Schedule B if required.	9a	
b	Qualified dividends (see page 25).	9b	
10	Capital gain distributions (see page 25).	10	
11a	IRA distributions. 11a	11b Taxable amount (see page 25).	11b	
12a	Pensions and annuities. 12a	12b Taxable amount (see page 26).	12b	
13	Unemployment compensation in excess of $2,400 per recipient and Alaska Permanent Fund dividends (see page 28).	13	
14a	Social security benefits. 14a	14b Taxable amount (see page 28).	14b	
15	Add lines 7 through 14b (far right column). This is your **total income.** ▶	15	$26,362

Adjusted gross income

16	Educator expenses (see page 30).	16	
17	IRA deduction (see page 30).	17	$1,500
18	Student loan interest deduction (see page 32).	18	
19	Tuition and fees deduction. Attach Form 8917.	19	
20	Add lines 16 through 19. These are your **total adjustments.**	20	$1,500
21	Subtract line 20 from line 15. This is your **adjusted gross income.** ▶	21	$24,862

For Disclosure, Privacy Act, and Paperwork Reduction Act Notice, see page 87.   Cat. No. 11327A   Form **1040A**

Form 1040A (2009)   Page **2**

Tax, credits, and payments	22	Enter the amount from line 21 (adjusted gross income).		22	$24,862
	23a	Check if: ☐ **You** were born before January 2, 1945, ☐ Blind ☐ **Spouse** was born before January 2, 1945, ☐ Blind Total boxes checked ▶ 23a			
	b	If you are married filing separately and your spouse itemizes deductions, see page 34 and check here ▶ 23b		☐	

Standard Deduction for—

- **People who checked any box on line 23a, 23b, or 24b or who can be claimed as a dependent, see page 34.**
- **All others:**

Single or Married filing separately, $5,700

Married filing jointly or Qualifying widow(er), $11,400

Head of household, $8,350

	24a	Enter your **standard deduction** (see left margin).		24a	$5,700
	b	If you are increasing your standard deduction by certain real estate taxes or new motor vehicle taxes, attach Schedule L and check here (see page 34) ▶ 24b		☐	
	25	Subtract line 24a from line 22. If line 24a is more than line 22, enter -0-.		25	$19,162
	26	**Exemptions.** If line 22 is $125,100 or less and you did not provide housing to a Midwestern displaced individual, multiply $3,650 by the number on line 6d. Otherwise, see page 34.		26	$3,650
	27	Subtract line 26 from line 25. If line 26 is more than line 25, enter -0-. This is your **taxable income.**	▶	27	$15,512
	28	**Tax,** including any alternative minimum tax (see page 35).		28	$1,909
	29	Credit for child and dependent care expenses. Attach Form 2441.	29		
	30	Credit for the elderly or the disabled. Attach Schedule R.	30		
	31	Education credits from Form 8863, line 29.	31		
	32	Retirement savings contributions credit. Attach Form 8880.	32		
	33	Child tax credit (see page 38).	33		
	34	Add lines 29 through 33. These are your **total credits.**		34	$0
	35	Subtract line 34 from line 28. If line 34 is more than line 28, enter -0-.		35	$1,909
	36	Advance earned income credit payments from Form(s) W-2, box 9.		36	
	37	Add lines 35 and 36. This is your **total tax.**	▶	37	$1,909
	38	Federal income tax withheld from Forms W-2 and 1099.	38	$3,276	
	39	2009 estimated tax payments and amount applied from 2008 return.	39		

If you have a qualifying child, attach Schedule EIC.

	40	Making work pay and government retiree credits. Attach Schedule M.	40		
	41a	**Earned income credit (EIC).**	41a		
	b	Nontaxable combat pay election. 41b			
	42	Additional child tax credit. Attach Form 8812.	42		
	43	Refundable education credit from Form 8863, line 16.	43		
	44	Add lines 38, 39, 40, 41a, 42, and 43. These are your **total payments.**	▶	44	$3,276

Refund Direct deposit? See page 64 and fill in 46b, 46c, and 46d or Form 8888.	45	If line 44 is more than line 37, subtract line 37 from line 44. This is the amount you **overpaid.**		45	$1,367
	46a	Amount of line 45 you want **refunded to you.** If Form 8888 is attached, check here ▶ ☐ 46a			$1,367
	▶ b	Routing number ☐☐☐☐☐☐☐☐☐ ▶ c Type: ☐ Checking ☐ Savings			
	▶ d	Account number ☐☐☐☐☐☐☐☐☐☐☐☐☐☐☐☐☐			
	47	Amount of line 45 you want **applied to your 2010 estimated tax.**	47	$0	
Amount you owe	48	**Amount you owe.** Subtract line 44 from line 37. For details on how to pay, see page 66.	▶	48	$0
	49	Estimated tax penalty (see page 66).	49		

Third party designee	Do you want to allow another person to discuss this return with the IRS (see page 67)? ☐ **Yes.** Complete the following. ☑ **No**

Designee's name ▶	Phone no. ▶	Personal identification number (PIN) ▶ ☐☐☐☐☐

Sign here

Joint return? See page 17.

Keep a copy for your records.

Under penalties of perjury, I declare that I have examined this return and accompanying schedules and statements, and to the best of my knowledge and belief, they are true, correct, and accurately list all amounts and sources of income I received during the tax year. Declaration of preparer (other than the taxpayer) is based on all information of which the preparer has any knowledge.

Your signature *Jennifer Crum*	Date 4/14	Your occupation Assistant Manager	Daytime phone number (410)-286-2594
Spouse's signature. If a joint return, **both** must sign.	Date	Spouse's occupation	

Paid preparer's use only

Preparer's signature ▶	Date	Check if self-employed ☐	Preparer's SSN or PTIN
Firm's name (or yours if self-employed), address, and ZIP code ▶		EIN Phone no.	

Form **1040A**

Schedule 1
(Form 1040A)

Department of the Treasury—Internal Revenue Service

Interest and Ordinary Dividends for Form 1040A Filers (99)

OMB No. 1545-0074

Name(s) shown on Form 1040A

Jennifer Crum

Your social security number

123 45 6789

Part I

Interest

(See back of schedule and the instructions for Form 1040A, line 8a.)

Note. If you received a Form 1099-INT, Form 1099-OID, or substitute statement from a brokerage firm, enter the firm's name and the total interest shown on that form.

1 List name of payer. If any interest is from a seller-financed mortgage and the buyer used the property as a personal residence, see back of schedule and list this interest first. Also, show that buyer's social security number and address.

		Amount	
Employees Credit Union	1	$1,624	

2 Add the amounts on line 1. | 2 | $1,624 |

3 Excludable interest on series EE and I U.S. savings bonds issued after 1989. Attach Form 8815. | 3 | |

4 Subtract line 3 from line 2. Enter the result here and on Form 1040A, line 8a. | 4 | $1,624 |

Part II

Ordinary dividends

(See back of schedule and the instructions for Form 1040A, line 9a.)

Note. If you received a Form 1099-DIV or substitute statement from a brokerage firm, enter the firm's name and the ordinary dividends shown on that form.

5 List name of payer. | | Amount |
| | 5 | |

6 Add the amounts on line 5. Enter the total here and on Form 1040A, line 9a. | 6 | |

For Paperwork Reduction Act Notice, see Form 1040A instructions. Cat. No. 12075R Schedule 1 (Form 1040A)

The QUICK START *exercises in each section contain solutions to help you get started.*

Find the adjusted gross income for each of the following people. (See Example 1.)

QUICK START

Name	Income from Jobs	Interest	Misc. Income	Dividend Income	Adjustments to Income	Adjusted Gross Income
1. R. Jacob	$22,840	$234	$1209	$48	$1200	$23,131
$22,840 + $234 + $1209 + $48 − $1200 = $23,131						
2. K. Chandler	$68,156	$285	$73	$542	$317	$68,739
$68,156 + $285 + $73 + $542 − $317 = $68,739						
3. The Hanks	$21,380	$625	$139	$184	$618	_____
4. The Jazwinskis	$33,650	$722	$375	$218	$473	_____
5. The Brashers	$38,643	$1020	$3820	$1050	$0	_____
6. The Claxtons	$93,680	$3247	$8115	$2469	$2800	_____
7. The Wheats	$21,370	$420	$0	$0	$0	_____
8. Tiny Peyton	$68,540	$1290	$480	$318	$1840	_____

Find the amount of taxable income and the tax owed for each of the following people. Use the tax rate schedule. The letter following the names indicates the marital status, and all married people are filing jointly. (See Examples 2 and 3.)

QUICK START

Name	Number of Exemptions	Adjusted Gross Income	Total Deductions	Taxable Income	Tax Owed
9. R. Rodriguez, S	1	$36,840	$2460	$27,490	$3706
$36,840 − $5700 − $3650 = $27,490; $835 + .15 × ($27,490 − $8350) = $3706					
10. S. Simpson, S	1	$26,190	$1248	$16,840	$2108.50
$26,190 − $5700 − $3650 = $16,840; $835 + .15 × ($16,840 − $8350) = $2108.50					
11. The Pacas, M	2	$72,450	$6040	_____	_____
12. The Laytons, M	4	$65,290	$8040	_____	_____
13. The Jordans, M	3	$99,500	$14,320	_____	_____
14. P. Jong, Head of Household	4	$162,370	$12,480	_____	_____
15. K. Tang, Married Filing Separately	2	$85,332	$8170	_____	_____

⚠ indicates an exercise that is related to the Case in Point feature.

Name	Number of Exemptions	Adjusted Gross Income	Total Deductions	Taxable Income	Tax Owed
16. G. Begay, Head of Household	4	$58,332	$8180	_____	_____
17. D. Kien, Head of Household	2	$82,650	$8100	_____	_____
18. L. Dimon, M	2	$262,680	$18,350	_____	_____

Find the tax refund or tax due for the following people. The letter following the names indicates the marital status. Assume a 52-week year and that married people are filing jointly. (See Example 4.)

QUICK START

Name	Taxable Income	Federal Income Tax Withheld from Checks	Tax Refund or Tax Due
19. L. Karecki, S	$78,500	$1516 monthly	$2379.50 tax refund
$18,192 − $15,812.50 = $2379.50 refund			
20. K. Turner, S	$32,060	$347.80 monthly	_____
21. M. Hunziker, S	$23,552	$72.18 weekly	_____
22. The Fungs, M	$38,238	$119.27 weekly	_____
23. The Todds, M	$202,100	$3200 monthly	_____
24. S. Benson, HH	$160,300	$720 weekly	_____

25. List four sources of income for which an individual might receive W-2 and 1099 forms. (See Objective 2.)

26. List four possible tax deductions, and explain the effect that a tax deduction will have on taxable income and on income tax due. (See Objective 5.)

Find the tax in the following application problems.

27. MARRIED—INCOME TAX The Tobins had an adjusted gross income of $98,700 last year. They had deductions of $2820 for state income tax, $490 for city income tax, $4400 for property tax, $5800 in mortgage interest, and $1450 in contributions. They file a joint return and claim 5 exemptions.

27. _____

28. SINGLE—INCOME TAX Diane Bolton works at The Doll House and had an adjusted gross income of $34,975 last year. She had deductions of $971 for state income tax, $1864 for property tax, $3820 in mortgage interest, and $235 in contributions. Bolton claims one exemption and files as a single person.

28. _____

29. Carol Ridgeway has an adjusted gross income of $73,200 and files as head of household since she has a dependent, 9-year-old daughter. Her deductions are $7143.

29. _____

30. MARRIED—INCOME TAX The Hernandez family had an adjusted gross income of $48,260 last year. They had deductions of $1078 for state income tax, $253 for city income tax, $3240 for property tax, $5218 in mortgage interest, and $386 in contributions. They claim three exemptions and file a joint return.

30. _____

31. HEAD OF HOUSEHOLD Martha Spencer, owner of The Doll House, had wages of $73,800, dividends of $385, interest of $1672, and adjustments to income of $1058 last year. She had deductions of $877 for state income tax, $342 for city income tax, $4986 for property tax, $5173 in mortgage interest, and $1800 in contributions. She claims four exemptions and files as head of household.

31. _____

32. HEAD OF HOUSEHOLD John Walker had wages of $48,200, other income of $2892, dividends of $340, interest of $651, and a regular IRA contribution of $2000 last year. He had deductions of $1163 for taxes, $5350 in mortgage interest, and $540 in contributions. Walker claims two exemptions and files as head of household.

32. _____

33. MARRIED John and Vicki Karsten had combined wages and salaries of $64,280, other income of $5283, dividend income of $324, and interest income of $668. They have adjustments to income of $2484. Their itemized deductions are $7615 in mortgage interest, $2250 in state income tax, $3300 in real estate taxes, and $1219 in charitable contributions. The Karstens filed a joint return and claimed 3 exemptions.

33. _____

34. HEAD OF HOUSEHOLD   Jayne Binyan is single with one dependent. She is the chief financial officer at the university where she works, and her salary is $173,400. She has other income of $2800, interest income of $8400, and an adjustment to income of $6000 for a 401K retirement plan at work. Her itemized deductions are $14,380 in mortgage interest, $4820 in state income tax, $7800 in real estate taxes, and $6800 in charitable contributions.

34. _____

QUICK CHECK ANSWERS

1. $98,950

2. $39,950; $5157.50

3. $29,500; $3950

4. (a) $39,900   **(b)** $5387.50   **(c)** $6720
(d) overpaid by $1332.50

13.3 Fire Insurance

OBJECTIVES

1 Define the terms *policy, coverage, face value*, and *premium*.
2 Find the annual premium for fire insurance.
3 Use the coinsurance formula.
4 Understand multiple-carrier insurance.
5 List additional types of insurance coverage.

case IN point ▶

Martha Spencer owns the building in which The Doll House is located. A fire in that building could leave her in financial ruin. Although she hopes that there is never a fire, she carries fire insurance to protect her business in the event there is one.

Insurance protects against risk. For example, there is only a slight chance that a particular building will be damaged by fire in any year. However, the financial loss from a fire could be devastating to the owner. Therefore, people and companies pay a small fee each year to an insurance company to protect them against catastrophic losses. The insurance company collects money from many different people and companies that buy insurance and pays money to the few who suffer damages.

Insurance is important. For example, a bank requires that fire insurance be purchased on a building (or home) before it will lend the funds to the buyer. Most states require automobile drivers to buy a minimum amount of car insurance before driving. Firms large and small buy liability insurance to protect against a lawsuit or a **catastrophic event** that would be financially damaging to the company. Parents buy life insurance to support their kids in the event of a parent's untimely death. In fact, it is rare for individuals and businesses not to carry insurance for protection.

The following figure shows that most home fires begin in the kitchen. As a result, experts recommend that everyone keep a fire extinguisher in the kitchen. They also recommend that every home have fire alarms so that anyone in a burning home quickly becomes aware of the fire.

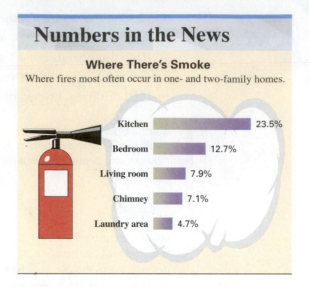

Numbers in the News

Where There's Smoke
Where fires most often occur in one- and two-family homes.

Kitchen	23.5%
Bedroom	12.7%
Living room	7.9%
Chimney	7.1%
Laundry area	4.7%

Individuals buy insurance to protect against losses due to fire, theft, illness or health problems, disability, car wrecks, lawsuits, and even death. Companies buy insurance to protect against losses due to fire, automobile accidents, employee illnesses, lawsuits, and worker accidents on the job. In this section, we talk about fire insurance.

OBJECTIVE 1 Define the terms *policy, coverage, face value,* **and** *premium.* The contract between the owner of a building and an insurance company is called a **policy** or an **insurance policy**. A basic fire policy provides **coverage** or protection for both the owner of the building and the company that holds the mortgage on the building. The owner of a building can also purchase coverage on the contents of the building and liability insurance in the event someone is injured while on the property. Homeowners often purchase a **homeowner's policy**, which includes all of these coverages. The graph below shows that the cost of homeowner's insurance continues to increase. However, it is important to note that most of the increase in cost is due to inflation.

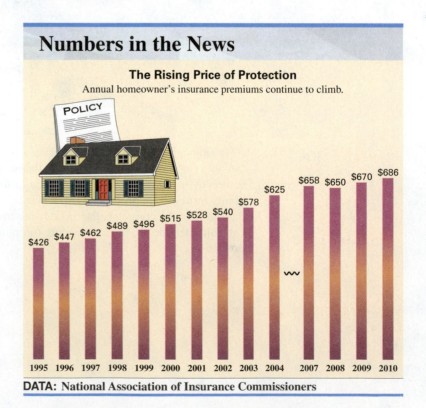

Numbers in the News

The Rising Price of Protection
Annual homeowner's insurance premiums continue to climb.

Year	1995	1996	1997	1998	1999	2000	2001	2002	2003	2004	2007	2008	2009	2010
Premium	$426	$447	$462	$489	$496	$515	$528	$540	$578	$625	$658	$650	$670	$686

DATA: National Association of Insurance Commissioners

The dollar value of the insurance coverage provided on a building is called the **face value** of the policy. The annual cost of the policy is called the **premium**. The premium is usually calculated based on factors such as age of the building, materials used in the construction of the building, crime rate of the neighborhood, presence of any safety features such as a sprinkler system, security system, and history of previous insurance claims on the property.

OBJECTIVE 2 Find the annual premium for fire insurance. The amount of the premium charged by the insurance company depends on several factors. Among them are the type of construction of the building, the contents and use of the building, the location of the building, and the type and location of any fire protection that is available. Wood frame buildings generally are more likely to be damaged by fire than masonry buildings and thus require a higher premium.

Building classifications are assigned to building types by insurance company employees called **underwriters**. These building categories are usually designated by letters such as A, B, and C. Underwriters also assign ratings called **territorial ratings** to each area that describe the quality of fire protection in the area. Although fire insurance rates vary from state to state, the rates in the following table are typical.

Annual Rates for Each $100 of Insurance

	BUILDING CLASSIFICATION					
	A		B		C	
TERRITORIAL RATING	BUILDING	CONTENTS	BUILDING	CONTENTS	BUILDING	CONTENTS
1	$.25	$.32	$.36	$.49	$.45	$.60
2	$.30	$.44	$.45	$.55	$.54	$.75
3	$.37	$.46	$.54	$.60	$.63	$.80
4	$.50	$.52	$.75	$.77	$.84	$.90
5	$.62	$.58	$.92	$.99	$1.05	$1.14

Finding the Annual Fire Insurance Premium

EXAMPLE 1

The Doll House is in a building rated class C. It is in territory 4. Find the annual premium if the replacement cost of the building is $640,000 and the contents are valued at $186,500.

SOLUTION

Building:

$$\text{Replacement cost in hundreds} = \$640,000 \div 100 = \mathbf{6400}$$
$$\text{Insurance premium for the building} = \mathbf{6400} \times \$.84 = \$5376$$

Contents:

$$\text{Replacement cost in hundreds} = \$186,500 \div 100 = \mathbf{1865}$$
$$\text{Insurance premium for contents} = \mathbf{1865} \times \$.90 = \$1678.50$$

Total premium: $5376 + $1678.50 = **$7054.50**

> **QUICK CHECK 1**
>
> A commercial building has a replacement cost of $1,480,000 and contents valued at $110,000. It has a classification of B and a territory rating of 5. Find the annual premium.

OBJECTIVE 3 Use the coinsurance formula. Most fires damage only a portion of a building and the contents. Since complete destruction of a building is rare, many owners save money by buying insurance for only a portion of the value of the building and contents. Realizing this, insurance companies place a **coinsurance clause** in almost all fire insurance policies. Effectively, the business assumes part of the risk of a loss under coinsurance.

Replacement cost refers to the cost to replace (rebuild) a building in the event it is completely destroyed. It may surprise you to learn that the replacement cost for an older building is often greater than the fair market value, since new construction costs often exceed the value of older buildings.

Most fire insurance contracts have an 80% coinsurance clause. This clause requires the owner of the building to have an insurance policy in effect with a face value that is at least 80% of the replacement cost of the building. If the policy has a face value greater than 80%, then the insurance companies pays for all losses caused by a fire. On the other hand, if the face value is less than 80%, then the insurance company will pay only a portion of any loss. The most the insurance company will pay is the smaller amount of the loss on the face value of the policy.

> **Finding Amount Insurance Will Pay**
>
> $$\begin{pmatrix} \text{Amount insurance company} \\ \text{will pay (assuming 80\% coinsurance)} \end{pmatrix} = \text{Amount of loss} \times \frac{\text{Amount of policy}}{80\% \text{ of replacement cost}}$$

Using the Coinsurance Formula

 EXAMPLE 2

Dayton Properties owns a small apartment building with a replacement cost of $760,000. The fire insurance policy has an 80% coinsurance clause and a face value of $570,000. A fire started in the kitchen of a tenant and swept through three apartments, resulting in $144,000 in losses. Find the amount of the loss that the insurance company will pay.

SOLUTION

The policy must have a face value of at least 80% of $760,000 or $608,000 in order to receive the payment for the entire loss. Since the face value of $570,000 is less than 80% of the replacement cost, the company will pay only the following portion of the loss.

$$\text{Amount insurance company pays} = \$144,000 \times \frac{\$570,000}{\$608,000} = \$135,000$$

$$\text{Amount not paid by insurance company} = \$144,000 - \$135,000 = \$9000$$

Stetson is responsible for $9000.

The calculator solution to this example uses chain calculations and parentheses to set off the denominator. The result is then subtracted from the fire loss.

144,000 ✕ 570,000 ÷ ((80 % ✕ 760,000)) = 135,000

144,000 − 135,000 = 9000

Note: Refer to Appendix B for calculator basics.

> **QUICK CHECK 2**
>
> A real estate investment trust owns an office building with a replacement cost of $8,400,000 that is insured for $5,600,000. Find the amount of the loss paid for by the insurance company if a fire causes $2,300,000 in losses and the policy has an 80% coinsurance feature.

Finding the Amount of Loss Paid by the Insurance Company

 EXAMPLE 3

A Swedish investment group owns a warehouse with a replacement cost of $3,450,000. The company has a fire insurance policy with a face value of $3,400,000. The policy has an 80% coinsurance feature. If the firm has a fire loss of $233,500, find the part of the loss paid by the insurance company.

SOLUTION

$$80\% \text{ of replacement cost} = .80 \times \$3,450,000 = \$2,760,000$$

The business has a fire insurance policy with a face value of more than 80% of the value of the store. Therefore, the insurance company pays the entire $233,500 loss.

> **QUICK CHECK 3**
>
> A plumbing company owns its own building with a replacement cost of $1,600,000. A fire results in damages of $445,000. Find the amount the insurance company will pay if the company has $1,400,000 in insurance coverage.

OBJECTIVE 4 Understand multiple-carrier insurance. A business may have fire insurance policies with several companies at the same time. Perhaps additional insurance coverage was purchased over a period of time, as new additions were made to a factory or building complex. Or perhaps the building is so large that one insurance company does not want to take the entire risk by itself, so several companies each agree to take a portion of the insurance coverage and thereby share the risk. In either event, the insurance coverage is divided among **multiple carriers**. When an insurance claim is made against multiple carriers, each insurance company pays its fractional portion of the total claim on the property.

Understanding Multiple-Carrier Insurance   **EXAMPLE 4**

Youngblood Apartments has an insured loss of $1,800,000 while having insurance coverage beyond its coinsurance requirement. The insurance is divided among Company A with $5,900,000 coverage, Company B with $4,425,000 coverage, and Company C with $1,475,000 coverage. Find the amount of the loss paid by each of the insurance companies.

SOLUTION

Start by finding the total face value of all three policies.

$$\$5,900,000 + \$4,425,000 + \$1,475,000 = \textbf{\$11,800,000 } \text{total face value}$$

$$\text{Company A pays } \frac{\$5,900,000}{\$11,800,000} = \frac{1}{2} \text{ of the loss}$$

$$\text{Company B pays } \frac{\$4,425,000}{\$11,800,000} = \frac{3}{8} \text{ of the loss}$$

$$\text{Company C pays } \frac{\$1,475,000}{\$11,800,000} = \frac{1}{8} \text{ of the loss}$$

Since the insurance loss is $1,800,000, the amount paid by each of the multiple carriers is

$$\text{Company A } \frac{1}{2} \times \$1,800,000 = \$900,000$$

$$\text{Company B } \frac{3}{8} \times \$1,800,000 = \$675,000$$

$$\text{Company C } \frac{1}{8} \times \$1,800,000 = \underline{\$225,000}$$

$$\text{Total loss} = \$1,800,000$$

QUICK CHECK 4

A fully insured bank has $780,000 in fire damage. The coverage is divided between Company A ($1,200,000) and Company B ($800,000). Find the amount of the loss paid by each company.

If the coinsurance requirement is not met, first find the total amount of the loss paid by the insurers. Then find the amount paid by each, as shown in Example 5.

Understanding Partial Coverage and Multiple Carriers   **EXAMPLE 5**

The fire damage to a small shopping center with a replacement cost of $4,800,000 was limited to $420,000 thanks to an advanced sprinkler system. The insurance coverage is divided between Company A ($2,000,000) and Company B ($1,200,000). Find the amount of the loss paid by each, assuming management had full coverage.

SOLUTION

$$80\% \text{ of } \$4,800,000 = \textbf{\$3,840,000}$$
$$\text{Total insurance coverage} = \$2,000,000 + \$1,200,000 = \textbf{\$3,200,000}$$

Since the total insurance coverage is less than 80% of the replacement cost of the building, the insurance companies will pay only a portion of the total damages.

$$\text{Amount paid by insurance: } \$420,000 \times \frac{\$3,200,000}{\$3,840,000} = \textbf{\$350,000}$$

$$\text{Paid by Company A: } \frac{\$2,000,000}{\$3,200,000} \times \textbf{\$350,000} = \$218,750$$

$$\text{Paid by Company B: } \frac{\$1,200,000}{\$3,200,000} \times \textbf{\$350,000} = \$131,250$$

QUICK CHECK 5

An office building with a replacement cost of $800,000 has fire damage of $100,000. The insurance coverage is divided between Company 1 ($300,000) and Company 2 ($200,000). First **(a)** find the amount covered by insurance, then **(b)** find the amount paid by each company.

The amount of money paid for insurance premiums by businesses is often small compared with other business expenses. Likewise, the average household pays only a small portion of its budget for insurance premiums. The following chart shows the percent of total household spending going to pay for insurance coverage.

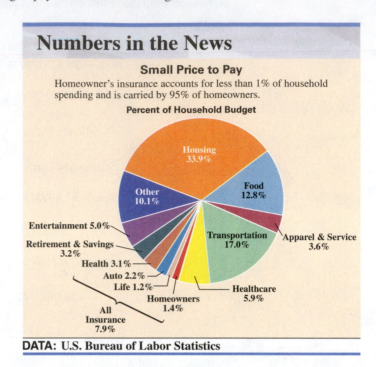

Numbers in the News

Small Price to Pay

Homeowner's insurance accounts for less than 1% of household spending and is carried by 95% of homeowners.

Percent of Household Budget

- Housing 33.9%
- Food 12.8%
- Apparel & Service 3.6%
- Transportation 17.0%
- Healthcare 5.9%
- Homeowners 1.4%
- Life 1.2%
- Auto 2.2%
- Health 3.1%
- Retirement & Savings 3.2%
- Entertainment 5.0%
- Other 10.1%
- All Insurance 7.9%

DATA: U.S. Bureau of Labor Statistics

OBJECTIVE 5 List additional types of insurance coverage. There are many other types of insurance coverages available as you can see.

Disability insurance pays monthly payments in event of disability.

Homeowner's insurance pays a homeowner in the event of fire, theft, or accidents.

Liability insurance protects business owners against lawsuit.
Long-term care insurance pays for nursing home costs.

Medical insurance pays for medical expenses.

Renter's insurance protects a renter against loss of his personal property.

Worker's compensation pays employees for injuries while on the job.

In our society, individuals, families, and business managers face risk. Experts believe that it is very important to realize where you have real risk and to cover at least some portion of that risk using insurance. Of course, it always pays to shop around to find the best deal, and finding the best insurance coverage is no different. Shop and compare to find the coverage that is best for you.

13.3 Exercises

The QUICK START *exercises in each section contain solutions to help you get started.*

Find the total annual premium for each of the following. Use the table on page 577. (See Example 1.)

QUICK START

	Territorial Rating	Building Classification	Building Value	Contents Value	Total Annual Premium
1.	2	B	$280,000	$80,000	$1700
2.	5	A	$220,500	$105,000	$1976.10
3.	1	C	$285,000	$152,000	_____
4.	4	C	$2,325,000	$111,500	_____
5.	5	B	$782,600	$212,000	_____
6.	3	A	$596,400	$206,700	_____

Find the amount to be paid by the insurance company in the following problems. Assume that each policy includes an 80% coinsurance clause. (See Examples 2 and 3.)

QUICK START

	Replacement Cost of Building	Face Value of Policy	Amount of Loss	Amount Paid
7.	$1,450,000	$850,000	$96,000	$70,344.83

$1,450,000 \times .8 = \$1,160,000$ (80%); $\frac{\$850,000}{\$1,160,000} \times \$96,000 = \$70,344.83$

8.	$187,400	$140,000	$10,850	$10,132.07

$187,400 \times .8 = \$149,920$ (80%); $\frac{\$140,000}{\$149,920} \times \$10,850 = \$10,132.07$

9.	$287,000	$232,500	$19,850	_____
10.	$780,000	$585,000	$10,400	_____
11.	$218,500	$195,000	$36,500	_____
12.	$750,000	$500,000	$56,000	_____

Find the amount paid by each insurance company in the following problems involving multiple carriers. Assume that the coinsurance requirement is met. (See Example 4.)

QUICK START

	Insurance Loss	Companies	Coverage	Amount Paid
13.	$80,000	Company 1	$750,000	$60,000
		Company 2	$250,000	$20,000

$\frac{750,000}{1,000,000} \times \$80,000 = \$60,000$; $\frac{250,000}{1,000,000} \times \$80,000 = \$20,000$

14.	$360,000	Company A	$1,200,000	_____
		Company B	$800,000	_____

indicates an exercise that is related to the Case in Point feature.

	Insurance Loss	*Companies*	*Coverage*	*Amount Paid*
15.	$650,000	Company 1	$1,350,000	_____
		Company 2	$1,200,000	_____
		Company 3	$450,000	_____
16.	$1,600,000	Company A	$4,800,000	_____
		Company B	$800,000	_____
		Company C	$2,400,000	_____

Find the annual fire insurance premium in each of the following application problems.
Use the table on page 577.

QUICK START

17. **COMMERCIAL BUILDING**   Home Depot owns a building with a replacement cost of
$1,400,000 and with contents of $360,000. The building is class C with a territorial
rating of 5.

17. $18,804

$14,000 × 1.05 = $14,700; 3600 × $1.14 = $4104
$14,700 + $4104 = $18,804

18. **FIRE INSURANCE PREMIUM**   Martha Spencer, owner of The Doll House, owns a class-B
building with a replacement cost of $165,400. Contents are valued at $128,000. The territorial rating is 3.

18. _____

19. **AIRPLANE HANGAR**   Valley Crop Dusting owns an airplane hanger located in a class-B
area. It has a replacement cost of $107,500. Contents are worth $39,800. The territorial
rating is 2.

19. _____

20. **INDUSTRIAL BUILDING INSURANCE**   London's Dredging Equipment is in a class-C
building with a territorial rating of 4. The building has a replacement cost of $305,000 and
the contents are worth $682,000.

20. _____

21. Describe three factors that determine the premium charged for fire insurance.
(See Objective 2.)

22. Explain the coinsurance clause and describe how coinsurance works. (See Objective 3.)

In the following application problems, find the amount of the loss paid by (a) the insurance
company and (b) the insured. Assume an 80% coinsurance clause.

QUICK START

23. **FIRE LOSS**   The Doll House is located in a building with a
replacement cost of $328,500, but Martha Spencer insured it for
only $200,000 in order to save money on insurance premiums. An
electrical short causes a fire that results in $180,000 in damage.

(a) $136,986.30

(b) $43,013.70

(a) $328,500 × .8 = $262,800; $\frac{$200,000}{$262,800}$ × $180,000 = $136,986.30
(b) $180,000 − $136,986.30 = $43,013.70

24. **GIFT-SHOP FIRE LOSS**   Indonesian Wonder gift shop has a replacement cost of $395,000. The shop is insured for $280,000. Fire loss is $22,500.

(a) _____

(b) _____

25. **SALVATION ARMY LOSS**   The main office of the Salvation Army suffers a loss from fire of $45,000. The building has a replacement cost of $550,000 and is insured for $300,000.

(a) _____

(b) _____

26. **FOURPLEX**   Fang Li purchased a fourplex that has a replacement cost of $185,000. She insures it for $111,000 and has a fire loss of $28,000 when a smoker accidently starts a fire.

(a) _____

(b) _____

In the following application problems, find the amount paid by each of the multiple carriers. Assume that the coinsurance requirement has been met.

QUICK START

27. **COINSURED FIRE LOSS**   C. Wood Plumbing had an insured fire loss of $548,000. It has insurance coverage as follows: Company A, $600,000; Company B, $400,000; and Company C, $200,000.

   A: $\frac{600,000}{1,200,000} \times \$548,000 = \$274,000$

   B: $\frac{400,000}{1,200,000} \times \$548,000 = \$182,666.67$

   C: $\frac{200,000}{1,200,000} \times \$548,000 = \$91,333.33$

   A: $274,000 _____

   B: $182,666.67 _____

   C: $91,333.33 _____

28. **COINSURED FIRE LOSS**   Beacon Cycles had an insured fire loss of $68,500. It has insurance as follows: Company 1, $60,000; Company 2, $40,000; and Company 3, $30,000.

   1: _____

   2: _____

   3: _____

29. **MAJOR FIRE LOSS**   Gold's Gym had fire insurance coverage as follows: Company 1, $360,000; Company 2, $120,000; and Company 3, $240,000. The gym has an insured fire loss of $250,000.

   1: _____

   2: _____

   3: _____

30. **MULTIPLE CARRIERS**   Tokyo International had an insured fire loss of $2,100,000. The company has insurance as follows: Company A, $2,000,000; Company B, $1,750,000; Company C, $1,250,000.

   A: _____

   B: _____

   C: _____

Find the amount paid by each of the multiple carriers in the following two problems. Note that the coinsurance requirement has not been met.

31. **PARTIAL COVERAGE**   A building with a replacement cost of $1,200,000 has fire damages of $420,000. The insurance coverage is split between Company A ($200,000) and Company B ($300,000). Find **(a)** the amount of the loss covered and **(b)** amount paid by each company.

(a) _____

(b) _____

32. **PARTIAL COVERAGE**   Family Dollar owns a building with a replacement cost of
    $1,800,000 that has fire and smoke damages of $310,000. The insurance coverage is split
    between Company 1 ($1,000,000) and Company 2 ($400,000). Find **(a)** the amount of the
    loss covered and **(b)** the amount paid by each company.

(a) _____

(b) _____

QUICK CHECK ANSWERS

1. $14,705   2. $1,916,666.67

3. $445,000

4. Company A—468,000;
   Company B—$312,000

5. **(a)** $78,125
   (b) Company A—$46,875;
   Company B—$31,250

13.4 Motor-Vehicle Insurance

OBJECTIVES

1 Describe the factors that affect the cost of motor-vehicle insurance.
2 Define liability insurance.
3 Define property damage insurance.
4 Describe comprehensive and collision insurance.
5 Define no-fault and uninsured motorist insurance.
6 Apply youthful-operator factors.
7 Find the amounts paid by the insurance company and the insured.

case IN point ▶ Martha Spencer owns a van that is used by employees of The Doll House. She insures her van, since an employee may be involved in an accident that hurts someone or damages property. Knowing that injuries can result in huge medical costs, Spencer carries more than the state-required minimum liability insurance.

OBJECTIVE 1 Describe the factors that affect the cost of motor-vehicle insurance.
Automobile insurance is one of the most common types of insurance. Banks or credit unions that finance automobiles require borrowers to buy automobile insurance. Many states require automobile insurance for people living and driving in those states. As you can see from the graph, the average cost of car insurance increased sharply for several years but has leveled off recently.

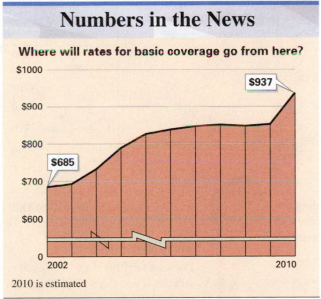

Numbers in the News

Where will rates for basic coverage go from here?

$937

$685

2002   2010

2010 is estimated

DATA: National Association of Insurance Commissioners; Insurance Information Institute

The **premium**, or cost, of an insurance policy is determined by **actuaries** who work for the insurance company. Actuaries look at the frequency and severity of accidents based on several factors, including

• location of the insured vehicle,
• age and sex of the driver,
• miles driven, and
• driving history of the driver.

These factors help measure the risk of insuring a particular driver, which is used to determine the premium. For example, drivers between 16 and 25 years of age are more likely to be involved in accidents and are therefore charged a higher premium. Some automobiles are more likely to be stolen than others, resulting in higher premiums for their owners. Several automobile coverages are now discussed.

OBJECTIVE 2 Define liability insurance. **Liability** or **bodily injury insurance** protects the insured in case he or she injures someone with a car. Many states have minimum amounts of liability insurance coverage set by law. The amount of liability insurance is expressed as a fraction, such as 15/30. The fraction 15/30 means that the insurance company will pay up to $15,000 for injury to one person, and a total of $30,000 for injury to two or more persons in the same accident.

However, many experts recommend liability limits of at least 100/300. The reason is that they are aware that a single driving mistake can be very costly, as shown in the following newspaper clipping.

One Accident affects Life

Thomas Garcia has driven for 10 years and has never had an accident or a speeding ticket. However, his life changed instantly when he accidently ran through a stop sign and hit a car driven by a nurse. She is now disabled and can no longer work. Garcia's policy limits of 25/50 are not nearly enough to pay her bills, and her lawyer is taking Garcia to court. Garcia wishes that he had carried higher liability limits.

The following table shows typical premium rates for various amounts of liability coverage. Included in the cost of the liability insurance is **medical insurance** for the driver and passengers in case of injury. For example, the table column 15/30 shows that the insured can also receive reimbursement for up to $1000 of his or her own medical expenses in an accident. Insurance companies divide the nation into territories based on past claims in all areas. Four territories are shown here. All tables in this section show annual premiums.

Liability (Bodily Injury) and Medical Insurance (Per Year)

	LIABILITY AND MEDICAL EXPENSE LIMITS				
TERRITORY	15/30 $1000	25/50 $2000	50/100 $3000	100/300 $5000	250/500 $10,000
1	$207	$222	$253	$282	$308
2	269	302	341	378	392
3	310	314	375	398	459
4	340	362	375	398	445

Finding the Liability and Medical Premium

EXAMPLE 1

case IN point

Martha Spencer, owner of The Doll House, is in territory 2 and wants 100/300 liability coverage. Find the amount of the premium for this coverage and the amount of medical coverage included.

SOLUTION

Look up territory 2 and 100/300 coverage in the liability and medical insurance table to find an annual premium of $378 just for liability and medical coverage. This cost includes $5000 medical coverage.

> **QUICK CHECK 1**
>
> Find the annual cost, for a person living in territory 4, for 250/500 liability coverage with $10,000 in medical insurance.

OBJECTIVE 3 Define property damage insurance. Liability coverage pays if you injure someone. **Property damage coverage** pays if you damage someone else's property such as an automobile or a building. The following table shows the annual cost for various **policy limits** on property damage. You are responsible for damages above the policy limit.

Property Damage Insurance (Per Year)

	PROPERTY DAMAGE LIMITS			
TERRITORY	$10,000	$25,000	$50,000	$100,000
1	$88	$93	$97	$103
2	168	192	223	251
3	129	134	145	158
4	185	203	236	262

Finding the Premium for Property Damage

EXAMPLE 2

Find the annual premium if Martha Spencer, in territory 2, wants property damage coverage of $50,000.

SOLUTION

Property damage coverage of $50,000 in territory 2 requires a premium of $223.

QUICK CHECK 2

Find the premium for $100,000 in property damage coverage for a person living in territory 4.

OBJECTIVE 4 Describe comprehensive and collision insurance. **Comprehensive** insurance pays for damages to the insured's vehicle caused by a fire, by theft of the automobile, by vandalism (e.g., someone purposefully scratches off paint), by a tree falling onto the automobile, and by other similar events. In general, comprehensive insurance pays for damages that are not covered by collision insurance.

Collision insurance pays for repairs to the insured's vehicle when it is involved in a collision with another object.

You choose the **deductible** for both comprehensive and collision insurance when you purchase the insurance. Common deductibles for each coverage range anywhere from $200 to $2000. Higher deductibles result in a lower insurance premium. However, higher deductibles require you to pay more out of your pocket when the vehicle is damaged. So, be careful to choose a deductible that you can afford.

In the event of damages to your automobile, you pay the deductible and the insurance company pays the balance. For example, assume a tree falls on your car during a storm and that you have a $1000 deductible on your comprehension coverage. The amount that must be paid by the insured and the insurance company are shown.

$$
\begin{array}{lr}
\text{Damages to your automobile} & \$3480 \\
\text{Deductible you must pay} & -1000 \\
\hline
\text{Insurance company pays} & \mathbf{\$2480}
\end{array}
$$

Note: States require that car owners purchase liability insurance but do not require them to purchase comprehension or collision insurance. However, the firm lending you money to buy a car requires that you buy comprehension and collision insurance so that it does not lose money in the event the vehicle is damaged.

The table that follows shows typical rates for comprehensive and collision insurance, each with a $1000 deductible. The rates are determined by actuaries based on the territory in which you live, the age group of your vehicle, and the symbol based on the cost to repair your specific vehicle. Age group 1 is a vehicle that is less than 2 years of age. Age group 2 is a vehicle that is at least 2 but less than 3 years of age, and so on. Age group 6 is a vehicle 6 years of age or older.

Comprehensive and Collision Insurance (Per Year)

TERRITORY	AGE GROUP	COMPREHENSIVE ($1000 DEDUCTIBLE) SYMBOL			COLLISION ($1000 DEDUCTIBLE) SYMBOL		
		6	7	8	6	7	8
1	1	$58	$64	$90	$153	$165	$184
	2, 3	50	56	82	135	147	171
	4, 5	44	52	76	116	128	147
	6	34	44	64	92	110	128
2	1	$26	$28	$40	$89	$95	$104
	2, 3	40	52	68	80	86	98
	4, 5	20	24	34	71	77	86
	6	30	36	45	95	103	115
3	1	$70	$78	$108	$145	$157	$174
	2, 3	60	66	90	128	139	162
	4, 5	52	64	92	111	122	139
	6	48	59	63	110	132	157
4	1	$42	$46	$66	$97	$104	$124
	2, 3	36	40	58	87	94	107
	4, 5	32	38	54	77	84	94
	6	60	68	84	140	158	166

Finding the Comprehensive and Collision Premiums

EXAMPLE 3

Martha Spencer, owner of The Doll House, is in territory 2 and has a 2-year-old minivan that has a symbol of 8. Use the comprehensive and collision insurance table to find the cost for **(a)** comprehensive coverage and **(b)** collision coverage.

SOLUTION

(a) The cost of comprehensive coverage is $68.

(b) The cost of collision coverage is $98.

> **QUICK CHECK 3**
>
> Find the premium for **(a)** comprehensive and **(b)** collision coverage for a 3-year-old vehicle in territory 4 and symbol 8.

OBJECTIVE 5 Define no-fault and uninsured motorist insurance. Some states have **no-fault** laws. Under no-fault insurance, all medical expenses and costs associated with an accident are paid to each individual by *his or her own insurance company*, no matter who is at fault. Legislators and insurance companies argue that no-fault insurance removes lawyers, courts, and juries from the process and results in quicker, less costly settlements. Others (including trial lawyers) argue that no-fault insurance leaves accident victims unable to recover all of their damages.

Most states do not have no-fault laws, thereby requiring the insurance company of the person at fault to pay for damages. A potential problem in these states is that the motorist who caused an accident either has no insurance at all or has too little insurance for the damages that occurred. **Uninsured motorist insurance** protects a vehicle owner from financial liability when hit by a driver with no insurance. **Underinsured motorist insurance** provides protection to a vehicle owner when hit by a driver who has *too little* insurance. Typical costs for uninsured motorist insurance are shown in the table at the left.

Uninsured Motorist Insurance (Per Year)

TERRITORY	BASIC LIMIT
1	$66
2	$44
3	$76
4	$70

Determining the Premium for Uninsured Motorist Coverage

EXAMPLE 4

Martha Spencer, in territory 2, wants uninsured motorist coverage. Find the premium in the uninsured motorist insurance table.

SOLUTION

The premium for uninsured motorist coverage in territory 2 is $44.

> **QUICK CHECK 4**
>
> Find the annual cost of uninsured motorist coverage in territory 1.

OBJECTIVE 6 Apply youthful-operator factors. Sometimes young people think they are being charged *far too much* for automobile insurance. Insurance companies base their rates on probabilities calculated from statistical data. The graph below shows that drivers under 25 are far more likely to be involved in a fatal automobile accident than drivers 25 or older. Therefore, insurance companies charge higher rates for **youthful** compared to **adult** drivers. The age at which a youth becomes an adult varies from company to company. Generally, drivers under 25 are considered youthful drivers, and drivers 25 or older are considered adults.

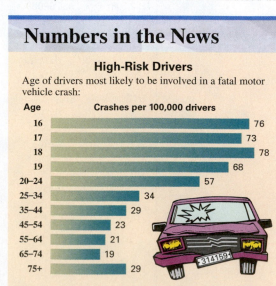

Numbers in the News

High-Risk Drivers

Age of drivers most likely to be involved in a fatal motor vehicle crash:

Age	Crashes per 100,000 drivers
16	76
17	73
18	78
19	68
20–24	57
25–34	34
35–44	29
45–54	23
55–64	21
65–74	19
75+	29

DATA: National Safety Council

The following table shows typical youthful-operator factors based on age and on whether or not the operator has taken driver's training. You can see that the factors are much higher for youthful operators who have not taken driver's training. The steps to apply these factors follow.

1. Determine the total premium for all coverages desired.

2. Multiply the total premium by the youthful-operator factor from the table.

Youthful-Operator Factor

AGE	WITH DRIVER'S TRAINING	WITHOUT DRIVER'S TRAINING
20 or less	2.35	2.95
21–25	2.10	2.40

Using the Youthful-Operator Factor

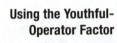

Janet Ito lives in territory 4, is 22 years old, has had driver's training, has never received a ticket or been involved in an accident, and drives a 5-year-old car with a symbol of 7. She wants a 25/50 liability policy, a $10,000 property damage policy, a comprehensive and collision policy, and uninsured motorist coverage. Find her annual insurance premium using the tables in this section.

SOLUTION

1. Determine the total premium for all coverages desired.

25/50 liability insurance	$362
$10,000 property damage	185
Comprehensive insurance	38
Collision	84
Uninsured motorist	+ 70
Subtotal	**$739**

2. Multiply the premium by the youthful-operator factor from the table.

$$\$739 \times 2.10 = \$1551.90$$

The calculator solution to this example uses parentheses and chain calculations.

(362 + 185 + 38 + 84 + 70) × 2.10 = 1551.9

QUICK CHECK 5

Scott Burch is 20, lives in territory 3, has not had driver's training, and drives a 3-year-old car with a symbol of 6. He wants the following coverages: 100/300 liability, $5000 medical, $50,000 property damage, uninsured motorist, and both comprehensive and collision insurance. Find the annual premium.

OBJECTIVE 7 Find the amounts paid by the insurance company and the insured. If you are at fault in an automobile accident and the damages *exceed the limits* on your insurance policy, you *may be personally liable* for the excess. You can help avoid this situation if you increase the liability and property damage limits on your policy. Sometimes, it does not cost much to increase your liability limits. For example, the additional cost of increasing liability coverage in territory 1 from 50/100 to 100/300 is only $29 per year ($282 − $253).

Finding the Amounts Paid by the Insurance Company and the Insured

EXAMPLE 6

James Benson has 25/50 liability limits, $25,000 property damage limits, and $500 deductible collision insurance. While on vacation, he was at fault in an accident that caused $5800 damage to his car, $3380 in damage to another car, and severe injuries to the other driver and his passenger. A subsequent lawsuit for injuries resulted in a judgment of $45,000 and $35,000, respectively, to the other parties. Find the amounts that the insurance company will pay for **(a)** repairing Benson's car, **(b)** repairing the other car, and **(c)** paying the court judgment resulting from the lawsuit. **(d)** How much will Benson have to pay the injured parties?

SOLUTION

(a) The insurance company will pay $4800 (**$5800 − $1000 deductible**) to repair Benson's car.

(b) Repairs on the other car will be paid to the property damage limits ($25,000). Here, the total repairs of $3380 are paid.

(c) Since more than one person was injured, the insurance company pays the limit of $50,000 ($25,000 to each of the two injured parties).

(d) Benson is liable for $30,000 (**$80,000 − $50,000**), the amount awarded over the insurance limits.

QUICK CHECK 6

Janet Yahn has the following coverages: 50/100 liability, $3000 medical, $25,000 property damage, and $500 deductible collision. She runs through a stop sign and hits a van with a value of $12,200. The van is destroyed and the cost to repair Yahn's car is $8600. The driver of the van had medical costs of $68,000 and Yahn had medical costs of $2800. Find each cost Yahn must pay.

13.4 Exercises

The **QUICK START** exercises in each section contain solutions to help you get started.

Find the annual premium for the following. (See Examples 1–5.)

QUICK START

Name	Territory	Age	Driver Training?	Liability	Property Damage	Comprehensive Collision Age Group	Symbol	Uninsured Motorist?	Annual Premium
1. Smyth	3	42	No	50/100	$25,000	2	7	Yes	$790
$375 + $134 + $66 + $139 + $76 = $790									
2. Thompson	4	20	Yes	25/50	$25,000	4	7	No	$1648.80
$362 + $203 + $38 + $84 = $687; $687 × 2.4 = $1648.80									
3. Shraim	3	52	No	250/500	$50,000	2	8	Yes	_____
4. Waldron	2	67	No	50/100	$100,000	1	6	Yes	_____
5. Applegate	4	35	No	100/300	100	1	6	Yes	_____
6. Rodriguez	1	24	Yes	50/100	50	3	8	Yes	_____

7. Describe four factors that determine the premium on an automobile insurance policy. (See Objective 1.)

8. Explain in your own words the difference between liability (bodily injury) and property damage. (See Objectives 2 and 3.)

Solve the following application problems.

QUICK START

9. **ADULT AUTO INSURANCE** Bill Poole is 47 years old, lives in territory 4, and drives a 2-year-old car with a symbol of 7. He wants 250/500 liability limits, $100,000 property damage limits, comprehensive and collision insurance, and uninsured motorist coverage. Find his annual insurance premium.

   $445 + $262 + $40 + $94 + $70 = $911

   9. $911

 10. **ADULT AUTO INSURANCE** Martha Spencer, owner of The Doll House, is thinking about moving from a house in territory 2 to a house in territory 3 and wants to know the effect on the insurance costs for her new car. She currently lives in territory 2 and the car has symbol 7. Her coverages are 250/500 for liability, $100,000 for property damage, comprehensive, collision, and uninsured motorist. She is 53 years old. Find the change in annual cost.

   10. _____

 indicates an exercise that is related to the Case in Point feature.

11. **YOUTHFUL-OPERATOR AUTO INSURANCE** Brandy Barrett is 23 years old, took a driver's education course, lives in territory 1, and drives a 4-year-old vehicle with a symbol of 6. She wants 50/100 liability limits, $25,000 property damage limits, comprehensive and collision insurance, and uninsured motorist coverage. Find her annual insurance premium.

11. _____

12. **YOUTHFUL OPERATOR—NO DRIVER'S TRAINING** Karen Roberts' father gave her a new Honda Accord to use at college under the condition she pay her own insurance. She is 17, has not had driver's training, lives in territory 1, and her vehicle has a symbol of 6. She wants 50/100 liability limits, $25,000 property damage limits, comprehensive and collision insurance, and uninsured motorist coverage. Find her annual insurance premium.

12. _____

13. **BODILY INJURY INSURANCE** Suppose your bodily injury policy has limits of 25/50 and you injure a person on a bicycle. The judge awards damages of $36,500 to the cyclist. **(a)** How much will the company pay? **(b)** How much will you pay?

(a) _____
(b) _____

14. **BODILY INJURY INSURANCE** Three years ago Martha Spencer, owner of The Doll House, lost control of her car while trying to find her cell phone and forced another driver off the road. The court awarded $28,000 to the driver of the other car and $8000 to a passenger of the other car. Spencer had limits of 15/30. **(a)** Find the amount the insurance company paid. **(b)** Find the amount Spencer had to pay.

(a) _____
(b) _____

15. **MEDICAL EXPENSES AND PROPERTY DAMAGE** Wes Hanover accidentally backed into a parked car. He caused $4300 in damage to the car, and Hanover's passenger needed stitches in her forehead, which cost $850. Hanover had 15/30 liability limits, $1000 medical expense, and property damage of $10,000. Find the amount paid by the insurance company for **(a)** damages to the automobile and **(b)** medical expenses.

(a) _____
(b) _____

16. **MEDICAL EXPENSES AND PROPERTY DAMAGE** Jessica Wallace backed into a new Mercedes and caused $12,800 in damage to the car. She also injured the vertebrae in her neck, requiring surgery costing $48,200. She had 50/100 liability limits, $10,000 in property damage, and $3000 in medical expense coverage. Find the amount paid by the insurance company for **(a)** damages to the automobile and **(b)** medical expenses.

(a) _____
(b) _____

17. **INSURANCE COMPANY PAYMENT** A reckless driver caused Sandy Silva to collide with a car in another lane. Silva had 50/100 liability limits, $25,000 property damage limits, and collision coverage with a $100 deductible. Silva's car had damage of $1878, while the other car suffered $6936 in damages. The resulting lawsuit gave injury awards of $60,000 and $55,000, respectively, in damages for personal injury to the two people in the other car. Find the amount that the insurance company will pay for **(a)** repairing Silva's car, **(b)** repairing the other car, and **(c)** personal injury damages. **(d)** How much must Silva pay beyond her insurance coverage, including the collision deductible?

(a) _____
(b) _____
(c) _____
(d) _____

18. **INSURANCE PAYMENT** Bob Armstrong lost control of
his car and crashed into another car. He had 15/30 liability limits, $10,000 property damage limits, and collision
coverage with a $100 deductible. Damage to Armstrong's
car was $2980; the other car, with a value of $22,800, was
totaled. The results of a lawsuit awarded $75,000 and
$45,000, respectively, in damages for personal injury to
the two people in the other car. Find the amount that the
insurance company will pay for **(a)** repairing Armstrong's car, **(b)** repairing the other car,
and **(c)** personal injury damages. **(d)** How much must Armstrong pay beyond his
insurance coverage?

(a) _____

(b) _____

(c) _____

(d) _____

19. Explain why insurance companies charge a higher premium for auto insurance sold to a
youthful operator. Do you think this is fair? (See Objective 6.)

20. Property damage pays for damage caused by you to the property of others. Since the average cost of a new car today is over $20,000, what amount of property damage coverage
would you recommend to a friend who owns her own business?

QUICK CHECK ANSWERS

1. $445
2. $262
3. (a) $58 (b) $107
4. $66
5. $2380.65
6. $1000 to repair her own car; $18,000 for medical expenses of other driver

13.5 Life Insurance

OBJECTIVES

1 Understand life insurance that does not accumulate cash value.
2 Understand life insurance that accumulates cash value.
3 Find the annual premium for life insurance.
4 Use premium factors with different modes of premium payment.

case IN point ▶ Martha Spencer owns the Doll House. Recently divorced, she worries about her two children should she become ill, disabled, or die. As a result, she carries medical insurance, disability insurance, and $250,000 in life insurance.

There is no doubt about it: Insurance is expensive! Yet, most of us need insurance (car, home, medical, disability, and life insurance). The graph on the left below shows that about one out of every five) adults have found themselves in a situation where they wished they had more insurance. The figure on the right illustrates that many adults are insured through an employer.

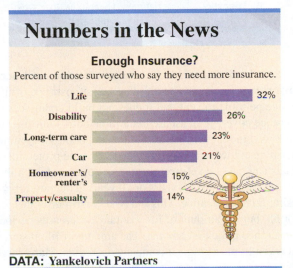

Numbers in the News

Enough Insurance?
Percent of those surveyed who say they need more insurance.

Life	32%
Disability	26%
Long-term care	23%
Car	21%
Homeowner's/renter's	15%
Property/casualty	14%

DATA: Yankelovich Partners

Numbers in the News

You're Covered
Nearly 85% of adults are insured through their employer or their spouse's employer. Those who say their coverage includes:

Medical	89%
Dental	55%
Vision	43%
Mental health	22%
Long-term disability	20%
Life	17%
Short-term disability	15%

DATA: Aragon Consulting Group

People buy **life insurance** to pay for their own burial expenses, to pay off a home mortgage or a car loan, to provide for a spouse and/or children, or to pay for their children's future college expenses. Some forms of life insurance build up a cash retirement value; other forms do not. Life insurance can also be important for the owner(s) of a business. Upon the death of the business owner, life insurance proceeds can provide a company with enough money to continue until it can be sold. Alternatively, life insurance proceeds can be used by one partner of a firm to buy out the ownership interest of a deceased partner.

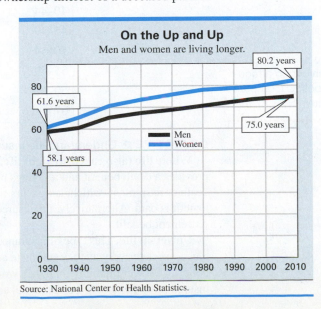

On the Up and Up
Men and women are living longer.

80.2 years
61.6 years
75.0 years
58.1 years

Men
Women

Source: National Center for Health Statistics.

In general, insurance rates have decreased markedly over the past 30 years for two reasons: People are living longer, as shown in the graph on the previous page, and costs have fallen due to increasing competition. The increase in competition is partly a result of sales of insurance using the Internet, which lowers costs and increases the availability of information about prices. Competition often, but not always, results in reduced prices to consumers.

The following table shows the most common causes of death in the United States and includes suggestions to reduce the risk of death by each. Notice that our health risks can be reduced by doing just a few things: quit smoking, lose weight, exercise more, eat more vegetables, eat less red meat and sugar (e.g., candy and soda), and reduce salt intake. That's it! Act on these things and you will probably live longer and have a healthier, more active life.

Biggest Causes of Death	To Reduce Risk:
1. **Heart disease**	Quit smoking, lose weight, eat more fish and less red meat, increase physical activity
2. **Cancer**	Eat more vegetables, fruit, and fish
3. **Accidents**	Do not drink and drive
4. **Stroke**	Quit smoking, reduce salt in diet, increase physical activity
5. **Lung disease**	Quit smoking, increase physical activity
6. **Diabetes**	Eat more vegetables, lose weight, increase physical activity, avoid simple sugars such as candy

Source: National Institute of Health Statistics, 2007.

OBJECTIVE 1 Understand life insurance that does not accumulate cash value.

Term insurance. Term insurance is the lowest-cost type of life insurance. It provides the most insurance per dollar spent, but it does not build up any cash values for retirement. This type of insurance coverage is usually renewable until some age, such as 70, when the insured is no longer allowed to renew it. As a result, most people discontinue term insurance before they die. Still, term insurance is a low-cost way to provide protection against an early death.

Individuals can buy a **level-premium** term policy in which the premium remains constant for a period of time, such as 10 years or 20 years. Thereafter, premiums increase rapidly.

Decreasing term insurance. This is a type of term insurance with fixed premiums commonly to age 60 or 65, but the amount of life insurance decreases periodically. An example of this is a mortgage insurance policy on a home. The amount of life insurance on the owner decreases as the amount owed to the mortgage company decreases. Many large companies provide decreasing term insurance to employees as a benefit. The table provides an example of the benefits of one particular decreasing term policy.

Example of Death Benefits for a Decreasing Term Policy with a Premium of $11 per Month

AGE	AMOUNT OF LIFE INSURANCE
Under 29	$160,000
30–34	$140,000
35–39	$120,000
40–44	$100,000
45–49	$72,000
50–54	$44,000
55–59	$28,000
60–66	$16,000
67 and over	$0

OBJECTIVE 2 Understand life insurance that accumulates cash value.

Whole life (also called **straight life, ordinary life**, or **permanent**). This type of insurance provides a death benefit and a savings plan. The insured commonly pays a constant premium until death or retirement, whichever occurs first. If the policy is in force at the time of death, a death benefit is paid. Alternatively, the insured may choose to convert the accumulated **cash value** to a retirement benefit.

Universal life. This type of insurance provides the life insurance protection of term insurance plus a tax-deferred way to accumulate assets. It sometimes allows people to establish a permanent policy at a lower premium than they would have to pay under a whole life policy, and it gives the insured more flexibility. For example, universal life can help a family obtain more insurance when young children are at home and then help accumulate savings later after the children are grown. The portion of the premium going into retirement benefits receives money market interest rates and often has a guaranteed minimum rate of return regardless of what happens to market rates.

Variable life. This type of insurance allows the policyholder to make choices among several investment options. It places the investment risk on the policyholder by allowing the insured to invest in any of the following: money market funds, bond funds, stock funds, or a combination of the three.

Limited-payment life insurance. Limited-payment life is similar to whole life insurance, except that premiums are paid for only a fixed number of years, such as 20. This type of insurance is thus often called 20-pay life, representing payments for 20 years. The premium for limited-payment life is higher than that for whole life policies. Limited-payment life is most appropriate for athletes, actors, and others whose income is likely to be high for several years and then decline.

Endowment policies are the most expensive type of policy since they accumulate cash more rapidly than the other types of life insurance. These policies guarantee payment of a fixed amount of money to a given individual, whether or not the insured lives. Endowment policies might be taken out by parents to guarantee a sum of money for their children's college education. Because of the high premiums, this is one of the least popular types of policies today.

Quick TIP ▼

Limited-payment and endowment policies cost more, but they accumulate money to be used later in life.

OBJECTIVE 3 Find the annual premium for life insurance. Calculation of life insurance rates by actuaries is based on statistical data involving death rates, interest rates, and other factors. Women tend to live a few years longer than men, so a woman pays a lower life insurance premium than a man of the same age. Incidentally, women are more likely to be disabled than men and therefore have higher disability insurance rates than men. Use the actual age of a man to find the premium factor in the table below. However, subtract 5 from the age of a woman before finding the premium factor in the table. Remember, life insurance costs differ significantly from company to company. As always, it pays to be a knowledgeable consumer and shop for the best deal.

Quick TIP ▼

Individuals with health problems must pay substantially more for life insurance than healthy individuals. Other factors that increase life insurance premiums include smoking and even some hobbies such as scuba diving or bungee jumping.

Annual Premium Rates* Per $1000 of Life Insurance

AGE	10-YEAR LEVEL PREMIUM TERM	WHOLE LIFE	UNIVERSAL LIFE	20-PAY LIFE
20	1.60	4.07	3.48	12.30
21	1.65	4.26	3.85	12.95
22	1.69	4.37	4.10	13.72
23	1.73	4.45	4.56	14.28
24	1.78	4.68	4.80	15.95
25	1.82	5.06	5.11	16.60
30	1.89	5.66	6.08	18.78
35	2.01	7.68	7.45	21.60
40	2.56	12.67	10.62	24.26
45	3.45	19.86	15.24	28.16
50	5.63	26.23	21.46	32.59
55	8.12	31.75	28.38	38.63
60	14.08	38.42	36.72	45.74

*For women, subtract 5 years from the actual age. For example, rates for a 30-year-old woman are shown for age 25 in the table.

Finding Annual Premium

Annual premium = Number of thousands × Rate per $1000

Finding the Life Insurance Premium

EXAMPLE 1

case in point

Martha Spencer became the primary source of income for her family at age 35 after her divorce. At that time, she decided that she needed $250,000 in life insurance to pay off the mortgage on her home, to repay some loans at her business, and to provide for her children. Find her annual premium for **(a)** a 10-year level premium term policy, **(b)** a whole life policy, **(c)** a universal life policy, and **(d)** a 20-pay life plan.

SOLUTION

First, divide the desired amount of life insurance by $1000 to find the number of thousands.

$250,000 ÷ $1000 = 250 thousands

Quick TIP ▼

Use the actual age of a man when using the table of premiums. However, subtract 5 from the age of a woman before using the table.

Since Spencer is a woman, subtract 5 from her actual age before using the table $(35 - 5 = 30)$. Look in the table at age 30 for the rates for each type of insurance.

(a) 10-year level premium term $250 \times \textbf{1.89} = \$472.50$

(b) Whole life $250 \times \textbf{5.66} = \$1415$

(c) Universal life $250 \times \textbf{6.08} = \$1520$

(d) 20-pay life $250 \times \textbf{18.78} = \$4695$

Spencer wanted to buy universal life because of the savings feature, which would help her save for retirement. However, she purchased the level premium term instead, since her income was limited and the level term policy was much cheaper.

QUICK CHECK 1

James Liberty is 50 and wants to buy $300,000 in life insurance. Find the annual cost for **(a)** 10-year level premium term, **(b)** whole life, **(c)** universal life, and **(d)** 20-pay life.

OBJECTIVE 4 Use premium factors with different modes of premium payment. Many companies give the insured the option of paying the premium semiannually, quarterly, or monthly. For this convenience, the policyholder *pays an additional amount* that is determined by a **premium factor**. The following table shows typical premium factors.

Premium Factors

MODE OF PAYMENT	PREMIUM FACTOR
Semiannually	.51
Quarterly	.26
Monthly	.0908

Using a Premium Factor **EXAMPLE 2**

The annual insurance premium on a $200,000 10-year level premium term life policy for Jane Rodriguez is $378. Use the premium factors table to find the amount of premium and the total annual cost if she pays **(a)** semiannually, **(b)** quarterly, or **(c)** monthly.

SOLUTION

	Premium	**Annual Cost**
(a) Semiannually:	$\$378 \times \textbf{.51} = \$192.78$	$\$192.78 \times \textbf{2 payments/year} = \$385.56$
(b) Quarterly:	$\$378 \times \textbf{.26} = \$98.28$	$\$98.28 \times \textbf{4 payments/year} = \$393.12$
(c) Monthly:	$\$378 \times \textbf{.0908} = \$34.32$ (rounded)	$\$34.32 \times \textbf{12 payments/year} = \$411.84$

QUICK CHECK 2

The annual premium on a life insurance policy is $470. Find the premium if payments are made **(a)** semiannually, **(b)** quarterly, and **(c)** monthly.

Pricing Life Insurance **EXAMPLE 3**

Shauna Jones has decided to buy $100,000 in life insurance to make sure that her kids will have funds if something happens to her. Jones is 28 and in good health. Find the monthly premium for **(a)** 10-year level premium term and **(b)** universal life.

SOLUTION

(a) 10-year level premium term:

premium factor for monthly payment

$$\text{Monthly premium} = (\$100 \times 1.73) \times .0908 = \textbf{\$15.71} \quad \textbf{(rounded)}$$

(b) Universal life:

premium factor for monthly payment

$$\text{Monthly premium} = (\$100 \times 4.56) \times .0908 = \textbf{\$41.40} \quad \textbf{(rounded)}$$

QUICK CHECK 3

Darryl Foster is 40 years old and wants to buy $400,000 of whole life insurance. Find the quarterly premium.

13.5 Exercises

The **QUICK START** exercises in each section contain solutions to help you get started.

Find the annual premium, the semiannual premium, the quarterly premium, and the monthly premium for each of the following. (Note: Subtract 5 years for women.) Round to the nearest cent.

QUICK START

	Face Value of Policy	Age of Insured	Sex of Insured	Type of Policy	Annual Premium	Semi-annual Premium	Quarterly Premium	Monthly Premium
1.	$100,000	45	F	Term	$256	$130.56	$66.56	$23.24

$100 \times \$2.56 = \$256$; $\$256 \times .51 = \$130.56$; $\$256 \times .26 = \$66.56$; $\$256 \times .0908 = \$23.24$

2.	$60,000	30	M	Whole life	$339.60	$173.20	$88.30	$30.84

$60 \times \$5.66 = \$339.60$; $\$339.60 \times .51 = \$173.20$; $\$339.60 \times .26 = \$88.30$; $\$339.60 \times .0908 = \$30.84$

	Face Value of Policy	Age of Insured	Sex of Insured	Type of Policy	Annual Premium	Semi-annual Premium	Quarterly Premium	Monthly Premium
3.	$35,000	40	M	20-pay life	_____	_____	_____	_____
4.	$60,000	50	F	20-pay life	_____	_____	_____	_____
5.	$85,000	30	M	Universal life	_____	_____	_____	_____
6.	$150,000	60	M	Term	_____	_____	_____	_____
7.	$75,000	21	M	Whole life	_____	_____	_____	_____
8.	$80,000	35	F	Term	_____	_____	_____	_____
9.	$65,000	60	M	20-pay life	_____	_____	_____	_____
10.	$50,000	45	F	Universal life	_____	_____	_____	_____

11. Compare level premium term insurance to universal life insurance. Which would you prefer for yourself? Why? (See Objectives 1 and 2.)

12. Describe premium factors and how they are used. How often do you prefer paying an insurance premium: annually, semiannually, quarterly, or monthly? (See Objective 4.)

indicates an exercise that is related to the Case in Point feature.

Solve the following application problems.

QUICK START

13. **LIFE INSURANCE** Bill Able married on his 25th birthday. He adopted the child his wife had from a previous marriage and wanted to care for the child as his own. To protect his new family against the loss of income in the event of his death, he purchased $200,000 in 10-year level premium term. Find the annual cost.

   13. <u>$364</u>

   $200,000 ÷ $1000 = 200$
   $200 \times 1.82 = \$364$

14. **WHOLE LIFE INSURANCE** Jessica Smith buys a whole life policy with a face value of $100,000 at age 35. Find the annual premium.

   14. _____

15. **KEY EMPLOYEE INSURANCE** Martha Spencer owns the Doll House and has a 35-year-old key male employee whom she wants to insure for $50,000. Find the annual premium **(a)** for 10-year level term and **(b)** for whole life.

   (a) _____
   (b) _____

16. **20-PAY LIFE POLICY** Luan Lee buys a $100,000, 20-pay life policy at age 45. Her son Bryan is the beneficiary and will collect the face value of the policy. **(a)** Find the annual premium. **(b)** How much will Bryan get if his mother dies after making payments for 12 years?

   (a) _____
   (b) _____

17. **WHOLE LIFE INSURANCE** Find the total premium paid over 30 years for a whole life policy with a face value of $20,000. Assume that the policy is taken out by a 25-year-old man.

   17. _____

18. **UNIVERSAL LIFE INSURANCE** Richard Gonsalves takes out a universal life policy with a face value of $50,000. He is 40 years old. Find the monthly premium.

   18. _____

19. **PREMIUM FACTORS** The annual premium for a whole life policy is $872. Using premium factors, find **(a)** the semiannual premium, **(b)** the quarterly premium, and **(c)** the monthly premium.

   (a) _____
   (b) _____
   (c) _____

20. **PREMIUM FACTORS** A universal life policy has an annual premium of $2012. Use premium factors to find **(a)** the semiannual premium, **(b)** the quarterly premium, and **(c)** the monthly premium.

   (a) _____
   (b) _____
   (c) _____

QUICK CHECK ANSWERS

1. (a) $1689 **(b)** $7869 **(c)** $6438   **3.** $1317.68
   (d) $9777

2. (a) $239.70 **(b)** $122.20 **(c)** $42.68

Chapter 13 | Quick Review

Chapter Terms *Review the following terms to test your understanding of the chapter. For each term you do not know, refer to the page number found next to that term.*

1099 forms [p. 560]
actuaries [p. 585]
adjusted gross income [p. 560]
adult operator [p. 588]
assessed value [p. 551]
assessment rate [p. 551]
bodily injury coverage [p. 586]
cash value [p. 596]
casualty or theft losses [p. 565]
catastrophic event [p. 575]
coinsurance clause [p. 577]
collision insurance [p. 587]
comprehensive insurance [p. 587]
contributions [p. 560]
coverage [p. 576]
decreasing term insurance [p. 596]
deductible [p. 587]
dependent [p. 562]
disability insurance [p. 580]
dollars per $100 [p. 552]
dollars per $1000 [p. 553]

endowment policies [p. 597]
face value [p. 577]
fair market value [p. 551]
Form 1040A [p. 566]
gifts to charity [p. 565]
head of household [p. 562]
homeowner's policy [p. 576]
income tax [p. 559]
individual retirement account (IRA) [p. 560]
insurance [p. 550]
insurance policy [p. 576]
interest [p. 565]
Internal Revenue Service [p. 560]
IRS [p. 560]
itemized deductions [p. 564]
level-premium term insurance [p. 587]
liability insurance [p. 580]
life insurance [p. 595]
limited-payment life insurance [p. 597]

long-term care insurance [p. 580]
medical and dental expenses [p. 564]
medical insurance [p. 580]
mills [p. 553]
miscellaneous deductions [p. 565]
multiple carriers [p. 578]
no-fault insurance [p. 588]
ordinary life insurance [p. 596]
permanent life insurance [p. 596]
personal exemptions [p. 562]
policy [p. 576]
policy limits [p. 586]
premium [p. 577]
premium factor [p. 598]
property damage insurance [p. 586]
property-tax rate [p. 552]
renter's insurance [p. 580]
replacement cost [p. 577]

Schedule 1 (Form 1040A) [p. 566]
standard deduction [p. 562]
straight life insurance [p. 596]
tax deduction [p. 564]
tax preparation [p. 565]
taxable income [p. 562]
taxes [p. 550]
term insurance [p. 596]
territorial ratings [p. 577]
underinsured motorist insurance [p. 588]
underwriters [p. 577]
uninsured motorist insurance [p. 588]
universal life policy [p. 596]
unreimbursed job expenses [p. 565]
variable life policy [p. 597]
W-2 forms [p. 560]
whole life insurance [p. 596]
worker's compensation [p. 580]
youthful operator [p. 588]

CONCEPTS

13.1 Fair market value and assessed value

The value of property is multiplied by a given percent to arrive at the assessed value.

Assessed value = **Assessment rate** × Market value

13.1 Tax rate

The tax rate formula is

$$\text{Tax rate} = \frac{\text{Total tax amount needed}}{\textbf{Total assessed value}}$$

13.1 Tax rates in different forms

1. **Percent**: multiply by assessed value.
2. **Dollars per $100**: move decimal point 2 places to the left in assessed value and multiply.
3. **Dollars per $1000**: move decimal point 3 places to the left in assessed value and multiply.
4. **Mills**: move decimal point 3 places to the left in rate and multiply by assessed value.

Use the formula

Property tax = Assessed value × **Tax rate**

EXAMPLES

The assessment rate is 30%; fair market value is $115,000; find the assessed value.

$$30\% \times \$115,000 = \$34,500$$

Tax amount needed: $3,864,400; total assessed value: $946,320,000; find the tax rate.

$$\frac{\$3,864,400}{\$946,320,000} = .00408 = .41\% \quad (\text{rounded})$$

Assessed value, $90,000; tax rate, 2.5%:

$$\$90,000 \times 2.5\% = \$2250$$

Tax rate, $2.50 per $100:

$$900 \times \$2.50 = \$2250$$

Tax rate, $25 per $1000:

$$90 \times \$25 = \$2250$$

Tax rate, 25 mills:

$$\$90,000 \times .025 = \$2250$$

CONCEPTS	EXAMPLES
13.2 Adjusted gross income Adjusted gross income includes wages, salaries, tips, dividends, and interest. Subtract IRA contributions and alimony.	Salary, $32,540; interest income, $875; dividends, $315; find adjusted gross income. $$\$32,540 + \$875 + \$315 = \$33,730$$
13.2 Standard deduction amounts The majority of taxpayers use the standard deduction allowed by the IRS.	$5700 for single taxpayers $11,400 for married taxpayers filing jointly or qualifying widow(er) $5700 for married taxpayers filing separately $8350 for head of household
13.2 Taxable income The larger of either the total of itemized deductions or the standard deduction is subtracted from adjusted gross income along with **$3650** for each personal exemption.	Single taxpayer, adjusted gross income, $38,500; itemized deductions, $3850; find taxable income. Note that itemized deductions are less than the standard deduction of $5700 and the personal exemption is **$3650**. $$\text{Taxable income} = \$38,500 - \$5700 - \$3650$$ $$= \$29,150$$
13.2 Tax rates There are six tax rates: 10%, 15%, 25%, 28%, 33%, and 35%.	Single: 10%; 15% over $8350; 25% over $33,950; 28% over $82,250; 33% over $171,550; 35% over $372,950 Married filing jointly: 10%; 15% over $16,700; 25% over $67,900; 28% over $137,050; 33% over $208,850; 35% over $372,950 Married filing separately: 10%; 15% over $8350; 25% over $33,950; 28% over $68,525; 33% over $104,425; 35% over $186,475 Head of household: 10%; 15% over $11,950; 25% over $45,500; 28% over $117,450; 33% over $190,200; 35% over $372,950
13.2 Balance due or a refund from the IRS If the total amount withheld by employers is greater than the tax owed, a refund results. If the tax owed is the greater amount, a balance is due.	Tax owed, $1253; tax withheld, $113 per month for 12 months. Find balance due or refund. $$\$113 \text{ withheld} \times 12 = \$1356 \text{ withheld}$$ $$\$1356 \text{ withheld} - \$1253 \text{ owed} = \$103 \text{ refund}$$
13.3 Annual premium for fire insurance The building and territorial ratings are used to find the premiums per $100 for the building and contents. The two are added.	Building value, $180,000; contents, $35,000. Premiums are: building, $.75 per $100; contents, $.77 per $100. Find the annual premium. $$\text{Building: } 1800 \text{ (hundreds)} \times \$.75 = \$1350$$ $$\text{Contents: } 350 \text{ (hundreds)} \times \$.77 = \$269.50$$ $$\text{Total premium: } \$1350 + \$269.50 = \$1619.50$$
13.3 Coinsurance formula Part of the risk of fire is taken by the insured. An 80% coinsurance clause is common. $$\begin{array}{l}\text{Loss paid by} \\ \text{insurance} \\ \text{company}\end{array} = \begin{array}{c}\text{Amount} \\ \text{of loss}\end{array} \times \frac{\text{Policy amount}}{80\% \textbf{ of replacement cost}}$$	Replacement cost, $250,000; policy amount, $150,000; fire loss, $40,000; 80% coinsurance clause; find the amount of loss paid by insurance company. $$\$40,000 \times \frac{\$150,000}{\$250,000} = \$30,000 \begin{pmatrix}\text{amount insurance} \\ \text{company pays}\end{pmatrix}$$

CONCEPTS	EXAMPLES
13.3 Multiple carriers Several companies insure the same property, which limits the risk of the insurance company, with each paying its fractional portion of any claim.	Insured loss, $500,000 Insurance is Company A with $1,000,000; Company B with $750,000; Company C with $250,000; find the amount of loss paid by each company. Total insurance: $$\$1,000,000 + \$750,000 + \$250,000 = \$2,000,000$$ Company A: $$\frac{1,000,000}{2,000,000} \times \$500,000 = \$250,000$$ Company B: $$\frac{750,000}{2,000,000} \times \$500,000 = \$187,500$$ Company C: $$\frac{250,000}{2,000,000} \times \$500,000 = \$62,500$$
13.4 Annual auto insurance premium Most drivers are required to purchase automobile insurance. The premium is determined by the types of coverage selected, the type of car, geographic territory, past driving record, and other factors.	Determine the premium: territory, 2; liability, 50/100; property damage, $50,000; comprehensive and collision, 3-year-old car with a symbol of 8; uninsured motorist coverage; driver is age 23 with driver's training. $341 — liability $223 — property damage 68 — comprehensive 98 — collision 44 — uninsured motorist $774 × 2.10 — youthful-operator factor = $1625.40
13.5 Annual life insurance premium There are several types of life policies. Use the table and multiply by the number of $1000s of coverage. Subtract 5 years from the age of women. Premium = Number of thousands × **Rate per $1000**	Find the premiums on a $50,000 policy for a 30-year-old man. (a) 10-year level premium term: 50 × **$1.89** = $94.50 (b) Whole life: 50 × **$5.66** = $283 (c) Universal life: 50 × **$6.08** = $304 (d) 20-pay life: 50 × **$18.78** = $939
13.5 Premium factors Life insurance premiums may be paid semiannually, quarterly, or monthly. The annual premium is multiplied by the premium factor to determine the premium amount.	The annual life insurance premium is $740. Use the table to find the (a) semiannual, (b) quarterly, and (c) monthly premiums. (a) Semiannual: $740 × **.51** = $377.40 (b) Quarterly: $740 × **.26** = $192.40 (c) Monthly: $740 × **.0908** = $67.19

case study

FINANCIAL PLANNING FOR PROPERTY TAXES AND INSURANCE

Baker's Pottery manufactures and sells ceramic pots of all types, shapes, and styles. Planning ahead, the company set aside $53,500 to pay property taxes, fire insurance premiums, and life insurance premiums on the company president. All of these premiums happen to be due in the same month. Find each of the following.

1. The company property has a fair market value of $1,990,000 and is assessed at 75% of this value. If the tax rate is $7.90 per $1000 of assessed value, find the annual property tax.

   1. _____

2. The building occupied by the company is a class-B building with a replacement cost of $1,730,000. The contents are worth $3,502,000 and the territorial rating is 4. Find the annual fire insurance premium.

   2. _____

3. The president of the company is a 50-year-old woman who lost the use of her legs in an automobile accident. She needs life insurance and the company buys a $250,000, 10-year level premium life insurance policy on her. Find the semiannual premium.

   3. _____

4. Find the total amount needed to pay property taxes, the fire insurance premium, and the semiannual life insurance premium.

   4. _____

5. How much more than the amount needed had the company set aside to pay these expenses?

   5. _____

INVESTIGATE

A recent article in *Consumer Reports* listed the top Web sites that offer to help a person shop for term life insurance. The article also lists dial-up services that offer a similar service. Use the Web to find information and prices for term life insurance to meet your personal life insurance needs and look at several types of life insurance products.

case _{IN} in point summary exercise

MATTEL INC.—TAXES AND INSURANCE

www.mattel.com

Facts:

- 1945: Founded by Elliot and Ruth Handler
- 1959: Barbie introduced
- 2004: More than one billion Barbies sold
- 2011: Sales over $5 billion

Antique dolls representing adults from the 17th and 18th centuries have been found, but they are very rare. Individual craftsmen in England made most of these earliest dolls. The craftsmen carved the dolls of wood, painted their features, and also designed the costumes for the dolls. Some of these earliest dolls are valued at more than $40,000.

The Barbie doll is the most popular fashion doll ever created. If all the Barbie dolls that have been sold since 1959 were placed head-to-toe, the dolls would circle the earth more than seven times. The most popular Barbie ever sold was the Totally Hair Barbie, which was introduced in 1992. With hair from the top of her head to her toes, more than 10 million of these dolls were sold, resulting in revenue of $100 million. With annual retail sales at an estimated $3.6 billion, Barbie is the #1 brand of doll for girls.

Martha Spencer started The Doll House and sells dolls around the world through her Web site. Her business has grown over the years, but she still carefully watches costs. She knows that she must control costs to be successful. Help her figure out some of these costs.

1. Spencer is looking at a building that she hopes to buy for what she believes is the fair market value of $310,000. However, the replacement cost is estimated to be $420,000. The assessment rate is 30% and the tax rate is $64 per $1000 of assessed value. Find the property tax for the year.

1. _____

2. Janet Chino, one of Spencer's employees, needs help estimating her income tax based on the following: wages—$28,410; interest—$212; ordinary dividends—$84; and IRA contribution—$500. Find the following: total income, adjusted gross income, taxable income, and income tax given that Chino is single and claims only 1 exemption. Use the tax rate schedules.

2. _____

3. Find the cost of fire insurance if the building in Question 1 is in territory 5 and has a building classification of C. The contents are valued at $145,000.

3. _____

4. Spencer purchases a new Toyota and buys 250/500 liability limits, $100,000 property damage, comprehensive, collision, and uninsured motorist. She is in territory 2 and the vehicle has symbol 8. Find the annual premium given that she is 35.

4. _____

5. Spencer is a 35-year old woman who is divorced and has two children. She decides to purchase $500,000 of life insurance to protect her children. Find the annual cost of 10-year level term.

5. _____

6. Find the total of all of the costs that Martha Spencer must pay. This total is only a small part of her total costs each year—clearly she has to sell a lot of dolls to pay her bills.

6. _____

Discussion Question: Is it important to pay taxes and also to buy insurance? Explain. What should happen to those who do not pay taxes? who do not buy required minimum amounts of insurance?

Chapter 13 Test

To help you review, the numbers in brackets show the section in which the topic was discussed.

Find the following property tax rates. **[13.1]**

Percent	Per $100	Per $1000
1. 5.76%	_____	_____
2. _____	_____	$93.50

Find the taxable income and the tax for each of the following people. The letter following the names indicates the marital status. **[13.2]**

Name	Number of Exemptions	Adjusted Gross Income	Total Deductions	Taxable Income	Tax
3. J. Spalding, S	2	$68,295	$5380	_____	_____
4. The Bensons, M	4	$43,487	$8315	_____	_____

Find the tax owed in the following problems.

5. Bradkin's Toggery owns property with a fair market value of $209,200. Property in the area is assessed at 30% of fair market value with a tax rate of 3.65%. Find the annual tax. **[13.1]**

5. _____

6. The Blakely family has an adjusted gross income of $98,316. They are married and file jointly with five exemptions and deductions of $8420. **[13.2]**

6. _____

7. Kari Heen had an adjusted gross income of $44,600 last year. She had deductions of $1280 for state income tax, $3620 for property tax, $3540 in mortgage interest, and $343 in contributions. Heen claims one exemption and files as a single person. **[13.2]**

7. _____

Find the annual fire insurance premium for the following. Use the table on page 577. **[13.3]**

8. Southside Plating owns a class-B building with a replacement cost of $780,000. Contents are valued at $128,600. The territorial rating is 5.

8. _____

9. A fourplex is valued at $220,000. The fire insurance policy (with an 80% coinsurance clause) has a face value of $150,000. If the building has a fire loss of $50,000, find the amount of the loss that the insurance company will pay.

9. _____

10. Dave's Body and Paint has an insurable loss of $72,000, while having insurance coverage beyond coinsurance requirements. The insurance is divided among Company A with $250,000 coverage, Company B with $150,000 coverage, and Company C with $100,000 coverage. Find the amount of the loss paid by each of the insurance companies.

A: _____

B: _____

C: _____

Find the annual motor-vehicle insurance premium for the following people. **[13.4]**

Name	Territory	Age	Driver Training?	Liability	Property Damage	Comprehensive Collision Age Group	Symbol	Uninsured Motorist?	Annual Premium
11. Ramos	3	18	Yes	15/30	$10,000	5	7	Yes	_____
12. Larik	1	42	No	50/100	$100,000	1	8	Yes	_____

Find the annual premium, the semiannual premium, the quarterly premium, and the monthly premium for each of the following life insurance policies. Use the tables in Section 13.5. **[13.5]**

	Annual	Semiannual	Quarterly	Monthly
13. Irene Chong, whole life, $28,000 face value, age 35	_____	_____	_____	_____
14. Gil Eckern, 20-pay life, $80,000 face value, age 40	_____	_____	_____	_____

Solve the following.

15. Betsy Monikens (age 28) and Jim Faber (age 30) recently married and need to buy both car and life insurance. They have one car, 4 years old, with symbol 7 and live in territory 2. Auto: 50/100 liability with $3000 in medical expense limits, $25,000 in property damage, comprehensive, $500 deductible collision, and uninsured motorist. Life: $100,000 10-year level term on Jim and $50,000 universal life on Betsy. Find the annual cost of **(a)** the auto insurance and **(b)** the life insurance. **[13.4 and 13.5]**

(a) _____

(b) _____

16. Jessie Hernandez's truck spun out of control on an icy road, causing an accident with another driver. Damages to his truck were $6400, damages to the other driver's vehicle were $8200, and the other driver had medical expenses of $12,900. Hernandez was not hurt and his policy showed that he had liability limits of 15/30, medical expenses of $1000, property damage of $10,000, no comprehensive or collision, and no uninsured motorist. Identify each of the costs he must pay. **[13.4]**

16. _____

appendix A

The Metric System

Today, the **metric system** is used just about everywhere in the world. In the United States, some industries are switching over to this improved system. The metric system is being taught in elementary schools, and it may eventually replace the current system.

A table on the **English system** is included here to refresh your memory. Notice that time is the same in both the English and metric systems.

LENGTH		WEIGHT	
1 foot	= 12 inches (in.)	1 pound (lb)	= 16 ounces (oz)
1 yard (yd)	= 3 feet (ft)	1 ton (T)	= 2000 pounds (lb)
1 mile (mi)	= 5280 feet (ft)		

CAPACITY		TIME	
1 cup (c)	= 8 fluid ounces	1 week (wk)	= 7 days
1 pint (pt)	= 2 cups	1 day	= 24 hours (hr)
1 quart (qt)	= 2 pints (pt)	1 hour (hr)	= 60 minutes (min)
1 gallon (gal)	= 4 quarts (qt)	1 minute (min)	= 60 seconds (sec)

1 meter

1 meter is 39.37 inches.

1 yard

1 yard is 36 inches.

inches

Prefixes in the Metric System

deca- = 10 times
kilo- = 1000 times
deci- = $\frac{1}{10}$ times
centi- = $\frac{1}{100}$ times
milli- = $\frac{1}{1000}$ times

OBJECTIVES

1 Learn the metric system.

2 Learn how to convert from one system to the other.

OBJECTIVE 1 Learn the metric system. The basic unit of length in the metric system is the **meter**. A meter is a little longer than a yard. For shorter lengths, the units **centimeter** and **millimeter** are commonly used. The prefix "centi" means hundredth, so 1 centimeter is one-hundredth of a meter. Thus

$$100 \text{ centimeters} = 1 \text{ meter} \quad \left(\textbf{or 1 centimeter} = \tfrac{1}{100} \textbf{ meter}\right)$$

The prefix "milli" means thousandth, so 1 millimeter means one-thousandth of a meter. Thus

$$1000 \text{ millimeters} = 1 \text{ meter} \quad \left(\textbf{or 1 millimeter} = \tfrac{1}{1000} \textbf{ meter}\right)$$

Meter is abbreviated m, centimeter is cm, and millimeter is mm.

Convert from centimeters to millimeters to meters by moving the decimal point, as shown in the following example.

Converting Length Measurements **EXAMPLE 1**

Convert the following measurements:

(a) 6.4 m to cm

(b) .98 m to mm

(c) 34 cm to m

SOLUTION

(a) A centimeter is a small unit of measure (a centimeter is about $\frac{1}{2}$ the diameter of a penny) and a meter is a large unit (a little over 3 feet), so many centimeters make a meter. Therefore, *multiply* by **100** to convert meters to centimeters.

$$6.4 \text{ m} = 6.4 \times \textbf{100} = 640 \text{ cm}$$

(b) Multiply by **1000** to convert meters to millimeters.

$$.98 \text{ m} = .98 \times \mathbf{1000} = 980 \text{ mm}$$

(c) A meter is a large unit of measure, and a centimeter is a smaller unit, so 34 cm is equivalent to a smaller number of meters. Thus, *divide* by **100** to convert centimeters to meters.

$$34 \text{ cm} = \frac{34}{\mathbf{100}} = .34 \text{ m}$$

QUICK CHECK 1

Convert 6 meters to millimeters and 3 centimeters to meters.

Long distances are measured in **kilometer** (km) units. The prefix "kilo" means one thousand. Thus,

$$1 \text{ kilometer} = 1000 \text{ meters} \quad \left(\text{or 1 meter} = \tfrac{1}{1000} \text{ kilometer}\right)$$

Since a meter is about a yard, 1000 meters is about 1000 yards, or 3000 feet. Therefore, 1 kilometer is about 3000 feet. One mile is 5280 feet, so 1 kilometer is about 3000/5280 of a mile. Divide 3000 by 5280 to find that 1 kilometer is about .6 mile.

The basic unit of volume in the metric system is the **liter** (L), which is a little more than a quart. You may have noticed that Coca Cola is sometimes sold in 2-liter plastic bottles. Again the prefixes "milli" and "centi" are used. Thus,

$$1 \text{ liter} = 100 \text{ centiliters}$$
$$1 \text{ liter} = 1000 \text{ milliliters}$$

Milliliter (mL) and **centiliter** (cL) are such small volumes that they find their main uses in science. In particular, drug doses are often expressed in milliliters.

Weight is measured in **grams** (g). A nickel weighs about 5 grams. **Milligrams** (mg; one-thousandth of a gram) and **centigrams** (cg; one-hundredth of a gram) are so small that they are used mainly in science. A more common measure is the **kilogram** (kg), which is 1000 grams. A kilogram weighs about 2.2 pounds.

$$1000 \text{ grams} = 1 \text{ kilogram}$$

1 liter   1 quart

A liter equals
1.06 quarts.

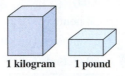

1 kilogram   1 pound

A kilogram equals
2.2 pounds.

Converting Weight Measurements   **EXAMPLE 2**

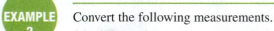

Convert the following measurements.

(a) 650 g to kg

(b) 9.4 L to cL

(c) 4350 mg to g

SOLUTION

(a) A gram is a small unit, and a kilogram is a larger unit. Thus, *divide* by **1000** to convert grams to kilograms.

$$650 \text{ g} = \frac{650}{\mathbf{1000}} = .65 \text{ kg}$$

(b) *Multiply* by **100** to convert liters to centiliters.

$$9.4 \text{ L} = 9.4 \times \mathbf{100} = 940 \text{ cL}$$

(c) *Divide* by **1000** to convert milligrams to grams.

$$4350 \text{ mg} = \frac{4350}{\mathbf{1000}} = 4.35 \text{ g}$$

QUICK CHECK 2

Convert 2 kilograms to grams and 700 centiliters to liters.

OBJECTIVE 2 Learn how to convert from one system to the other. Most Americans do not think in the metric system as easily as in the English system of feet, quarts, pounds, and so on. So, they find it necessary to convert from one system to the other. Approximate conversion can be made with the aid of the next table.

ENGLISH-METRIC CONVERSION TABLE

FROM METRIC	TO ENGLISH	MULTIPLY BY	FROM ENGLISH	TO METRIC	MULTIPLY BY
Meters	Yards	1.09	Yards	Meters	.914
Meters	Feet	3.28	Feet	Meters	.305
Meters	Inches	39.37	Inches	Meters	.0254
Kilometers	Miles	.62	Miles	Kilometers	1.609
Grams	Pounds	.00220	Pounds	Grams	454
Kilograms	Pounds	2.20	Pounds	Kilograms	.454
Liters	Quarts	1.06	Quarts	Liters	.946
Liters	Gallons	.264	Gallons	Liters	3.785

Converting Metric to English **EXAMPLE 3**

Convert the following measurements.

(a) 15 meters to yards

(b) 39 yards to meters

(c) 47 meters to inches

(d) 87 kilometers to miles

(e) 598 miles to kilometers

(f) 12 quarts to liters

SOLUTION

(a) Look at the table for converting meters to yards and find the number **1.09**. Multiply 15 meters by **1.09**.

$$15 \times 1.09 = 16.35 \text{ yards}$$

(b) Read the yards-to-meters row of the table. The number **.914** appears. Multiply 39 yards by **.914**.

$$39 \times .914 = 35.646 \text{ meters}$$

(c) 47 meters $= 47 \times \mathbf{39.37} = 1850.39$ inches

(d) 87 kilometers $= 87 \times \mathbf{.62} = 53.94$ miles

(e) 598 miles $= 598 \times \mathbf{1.609} = 962.182$ kilometers

(f) 12 quarts $= 12 \times \mathbf{.946} = 11.352$ liters

QUICK CHECK 3

Convert a speed limit of 70 miles per hour to kilometers per hour, and convert 3 pounds to grams.

Temperature in the metric system is measured in degrees **Celsius** or **centigrade** (abbreviated C). In the Celsius scale, water freezes at 0°C and boils at 100°C. This is more sensible than degrees **Fahrenheit** (abbreviated F) in use now, in which a mixture of salt and water freezes at 0°F, and 100°F represents the temperature inside the mouth of an individual: Gabriel Fahrenheit.

Converting from Fahrenheit to Celsius

Step 1 Subtract 32.

Step 2 Multiply by 5.

Step 3 Divide by 9.

These steps can be expressed by the following formula.

$$C = \frac{5(F - 32)}{9}$$

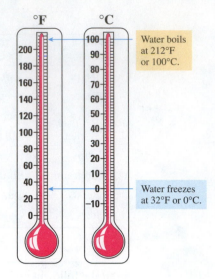

Water boils at 212°F or 100°C.

Water freezes at 32°F or 0°C.

Converting Fahrenheit to Celsius

EXAMPLE 4

Convert 68°F to Celsius.

SOLUTION

Use the steps on the previous page.

Step 1 Subtract 32: $68 - 32 = 36$
Step 2 Multiply by 5: $36 \times 5 = 180$

Step 3 Divide by 9: $\dfrac{180}{9} = 20$

Thus, 68°F = 20°C.

QUICK CHECK 4

Convert 85°F to Celsius.

Converting from Celsius to Fahrenheit

Step 1 Multiply by 9.
Step 2 Divide by 5.
Step 3 Add 32.

These steps can be expressed by the following formula.

$$F = \frac{9 \times C}{5} + 32$$

Converting Celsius to Fahrenheit

EXAMPLE 5

Convert 11°C to Fahrenheit.

SOLUTION

Use the previous steps.

Step 1 Multiply by 9: $9 \times 11 = 99$
Step 2 Divide by 5: $99 \div 5 = 19.8$
Step 3 Add 32: $19.8 + 32 = 51.8°F$

Thus, 11°C = 51.8°F.

QUICK CHECK 5

Convert 35°C to Fahrenheit.

appendix A Exercises

Convert the following measurements.

1. 68 cm to m _____

2. 934 mm to m _____

3. 4.7 m to mm _____

4. 7.43 m to cm _____

5. 8.9 kg to g _____

6. 4.32 kg to g _____

7. 39 cL to L _____

8. 469 cL to L _____

9. 46,000 g to kg _____

10. 35,800 g to kg _____

11. .976 kg to g _____

12. .137 kg to g _____

Convert the following measurements. Round to the nearest tenth.

13. 36 m to yards _____

14. 76.2 m to yards _____

15. 55 yards to m _____

16. 89.3 yards to m _____

17. 4.7 m to feet _____

18. 1.92 m to feet _____

19. 3.6 feet to m _____

20. 12.8 feet to m _____

21. 496 km to miles _____

22. 138 km to miles _____

23. 768 miles to km _____

24. 1042 miles to km _____

25. 683 g to pounds _____

26. 1792 g to pounds _____

27. 4.1 pounds to g _____

28. 12.9 pounds to g _____

29. 38.9 kg to pounds _____

30. 40.3 kg to pounds _____

31. One nickel weighs 5 grams. How many nickels are in 1 kilogram of nickels?

    31. _____

32. Seawater contains about 3.5 grams of salt per 1000 milliliters of water. How many grams of salt do 5 liters of seawater contain?

    32. _____

33. Helium weighs about .0002 gram per milliliter. A balloon contains 3 liters of helium. How much does the helium weigh?

    33. _____

34. About 1500 grams of sugar can be dissolved in 1 liter of warm water. How much sugar can be dissolved in 1 milliliter of warm water?

    34. _____

35. Find your height in centimeters.

35. _____

36. Find your height in meters.

36. _____

Convert the following Fahrenheit temperatures to Celsius. Round to the nearest degree.

37. 104°F _____

38. 86°F _____

39. 536°F _____

40. 464°F _____

41. 98°F _____

42. 114°F _____

Convert each of the following Celsius temperatures to Fahrenheit.

43. 35°C _____

44. 100°C _____

45. 10°C _____

46. 25°C _____

47. 135°C _____

48. 215°C _____

In most cases today, medical measurements are given in the metric system. In each of the following problems, a doctor's prescription is given. Decide whether the dosage is or is not reasonable.

49. 1940 grams of Kaopectate after each meal

49. _____

50. 76.8 centiliters of cough syrup every 2 hours

50. _____

51. 943 milliliters of antibiotic every 6 hours

51. _____

52. 1.4 kilograms of vitamins every 3 hours

52. _____

QUICK CHECK ANSWERS

1. 6000 mm; .03 m

2. 2000 g; 7 L

3. 112.63 km per hour; 1362 g

4. 29.4°C (rounded)

5. 95°C

appendix B

Basic Calculators

OBJECTIVES

1 Learn the basic calculator keys.
2 Understand the C, CE, and ON/C keys.
3 Understand the floating decimal point.
4 Use the % and 1/x keys.
5 Use the x^2, y^x, and $\sqrt{}$ keys.
6 Use the $a^{b/c}$ key.
7 Solve problems with negative numbers.
8 Use the calculator memory function.
9 Solve chain calculations using order of operations.
10 Use the parentheses keys.
11 Use the calculator for problem solution.

Calculators are among the more popular inventions of the last four decades. Each year, better calculators are developed and their cost drops. The first all-transistor desktop calculator was introduced to the market in 1966. It weighed 55 pounds, cost $2500, and was slow. Today, these same calculations are performed quite well on a calculator costing less than $10, and today's $200 pocket calculators have more ability to solve problems than some of the early computers.

Many instructors allow their students to use calculators in business mathematics courses. Some require calculator use. Many types of calculators are available, from the inexpensive basic calculator to the more complex **scientific**, **financial**, and **graphing** calculators.

In this appendix, we discuss the basic calculator, which has a percent key, reciprocal key, exponent keys, square-root key, memory function, order of operations, and parentheses keys. In Appendix C, the financial calculator with its associated financial keys is discussed.

OBJECTIVE 1 Learn the basic calculator keys. Most calculators use **algebraic logic**. Some problems can be solved by entering number and function keys in the same order as you would solve a problem by hand. Other problems require a knowledge of the order of operations when entering the problem.

Quick TIP ▼
The various calculator models differ significantly. *Use the instruction booklet that came with your calculator* for specifics about that calculator if your answers differ from those in this section.

Using the Basic Keys

EXAMPLE 1

Perform the following operations.

(a) 12 + 25   (b) 456 ÷ 24

SOLUTION

(a) The problem 12 + 25 is entered as

[1] [2] [+] [2] [5] [=]

and 37 appears as the answer.

(b) Enter 456 ÷ 24 as

[4] [5] [6] [÷] [2] [4] [=]

and 19 appears as the answer.

QUICK CHECK 1

Find 279.04 ÷ 12.8.

OBJECTIVE 2 Understand the `C` **,** `CE` **and** `ON/C` **keys.** Most calculators have a `C` key. Pressing this key erases everything in most calculators and prepares them for a new problem. Some calculators have a `CE` key. Pressing this key erases only the number displayed, thus allowing for the correction of a mistake without having to start the problem over. Many calculators combine the `C` key and `CE` key and have an `ON/C` key. This key turns the calculator on and is also used to erase the calculator display. If the `ON/C` is pressed after the `=` key, or after one of the operation keys (`+`, `−`, `×`, `÷`), everything in the calculator is erased. If the wrong operation key is pressed, simply press the correct key and the error is corrected. For example, in 7 `+` `−` 3 `=` 4, pressing the `−` key cancels out the previous `+` key entry.

OBJECTIVE 3 Understand the floating decimal point. Most calculators have a **floating decimal** that locates the decimal point in the final result.

Calculating with Decimal Numbers **EXAMPLE 2**

Jennifer Videtto purchased 55.75 square yards of vinyl floor covering at $18.99 per square yard. Find her total cost.

SOLUTION

Proceed as follows.

$$55.75 \ \boxed{\times} \ 18.99 \ \boxed{=} \ 1058.6925$$

The decimal point is automatically placed in the answer. Since money answers are usually rounded to the nearest cent, the answer is $1058.69.

QUICK CHECK 2

Find the cost of 7 boxes of paper costing $24.87 each.

To use a machine with a floating decimal, enter the decimal point as needed. For example, enter $47 as

$$\boxed{4}\ \boxed{7}$$

with no decimal point, but enter $.95 as follows.

$$\boxed{.}\ \boxed{9}\ \boxed{5}$$

One problem in utilizing a floating decimal is shown by the following example.

Placing the Decimal Point in Money Answers **EXAMPLE 3**

Add $21.38 and $1.22.

SOLUTION

$$21.38 \ \boxed{+} \ 1.22 \ \boxed{=} \ 22.6$$

The final 0 is left off. Remember that the problem deals with dollars and cents, and write the answer as $22.60.

QUICK CHECK 3

Add 95.07 and 100.33.

OBJECTIVE 4 Use the `%` **and** `1/x` **keys.** The `%` key moves the decimal point two places to the left when used following multiplication or division.

Using the `%` **Key** **EXAMPLE 4**

Find 8% of $4205.

SOLUTION

$$4205 \ \boxed{\times} \ 8 \ \boxed{\%} \ \boxed{=} \ 336.4 = \$336.40$$

QUICK CHECK 4

Find the real estate commission of 6% on a home sold for $235,000.

The `1/x` key replaces a number with the reciprocal of that number.

Using the $\boxed{1/x}$ Key Find the inverse or reciprocal of 40.

SOLUTION

$$40 \boxed{1/x} .025$$

> **QUICK CHECK 5**
> Find the inverse of 80.

OBJECTIVE 5 Use the $\boxed{x^2}$, $\boxed{y^x}$, and $\boxed{\sqrt{}}$ keys. The product of 3 × 3 can be written as follows.

The exponent (2 in this case) shows how many times the base is multiplied by itself (multiply 3 by itself or 3 × 3). The $\boxed{x^2}$ key can be used to quickly find the square of a number.

Using the $\boxed{x^2}$ Key Find 5^2 and 8.5^2.

SOLUTION

$$5 \boxed{x^2} 25 \qquad \text{and} \qquad 8.5 \boxed{x^2} 72.25$$

> Pushing $\boxed{=}$ is usually not necessary when using the $\boxed{x^2}$ key.

> **QUICK CHECK 6**
> Find 25^2.

The $\boxed{y^x}$ key raises any base number y to a power x. Use as follows.
1. Enter the base number first.
2. $\boxed{y^x}$
3. Enter the exponent.
4. $\boxed{=}$

Using the $\boxed{y^x}$ Key Find 5^3.

SOLUTION

$$5 \boxed{y^x} 3 \boxed{=} 125$$

> **QUICK CHECK 7**
> Find 4.8^3.

Since $3^2 = 9$, the number 3 is called the **square root** of 9. Square roots of numbers are written with the symbol $\sqrt{}$.

$$\sqrt{9} = 3$$

Using the $\boxed{\sqrt{}}$ Key Find each square root.
(a) $\sqrt{144}$ **(b)** $\sqrt{20}$

SOLUTION

(a) Enter

$$144 \boxed{\sqrt{x}}$$

and 12 appears in the display. The square root of 144 is 12.

(b) The square root of 20 is

$$20 \;\boxed{\sqrt{x}}\; 4.472136$$

which may be rounded to the desired position.

OBJECTIVE 6 Use the $\boxed{a^{b/c}}$ key. Many calculators have an $\boxed{a^{b/c}}$ key that can be used for problems containing fractions and mixed numbers. A mixed number is a number with both a whole number and a fraction, such as $7\frac{3}{4}$, which equals $7 + \frac{3}{4}$. The rules for adding, subtracting, multiplying, and dividing both fractions and mixed numbers are given in Chapter 2. Here, we simply show how these operations are done on a calculator.

Using the $\boxed{a^{b/c}}$ Key with Fractions

Solve the following.

(a) $\dfrac{6}{11} + \dfrac{3}{4}$ **(b)** $\dfrac{3}{8} \div \dfrac{5}{6}$

Quick TIP ▼

The calculator automatically shows fractions in lowest terms and as mixed numbers when possible.

SOLUTION

(a) $6 \;\boxed{a^{b/c}}\; 11 \;\boxed{+}\; 3 \;\boxed{a^{b/c}}\; 4 \;\boxed{=}\; 1\dfrac{13}{44}$

(b) $3 \;\boxed{a^{b/c}}\; 8 \;\boxed{\div}\; 5 \;\boxed{a^{b/c}}\; 6 \;\boxed{=}\; \dfrac{9}{20}$

Using the $\boxed{a^{b/c}}$ Key

Solve the following.

(a) $4\dfrac{7}{8} \div 3\dfrac{4}{7}$ **(b)** $\dfrac{5}{3} \div 27.5$ **(c)** $65.3 \times 6\dfrac{3}{4}$

SOLUTION

(a) $4 \;\boxed{a^{b/c}}\; 7 \;\boxed{a^{b/c}}\; 8 \;\boxed{\div}\; 3 \;\boxed{a^{b/c}}\; 4 \;\boxed{a^{b/c}}\; 7 \;\boxed{=}\; 1\dfrac{73}{200}$

(b) $5 \;\boxed{a^{b/c}}\; 3 \;\boxed{\div}\; 27.5 \;\boxed{=}\; 0.060606061$

(c) $65.3 \;\boxed{\times}\; 6 \;\boxed{a^{b/c}}\; 3 \;\boxed{a^{b/c}}\; 4 \;\boxed{=}\; 440.775$

OBJECTIVE 7 **Solve problems with negative numbers.** There are several calculations in business that result in a **negative number**, or **deficit amount**.

Working with Negative Numbers

The amount in the advertising account last month was $4800, while $5200 was actually spent. Find the balance remaining in the advertising account.

SOLUTION

Enter the numbers in the calculator.

$$4800 \;\boxed{-}\; 5200 \;\boxed{=}\; -400$$

The minus sign in front of the 400 indicates that there is a deficit or negative amount. This value can be written as $-\$400$ or sometimes as ($400), which indicates a negative amount. Some calculators place the minus sign after the number, as $400-$.

Negative numbers may be entered into the calculator by using the $\boxed{-}$ key before entering the number. For example, if $3000 is now added to the advertising account in Example 11, the new balance is calculated as follows.

$$\boxed{-}\ 400\ \boxed{+}\ 3000\ \boxed{=}\ 2600$$

The new account balance is $2600.

The $\boxed{+/-}$ key can be used to change the sign of a number that has already been entered. For example, 520 $\boxed{+/-}$ changes +520 to −520.

OBJECTIVE 8 Use the calculator memory function. Many calculators feature memory keys, which are a sort of electronic scratch paper. These **memory keys** are used to store intermediate steps in a calculation. On some calculators, a key labeled $\boxed{M}$ or $\boxed{STO}$ is used to store the numbers in the display, with $\boxed{MR}$ or $\boxed{RCL}$ used to recall the numbers from memory.

Other calculators have $\boxed{M+}$ and $\boxed{M-}$ keys. The $\boxed{M+}$ key adds the number displayed to the number already in memory. For example, if the memory contains the number 0 at the beginning of a problem, and the calculator display contains the number 29.4, then pushing $\boxed{M+}$ will cause 29.4 to be stored in the memory (the result of adding 0 and 29.4). If 57.8 is then entered into the display, pushing $\boxed{M+}$ will cause

$$29.4 + 57.8 = 87.2$$

to be stored. If 11.9 is then entered into the display, with $\boxed{M-}$ pushed, the memory will contain

$$87.2 - 11.9 = 75.3$$

The $\boxed{MR}$ key is used to recall the number in memory as needed, with $\boxed{MC}$ used to clear the memory.

Scientific calculators typically have one or more **memory registers** in which to store numbers. These memory keys are usually labeled $\boxed{STO}$ for store and $\boxed{RCL}$ for recall. For example, 32.5 can be stored in memory register 1 by

$$32.5\ \boxed{STO}\ 1$$

or it can be stored in memory register 2 by 32.5 $\boxed{STO}$ 2, and so forth. Values are retrieved from a particular memory register by using the $\boxed{RCL}$ key followed by the number of the register. For example, $\boxed{RCL}$ 2 recalls the contents of memory register 2.

With a scientific calculator, a number stays in memory until it is replaced by another number or until the memory is cleared. The contents of the memory are saved even when the calculator is turned off.

> **Quick TIP ▼**
> Always clear the memory before starting a problem; not doing so is a common error.

Using the Memory Registers   **EXAMPLE 12**

An elevator technician counted the number of people entering an elevator and also measured the weight of each group of people. Find the average weight per person.

NUMBER OF PEOPLE	TOTAL WEIGHT
6	839 pounds
8	1184 pounds
4	640 pounds

SOLUTION

First find the weight of all three groups and store in memory register 1.

$$839\ \boxed{+}\ 1184\ \boxed{+}\ 640\ \boxed{=}\ 2663\ \boxed{STO}\ 1$$

Then find the total number of people.

$$6 \boxed{+} 8 \boxed{+} 4 \boxed{=} 18$$

Finally, divide the contents of memory register 1 by the 18 people.

$$\boxed{\text{RCL}} \ 1 \boxed{\div} 18 \boxed{=} 147.94444 \text{ pounds}$$

This value can be rounded as needed.

QUICK CHECK 12

The following animals were brought to the market: 7 calves with a total weight of 2989 pounds; 10 calves with a total weight of 4490 pounds; and 17 calves with a total weight of 6953 pounds. Find the average weight of a calf to the nearest tenth of a pound.

OBJECTIVE 9 Solve chain calculations using order of operations. Long calculations involving several operations (adding, subtracting, multiplying, and dividing) must be done in a specific sequence called the **order of operations** and are called **chain calculations**. The logic of the following order of operations is built into most scientific calculators and can help us work problems without having to store a lot of intermediate values.

Order of Operations

Step 1   Do all operations inside parentheses first.

Step 2   Simplify any expressions with exponents and find any square roots.

Step 3   Multiply and divide from left to right.

Step 4   Add and subtract from left to right.

Using the Order of Operations Solve the following.

(a) $3 + 7 \times 9\dfrac{3}{4}$ **(b)** $42.1 \times 5 - 90 \div 4$

SOLUTION

Most calculators automatically keep track of the order of operations for us.

(a) $3 \boxed{+} 7 \boxed{\times} 9 \boxed{\text{a}^{\text{b/c}}} 3 \boxed{\text{a}^{\text{b/c}}} 4 \boxed{=} 71\dfrac{1}{4}$

(b) $42.1 \boxed{\times} 5 \boxed{-} 90 \boxed{\div} 4 \boxed{=} 188$

QUICK CHECK 13

Solve $9^2 + 2.7 \cdot 14$.

OBJECTIVE 10 Use the parentheses keys. The parentheses keys can be used to help establish the order of operations in a more complex chain calculation. For example, $\dfrac{4}{5 + 7}$ can be written as $\dfrac{4}{(5 + 7)}$, which can be solved as follows.

left-parenthesis key

$$4 \boxed{\div} \boxed{(} 5 \boxed{+} \boxed{7} \boxed{)} \boxed{=} 0.3333333$$

right-parenthesis key

Using Parentheses Solve the following problem.

$$\frac{16 \div 2.5}{39.2 - 29.8 \times .6}$$

SOLUTION

Think of this problem as follows:

$$\frac{(16 \div 2.5)}{(39.2 - 29.8 \times .6)}$$

Using parentheses to set off the numerator and denominator will help you minimize errors.

$$\boxed{(}\ 16\ \boxed{\div}\ 2.5\ \boxed{)}\ \boxed{\div}\ \boxed{(}\ 39.2\ \boxed{-}\ 29.8\ \boxed{\times}\ .6\ \boxed{)}\ \boxed{=}\ 0.3001876$$

QUICK CHECK 14

Solve $\dfrac{5^3 - 16}{253 - 4^2 \cdot 9}$

OBJECTIVE 11 Use the calculator for problem solution. Scientific calculators are great tools to help you solve problems.

Finding Sale Price **EXAMPLE 15**

A digital camera with an original price of $560 is on sale at 10% off. Find the sale price.

SOLUTION

If the discount from the original price is 10%, then the sale price is 100% − 10% of the original price.

$$560\ \boxed{\times}\ \boxed{(}\ 100\ \boxed{-}\ 10\ \boxed{)}\ \boxed{\%}\ \boxed{=}\ 504$$

On some calculators the following keystrokes will also work.

$$560\ \boxed{-}\ 10\ \boxed{\%}\ \boxed{=}\ 504$$

The sale price is $504.

QUICK CHECK 15

Find the price of a new home that was originally priced at $239,000 if the price was reduced by 15%.

Applying Calculator Use to Problem Solving **EXAMPLE 16**

A home buyer borrows $86,400 at 10% on a cottage, for 30 years. The monthly payment on the loan is $8.78 per $1000 borrowed. Annual taxes are $780, and fire insurance is $453 a year. Find the total monthly payment including taxes and insurance.

SOLUTION

The monthly payment is the *sum* of the monthly payment on the loan *plus* monthly taxes *plus* monthly fire insurance costs. The monthly payment on the loan is the number of thousands in the loan (86.4) times the monthly payment per $1000 borrowed (8.78).

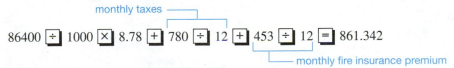

monthly taxes

$$86400\ \boxed{\div}\ 1000\ \boxed{\times}\ 8.78\ \boxed{+}\ 780\ \boxed{\div}\ 12\ \boxed{+}\ 453\ \boxed{\div}\ 12\ \boxed{=}\ 861.342$$

monthly fire insurance premium

To the nearest cent, this amount rounds to $861.34.

QUICK CHECK 16

An investor borrows $1,200,000 on a piece of commercial property. The monthly payment on the loan is $8.43 per $1000 of debt. Annual taxes and insurance are $28,200 and $6240, respectively. Find the monthly payment.

Applying Calculator Use to Problem Solving **EXAMPLE 17**

A Japanese company produces robotic dogs for the retail market. The dogs talk, cock their heads, bark, and walk. The company sells the robotic dogs to distributors for $256.80 each.

(a) Find the revenue to the manufacturer if the company sells 26,340 robotic dogs.

(b) Find the final price to the customer if the robotic dogs are marked up an average of 87% on cost.

SOLUTION

(a) Revenue = Number sold × Price of each

26340 ☒ 256.80 ▣ 6764112   or $6,764,112

(b) Sales price = Cost × (1 + Markup percent)

256.80 ☒ 1.87 ▣ 480.216   or   480.22

QUICK CHECK 17

It cost a manufacturer an average of $38.20 per pair for each of the 180,400 shoes produced in one month. The markup on the shoes is 35% based on cost. Find the total revenue to the company from the sale of the month's production.

appendix B Exercises

Solve the following problems on a calculator. Round each answer to the nearest hundredth.

1.
$$384.92$$
$$407.61$$
$$351.14$$
$$+ \quad 27.93$$

2.
$$85.76$$
$$21.94$$
$$+ \quad 39.89$$

3.
$$6850$$
$$321$$
$$+ \quad 4207$$

4.
$$781.42$$
$$304.59$$
$$+ \quad 261.35$$

5.
$$4270.41$$
$$- \quad 365.09$$

6.
$$3000.07$$
$$- \quad 48.12$$

7.
$$384.96$$
$$- \quad 129.72$$

8. $36.84 - 12.17$

9.
$$365$$
$$\times \quad 43$$

10.
$$27.51$$
$$\times \quad 1.18$$

11. 3.7×8.4

12. 62.5×81

13. $\dfrac{375.4}{10.6}$

14. $\dfrac{9625}{400}$

15. $96.7 \div 3.5$

16. $103.7 \div .35$

Solve the following chain calculations. Round each answer to the nearest hundredth.

17. $\dfrac{9 \times 9}{2 \times 5}$

18. $\dfrac{15 \times 8 \times 3}{11 \times 7 \times 4}$

19. $\dfrac{87 \times 24 \times 47.2}{13.6 \times 12.8}$

20. $\dfrac{2 \times (3 + 4)}{6 + 10}$

21. $\dfrac{2 \times 3 + 4}{6 + 10}$

22. $\dfrac{4200 \times .12 \times 90}{365}$

23. $\dfrac{640 - .6 \times 12}{17.5 + 3.2}$

24. $\dfrac{16 \times 18 \div .42}{95.4 \times 3 - .8}$

25. $\dfrac{14^2 - 3.6 \times 6}{95.2 \div .5}$

26. $\dfrac{9^2 + 3.8 \div 2}{14 + 7.5}$

Solve the following problems. Reduce any fractions to lowest terms or round to the nearest hundredth.

27. $7\dfrac{5}{8} \div \left(1 + \dfrac{3}{8}\right)$

28. $\left(5\dfrac{1}{4}\right)^2 \times 3.65$

29. $\left(\dfrac{3}{4} \div \dfrac{5}{8}\right)^3 \div 3\dfrac{1}{2}$

30. $\sqrt{6} \times \dfrac{3^2 + 2\frac{1}{2}}{7 \times \frac{5}{6}}$

31. Describe in your own words the order of operations to be used when solving chain calculations. (See Objective 9.)

32. Explain how the parentheses keys are used when solving chain calculations. (See Objective 10.)

Solve the following application problems on a calculator. Round each answer to the nearest cent.

33. Bucks County Community College Bookstore bought 397 used copies of a computer science book at a net cost of $46.40 each; 125 used copies of an accounting book at $38.40 each; and 740 used copies of a real estate text at $28.30 each. Find the total paid by the bookstore.

33. _____

34. Judy Martinez needs to file her expense account claims. She spent 5 nights at the Macon Holiday Inn at $104.19 per night and 4 nights at the Charlotte Super 8 motel at $86.80 per night. She then rented a car for 8 days at $36.40 per day. She drove the car 916 miles with a charge of $.28 per mile. Find her total expenses.

34. _____

35. In Virginia City, the sales tax is 6.5%. Find the tax on each of the following items: **(a)** a new car costing $17,908.43 and **(b)** a computer costing $1463.58.

(a) _____

(b) _____

36. Marja Strutz bought a two-year-old commercial fishing boat equipped for sardine fishing at a cost of $78,250. Additional safety equipment was needed at a cost of $4820, and sales tax of $7\frac{1}{4}$% was due on the boat and safety equipment. In addition she was charged a licensing fee of $1135 and a Coast Guard registration fee of $428. Strutz will pay $\frac{1}{3}$ of the total cost as a down payment and will borrow the balance. How much must she borrow?

36. _____

37. Becky Agnosti and her husband bought a small townhouse for $155,000. They paid $8000 down and agreed to make payments of $1002.80 per month for 30 years. By how much does the down payment and the sum of the monthly payments exceed the purchase price?

37. _____

38. Linda Smelt purchased a 20-unit apartment house for $620,000. She made a down payment of $150,000, which she had inherited from her parents, and agreed to make monthly payments of $5050 for 15 years. By how much does the sum of her down payment and all monthly payments exceed the original purchase price?

38. _____

39. Ben Hurd wishes to open a small repair shop but has only $32,400 in cash. He estimates that he will need $15,000 for equipment, $2800 for the first month's rent on a building, and about $28,000 operating expenses until the business is profitable. How much additional funding does he need?

39. _____

40. Koplan Kitchens wishes to expand their retail store. In order to do so, they must first purchase the $52,000 lot next door to them. They then anticipate $240,000 in construction costs plus an additional $57,000 for additional inventory. They have $100,000 in cash and must borrow the balance from a bank. How much must they borrow?

40. _____

41. A college bookstore buys a used textbook for $24.50 at the end of a semester and sells it at the beginning of the next semester for $60. Find the percent of markup on selling price to the nearest percent.

41. _____

42. A homebuilder spent the following when building a home: $37,800 for a cleared parcel of land with utility hookups, $59,600 for materials, and $24,300 for labor and other expenses. He then sold the home for $136,500. Find the percent markup over cost to the nearest percent.

42. _____

QUICK CHECK ANSWERS

1. 21.8
2. $174.09
3. 195.4
4. $14,100
5. .0125
6. 625
7. 110.592
8. 27
9. $1\frac{7}{16}$

10. $1\frac{5}{18}$
11. $1444.88
12. 424.5 pounds (rounded)
13. 118.8
14. 1
15. $203,150
16. $12,986
17. $9,303,228

appendix C

Financial Calculators

OBJECTIVES

1. Learn the basic conventions used with cash flows.
2. Learn the basic financial keys.
3. Understand which keys to use for a particular problem.
4. Use the calculator to solve financial problems.

Calculators are among the more popular inventions of recent times. The power and capability of calculators have increased significantly even as their cost has continued to fall. Today, programmable calculators costing less than $100 have more ability to solve problems than some of the early computers.

OBJECTIVE 1 Learn the basic conventions used with cash flows. There is a need to separate inflows of cash (cash received) from outflows of cash (cash paid out). The following convention is commonly used for this purpose and will be used throughout this appendix.

1. Inflows of cash (cash received) are **positive**.
2. Outflows of cash (cash paid out) are **negative**.

For example, assume that you are making regular investments into an account. Your payments are *outflows* of cash to you and should be considered *negative* numbers. The future value of your savings will eventually be returned to you as an inflow of cash, thereby as a positive number.

OBJECTIVE 2 Learn the basic financial keys. Financial calculators have special functions that allow the user to solve financial problems involving time, interest rates, and money. Many of the compound interest problems presented in this text can be solved using a financial calculator. Most financial calculators have financial keys similar to those shown below.

These keys represent the following functions (see Chapter 10 for a full definition of each term).

$\boxed{n}$—The number of compounding periods

$\boxed{i}$—The interest rate *per compounding period*

$\boxed{PV}$—Present value, the value in *today's* dollars

$\boxed{PMT}$—The amount of a level payment (for example, $625 per month); this is used for annuity type problems.

$\boxed{FV}$—Future value, the value at *some future date*

Note: Different financial calculators sometimes give slightly different answers to the same problems due to rounding.

OBJECTIVE 3 Understand which keys to use for a particular problem. Most simple financial problems require only four of the five financial keys described earlier. Both the number of compounding periods $\boxed{n}$ and the interest rate per compounding period $\boxed{i}$ *are needed for each financial problem*—these two keys will always be used. Which two of the remaining three financial keys ($\boxed{PV}$, $\boxed{PMT}$, and $\boxed{FV}$) are used depends on the particular problem. Using the convention described under Objective 1, one of these values will be negative and one will be positive. The process of solving a financial problem is to enter values for the three variables that are known, *then press the key for the unknown*, fourth variable.

For example, if you wish to know the future value of a series of known, equal payments, enter the specific values for ⎡n⎤, ⎡i⎤, and ⎡PMT⎤. Then press ⎡FV⎤ for the result. Or, if you wish to know how long it will take for an investment to grow to some specific value at a given interest rate, enter values for ⎡PV⎤, ⎡i⎤, and ⎡FV⎤. Then press ⎡n⎤ to find the required number of compounding periods.

Many financial calculators require that you enter a cash inflow as a positive number and a cash outflow as a negative number. Also, be sure to clear all values from the memory of your calculator before working a problem.

OBJECTIVE 4 Use the calculator to solve financial problems.

Finding *FV*, given *n*, *i*, and *PV* **EXAMPLE 1**

Barbara and Ivan Cushing invest $2500 that they received from the sale of the old family car in a stock mutual fund that has recently paid 8% compounded quarterly. Find the future value in 5 years if the fund continues to do as well.

SOLUTION

The present value of $2500 (a cash outflow is entered as a negative number) is compounded at 2% per quarter (8% ÷ 4 = 2%) for 20 quarters (4 × 5 = 20). Enter values for ⎡PV⎤, ⎡i⎤, and ⎡n⎤.

$$-2500 \; \boxed{PV} \; 2 \; \boxed{i} \; 20 \; \boxed{n}$$

Then press ⎡FV⎤ to find the compound amount at the end of 5 years.

$$\boxed{FV} \;\; \$3714.87, \text{ which is the future value}$$

> **QUICK CHECK 1**
>
> A lump sum of $28,000 is deposited in a retirement account paying 10% compounded quarterly. Find the future value in 10 years.

Finding *FV*, given *n*, *i*, and *PMT* **EXAMPLE 2**

Joan Jones plans to invest $100 at the end of each month in a mutual fund that she believes will grow at 9% per year compounded monthly. Find the future value at her retirement in 20 years.

SOLUTION

Two hundred forty payments (12 × 20 = 240) of $100 each (cash outflows entered as a negative number) are made into an account earning .75% per month (9% ÷ 12 = .75%). Enter values for ⎡n⎤, ⎡PMT⎤, and ⎡i⎤.

$$240 \; \boxed{n} \; -100 \; \boxed{PMT} \; .75 \; \boxed{i}$$

Press ⎡FV⎤ for the result.

$$\boxed{FV} \;\; \$66,788.69, \text{ which is the future value}$$

Quick TIP

The order in which data are entered into the calculator does not matter—just remember to press the financial key for the unknown value last.

> **QUICK CHECK 2**
>
> Benjamin Delton deposits $2500 at the end of each year into a retirement account paying 8% per year. Find the future value in 45 years.

Any one of the four values used to solve a particular financial problem *can be unknown*. Look at the next three examples in which the number of compounding periods ⎡n⎤, the payment amount ⎡PMT⎤, and the interest rate per compounding period ⎡i⎤, respectively, are unknown.

Finding *n*, given *i*, *PMT*, and *FV* **EXAMPLE 3**

Mr. Trebor needs $140,000 for a new farm tractor. He can invest $8000 at the end of each month in an account paying 6% per year compounded monthly. How many monthly payments are needed?

SOLUTION

The $8000 monthly payment (cash outflow) will grow at .5% per compounding period (6% ÷ 12 = .5%) until a future value of $140,000 (cash inflow at a future date) is accumulated. Enter values for ⎡PMT⎤, ⎡i⎤, and ⎡FV⎤.

$$-8000 \; \boxed{PMT} \; .5 \; \boxed{i} \; 140000 \; \boxed{FV}$$

Press $\boxed{\text{n}}$ to determine the number of payments.

$$\boxed{\text{n}} \quad \text{17 monthly payments of \$8000 each are needed}$$

Actually, 17 payments of $8000 each into an account earning .5% per month will grow to slightly more than $140,000.

$$-8000 \; \boxed{\text{PMT}} \quad .5 \; \boxed{\text{i}} \quad 17 \; \boxed{\text{n}}$$

Press $\boxed{\text{FV}}$ to determine the future value.

$$\boxed{\text{FV}} \quad \textbf{\$141,578.41}, \text{ which is the future value}$$

The 17th payment would need to be only

$$\$8000 - (\textbf{\$141,578.41} - \$140,000) = \$6421.59$$

to accumulate exactly $140,000.

QUICK CHECK 3

Black Coal, Inc., needs $1,280,000 for a new dredge. The firm can invest $21,200 at the end of each quarter in a fund earning 2% per quarter. Find the number of quarters needed to save up the required funds.

Finding *PMT*, given *n*, *i*, and *FV* Jane Abel wishes to have $1,000,000 at her retirement in 40 years. Find the payment she must make at the end of each quarter into an account earning 8% compounded quarterly to attain her goal.

SOLUTION

One hundred sixty payments ($40 \times 4 = 160$) are made into an account earning 2% per quarter ($8\% \div 4 = 2\%$) until a future value of $1,000,000 (cash inflow at a future date) is accumulated. Enter values for $\boxed{\text{n}}$, $\boxed{\text{i}}$, and $\boxed{\text{FV}}$.

$$160 \; \boxed{\text{n}} \quad 2 \; \boxed{\text{i}} \quad 1000000 \; \boxed{\text{FV}}$$

Press $\boxed{\text{PMT}}$ for the quarterly payment.

$$\boxed{\text{PMT}} \quad -\textbf{\$878.35}, \text{ which is the required quarterly payment of cash}$$

One hundred sixty payments of $878.35 at the end of each quarter into an account earning 8% compounded quarterly will grow to $1,000,000.

QUICK CHECK 4

Bill Watson has only 13 years until he retires and he wants to have $1 million at that time. He decides to make payments into a mutual fund at the end of each year, one that he hopes will earn 9% per year. Find the yearly payment needed.

Finding *i*, given *n*, *PV*, and *FV* Tom Fernandez bought 200 shares of stock in an oil company at $33.50 per share. Exactly three years later, he sold the stock at $41.25 per share. Find the annual rate, rounded to the nearest tenth of a percent, that Mr. Fernandez earned on this investment.

SOLUTION

In three years, the per-share price increased from a present value of $33.50 to a future value of $41.25. The purchase of the stock is a cash outflow, and the eventual sale of the stock is a cash inflow. It is not necessary to multiply the stock price by the number of shares—the interest rate indicating the return on the investment is the same whether 1 share or 200 shares are used. Enter values for $\boxed{\text{n}}$, $\boxed{\text{PV}}$, and $\boxed{\text{FV}}$.

$$3 \; \boxed{\text{n}} \quad -33.50 \; \boxed{\text{PV}} \quad 41.25 \; \boxed{\text{FV}}$$

Press $\boxed{\text{i}}$ for the annual interest rate.

$$\boxed{\text{i}} \quad \textbf{7.18}\%, \text{ or about 7.2\% per year}$$

Mr. Fernandez's return on his original investment compounded at 7.2% per year.

Interest rates can have a great influence on both individuals and businesses. Individuals borrow for homes, cars, and other personal items, whereas firms borrow to buy real estate, expand operations, or cover operating expenses. A small difference in interest rates can make *a large difference* in costs over time, as shown in the next example.

Comparing Monthly House Payments EXAMPLE 6

Hank and Francesca Wilson want to borrow $165,000 on a 30-year home mortgage. Find the monthly payment at interest rates of (**a**) 6% and (**b**) 8%. Find (**c**) the monthly savings at the lower rate and (**d**) the total savings if they make payments for the entire 30-year life of the mortgage.

SOLUTION

(**a**) Enter a present value of $165,000 (cash inflow) with 360 compounding periods (30 × 12 = 360) and a rate of .5% per month (6% ÷ 12 = .5) and press **PMT** to find the monthly payment.

$$165000 \; \boxed{PV} \; 360 \; \boxed{n} \; .5 \; \boxed{i}$$

PMT −**$989.26** is the monthly payment.

(**b**) Enter the values again using a rate of .66667% (8% ÷ 12 = .66667 rounded)

$$165000 \; \boxed{PV} \; 360 \; \boxed{n} \; .66667 \; \boxed{i}$$

PMT **$1210.72** is the monthly payment.

(**c**) Difference between payments = **$1210.72** − **$989.26**
= $221.46 per month

(**d**) Find the total difference in payments during the 30-year mortgage as follows.

$221.46 × 369 payments = $79,725.60

The lower rate will save a total of $79,725.60 in payments over the 30 years. Interest rates *do* make a difference!

Planning for Retirement EXAMPLE 7

Courtney and Nathan Wright plan to retire in 25 years and need $3500 per month for 20 years.

(**a**) Find the amount needed at retirement to fund the monthly retirement payments, assuming the funds earn 9% compounded monthly while payments are being made.

(**b**) Find the amount of the quarterly payment they must make for the next 25 years to accumulate the necessary funds, assuming earnings of 12% compounded quarterly during the accumulation period.

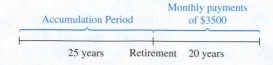
Accumulation Period   Monthly payments of $3500
25 years   Retirement   20 years

SOLUTION

(**a**) The accumulated funds at the end of 25 years are, at their retirement, a present value that must generate a cash inflow to the Wrights of $3500 per month for 240 months (20 × 12 = 240) assuming earnings of .75% per month (9% ÷ 12 = .75%). Enter values for **n**, **i**, and **PMT**.

$$240 \; \boxed{n} \; .75 \; \boxed{i} \; 3500 \; \boxed{PMT}$$

Press **PV** to find the amount needed at the end of 25 years.

PV **$389,007.34** is the amount they must accumulate

(b) The Wrights have 25 years of quarterly payments (100 payments that are cash outflows) in an account earning 3% per quarter (12% ÷ 4 = 3%) to accumulate a future value of $389,007.34. The question is what quarterly payment is required. Enter values for $\boxed{n}$, $\boxed{i}$, and $\boxed{FV}$.

$$100 \boxed{n} \; 3 \boxed{i} \; 389007.34 \boxed{FV}$$

Press $\boxed{PMT}$ to find the quarterly payment needed.

$\boxed{PMT}$ $640.57 is the required quarterly payment

Thus, the Wrights must make 100 end-of-quarter deposits of $640.57 each into an account earning 3% per quarter in order to subsequently receive 20 years of payments of $3500 per month, assuming 9% per year during the time that payments are made.

QUICK CHECK 7

Tom and Jane Blackstone plan to retire in 20 years. At that time, they believe they will need $60,000 per year for 25 years, not including income from Social Security. **(a)** If funds earn 7% per year during retirement, find the amount needed to fund their retirement when they retire, to the nearest dollar. **(b)** Find the end-of-the-year payment they must make for the next 20 years to have the needed amount at retirement, assuming funds earn 8% per year.

Using a financial calculator, solve the following problems for the missing quantity. Round dollar answers to the nearest cent, interest rates to the nearest hundredth of a percent, and number of compounding periods to the nearest whole number. Assume that any payments are made at the end of the period.

	n	i	PV	PMT	FV
1.	20	10%	$5800	—	_____
2.	7	8%	$8900	—	_____
3.	10	3%	_____	—	$12,000
4.	16	4%	_____	—	$8200
5.	7	8%	—	$300	_____
6.	25	2%	—	$1000	_____
7.	30	____	—	$319.67	$12,000
8.	50	____	—	$4718.99	$285,000
9.	360	1%	$83,500	_____	—
10.	180	.5%	$125,000	_____	—
11.	____	4%	$85,383	$5600	—
12.	____	2%	$3822	$100	—

Solve each of the following application problems.

13. Juanipa Manglimont inherited $23,500 from her father. She placed the money in a 5-year certificate of deposit earning 6% compounded quarterly. Find the future value at the end of 5 years.

13. _____

14. At the end of each month, Tina Ramirez has $50 taken out of her paycheck and invested in an account paying .5% per month. Find the future value at the end of 14 years.

14. _____

15. After a large down payment, Mr. and Mrs. Thrash borrowed $86,500 on a 30-year home loan at 9% per year. Find the monthly payment.

15. _____

16. Terrance Walker wishes to have $20,000 in 10 years when his son begins college. What payment must he make at the end of each quarter into an investment earning 10% compounded quarterly?

16. _____

17. The *Daily Gazette* needs $340,000 for a new printing press. The *Gazette* can invest $12,000 per month in an account paying .8% per month. Find the number of payments that must be paid before reaching the goal. Round to the nearest whole number.

17. _____

18. Cathy Cockrell anticipates that she will need $70,000 when her son Sam enters college. She can save $500 per month and earn 7% per year compounded monthly. How long will it take her to save the needed funds?

18. _____

19. Mr. and Mrs. Peters wish to build a home and must borrow $110,000 on a 30-year mortgage to do so. Find the highest acceptable annual interest rate, to the nearest tenth of a percent, if they cannot afford a monthly payment above $845.

19. _____

20. Jim Blalock needs to borrow $28,000 for a new work truck but cannot afford a payment of more than $700 per month. If a bank will finance the truck for 4 years, find the maximum interest rate Blalock can afford.

20. _____

QUICK CHECK ANSWERS

1. $75,181.79
2. $966,264.04
3. 40 quarters
4. $43,566.56
5. 8.7%

6. (a) $1061.87
   (b) $1174.68
   (c) $112.81
7. (a) $699,215
   (b) $15,279.39

answers to selected exercises

CHAPTER 1

Section 1.1 Exercises (Page 11)

1. seven thousand, forty **3.** thirty-seven thousand, nine hundred one **5.** four million, six hundred fifty thousand, fifteen **7.** 2070; 2100; 2000 **9.** 46,230; 46,200; 46,000 **11.** 106,050; 106,100; 106,000 **15.** 210 **17.** 2186 **19.** 1396 **21.** 983,493 **23.** 668 **25.** 2877 **27.** 21,546 **29.** 6,088,899 **31.** Totals horizontally: $293,267; $387,795; $426,869; $373,100; $1,481,031; Totals vertically: $269,761; $267,502; $206,932; $246,587; $244,616; $245,633; $1,481,031 **33.** 9374 **35.** 117,552 **37.** 1,696,876 **39.** 8,107,899 **41.** Estimate: 12,760; Exact: 12,605 **43.** Estimate: 600; Exact: 545 **45.** Estimate: 30,000; Exact: 29,986 **47.** $37 \times 18 = 666$; 66,600 **49.** $376 \times 6 = 2256$; 22,560,000 **51.** 1241 R1 **53.** 458 R21 **57.** 2385 R5 **59.** 58 R4 **61.** twenty-nine million, six hundred seventy-one thousand, three hundred **63.** three million, two hundred thousand **65.** 854,795 boxes **67.** 55,572,633 **69.** 200,000 chips **71.** 500 items per hour **73.** $3483 **75.** 6,533,000,000 pounds **77.** 2,771,000,000 pounds **79.** 6500 stores **81.** Dollar General; 8500 stores **83.** 2500 stores

Section 1.2 Exercises (Page 21)

1. 5208 sandwiches **3.** 100 billion fewer miles **5.** 383,250 veterans **7.** 8589 pounds **9.** $64 **11.** 6,098,400 square feet **13.** $378 **15.** $20,961 **17.** $375 **19.** 20 seats

Section 1.3 Exercises (Page 25)

1. thirty-eight hundredths **3.** five and sixty-one hundredths **5.** seven and four hundred eight thousandths **7.** thirty-seven and five hundred ninety-three thousandths **9.** four and sixty-two ten-thousandths **13.** 438.4 **15.** 97.62 **17.** 1.0573 **19.** 3.5827 **21.** $6.00 **23.** $.58 **25.** $1.17 **27.** 3.5; 3.52; 3.522 **29.** 2.5; 2.55; 2.548 **31.** 27.3; 27.32; 27.325 **33.** 36.5; 36.47; 36.472 **35.** .1; .06; .056 **37.** $5.06 **39.** $32.49 **41.** $382.01 **43.** $42.14 **45.** $.00 **47.** $1.50 **49.** $2.00 **51.** $752.80 **53.** $26 **55.** $0 **57.** $12,836 **59.** $395 **61.** $4700 **63.** $379 **65.** $722

Section 1.4 Exercises (Page 29)

1. $40 + 20 + 9 = 69$; 68.46 **3.** $6 + 4 + 5 + 7 + 2 = 24$; 23.82 **5.** $2000 + 5 + 3 + 7 = 2015$; 2171.414 **7.** $6000 + 500 + 20 + 8 = 6528$; 6666.061 **9.** $2000 + 70 + 500 + 600 + 400 = 3570$; 3451.446 **11.** 173.273 **13.** 59.3268 **17.** $15,138.19 **19.** $5.32 per pound **21.** $20 - 7 = 13$; 13.16 **23.** $50 - 20 = 30$; 31.507 **25.** $300 - 90 = 210$; 240.034 **27.** $8 - 3 = 5$; 4.848 **29.** $5 - 2 = 3$; 3.0198 **31.** $43,815.81

Section 1.5 Exercises (Page 35)

1. $100 \times 4 = 400$; 406.56 **3.** $30 \times 7 = 210$; 231.88 **5.** $40 \times 2 = 80$; 89.352 **7.** 1.9152 **9.** 9.3527 **11.** .002448 **13.** $152.63 **15.** $418.10 **17.** 8.075 **19.** 27.442 **21.** 57.977 (rounded) **25.** $14,790 **27.** 50.9 mpg **29.** 27 months **31.** (a) .43 inch (b) 4.3 inches **33.** $129.25 **35.** (a) $70.05 (b) $25.80

Case Study (Page 41)

1. $30,166 **2.** $5998 **3.** 162 guests; $6 left over **4.** $73.33 **5.** $644.25

Case in Point Summary Exercises (Page 42)

1. $2190.77 **2.** 19.5 hours; $168.68 **3.** $200.56; 213 customers **4.** $673.28; $14,280.19

Chapter 1 Test (Page 43)

1. 840 **2.** 22,000 **3.** 672,000 **4.** 50,000 **5.** 900,000 **6.** $606 **7.** $8399 **8.** $21.06 **9.** $364.35 **10.** $7246 **11.** 181.535 **12.** 498.795 **13.** 133.6 **14.** 3.7947 **15.** 15.8256 **16.** 8.0882 **17.** 11.56 **18.** 23.8 **19.** 4.25 **20.** $125.18 **21.** $3942.90 (rounded) **22.** 14,454 gallons saved **23.** $17.31 **24.** $.79 per pound (rounded) **25.** 253 seedlings

CHAPTER 2

Section 2.1 Exercises (Page 51)

1. $\frac{29}{8}$ **3.** $\frac{17}{4}$ **5.** $\frac{38}{3}$ **7.** $\frac{183}{8}$ **9.** $\frac{55}{7}$ **11.** $\frac{364}{23}$ **13.** $3\frac{1}{4}$ **15.** $2\frac{2}{3}$ **17.** $3\frac{4}{5}$ **19.** $13\frac{7}{11}$ **21.** $1\frac{62}{63}$ **23.** $7\frac{8}{25}$ **27.** $\frac{1}{2}$ **29.** $\frac{5}{8}$ **31.** $\frac{3}{5}$ **33.** $\frac{11}{12}$ **35.** 1 **37.** $\frac{7}{12}$ **41.** ✓ x ✓ x x ✓ x x **43.** ✓ ✓ ✓ ✓ ✓ x x ✓ **45.** ✓ ✓ x ✓ ✓ x ✓ ✓ **47.** ✓ x ✓ x x x x x

Section 2.2 Exercises (Page 57)

1. 16 **3.** 36 **5.** 48 **7.** 42 **9.** 24 **11.** 180 **13.** 480 **15.** 2100 **17.** 360 **21.** $\frac{2}{3}$ **23.** $\frac{1}{2}$ **25.** $\frac{17}{48}$ **27.** $1\frac{23}{36}$ **29.** $\frac{13}{14}$ **31.** $2\frac{1}{15}$ **33.** $2\frac{11}{36}$ **35.** $1\frac{13}{30}$ **37.** $\frac{9}{20}$ **39.** $\frac{7}{24}$ **43.** $\frac{23}{24}$ cubic yard **45.** $\frac{47}{60}$ inch **47.** $\frac{7}{24}$ of the contents **49.** $\frac{19}{24}$ of the debt **51.** $\frac{3}{16}$ inch **53.** $\frac{7}{24}$ **55.** work and travel; $\frac{1}{2}$ **57.** $\frac{1}{2}$ inch **59.** $\frac{1}{12}$ mile

Section 2.3 Exercises (Page 63)

1. $97\frac{4}{5}$ **3.** $80\frac{3}{4}$ **5.** $97\frac{7}{40}$ **7.** $53\frac{17}{24}$ **9.** $105\frac{107}{120}$ **11.** $7\frac{1}{8}$ **13.** $162\frac{1}{6}$ **15.** $9\frac{1}{24}$ **17.** $46\frac{23}{30}$ **19.** $\frac{7}{10}$ **23.** $116\frac{1}{2}$ inches **25.** 130 feet **27.** $1\frac{5}{8}$ cubic yards **29.** $22\frac{7}{8}$ hours

Section 2.4 Exercises (Page 71)

1. $\frac{3}{10}$ **3.** $\frac{99}{160}$ **5.** $\frac{9}{32}$ **7.** $4\frac{3}{8}$ **9.** $9\frac{1}{3}$ **11.** $\frac{1}{3}$ **13.** $4\frac{7}{12}$ **15.** $1\frac{7}{9}$ **17.** $\frac{3}{5}$ **19.** $1\frac{1}{2}$ **21.** $\frac{2}{3}$ **23.** $2\frac{2}{3}$ **25.** $\frac{3}{20}$ **27.** $8\frac{2}{5}$ **31.** $12 **33.** $18.75 **37.** 6¢ **39.** 36 yards **41.** 12 homes **43.** $2632\frac{1}{2}$ inches **45.** 2480 anchors **47.** 471 gallons **49.** 88 dispensers **51.** 5 trips

Section 2.5 Exercises (Page 77)

1. $\frac{3}{4}$ **3.** $\frac{6}{25}$ **5.** $\frac{73}{100}$ **7.** $\frac{17}{20}$ **9.** $\frac{17}{50}$ **11.** $\frac{111}{250}$ **13.** $\frac{5}{8}$ **15.** $\frac{161}{200}$ **17.** $\frac{12}{125}$ **19.** $\frac{3}{80}$ **21.** $\frac{3}{16}$ **23.** $\frac{1}{625}$ **27.** .25 **29.** .375 **31.** .667 (rounded) **33.** .778 (rounded) **35.** .636 (rounded) **37.** .88 **39.** .883 (rounded) **41.** .993 (rounded) **43.** (a) .667 (b) 91 quit smoking

Case Study (Page 81)

1. $288,000 **2.** $\frac{5}{12}$; $\frac{1}{4}$; $\frac{1}{12}$; $\frac{1}{16}$; $\frac{1}{16}$; $\frac{1}{8}$ **3.** Miscellaneous: $\frac{1}{8}$; Insurance: $\frac{1}{16}$; Advertising: $\frac{1}{16}$; Utilities: $\frac{1}{12}$; Rent: $\frac{1}{4}$; Salaries: $\frac{5}{12}$ **4.** 150°; 90°; 30°; 22.5°; 22.5°; 45°

Case in Point Summary Exercises (Page 82)

1. $193\frac{1}{2}$ inches **2.** $467\frac{5}{8}$ square inches **3.** $2805\frac{3}{4}$ square inches **4.** 4 side panels

Chapter 2 Test (Page 83)

1. $\frac{5}{6}$ **2.** $\frac{7}{8}$ **3.** $\frac{7}{11}$ **4.** $8\frac{1}{8}$ **5.** $4\frac{2}{3}$ **6.** $2\frac{2}{3}$ **7.** $\frac{31}{4}$ **8.** $\frac{94}{5}$ **9.** $\frac{147}{8}$ **10.** 30 **11.** 120
12. 72 **13.** $\frac{7}{8}$ **14.** $15\frac{1}{16}$ **15.** $36\frac{5}{16}$ **16.** 36 **17.** $1\frac{1}{2}$ **18.** $24\frac{1}{8}$ pounds
19. \$340 **20.** $35\frac{7}{8}$ gallons **21.** 64 blouses **22.** $\frac{5}{8}$ **23.** $\frac{41}{50}$
24. .25 inch **25.** .875 inch

CHAPTER 3

Section 3.1 Exercises (Page 91)

1. 25% **3.** 72% **5.** 203.4% **7.** 362.5% **9.** 87.5% **11.** .05% **13.** 345%
15. 3.08% **17.** .625 **19.** .65 **21.** .125 **23.** .125 **25.** .0025 **27.** .8475
29. 1.75 **31.** .5; 50% **33.** $\frac{7}{8}$; 87.5% **35.** $\frac{1}{125}$; .008 **37.** 10.5; 1050%
39. $\frac{13}{20}$; 65% **41.** $\frac{1}{200}$; .5% **43.** $.333\overline{3}$; $33\frac{1}{3}$% **45.** $2\frac{1}{2}$; 250% **47.** $\frac{17}{400}$;
.0425 **49.** .015; 1.5% **51.** $10\frac{3}{8}$; 10.375 **53.** $\frac{1}{400}$; .25% **55.** $\frac{3}{8}$; .375

Section 3.2 Exercises (Page 97)

1. 62 homes **3.** \$604 **5.** 4.8 feet **7.** 10,185 miles **9.** 182 cell phones
11. 148.44 yards **13.** \$5366.65 **17.** 238 people **19.** \$429.92
21. 44 females **23.** 8.95 ounces **25.** 4853 accidents **27. (a)** 28.6%
female **(b)** 313,099 female **29.** \$239.25 **31.** 2156 products
33. 1,628,894 units **35.** \$51,844.20 **37.** \$6296.40 **39.** \$199.89
41. \$87.58

Section 3.3 Exercises (Page 103)

1. 2120 **3.** 325 **5.** 2000 **7.** 4800 **9.** 44,000 **11.** 20,000 **13.** \$90,320
15. 1080 **17.** 312,500 **19.** 65,400 **21.** 40,000 **25.** 107.1 million
households **27.** 7761 students **29.** \$4500 **31.** \$2050 **33.** 1749 owners
35. \$185,500

Supplementary Exercises (Page 105)

1. 16 ounces **3.** \$288,150 **5.** 478,175 Mustangs **7.** 162 calories
9. \$39,000 **11.** 230 companies **13.** 55 companies

Section 3.4 Exercises (Page 109)

1. 10 **3.** 50 **5.** 28.3 **7.** 76 **9.** 4.1 **11.** 5.9 **13.** 1.3 **15.** 250 **17.** 27.8
21. 6.2% **23.** 2% **25.** 8.7% **27.** 65% **29.** 69.1%

Supplementary Exercises (Page 111)

1. 97 people **3.** 40% **5.** 1100 boaters **7.** \$370.14 **9.** \$568.80
11. 4% **13.** 4 million riders **15.** 62.1% **17.** China—12%; India—
55%; United States—40%; Indonesia—39%; Brazil—25%;
Pakistan—126% **19.** China—1,417,000,000; India—1,614,000,000
21. 5760 items **23.** \$5886 **25.** \$6528 **27.** 5742 deaths **29. (a)** 36%
(b) 64%

Section 3.5 Exercises (Page 119)

1. \$375 **3.** \$27.91 **5.** \$25 **7.** \$854.50 **11.** \$195,500 **13. (a)** \$950
(b) \$76 **15.** 842,857 restaurants **17.** \$66.12 **19.** 3,437,500
subscribers **21.** 21.4 million **23.** \$3864 **25.** \$145.24 million
27. 51.2 million **29.** 30,000 students **31.** 695 deaths **33.** 14,742
fewer unemployed

Case Study (Page 125)

Amazon.com—96.5%; Bank of America—\$17.24;
McDonald's—\$56.04; Wal-Mart Stores—\$54.12

Case in Point Summary Exercises (Page 126)

1. 3.2% **2.** \$1,181,640 **3.** \$13,488 **4.** \$82,976.25

Chapter 3 Test (Page 127)

1. 37.5% **2.** $\frac{7}{20}$ **3.** .024 **4.** $\frac{7}{50}$ **5.** 587.5% **6.** 300 home sales **7.** \$3.15
8. $\frac{6}{25}$ **9.** 1920 purchase orders **10.** $\frac{7}{8}$ **11.** \$.53 **12.** 224,000 units
13. \$20,654.98 **14.** 315.4 million people **15. (a)** 11% **(b)** \$4488

per year **16.** 75% **17.** \$186.25 **18.** 1200 backpacks **19.** 6.2%
20. \$1.47 billion

CHAPTER 4

Section 4.1 Exercises (Page 135)

1. 3 **3.** 31 **5.** 3 **7.** 7 **9.** 2 **11.** 30 **13.** 7.5 **15.** 10 **17.** 4 **19.** 1.5 **21.** 7
23. 1

Section 4.2 Exercises (Page 143)

1. $27 + x$ **3.** $22 + x$ **5.** $x - 4$ **7.** $x - 3\frac{1}{2}$ **9.** $3x$ **11.** $\frac{3}{5}x$ **13.** $\frac{9}{x}$ **15.** $\frac{16}{x}$
17. $2.1(4 + x)$ **19.** $7(x - 3)$ **21.** $12y$ **23.** $472 - x$ **25.** $73 - x$
27. $\frac{20,210}{x}$ **29.** $21 - x$ **31.** 13 **33.** 1.5 **35.** 1 **37.** $1\frac{3}{7}$ **39.** 59 stereos
41. 207 employees **43.** \$20,500 **45.** \$30,000 office; \$105,000
retail **47.** 3 new; 19 experienced **49.** 81 Altimas; 39 Sentras

Section 4.3 Exercises (Page 151)

1. \$586.50 **3.** \$10,080 **5.** \$16.50 **7.** 14 **9.** 2250 **11.** 151.2
13. \$749.86 **15.** 7.5 **17.** 7 **19.** 24,000 **21.** $L = \frac{A}{W}$ **23.** $V = \frac{nRT}{P}$
25. $P = \frac{M}{(1 + i)^n}$ **27.** $i = \frac{A - P}{P}$ **29.** $D = \frac{M - P}{MT}$ **31.** $h = \frac{2A}{b + B}$
33. \$2.40 **35.** \$93.80 **37. (a)** \$427 **(b)** \$502.50 **39.** \$236 million
41. \$2.29 **43.** \$644,400 **45.** \$390 **47.** .13, or 13% **49.** 4 years
51. \$4000 **53.** \$4500

Section 4.4 Exercises (Page 161)

1. $\frac{9}{32}$ **3.** $\frac{27}{1}$ **5.** $\frac{4}{3}$ **7.** $\frac{3750}{1}$ **9.** $\frac{225}{1}$ **11.** $\frac{8}{5}$ **13.** $\frac{1}{6}$ **15.** $\frac{4}{15}$ **17.** $\frac{9}{2}$ **19.** T **21.** F **23.** F
25. F **27.** F **29.** F **31.** T **33.** T **35.** F **37.** T **39.** 7 **41.** 72 **43.** 105
45. $3\frac{1}{2}$ **47.** 24 **49.** 8 **53.** 1575 tickets **55.** \$516,000 **57.** \$360
59. 2.6°F **61.** 1020 miles **63.** \$713,211.20 **65.** \$128,000
67. 350 miles **69.** 3,500,000 cubic meters **71.** \$214.26 U.S.

Case Study (Page 167)

1. \$10,460; \$16,400 **2.** \$3000 **3.** Answers will vary.

Case in Point Summary Exercises (Page 168)

1. Answers will vary, but here are some obvious things: Sales
of light trucks have increased dramatically since 1985, but sales
of cars have fallen off. Sales of both light trucks and cars fell
sharply in 2009. General Motors has a lot of competition and
was only slightly larger than Ford or Toyota in 2009. **2.** 60,720
vehicles **3.** 128,490 vehicles **4.** 22,756 vehicles

Chapter 4 Test (Page 171)

1. 51 **2.** 50.7 **3.** 16.3 **4.** $5\frac{1}{4}$ **5.** 258 **6.** 136 **7.** 56 **8.** $13\frac{1}{2}$ **9.** 7 **10.** $1\frac{2}{3}$
11. 21 **12.** 3.6 **13.** $I = 504$ **14.** $S = 324$ **15.** $G = 3183.6$
16. $M = 493.50$ **17.** $R = .05$ **18.** $A = 12,000$ **19.** $D = 200$
20. $I = 75$ **21.** $d = .84$ **22.** $I = 120$ **23.** $\frac{A}{L}$ **24.** $\frac{d}{t}$ **25.** $\frac{I}{PR}$ **26.** $\frac{P - 1}{T}$
27. $\frac{A - P}{PR}$ **28.** $\frac{D}{1 - DT}$ **29.** $\frac{1}{5}$ **30.** $\frac{9}{22}$ **31.** $\frac{8}{5}$ **32.** $\frac{1}{6}$ **33.** $\frac{7}{12}$ **34.** $\frac{1}{6}$ **35.** true
36. false **37.** false **38.** true **39.** true **40.** true **41.** 175 **42.** 39 **43.** 5
44. 27 **45.** 8 **46.** 32 **47.** $\frac{7}{2}$ or $3\frac{1}{2}$ **48.** $\frac{15}{2}$ or $7\frac{1}{2}$ **49.** 12 **50.** 47 **51.** 60
52. 8 **53.** 15 **54.** 2 **55.** 45; 46 **56.** 119; 121 **57.** \$1.74 **58.** 19 men;
28 women **59.** \$2056 **60.** \$430,000 **61.** \$12 **62.** \$114.25 **63.** \$16
64. \$1200

Cumulative Review: Chapters 1–4 (Page 175)

1. 65,500 **3.** 78.4 **5.** 3609 **7.** 24,092 **9.** 85 **11.** 35.174 **13.** 12.218
15. \$98 **17.** \$31,658.27 **19.** $\frac{8}{9}$ **21.** $7\frac{2}{15}$ **23.** $13\frac{13}{24}$ **25.** 3 **27.** $12\frac{1}{2}$ square
feet **29.** 130 feet **31.** $\frac{13}{20}$ **33.** 87.5% **35.** 2170 home loans **37.** 25%
39. 1.03% **41.** 97,757 copies **43.** 45,000% **45. (a)** 83% **(b)** 1.909
billion pounds **47.** .69 billion pounds **49.** 6 **51.** $7\frac{1}{5}$ **53.** $l = \$337.5$
55. $R = .07$ **57.** $T = \frac{I}{PR}$ **59.** $P = \frac{M}{(1 + i)^n}$ **61.** $\frac{20}{29}$ **63.** $\frac{7}{20}$ **65.** 46
67. \$111.97 **69.** \$10,924

CHAPTER 5

Section 5.1 Exercises (Page 189)

1. $14.20 **3.** $20.00 **5.** $17.10 **7.** $21.90 **9.** Mar. 8; $380.71; Nola Akala; Tutoring; 3971.28; 79.26; 4050.54; 380.71; 3669.83 **11.** Dec. 4; $37.52; Paul's Pools; Chemicals; 1126.73; 1126.73; 37.52; 1089.21 **17.** Oct. 10; $39.12; County Clerk; License; 5972.89; 752.18; 23.32; 6748.39; 39.12; 6709.27 **19.** 9412.64; 8838.86; 8726.71; 9479.99; 10,955.68; 10,529.13; 9891.20; 9825.58; 9577.41; 9913.26; 9462.76 **21.** 574.86; 384.36; 462.65; 620.07; 581.31; 405.43; 784.71; 587.51; 562.41; 487.41; 1209.76

Section 5.2 Exercises (Page 197)

1. $1595.36 **3.** $1387.67 **5.** $1352.98 **7.** $203.86 **9.** $66.48 **11.** $1064.72 **13.** $991.89 **15.** $972.05 **17.** $60.21 **19.** $29.62

Section 5.3 Exercises (Page 203)

1. $4870.24 **3.** $7690.62 **5.** $18,314.72 **11.** 421, $371.52; 424, $429.07; 427, $883.69; 429, $35.62; $1719.90; $6875.09; 701.56; 421.78; 689.35; 8687.78; 1719.90; $6967.88; $6965.92; 8.75; 6957.17; 10.71; $6967.88 **13.** 765, $63.24; 768, $135.76; $199.00; $5636.51; 220.16; 5856.67; 199.00; $5657.67; $5858.85; 209.30; 5649.55; 8.12; $5657.67

Case Study (Page 209)

1. $8178.46 **2.** $204.46 **3.** $9810.36 total of checks outstanding **4.** $4882.58 deposits not recorded **5.** $7274.56

Case in Point Summary Exercises (Page 210)

Checks Outstanding $763—$723.35, $764—$3290.41; Total $4013.76; $13,272.17, 0, $13,272.17, −$4013.76, $9258.41; $9266.79, −$8.95, $9257.84, $.57, $9258.41

Chapter 5 Test (Page 213)

1. $19.90 **2.** $9.40 **3.** $17.40 **4.** Aug. 6; $6892.12; WBC Broadcasting; Airtime; $16,409.82; 16,409.82 764; 6892.12; 9517.70 **5.** Aug. 8; $1258.36; Lakeland Weekly; Ad; 9517.70; 1572.00; 11,089.70; 1258.36; 9831.34 **6.** Aug. 14; $416.14; W. Wilson; Freelance Art; 9831.34; 10,000.00; 19,831.34; 416.14; 19,415.20 **7.** $1709.55 **8.** $81.99 **9.** $1627.56 **10.** $56.96 **11.** $1570.60 **12.** $5482.18 current balance

CHAPTER 6

Section 6.1 Exercises (Page 223)

1. 40; 0; $12.15 **3.** 38.75; 0; $28.05 **5.** 40; 5.25; $17.22 **7.** $329.60; $92.70; $422.30 **9.** $380; $160.31; $540.31 **11.** $13.20; $347.60; $0; $347.60 **13.** $21.60; $576.00; $97.20; $673.20 **15.** $13.77; $367.20; $58.52; $425.72 **17.** 50.5; 10.5; $4.75; $479.75; $49.88; $529.63 **19.** 53.5; 13.5; $6.25; $668.75; $84.38; $753.13 **21.** 35; 6; $14.10; $329.00; $84.60; $413.60 **23.** 39.5; 3.75; $16.20; $426.60; $60.75; $487.35 **25.** 39.75; 3.5; $32.25; $854.63; $112.88; $967.51 **29.** $443.08; $886.15; $1920; $23,040 **31.** $1200; $2400; $2600; $62,400 **33.** $1660; $1798.33; $3596.67; $43,160 **35.** $387 **37.** $467.25 **39.** $832 **41.** $788.80 **43.** $556.32 **45. (a)** $1260 biweekly **(b)** $1365 semimonthly **(c)** $2730 monthly **(d)** $32,760 annually

Section 6.2 Exercises (Page 233)

1. $93.12 **3.** $153.60 **5.** $49.80 **7.** $52.68 **11.** $353.60 **13.** $371.90 **15.** $397.48 **17.** $471.50 **19.** $608.10 **21.** $421.65 **23.** $1405 **25.** $688.40 **27.** $478.10 **29.** $628.61

Section 6.3 Exercises (Page 239)

1. $26.04; $6.09 **3.** $28.72; $6.72 **5.** $52.99; $12.39 **7.** $189.39 **9.** $308.99 **11.** $41.56 **13.** $368.80; $76.07; $444.87; $27.58; $6.45; $4.45 **15.** $568; $106.50; $674.50; $41.82; $9.78; $6.75 **17.** $467.20; $122.64; $589.84; $36.57; $8.55; $5.90 **19. (a)** $24.07 **(b)** $5.63 **21. (a)** $95.67 **(b)** $22.38 **(c)** $15.43 **23.** $7221.60; $1688.92 **25.** $3609; $844.04 **27.** $3328.61; $778.46

Section 6.4 Exercises (Page 251)

1. $101 **3.** $22 **5.** $85 **7.** $39 **9.** $11 **11.** $33 **13.** $6.87 **15.** $28.00 **17.** $69.11 **19.** $35.73; $8.36; $0; $532.19 **21.** $217.78; $50.93; $397.24, $2846.58 **23.** $141.16; $33.01; $156.54; $1946.12 **25.** $184.21; $43.08; $192.24; $2551.53 **27.** $232.70; $54.42; $669.40; $2796.66 **29.** $110.76; $25.90; $348.78; $1301.00 **35.** $8748.05 **37.** $53,332.52 **39.** $44,323.10 **41.** $691.67 **43.** $568.17 **45.** $3839.87

Case Study (Page 258)

1. $818 **2.** $368.10 **3.** $1186.10 **4.** $73.54 **5.** $17.20 **6.** $185.58 **7.** $11.86 **8.** $52.19 **9.** $608.73

Case in Point Summary Exercises (Page 259)

1. Betinez: $245.00; $15.19; $3.55; $3.68; $7.52; $2.45; $212.61 Parton: $581.88; $36.08; $8.44; $13.85; $17.86; $5.82; $474.83 Dickens: $280.50; $17.39; $4.07; $18.28; $8.61; $2.81; $219.34 **2.** $450; $205.92; $655.92; $40.67; $9.51; $23.53; $20.14; $6.56; $490.51 **3.** FICA—$218.66; Medicare—$51.14; Federal Taxes—$55.31; Total—$325.11 **4.** State Income Tax—$54.13; State disability insurance—$17.64; Total—$71.77

Chapter 6 Test (Page 261)

1. 40; 6.5; $537.30 **2.** 40; 7.5; $440.75 **3. (a)** $655 weekly **(b)** $1310 biweekly **(c)** $1419.17 semimonthly **(d)** $2838.33 monthly **4.** $425 **5.** $3532.50 **6. (a)** $576.60 **(b)** $134.85 **7. (a)** $477.40 **(b)** $134.85 **8.** $17 **9.** $26 **10.** $113 **11.** $25 **12.** $3 **13.** $1525.55 **14.** $749.76 **15.** $568.10 **16. (a)** $31.90 **(b)** $7.46 **(c)** $5.14 **17. (a)** $162.71 **(b)** $38.42 **18. (a)** $4552.55 **(b)** $1064.71 **19. (a)** $5255.20 **(b)** $1229.04 **20.** $2246.54

CHAPTER 7

Section 7.1 Exercises (Page 271)

1. $226.80 **3.** $126.36 **5.** $3610.36 **7.** $4935.88 **9.** $57.00 **11.** $28.40 **13.** $501.20 **15.** foot **17.** pair **19.** kilogram **21.** case **23.** drum **25.** liter **27.** gallon **29.** cash on delivery **33.** $.9 \times .8 = .72$ **35.** $.9 \times .9 \times .9 = .729$ **37.** $.75 \times .95 = .7125$ **39.** $.6 \times .7 \times .8 = .336$ **41.** $.5 \times .9 \times .8 \times .95 = .342$ **43.** $267.52 **45.** $14.02 **47.** $722.93 **49.** $218.88 **51.** $16.83 **53.** $714.42 **55.** $972 **57.** $640 **63.** $182.24 **65. (a)** 20/15 **(b)** $4.08 **67. (a)** 15/20 **(b)** $.55 **69.** $1280.45 **71.** $56, 677 **73.** $326.40 undercharged

Section 7.2 Exercises (Page 277)

1. .72; 28% **3.** .68; 32% **5.** .504; 49.6% **7.** .5184; 48.16% **11.** $720 **13.** $2280 **15.** $388 **17.** $5933.81 **19.** $89.30 **21.** $207.09 **23. (a)** $25.89 wholesale **(b)** $28.76 retailer's price **(c)** $2.87

Section 7.3 Exercises (Page 283)

1. May 14; June 3 **3.** July 25; Sept. 8 **5.** Oct. 1; Oct. 11 **7.** $1.70; $92.20 **9.** $0; $81.25 **11.** $21.60; $1120.55 **15.** $4542.69 **17.** $1798.92 **19. (a)** Jan. 28; Feb. 7; Feb. 17 **(b)** Mar. 9 **21. (a)** Apr. 25 **(b)** May 5

Section 7.4 Exercises (Page 289)

1. Mar. 10; Mar. 30 **3.** Dec. 22; Jan. 11 **5.** June 16; July 6
7. $20.47; $661.81 **9.** $0; $785.64 **11.** $229.60; $11,250.40
13. $.72; $23.23 **17. (a)** Dec. 13 **(b)** $2334.93 **19.** $6586.09
21. $1495.58 **23. (a)** $1467.39 **(b)** $549.51 **25. (a)** June 10
(b) June 30 **27.** $1509.75 due **29. (a)** $3350.52 **(b)** $1052.06

Case Study (Page 295)

1. $1151.92 **2.** $78.56 **3.** 17.7%

Case in Point Summary Exercises (Page 296)

1. $17,750.66 **2.** October 15 **3.** November 4 **4.** $17,966.52
5. $10,309.28; $8189.76

Chapter 7 Test (Page 297)

1. $225.65 **2.** $784.80 **3. (a)** .63 **(b)** 37% **4. (a)** .576 **(b)** 42.4%
5. Mar. 15 **6.** May 30 **7.** Jan. 15 **8.** Dec. 19 **9. (a)** $788.80 **(b)** $773.02
(c) $811.77; $560; $52; $101.20; $75.60; $788.80; $15.78; $773.02;
$811.77 **10.** $91,300.78 **11. (a)** July 20 **(b)** $3041.28 **12.** $437.48
13. (a) Builders Supply **(b)** $1.91 **14. (a)** $1762.20 **(b)** $1780 full
amount **15.** $2527.08 **16. (a)** $1882.59 **(b)** $1900.39

CHAPTER 8

Section 8.1 Exercises (Page 305)

1. 140%; $4.96; $17.36 **3.** 100%; 20%; $27.17; $5.43 **5.** 100%;
130%; $168.00; $218.40 **7.** $2.70; $11.70 **9.** 60%; $19.20
11. $61.44; 40% **13.** $33.80; 25% **17.** $148.64 markup **19.** $12.95
selling price **21.** $221.40 selling price **23. (a)** $95.96 **(b)** 25%
(c) 125% **25. (a)** 126% **(b)** $567 selling price **(c)** $117 markup

Section 8.2 Exercises (Page 313)

1. 75%; $21.00; $28.00 **3.** 58%; 42%; $105.00 **5.** 50%; 100%;
$2025; $4050 **7.** $1920; $2400.00 **9.** $8.46; $22.26; 61.3%
11. $750; $1050; 28.6% **13.** 50% **15.** 15.3% **19. (a)** $1250 selling
price **(b)** $812.50 cost **(c)** 65% **21. (a)** $1507 **(b)** $577 **(c)** 38.3%
(d) 62.0% **23.** $1.13

Supplementary Exercises (Page 315)

1. $559.52 **3.** 19.1% **5.** $6.98 **7.** $119 **9. (a)** 76% **(b)** $147.89
(c) $35.49 **11. (a)** $32.40 **(b)** 25.9% **13. (a)** $24.90 **(b)** 12.5%
(c) 14.2% **15.** $35.00

Section 8.3 Exercises (Page 321)

1. 25%; $645 **3.** 30%; $18.48 **5.** 20%; $5.20 **7.** $120; $20; none
9. $16; $22; $6 **11.** $385; $250; $60 **15.** 41% **17.** $30.01 operating
loss **19. (a)** $77.15 operating loss **(b)** $18.77 absolute loss

Section 8.4 Exercises (Page 329)

1. $22,673 **3.** $60,568 **5.** 2.83; 2.81 **7.** 3.59; 3.52 **9.** 4.69; 4.66
11. $182; $195; $170 **13.** $2352; $2385; $2312.50 **17.** 5.43 turnover
at cost **19. (a)** $508.50 weighted-average method **(b)** $562.50
FIFO **(c)** $520 LIFO **21. (a)** $1251.20 weighted-average method
(b) $1430 FIFO **(c)** $1040 LIFO **23.** $30,660

Case Study (Page 337)

1. $125 original selling price **2.** $2062.50 total selling price
3. $375 operating loss **4.** none

Case in Point Summary Exercises (Page 338)

1. Steep Alpine $293; Cliff Hoppers $327 **2.** Steep Alpine
$404.34; Cliff Hoppers $451.26 **3.** $9109 **4.** .54 **5.** Steep Alpine
$242.60; Cliff Hoppers $270.76 **6.** $1804.94 operating loss
7. Discussion may vary, but either is acceptable.

Chapter 8 Test (Page 341)

1. (a) 20 **(b)** 120 **(c)** 76.80 **2. (a)** 138 **(b)** 365.50 **(c)** 138.89
3. (a) 80 **(b)** 20 **(c)** 33.60 **4. (a)** 75 **(b)** 25 **(c)** 18.45 **5.** 20%
6. 50% **7.** $200; $14; none **8.** $72; $99; $27 **9.** 5.76; 5.73 **10.** $25
selling price per pair **11.** $4200 **12.** 40% **13. (a)** $37.99 **(b)** 19.0%
(rounded) **(c)** 23.5% **14.** 28% **15. (a)** $131.10 operating loss
(b) $45.60 absolute loss **16.** $130,278 average inventory
17. $12,978 weighted-average method **18. (a)** $11,775 FIFO
(b) $13,350 LIFO

Cumulative Review Chapters 5–8 (Page 343)

1. $1958.20 **3.** $1749.75 **5.** $1727.88 **7.** $4359.38 **9.** $240.47
11. 62.2% **13.** Nov. 15; Dec. 5 **15.** $400; $280; $32 **17.** $93.11
(rounded) **19.** 12.88 turnover at cost **21.** $6489 weighted-average
method

CHAPTER 9

Section 9.1 Exercises (Page 353)

1. $209; $4009 **3.** $440; $5940 **5.** 68 **7.** 99 **9. (a)** $2493.15
(b) $2527.78 **(c)** $34.63 **11. (a)** $1091.10 **(b)** $1106.25 **(c)** $15.15
13. Helen Spence **15.** Donna Sharp **17.** 90 days **19.** Jan. 25
21. Oct. 18; $5064 **23.** May 9; $6591.38 **25. (a)** $138,750
(b) $2,138,750 **27.** $16,800 **29. (a)** Oct. 3 **(b)** $7008.41
31. (a) Sept. 6 **(b)** $84,200 **33.** $86.17 **35. (a)** Sept. 30
(b) $136,106.67

Section 9.2 Exercises (Page 361)

1. $14,000 **3.** $5040 **5.** $10,800 **7.** 11.8% **9.** 9.5% **11.** 7.5%
13. 120 days **15.** 62 days **17.** 5 months **19.** $10,200 **21.** 9.5%
23. 10.75% **25. (a)** $10,800 **(b)** $11,250 **27.** 76 days **29.** 4%
31. (a) $12,000 **(b)** $1200 **33.** 208 days **35. (a)** 10.75% **(b)** 11.4%

Section 9.3 Exercises (Page 371)

1. $234; $7566 **3.** $950; $18,050 **5.** $408.33; $21,991.67 **7.** Jun. 20;
$6248 **9.** Dec. 9; $9572.92 **11.** Feb. 8; $23,600 **13. (a)** $220
(b) $5780 **15.** 200 days **17.** 10% **19.** $7891.30 **21. (a)** $3780
(b) 13.3% **23.** 105 days **25. (a)** 166,107,382.60 yen **(b)** 8.1%
27. (a) $11,262.50 **(b)** 8.9% **29. (a)** $24,625,000 **(b)** $25,000,000
(c) $375,000 **(d)** 6.09%

Section 9.4 Exercises (Page 381)

1. 107 days **3.** 53 days **5.** $10,179 **7.** $24,812.50 **9.** $6362.75;
37 days; $78.47; $6284.28 **11.** $2044; 49 days; $33.39; $2010.61
13. $17,355; 42 days; $228.43; $17,571.57 **15.** $30,829.37;
83 days; $814.09; $31,285.91 **17. (a)** $4968 **(b)** $367,632
19. (a) $238,750 **(b)** 93 days **(c)** $5166.67 **(d)** $244,833.33
21. (a) $311,250 **(b)** $304,713.75 **23. (a)** $24,150 **(b)** $538.46
(c) $24,461.54 **(d)** 6.71%

Supplementary Exercises (Page 385)

1. (a) $660 **(b)** $18,660 **3.** $96,000 **5.** 200 days **7. (a)** $750
(b) $20,750 **9.** 12.1% **11.** Apr. 12; $9,475,000 **13.** $15,000
15. $18,208.12 **17. (a)** $1711.11 **(b)** $29,711.11 **(c)** 130 days
(d) $1180.19 **(e)** $28,530.92 **19. (a)** $3843.89 **(b)** $72,191.09
(c) $4191.09 **(d)** $347.20

Case Study (Page 393)

3. (a) $1,037,500 **(b)** $78,292,500 **(c)** 2.65%

Case in Point Summary Exercises (Page 394)

1. $7727.27; $92,727.27 **2.** $7437.50; $92,437.50 **3.** Simple
interest loan from Union Bank; $289.77 **4.** Bank One—10.91%;
Union Bank—10.50%

Chapter 9 Test (Page 395)

1. $1020.83 **2.** $508.75 **3.** $137.50 **4.** $148.06 **5.** $13,013.01
6. $25,575.75 **7.** $11.19 **8.** 9.2% **9.** 333 days **10.** $43,000
11. $26,595.74 **12.** $359.33; $9440.67 **13.** $162.29; $10,087.71
14. (a) $14,550 **(b)** 9.3% **15.** $28,626.58 **16.** $9034.40
17. (a) $19,812.50 **(b)** $20,000 **(c)** $187.50 **(d)** 3.79%
18. 44 days; $144.07; $9285.93 **19. (a)** $452.81 **(b)** $8997.19
(c) loses $2.81

CHAPTER 10

Section 10.1 Exercises (Page 407)

1. $16,325.87; $4325.87 **3.** $30,906.76; $2906.76 **5.** $40,841.23;
$8491.23 **7.** $28,949.25; $14,449.25 **9.** $60,476.40; $15,476.40
11. $1296; $1417.39; $121.39 **13.** $1440; $2606.60; $1166.60
15. (a) $11,431.57 **(b)** $2931.57 **17. (a)** $5707.08 **(b)** $1207.08
19. (a) 31,669.25 yuan **(b)** 6669.25 yuan **21.** $966
23. (a) $1,777,622 **(b)** $377,622 **25. (a)** $28,137.75 **(b)** $50,819.75
(c) $22,682 **27. (a)** $8787.45 **(b)** $10,079.40 **(c)** second is larger

Section 10.2 Exercises (Page 417)

1. $39.75 **3.** $50.48 **5.** $101.88 **7.** $4763.41 **9.** $17,412.96
13. (a) $3284.75 **(b)** $24.75 **15. (a)** $11,638.49 **(b)** $118.49
17. $4420.65; $4647.29 **19. (a)** $901,988.58 **(b)** $101,988.58
21. $4700 **23.** Loss of $397.50 **25. (a)** $187,345.53 **(b)** $191,129.64
(c) $3784.11

Section 10.3 Exercises (Page 425)

1. $10,327.33; $1972.67 **3.** $7674.01; $1675.99 **5.** $9792.06;
$9060.94 **7. (a)** $26,444.80 **(b)** $13,555.20 **9.** $3503.40
11. (a) $793,054 **(b)** $592,618 **13. (a)** $26,620 **(b)** $20,989.60

Case Study (Page 429)

1. $4,053,386; $3,016,084 **2.** $2,539,384; $1,889,530
3. $2,798,295; $2,082,183 **4.** $2,539,384; $1,889,530;
$2,798,295; $2,082,183; $4,053,386; $3,016,084

Case in Point Summary Exercises (Page 430)

1. 2006—$4,235,680; 2007—$7,891,680; 2008—$8,550,370;
2009—$1,768,026; 2010 projected—$480,000 **2.** $5,030,500; not
enough to offset 2007 loss **3. (a)** $18,210,076 **(b)** $8,537,612

Chapter 10 Test (Page 431)

1. $18,649.23; $9949.23 **2.** $16,127.04; $4127.04 **3.** $13,170.42;
$3370.42 **4.** $18,556.38; $6056.38 **5.** $50.52 **6.** $530.60 **7.** $286.28
8. $7509.25 **9.** $10,380.83 **10.** $38,291.99 **11.** $16,077.25
12. $4120.01 **13.** $5399.30 **14.** $38,680.72 **15.** Loss of $676
16. Loss of $1625 **17. (a)** $4408.99 **(b)** $3801.87
18. (a) $15,173.40 **(b)** $13,481.41 **19. (a)** $283,233.48
(b) $206,955.87 **20. (a)** $59 million **(b)** $93 million

Cumulative Review: Chapters 9–10 (Page 433)

1. $272 **3.** $8500.11 **5.** 9.5% **7.** 80 days **9.** $270; $8730 **11.** $4875
13. $1947.90 **15.** $86.07; $12,686.07 **17.** $583.49; $416.51
19. $1250; $23,750 **21.** $10,871.40 **23.** $20.01

CHAPTER 11

Section 11.1 Exercises (Page 443)

1. $25,319.14; $9119.14 **3.** $201,527.78; $51,527.78
5. $139,509.30; $41,509.30 **7.** $7603.12; $1603.12
9. $207,485.32; $36,485.32 **11.** $51,985.25; $6385.25
15. (a) $423,452.16 **(b)** $290,452.16 **17. (a)** $11,277.89
(b) $3277.89 **19.** $44,502

Section 11.2 Exercises (Page 451)

1. $14,762.54 **3.** $30,493.92 **5.** $18,991.59 **9.** $810,043.65
11. (a) $70,016.48 **(b)** $9983.52 **13. (a)** $48,879.76 **(b)** No
15. (a) First offer **(b)** $2769.99 **17.** $151,694.02

Section 11.3 Exercises (Page 457)

1. $2784.12 **3.** $715.29 **5.** $2271 **7.** $183.22 **11. (a)** $144,026
(b) $55,844 **13. (a)** $3860 **(b)** $845,600 **15.** $12,649.20
17. (a) $53,383 **(b)** $37,559 **19. (a)** $1200 **(b)** $6511.80
(c)

Payment Number	Amount of Deposit	Interest Earned	Total in Account
1	$6511.80	$0	$6511.80
2	$6511.80	$260.47	$13,284.07
3	$6511.80	$531.36	$20,327.23
4	$6511.80	$813.09	$27,652.12
5	$6511.80	$1106.08	$35,270.00
6	$6511.80	$1410.80	$43,192.60
7	$6511.80	$1727.70	$51,432.10
8	$6510.62	$2057.28	$60,000.00

21.

Payment Number	Amount of Deposit	Interest Earned	Total in Account
1	$713,625	$0	$713,625.00
2	$713,625	$10,704.38	$1,437,954.38
3	$713,625	$21,569.32	$2,173,148.70
4	$713,625	$32,597.23	$2,919,370.93

23. $1707 **25.** $6819.92

Supplementary Exercises (Page 461)

1. (a) $15,210.93 **(b)** $3210.93 **3. (a)** $77,985.46 **(b)** $37,985.46
5. $1,384,797.60 **7.** $106,216.95 **9.** $267,986.10

Payment Number	Amount of Deposit	Interest Earned	Total in Account
1	$267,986.10	$0	$267,986.10
2	$267,986.10	$21,438.89	$557,411.09
3	$267,996.02	$44,592.89	$870,000.00

11. (a) $286,748 **(b)** $6265.44

Section 11.4 Exercises (Page 471)

1. $4.00 **3.** $0 **5.** 178,700 **7.** 47 **9.** $1.90 **11.** 6.3% **13.** $.40 **15.** −$.17
17. $51.04 **19.** $12,384 ; $128 **21.** $3950; $56 **23.** $2754; $0
27. 2.5% **29.** 3.5% **31.** 1.7% **33.** 32 **35.** 14 **37.** 41 **39.** .85; 2.5%
41. $15,120 **43. (a)** $15,326.80 **(b)** $17,866.85 **(c)** $2540.05

Section 11.5 Exercises (Page 481)

1. $1065.00 **3.** May 15, 2016 **5.** 4.749% **7.** $51,325 **9.** $91,783.20
11. $260,750 **15. (a)** $4,135,200 **(b)** $270,000 **(c)** 6.5%
17. (a) $18,637.35 **(b)** $1387.50 **(c)** 7.4% **19. (a)** $3600
(b) $97,151.40

Case Study (Page 486)

1. $620,703.67 **2.** $97,090.40 **3.** $67,090.40 **4.** $658,703.61
5. Almost, about $38,000 short. **6.** Answers will vary.

Case in Point Summary Exercises (Page 487)

1. $7560 **2.** $856,421.07 **3.** $20,467,000 **4.** $1,637,360
5. $1,053,090 **6.** $499,455

Chapter 11 Test (Page 489)

1. $9897.47 **2.** $126,595.71 **3.** $930,909 **4.** $86,210.18
5. $67,880.28 **6.** $47,575.42 **7.** $6801.69 **8.** $39,884.63
9. $21,316.12 **10.** $264,795.02 **11.** $22,696.72 **12.** $24,683.07
13. $8702 **14.** $8395 **15.** $5835.60 **16.** $17,976 **17.** $22,492
18. $2322 **19.** (a) $9120 (b) $304 **20.** (a) $24,025 (b) $1050
(c) 4.4% **21.** Highest and lowest prices for the year were $65.90
and $20.10. Weekly volume was 7,451,500 shares. Dividend yield
is .8% of current price. PE ratio is 27. Stock closed at $63.44. The
stock price was up $1.23 for the week. Earnings were $5.47 last
year and are expected to be $2.53 this year and $2.89 next year.
The last quarterly dividend was $.12 per share. **22.** Annual interest
is 7.950% of $1000 = $79.50 per bond. Bond matures on June
15, 2018. Bond closed at $1173.89. Yield to maturity is 5.369%.
Estimated volume for the week is $209,183,000.

CHAPTER 12

Section 12.1 Exercises (Page 499)

1. $51.40 **3.** $15.02 **5.** October, $6.12; $419.17; November, $419.17,
$5.87, $541.68; December, $541.68, $7.58, $529.22; January,
$529.22, $7.41, $211.71 **9.** $20.42 **11.** $4.87 **13.** $17.30
15. (a) $104 (b) $65 (c) $39 **17.** (a) $2641.56 (b) $39.62
(c) $2885.84 **19.** (a) $312.91 (b) $4.69 (c) $285.94 **21.** (a) $139.71
(b) $2.10 (c) $74.32

Section 12.2 Exercises (Page 507)

1. $2050; $250 **3.** $180; $30 **5.** $3543; $643 **7.** 8.1% **9.** 11.6%
11. 15.4% **13.** 12.25% **15.** 10.25% **17.** 11.25% **21.** (a) $59,840
(b) $83,966.60 (c) $9166.60 (d) 9.9% **23.** (a) 13.3% (b) 13%
25. 10.00% **27.** (a) $18,800 (b) $25,600 (c) $4800 (d) 11.25%
29. (a) 732,212.32 pesos (b) 13.75% **31.** (a) 97,689.60 (b) 10.75%

Section 12.3 Exercises (Page 515)

1. $8307.31; $307.31 **3.** $9198.18; $698.18 **5.** $9862.15; $507.15
7. $231 **9.** $103.18 **11.** $28.38 **15.** (a) $415.33 (b) $9315.33
17. (a) $69,936.02 (b) $2286.02 **19.** (a) $41,176.11 (b) $1876.11
21. (a) $17.31 (b) $457.69 **23.** (a) $1700 (b) $170 (c) $5980
25. (a) $87,716.70 (b) $10,916.70 (c) $4930.12 (d) $43,547.68

Section 12.4 Exercises (Page 523)

1. $1703.13 **3.** $404.73 **5.** $4185.60 **7.** $161.93 **9.** $147.61; $899.62
11. $321.96; $3454.08 **13.** $255.45; $3577 **17.** (a) $1900.70
(b) $13,628
19.

Payment Number	Amount of Payment	Interest for Period	Portion to Principal	Principal at End of Period
0	—	—	—	$4000.00
1	$1207.68	$320.00	$887.68	$3112.32
2	$1207.68	$248.99	$958.69	$2153.63
3	$1207.68	$172.29	$1035.39	$1118.24
4	$1207.70	$89.46	$1118.24	$0

21.

Payment Number	Amount of Payment	Interest for Period	Portion to Principal	Principal at End of Period
0	—	—	—	$14,500.00
1	$374.83	$132.92	$241.91	$14,258.09
2	$374.83	$130.70	$244.13	$14,013.96
3	$374.83	$128.46	$246.37	$13,767.59
4	$374.83	$126.20	$248.63	$13,518.96
5	$374.83	$123.92	$250.91	$13,268.05

23.

Payment Number	Amount of Payment	Interest for Period	Portion to Principal	Principal at End of Period
0	—	—	—	$35,000.00
1	$1196.30	$408.33	$787.97	$34,212.03
2	$1196.30	$399.14	$797.16	$33,414.87
3	$1196.30	$389.84	$806.46	$32,608.41
4	$1196.30	$380.43	$815.87	$31,792.54
5	$1196.30	$370.91	$825.39	$30,967.15

Section 12.5 Exercises (Page 533)

1. $2266.10 **3.** $1111.08 **5.** $599.68 **9.** $802.53 **11.** $2516.88
13. $873.82 **15.** Yes, qualified
17. Monthly payment = 122.5 × $9.28 = $1136.80

Payment Number	Total Payment	Interest Payment	Principal Payment	Balance of Principal
0	—	—	—	$122,500.00
1	$1136.80	$765.63	$371.17	$122,128.83
2	$1136.80	$763.31	$373.49	$121,755.34

Case Study (Page 539)

1. $495.00; $419.94; $950.53; $149.45; $2014.97 **2.** $2014.97;
$215.00; $290.00; $279.17; $2799.14 **3.** $392.32; $285.61;
$695.83; $149.45; $187.00; $290.00; $279.17; $2279.38
4. $519.76

Case in Point Summary Exercises (Page 541)

1. $1715 **2.** $229,875; $76,625 **3.** $100,000 **4.** $1849.65
5. $749.65

Chapter 12 Test (Page 543)

1. $20,900 **2.** $932.56 **3.** 11.75% **4.** 12.25% **5.** 11% **6.** $4364.31
7. (a) $235.51 (b) $2502.17 **8.** $4811.72 **9.** $1924.50 **10.** $864.50
11. $1209.69 **12.** $629.48 **13.** (a) $6441.72 (b) $1,295,509.60
14. (a) $1398.24 (b) $360,577.60

Cumulative Review: Chapters 11–12 (Page 545)

1. $9214.23; $1214.23 **3.** $17,855.03; $2855.03 **5.** $13,367.29
7. $403.45 **9.** (a) $11,957.94 (b) $27,257.87 **11.** (a) $2345
(b) 15 (c) 1.5% **13.** (a) $3098.48 (b) $298.48 (c) $2300
(d) 12.00% **15.** (a) $2118.14 (b) $3017.68 **17.** (a) $14,570
(b) $14,952.46 **19.** $13,327.06

CHAPTER 13

Section 13.1 Exercises (Page 555)

1. $34,000 **3.** $71,150 **5.** $325,125 **7.** .3% **9.** 8% **11.** 3%
13. (a) $4.84 (b) $48.40 (c) 48.4 **15.** (a) 7.08% (b) $7.08
(c) 70.8 **19.** $5861.60 **21.** $5384.40 **23.** $5978.70 **25.** $6295.08
27. $262,145 **29.** (a) The second parish (b) $75.24

Section 13.2 Exercises (Page 571)

1. $23,131 **3.** $21,710 **5.** $44,533 **7.** $21,790 **9.** $27,490; $3706
11. $53,750; $7227.50 **13.** $74,230; $10,932.50 **15.** $69,862;
$13,693.11 **17.** $67,000; $11,602.50 **19.** $2379.50 tax refund
21. $638.06 tax refund **23.** $6451.50 due **27.** $8988.50 **29.** $9240
31. $6607.75 **33.** $5575.55

Section 13.3 Exercises (Page 581)

1. $1700 **3.** $2194.50 **5.** $9298.72 **7.** $70,344.83 **9.** $19,850
11. $36,500 **13.** $60,000; $20,000 **15.** $292,500; $260,000;

$97,500 **17.** $18,804 **19.** $702.65 **23. (a)** $136,986.30
(b) $43,013.70 **25. (a)** $30,681.82 **(b)** $14,318.18 **27. A:** $274,000
B: $182,666.67 **C:** $91,333.33 **29. 1:** $125,000 **2:** $41,666.67
3: $83,333.33 **31. (a)** $218,750 **(b) A:** $87,500; **B:** $131,250

Section 13.4 Exercises (Page 591)

1. $790 **3.** $932 **5.** $869 **9.** $911 **11.** $1201.20 **13. (a)** $25,000;
(b) $11,500 **15. (a)** $4300; **(b)** $850 **17. (a)** $1778; **(b)** $6936;
(c) $100,000; **(d)** $15,100

Section 13.5 Exercises (Page 599)

1. $256; $130.56; $66.56; $23.24 **3.** $849.10; $433.04; $220.77;
$77.10 **5.** $516.80; $263.57; $134.37; $46.93 **7.** $319.50; $162.95;
$83.07; $29.01 **9.** $2973.10; $1516.28; $773.01; $269.96 **13.** $364
15. (a) $100.50 **(b)** $384 **17.** $3036 **19. (a)** $444.72 **(b)** $226.72
(c) $79.18

Case Study (Page 604)

1. $11,790.75 **2.** $39,940.40 **3.** $439.88 **4.** $52,171.03 **5.** $1328.97

Case in Point Summary Exercises (Page 605)

1. $5952 **2.** $2410.90 **3.** $6063 **4.** $831 **5.** $945 **6.** $13,791

Chapter 13 Test (Page 607)

1. $5.76; $57.60 **2.** 9.35%; $9.35 **3.** $55,295; $10,011.25
4. $17,487; $1788.05 **5.** $2290.74 **6.** $9541.50 **7.** $4407.55
8. $8449.14 **9.** $42,613.64 **10. A:** $36,000 **B:** $21,600

C: $14,400 **11.** $1086.55 **12.** $696 **13.** $158.48; $80.82; $41.20;
$14.39 **14.** $1940.80; $989.81; $504.61; $176.22
15. (a) $678 **(b)** $417 **16.** $6400 to repair his truck

APPENDICES

Appendix A Exercises (Page A-5)

1. .69 m **3.** 4700 mm **5.** 8900 g **7.** .39 L **9.** 46 kg **11.** 976 g
13. 39.2 yards **15.** 50.3 m **17.** 15.4 feet **19.** 1.1 m **21.** 307.5 miles
23. 1235.7 km **25.** 1.5 pounds **27.** 1861.4 g **29.** 85.6 pounds
31. 200 nickels **33.** .6 g **37.** 40°C **39.** 280°C **41.** 37°C **43.** 95°F
45. 50°F **47.** 275°F **49.** Not reasonable **51.** Not reasonable

Appendix B Exercises (Page B–9)

1. 1171.60 **3.** 11,378 **5.** 3905.32 **7.** 255.24 **9.** 15,695 **11.** 31.08
13. 35.42 **15.** 27.63 **17.** 8.1 **19.** 566.1397059 = 566.14 (rounded)
21. .625 = .63 (rounded) **23.** 30.57004831 = 30.57 (rounded)
25. 0.915966387 = .92 (rounded) **27.** $5\frac{6}{11}$
29. .493714286 = .49 (rounded) **33.** $44,162.80
35. (a) $1164.05 rounded **(b)** $95.13 rounded **37.** $214,008
39. $13,400 **41.** 59%

Appendix C Exercises (Page C–7)

1. $39,019.50 **3.** $8929.13 **5.** $2676.84 **7.** 1.5% **9.** $858.89
11. 24 **13.** FV = $31,651.09 **15.** PMT = $696 **17.** n = 26
19. i = 8.5%

glossary

401 (k): A retirement plan for individuals working for private-sector companies.

403 (b): A retirement plan for employees of public schools and certain tax-exempt organizations.

A

Absolute, or gross, loss: The loss resulting when the selling price is less than the cost.

Accelerated depreciation: A technique to increase the depreciation taken during the early years of an asset's useful life.

Accelerated mortgages: Mortgages with payoffs of less than 30 years, such as 15, 20, or 25 years.

Accountant: A person who maintains financial data for a firm or individual and then prepares the income tax return.

Accounts payable: A business debt that must be paid.

Accumulated depreciation: A running balance or total of the depreciation to date on an asset.

Acid-test ratio: The sum of cash, notes receivable, and accounts receivable, divided by current liabilities.

ACRS (Accelerated cost recovery system): A depreciation method introduced as part of the Economic Recovery Tax Act of 1981.

Actual rate of interest: The true annual percentage rate that can be used to compare loans.

Actuary: A person who determines insurance premiums.

Addends: The numbers added in an addition problem.

Addition rule: The same number may be added or subtracted on both sides of an equation.

Adjustable rate mortgage: A home loan where the interest rate is adjusted up or down depending on a benchmark interest rate.

Adjusted bank balance: The actual current balance of a checking account after reconciliation.

Adjusted gross income: An individual's or family's income for a year, including all sources of income, and after subtracting certain expenses, such as moving expenses and sick pay.

Algebraic logic: Rules used by most calculators for entering and evaluating arithmetic expressions.

Allowances: The number of allowances claimed by a taxpayer affects the amount withheld for income taxes.

American Express: A widely accepted credit card that requires an annual fee.

Amortization table: A table showing the level (unchanging) payment necessary to pay in full a loan for a specific amount of money including interest over a specific length of time.

Amortize: The process of paying off a loan with a sequence of periodic payments over a period of time.

Amount of an annuity: The future value of the annuity.

Amount of depreciation: The dollar amount of depreciation taken. This is usually an annual figure.

Annual meeting: Corporations have annual meetings for stockholders.

Annual percentage rate (APR): The true annual percentage rate which can be used to compare loans. The federal Truth-in-Lending Act requires lenders to state the APR.

Annual percentage rate table: A table used to find the annual percentage rate (APR) on a loan or installment purchase.

Annual rate of depreciation: The percent or fraction of the depreciable amount or declining balance to be depreciated each individual year of an asset's useful life.

Annuity: Periodic payments of a given, fixed amount of money.

Annuity due: An annuity whose payments are made at the beginning of a time period.

APR (Annual percentage rate): The true annual percentage rate that can be used to compare loans. It is required by the federal Truth-in-Lending Act.

"AS OF": A later date that appears on an invoice. The given sales terms may start at this time.

Assessed value: The value of a piece of property. Set by the county assessor, assessed value is used in figuring property taxes.

Assessment rate: The assessed valuation of a property is found by multiplying the fair market value by the assessment rate.

Asset: An item of value owned by a firm.

ATM (Automated teller machine): A machine that allows bank customers to make deposits, withdrawals, and fund transfers.

Automatic savings transfer account: A bank account that automatically transfers funds from one account to another.

Average: *See* mean.

Average cost method: An inventory valuation method whereby the cost of all purchases during a time period is divided by the number of units purchased.

Average daily balance method: A method used to calculate interest on open-end credit accounts.

Average inventory: The sum of all inventories taken divided by the number of times inventory was taken.

Average owner's equity: Sum of owner's equity at the beginning and end of the year divided by 2.

B

Bad checks: A check that is not honored because there are insufficient funds in the checking account.

Balance brought forward (Current balance): The amount left in a checking account after previous checks written have been subtracted.

Balanced: In agreement. When the bank statement amount and the depositor's checkbook balance agree, they are balanced.

Balance sheet: A summary of the financial condition of a firm at one point in time.

Bank discount: A bank fee charged on a note. It is subtracted from the face value to find the proceeds loaned.

Banker's interest: A method used to calculate interest by dividing exact days by 360.

Banker's ratio: *See* current ratio.

Bank statement: A monthly statement prepared by a bank that lists all charges and deposits to a checking account. Historically banks mailed the statements, but many people now look at their monthly statements on the web.

Bankrupt: A company or individual whose liabilities exceed assets can declare bankruptcy, which is a legal process of working with debtors to pay off debts.

Bar code: A code placed on the side of a product that allows it to be scanned and then recognized and priced by a computer system.

Bar graph: A graph using bars to compare various numbers.

Base: The starting point or reference point or that to which something is being compared.

bbl.: Abbreviation for *barrel*.

Bimodal: A set of data with two modes.

Blank endorsement: A signature on the back of a check by the person to whom the check is made.

Board of directors: A group of people who represent the stockholders of a corporation.

Bodily injury insurance: A type of automobile insurance that protects a driver in case he or she injures someone with a car.

Bond: A contractual promise by a corporation, government entity, or church to repay borrowed money at a specified rate and time.

Book value: The cost of an asset minus depreciation to date.

Break-even point: The cost of an item plus the operating expenses associated with the item. Above this amount a profit is made; below it, a loss is incurred.

Broker: A person who sells stocks, bonds, and other investments owned by others.

Business account: The type of checking account used by businesses.

bx.: Abbreviation for *box*.

C

C: Roman numeral for 100.

Canceled check: A check is canceled after the amount of the check has been transferred from the payer's bank account into the account of the receiver of the check.

Cancellation: A process used to simplify multiplication and division of fractions.

Capital: The amount of money originally invested in a firm. The difference between the total of all the assets and the total of all the liabilities is called the capital or net worth.

Capital gains: Profits made on investments such as stocks or real estate.

cart.: Abbreviation for *carton*.

Cash discount: A discount offered by the seller allowing the buyer to take a discount if payment is made within a specified period of time.

Cashier's check: A check written by a financial institution, such as a bank, that is guaranteed by the institution.

Cash value: Money that has built up in an ordinary life insurance policy.

Casualty or theft loss: Loss due to a casualty (e.g., fire) or theft that is deductible on a personal income tax return.

Catastrophic event: A major (harmful) event that occurs rarely. For example, a financial crisis is a catastrophic event that can devastate the finances of families.

Centi-: A prefix used in the metric system meaning hundredth. (For example, a centiliter is one one-hundredth of a liter.)

Centimeter: One one-hundredth of a meter. There are 2.54 centimeters to an inch.

Central tendency: The middle of a set of data.

Certificate of deposit (CD): A savings account in which a minimum amount of money must be deposited and left for a minimum period of time.

Chain calculations: Long calculations done on a calculator.

Chain discount: Two or more discounts that are combined into one discount.

Check 21 Act: A federal law that took effect in October 2004 and allows banks to take electronic photos of all cancelled checks and exchange checks electronically, so the banks no longer have to mail cancelled checks.

Check register: A table usually found in a checkbook that is used by the check writer to list all checks written, deposits and withdrawals made, and ATM transactions.

Checks outstanding: Checks written that have not reached and cleared the bank as of the statement date.

Check stub: A stub attached to the check and retained as a record of checks written.

Circle graph: A circle divided into parts that are labeled and often colored or shaded to show data.

COD: A method of shipping goods that requires cash on delivery of goods.

Coinsurance: The portion of a loss that must be paid by the insured.

Collateral: Assets foreclosed on by a lender should the borrower default on payments.

Collision insurance: A form of automobile insurance that pays for car repairs in case of an accident.

Commission: A fee charged by a broker for buying and selling either stocks or bonds.

Commissions: Payments to an employee that represent a certain percent of the total sales produced by the employee's efforts.

Common denominator: Two or more fractions with the same denominator are said to have common denominators.

Common stock: Ownership of a corporation, held in portions called shares.

Comparative balance sheet: An analysis for two or more periods that compares asset categories such as cash.

Comparative income statement: A vertical analysis for two or more years that compares incomes or balance sheet items for each year analyzed.

Comparison graph (Comparative line graph): One graph that shows how several things relate.

Compensatory time (Comp time): Time off given to an employee to compensate for previously worked overtime.

Compound amount: The future value of an investment.

Compounding period: The interval of time at which interest is added to the account. For example, interest compounded quarterly results in interest being added to the account every quarter.

Compound interest: Interest charged or received on both principal and interest.

Comprehensive insurance: A form of automobile insurance that pays for damage to a car caused by fire, theft, vandalism, and weather.

Consolidated statement: A financial statement showing the combined results of all subsidiaries of a firm.

Consumer price index (CPI): A measure of the cost of living calculated by the government and used to estimate inflation.

Continuous inventory systems: Inventory systems that continuously monitor inventory levels.

Conventional loan: A loan made by a bank, savings and loan, or other lending agency that is not guaranteed or insured by the federal government.

Corporation: A form of business that gives the owners limited liability.

Cosign: Signing a loan with someone else. Parents sometimes cosign at the bank on a car loan applied for by their son or daughter. The cosigner must pay back the loan if the primary borrower does not.

Cost: The total cost of an item, including shipping, insurance, and other charges. Most often, the cost is the basis for calculating depreciation of an asset.

Cost (Cost price): The price paid to the manufacturer or supplier after trade and cash discounts have been taken. This price includes transportation and insurance charges.

Cost of goods sold: The amount paid by a firm for the goods it sold during the time period covered by an income statement.

Cost of living index: A measure of the cost of living calculated by the government and used to estimate inflation. It is the same as the consumer price index or CPI.

Country club billing method: A billing method that provides copies of original charge receipts to the customer.

cpm.: Abbreviation for *cost per thousand*.

Credit card (transactions): The purchase or sale of goods or services using a credit card in place of cash or a check.

Credit history: The history built up by an individual when purchasing things and making payments. A lender checks a person's credit history before making a loan.

Credit score: Three national credit-reporting agencies (Equifax, TransUnion, and Experian) keep financial records on U.S. citizens and calculate a credit score on each indicating the creditworthiness of that individual. Also called a FICO score.

Credit union: A financial institution similar to a bank, except that it is owned by its member customers.

Credit union share draft account: A credit union account that may be used as a checking account.

Cross-products: The equal products obtained when each numerator of a proportion is multiplied by the opposite denominator.

cs.: Abbreviation for *case*.

ct.: Abbreviation for *crate*.

ctn.: Abbreviation for *carton*.

Current assets: Cash or items that can be converted into cash within a given period of time, such as a year.

Current liability: Debts that must be paid by a firm within a given period of time, such as a year.

Current ratio: The quotient of current assets and current liabilities.

Current yield: The annual dividend per share of stock divided by the current price per share.

cwt.: Abbreviation for *per hundredweight* or *per one hundred pounds*.

D

Daily interest charge: The amount of interest charged per day on a loan.

Daily overtime: The amount of overtime worked in a day.

Debit card: A card that results in a debit to a bank account when the card is used for a purchase.

Decimal: A number written with a decimal point, such as 4.3 or 7.22.

Decimal equivalent: A decimal that has the same value as a fraction.

Decimal point: The starting point in the decimal system (.).

Decimal system: The numbering system based on powers of 10 and using the 10 one-place numbers 0, 1, 2, 3, 4, 5, 6, 7, 8, and 9, which are called *digits*.

Declining-balance depreciation: An accelerated depreciation method.

(200%) Declining-balance method: An accelerated method of depreciation using twice, or 200% of, the straight-line rate.

Decrease problem (Difference problem): A percentage problem in which something is taken away from the base. It may require you to find the base.

Decreasing term insurance: A form of life insurance in which the insured pays a fixed premium until age 60 or 65, with the amount of life insurance decreasing periodically.

Deductible: An amount paid by the insured, with the balance of the loss paid by the insurance company.

Deductions: Amounts that are subtracted from the gross earnings of an employee to arrive at the amount of money the employee actually receives.

Defaulting on debt: Failure to pay back a debt.

Deflation: Occurs when prices of goods and services fall over time.

Denominator: The number below the line in a fraction. For example, in the fraction $\frac{7}{9}$, 9 is the denominator.

Dependents: An extra deduction is allowed on income taxes for each dependent.

Deposits in transit: Deposits that have been made but have not yet been recorded by a bank.

Deposit slip: A slip for listing all currency and checks that are part of a deposit into a bank account.

Depreciable amount: The amount of an asset's value that can be depreciated.

Depreciation: The decrease in value of an asset caused by normal use, aging, or obsolescence.

Depreciation schedule: A schedule or table showing the depreciation rate, amount of depreciation, book value, and accumulated depreciation for each year of an asset's life.

Difference (Remainder): The answer in a subtraction problem.

Differential piece rate: A rate paid per item that depends on the number of items produced.

Digits: One-place numbers in the decimal system. They are 0, 1, 2, 3, 4, 5, 6, 7, 8, and 9.

Direct deposit: Allows deposits (such as payroll) to be made directly into your account.

Direct payment: Allows you to authorize electronic payments from your account.

Disability coverage: Insurance coverage in the event of a disability.

Discount: (1) To reduce the price of an item. (2) The amount subtracted from the face value of a note to find the proceeds loaned.

Discount broker: A stockbroker who charges a reduced fee to customers (and, generally, reduced services).

Discount date: The last date on which a cash discount may be taken.

Discounting a note: Cashing or selling a note at a bank before the note is due from the maker.

Discount method of interest: A method of calculating interest on a loan by subtracting the interest from the amount of the loan. The borrower receives the amount borrowed less the discounted interest.

Discount period: The discount period is the period from the time of sale of a note to the note's due date.

Discount rate: The discount rate is a percent that is multiplied by the face value and time to find bank discount.

Discover: A credit card that sometimes pays the card holder back a percentage of the amount charged.

Distributive property: The property that states the product of the sum of two numbers equals the sum of the individual products; that is $a(b + c) = ab + ac$.

Dividend: (1) The number being divided by another number in a division problem. (2) A return on an investment; money paid by a company to the holders of stock.

Divisor: The number doing the dividing in a division problem.

Double-declining balance: A method of accelerated depreciation that doubles depreciation in the early years compared to straight-line depreciation.

Double time: Twice the regular hourly rate. A premium often paid for working holidays and Sunday.

Dow Jones Industrial Average: A frequently quoted average price of the stocks of 30 large industrial companies.

doz.: Abbreviation for *dozen*.

Draw: A draw is an advance on future earnings.

Drawing account: An account from which a salesperson can receive payment against future commissions.

drm.: Abbreviation for *drum*.

E

ea.: Abbreviation for *each*.

Effective rate: The true rate of interest.

Effective rate of interest: The true annual percentage rate that can be used to compare loans. It is required by the federal Truth-in-Lending Act.

Electronic banking: Banking activities that take place over a network, such as the World Wide Web.

Electronic bill pay: Allows bills to be paid using the Internet.

Electronic commerce: Purchases that take place over a network, such as the World Wide Web.

Electronic funds transfer: Moving money electronically over a network, such as the World Wide Web.

Electronic payment: Bills that are paid using the Internet.

Electronic product code: A tag on a product that includes information about that product. It may succeed the bar code.

End-of-month dating (EOM): A system of cash discounts in which the time period begins at the end of the month the invoice is dated. *Proximo* and *prox.* have the same meaning.

Endowment policy: A life insurance policy guaranteeing the payment of a fixed amount of money to a given individual whether or not the insured person lives.

Equation: Two algebraic expressions that are equal to one another.

Escrow account into which monies are paid: *See* impound account.

Exact interest: A method of calculating interest based on 365 days per year.

Exchange traded funds (ETFs): These funds are similar to mutual funds except they are not as actively managed. A particular ETF tries to match the performance of an index such as the Dow Jones Averages or perhaps a market sector such as energy.

Executive officers: The top few officers in a corporation.

Expenses: The costs a firm must pay to operate and sell its goods or services.

Extension total: The number of items purchased times the price per unit.

Extra dating (ex., x): Extra time allowed in determining the net payment date of a cash discount.

F

Face value: The amount shown on the face of a note.

Face value of a bond (Par value of a bond): The amount the company has promised to repay.

Face value of a policy: The amount of insurance provided by the insurance company.

Factoring: The process of selling accounts receivable for cash.

Factors: Companies that buy accounts receivable.

Fair Labor Standards Act: A federal law that sets the minimum wage and also a 40-hour workweek.

Fair market value: The price for which a piece of property could reasonably be expected to be sold in the market.

FAS (Free alongside ship): A method of shipping goods in which the seller of goods pays for transportation of the goods to the port from which they will be shipped. The buyer of the goods must pay for all costs in moving the goods from the shipping port to his facility.

Federal Insurance Contributions Act (FICA): An emergency measure passed by Congress in the 1930s that established the so-called social security tax. *See* FICA tax.

Federal Reserve Bank: Today, all banks are part of the Federal Reserve system. The Federal Reserve is our national bank.

Federal Truth-in-Lending Act: An act passed in 1969 that requires all interest rates to be given as comparable percents.

Federal Unemployment Tax Act (FUTA): An unemployment insurance tax paid entirely by employers to the federal government for administrative costs of federal and state unemployment programs.

FHA loan: A real estate loan that is insured by the Federal Housing Administration, an agency of the federal government.

FICA tax (Social Security tax): The amount of money deducted from the paychecks of almost all employees, used by the federal government to pay pensions to retired people, survivors' benefits, and disability.

FICO: Three national credit-reporting agencies (Equifax, TransUnion, and Experian) keep financial records on U.S. citizens and calculate a credit score on each indicating the creditworthiness of that individual. Also called a credit score.

FIFO: A method of inventory accounting in which the first items received are considered to be the first ones shipped.

Finance charge: The difference between the cost of something paid for in installments and the cash price.

Financial ratio: A number found using financial data that is used to compare different companies within the same industry.

Fixed assets: Assets owned by a firm that will not be converted to cash within a year.

Fixed liabilities: Items that will not be paid off within a year.

Fixed-rate loan: A loan made at a fixed, stated rate of interest.

Flat-fee checking account: A checking account in which the bank supplies check printing, a bank charge card, and other services for a fixed charge per month.

Float: The time between an actual deposit to an account and the moment those funds are available for use.

Floating decimal: A feature on most calculators that positions the decimal point where it should be in the final answer.

FOB (Free on board): A notation sometimes used on an invoice. "Free on board shipping point" means the buyer pays for shipping. "Free on board destination" means the seller pays for shipping.

Foreclose: The process by which a lender takes back the property when payments are not made.

Form 941: The Employer's Quarterly Federal Tax Return form that must be filed by the employer with the Internal Revenue Service.

Form 1040A: The form used by most federal income tax payers.

Form 1040EZ: A simplified version of the 1040A federal income tax form.

Fraction: An indication of a part of a whole. (For example, $\frac{3}{4}$ means that the whole is divided into 4 parts, of which 3 are being considered.)

Frequency distribution table: A table showing the number of times one or more events occur.

Fringe benefits: Benefits offered by an employer, not including salary, that can include medical, dental, life insurance, and day care for employee's children.

Front-end rounding: Rounding so that all digits are changed to zero except the first digit.

Future amount: The value of an investment at a future date. It is the same as future value.

Future value: The value, at some future date, of an investment.

G

GI (VA) loan: A loan guaranteed by the Veterans Administration and available only to qualified veterans.

Grace period: The period between the due date of a payment and the time the lending institution assesses a penalty for the payment being late, usually a few days after the payment is due.

Gram: The unit of weight in the metric system. (A nickel weighs about 5 grams.)

Graph: A visual presentation of numerical data.

Gr. gro. (Great gross): Abbreviation for 12 gross ($144 \times 12 = 1728$).

Gro.: Abbreviation for *gross*.

gross: A dozen dozen, or 144 items.

Gross earnings: The total amount of money earned by an employee before any deductions are taken.

Gross loss: *See* absolute loss.

Gross profit: The difference between the amount received from customers for goods and what the firm paid for the goods.

Gross profit on sales: *See* gross profit.

Gross sales: The total amount of money received from customers for the goods or services sold by the firm.

H

Half-year convention: Method of depreciation used for the first year the property is placed in service.

Head of household: An unmarried person who has dependents can use the head of household category when filing income taxes.

High: The highest price reached by a stock during the day.

Homeowner's policy: An insurance policy that covers a home against fire, theft, and liability.

Horizontal analysis: An analysis that shows the amount of any change from last year to the current year, both in dollars and as a percent.

I

Identity theft: When someone gathers enough information about you to fraudulently establish credit cards or borrow money using your name and personal information.

Impound account (Escrow account): An account at a lending institution into which taxes and insurance are paid on a monthly basis by a borrower on real estate. The lender then pays the tax and insurance bills from this account when they become due.

Improper fraction: A fraction with a numerator larger than the denominator. (For example, $\frac{7}{5}$ is an improper fraction; $\frac{1}{9}$ is not.)

Incentive rate: A payment system based on the amount of work completed.

Income statement: A summary of all the income and expenses involved in running a business for a given period of time.

Income tax: The tax based on income that both individuals and corporations are required to pay to the federal government and sometimes to a state.

Income tax withholding: Federal income tax that the employer withholds from gross earnings.

Income-to-monthly-payment ratio: A ratio used to determine from an income standpoint whether a prospective borrower meets the lender's qualifications.

Increase problem (Amount problem): A percentage problem in which something has been added to the base. Usually the base must be found.

Index fund: A mutual fund that holds the stocks that are in a particular market index such as the Dow Jones Industrial Average.

Indicator words: Key words that help indicate whether to add, subtract, multiply, or divide.

Individual retirement account (IRA): An account designed to help people prepare for future retirement.

Inflation: Inflation results in a continuing rise in the cost of goods and services. *See* consumer price index (CPI).

Installment loan: A loan that is paid off with a sequence of periodic payments.

Insurance: Individuals and firms purchase insurance from insurance companies to protect them in the event of an unexpected loss.

Insured: A person or business that has purchased insurance.

Insurer: The insurance company.

Intangible assets: Assets such as patents, copyrights, or customer lists that have a value that cannot be immediately converted to cash, unlike jewelry or stocks.

Interest: A charge paid for borrowing money or a fee received for lending money.

Interest-bearing checking account: A checking account that earns interest.

Interest-in-advance notes: *See* simple discount note.

Interest rate per compounding period: Interest rates are usually given on an annual basis; however the interest rate per compounding period is needed when making many financial calculations.

Interest rate spread: The difference between the interest rate paid to depositors and the rates charged to borrowers by the same lender.

Internal Revenue Service: The branch of the U.S. federal government responsible for collecting taxes.

Internet banking: Banking done over the Internet.

Inventory: The value of the merchandise that a firm has for sale on the date of balance sheet.

Inventory-to-net-working-capital ratio: Inventory divided by working capital, where working capital is current assets minus current liabilities.

Inventory turnover: The number of times during a certain time period that the average inventory is sold.

Inventory turns: The number of times a year that a firm turns over its average inventory.

Invoice: A printed record of a purchase and sales transaction.

Invoice amount: List price minus trade discounts.

Invoice date: The date an invoice is printed.

Itemized billing method: A billing method that provides an itemization of the customer's charge purchases but not copies of the original charge receipts.

Itemized deductions: Tax deductions, such as interest, taxes, and medical expenses, that are listed individually on a tax return in order to affect the total amount of taxes payable at the end of the year.

J

Joint return: An income tax return filed by both husband and wife.

K

Kilo-: A prefix used in the metric system to represent 1000.

Kilogram: A unit of weight in the metric system meaning 1000 grams. One kilogram is about 2.2 pounds.

Kilometer: One thousand meters. A kilometer is about .6 mile.

L

Late fees: Fees required because payments were made after a specific due date.

Least common denominator: The smallest whole number that all the denominators of two or more fractions evenly divide into. (For example, the least common denominator of $\frac{3}{4}$ and $\frac{5}{6}$ is 12.)

Left side: The left-hand side of an equation.

Level premium: A level premium insurance policy is one with a level premium throughout its life.

Liability: An expense that must be paid by a firm.

LIFO: A method of inventory accounting in which the most recent items received are considered to be the first ones shipped.

Like fractions: Fractions with the same denominator.

Like terms: Two terms in an algebraic expression with the same variable can be added together (combined). For example, $2x + 5x = 7x$.

Limited liability: A form of protection that shields a company and its shareholders from having to pay large sums of money in the event that the company loses a lawsuit.

Limited-pay life insurance: Life insurance for which premiums are paid for only a fixed number of years.

Line graph: A graph that uses lines to compare numbers.

Liquid assets: Cash or items that can be converted to cash quickly.

Liquidity: The ability of a firm or individual to raise cash quickly without being forced to sell assets at a loss.

List price: The suggested retail price or final consumer price given by the manufacturer or supplier.

Liter: A measure of volume in the metric system. One liter is a little more than one quart.

Loan amount: The amount of a loan.

Loan reduction schedule: *See* repayment schedule.

Long-term care coverage: Insurance that pays for long-term care such as nursing home expenses.

Long-term liabilities: Money owed by a firm that is not expected to be paid off within a year.

Long-term notes payable: The total of all debts of a firm, other than mortgages, that will not be paid within a year.

Low: The lowest price reached by a stock during the day.

Lowest terms: The form of a fraction if no number except the number 1 divides evenly into both the numerator and denominator.

M

M: Roman numeral for 1000.

MACRS (Modified accelerated cost recovery system): A depreciation method introduced as part of the Tax Reform Act of 1986.

Maintenance charge per month: The charge to maintain a checking account (usually determined by the minimum balance in the account).

Maker of a note: A person borrowing money from another person.

Manufacturers: Businesses that buy raw materials and component parts and assemble them into products that can be sold.

Margin: The difference between cost and selling price.

Marital status: An individual can claim married, single, or head of household when filing income taxes.

Markdown: A reduction from the original selling price. It may be expressed as a dollar amount or as a percent of the original selling price.

Marketing channels: The path of products and services beginning with the manufacturer and ending with the consumer.

Markup (Margin, Gross profit): The difference between the cost and the selling price.

Markup on cost: Markup that is calculated as a percent of cost.

Markup on selling price: Markup that is calculated as a percent of selling price.

Markup with spoilage: The calculation of markup including deduction for spoiled or unsaleable merchandise.

MasterCard: A credit-card plan (formerly known as Master-Charge).

Maturity value: The amount that a borrower must repay on the maturity date of a note.

Mean: The sum of all the numbers divided by the number of numbers.

Median: A number that represents the middle of a group of numbers.

Medical insurance: Insurance providing medical protection in the event of accident or injury.

Medicare tax: The amount of money deducted from the paychecks of almost all employees, used by the federal government to pay for Medicare.

Memory function: A feature on some calculators that stores results internally in the machine for retrieval and future use.

Merchant batch header ticket: The bank form used by businesses to deposit credit-card transactions.

Meter: A unit of length in the metric system that is slightly longer than 1 yard.

Metric system: A system of weights and measures based on decimals, used throughout most of the world. It is gradually being adopted in the United States.

Milli-: A prefix used in the metric system meaning thousandth. (For example, a milligram is one one-thousandth of a gram.)

Millimeter: One one-thousandth of a meter. There are 25.4 millimeters to an inch.

Mills: A way of expressing a real estate tax rate that is based on thousandths of a dollar.

Minuend: The number from which another number (the subtrahend) is subtracted.

Mixed number: A number written as a whole number and a fraction. (For example, $1\frac{3}{4}$ and $2\frac{5}{9}$ are mixed numbers.)

Mode: The number that occurs most often in a group of numbers.

Modified accelerated cost recovery system: *See* MACRS.

Money market account: An interest-bearing account offered by many banks, savings and loans, and brokerage firms. These accounts pay interest but allow the user to draw funds out without penalty.

Money order: A document that looks similar to a check and is issued by a bank, other financial institution, or a retail store that is often used in place of cash.

Mortgage: A loan on a home.

Mortgages payable: The balance due on all mortgages owed by a firm.

Multiple carrier insurance: The sharing of risk by several insurance companies.

Multiplicand: A number being multiplied.

Multiplication rule: The same nonzero number may be multiplied or divided on both sides of an equation.

Multiplier: A number doing the multiplying.

Mutual fund: A mutual fund accepts money from many different investors and uses it to purchase stocks or bonds of numerous companies.

N

NASDAQ composite index: A commonly quoted stock index composed of the stock prices of several technology companies.

Negative numbers: Numbers that are the opposite of positive numbers.

Net cost: The cost or price after allowable discounts have been taken. *See* net price.

Net cost equivalent: The decimal number derived from the complement of the single trade discount. This number multiplied by the list price gives the net cost.

Net earnings: The difference between gross margin and expenses. After the cost of goods and operating expenses are subtracted from total sales, the remainder is net profit.

Net income: The difference between gross margin and expenses.

Net pay: The amount of money actually received by an employee after deductions are taken from gross pay.

Net payment date: The date by which an invoice must be paid.

Net price: The list price less any discounts. *See* net cost.

Net proceeds: The amount received from the bank for a discounted note.

Net profit: *See* net earnings.

Net sales: The value of goods bought by customers after the value of goods returned is subtracted.

Net worth (Capital, Stockholder's equity, Owner's equity): The difference between assets and liabilities.

No-fault insurance: A guarantee of reimbursement (provided by the insured's own insurance company) for medical expenses and costs associated with an accident no matter who is at fault.

Nominal rate: The interest rate stated in connection with a loan. It may differ from the annual percentage rate.

Nonsufficient funds (NSF): When a check is written on an account for which there is an insufficient balance, the check is returned to the depositor for nonsufficient funds.

No scrap value: The value of an item is assumed to be zero at the end of its useful life.

Notes payable: The value of all notes owed by a firm.

Notes receivable: The value of all notes owed to a firm.

NOW account (Negotiable order or withdrawal): Technically a savings account with special withdrawal privileges. It looks the same and is used the same as a checking account.

Numerator: The number above the line in a fraction. (For example, in the fraction $\frac{5}{8}$, 5 is the numerator.)

O

Odd lot: Fewer than 100 shares of stock.

Open-end credit: Credit with no fixed number of payments. The consumer continues making payments until no outstanding balance is owed.

Operating expenses (Overhead): Expenses of operating a business. Wages, salaries, rent, utilities, and advertising are examples.

Operating loss: The loss resulting when the selling price is less than the break-even point.

Ordered array: A list of numbers arranged from smallest to largest.

Order of operations: The rules that are used when evaluating long arithmetic expressions.

Ordinary annuity: An annuity whose payments are made at the end of a given period of time.

Ordinary dating: A method for calculating the discount date and the net payment date. Days are counted from the date of the invoice.

Ordinary interest: A method of calculating interest, assuming 360 days per year. *See* banker's interest.

Ordinary life insurance (Whole life insurance, Straight life insurance): A form of life insurance whereby the insured pays a constant premium until death or retirement, whichever occurs sooner. Upon retirement, monthly payments are made by the company to the insured until the death of the insured.

Other expenses: Certain expenses that are deductible on a personal income tax return.

Overdraft: An event that results when there is not enough money in a bank account to cover a check that is written from that account.

Overhead: Expenses involved in running a firm. *See* operating expenses.

Over-the-limit fees: Fees charged when the balance on a credit-card account exceeds the account's credit limit.

Overtime: The number of hours worked by an employee in excess of 40 hours per week.

Owner's equity: *See* net worth.

P

Part: The result of multiplying the base times the rate.

Partial payment: A payment made on an invoice that is less than the full amount of the invoice.

Partial product: Part of the process of getting the answer in a multiplication problem.

Par value of a bond: *See* face value of a bond.

Passbook account: A type of savings account for day-in and day-out savings.

Pay by phone: Bill payments authorized by phone.

Payee: The person who lends money and will receive repayment on a note.

Payer of a note: A person borrowing money from another person. *See* maker of a note.

Payroll: A record of the hours each employee of a firm worked and the amount of money due each employee for a given pay period.

Payroll card: A card maintained by employers showing the name of employee, dates of pay period, days, times, and hours worked.

Payroll ledger: A chart showing all payroll information.

Percent (Rate): Some parts of a whole: hundredths, or parts of a hundred. (For example, a percent is one one-hundredth. Two percent means two parts of a hundred, or $\frac{2}{100}$.)

Percentage method: A method of calculating income tax withholding that is based on percentages.

Per debit charge: A charge per check (usually continues regardless of the number of checks written).

Periodic inventory: A physical inventory taken at regular intervals.

Permanent life insurance: Life insurance that can be continued until death, no matter the age at the time of death.

Perpetual inventory: A continuous inventory system normally involving a computer.

Personal account: The type of checking account used by individuals.

Personal computer banking: Banking using a personal computer and the Internet.

Personal exemption (Exemption): A deduction allowed each taxpayer for each dependent and the taxpayer himself or herself.

Personal identification number (PIN): A lettered or numbered code that allows a person with a credit or debit card to gain access to credit or cash.

Personal property: Property such as a boat, a car, or a stereo.

Piecework: A method of pay by which an employee receives so much money per item produced or completed.

Plant assets: *See* fixed assets.

Point-of-sale terminal: A machine that allows a customer to make purchases using a credit or debit card.

Policy: A contract outlining the insurance agreement between an insured and an insurance company.

Policy limits: The maximum amount that an insurance company will pay as defined in the policy.

Postdating: Dating in the future; on an invoice, "AS OF" dating.

pr.: Abbreviation for *pair*.

Preferred stock: A type of stock that offers investors certain rights over holders of common stock.

Premium: The amount of money charged for insurance policy coverage.

Premium factor: A factor used to adjust an annual insurance premium to semiannually, quarterly, or monthly.

Premium payment plan: An additional payment for extra service such as overtime.

Prepaid card: A card on which a user has stored monetary value which allows her to make purchases.

Present value: The amount that must be deposited today to generate a specific amount at a specific date in the future.

Price-earnings (PE) ratio: The price per share divided by the annual net income per share of stock.

Prime interest rate: The interest rate banks charge their largest and most financially secure borrowers.

Prime number: A number that can be divided without remainder by exactly two distinct numbers: itself and 1.

Principal: The amount of money either borrowed or deposited.

Privately held corporation: A corporation that has relatively few owners, or perhaps a single owner. Its stock is not traded on a large exchange such as the New York Stock Exchange.

Proceeds: The amount of money a borrower receives after subtracting the discount from the face value of a note.

Product: The answer in a multiplication problem.

Promissory note: A business document in which one person agrees to repay money to another person within a specified amount of time and at a specified rate of interest in exchange for money borrowed.

Proper fraction: A fraction in which the numerator is smaller than the denominator. (For example, $\frac{2}{3}$ is a proper fraction; $\frac{9}{5}$ is not.)

Property damage insurance: A type of automobile insurance that pays for damages that the insured causes to the property of others.

Proportion: A mathematical statement that two ratios are equal.

Proprietorship: Stockholder's equity.

Proximo (Prox.): *See* end-of-month dating.

Publicly held corporations: Corporations that are owned by the public and have stock that trades freely.

Purchase invoice: A list of items purchased, prices charged for the items, and payment terms.

Q

Qualifying for a loan: A person applying for a loan is said to qualify if his or her credit history, income, and financial statement satisfy the requirements of the lending institution.

Quick ratio: The quotient of liquid assets and current liabilities.

Quota: An expected level of production. A premium may be paid for surpassing quota.

Quotient: The answer in a division problem.

R

Radio frequency identification (RFID): A chip that responds to an electronic scan with information about the product.

Rate: Parts of a hundred. *See* percent.

Rate of interest: The percent of interest charged on a loan for a certain time period.

Ratio: A comparison of two (or more) numbers, frequently indicated by a common fraction.

Real estate: Real property such as a home or a parcel of land.

Receipt-of-goods dating (ROG): A method of determining cash discounts in which time is counted from the date that goods are received.

Reciprocal: A fraction formed from a given fraction by interchanging the numerator and denominator.

Reconciliation: The process of checking a bank statement against the depositor's own personal records.

Recourse: Should the maker of a note not pay, the bank may have recourse to collect from the seller of the note.

Recovery classes: Classes used to determine depreciation under the modified accelerated cost recovery system.

Recovery period: The life of property depreciated under the accelerated cost recovery system.

Recovery year: The year of life of an asset when using the MACRS method of depreciation.

Reduced net profit: The situation that occurs when a markdown decreases the selling price to a point that is still above the break-even point.

Refinance: Borrowers can go to a lender and refinance their existing loan with a different interest rate, period, and payment.

Regulation DD: A Federal Reserve System document that specifies how interest paid to savers is to be calculated.

Regulation Z: A Federal Reserve System document that implements the Truth-in-Lending Act.

Renter's coverage: Insurance that covers only the possessions of a renter and not the house or apartment in which the possessions are kept.

Repayment schedule: A schedule showing the amount of payment going toward interest and principal and the balance of principal remaining after each payment is made.

Repeating decimals: Decimal numbers that do not terminate but that contain numbers that repeat themselves.

Replacement cost: The cost of replacing a property that is completely destroyed.

Repossess: The taking back of property by a lender when payments have not been made to the lender.

Residual value: *See* scrap value.

Restricted endorsement: A signature or imprint on the back of a check that limits the ability to cash the check.

Retailer: A business that buys from the wholesaler and sells to the consumer.

Retail method: A method used to estimate inventory value at cost that utilizes both cost and retail amounts.

Returned check: A check that was deposited and then returned due to lack of funds in the payer's account.

Return on average total assets: Net income divided by average total assets.

Returns: The total value of all goods returned by customers.

Revolving charge account: A charge account that never has to be paid off.

Right side: The right-hand side of an equation.

Risk: The potential of losing part or all of an investment.

Roth IRA: Contributions to a Roth Individual Retirement Account (Roth IRA) are not deductible when made. However, funds in the account grow tax free and withdrawals are not taxed once the account holder reaches a certain age.

Rounding off: The reduction of a number with more decimals to a number with fewer decimals.

Rounding whole numbers: Reduction of the number of nonzero digits in a whole number.

Round lot: A multiple of 100 shares of stock.

Rule of 78: A method of calculating a partial refund of interest that has already been added to the amount of a loan. This calculation is done when the loan is paid off early.

S

Salary: A fixed amount of money per pay period.

Salary plus commission: Earnings based on a fixed salary plus a percent of all sales.

Sale price: The price of an item after markdown.

Sales invoice: *See* purchase invoice.

Sales tax: A tax placed on sales to the final consumer. The tax is collected by the state, county, or local government.

Salvage value: *See* scrap value.

Savings account: An interest-paying account that allows day-to-day savings and withdrawals.

Schedule 1: The part of the 1040A federal tax form that is used to list all interest and dividends.

Scrap value (Salvage value): The value of an asset at the end of its useful life. For depreciation purposes, this is often an estimate.

SDI deduction: State disability insurance pays the employee in the event of disability and is paid for by the employee.

Self-employed people: People who work for themselves instead of for the government or for a private company.

Series discount: *See* chain discount.

Shift differential: A premium paid for working a less desirable shift, such as the swing shift or the graveyard shift.

Simple discount note: A note in which the interest is deducted from the face value in advance.

Simple interest: Interest received on only the principal.

Simple interest note: A note in which interest = principal × interest rate × time in years.

Single discount equivalent: A series, or chain, discount expressed as a single discount.

Single return: An income tax return filed by a single person.

Sinking fund: A fund set up to receive periodic payments in order to pay off a debt at some time in the future.

sk.: Abbreviation for *sack*.

Sliding scale: Commissions that are paid at increasing levels as sales increase.

Smart card: A card with a microchip that receives electronic signals, makes calculations, and sends signals. It is sometimes used for identification.

Social Security tax: *See* FICA tax.

Solution: The number that makes an equation true when it is substituted in place of the variable.

Special endorsement: A signature on the back of a check that passes the ownership of the check to someone else.

Specific identification method: An inventory valuation method that identifies the cost of each item.

Split-shift premium: A premium paid for working a split shift, for example, for an employee who is on 4 hours, off 4 hours, and then on 4 hours.

Square root: One of two equal positive factors of a number.

Stafford loan: A loan taken out by college students to help pay tuition.

Standard deduction: A tax preparer may use the higher of the itemized deductions or the standard deduction established by the government.

Stated rate: The interest rate stated in connection with a loan. It may differ from the annual percentage rate.

State income tax: An income tax that is paid to a state government on income earned in that state.

Statement: Usually sent out monthly by the bank, a list of all charges and deposits made against and to a checking account.

Statistics: Refers both to data and to the techniques used in analyzing data.

Stock: A form of ownership in a corporation that is measured in units called *shares*.

Stockbroker: A person who buys and sells stock at the stock exchange.

Stock exchange: An institution where stock shares are bought and sold.

Stockholders: Individuals who own stock in a particular company.

Stockholder's equity: *See* net worth.

Stock ratios: Ratios calculated from the financial statements of a company—used to determine the financial health of the firm.

Stock turnover: *See* inventory turnover.

Stop payment: A request from a depositor that the bank not honor a check that the depositor has written.

Straight commission: A salary that is a fixed percent of sales.

Straight life insurance: *See* ordinary life insurance.

Straight-line depreciation: A depreciation method in which depreciation is spread evenly over the life of the asset.

Substitution: Method for checking the solution to an equation.

Subtrahend: The number being subtracted or taken away in a subtraction problem.

Sum: The total amount; the answer in addition.

Sum-of-the-years'-digits method: An accelerated depreciation method that results in larger amounts of depreciation taken in earlier years of an asset's life.

Supply chain: The chain of businesses and processes involved with moving raw materials, components, and final goods to the end user.

T

Tangible assets: Assets such as a car, machinery, or computers.

Taxable income: Adjusted income subject to taxation.

Tax deduction: Any expense that the Internal Revenue Service allows taxpayers to subtract from adjusted gross income.

Taxes: Individuals and corporations must pay taxes to government entities such as schools, cities, counties, states, and the federal government. Here are a few of the many types of taxes: sales taxes, property taxes, gasoline taxes, income taxes, and estate taxes.

Tax preparation: The preparation of an income tax return that is then sent to the Internal Revenue Service.

T-bill: A short-term note issued by the federal government that pays interest to the note holder. Issuing T-bills allows the federal government to raise cash without having to borrow the money from a bank and pay interest.

Telephone transfer account: An interest-bearing checking account into which funds may be transferred by the customer over the telephone.

Term: A number, variable, or product or division of a number and a variable, such as $5x$ or $7 + b$.

Term insurance: A form of life insurance providing protection for a fixed length of time.

Term of an annuity: The length of time that an annuity is in effect.

Term of a note: The length of time between the date a note is written and the date the note is due.

Terms: The area of an invoice where cash discounts are indicated if any are offered. The words "terms discount" are often used in place of "cash discount."

Territorial ratings: Ratings used by insurance companies that describe the quality of fire protection in a specific area.

Texting: Text sent to a cell phone. Some banks communicate with account holders using texting.

Time-and-a-half rate: One and one-half times the normal rate of pay for any hours worked in excess of 40 per week.

Time card: A card filled out by an employee that shows the number of hours worked by that employee.

Time deposit account: A savings account in which the depositor agrees to leave money on deposit for a certain period of time.

Time rate: Earnings based on hours worked, not for work accomplished.

Total installment cost: Includes the down payment plus the sum of all payments.

Total revenue: The total of all revenue from all sources.

Trade discount: A discount offered to businesses. This discount is expressed either as a single discount (like 25%) or a series discount (like 20/10) and is subtracted from the list price.

Traditional banking: A method of banking involving the use of paper checks and check registers to record deposits and checks.

Transaction register: Shows the checks written and deposits made on a checking account.

True rate of interest: *See* effective rate of interest.

Turnover at cost: The cost of goods sold, divided by the average inventory at cost.

Turnover at retail: Sales, divided by the average inventory at retail.

U

Underinsured motorist: A motorist who does not carry enough insurance to cover the costs of an accident.

Underwater: The situation where homeowners owe more on their home than it is worth.

Underwriters: Term applied to any insurer. Usually associated with an insurance company.

Unearned interest: Interest that a company has received but has not yet earned so that it is not shown in revenues.

Uniform product code (UPC): The series of black vertical stripes seen on products in stores that cashiers scan. Also called the *bar code*.

Uninsured motorist insurance: Insurance coverage that covers the insured when involved in an accident with a driver who is not insured.

United States Rule: The rule by which a loan payment is first applied to the interest owed, with the balance used to reduce the principal amount of the loan.

Unit price: The cost of one item.

Units-of-production: A depreciation method by which the number of units produced determines the depreciation allowance.

Universal life policy: A policy whose premiums flow into a general account from which the insurance company makes investments.

Unlike fractions: Fractions with different denominators.

Unlike terms: Two terms in an algebraic expression that do not have the same variables, so they cannot be added together. For example, $2x + 5y$ cannot be combined into one term.

Unpaid-balance method: A method used to calculate interest on open-end credit accounts.

Unreimbursed job expenses: Certain expenses that are deductible on a personal income tax return.

Useful life: The estimated life of an asset. The Internal Revenue Service gives guidelines of useful life for depreciation purposes.

V

Valuation of inventory: Determining the value of merchandise in stock. Four common methods are specific-identification, average cost, FIFO, and LIFO.

Variable: A letter that stands for a number.

Variable commission: A commission whose rate depends on the total amount of the sales.

Variable interest rate loan: A loan on which the interest rate can go up or down.

Variable life policy: A life insurance policy that allows the owner to invest the funds within the policy in different types of investments.

Verbal form: Word form (the form of numbers expressed in words).

Vertical analysis: The listing of each important item on an income statement as a percent of total net sales or each item on a balance sheet as a percent of total assets.

Visa: A credit-card plan (formerly known as Bank Americard).

W

Wage: A rate of pay expressed as a certain amount of dollars per hour.

Wage bracket method: A method of calculating income tax withholding that is based on tables that list income ranges.

Weighted average method: A method for calculating the arithmetic mean for data where each value is weighted (or multiplied) according to its importance.

Whole life insurance: *See* ordinary life insurance.

Whole number: A number made up of digits to the left of the decimal point.

Wholesaler: A business that buys directly from the manufacturer or other wholesalers and sells to the retailer.

Withholding allowance: An allowance for the employee, spouse, and dependents that determines the amount of withholding tax taken from gross earnings.

Withholding tax: The money withheld from an employee's paycheck and deposited to the account of the employee with the federal or state government to cover the amount of income tax owed by the employee.

With recourse: An understanding that the seller of a note is responsible for payment of the note if the original maker of the note does not make payment. The note is sold with recourse.

Worker's compensation: Insurance purchased by companies to cover employees against work-related injuries.

W-2 form: The wage and tax statement given to the employee each year by the employer.

W-4 form: A form usually completed at the time of employment, on which an employee states the number of withholding allowances being claimed.

Y

Yield to maturity: The equivalent interest rate yield to the maturity of a bond or other financial instrument.

Youthful operator: A driver of a motor vehicle who is under a certain age, usually 25.

index

acknowledgments

Page xxi, group of students studying/Getty Royalty Free

Page 1, Subway sandwich shop/Beth Anderson

Page 6, Subway drink cup/Beth Anderson

Page 7, Ford Escape/Stan Salzman

Page 8, baseball card/Lana Sundman/Alamy

Page 12, washer and dryer/© Scott Leigh/iStockphoto

Page 14, parachute jumpers/PhotoDisc

Page 15, rafters on river/Shutterstock

Page 17, child filling water jugs/Getty Images

Page 18, family moving out/David Sacks/Getty Images, Inc.

Page 20, Jared Fogle with big pants/AP Wideworld Photo

Page 20, Subway napkin/Beth Anderson

Page 21, Subway sandwiches/Beth Anderson

Page 21, Iwo Jima flag/Joe Rosenthal/Corbis

Page 21, Army WWII/Beth Anderson

Page 21, girl on laptop/Shutterstock

Page 23, candy bar/Beth Anderson

Page 25, soda cans/Shutterstock

Page 25, frozen-type pizza/iStockphoto

Page 28, deposit slips/iStockphoto

Page 30, waitress with tapas and beer/Richard Nowitz/ National Geographic Image Collection

Page 31, Subway/Beth Anderson

Page 36, Toyota Prius/Shutterstock

Page 42, Subway/Beth Anderson

Page 45, Home Depot storefront/Don Smetzer/Photo Edit

Page 45, Blueprint of Kitchen, Getty Images – Thinkstock

Page 46, kitchen cabinets/PhotoEdit Inc.

Page 47, built-in microwave oven/iStockphoto

Page 52, gold Chains/Shutterstock

Page 59, sprinter/Shutterstock

Page 59, students/Doug Menuez/Getty Images, Inc.

Page 60, students if a coffee shop/Shutterstock

Page 68, chocolate/Oat-Chip cookie/Shutterstock

Page 72, woman using hairdryer/Shutterstock

Page 72, Carpet store/Getty Images

Page 74, Visine/Getty Images

Page 74, snowmobile/Tom Stack & Associates, Inc.

Page 82, woman shopping at Home Depot/Photo Disk

Page 84, wedding cake/Shutterstock

Page 85, Century 21 sign/Beth Anderson

Page 88, woman making business presentation/Shutterstock

Page 93, modest home/PhotoEdit Inc.

Page 94, unemployment line/The Image Works

Page 98, Navy Ship/U.S. Navy

Page 98, girl screaming with cell phone while driving car/Shutterstock

Page 98, nurse with baby/Photo Researchers, Inc.

Page 99, GM sales in China/STR/AFP/Getty Images

Page 99, NFL Superbowl ad cost/Digital Vision

Page 100, Country Store household items/iStockphoto

Page 108, marathon runner/The Image Works

Page 109, women in military/AP Wideworld Photo

Page 110, woman on motorcycle/iStockphoto

Page 110, wind turbines/Shutterstock

Page 111, exotic birds/iStockphoto

Page 111, sport store/© Richard Ransier/Corbis All Rights Reserved

Page 113, totaled car/Shutterstock

Page 116, white lab mouse/Tetra Images/Getty Images

Page 117, running shoes/© Dorling Kindersley

Page 121, car in showroom, Shutterstock

Page 121, student, Shutterstock

Page 122, Chiquita bananas/Shutterstock

Page 126, Case Study Century 21/Beth Anderson

Page 126, Honda Civic/Shutterstock

Page 128, Golf course

Page 140, shark cage/Shutterstock

Page 143, Green Giant Nursery/Shutterstock

Page 129, Chevy Volt/Ethan Miller/Getty Images Inc.

Page 139, Chevy Impala/© DMAAKA Images /Alamy

Page 140, nursery/iStockphoto

Page 146, Motorcycle Store front/Courtesy of Gary Clendenen

Page 149, fishing lure/iStockphoto.com

Page 153, refrigerator/Courtesy of Gary Clendenen

Page 154, pizza/Courtesy of Gary Clendenen

Page 155, antique store/Courtesy of Gary Clendenen

Page 157, Burger King/Getty Images Inc.

Page 159, lettuce/Ian O'Leary © Dorling Kindersley

Page 162, apartments/Courtesy of Gary Clendenen

Page 163, health food store/Courtesy of Gary Clendenen

Page 164, school in China/Courtesy of Gary Clendenen

Page 167, clothing boutique/Getty Images

Page 168, GM sign/Almay

Page 181, rose garden/iStockphoto

Page 183, Walmart/Courtesy of Gary Clendenen

Page 194, garden center/Thinkstock

Page 197, mechanic/iStockphoto

Page 197, nursery/Shutterstock

Page 198, bicycle shop/ThinkStock

Page 197, studio family portrait/iStockphoto

Page 209, mechanic/iStockphoto

Page 210, rose/Thinkstock

Page 215, Starbucks store/Beth Anderson

Page 217, coffeeshop/iStockphoto

Page 229, mechanic changing tire Getty Images, Inc. – Jupiter Images

Page 230, house/Shutterstock

Page 231, muffins/Thinkstock

Page 235, Social Security Office/

Page 242, W-4/iStockphoto

Page 248, couple/Shutterstock

Page 253, travel agency/© Danita Delimont/Alamy

Page 263, home furnishing store/Courtesy of Gary Clendenen

Page 267, pots and pans/Shutterstock

Page 268, George Foreman/Jeremy O'Donnell/Getty Images Inc.

Page 268, Stove/

Page 273, Zune/Shutterstock

Page 273, elderly woman with walker/Shutterstock

Page 273, home beverage fountain/iStock photo

Page 274, tap shoes/Shutterstock

Page 275, kitchen sink/Thinkstock

Page 276, coffeemaker/© Susan Van Etten/PhotoEdit

Page 278, calculator/Getty Images

Page 280, Hershey products/Beth Anderson

Percent Formula	$\text{Part} = \text{Base} \times \text{Rate}$ or $P = B \times R$ or $P = BR$
Markup Formula	$\text{Cost} + \text{Markup} = \text{Selling price}$ or $C + M = S$
Converting Markup Percent on Cost to Selling Price	$\dfrac{\text{Markup on}}{\text{selling price}} = \dfrac{\text{Markup on cost}}{100\% + \text{Markup on cost}}$
Converting Markup Percent on Selling Price to Cost	$\dfrac{\text{Markup on}}{\text{cost}} = \dfrac{\text{Markup on selling price}}{100\% - \text{Markup on selling price}}$

Terms Associated with Loss

Original Selling Price

$ Cost	$ Operating Expenses	$ Net Profit

Selling Price   Absolute Loss   Breakeven Point

Selling Price   Operating Loss

Selling Price   Reduced Net Profit

Stock Turnover	$\text{Turnover at retail} = \dfrac{\text{Retail sales}}{\text{Average inventory at retail}}$ $\text{Turnover at cost} = \dfrac{\text{Cost of goods sold}}{\text{Average inventory at cost}}$
Simple Interest	The *simple interest*, I, on a principal of P dollars at a rate of interest R per year for T years is given by $I = PRT$.

Number of Days in Each Month

31 Days		30 Days	28 Days
January	August	April	February
March	October	June	(29 days in leap year)
May	December	September	
July		November	

Types of Interest

The method for forming the *time fraction* used for T in the formula $I = PRT$ is summarized as follows:

The *numerator* is the *exact number* of days in a loan period.
The *denominator* is one of the following:
- *exact interest* assumes 365 days in a year and uses 365 as denominator.
- *ordinary*, or *banker's interest* assumes 360 days in a year and uses 360 as denominator.

Interest, Principal, Rate, and Time Formulas

Interest: $I = PRT$ Principal: $P = \dfrac{I}{RT}$ Rate: $R = \dfrac{I}{PT}$

Time: Time in days $= \dfrac{I}{PR} \times 360$ Time in years $= \dfrac{I}{PR}$

Maturity Value   The *maturity value* M of a loan having a principal P and interest I is given by $M = P + I$.

Simple Interest and Simple Discount

	Simple Interest Note	Simple Discount Note
	I = Interest	B = Discount
	P = Principal (face value)	P = Proceeds
	R = Rate of interest	D = Discount rate
	T = Time, in years or fraction of a year	T = Time, in years or fraction of a year
	M = Maturity value	M = Maturity value
Face value	Stated on note	Same as maturity value
Interest charge	$I = PRT$	$B = MDT$
Maturity value	$M = P + I$	Same as face value
Amount received by borrower	Face value or principal	Proceeds: $P = M - B$
Identifying phrases	Interest at a certain rate	Discounted at a certain rate
	Maturity value greater than face value	Proceeds
		Maturity value equal to face value
True annual interest rate	Same as stated rate R	Greater than stated rate D

Compound Interest   If P dollars are deposited at a rate of interest t per period for n periods, then the *compound amount* M, or the final amount of deposit, is

$$M = P(1 + i)^n$$

The interest earned I is

$$I = M - P$$

(Use the compound interest table.)